Awakening Lives

*For Vera,
with best
regards,*

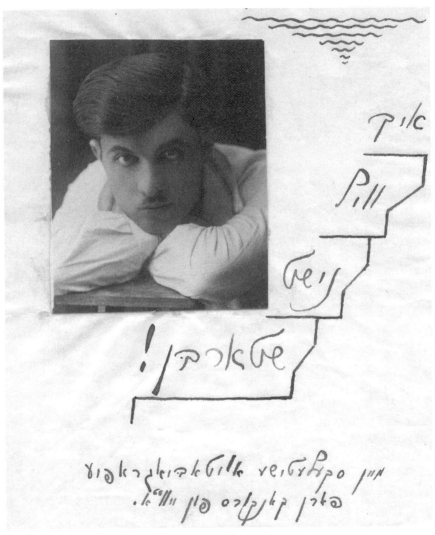

First page of "I Do Not Want to Die!: My Skeletal Autobiography for the YIVO Contest,"
1934.

AWAKENING LIVES

Autobiographies of Jewish Youth in Poland before the Holocaust

edited by
Jeffrey Shandler

with an introduction by
Barbara Kirshenblatt-Gimblett, Marcus Moseley, and
Michael Stanislawski

Published in cooperation with
The YIVO Institute for Jewish Research

Yale University Press
New Haven and London

*This project was supported by a grant from the National Endowment for the Humanities,
an independent federal agency. Major funding was also provided by the Smart Family
Foundation and the Sol and Lillian Goldman Foundation. Additional contributions were
received from Roger S. and Julie Baskes; Walter and Esther Hautzig, in honor of Ron and
Nancy Kraus; the Jewish Theological Seminary of America, in honor of Fanya Heller; and
Lawrence and Helaine Newman. YIVO is grateful to all donors whose generous support has
made the publication of this volume possible.*

Designed by Adam Freudenheim
Set by SNP Best-set Typesetter Ltd., Hong Kong
Printed in the United States of America

Library of Congress Cataloging-in-Publication Data

    Awakening lives: autobiographies of Jewish youth in Poland before the
Holocaust / edited by Jeffrey Shandler; with an introduction by Barbara
Kirshenblatt-Gimblett, Marcus Moseley, and Michael Stanislawski.
      p. cm.
    "Published in cooperation with The YIVO Institute for Jewish Research".
    ISBN 0-300-09277-6
    1. Jews—Poland—Biography. 2. Jewish youth—Poland—Biography.
3. Poland—Biography. I. Title: Autobiographies of Jewish youth in Poland before
the Holocaust. II. Shandler, Jeffrey.
DS135.P63 A1238 2002
920'.0092995033288'0835—dc21

        2002002660

A catalogue record for this book is available from the British Library
10 9 8 7 6 5 4 3 2 1

CONTENTS

The Autobiographies

ACKNOWLEDGMENTS

The history of YIVO's youth autobiographies project extends over much of the institute's history. The realization of this volume is indebted to the efforts of many individuals, united by their commitment to see that these unique documents of Polish Jewish life become available to a wide audience.

YIVO's plans to publish selected texts from the youth autobiography contests date back to the prewar years. As director of the *Yugntforshung* reseach project, Max Weinreich intended the publication of these autobiographies to supplement the scholarly material that the project generated, such as his own methodological study of 1935, *Der veg tsu undzer yugnt*. These plans came to an end with the destruction of YIVO's headquarters in Vilna during World War II.

After the war, some of the autobiographies and other *Yugntforshung* materials were recovered by YIVO, now headquartered in New York. There, work on the youth autobiographies project was undertaken by sociologist Moshe Kligsberg. Under a grant received from the U.S. Department of Health, Education and Welfare, Kligsberg compiled an index of the collection and drafted summaries of about half of the autobiographies in YIVO's possession. These provided a key to the collection for other scholars, and they also formed the basis of Kligsberg's own studies of the material.

In 1990 YIVO initiated a plan to prepare an English-language anthology of these autobiographies. The project, designed by literary scholar Marcus Moseley, was awarded a major grant from the National Endowment for the Humanities. An interdisciplinary group of scholars of Eastern European Jewry was convened to serve as the project's editoral committee. The initial committee, headed by Moseley, included historians Lucjan Dobroszycki and Michael Stanislawski; political scientist Jan Gross; YIVO's executive director at the time, Samuel Norich; the institute's head archivist, Marek Web; and Rachel Wizner, a doctoral candidate in Jewish history. Wizner took on the task of completing Kligsberg's inventory of the autobiographies; based on her work, the editorial committee selected the texts to be translated. In addition, Wizner coordinated the committee's activities and oversaw the preparation of draft translations of the texts. The translators who worked on this project include Rena Borow, Dobrochna Dyrcz-Freeman, Regina Grol-Prokopczyk, Chana Mlotek, Fruma Mohrer, Alex Molot, Elinor Robinson, Rosaline Schwartz, Daniel Soyer, Michael Taub, Andrej Tumowski, John Weeks, and Sheva Zucker.

Other YIVO staff members played vital roles in bringing the project toward completion, including Michael Steinlauf, during his tenure as senior research fellow, Lisa Epstein, when she served as director of research, and administrative assistants Portia Auguste-Smith and Chava Boylan. In 1998 folklorist Barbara Kirshenblatt-Gimblett and Yiddish studies scholar Jeffrey Shandler joined the editorial committee. Shandler took on the task of preparing the volume for publication: planning the format of the volume, editing the draft translations and the introduction, and preparing the annotations. He was assisted in his work by Jan Gross, who reviewed the translations from Polish, and by YIVO staff members Paul Glasser and Beatrice Weinreich, who reviewed the translations from Yiddish and Hebrew; additional research was prepared by Natalia Aleksiun (who researched the volume's chronology and map), Michał Chajn, Jocelyn Cohen, and Kalman Weiser. Others who generously offered their assistance with challenging editorial questions include Zachary Baker, Alina Cała, David Engel, Krysia Fisher, Marvin Herzog, Jim Hoberman, Ezra Mendelsohn, Chana Mlotek, Edna Nahshon, Mordkhe Schaechter, Nancy Sinkoff, and Aaron Taub. YIVO staff member Shaindel Fogelman played an invaluable role in preparing the typescript for publication.

The editorial committee wishes to thank Carl Rheins, executive director of YIVO, and his executive assistant, Marilyn Goldfried, as well as Andrea Sherman and Kathy Anderson for all their efforts on behalf of the publication of this volume. The volume's copy editor, Judith Wardman, brought an attentive eye to this project's linguistic and stylistic complexities. It has been a special pleasure to work with Adam Freudenheim, our editor at Yale University Press, who has brought great enthusiasm and thoughtfulness to the project.

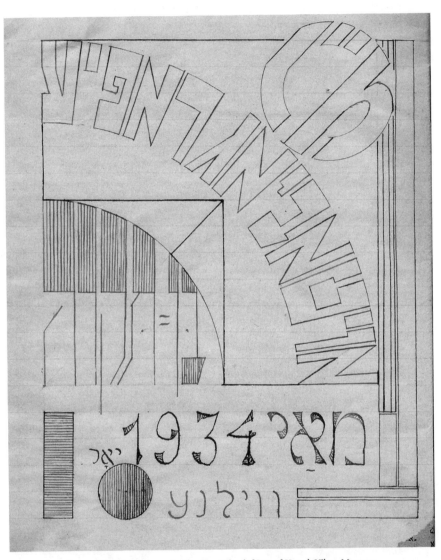

Cover of "My Autobiography," by Ben-Tikvah [Son of Hope], Vilna, May 1934.

Introduction

Barbara Kirshenblatt-Gimblett,
Marcus Moseley, and Michael Stanislawski

This volume presents the public with a selection of remarkable documents previously known only to professional scholars of East European Jewry: hundreds of unpublished autobiographies written by Polish Jewish adolescents in the decade before the Holocaust. These are singular documents of Jewish life in Eastern Europe during the years between the two World Wars, and they were gathered in a most unusual manner: through a series of competitions held in 1932, 1934, and 1939 by the YIVO Institute for Jewish Research. Scholars at YIVO invited Jews between the ages of sixteen and twenty-two years old to write their life histories and send them to the institute's headquarters in Vilna, so as to help researchers "become fully aware of the life of the Jewish youth."[1] YIVO offered prizes for those autobiographies judged to be the best ones; in exchange, their authors provided YIVO with prized information about their experiences, thoughts, and feelings. Indeed, more than a half-century after they were written, these autobiographies offer us insights into Jewish life in interwar Eastern Europe unlike any other source. In addition, the research initiative that inspired their writing and the historical moment that they embody provide rich material for understanding adolescence, autobiography writing, and the special challenges faced by diaspora and minority cultures.

The context in which these autobiographies were created not only informed their authors' writing but was strategic to the inception of this project. During the years between the two World Wars the Polish Republic was home to Europe's largest Jewish population. For all its citizens, life in interwar Poland was strikingly different from the period both before and after. In 1919 the Versailles Treaty redrew the map of Eastern Europe. As a result—after one-and-a-half centuries of a divided existence under the rule of Prussia, tsarist Russia, and the Habsburg Empire—Poland was reunited and declared an independent republic. Following the violent upheavals of World War I and its immediate aftermath, this new state promised greater political stability and democratic rule, and it also offered unprecedented opportunities to Poland's diverse ethnic communities, including its Jews.

The second largest ethnic minority in Poland, Jews comprised about ten percent of Poland's population (according to the 1931 census, there were 3,114,000 Jews in Poland, which had a total population of 31,916,000). Like all its other citizens, Jews were given the right to vote in elections, to organize their own political parties, and to run for office. Poland's public schools gave young Jews access to modern education unknown to previous generations. The constitution of the Polish Republic also stipulated that ethnic minorities had the right to establish their own press and publishing houses, cultural institutions, and educational systems in their own languages. Marshal Józef Piłsudski, a military hero and Poland's popular head of state from 1926 until his death in 1935, supported minority rights and called for interethnic tolerance.[2]

But the optimism many Jews felt at the beginning of the Polish Republic dimmed over time. During the 1930s, worldwide economic depression, the rise of fascism abroad, and growing anti-Semitism at home made life increasingly onerous for Polish Jews. Many of them sought to immigrate, though restrictive quotas made immigration to America, Palestine, and other countries possible for only a very few. In the late 1930s future prospects seemed dim for most Polish Jews, but the terrible fate that awaited them during World War II was beyond their imagining. The war brought an end to the Polish Republic, and by 1945 nine-tenths of Polish Jewry had been murdered.

For reasons that are, perhaps, quite understandable, the audience for works on the destruction of Polish Jewry still far outpaces the audience for works on the history and culture of this community before its demise. In recent decades, though, scholars have attempted to study Polish Jewish life before the Holocaust without looking through lenses tinted by nostalgia or horror, personal or familial loyalty, political or religious commitment, and endeavoring to avoid the dangers of hindsight—that is, of judging Jews living in prewar Poland in light of what we know of their subsequent fate.[3] The work of these scholars reveals the intense and often fractious vitality of interwar Polish Jewry.

This volume contributes to these efforts by presenting the rich complexity of ordinary young Jews' lives as they understood themselves during this remarkable period. As scholars of the period have already demonstrated, the diverse society of Polish Jewry was considerably transformed by the sudden impact of multiple modernizing forces—political reforms, religious innovation, linguistic adaptation, social and economic restratification—in the years immediately following World War I. The generations of Polish Jews who came of age in the interwar years were, consequently, quite different from their parents. While all generations mark a transition from one cohort to the next, the extent of political upheaval, economic disarray, social mobility (both downward and upward), and innovative political and religious ideologies encountered by interwar Polish Jews was unprecedented.

Therefore, it is not surprising to find a gulf separating the generation of Jews represented by the autobiographies in this volume, who were born just before, during, or immediately after World War I, from their parents, who were born in the relatively more stable 1890s or during the first years of the twentieth century. When this older generation was young—to cite only a few examples—there was no Polish republic to relate to as citizens, no compulsory public educational system, little industrialization, much more limited political mobilization, no sustained worldwide Depression, no local fascists or widespread (albeit clandestine) communist organizations, and virtually no organized Jewish "Orthodoxy." But their children had to grapple with these sudden, new developments as well as with all the usual vicissitudes of adolescent life. To these young people the dislocations they experienced seemed to have both positive and negative consequences, full of uncharted dangers and unprecedented aspirations.

The YIVO Institute, which solicited these autobiographies in an effort to understand this generation of young Jews and assist them in their struggles, was itself an exemplary innovation of Jewish society in interwar Poland. Founded in Vilna in 1925, YIVO pioneered the modern scholarly study of East European Jewish life from an interdisciplinary perspective, bringing together historians, linguists, psychologists, economists, folklorists, and sociologists. Within a few years of its creation, the institute established a special division for the study of youth, known in Yiddish as *Yugntforshung*, or *Yugfor* for short. Under the leadership of YIVO's research director, the linguist Max Weinreich, *Yugfor* conceived and oversaw these autobiography competitions as its main project.

YIVO's approach to the study of Jewish youth was rooted in an ideology that had distinct intellectual and political implications. Though interested in studying Jewish traditions, YIVO was an ardently secular institution. It not only functioned in Yiddish, the traditional vernacular of East European Jews, but considered the cultivation of Yiddish language and culture to be central to its mission. Moreover, while organized as a professional research institute, YIVO had a strong populist agenda and sought ways to engage and to serve the general Jewish community. And, unlike many other Jewish cultural institutions, which placed their hopes on the future of Jewry else- where, YIVO was committed to legitimating and sustaining Jewish life in Eastern Europe. In this regard, YIVO epitomized the diaspora nationalist ideology of *doikeyt* (Yiddish for "hereness"), an East European Jewish political principle that championed the legitimacy of Jewish communities wherever they were found. *Doikeyt* offered an alternative to Zionism or territorialism, which repudiated the diaspora and advocated the creation of a new and separate Jewish polity.[4]

YIVO's larger aspirations are reflected in the way that *Yugfor* invited participation in its autobiography contests. The institute urged contestants to write in detail about their earliest memories, their childhood experiences, their relations with their parents and siblings, their sexual development, their education and work experiences, as well as what they read, what they thought, what they hoped for in the future. Responding to these instructions, participants offered extensive and sometimes surprisingly candid accounts of their lives, which reflect great depth of insight and diversity of experience.

Indeed, those who entered YIVO's youth autobiography contests were not limited to the institute's core constituency of secular Yiddishists and diaspora nationalists. Over the course of the three contests, YIVO received autobiographies from Jewish youth in more than a dozen countries. And while most of the entries came from Poland, these authors range over virtually the entire spectrum of Polish Jewry: Orthodox, communist, Bundist, and Zionist (left, right, and center); rich, poor, and in-between; Yiddishists, Hebraists, Polonophiles; rural, small-town, and large-city residents; in almost every possible permutation and combination.[5]

Virtually each of these autobiographies, therefore, challenges generalizations that both scholars and lay people have made about interwar Polish Jewry. The young lives detailed in these texts were as jumbled and convoluted and essentially impervious to simple categorization as our own. These texts caution against simplifying the experiences of Polish Jewish youth by fitting them neatly into such categories as religious vs. secular, socialist vs. Zionist, rich vs. poor—dichotomies that not only oversimplify the past but distort it.

Thus, historians note that this generation of Polish Jews was highly politicized, whether active in specifically Jewish movements—the various Zionist parties, the Jewish Workers' Bund, the Orthodox Agudas Yisroel, and so on—or in Poland's communist and socialist parties. But these autobiographies reveal a far more nuanced and intellectually challenging picture of political mobilization and stratification. Jewish adolescents regularly crossed the boundaries of political and religious movements, both privately and in public. Some autobiographies report members of one political movement secretly attending meetings of another and then switching allegiances; they describe young men and women serially or even simultaneously belonging to rival political organizations due to their convictions, doubts, changing perceptions of political realities, or even romantic attractions to other members.

In some of these life histories, political engagement is articulated as a series of crises of faith. The autobiography of a twenty-two-year-old young man writing under the pseudonym "The Stormer," for example, recounts his traditional study of rabbinics in a small-town yeshiva, followed by recruitment into a communist cell by one of his cousins in the city of Łódź. (In something of an epitomizing moment, he writes of making a trip home for Passover, packing into his bag both illegal political propaganda that his cousin gives him to distribute to the local young people and a bottle of kosher wine for his family.) He then offers accounts of training with the Jewish sports organization Maccabi, a visit to a Zionist training farm run by Hashomer Hatsa'ir, trade union activism, as well as a remarkable—though ultimately unsuccessful—journey through Poland, Romania, and Bulgaria in an attempt to emigrate illegally to Palestine.

Just as these autobiographies evince highly idiosyncratic, hybridized political profiles, they reflect similarly complex educational backgrounds, including self-instruction as well as formal schooling. Typically, these authors describe attending more than one kind of school, sometimes simultaneously, thereby garnering complementary, if not contradictory, instruction. The nineteen-year-old autobiographer known to us as "Esther" writes with equal passion about attending a newly established Beys Yaakov school, which provided an elementary education for Orthodox Jewish girls, and about the intellectual discoveries she makes in the local Polish public school; she is as inspired by the words of Sara Schenirer, the founder of the Beys Yaakov schools, as she is by the verses of the nineteenth-century Polish romantic poet Adam Mickiewicz, a volume of which she requests as an award after making a public speech on Piłsudski's name-day.

Nor can these authors be readily characterized as Yiddishists, Hebraists, or Polonophiles, simply by virtue of the language in which they chose to compose their autobiography. Many offer accounts of the challenges, as well as the delights, of living in a complexly multilingual society. One autobiography, written in 1934 by a twenty-year-old young man from a small town in central Galicia, begins with the very question of language choice:

As I sit down to write my autobiography, I don't actually know which language to use: Yiddish, Hebrew, or even Polish. There are issues that I think about in Yiddish; these are primarily matters connected to daily life. I think about questions concerning Palestine and Zionism in Hebrew. Then there are also many issues that I think about in Polish: things that have to do with school, Polish history, world history, and the like. I've decided, however, to write in Yiddish, as I expect that my autobiography will consist of my everyday experiences.[6]

Similarly, the gap between parents and their children, described so prominently in many of these autobiographies, appears to be not so much ideological as experiential, born of the rapid social, economic, and political changes in interwar Poland. Most of the autobiographies describe an increasingly grim economic reality that weighed heavier on the authors as they came of age and faced the challenge of making their own way in the world. These autobiographies portray progressive impoverishment, experienced by so much of interwar Polish Jewry, in ways often not communicated as effectively in literary accounts or memoirs written after World War II, whose authors sometimes tend to romanticize their material circumstances in retrospect. Quite a few of the autobiographers also offer extensive accounts of child neglect and even child abuse, challenging idealized stereotypes of "Jewish family values." Such episodes are likewise seldom encountered in postwar accounts. Often written by a family's sole survivor, these accounts are generally more likely to eulogize relatives lost during the Holocaust.[7]

Another surprise in light of other accounts of this period, especially postwar memoirs, is how little attention the autobiographers represented here devote to the encounter with anti-Semitism in everyday life, as opposed to the large-scale anti-Semitism that restricted social and professional mobility, as well as access to advanced schooling or to professional careers. Indeed, more than one autobiography in this volume juxtaposes the author's personal friendship with a non-Jew against the larger societal backdrop of growing intolerance. Finally, there is little in these autobiographies about the rise of Nazism in Germany and its possible implications for Poland. This is true even in those life histories written in 1939, such as the work of the twenty-year-old author known to us as "G.W.," who writes at the end of his autobiography: "Young people live with hope and faith in a bright future. Those who are deeply convinced, believe. But there is a question as to when that day will come. When do we stop hoping? No one has determined this yet."

This is perhaps the most striking lesson of these texts. It is virtually impossible for the reader today to ponder the lives of East European Jews in these years without reflecting on the horrors that would soon come. For the reader knows what was unknowable for the authors: that they would most likely be murdered only a short time after writing these life stories. Or, if they were fortunate enough to be part of the fraction of Polish Jewry that survived the Holocaust, they would witness the cruel and unfathomable killings of their parents, siblings, friends, teachers—the destruction of their society and culture as a whole. Even some of the most ardent Zionists among them, committed in principle to the belief that there was no future for Polish Jewry, were nonetheless unmistakably hopeful about their own futures. Indeed, the extent of the hopefulness of these accounts may be their most unsettling characteristic. And yet, the more difficult it is for us to fathom today how the autobiographers in this volume could not have seen what was ahead, the more valuable are their accounts.

THE INTELLECTUAL BACKGROUND OF YIVO'S AUTOBIOGRAPHY CONTESTS

YIVO's decision to study Jewish adolescents during the 1930s—and to do so by encouraging them to enter an autobiography contest—was unusual on several counts. After all, the authors of these accounts were neither professional writers nor famous figures, and they were too young to have achieved much of note. Rather, they were ordinary individuals who spoke in their own voices about their everyday lives at a critical historical moment. Writing at a turning point in their lives, their personal histories were defined throughout by the experience of coming of age. At the conclusion of her autobiography, for example, "Esther" reflects, "Perhaps this autobiography will change the course of my life. This is something new for me. I have never before examined my life seriously."

Adolescents were of special interest to YIVO because they held the future of Jewish life in their hands. Many young Polish Jews, facing a desperate present and a bleak future in the 1930s, were eager to emigrate, an option that deeply troubled Max Weinreich, who was committed to a Jewish future in Eastern Europe. Writing about the *Yugfor* project in 1935, he asserted that the saying "He who holds the youth, holds the future" had become banal and needed to be replaced by the more fitting epigram: "He who holds the future, holds the youth."[8]

YIVO's ultimate goal was to enable a Jewish future in Eastern Europe, no matter how unpromising the immediate prospects. The key to the institute's own survival was the very generation that Weinreich proposed to study. YIVO hoped that contestants would become more involved in its work and offered to send them the institute's newsletter, *Yedies fun YIVO*. YIVO also encouraged contestants to maintain contact with the institute in the future and later asked them to send YIVO materials regarding their towns and regions.

The study of youth was thus a matter of ideological urgency. For several decades, social and political movements had been mobilizing European youth, including growing numbers of Jews, by offering them a total and alternative way of life, the chance to continue their development after they left school, and a program for the future. Weinreich understood the power of these movements from his own experience in SKIF, the Bund's youth movement. Consistent with the view that youngsters first became interested in political movements by about the age of seventeen, the autobiography contests specified that contestants had to be between the ages of sixteen and twenty-two, thereby defining "youth" as the period from political awakening to self-sufficient adulthood.[9] This historically conditioned phase in the life cycle was fundamental to youth research as an interdisciplinary field of study familiar to Weinreich. What Viennese scholars termed *Jugendforschung* had developed in relation to the historical unfolding of its subject, beginning with the emergence of youth movements in Central Europe in the 1890s. Youth research thus signaled the convergence of a developmental stage—adolescence—and an historically specific social formation: youth movements and youth culture.[10]

Weinreich formally launched YIVO's *Yugntforshung* project on 1 June 1934. He had only recently returned to Vilna from more than a year abroad, where he had been involved in a variety of scholarly encounters that were fundamental to the design of *Yugfor*'s goals and methodology.[11] During the 1932–33 academic year he studied the impact of culture on personality at Yale University with anthropologist Edward Sapir and sociologist John Dollard. During the fall of 1933 Weinreich studied child and adolescent psychology at the University of Vienna with Charlotte Bühler. While in Vienna, he also met with Siegfried Bernfeld, a psychoanalyst specializing in adolescence.[12]

Bernfeld's work was to prove especially influential on Weinreich's study of Jewish youth. Psychoanalysis, which was of great interest to Weinreich, had concentrated almost entirely on adults in relation to their early childhood. The field had paid relatively little attention to puberty, which Bernfeld defined broadly as the period between twelve and twenty years old—that is, the period between childhood and adulthood, from the onset of a significant increase in libido to independence. He recognized not only phases within this extended period of "adolescence," but also the cultural and historical specificity of any periodization of the life cycle.[13] Wedding radical politics with psychoanalysis, Bernfeld believed that youth culture comprised a distinct social alternative for young people, which offered an implicit critique of authoritarian and regimented middle-class life at home and in school.[14]

Consistent with his commitment to the social emancipation of youth, Bernfeld believed that qualitative rather than experimental studies were in order. That is, the best evidence would come from young people themselves—their diaries, journals, autobiographies, letters, and literary and artistic efforts, rather than from controlled psychological studies. In this spirit, Bernfeld established the Archive for Jewish Youth Culture in 1913 and the Jewish Institute for Youth Culture and Education in 1922, both based in Vienna. Bernfeld is credited as the first person to bring a multidisciplinary perspective to youth research and a psychoanalytic approach to pedagogy.[15]

On his return to Vilna, Weinreich attempted to place YIVO at the forefront of social scientific research by applying the theories and methods that he had encountered in New Haven and Vienna to the study of contemporary Jewish life in Eastern Europe.[16] YIVO's *Yugfor* project not only attempted to align European and American scholarly approaches to the study of Jewish adolescents; it also marked a threshold in the development of the institute's overall approach to the study of Jews. When it was founded in 1925, YIVO's research priorities were philological and historical. Consistent with the goal of "rescuing from loss and oblivion the relics of the Jewish past and the gems of Jewish folk creation,"[17] the first major project of YIVO's Department of Psychology and Pedagogy was the collection of detailed memoirs of *kheyder*, the traditional school where Jewish children began their religious instruction, learning to read Hebrew and to recite prayers. During 1927–28, researchers elicited information from respondents ranging in age from nineteen to eighty by means of questionnaires published in *Yedies fun YIVO*. Elderly informants, fully formed adults with long memories, were valued as repositories of cultural information, though not as subjects to be studied in themselves.

But by 1930 Weinreich had started to reorient the agenda of YIVO's Department of Psychology and Pedagogy by making the "psyche of the Jewish child" a research topic.[18] Two years later, the first autobiography contest proceeded from the idea that the adolescent, a person in the process of becoming, was a valuable subject of study in his or her own right. By the end of the second autobiography contest, held in 1934, YIVO formally launched *Yugfor* as a major research project. In contrast with the earlier *kheyder* initiative, *Yugfor* would focus on individuals and on a pivotal point in their personal development, rather than on collective experience within an institution. Also, YIVO would study contemporary Jewish life, rather than the past. The research would be based on documents that young people themselves created, rather than on their answers to someone else's questions. The contest instructions did, of course, guide the autobiographers, but above all they encouraged contestants to speak freely about their lives.

Over the course of YIVO's three youth autobiography contests the number of submissions and their geographic range increased. The first contest, held in 1932, was addressed to "the Jewish youth of Vilna and the Vilna region." Thirty-four young people responded.[19] The second contest, held in 1934, attracted 304 entries from twelve countries, far exceeding the institute's expectations.[20] So pleased was YIVO with the response that the deadline was extended by several months so that more young people could enter, and the number of prizes was increased.[21] The third contest, which was announced in the fall of 1938, brought in 289 submissions.[22] Cash prizes for this contest ranged from 150 zloty (about 30 U.S. dollars) for first prize to 25 zloty (about 5 dollars) for fifth and sixth prize. These were substantial sums in Poland at the time, considering that some of the contestants did not even have enough money to buy the stamps to mail in their autobiographies. YIVO publications were to be awarded to the remaining nineteen winners. All in all, the three contests yielded 627 autobiographies, in addition to diaries, journals, letters, photographs, drawings, literary efforts, and other materials. YIVO researchers followed up on some of the autobiographies and interviewed some of their authors' parents and teachers.[23]

The autobiography contests suited Weinreich's goals for several reasons. First, YIVO was a young institution with meager resources, and contests were an inexpensive and efficient way to collect a vast amount of data. Moreover, such contests were already an established practice in Polish sociology. The Institute for Social Economy in Warsaw collected 800 autobiographies of the unemployed in 1931 and about 500 peasant autobiographies in 1933, to cite only two examples.[24] As a result of such efforts, "the collection of autobiographies agglomerated in the archives of Polish research institutes is quantitatively and qualitatively unique."[25] Furthermore, Polish sociology in this period also focused on contemporary life and "the young generation."

It was Florian Znaniecki, the founder of modern sociology as an academic discipline in interwar Poland, who encouraged the collecting of autobiographies. *The Polish Peasant in Europe and America*, coauthored by Znaniecki and William I. Thomas at the University of Chicago, was exemplary for its use of personal documents. This multi-volume work, published between 1918 and 1920, includes 10,000 letters exchanged between Polish peasants who had immigrated to Chicago and the families they left behind in Poland, as well as a lengthy autobiography of a Polish immigrant. Not only did Weinreich admire *The Polish Peasant*, but he also published

Table of Statistics

In his postwar studies of YIVO's youth autobiography contests of the
1930s, sociologist Moshe Kligsberg tabulated the following statistics,
based on the extant materials housed in the YIVO Archives in New York.*
These represent slightly less than half of all the autobiographies originally
submitted to YIVO; most of the others were destroyed during World War
II or missing after the war. Others not included in his statistical survey are
autobiographies sent from outside Poland, as well as texts for which some
information was missing or which were otherwise incomplete.

Total number of autobiographies surveyed: 302   *out of 627 (48.2%)*
    1932 contest: 17 (5.6% of survey)   *out of 34 (50%)*
    1934 contest: 176 (58.3% of survey)   *out of 304 (57.9%)*
    1939 contest: 109 (36.1% of survey)   *out of 289 (37.7%)*

Language of autobiographies
    Yiddish: 223 (73.8%)
    Polish: 71 (23.6%)
    Hebrew: 8 (2.6%)

Length of autobiographies
    Average length: 59 pages ("of standard notebook size")
    Longest autobiography: 800 pages
    (The required minimum was 25 pages.)

Sex of authors
    Male: 236 (78%)
    Female: 66 (22%)

---

* Adapted from Moses Kligsberg, "Child and Adolescent Behavior under Stress:
An Analytical Guide to a Collection of Autobiographies of Jewish Young Men and
Women in Poland (1932–1939) . . ." [report] (New York: YIVO, 1965), p. 10.

"A Study of Jewish Youth: Program and Method" in 1935 in *Przegląd
socjologiczny*, the Polish sociology journal founded by Znaniecki.

The theoretical justification for using personal documents rested on
the sociological importance that Znaniecki and Thomas accorded the
individual as a totality, the primacy of experience, and a view of socializa-
tion "as the product of a continual interaction of individual consciousness

and the objective social reality."[26] It followed that "personal life-records, as complete as possible, constitute the *perfect* type of sociological material," despite the practical difficulties of gathering enough diaries and processing the massive amount of material generated by autobiography contests.[27]

Moreover, Weinreich valued autobiographies for what they could reveal about the impact of culture on personality, particularly from a psychoanalytic perspective. Such evidence would allow Weinreich to test the thesis guiding YIVO's *Yugfor* project, which he had termed the "nationality" problem. This problem expressed itself in the double insecurity of the Jewish child: "First, the child discovers that he is Jewish and that he belongs to a disadvantaged group." Second, "the adolescent begins to deliberate earnestly about his place in the community and his own future," only to be thwarted by discrimination from realizing his aspirations.[28]

Through their autobiographies, Jewish youth would speak in their own voice about this experience. As Weinreich declared, "To understand the situation, we must listen to the voice of youth themselves; they alone must tell about their psychological and social problems."[29] Youth would be taken seriously as experts on themselves. It was Weinreich's hope that their personal revelations would illuminate how the psychology of a national group develops in response to the situation of disadvantage. The crisis in Eastern Europe, as he saw it, was an unbridgeable generation gap. The autobiographies would provide a solid research foundation for addressing this crisis.

Seeking the participation of the full range of Jewish youth, announcements for all three contests stressed that education, class, occupation, or political affiliation were of no consequence. "Bad style" or the ordinariness of their lives was no obstacle to winning a prize: "Don't think that only an individual with extraordinary experiences can enter." Submissions would be judged on sincerity, accuracy, and detail: "Don't think that little things are not important." If anything, contestants were warned not to make their autobiographies "more interesting" by making things up or using flowery language; it was better to be candid and direct. As for the length of the submissions, the more the better and not less than twenty-five pages of a notebook.[30] (Very few submissions kept to the minimum length; many were as long as the lengthier autobiographies in this volume and several even longer.)

To encourage the autobiographers to write about intimate details of their lives, YIVO guaranteed them anonymity. The only information the contestants needed to provide was age, gender, and a pseudonym of some kind. The writer's real name and address were to appear only inside a sealed envelope that was to be submitted with the autobiography. That envelope would be opened only after the prizes had been decided so that the awards could be mailed to the winners. Any writer who did not wish to reveal his or her real name under any circumstances was offered the option of providing an address to which a prize could eventually be sent.

While contestants were free to choose what to write about, the guidelines for the first contest encouraged them to address the following topics:

> You and your family, war years, teachers, schools and what they gave you. Boyfriends, girlfriends. Youth organizations, [political] party life, and what they gave you. How you came to your occupation or how you are planning to come to your occupation. What events in your life made the greatest impression on you.[31]

Announcements for the two subsequent contests added several additional guidelines: though writers could arrange their accounts as they wished, chronological order was recommended as the "easiest" approach. Small, but telling, adjustments were made to the list of topics that authors were encouraged to address. The announcement for the second contest added the instruction to reflect on "relationships" among family members and "relationships" among their friends. The specification of "relationships" is a subtle but important indication of what Weinreich had learned at Yale. [32] The announcement for the third contest, issued late in 1938, expressly encouraged the writers to reflect on the challenges they faced in "these difficult days."

Since the contest was a means of gathering personal documents, the announcement for the second contest took advantage of the opportunity to ask for diaries and told contestants that those who submitted diaries increased their chances of winning prizes for their autobiographies. Scholars had debated the relative value of different types of personal documents. Bühler, a psychologist, preferred diaries and biographies, considering autobiographies unreliable because they were personally authored after the fact. Dollard, a sociologist, favored life histories, because a trained researcher could elicit information from his subject that was directly relevant to his research. Biographies and oral histories were also more difficult to collect because they required professional researchers to create them. Autobiographies were the easiest to gather, particularly by means of contests. YIVO collected everything that it could.

The third of YIVO's youth autobiography contests was also the most international of the three. Announcements in many languages went out to Jewish youth throughout Europe, North and South America, Australia, South Africa, and Palestine. The instructions *Yugfor* issued in 1938 stipulated what contestants in the earlier contests had already assumed when they wrote in Yiddish, Polish, Hebrew, Russian, and German—namely, that "each contestant may write in the language most convenient for him."

Submissions for the third contest were due 1 May 1939, and the prizes were to be announced on 1 September of that year. [33] With a sense of mounting crisis, the announcement explained the purpose of the contest more fully:

> We want to become fully aware of the life of the Jewish youth in these difficult days. We want to know what barriers stand before the young man who wants to find his way in the world; what conflicts arise between him and both his immediate and general environment, as well as within himself. We want to know about the people who found it possible to overcome hardships and also about those who have not yet succeeded. When we shall be able to collect this material, we shall be able to learn a great deal, and it is quite possible that from the mistakes and failures of one individual as well as from the successes of another, we shall be able to make deductions for the whole of Jewish youth. [34]

Although contestants were again assured that "a bad literary style, an unpracticed pen are, therefore, no hindrances to participation in this contest and even to winning first prize," they were also admonished against waxing literary. Perhaps because some who entered in the previous contest had not heeded the advice to write in a plain and direct style, the announcement for the third contest stated in no uncertain terms that "YIVO does not propose to discover new writers through the medium of this competition." The tone of the announcement vacillated between patience in explaining the value of "little things"—"actually interesting sociological and psychological conclusions may often be derived just from such details"—to impatience with "general statements about 'hard times' and the 'lost generation.'" Length was encouraged "so that the personality of the writer may become clearer." Psychological insight was prized above all. These personal documents were not intended to provide ethnographic descriptions of daily life per se; they were to reveal the inner life of Jewish youth at a pivotal historical moment and place.

By all accounts, including the hundreds of inquiries and submissions and the enthusiasm expressed in the autobiographies themselves, Jewish youth welcomed the opportunity to pour out their hearts and reflect on their lives. No doubt the prospect of substantial cash prizes and the validation that would come with any prize, even a YIVO publication, as well as the possibility of seeing one's own words in print, intensified their interest.

Hoping that some of the contestants would want to collaborate on *Yugfor* in the future, YIVO sent them copies of Max Weinreich's *Der veg tsu undzer yugnt* (The Way to Our Youth), which the institute had published in 1935. This book drew on the autobiographies submitted to the first two contests and outlined the methodology for YIVO's youth research project. When he began work on *Der veg tsu undzer yugnt* in New Haven in 1933, Weinreich did not plan more than a long essay. It would set out his central theme (the psychology of belonging to a disadvantaged minority) and introduce the "new discipline of culture and personality to the study of East European Jews, and their youth in particular."[35] By the time he finished it in Vilna two years later, this book, as well as YIVO's youth research project, had come to epitomize the institute's commitment to the diaspora nationalist principle of *doikeyt*.

Der veg tsu undzer yugnt offered a psychological analysis of a generation that either assimilated, emigrated, or flocked to political organizations, particularly Zionist ones, in an effort to escape their hopeless circumstances. Difficult as it may be to understand his position today, Weinreich's diagnosis of the situation facing Jewish youth in Poland was psychological immaturity: they were simply running away from their problems. Facing the situation and dealing with it—the essence of *doikeyt*—was the only mature and healthy psychological response. Psychological analysis thus became the site of a displaced political subject, and the work of YIVO became the solution. Every document, demographic datum, photograph, questionnaire, folk song, book, artifact, and autobiography that YIVO added to its collection affirmed Jewish rootedness in Eastern Europe. Every effort to gather these materials, preserve and study them, and disseminate research based on them laid the ground for a Jewish future in Poland. Participation in the work of YIVO was a way of affirming being a Jew in Poland.[36]

It is, sadly, impossible to know what insights the Vilna YIVO would have gained from seeing the *Yugfor* project to its completion. On the very day YIVO planned to announce the winners of the third autobiography contest Germany invaded Poland, starting World War II. Weinreich was then en route to a conference in Brussels; unable to return to Vilna, he traveled to the United States, arriving on 19 March 1940. Immediately he moved YIVO's headquarters to its branch office in New York. During the war, YIVO was liquidated by the German army, which confiscated much of its vast library and archival collections and eventually murdered most of its staff. Some of the institute's most prized holdings were hidden or smuggled out by YIVO employees, often at great personal risk. A large part of YIVO's collections remained in Vilna, where they were seized by Soviet authorities when they took control of the Baltic states after the war;[37] still other materials were lost or destroyed. After the war the New York YIVO managed to reclaim 350 of these 627 autobiographies, along with other material that had been confiscated by the Germans; it is from these that the fifteen texts that appear in this volume were selected. During 1940 Weinreich tried to establish a Jewish youth project in the United States, but without success. Autobiography contests, however, continued to play an important role in YIVO's work. In 1942 YIVO solicited the best American Jewish immigrant autobiography on the theme "Why I Left Europe and What I Have Accomplished in America," and in 1946 the institute ran a contest among Jewish soldiers and veterans for the best essays on the subject "My Experiences and Observations as a Jew in World War II."[38]

As late as 1943 Weinreich stated in YIVO's academic journal, *YIVO-bleter*, that he planned to return to Vilna once the war was over and rebuild a YIVO that would have "two centers," one in New York and the other in Vilna.[39] That was not to be. By 1945 *YIVO-bleter* was mourning the destruction of European Jewry and with it the YIVO in Vilna and so many of those who had once sent it material, including the young participants in the autobiography contests: "In the destruction of our people, YIVO mourns its own disaster. The Jewish community in Eastern Europe, out of whose direct needs YIVO grew, has practically disappeared. There is practically no one left from the thousands of correspondents upon whom YIVO's network across Jewish cities and towns depended. Virtually none of the people who built YIVO by their daily efforts and by giving their heart and soul survive."[40]

THE LITERARY CONTEXT OF THE YIVO AUTOBIOGRAPHIES

In the 1930s, YIVO was primarily interested in these youth autobiographies for the information they could provide social scientists seeking to analyze contemporary, and increasingly urgent, societal problems. The *Yugfor* scholars did not value these texts as literary works—indeed, they discouraged the autobiographers from approaching the task as a creative writing exercise. Today, however, we read these autobiographies with a very different eye. The literary inclinations of their authors are not something we strive to set aside—indeed, this is key to what makes these life histories so compelling to read and to study. Therefore, it is especially important to consider the literary context in which these young writers crafted their autobiographies, for their efforts are as much a product of what their authors read, and how they read, as what they experienced.

Indeed, all of the autobiographies in this volume, however much they differ from one another, are the life histories of *readers*. The experience of

Cover of "A Description of My Life, Written Especially for the YIVO Contest," Vilna, 1932. The illustration's Hebrew inscription, "I was a wanderer on the paths of life," pays homage to Peretz Smolenskin's nineteenth-century *Bildungsroman, Hato'eh bedarkhei ha-ḥayyim* (The Wanderer on the Paths of Life).

reading secular literature occupies a prominent place in these life histories, and the act of reading is frequently depicted as a catalyst in their authors' lives. This is an especially important element of these texts, given that the genre of autobiography itself can be understood as the rereading of personal experience through the prism of fiction. The initiation into modern secular literature gave rise, in no small part, to the autobiographical impulse among European Jews. As scholars have frequently noted, there is almost no Jewish autobiographical literature prior to this encounter with European belles lettres.[41]

The notion of telling one's personal history through the narrative idioms of fiction, especially the novel, appears in Western literature as early as Rousseau.[42] Among East European Jews the impact of this kind of literature came relatively late, in comparison to their fellow Europeans. As a consequence, East European Jewry experienced centuries of Western European literary development within the span of a few generations, and it is only in the 1860s that rudimentary equivalents of the novel began to appear in Hebrew and Yiddish.[43] These were the work of a numerically insignificant, extremely marginalized avant-garde of aesthetic and ethical reformers known as *maskilim*, proponents of the *Haskalah*, or Jewish Enlightenment movement.

Maskilim and their ideological offspring thus encountered the treasury of Western literary tradition simultaneously, as one encounters works of fine art from the ancient to modern periods in a museum. In Hebrew and Yiddish periodicals of the second half of the nineteenth century, for example, it is not unusual to find within one volume translations of the Greek and Roman classics, of Nietzsche and Byron, discussions of Maeterlinck, Bergson, Goethe, Tolstoy, and so on. Or consider how the pioneering Yiddish and Hebrew modernist Y.L. Peretz recalls, in his memoirs, his introduction to the realm of Western literature as an adolescent: "The books had been shelved at random, with novels, scientific works, and serial romances all mixed up and scattered, especially the translations from the French— Alexandre Dumas, Eugene Sue, Victor Hugo, and so on. . . . Soon after, I came across the Napoleonic Code in Zanyavsky's translation. . . . I was amazed! Here were principles of law without the Talmud's ubiquitous Reuben and Simon!"[44] Continuing with Buckle's *History of Civilization in England* and works by the philosopher Edward von Hartmann and the biologist Carl Vogt, Peretz describes his experience during the mid-1860s. But this account could well have been taken from one of the YIVO autobiographers, writing seven decades later; it was as if many Jewish youth in the interwar period recapitulated the experience of the early pioneers of the Eastern European *Haskalah*. Consider, for example, the testimony of one autobiographer from the 1934 contest, a twenty-one-year-old male of hasidic background, who recalls his introduction to the world of literature, at the age of fifteen, in Bresler's library in Warsaw:[45]

> At the time I knew as much about literature as a Cossack knows how to recite the Psalms in Hebrew. The first works I read were by Mendele Mokher Seforim, Sholem Aleichem, and Linetski. . . . From day to day I became, so to speak, newly born. . . . Lermontov, Pushkin, Yesenin, Tagore, Baudelaire, Rainer Maria Rilke, Heinrich Heine—these writers showed me a bright, new world. . . . Then I started reading proletarian literature, all in Yiddish: Reisen, Rosenfeld, Vinchevsky, Leivik, Schwarzman, Broderzon, Mani-Leyb . . . , Hofstein, Kharik, Fefer, Kvitko, Markish, Bergelson. . . .[46]

And as his autobiography becomes, in effect, an inventory of his avid reading, the young author's list continues with works by Gorki, France, Barbusse, Tolstoy, Rolland, Shakespeare, Schopenhauer, Weininger, as well as others.

The centrality of the act of reading for this generation of East European Jews, as evinced in the YIVO autobiographies, is corroborated by statistics compiled by sociologist Moshe Kligsberg. After fleeing his native Poland, Kligsberg became a research associate at YIVO in New York in 1941. There he conducted the first postwar analysis of these youth autobiographies and published articles on them in English and Yiddish. Drawing on Polish population surveys of 1921 and 1931, Kligsberg estimates that there were some 450,000 Jews between the ages of fourteen to twenty during the interwar years. A member of this generation himself, he provides the following testimony:

> On the basis of many years of direct observation I can posit that at least two-thirds of us read books. On average we read one book a week (usually on a day off, Saturday or Sunday, the book was exchanged for another). There were, of course, some who read little, but to compensate for this, there were many more who devoured books, several a week or even on a daily basis. Thus, in the course of a year, Jewish youth in Poland read fifteen million books in their entirety—that is, every library was, on average, read through in the course of fifteen years.[47]

In these autobiographies, the act of reading almost invariably correlates with a marked turn toward introspection, a development associated with the discovery of a language with which to depict the inner self. It is thus no coincidence that these adolescents' initiation into literature was often accompanied by the decision to write a journal. The YIVO auto-biographies reveal a generation of diarists, and this regardless of gender—the private journal being a disproportionately female phenomenon in other cultures.[48] Indeed, so many diaries were submitted along with autobio-graphies in the 1932 and 1934 competitions that Max Weinreich addressed the special methodological issues raised by youth diaries in *Der veg tsu undzer yugnt.*[49]

The YIVO autobiographers offer most eloquent testimony with respect to the relationship between literature and self-awareness. "Esther," for example, who was born into a strict hasidic household, had to conspire with her mother to register for the library at the Polish school she attended, in defiance of her father's wishes. She writes of her experience:

> I devoted myself to reading with a passion. Within the red and blue covers of the library's books I found an enchanted world, filled with regal characters involved in wondrous tales that completely captivated my young mind. I read in secret, so as to escape my father's notice. It hurt me that he would not allow me to read. . . . And the more I read, the more I kept my thoughts a secret. . . . I became a world unto myself.

Esther's father was perhaps not altogether misguided in his extreme mis-givings concerning the books his daughter read—which included the lives of Christian martyrs, with whom she felt a degree of affinity—and the marked alteration in her behavior as a result of her reading. In a more stable cultural setting, the transmission of books from one generation to another often serves to consolidate the family unit and to establish connections between the family and the wider community. But it is clear from the testimony of Esther and many other YIVO autobiographers that for this generation reading performed precisely the opposite function. As she writes further on in her autobiography, Esther finds a surrogate mother in nature, a surrogate friend and confidante in her diary, and her links with family and community are increasingly attenuated as she becomes ever more absorbed in books.

This process is corroborated by the testimony of the autobiographer we know as "A. Greyno," a twenty-three-year-old member of the urban working class. His early youth is characterized by bouts of juvenile delinquency on the streets alternating with backbreaking work at the sewing machine in his parents' home, which doubled as their workshop:

> After working several weeks in a row without a break until bedtime, I managed to convince my mother to give me money to become a member

of the town's Tarbut library. I would sit up until very late at night by the oil-lamp, immersed in completely different, new worlds, unaware of the hours flying by, until I went to bed with a loving kiss to the pages of my book. I felt as if I had acquired a fresh, brand-new skin, and, without feeling any physical fatigue, I fell asleep with a smile of intellectual satisfaction on my face. . . . One by one, I broke with all of my friends. They seemed to me to be too common and ignorant. My life began to become monotonous. After a day of work at the sewing machine, I would slip quietly, like a shadow, into the library with a book tucked inside my jacket, then I'd read and read almost the entire night.

Peretz terms the library described in his memoirs as "'their' *beys-medresh*"—that is, it served young rebels such as himself as the secular equivalent of the traditional Jewish study-house.[50] In the YIVO autobiographies the library similarly emerges as a cultural institution of central importance. Many of the local headquarters of the various political youth movements made it a high priority to establish their own libraries of books in Yiddish, Hebrew, and Polish. Noting that few young Jews could afford to buy books of their own, Kligsberg characterizes these libraries as being among the most important communal institutions for Jewish youth living in small towns. He cites one YIVO autobiography contestant from Ostryna, a town with a community of about 1,000 Jews in the 1930s: "There are several people in our town, whose formal education consisted of little more than the *kheyder*, and yet they are quite cultivated and enlightened, all thanks to the library. . . . Here is their university, here is their inexhaustible source of knowledge. *The library has a holding of two thousand volumes.*"[51]

Indeed, it is clear from many of the YIVO autobiographies that the initial appeal of youth movements was often not so much ideological as it was motivated by a hunger for culture, especially for literature.[52] The youth movements' libraries not only supplied readers with books but served as sites of communal interaction. Here young people met friends and comrades, discussed what they were reading, worked together on political projects, wrote for organizational publications, and prepared literary evenings and amateur theatricals.[53]

Among the new modes of behavior associated with youth movements, Kligsberg highlights the significance of walking, either in small groups or in pairs. These walks were also of a decisively literary character, combining a heightened appreciation of nature with the discussion of literature. As described in several autobiographies in this volume, such walks manifest the belated romanticism characteristic of this generation of young Jews. But whereas Rousseau and Goethe's Werther, their literary role models, were

Cover of "My Biography," by N. Drori, 1934.

solitary walkers, walking provided these generally more sociable Jewish romantics with a shared intimacy: "Books were an especially beloved topic on these walks," Kligsberg notes. "For around such topics more open expression was given to personal, intimate moments, since every individual had his favorite literary heroes, with whom he would identify."[54]

Kligsberg thus suggests a direct connection between the reading and discussing of literature, of whatever genre, and the dawning of individualistic self-awareness through identification with literary "heroes." Moreover, this identification fostered the capacity to voice aspects of the inner life that, without the mediation of literature, would not and could not have come to light. In other words, the library and the political organization played no small role in teaching Jewish youth to think, speak, and write *autobiographically*.[55] Indeed, YIVO's records indicate that, following announcements of its autobiography competitions, several youth movements held discussions on the topic of "how to write one's life story." Given the intense intellectual atmosphere of these institutions and the consuming desire of Jewish youth in this period for self-actualization—or, as Kligsberg puts it, for "the consciousness that *you were something in and of yourself* (something, that is, that stood out from the collective)"[56] —such discussions were likely to have been fairly widespread and passionate.

Another striking feature that emerges from these autobiographies is the high proportion of these young Jews whose reading leads directly to writing.[57] An extraordinarily large number of the YIVO autobiographers mentioned (and sometimes submitted) personal journals and offered accounts of their first experiments in poetry and prose. Many incorporated examples of their youthful literary efforts within their autobiographies (see, for example, the life history in this volume by the author we know as "EM.TEPA"). The autobiography by twenty-year-old Ludwik Stöckel included an appendix of forty-two pages of poems and other annotations that were indexed to his lengthy life history. "Esther" reports that by the age of nineteen she had already written two novels, numerous poems, and a play that she staged on her own. Or consider the example of "J. Harefuler," nicknamed "Jakub the Poet" by his comrades, who describes writing his first poem—an introspective work inspired, perhaps, by the profound impression made on him by reading *Robinson Crusoe*:[58]

All these ideas, linked by my feelings and my vivid imagination, became literary material. The first poem I wrote during this period was inspired by my sad fate as a recluse. In this poem I depicted a young man alone on the open sea. . . . In the endless sea, I depicted life, and in the young man, myself. I gave it the title "Alone among the Waves."

The degree to which these young autobiographers internalized literary models and then held them up as a mirror—however much it offered an altered image of the self—is illustrated with remarkable emotional nuance in the autobiography of a seventeen-year-old who signs her text "Hanzi." The all-but-abandoned daughter of a pious mother and a heretical, unfaithful father, she goes about hungry, unwashed, dressed in filthy rags. Practically blind in one eye, she also suffers from a chronic skin disease and a crippling leg infection. Reading—whether chapters of the Bible or the latest works of Hebrew literature—emerges repeatedly as her most constant source of comfort and inspiration, eventually becoming a powerfully self-reflective act:

> In my reading I lingered increasingly over the descriptions of the heroes. The authors would describe the details of their external appearance and, in particular, their eyes, which were so expressive. Their eyes, their eyes! What were their eyes to them or to me? At such moments I felt a terrible contempt for myself and for everything around me, and in the mirror I saw my misfortune—ah!

This internalization of literary experience can even be inferred from those autobiographers who go out of their way to stress the *non*-literary nature of their life histories. Eighteen-year-old "Eter" begins her autobiography by stating: "Although what I am writing is not in the least like a novel, I will start with a prologue." And she concludes her life history with a highly literary epilogue: "All day long the same thought pounds inside my head. . . . Many times a day, I recite to myself Julian Tuwim's poem 'If Only . . .' I call it 'Hope'"—and she cites the poem in its entirety.

If one book spoke more directly than any other to the minds and hearts of the YIVO autobiographers it was *Jean Christophe*, French novelist Romain Rolland's monumental *Bildungsroman*, published between 1904 and 1912 (a book, it should be noted, that teems with Jewish motifs and characters, from Biblical figures to Dreyfusards). No other literary work is mentioned with greater frequency in these autobiographies. For many of these young men and women, reading *Jean Christophe* constituted a revelation.[59] Paeans to the novel and to Rolland appear frequently, such as the following, written in 1934 by a twenty-year-old living in Łódź at the conclusion of his autobiography: "I read the ten volumes; it took me three whole months. Finally I looked at the last pages and thought: 'Is this already the end?' Let us honor and respect people who have great hearts! I feel like shouting, 'Long live Romain Rolland!'" Another autobiographer, "J. Harefuler," even follows Rolland in titling a section of his account "Youth."

Employing such obviously literary models for the recasting of one's life history into narrative might be seen as compromising the veracity of these documents. Indeed, YIVO warned contestants against "tell[ing] fairy tales."[60] Such suspicion even appears to have crossed the minds of some of the autobiographers themselves. A similar equivocation may be discerned in the aforementioned twenty-year-old autobiographer's discussion of *Jean Christophe*: "Romain Rolland is faithful to reality. But to what extent is his reality ours? Ours is ugly and rotten. . . ."[61] Clearly, it would have been difficult *not* to perceive the glaring disparity between the world of which Rolland writes and the reality of impoverishment and persecution that pervaded Jewish life in interwar Poland. Yet it was precisely the consciousness of this disparity, gleaned through reading, that served this autobiographer as a catalyst for subjecting the self to scrutiny. These documents cast into cruel relief the painful contrast between the high cultural aspirations of the majority of the contestants and the degradation of their material existence. Indeed, the autobiographers vent their most ardent protests against the incompatibility of literature and life—doing so, of necessity, in literary rhetoric. For example, this highly stylized and "poetic" plaint by the young woman known to us as "Forget-me-not":

> What does life mean? Can I use this beautiful word to describe the hard and thorny road that I've traveled? Why is my life a long chain of suffering and struggle, an endless struggle to survive? For the first time I asked: Where is my home, my childhood, my youth, about which poets write so much?

Remarkably, Weinreich insisted that "with respect to the *great majority* of participants in our competition, the assertion is surely correct: The material that they sent is for them absolutely not literature, but *life*."[62] Weinreich sought "scientific" approaches to the study of Jewish youth through their autobiographies and other personal writings, working with the prevailing scholarly assumption that "artistic truth" and "scientific truth" are inherently incompatible. Given that he himself was an accomplished literary scholar,[63] the almost total absence of literary considerations in *Der veg tsu undzer yugnt* is all the more surprising. Indeed, when Weinreich does address the literary character of these documents his tone is defensive, even apologetic:

> [T]here is also a group of participants with *writerly* ambitions. The word "ambitions" should by no means be construed as pejorative. . . . There is a school of thought that maintains that autobiographers who have literary inclinations import specific defects into their documents. . . . Be

that as it may, we must emphasize that these "young lions," literary prodigies, constitute an extreme minority among the writers of the autobiographies in the YIVO collections.[64]

In his discussion of "'Lies' in an Autobiography," Weinreich praises the social scientific value of the autobiography of "Vladek," published by Thomas and Znaniecki in *The Polish Peasant in Europe and America*, precisely because the author's limited education spared him from "excessive 'waxing literary.'" Weinreich calls attention to the problems this tendency poses for scholars analyzing autobiographies:

> The metaphor and image take pride of place, thus eclipsing the content of what is depicted. What is worse, these metaphors and images are not infrequently *borrowed*, adopted ready-made; these writers confirm the maxim of Henryk Sienkiewicz, that on occasion it is not the head that guides the pen, but the pen that guides the head.[65]

But how can one conceive of any form of written document, autobiographical or otherwise, that does not "borrow" from a shared discourse of metaphors, analogies, images, and so on? Importing literary models, apparent to a greater or lesser degree in all of the YIVO autobiographies, was essential not only for writing these documents, but for the sense of self that existed prior to taking the pen in hand. As Philippe Lejeune observes, "The autobiographer could not realize himself other than by imitating people who imagined what it was like to be an autobiographer."[66]

In addition to their often copious reading and youthful literary endeavors, there were, of course, other influences at work on the personal narratives that YIVO's young autobiographers fashioned during the 1930s. Following the institute's suggestion that they organize their texts chronologically, many begin with their own earliest memories. Others, however, start with stories about their birth and infancy that are clearly the product of family lore rather than personal recollection. And, despite YIVO's admonition that "the contest requires an autobiography, not an editorial," some authors occasionally lapse into diatribes that reflect their political indoctrination. While Weinreich and his colleagues in Vilna might well have seen these, too, as problematic "borrowings," they provide the reader of these deeply personal texts with an unrivaled glimpse into the full range of influences—literary, pedagogical, psychological, political, experiential—that forged these adolescents' emerging sense of self.

Indeed, we approach these autobiographies today quite differently than did their original audience of YIVO scholars. They sought to strengthen the future of Polish Jewry; we are interested in understanding its recent past. Their scholarly agenda was shaped by social science disciplines, especially psychology and sociology; our approach also includes the interests of historians, literary scholars, and folklorists. Our approach to these auto-biographies is also distinguished by the fact that their authors were among the very first to write about their generation. Their life histories have since joined an extensive corpus of literary works, histories, and communal and personal testimonies about East European Jewish life before World War II. During the final decades of the twentieth century, personal documents of this generation attained an unprecedented prominence, as Holocaust survivors began to offer public testimonies of their prewar and wartime experiences. In fact, many Holocaust survivors alive today could have entered YIVO's contests. But it is hard to imagine how their experiences as adolescents in the 1930s could ever be recaptured now, so overshadowed are those years by the tragedy of the Holocaust. Through these autobiographies, we can discover the wide range of young Jews' experience in that fervid time and place as described in their own words, as they were coming of age. In ways unforeseen by these young authors and the scholars who encouraged them to write, we glimpse an exceptional generation as they arrive at the threshold of adulthood. Most would not live to cross that threshold, and those who survived the Holocaust went on to lead lives markedly different from their prewar existence. In this sense, these adolescents and their per-sonal histories epitomize Jewish life in Poland's interwar period in its sudden newness and its great anxieties as well as its great hopes.

Notes

1 Announcement for YIVO autobiography contest, flier: English version [Vilna, 1938], unpaginated.
2 On Jewish life in interwar Poland, see Hirsz Abramowicz, *Profiles of a Lost World: Memoirs of East European Jewish Life before World War II*, trans. Eva Zeitlin Dobkin (Detroit: Wayne State University Press, 1999); Lucy S. Dawidowicz, *The Golden Tradition: Jewish Life and Thought in Eastern Europe* (New York: Schocken, 1984); Lucjan Dobroszycki and Barbara Kirshenblatt-Gimblett, *Image before My Eyes: A Photographic History of Jewish Life in Poland before the Holocaust* (New York: Schocken, 1994); Joshua A. Fishman, ed., *Studies of Polish Jewry 1919–1939: The Interplay of Social, Economic and Political Factors in the Struggle of a Minority for Its Existence* [Yiddish and English] (New York: YIVO, 1974); Celia Stopnicka Heller, *On the Edge of Destruction: Jews of Poland between the Two World Wars* (Detroit: Wayne State University Press, 1994); Jack Kugelmass and Jonathan Boyarin, eds., *From a Ruined Garden: The Memorial Books of Polish Jewry* (New York:

Schocken, 1983); Ezra Mendelsohn, *The Jews of East Central Europe between the World Wars* (Bloomington: Indiana University Press, 1983).

3 The tension between objective description and retroactive romanticization is itself a centuries-old phenomenon in the historiography of Polish Jewry. In the late seventeenth century, Nathan Hannover, the most important Jewish chronicler of the devastation wreaked on Polish Jews during the Chmielnicki Uprising of 1648, added an appendix to his account that lionized the purity and righteousness of the communities that were destroyed. Similarly, after extensive destruction of East European Jewish life and culture during World War I, the Russian and Ukrainian civil wars, and the Soviet-Polish War, fiction writers, memoirists, and sermonizers immortalized the *shtetl* (i.e., the East European small town where the majority of Polish Jews once lived) as "a world that is no more." These literary re-creations, however stylistically brilliant and psychologically compelling, are extremely problematic in terms of historical accuracy, and their influence on the "collective memory" of East European Jewry has been extensive. For a further discussion of the *shtetl* as a subject of Jewish literature, see the introduction to Ruth R. Wisse, ed., *A Shtetl and Other Yiddish Novellas* (New York: Behrman House, 1983). For a related analysis of the *shtetl* as a paradigm in a landmark work of post-World War II American anthropology on East European Jewry, see Barbara Kirshenblatt-Gimblett's introduction to Mark Zborowski and Elizabeth Herzog, *Life Is with People: The Culture of the Shtetl* (New York: Schocken, 1995 [1952]).

4 A concise history of YIVO appears in *Guide to the YIVO Archives*, eds. Fruma Mohrer and Marek Web (Armonk, N.Y.: M.E. Sharpe, 1998), pp. xi–xxi; a lively description of the Vilna YIVO during the year before the start of World War II appears in Lucy S. Dawidowicz, *From That Place and Time: A Memoir, 1938–1947* (New York: W.W. Norton, 1989); see pp. 77–100. On diaspora nationalism, see Ezra Mendelsohn, *On Modern Jewish Politics* (New York: Oxford University Press, 1993), pp. 18–19.

5 The only groups that do not seem to be represented in the contests are the most highly polonized of Polish Jews—who had ceased to regard themselves as Jews in any meaningful way, and therefore would have little, if any, reason to contribute to a Jewish autobiography contest—and, on the other extreme, those yeshiva students who would have considered the very act of participating in such a contest to be heretical.

6 YIVO Archives, Record Group 4, Autobiography 3770, p. 1; translator: Daniel Soyer.

7 It should be noted, though, that descriptions of poverty and child abuse are a mainstay of *Haskalah* fiction and memoir. This similarity might reflect a parallel sense of social and cultural self-consciousness on the part of young writers during periods of cultural upheaval, or it might indicate that the writers of the YIVO autobiographies were addressing in their own life histories issues raised in works they were reading by Jewish writers of a previous generation.

8 Maks Vaynraykh, *Der veg tsu undzer yugnt: yesoydes, metodn, problemen fun yidisher yugnt-forshung* [*The Way to Our Youth: Foundations, Methods, and Problems of Jewish Youth Research*] (Vilna: YIVO, 1935), p. 12.

9 See Philip Lee Utley, *Siegfried Bernfeld: Left-wing Youth Leader, Psychoanalyst, and Zionist, 1910–April, 1918*, Ph.D. dissertation, University of Wisconsin-Madison, 1975. Utley notes (p. 5) that the German term *Jugend* corresponds neither to "youth" nor to "adolescence," but rather to a broader period, from the ages of fourteen to twenty-one.

10 See Peter Dudek, *Jugend als Objekt der Wissenschaften: Geschichte der Jugendforschung in Deutschland und Osterreich* (Opladen: Westdeutscher Verlag, 1990).

11 "YIVO's Youth Research (*Yugfor*)" [Yiddish], *Yedies fun YIVO* 4–5 (45–46), April–May 1934, pp. 1–3.

12 On Weinreich's studies with Sapir, see Barbara Kirshenblatt-Gimblett, "Coming of Age in the Thirties: Max Weinreich, Edward Sapir, and Jewish Social Science," *YIVO Annual* 23 (1996): pp. 1–104.

13 See Siegfried Bernfeld, "Types of Adolescence," *The Psychoanalytic Quarterly* 7 (1938): pp. 243–53.

14 A follower of Gustav Wyneken, Bernfeld had been active in German Jewish youth movements and shared with Wyneken the utopian view that youth was not just a transition or developmental stage, but a distinctive formation. See Siegfried Bernfeld, "Ein Institut für Psychologie und Soziologie der Jugend. (Archiv für Jugendkultur). Entwurf zu einem Programm," *Annalen der Natur- und Kulturphilosophie* 13, Wilhelm Ostwald and Rudolf Goldscheid, eds. (Leipzig: Verlag Unesma G.M.B.H., 1917): pp. 217–51. See also Siegfried Bernfeld, *Das jüdische Volk und sein Jugend* (Berlin, Vienna, Leipzig: R. Loewit Verlag, 1919).

15 By the time Weinreich met with him in Vienna in 1934, Bernfeld was no longer working on Jewish youth research and agreed to turn his archives over to YIVO. Two years later Weinreich began publishing his Yiddish translation of Freud's *Vorlesungen zur Einführung in die Psychoanalyse* (*Araynfir in psikhoanaliz*, published by YIVO in three parts in 1936, 1937, 1938; this was about half of what Weinreich projected to translate and publish of Freud's work). Freud accepted Weinreich's invitation to join YIVO's *kuratorium* (honorary board of trustees) in 1930.

16 This was easier said than done, given the differences in American and European disciplinary formations. The interdisciplinary social science that Weinreich had encountered in the United States, which depended heavily on American anthropology, could not be transferred wholesale to Europe, just as *Jugendforschung* had no precise analog in the United States, Stanley Hall's child study movement notwithstanding. See G. Stanley Hall, *Adolescence and Its Psychology and Its Relations to Physiology, Anthropology, Sociology, Sex, Crime, Religion and Education*, 2 vols. (New York: D. Appleton, 1904.) Though Hall, who was trained in experimental psychology, was sympathetic to psychoanalysis, his evolutionary views (ontology recapitulates phylogeny) and biological determinism stood in sharp contrast to Weinreich's approach.

17 "An Appeal to the Jews of America" from the Friends of the Yiddish Scientific Institute [1930]. YIVO Archives, Record Group 100, Sapir/Weinreich correspondence, YIVO New York, series: Amopteyl (American Branch).

18 "It [YIVO] is making researches into the peculiarities of the psyche of the Jewish child" ("An Appeal to the Jews of America" from the Friends of the Yiddish Scientific Institute [1930]). Also, "development of the Jewish child" is identified as a research topic in Nahum Shtif et al., *Di organizatsye fun der yidisher visnshaft* [*The Organization of Jewish Research*] (Vilna: Tsentraler Bildungs Komitet / Vilner Bildungs Gezelshaft, 1925), p. 39.

19 For an announcement of this contest, see *Yedies fun YIVO* 3 (38), May 1932, n.p. *Yedies fun YIVO* 2 (41), March 1933, p. 7, reports thirty-four entrants. Elsewhere, thirty-five are reported.

20 In addition to Poland, which provided the great majority of entries, YIVO received autobiographies from Austria (nine entries), Latvia (eight), Palestine (seven), Romania (six), Germany (four), Czechoslovakia (three), and one each from Hungary, France, Syria, United States, and South America.

21 YIVO Archives, Record Group 4, folder 3887, document no. 151019.

22 YIVO attempted to reach as many Jewish communities as possible through its own network of Friends of YIVO, including Jews in Lithuania, Latvia, and Estonia; Finland, Sweden, and Denmark; France, England, and Switzerland; Romania, Czechoslovakia,

Yugoslavia, and Bulgaria; United States and Canada; Argentina, Peru, Chile, and Mexico; Australia and South Africa; and Palestine. The call for submissions went out in several languages, and YIVO requested that the announcement be translated into other languages.

23 "Ershter proyekt far a gliderung fun der yugnt-forshung" (YIVO Archives, Record Group 4, folder 3880, document no. 150751) indicates that the researchers supplemented a selection of about six autobiographies by talking with the authors, their parents, friends, and others, as well as by family correspondence. The researchers also collected magazines, literature, letters, poetry, and diaries, including diaries that were specially commissioned.

24 Eileen Markley Znaniecka, "Current Sociology in Poland," *American Sociological Review* 2, no. 1–6 (1937): p. 422.

25 Eileen Markley Znaniecka, "Eastern European Sociology: A Polish Sociology," in *Twentieth Century Sociology*, George Gurvitch and Wilbert Ellis Moore, eds. (New York: Philosophical Library, 1945), pp. 703–17.

26 William I. Thomas and Florian Znaniecki, *The Polish Peasant in Europe and America* (New York: Knopf, 1927), vol. 2, p. 1831.

27 Ibid., vol. 2, p. 1832.

28 Max Weinreich, "Culture and Personality among the Eastern Jews and Their Relation to the General Problems of Social Science" [proposal: typescript], May 1933, document no. 171A, p. 5.

29 "Yugtforshung (yugfor) fun Yivo," *Yedies fun YIVO* 1–3 (42–44), January–March 1934, p. 5.

30 Announcement for YIVO autobiography contest, flier: English version [Vilna, 1938], unpaginated.

31 Ibid.

32 "Competition for the Best Autobiography of a Jewish Youth" [Yiddish], *Yedies fun YIVO* 1–3 (42–44), January–March 1934, p. 6.

33 YIVO continued to receive submissions to the last youth autobiography contest as late as March 1940; see [list kept by Khana Pitchatcher-Man], YIVO Archives, Record Group 4, folder 3879, document no. 150741.

34 Announcement for YIVO autobiography contest, flier: English version [Vilna, 1938], unpaginated.

35 Vaynraykh, *Der veg tsu undzer yugnt*, pp. 19–21; on the discussion of the volume's central theme, see p. 192. Although no definitive study of the autobiographies ever appeared, sociologist Moshe (Moses) Kligsberg provided content analyses in several studies: Moses Kligsberg, "Socio-psychological Problems Reflected in the YIVO Autobiography Contests," *YIVO Annual of Jewish Social Science* 1 (1946): pp. 242–59; Moses Kligsberg, "Child and Adolescent Behavior under Stress: An Analytical Guide to a Collection of Autobiographies of Jewish Young Men and Women in Poland (1932–1939) . . ." [report] (New York: YIVO, 1965); Moshe Kligsberg, "The Jewish Youth Movement in Interwar Poland: (A Sociological Study)" [Yiddish], in *Studies of Polish Jewry 1919–1939*, ed. Joshua A. Fishman (New York: YIVO, 1974), pp. 137–228. Kligsberg's earliest work on the autobiographies appears to be two reports prepared for Max Weinreich, dated 1940; see YIVO Archives, Record Group 4, folder 3876 alef, document no. 150663 alef.

36 Weinreich acknowledged in 1934 that "Never was the situation of youth as complicated as it is today." The following year, in *Der veg tsu undzer yugnt*, he mentions how Jews in Germany, Austria, and Hungary, among other places, were losing their jobs because of

Hitler's Aryan policies. Unemployed youth were prime candidates for revolutionary movements and emigration.

37 Materials related to the YIVO youth autobiography contests recently recovered from Vilna and sent to YIVO's headquarters in New York include contest correspondence, some thirty-nine additional complete autobiographies, as well as interviews, diaries, fragments of autobiographies and other related items. On the history of YIVO's collections during and after World War II, see David E. Fishman, "Embers Plucked from the Fire: The Rescue of Jewish Cultural Treasures in Vilna" [pamphlet] (New York: YIVO, 1996).

38 See Daniel Soyer, "Documenting Immigrant Lives at an Immigrant Institution: Yivo's Autobiography Contest of 1942," *Jewish Social Studies* 5, no. 3 (spring/summer 1999): pp. 218–43. An extended selection from one of these autobiographies, written by Israel Pressman, appears in English translation as "Roads That Passed: Russia, My Old Home," *YIVO Annual* 22 (1995): pp. 1–80.

39 Maks Vaynraykh, "YIVO during a year of destruction" [Yiddish], *YIVO-bleter* 21, no. 1 (January–February 1942): p. 98.

40 "In memoriam" [Yiddish], *YIVO-bleter* 26 (July–December 1945): p. 3.

41 See Marcus Moseley, *Jewish Autobiography in Eastern Europe*, Ph.D. dissertation, Oxford University, 1990, esp. pp. 49–84.

42 See Philippe Lejeune, *L'autobiographie en France* (Paris: A. Colin, 1971), pp. 63–66.

43 On the emergence of modern Yiddish and Hebrew novels in mid-nineteenth-century Eastern Europe, see Dan Miron, *A Traveler Disguised: The Rise of Modern Yiddish Fiction in the Nineteenth Century* (New York: Schocken, 1973); Israel Ginzburg, *A History of Jewish Literature: Haskalah at Its Zenith*, trans. Bernard Martin (Cincinnati: Hebrew Union College Press/New York: KTAV, 1978); Israel Ginzburg, *A History of Jewish Literature: The Haskalah Movement in Russia*, trans. Bernard Martin (Cincinnati: Hebrew Union College Press/New York: KTAV, 1978).

44 *The I.L. Peretz Reader*, ed. Ruth Wisse (New York: Schocken, 1990), pp. 344–45.

45 The same Bresler's library, located on Nowolipki Street, was to provide the Yiddish writers Israel Joshua Singer and Isaac Bashevis Singer, two brothers of similar background to the author of this autobiography, with their first acquaintance with secular literature. See Isaac Bashevis Singer, *Love and Exile* (Garden City, N.Y.: Doubleday, 1984), pp. 26–29.

46 YIVO Archives, Record Group 4, Autobiography 3752, pp. 10–13, passim; translator: Elinor Robinson.

47 Kligsberg, "The Jewish Youth Movement in Interwar Poland," p. 169. According to Kligsberg, the largest category of books read was belletristic.

48 See Philippe Lejeune, *Le moi des demoiselles: enquête sur le journal de jeune fille* (Paris: Editions du Seuil, 1993), passim.

49 See Vaynraykh, *Der veg tsu undzer yugnt*, pp. 149–61.

50 *The I.L. Peretz Reader*, p. 343.

51 Kligsberg, "The Jewish Youth Movement in Interwar Poland," p. 165. Emphasis in original.

52 Compare Ezra Mendelsohn's appraisal of the YIVO autobiographies in his *Zionism in Poland: The Formative Years, 1915–1926* (New Haven and London: Yale University Press, 1981), pp. 338–44.

53 See Kligsberg, "The Jewish Youth Movement in Interwar Poland," p. 174.

54 Ibid., p. 175.

55 One could argue that in this regard these institutions performed a function somewhat akin to the contemporary "autobiographical workshop." See Philippe Lejeune, "Teaching People to Write their own Life Story," in his *On Autobiography*, ed. Paul John Eakin, trans. Katherine Leary (Minneapolis: University of Minnesota Press, 1989), pp. 216–32.

56 Kligsberg, "The Jewish Youth Movement in Interwar Poland," p. 174.

57 See ibid., p. 171.

58 On the role of *Robinson Crusoe* in fostering autobiographical consciousness, see Ian Watt, *The Rise of the Novel: Studies in Defoe, Richardson, and Fielding* (Berkeley: University of California Press, 1957), pp. 89–92.

59 The universal appeal of *Jean Christophe* for adolescents of this generation is attested to by none other than Jean-Paul Sartre, who recalls the intoxicating effect the novel had upon him as a twenty-year-old. See Sartre, *The War Diaries (November 1939/March 1940)*, trans. Quintin Hoare (New York: Pantheon, 1984), p. 73.

60 Announcement for YIVO autobiography contest, flier: English version [Vilna, 1938], unpaginated.

61 YIVO Archives, Record Group 4, Autobiography 3701, pp. 44–45; translator: Elinor Robinson.

62 Vaynraykh, *Der veg tsu undzer yugnt*, p. 140, emphasis in original.

63 See, for example, Maks Vaynraykh, *Bilder fun der yidisher literaturgeshikhte fun di onheybn biz Mendele Moykher-sforim* [Moments from the History of Yiddish Literature from its Beginnings to Mendele Mokher Seforim] (Vilna: Tomer Press, 1928).

64 Vaynraykh, *Der veg tsu undzer yugnt*, pp. 140–42, emphasis in original. Note that, in contrast to much of American culture, "ambition" and "ambitious" were, until very recently, highly pejorative terms in European high culture.

65 Vaynraykh, *Der veg tsu undzer yugnt*, p. 145. Weinreich's equivocations concerning the literary aspect of these documents is evinced in his own Yiddish coinage of the term *literatureven*, "to wax literary." In his usage, the term carries a somewhat pejorative accent.

66 Lejeune, *L'autobiographie en France*, p. 47. The YIVO autobiographies are by no means the sole example of this close interdependency of life and literature in autobiographical writing. Consider, for instance, the personal history of Richard Wright, another member of a disadvantaged minority writing in the middle decades of the twentieth century, who describes the effort to compose his autobiography as an effort "to try to build a bridge of words between me and that world outside, that world that was so distant and elusive that it seemed unreal. I would hurl words into the darkness and wait for an echo, and if an echo sounded, no matter how faintly, I would send other words to march, to fight, to create a sense of the hunger for life that gnaws in us all, to keep alive in our hearts a sense of the inexpressibly human." (*Black Boy [American Hunger]*, [New York: Harper Perennial, 1993], p. 452.)

EDITOR'S NOTE

The fifteen autobiographies translated for this volume were selected from among some 300 entries written by Polish Jews for YIVO's youth auto-biography contests of 1932, 1934, and 1939, which are currently housed in the YIVO Archives in New York. (Although the 1934 and 1939 contests were international in scope, the great majority of entrants to all three contests were from Poland.) While this selection presents authors from a consid-erable range of backgrounds, experiences, and ideological convictions, offering a representative sampling of these categories has not been the primary goal of its compilers. Rather, the foremost concern has been to provide autobiographies that make for compelling reading.

In translating these texts from Yiddish, Polish, and Hebrew into English, our goal has been to offer renderings that convey the authors' different styles, which reflect their various personalities, levels of education, and writing talents. All texts are translated in full, with minor exceptions; in a few instances, a word, phrase, or sentence has been omitted due to prob-lems in clarity. Occasional factual errors (e.g., the correct title of a person-ality or literary work) have been corrected in the text without comment. Occasional glosses or other information are inserted in the text in square brackets.

Names of political leaders, professional writers, and other well-known figures are given according to authoritative spellings. Jewish names usually written in Yiddish or Hebrew are generally romanized according to spellings used in the *Encyclopedia Judaica*. Personal names of friends, family, and acquaintances appearing in those autobiographies written in Polish are spelled as in the original text. Personal names in the Yiddish and Hebrew texts are rendered according to the YIVO standard for romanization, with the exception of names that have familiar English spellings and are pro-nounced the same in Yiddish or Hebrew (e.g., Esther, not Ester). Also, Polish names mentioned in Yiddish or Hebrew texts are spelled according to Polish orthography (e.g., Staś, not Stash). Whenever authors requested that YIVO substitute pseudonyms for the names of individuals mentioned in their autobiographies we have done so, and we indicate these names when they first appear thus: Yosl°. With the exception of cities such as Warsaw, Vilna, and Cracow, which have familiar English spellings, place names are rendered according to their official spelling during the interwar years.

In keeping with YIVO's original commitment to contestants, their identities remain anonymous except when an author has given YIVO permission to use his actual name. In all other instances the autobiographers are identified by the pseudonyms they supplied when they entered the contests. To ensure their anonymity, these authors' home towns (with the exception of major cities such as Warsaw and Łódź) have been replaced by the editor with a letter chosen at random (e.g., "the town of D."). Endnotes indicate the province in which these towns are located, together with their Jewish and total populations during the interwar years, when known.

At the end of this volume a brief epilogue provides what information is known about the fates of these fifteen autobiographers during and after World War II. Endnotes to each autobiography follow, providing information on the original manuscripts, and short explanations of historical events, Jewish customs, etc., as well as clarifications of some textual features. The endnotes also identify citations from sacred texts and references to literary works and other publications; when known, information on translations of books not originally written in Yiddish, Polish, or Hebrew into those languages are offered as an indication of editions that may have been read by the autobiographers. Short biographies of writers, political leaders, religious leaders, and other prominent figures mentioned in the autobiographies appear in the Personalities appendix; brief descriptions of political parties, youth organizations, educational movements, and philanthropic and cultural institutions appear in the Organizations appendix; and the Glossary provides definitions of foreign terms and expressions.

1914–1939: A CHRONOLOGY

1914

- **August:** World War I begins.
- The American Jewish Joint Distribution Committee is organized to provide relief for Jewish victims of the war in Europe.
- Plans to establish the Hebrew University in Jerusalem are initiated.

1915

- The German army occupies Warsaw and Vilna during its offensive against Russia.
- The Jewish Legion is created to join the Allies' campaign to liberate Palestine from Turkish control.
- The author Yitskhok Leybush Peretz dies in Warsaw.

1916

- German and Austrian occupation forces establish a semi-autonomous Polish state on territories formerly held by Russia; this state is dissolved the following year.
- The author Sholem Aleichem dies in New York City.
- The international Zionist socialist youth movement Hashomer Hatsa'ir is founded.
- The Vilna Troupe, a Yiddish theater company, is founded.

1917

- Sara Schenirer opens the first Beys Yaakov school for Orthodox Jewish girls in Cracow.
- The Polish division of the Bund, the Jewish socialist party, is founded in Lublin.
- Habimah, a Hebrew theater company, is founded in Moscow.

- **March:** Following the February Revolution, Tsar Nikolai II abdicates the Russian throne. Aleksandr Kerenskii heads a provisional Russian government.
- **2 November:** The British government issues the Balfour Declaration, stating that it views "with favor the establishment in Palestine of a national home for the Jewish People."
- **November:** The Bolsheviks seize power in Russia, replacing the provisional government.

1918

- **January:** A Jewish Commissariat, a government agency overseeing Jewish cultural affairs, is established in Soviet Russia.
- **10 November:** Marshal Józef Piłsudski returns to Poland, after being imprisoned in Germany, and is appointed the Polish chief of state and commander in chief of the newly reestablished Polish Army.
- **11 November:** World War I ends.
- **27 December:** The Uprising of Great Poland against German military occupation begins.

1919

- Ukrainian forces led by nationalist leader Symon Petliura massacre thousands of Jewish civilians in Ukraine.
- Tsukunft ("Future"), the Bund's youth movement, is founded in Poland.
- **26 January:** The Constitutional Sejm is elected and begins the task of preparing the national laws of the Polish Republic.
- **January:** The Communist Party of Poland is declared illegal.
- **16 February:** The Uprising of Great Poland ends with an armistice signed in Trewir.
- **February:** The Polish-Soviet War begins with a Polish offensive in Ukraine.
- **28 June:** The Versailles Peace Treaty is signed, establishing the provisional boundaries of the Polish Republic. At Versailles, Poland signs the Minorities Treaty, promising to protect the rights of ethnic and religious minorities within its borders.

1920

- The British mandatory government begins issuing certificates for legal immigration to Palestine.
- Polish military officials establish a detention camp in Jablonna for Jewish officers of the Polish Army, whose loyalty is considered suspect, during the Polish-Soviet War.

- **August**: The Battle of Warsaw. The Polish Army, retreating from an offensive against Soviet forces in Ukraine, defends Warsaw against the Red Army.
- **October:** The Polish military takes over Vilna and its environs, leading to the proclamation of an independent Republic of Central Lithuania.

1921

- Census figures report that there are over 2,853,000 Jews in Poland. Jews are the country's second largest ethnic minority (after Ukrainians), comprising slightly more than ten percent of the population.
- The Central Yiddish School Organization, a secular Yiddish-language school system, is formed in Poland.
- TOZ, the Society for Safeguarding the Health of the Jewish Population, is created in Poland.
- **17 March:** The Constitutional Sejm ratifies Poland's national constitution. Known as the "March Constitution," it declares Poland to be a democratic republic governed by a bicameral parliament, which consists of the Sejm (lower house) and the Senate (upper house).
- **18 March:** The Treaty of Riga is signed, ending the Polish-Soviet War.

1922

- The Bloc of National Minorities is established, promoting cooperation among Jewish, Slavic, and German minorities in the Sejm. The Polish majority views the Bloc as an anti-Polish measure.
- **January**: The parliament of the Republic of Central Lithuania votes to incorporate its state into Poland.
- **December:** Gabriel Narutowicz, the first president of the Polish Republic, is assassinated. Four days later, Stanisław Wojciechowski is elected president.

1923

- Betar, a right-wing Zionist youth movement, is founded in Riga.
- Polish prime minister Władysław Grabski introduces tax laws and other economic policies that impose severe financial burdens on small businesses.
- Gordonia, a Zionist youth movement, is founded in Galicia.

1924

- A Jewish student is tried in Lwów on trumped-up charges that he conspired to assassinate President Wojciechowski.

- The United States enacts legislation severely restricting emigration from Southern and Eastern Europe.
- CENTOS, a network of orphanages for children in Poland, is established.

1925
- The YIVO Institute for Jewish Research is established in Vilna.
- A Concordat between the Pope and the government of Poland is signed, granting extensive privileges to clergy and providing the Roman Catholic Church with almost full administrative and legal autonomy.
- **4 July:** The Polish government signs an agreement with representatives of Galician Jewry regarding the religious and cultural rights of Polish Jews.

1926
- Morgnshtern, the Bund's sports organization for Jewish youth, is established in Poland.
- **12–14 May:** Piłsudski leads a military takeover of the Polish government. He and his followers establish the authoritarian Sanacja regime, which limits the power of Poland's parliament. This regime remains in power in Poland until the beginning of World War II.
- **1 June:** The Polish parliament elects Ignacy Mościcki as the president of the Polish Republic.
- **December:** The Camp for a Greater Poland, a radical right-wing political organization, is established by Roman Dmowski to revitalize the National Democratic (Endek) Party.

1928
- The Soviet Union begins promoting Jewish settlement in the far eastern region of Birobidzhan, part of an effort to establish Jewish agricultural colonies.
- **February:** The Institute of Judaic Studies opens in Warsaw.

1929
- A coalition of center-left political parties is established in Poland, in an effort to replace the Sanacja regime with a democratic government. The Sanacja regime arrests the leaders of this coalition during the following year.
- **October:** The Great Depression begins with the stock market crash on Wall Street.

1931

- Census figures report that there are over 3,114,000 Jews in Poland, comprising ten percent of the population.

1932

- Poland and the Soviet Union sign a non-aggression treaty.
- The YIVO Institute announces its first autobiography contest for Jewish youth.

1933

- The Camp for a Greater Poland is declared illegal by the Polish government.
- **30 January:** Nazi Party leader Adolf Hitler is appointed Chancellor of Germany.

1934

- The National Radical Camp, a Polish fascist organization, is founded. It adopts some of the tactics of the Italian fascists and the Nazis, organizes fighting squads, attacks Jews and leftist politicians, destroys Jewish property.
- Poland and Germany sign a non-aggression treaty.
- The YIVO Institute announces its second autobiography contest for Jewish youth.
- The Polish government denounces the Minorities Treaty.
- Falanga, a fascist youth movement sponsored by the National Radical Camp, is established in Poland.
- The Sanacja regime establishes a concentration camp for political prisoners in Bereza Kartuska.
- The Soviet Union declares Birobidzhan a Jewish autonomous region.

1935

- The YIVO Institute convenes an international conference of scholars to mark its tenth anniversary and establishes a training program for young scholars in the field of Jewish social science.
- **23 April:** The Polish parliament adopts the "April constitution," granting more power to the president of Poland. This constitution is planned as a compromise between a parliamentary democracy and a more authoritarian government.
- **12 May:** Piłsudski dies.

1936

- Polish university students establish "bench ghettos," restricting where Jewish students may sit in classes. Jewish students respond by standing during classes.
- The YIVO Institute establishes rules for standard Yiddish orthography.
- Meir Bałaban, the founder of modern historiography of Polish Jewry, is named associate professor of Jewish history at Warsaw University. His is the first chair in Jewish history in a Polish university.
- The Spanish Civil War begins.
- **March:** During a pogrom in Przytyk three Jews are killed and dozens wounded. When a Pole is killed in subsequent clashes with Jewish defense groups his assailant is jailed, provoking a general strike by Jewish workers throughout Poland.
- **April:** The Polish government passes a law limiting the practice of kosher slaughter of animals.
- **August:** The Polish Ministry of Commerce requires all shop signs to include the owner's name; this is widely perceived as stigmatizing Jewish-owned businesses.

1937

- Boycotts of Jewish businesses receive the official approval of Polish prime minister Felicjan Sławoj-Skaładowski.
- **February:** The Sanacja regime establishes the Camp of National Unity, an authoritarian political organization, in an effort to consolidate support for the government in the wake of Piłsudski's death.

1938

- The YIVO Institute announces its third autobiography contest for Jewish youth.
- Lithuania restores diplomatic relations with Poland.
- **March:** Germany invades and annexes Austria.
- **September:** At the Munich Conference, Italy, France, and Great Britain agree to Germany's annexation of the Sudetenland, in western Czechoslovakia. At this conference, Poland demands the return of Cieszyn Silesia and the following month occupies Zaolzie, the region within this territory most densely populated by Poles.
- **October:** Between 14,000 and 17,000 Jews who are Polish citizens residing in Germany are deported to western Poland.
- **November:** Herszel Grynszpan, a Jewish student, assassinates German ambassador Ernst vom Rath in Paris, protesting Germany's expulsion of Polish Jews. Purportedly as an act of collective punishment of

German Jewry for Grynszpan's action, the Nazi Party stages two days of anti-Jewish riots throughout Germany and Austria. During these riots, known as *Kristallnacht*, dozens of synagogues are destroyed, thousands of Jewish homes looted, ninety-one Jews are killed, and tens of thousands of Jews are arrested.

1939

- Hitler demands the return of Gdańsk and a highway through the Polish "corridor" between Germany to East Prussia. The Polish government rejects this demand.
- **17 May:** Great Britain issues a White Paper proposing the creation of an independent Palestinian state, restricting Jewish immigration to Palestine, and prohibiting the sale of land there to Jews.
- **May:** France and Poland sign an agreement, in which France promises military assistance to Poland in case of German aggression.
- **23 August:** Germany and the Soviet Union sign the Ribbentrop-Molotov Pact in Moscow; secretly, the two countries agree to divide Poland through military occupation.
- **25 August:** Poland and Great Britain sign the Treaty of Mutual Assistance in London in response to the Ribbentrop-Molotov Pact.
- **1 September:** Germany invades Poland; World War II begins.
- **17 September:** Soviet forces occupy eastern Poland.

INTERWAR POLAND

BALTIC SEA

LITHUANIA

GERMANY

GERMANY

GERMANY

DANZIG

Sopot

POMORZE

Ciechocinek

POZNAŃ

• Poznań

POZNAŃ

• Zbąszyń

Rawicz

ŁÓDŹ

Radogoszcz

• Łódź

Studzieniec

WARSAW

Warsaw

Otwock

Góra Kalwaria

Skarżysko Kamienna

Żarnów

Końskie • Wierzbnik

Kielce • Opatów • Ostrowiec

Sandomierz

KIELCE

Działoszyce •

Rozwadów • Nisko

Rudnik

Leżajsk

• Cracow • Wieliczka

ŚLĄSK

CRACOW

• Nowy Sącz

Szczawnica •

Niemojki •

• Siedlce

• Brześć

Międzyrzec

LUBLIN

Kazimierz

• Sieniawa

• Jarosław Lw

LWÓW • Przemyśl

• Iwonicz

Lv

Panevėžys •

• Kaunas

Grodno •

BIAŁYSTOK

CZECHOSLOVAKIA

Vienna •

HUNGARY

Debrecen •

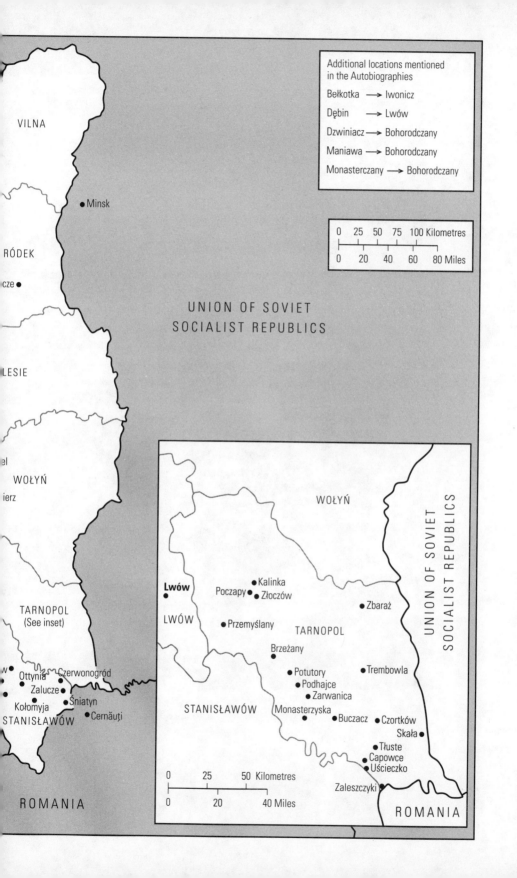

VILNA

● Minsk

RÓDEK

cze ●

UNION OF SOVIET
SOCIALIST REPUBLICS

LESIE

el

WOŁYŃ

ierz

TARNOPOL
(See inset)

w ●
  Ottynia ● ● Czerwonogród
    Zalucze ●
  Kołomyja ● Śniatyn
STANISŁAWÓW   ● Cernăuţi

ROMANIA

Additional locations mentioned
in the Autobiographies

Bełkotka ⟶ Iwonicz

Dębin ⟶ Lwów

Dzwiniacz ⟶ Bohorodczany

Maniawa ⟶ Bohorodczany

Monasterczany ⟶ Bohorodczany

| 0 | 25 | 50 | 75 | 100 Kilometres |
| 0 | 20 | 40 | 60 | 80 Miles |

WOŁYŃ

UNION OF SOVIET
SOCIALIST REPUBLICS

Lwów
●   Poczapy ● ● Kalinka
         ● Złoczów
LWÓW
                ● Zbaraż
    ● Przemyślany
                TARNOPOL
       ● Brzeżany

        ● Potutory   ● Trembowla
        ● Podhajce
           ● Zarwanica
STANISŁAWÓW Monasterzyska
        ●   ● Buczacz ● Czortków
                        Skała ●
                ● Tłuste
                Capowce
                ● Uścieczko
       Zaleszczyki ●

| 0 | 25 | 50 Kilometres |
| 0 | 20 | 40 Miles |

ROMANIA

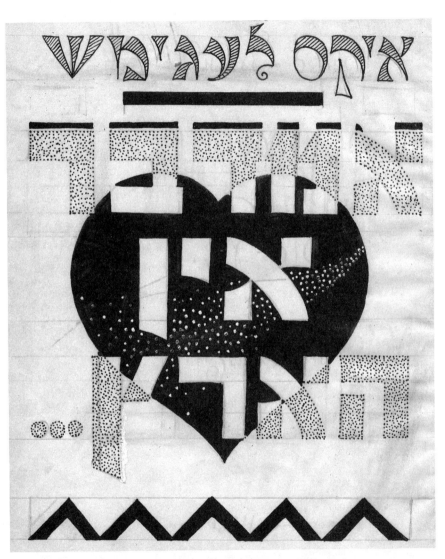

Cover of "A Desert in My Heart . . . ," by X. Legimsh, 1934.

The Autobiographies

1

S. Etonis

Contest year: 1932 • Language: Yiddish
Year of birth: 1910 • Age: [22] • Sex: Male

I was born on 4 December 1910 in R., a small town near Minsk. My parents are respectable and well-to-do members of the community.

I had just turned four when the well-known World War broke out. Out of fear for our safety our family moved to Minsk. I don't remember exactly what life was like in Minsk. I have only two recollections from that period. The first was the fear I felt because my father was a deserter. We children dreaded the Russian words *strazhnik* [guard] and *gradavoi* [policeman]. Father didn't sleep at home. When he would come quietly into the house before nightfall, I would gather—from the gestures and whispering and cautious, sidelong glances of my mother and my late grandmother—that something secret was happening, which was being kept from us children. The word *strazhnik*, which came up often during their secretive conversations, would fill us children with dread.

My second recollection of this period is that by then I had begun to attend *kheyder*. At first I was sent to *kheyder* together with the son of a nearby neighbor. This boy acted as though he was my superior. His family, which was friendly with ours, could barely convince him to take me to *kheyder*. But the teacher liked me. Once, when Mother came to *kheyder*, the teacher praised me, gave me an affectionate pat on the back, and said to her, "I predict that one day he is going to amount to something. He has a good head on his shoulders."

The war dragged on. Father could no longer support us, so he reported to the military. Mother, my sister, and I returned to R., where scarcely two years earlier we had left behind, unprotected, all that we owned. The children there gave me a hearty welcome. They came over to visit us, looked at me with curiosity, and listened eagerly to the stories I told them about the *kheyder* in Minsk.

Within a few weeks, my friends and I began to attend a different school, a *shule*, which had been established in our town. This educational institution bore some resemblance to a modern *kheyder*. The teacher, a local young man, was a "progressive." He taught us to read and write Hebrew from a textbook, as well as to recite prayers. We didn't sit at tables but on real school benches. Every Friday we would gather in the teacher's room and sing songs. Naturally, there were Hebrew songs, such as "The Little Room," "Sleep, My Child," "Mother, Mother," as well as other children's songs, and at the end we sang "Hatikvah."

During the second term in the winter of 1916–17, this teacher stopped coming to us. The local Jewish community leaders brought in a new teacher, whom we later nicknamed the Black Hat, because he wore a crooked, crumpled old hat, typical of a *maskil*. His school was neither a *kheyder* nor a *shule*, but a combination of both. Although he considered himself a modern Jew, he was, in fact, just like the men who did nothing more than hang around the synagogue all day. Mostly we studied Torah with smatterings of Rashi commentaries, the beginning of the Prophets, and we also reviewed the weekly Torah reading. But this teacher didn't last long with us. We sensed his weakness and showed him little respect. We often engaged him in political discussions about the Tsar, the war, and the relative strength of the Russians and the Germans. The older boys would tell stories they had heard at home. They would "debate" with the teacher, while we younger boys listened with much greater curiosity and concentration than usual.

And so passed the winter of 1916–17. At the end of the winter fresh, new political winds began to blow. Rumors began to spread in our town that there was going to be some sort of revolution somewhere, which would bring happiness to the world. This was the subject of intense discussion. Even our teacher discussed the revolution with us. Finally, the much-anticipated revolution broke out. There were demonstrations in the town. Festive processions of people marched through the streets, shouting for joy, drunk with excitement. At the time I didn't understand what a revolution was. All I knew was that the Tsar had been "overthrown," and that everyone was now happy and content. So I was happier. At this point I became convinced that the revolution was indeed a good thing.

Once, after we boys felt sure that our parents were no more satisfied with the teacher than we were, we decided to stage a "strike." One day, without discussing it with anyone, we didn't show up in *kheyder*. We all went off with our books to the nearby woods, where we heard soldiers approaching with artillery and machine guns. When I came home in the evening I was asked why I hadn't gone to *kheyder* that day. I answered directly: "Because the teacher isn't any good. I haven't learned anything from him." Still, they were rather angry with me: "What do you mean by not going to *kheyder*?" However, the next day our parents got together and fired the teacher. We boys were victorious.

But what to do now about finding another teacher? The idea of our studying with a traditional *melamed* did not, after all, sit well with the men of the community. So they considered going to the city to find us a teacher. In the meantime, there was a simple mechanic in our town who was rumored to be a *maskil*; he was always reading modern Hebrew books and was an expert on Hebrew grammar. After thinking it over, he offered to quit his job and become our teacher. This did not please the "intellectual" mothers. They claimed that a mechanic couldn't be their children's teacher. This led to a split: some of the parents entrusted their children to a semi-traditional teacher, who taught them modern Hebrew, with Hebrew as the language of instruction. The rest of the parents, including my father, decided to hire the mechanic to be our teacher.

The first class took place in our house. I remember that when the teacher came to the house he spotted the first volume of the Hebrew children's reader *Ha-lashon* [The Language] on the table. He called me over and asked, "What does *Ha-lashon* mean?" Without hesitating, I answered, "the tongue."

Our teacher was truly an expert in grammar. He would cover entire walls with conjugations and declensions. He barely allowed a single word of the Bible to escape grammatical analysis. By then I was also taking lessons in secular subjects with another teacher. I studied Russian, arithmetic, and eventually geography.

After the revolution we had several changes of government. At first, complete anarchy reigned. Peasants from the surrounding villages came into our town and staged a full-fledged pogrom against Jews. The peasants robbed, beat, and smashed anyone and anything that fell into their hands. Jews were afraid to go outside; we feared for our lives. No one stood up to the raging pogromists, who did whatever they pleased. Finally, a few soldiers happened to pass through our town, and their officer, who was a good man, drove away the wild peasant bands.

Next, the Kerenskii regime was in power; then, for a short time, the Germans; and finally, the Bolsheviks. It was the end of 1918. These were hungry times. No one had any bread. There was no wheat to be found. Mother baked cakes from oat flour; they were full of husks and chaff that scratched our tongues and throats. Nevertheless, they nourished us. I used to bring these cakes to *kheyder*. The poor children didn't even have that. I used to trade these cakes for various toys, such as exploded cartridges, shells, and caps that the other children would collect from the soldiers.

By then we had a new teacher; this one was a former merchant. When he came to our town he was homeless. During the war he had left his home and wandered from place to place until he arrived in our town and became a *melamed* out of necessity. His daughter taught secular subjects to me and the other children.

We all loved our new teacher. He inspired us to be diligent, so much so that many children even came after school hours to learn more. He never refused them. He greatly enjoyed teaching us. Within the limits of my understanding, I learned a great deal of Bible from him. We studied all of it, even those sections that are in Aramaic. I memorized much of the Book of Proverbs, many chapters of Psalms, Isaiah, and so forth.

Once, I remember, the teacher was talking to my father about hard times, about his terribly difficult situation. He let out a deep, broken sigh and said, "What can we do? We have only one way out: to rely on the One in Heaven. As the Bible says, 'Cast your burden upon the Lord.'" Turning to me, he said, "Well?" and I answered, "And He will sustain you."

Some time passed under the reign of the Bolsheviks. Suddenly, rumors began to circulate that the Poles were moving closer to us. Of course, every rumor made its way to *kheyder*. We boys used to whisper to each other about the Poles. We had strange ideas about the Poles in general and about their language in particular. Some years earlier—when we were studying with our first teacher, the young man from our town—our school had been located in the house of a Pole. We used to see him in his workshop, where he made coffins. He would teach his son from a strange book, which was unintelligible to us, but the man couldn't get his son to study. We recalled this now; Poles seemed even more mysterious and obscure.

Once, a boy told us that Polish was not a strange language. It was just like Russian, only you had to say *mleko* instead of *moloko* (milk), and *mięso* instead of *miaso* (meat)—that was all there was to it.

The rumors grew. In the summer of 1919, unit after unit of Russian soldiers began to pass through our town. Disorganized, shabby, weak, and hungry, they trudged through town. Finally, we were rid of the Red Army. The town then established a self-defense group that, although full of fear itself, "maintained order in the town." Everyone was frightened and anxious. No one knew what would happen next. Some said that the Reds were coming back, while others claimed the opposite, that the Poles were coming for sure.

One day, as we were studying in *kheyder*, there was a sudden commotion. Mothers came running to get their children. The town was in turmoil. Four Polish cavalrymen had arrived. By evening, the streets were full of Polish soldiers. The officers summoned a few community leaders, my father among them, and ordered them to bring oats for the soldiers' horses. At first, when the soldiers led these men through the town, there was panic. Stories circulated that they were being taken as hostages. When people found out the real reason they'd been summoned, everyone breathed easier. Indeed, now everyone was calm. People gathered around and chatted comfortably with the soldiers.

Then a sudden, strong blast, like a clap of thunder, shattered the calm. Immediately afterward, there was a long mournful whistle, and after that, as though flying behind it, came a second terrible blast that rattled the window panes. People panicked. It was artillery fire. People ran amok, not knowing where to go.

The soldiers assembled right away. Suddenly, the streets were completely empty. It seemed like a ghost town. Here and there people could be seen moving like shadows along the walls. Outside, fire from rifles, machine guns, and cannons thundered and hailed. The battle raged through the town in full force. Our entire block gathered in a nearby cellar that was well fortified. It was filled to capacity. Women became hysterical. We children trembled with terror. In the middle of the night, a steady rain began to fall, with thunder and lightning. It was difficult to distinguish the thunder from the cannons. Each blast was accompanied by the women's mournful cries and hysteria. The men gathered and recited psalms together. I joined in, repeating those psalms I knew by heart. This recitation was so heartfelt, so intense, so full of pleading, that even now I can remember how it felt.

At daybreak the din quieted down and the rain stopped. A few brave men made their way out to the courtyard and, through the cracks in the gate, stole a glimpse of what was outside. At the same time, we suddenly heard strange, ferocious cries, like the roar of wild animals. Minutes later the street near the cellar was filled with soldiers from both sides. They brandished their swords, which flashed in the dim predawn light. The two sides made wild, animal-like cries as they fought face to face, eye to eye. In the end the Poles won, and the Bolsheviks retreated in great haste.

The house above the cellar where we were hiding had been damaged and was turned into a temporary hospital. The wounded were brought in, one after the other. Their wounds, dripping with blood, were swathed in bandages. Many of the men were only half-conscious, near death. A rattle would escape from their throats and they would lie motionless, silent forever. Others were somehow revived in time and brought back to consciousness.

The officers set about calming the townspeople. Promising that there would be peace and quiet, they told us to leave the cellars. We went out into the open air. We still heard gunshots in the streets, but there was no

more cannon fire. After that there was a week of "calm." Unit after unit of
soldiers moved through town each day. Wherever they found something
they wanted they took it, without asking any questions. Nothing helped:
not crying, not begging for mercy.

At the end of the week we could tell that something was bothering the
Polish soldiers, we could sense their confusion and restlessness. From a distance, we heard shells exploding. Then came a rumor that there would
be another battle in town the following day. This time we didn't stay. Our
family and a few others moved to a small estate fifteen kilometers away.
Having nothing to eat but potatoes, we simply went hungry.

The Red Army retreated again, and we returned to our town, which lay
in ruins. Here, a broken window pane; there, a wall full of holes—the war
was still on! The Poles had taken charge. This led to a spate of arrests. Some
Jewish boys were detained, supposedly on suspicion of being communists.
They were savagely tortured. Nevertheless, some time passed and things
quieted down. We began to get used to living with our new neighbors.
People returned to their usual affairs, and once again life seemed normal.
We children went back to *kheyder* and met again with our teacher and our
friends.

Each of us children formed his own impressions of the war based on his
own perspective—where he was, what he had experienced. It seems to me
that the various experiences I'd had during the war somehow made me
much tougher and more mature. At the same time, though, they left
me broken. From earliest childhood I had been taught to believe that killing
a person is the most terrible of crimes, that shedding human blood is the
most shameful deed possible. And then it was my fate to see, with my own
eyes, dead bodies lying in the street like garbage, lying in their own blood
as if it were dirty water. And, furthermore, I couldn't understand why. This
wound, perhaps the very first one on my pure and innocent soul, has still
not healed completely.

Meanwhile, the years went on and moved into the infinite abyss of the
past. I began to enjoy reading. I simply devoured children's books in
Hebrew. Sometimes I even read books that weren't written for children. Any
free time I had I spent "lying around with books," as they used to say at
home. At the same time my religious feelings began to develop. I insisted
on getting up with my father before dawn to go to the special early-morning
service, and this gave me great pleasure. I felt somehow more heroic, better
than the others, when I went to the *beys-medresh* during the wintry mornings, while everything around us was still asleep and wrapped in the thick
gray of dawn. No one could talk me out of it. I insisted on getting up before
dawn and praying with the first *minyan*.

The end of the winter of 1920 arrived. I was between nine and ten years old. At this time something happened that came as a deep shock and shattered my young life. My mother, whom I loved so much, upon whom I lavished so many warm kisses, suddenly became ill. Two weeks later, she passed away.

Her final moments will remain in my memory forever. The image of her face during the last days of her life is constantly before me. She lay in bed, her face flushed, her eyes bloodshot, looking aimlessly into the distance. Most of the time she was no longer lucid. The last time that I walked past her bed, her gaze rested on me. She called me to her side, took my hand, and wept bitterly. It seemed she was already aware that these were her last moments. She already felt the wings of the Angel of Death, who tormented her with such pain. At that moment I felt a strange tightness in my throat. I was unable to utter a single word and couldn't bear to have her burning eyes on me. Then suddenly I collapsed upon her bed. I put my face next to hers and kissed her ferociously, again and again. The others in the house tore me away from her; we weren't supposed to excite her. I was led out of the room.

It was the day before Passover. Mother was near death. Two doctors had been brought from Minsk, and they were attending to her. I was taken to my uncle's house and not allowed to return home. All day long I recited psalms, covering the book with tears of grief. I gave the rubles I had saved to the poor. I would constantly ask the others, "What's new? How's Mother doing?" But they all gave vague and ambiguous answers, just to keep me calm. The next morning I jumped out of bed and my first question was, "How is Mother?" My uncle and aunt looked at each other and were silent with grief. Again I demanded, "How does Mother feel?" Then the door opened and Father entered. He looked pale and broken. I ran to him: "How is Mother?" He was silent and bitter. I looked deep into his eyes and waited for a response. But instead of answering he burst into heartbroken sobs. He seized me in his arms, pressed me close, and whispered through his tears, "You have no mother anymore." I didn't understand what he was saying. I couldn't imagine it. I didn't want to believe it. How was it possible? How could it be? My mother, my mother—I would never see her again? All was lost. Nothing mattered any more. What good were the psalms I'd said, the charity I'd given?

They took me to the *beys-medresh*. From all sides people looked at me with compassion. I felt such deep sympathy from everyone. I felt somehow that everyone now regarded me differently than they had before. And then, at the end of the service, they brought me up to the pulpit, gave me a prayerbook, and told me to recite Kaddish. Then I felt different from usual, different from normal, different from everyone else. On that day I became an orphan!

And from that time on, I did, in fact, become different. Mother's death left me in a strangely serious and pensive state. I began to prefer being by myself. When I played, I never allowed myself to enjoy it fully. I somehow thought that my being cheerful dishonored my mother's memory. When I did sometimes let myself take part in happy, childish games, I always took myself to task afterwards, upset that I'd forgotten my dead mother.

The Poles were now in power. They continued to make false accusations that the Jews were communists. Once, a group of young people gathered in the nearby woods to rehearse a play, *The Selling of Joseph*, that they wanted to perform in town. They were all arrested, charged with holding a communist meeting, and sent under guard to Minsk.

At first, no one took their arrest seriously, because they knew that the young people under arrest didn't have the slightest connection with communism. But then the investigation turned very serious. The Poles simply decided that these twenty or so young people were to be shot. The town was plunged into grief. Mothers ran to the holy ark in the synagogue and to the cemetery, where they offered up endless prayers. The town rabbi became consumed with the cause, knocking on the door of every high-ranking government official and Jewish community leader. Finally, after much arduous effort, torment, and anxiety, the young people managed to be set free.

A few months passed, and there were more upheavals. The Poles retreated and the Bolsheviks returned. And a few months later, the Poles drove the Reds out of town again. Some of the Jews shrugged their shoulders. "War is something of a game for them," they would say. "One comes and the other goes. We don't remember anything like this happening during our lifetime." Finally came the well-known Treaty of Brest-Litovsk, and the border with Russia stood half a kilometer from our town.

By then most of my friends from *kheyder* and I were studying at the preparatory yeshiva. The town rabbi took direct charge over us. He was a Jew of great piety and devotion. His greatest concern was that we children, who came from proper and respectable families, be brought up as observant Jews. He spent a great deal of time with us, testing us frequently and often giving us personal instruction. He constantly told us stories about great sages, righteous men, and so on.

However, I was becoming increasingly interested in secular literature. As soon as I came home from the *beys-medresh*, where we studied, I would start reading. I had already read Smolenskin and even Berdyczewski, as well as various other Hebrew books and monthly journals for young people,

which I found in the town library. I also began to read Yiddish books, especially humorous novels. I loved books that poked fun at yeshivas and
hasidim. But these books didn't affect me; on the contrary, I myself made
fun of the same things and enjoyed the stories that the authors had
invented. Someone told the rabbi what I was reading. He gave me a stern
lecture about wasting time on nonsense and told my father not to let me
read such things. But Father wasn't strict or overly fanatical, and he didn't
stop me from reading.

Our town began to get accustomed to life near the border. A company
of soldiers was stationed in town to guard the border. The townspeople
started to get used to their presence, and this led to smuggling goods across
the border. Everyone and his brother, kith and kin, young and old alike,
started doing business at the border. It teemed with all sorts of merchants
and brokers, suppliers and buyers. They bought and sold everything: precious stones, saccharin, clothing, textiles.

You didn't have to know much about the merchandise, because no matter
how much you might have overpaid for it, you were still sure to make a
one-hundred-percent profit when the goods were sent up to the "place"—
that is, to Minsk—and you got your "return." The "return" always came
in the form of something valuable—money, gold, furs, jewels, and many
other such items—things that even a wealthy person could never have
dreamed of.

Trading at the border became a risky business, like playing roulette. Yet
everyone, from the poorest to the richest, was involved. Really, how could
you not get involved in this game, when you could become rich overnight,
in a few hours? You delivered the merchandise, and the next day you got
one-hundred- or (without exaggeration) one-thousand-percent profit, and
often even more. The game attracted everyone. It influenced everything. A
new smugglers' language developed; there were wordless or tight-lipped
insinuations, winks and gestures, secrets and hints.

And the town did prosper. There were no poor people to be found
anywhere. People who were once poor now wore costly furs and rings with
precious stones, and everyone was happy. Wealth also encouraged people
to aspire to be high-brow. It became fashionable to send children off to
the *gymnasium* in Vilna. All the young people who were up to it went off
to the city. However, they all did poorly in their studies. They had more
than enough money, so most of them had a good time and didn't give their
studies a second thought.

This atmosphere led to moral corruption and empty frivolity. All that
people thought about was the border, their "return," precious stones, and
so on. No one knew or cared about anything else. The town rabbi, whose

great spiritual influence held sway over us yeshiva boys, was deeply worried
that we might catch "border fever." And he was right. I remember how
tempted I was to go off to the "place." I simply couldn't control myself and
begged to be allowed to go to "the other side" with some "stones." The rabbi
wanted to remove us from this environment and pleaded with our parents
to send us away to a yeshiva. He was particularly insistent with my father.
One day, early in the summer of 1922, when he was making a trip to
Baranowicze, he simply snatched me from my house and took me to the
yeshiva there.

At first, when there had been talk about my leaving home, I was completely thrilled. The prospect of going far away excited me, and I said that
I was eager to travel. But when the moment of my departure arrived, I
suddenly felt so sad that I wanted to call off the trip, but it was too late for
that. My pride was at stake. So, against my own will, I left.

The yeshiva in Baranowicze, which is still there today, consists of several
levels of classes, leading up to independent study. It was the beginning of
the term. The other students had not yet returned from their homes. The
beys-medresh, where we studied, was still empty. The lecterns were scattered
about in disorder. Here and there lay an open volume of the Talmud or a
book missing its covers. Everything seemed so melancholy, so lonely. My
spirits, which were none too high at the start of the trip, sank even further
after I entered the beys-medresh. I was gripped by terrible homesickness. I
felt a strange bitterness in my throat and a weakness in my heart, and I burst
into tears. Seeing this, the rabbi asked me why I was crying. I tried to dismiss
it by saying simply, "Oh, nothing, nothing in particular."

Eventually, I was assigned a "reading." I studied a section of the Gemara
and then repeated it before the rosh-yeshiva. Apparently he was pleased
with my "reading"; he assigned me to the fourth level. In all, there were
five levels of classes; this showed that I was quite precocious for an eleven-
year-old.

However, I had decided not to stay there. I was ashamed to say that I
wanted to go home, so I found a pretext. I said that the lodgings that had
been rented for me were too expensive, and that I had to go home in order
to figure out what to do. The rabbi understood my real motive. He didn't
want to press me too hard. Instead, he tried to influence me indirectly by
taking me to the rosh-yeshiva. The mazhgiekh was also there. The rabbi told
them that I wanted to leave. The rosh-yeshiva tried to persuade me not to
go, as did the mazhgiekh. But it was all in vain. I held firm to my wish to
leave.

The mazhgiekh tried to prevail on me to stay. "This is Satan's doing. He
has interfered here," he declared. Satan was dragging me into the gutter,

into a wanton existence. I must gain control over him. As soon as I heard the word "Satan" my resolve to go home wavered. I remembered a story that I had read about a nobleman and a peasant's son. The peasant pulled the boy toward himself, while Satan pulled him toward the nobleman. I imagined the whole scene: I saw Satan tugging at me, and that I must overcome him. I mustn't heed him but must drive him away and remain at the yeshiva. I had almost made up my mind to stay. But suddenly my homesick, childish heart tugged at me again, and I had another good cry. After we left the *rosh-yeshiva*'s quarters, I said to the rabbi once again, "I don't want to stay here!"

We went back home, stopping on the way in Vilna. There I met many of the *gymnasium* students from my home town. In a strange way, I felt I could actually have stayed in Vilna. There was something appealing about the students' caps and uniforms. Everything there seemed so nice, so pleasant. But in a few days I left for home.

The Jewish community there had hired a new *rosh-yeshiva*, and we began to study with him. I did very poorly the entire term. My mind wandered. While the *rosh-yeshiva* was speaking, I didn't hear a word. I was absorbed in my thoughts; I would fantasize and daydream. The *rosh-yeshiva* noticed this, and often he would stop in the middle of the lesson and ask me, "So, what's happening in Warsaw?"—suggesting that I was somewhere in Warsaw and not at the lesson. I dreamed about everything, especially about the future. I would imagine how I might look if I were a *gymnasium* student. I fantasized about the way that they dressed and carried themselves.

The year went by, and once again the rabbi tried to persuade our parents to send us away to a yeshiva. "It's not good for them to be at home. They're getting spoiled." In the summer of 1923, six of us left for—or, more accurately, were taken to—the yeshiva in Baranowicze. Before setting out, my friends warned me not to "go crazy" and not, for heaven's sake, to study *musar*. In short, I should be sure to remain a decent human being.

This time, studies were well underway when we arrived in Baranowicze. I remembered everything that had happened the previous year. I won't deny that returning to Baranowicze had little appeal for me. But this time there were six of us. Each was ashamed to tell the others that he harbored the same desire to go home.

That summer I continued to do poorly in my studies. Here, too, I still daydreamed, thinking about days gone by and days to come. Yet here I also discovered all sorts of new things. There seemed to be something interesting at every turn. Back home, we didn't have a formal yeshiva, just a place where the local boys studied. But here were young men who had come from all over Poland, some the likes of which I had never seen before.

I was interested in all of them—their speech, their clothes, their entire way of life.

The first time we studied *musar*, I recalled my friends' warnings and wanted to withdraw from the yeshiva. However, I was intrigued by the arcane nature of this subject, which was unfamiliar to me. I hesitated and in the end remained at the yeshiva. When we gathered to study *musar*, some students wept or shouted, while others only intoned a sad and pious chant. The study of *musar* made a strange impression on me, and I was reluctant to pass judgment on it, even as it applied to me. Yet I knew I mustn't even pick up a book of *musar*, lest I become a "fanatic."

My friends from the town of R. and I barely made it through the summer. Every day we'd get together and count the remaining weeks and days of the term. When the month of Elul finally arrived, we all laughed happily and talked about going home. We were saddened only by the thought that we would have to come back here again in the winter.

We studied there for another year and a half without much enthusiasm. In the winter of 1924–25, three of our group of six didn't return to Baranowicze. They went to Vilna, supposedly to the Ramayles Yeshiva, but their true intent was to pursue secular studies. Two other boys and I went back to Baranowicze. I also wanted to study secular subjects and often recalled the *gymnasium* uniforms with their peaked caps. Nevertheless, I decided to go back to the yeshiva for a few more terms. In any case, I thought, as the youngest of all my friends, I would catch up with them.

That year, however, I unexpectedly experienced a complete internal upheaval. During this time, I became much more mature and self-aware. I began to think differently and to acquire new views about life. This came about because of a friend I had. He was a person of rare gifts, but he was not without faults. At the yeshiva he was considered to be a heretic and was harassed for this. And then a remarkable thing happened: I have to admit that it was, in fact, because of this "heretical" friend that I became a religious person.

My friend was actually both a heretic and a believer. He had a restless, inquisitive spirit. He was never satisfied with what he was taught or shown. He explored on his own; he wanted to find his own way. For this reason, his moods changed frequently. There were moments when he was ecstatic with piety, wildly fanatical. And then there were times when he would flagrantly disobey Jewish law. You had to know him.

My "heretical" friend had a strange weakness, a passion for one thing: the study of *musar*! He studied with a strange enthusiasm, with great exal- tation and fervor. Some said that he was passing himself off as a disciple of *musar* in order to shield himself from the suspicions of others. But this view of him was completely false from beginning to end. He studied *musar* because it provided his yearning soul with relief. There he sometimes found comfort, encouragement, and exaltation for his troubled soul.

I began to study with this friend, whose name was Shloyme. The yeshiva administrators didn't approve of my becoming his study partner, but I especially wanted to do this because he was very gifted.

There are different types of friendships in yeshiva: There are friends who are especially suitable as study partners but with whom you have no other common interests. Then there are friends that are only for life outside of studying; they aren't gifted as students or aren't compatible with you. And in very rare instances you find a friend who is well suited to you, with whom you have a bond, both for study and for friendship, for intimate companionship. For me, Shloyme was this last type of perfect friend. Not only did I study with him, but after our scheduled study periods we also chatted about all sorts of things, personal as well as general. And it was because of our conversations that I became a truly different person.

Shloyme was already much more mature than I was, more developed. He had already read a great deal, and he had an understanding of serious literature and specific, well-formed views of life. Shloyme also read newspapers, he understood the articles well, and was even well-versed in politics. I, however, was still, on the whole, almost completely raw and undeveloped. I never thought about outlooks on life. I almost never read newspapers, except for the humor sections. In general, I was not well-versed in serious issues. Even my religious feelings, which had glowed within me since earliest childhood, were beginning to grow dimmer, weaker, paler; they were on the verge of being extinguished.

My conversations with Shloyme began as casual discussions of current events. With time our talks developed, becoming deeper, more serious. We talked about great sages, famous people, literature, writers, life, *musar*, faith, and so on. At first I was the weaker one. For the most part, I did the listening and he did the talking. I did know a great deal about Hebrew and Yiddish literature, as I had read constantly back home. What I lacked, however, was my own critical understanding. I wasn't bold enough to express my own opinion of a text, while Shloyme spoke readily about writers and books.

I knew very little about *musar*, because I had never really studied it in earnest. Now my heretical friend began to reproach me for not devoting myself to it. "After all," he said, "*musar* delights the heart of man. It is a source of feeling and deep thoughts." I got over my fears and, little by little,

I began to look at *musar* literature. I began to study *musar* and was drawn into it. New worlds unfolded before me, new concepts, new ideas. Somehow I began to see before me an opening onto a broader path, a broader perspective. Now I, too, I often became absorbed in my thoughts. I sensed that my thinking and dreaming were actually part of my whole self; they were embedded entirely within me. I no longer dreamed about days gone by or far-off days to come, but about the present. I often looked within myself to take stock: Which path was I to follow in life? Toward what end was I actually striving? What were my obligations?

And the more I turned inward, the more I began to realize how small I was and how limited and narrow my ideas were. I saw even broader horizons before me. At one point my inner thoughts reached a climax. I was studying *musar* intensively, with much feeling and reflection. Suddenly I experienced sensations that I had suppressed, welling up inside me. I couldn't control them. I felt a strange pressure, an inner anxiety. I didn't know exactly what it was. I could only sense a call within me that demanded I make a radical change. And indeed, this became a turning point in my life. I "took myself in hand," so to speak.

I began to live in earnest, in a more responsible and deliberate manner. First, I buckled down and studied with great diligence, both before and after classes, whenever I had the opportunity. I purchased *The Examination of the World* by Rabbi Jedaiah Ha-Penini, a renowned medieval philosopher, and began to study his work. I immersed myself in *Duties of the Heart* and studied the "Eight Chapters" by Maimonides and other philosophical works.

From then on, my way of thinking, my perspective, changed completely. I eliminated my former frivolous thoughts, and my faith was renewed and grew stronger. It moved away from childish naiveté and became a self-aware, thoughtful, and earnest belief. I became more religious than I had been before, though I still wasn't like all the others in the yeshiva. I had my own religious practices, my own ways. I refrained from doing things that others at the yeshiva did without any qualms. However, I had moved far beyond the rest of the boys in other respects. Although we were forbidden to do so, I loved to read secular books. I didn't read them in the yeshiva, for I had no time to do anything there but study. But when I went back home for Passover I began reading these books again. Now, though, I read in a completely different way than I had before. I wanted to understand what I was reading. I had to make my own critique of each book, form my own impressions and judgments. At the time I was reading works by Ahad Ha-Am and Bialik, the most serious Hebrew literature. I was also reading Lilienblum's *Sins of My Youth*. I found him rather petty. It seemed to me that his book only made him appear ridiculous. I saw life in the yeshiva, and religious life in general, in quite a different light!

I remained in Baranowicze until the summer of 1926. My friend Shloyme was no longer there, but I continued to manage on my own. I had several other close friends with whom I got along. But my way of thinking didn't always agree with their view, and this led to some amicable disputes among us. The *mazhgiekh* also noticed that I had changed. Although he couldn't tell what had taken place within me, he could still see that I was different from before. Indeed, he once said to me in private, "I've noticed that you're already sitting on the wagon. Now you must grow stronger and see to it that you travel further."

That summer I went home, where I studied Polish and read a great deal. I hadn't forgotten how to imagine, how to dream. In general, the atmosphere in town was very far removed from yeshiva, and especially so from my philosophy. My former friends had gone off in different directions. Some of them went into business. Others were to be found in the Hebrew teachers' seminary or attending *gymnasium*. Still, we all belonged to the same social circle in the town. When I was in their company, I joined in their pastimes. But when I was alone my thoughts were completely different from theirs, and I enjoyed the time I spent by myself. Sometimes I would think about serious problems or drift off into the distance on a wave of fantasy. I also began to write many different kinds of poetry. In general I had a weakness for poets, writers, famous people. I fantasized about becoming world-renowned.

Winter came. I decided to go to the yeshiva in Raduń. My friends and acquaintances in town tried to dissuade me from going. "What's the point of yeshiva?" they argued. "How can studying contribute to your life? You have to think about making a living." But I paid little heed to all their arguments. I viewed these people as Lilliputian, petty folk, who looked for the material purpose in everything and had no higher ideals. And so I left.

In Raduń I studied very diligently and soon made new friends. I was satisfied with my situation and didn't want to think about what practical ends might come from my studies. I studied because I wanted to know how to study. I studied because I understood that I had to study.

Several years passed. I became older, wiser, more mature. I experienced many inner struggles. More than once I stood on the brink of abandoning my faith, on the verge of crossing the threshold. And yet, at the last moment, I would step back and throw myself once more into the whirl of yeshiva life. I experienced a great deal during the years 1927–30. I underwent more profound internal development. I had the opportunity to discover the great wide world. In 1928 I spent a few weeks in the bustling town of Sopot. I saw with my own eyes what life is like in the world today. And after all these encounters and struggles, I still retained my deep religious convictions. At this time, I also started to give speeches in public; I'm told that I have some talent for public speaking.

It was 1930; I was already twenty years old. In spite of myself, I kept wondering: What would be my future? What could I possibly do? I didn't want to become a rabbi. First of all, the profession didn't appeal to me. I thought about this in particular, because a wave of materialism had swept through the yeshiva. Students there began to study the *Yoreh De'ah*, because they wanted to be sure to be able to make a living. But I felt that if I turned my knowledge of Torah into "a spade with which to dig," then all the studying I had done during the best years of my youth would be greatly compromised. I had approached my studies differently from all the others—without a practical purpose in mind, without a materialistic goal. I studied only out of conviction. In a certain sense, perhaps, it could be called *lishmah*—that is, for its own sake.

I gave this issue more serious thought, until I decided what new path my life should take. Finally, after much consideration and introspection, I did not return to the yeshiva in the winter of 1931–32. I stayed in our town, where I found a position teaching Jewish religion in the public school. I began to study secular subjects on my own. At the same time, by the way, I also taught a daily page of Talmud to men in the community. This was my plan: I would get as much secular education as was required in order to find a position anywhere, whether in a public or a private school. There was no one in town to teach me. The teachers in the public schools had only an elementary education. Still, I wanted to complete the entire course of studies in a *gymnasium*.

Once again, life in our town seemed unappealing. I decided to move to the city. And so this past summer I came to Vilna, where I prepared myself for the eighth form of *gymnasium*, working hard all summer. Of all my studies, I most enjoyed the poetry of Mickiewicz, which often stirred my own suffering soul. When I look at myself, I see that I am at heart a romantic rather than a realist.

It's not yet clear whether or not I will succeed in getting into the eighth form. Rumor has it that the ministry of education won't permit any new admissions into the eighth form. And I'm faced with another difficult problem here, one of finances. The economic crisis has affected my father as well. He can't support me in Vilna, so I have to find a way to earn money myself. It's difficult. This is how things stand today. What will happen later I cannot, of course, foresee. Life is full of complicated surprises, and I can't know what surprises will come my way.

I wrote this autobiography in snatches, whenever I had a free moment. This summer I was so busy preparing for the examinations that I didn't have even a minute of free time. Therefore there are some inaccuracies. Things about which I should have written more I sometimes said too little, and what should have been shorter I perhaps made too long. Because of my circumstances, I ask your forgiveness.

2

Khane

Contest year: 1932 • Language: Yiddish
Year of birth: [1912] • Age: 20 • Sex: Female

I'd like to give a short explanation about my autobiography, which consists of seventy pages filled with my twenty years of girlhood. I wrote very poorly— besides a bad style, the words are unclear. This is due, perhaps, to the poor conditions under which I wrote: right after coming home from work I would sit down, tired and hungry, and write, always with a headache. Naturally, in such a state my mind is too lazy to work. When I learned of the autobiography contest I saw it as a happy coincidence, because in recent years, as I came to know more about the world, I dreamed of writing an autobiography. Now the opportunity to do so has arrived. I don't think that my life story is extraordinary, though I do believe that there aren't many like it. But I do have doubts as to whether you will be able to understand what I have written. I have written what is important in my life that remains with me. I haven't written the most important and most interesting things about the three years of my life and work in the party. I don't know why I have done this; perhaps because I didn't want to reveal secret things about the party. If anything isn't clear, I would be glad to provide clarification.

Respectfully,

    [Khane]

*E*ven before I came into the world, my parents had been to the rabbi twice for a divorce. Apparently, however, it was fated that I be born to these two people, who had known so little joy in their lives, and so I prolonged their unhappy life together.

My mother came from a small town in Lithuania. Her parents were moderately wealthy, but they were primitive people who couldn't give her a proper education. She was a simple girl, but she attracted attention with her liveliness and physical beauty, and everyone loved her.

By chance she met my father, who came from Poland, and he liked her at once. Because he couldn't get along with his stepmother, my father had left home, become a peddler, and lived on his own. Father told Mother's parents that he wanted to marry their daughter; they agreed and were especially happy that he didn't ask for any dowry. They owned two houses; they lived in one, while they were keeping the second for another daughter, who wasn't as attractive as my mother. Mother was seventeen years old when she got married and moved to Poland with Father. Young, pretty, and in her prime, it was hard for her to part with her girlish freedom and become a slave to her husband.

Father was by nature a bad man, and he tormented Mother terribly in order to prove his masculine superiority. He ignored her feelings and desires, and her whole life became dependent on his will. From the very beginning, their life together consisted of quarreling, fighting, and running away from home.

I was their second daughter. My parents' life together became more and more difficult. Now Mother had to fight with Father on our behalf as well. Our financial situation was also not very good. Father took little interest in us and vented his frustrations at Mother. Recognizing the hardships that faced her family, Mother had to leave us and become a breadwinner, just like her husband. She used to go from one courtyard to the next buying second-hand goods. She also sold fruit, eventually dealing with whole orchards. Mother ran the entire business from beginning to end; she used to harness the horses herself and go to town to sell the fruit at the market. The orchard became our cradle. We used to lie in the straw among the fruit or on a board under the wagon when Mother went to the market.

When I was still in diapers, my mother more than once put me in a stranger's wagon at the market. In the confusion, the stranger would drive off with me, and when Mother realized what had happened she would go berserk. They would search for me well into the night until I was found.

That is all I know about my parents and the first three years of my life.

Until I was three years old, I didn't feel anything. Though I don't remember them, I know they were peaceful years, perhaps the happiest years of my life. When I was three years old, my heart began to feel, my eyes to see, and my mind to remember.

My earliest memory of our impoverished home is of a Friday night. I was lying on the oven and looking at the two Sabbath candles on the table.

My earliest feeling was love for my mother. That Sabbath eve was the end of my three happy years. It was 1914, and the next day the bloody World War broke out. Father was drafted and sent to the front.

By this time we were three sisters. The oldest was six years old and the youngest barely a month old. Mother raised us and kept us fed. With her energy and her deep love for us, she feared nothing, not even looking death straight in the eye. She transported illegal goods in the middle of the night, and when she heard shots behind her, she continued on her way without even turning around. She did all sorts of hard work to keep us from going hungry, and she had to raise us as well. Life was hard; food was very expensive and difficult to come by. Mother used to go away for days at a time and leave us in the house. I was so hungry that I would eat pieces of coal and raw potatoes. Once, while looking for a way to quiet my hunger, I found some saccharin and ate it. I nearly poisoned myself, and Mother barely managed to save me.

The war raged closer and closer to us (we were near the Lithuanian border). We lived outside of town in a field. We trembled when we heard shots nearby; the windowpanes rattled, and the whole house seemed to dance. The town was anxious. Every so often there would be rumors that the fighting was getting nearer, that the war was approaching our town. By this time there was no way to earn a living. Life came to a standstill. The fear that "they" would come and massacre the entire town kept people from leaving their houses. Mother was also afraid to let us out in the field. She had no choice but to sit there with us and starve. I didn't even mind going hungry, because Mother was there with us.

Once, in the middle of the night, we heard loud movements near our door—rustling, banging, crashing. Mother hung a sack over the window, and all four of us lay in bed, trembling. In the morning, as soon as it was light, we were shocked to see what had happened! The windowpanes were all broken, and horses poked their heads in through the windows. All around the house, horses had been tethered. Cossacks had arrived overnight and set up their camp nearby. For two or three days we were trapped behind a thick wall of horses and couldn't get out. We were afraid to show any signs of life. Our situation was desperate. We were caught between the danger of being trampled under the horses' hooves and dying of starvation. Mother gave us whatever there was to eat in the house. She herself fasted. Fortunately, the Cossacks were forced to retreat as the Germans approached. Then some people remembered the woman and her three children. When they entered the house, they found Mother unconscious and us children in bed crying, weak from hunger.

When Mother came to, the town was astir with the news that the Germans were coming. Rotten potatoes gathered from the fields (our only nourishment at the time) weren't enough to still our hunger, and even this supply soon ran out. People began to flee the town, heading to any place that seemed out of the war's reach.

Mother realized that we also had nothing to lose; we could find hunger anywhere. So she sold everything in the house, saving only a few shirts for each of us, and we went to Panevėžys. I remember how I cried when the clock was taken off the wall. My only pleasure in life had been listening to it strike the hour.

When we arrived in Panevėžys, we were shown to a small synagogue, which was being used to house the homeless. This was our new home. Mother immediately went out to earn some money; she did laundry, washed floors, and tended to the sick. We no longer suffered from hunger. Every day new families arrived at the synagogue, having fled their homes just as we had. It got very crowded. At night you couldn't even find a place to stand. The floor was like a big bed, on which dozens of refugees found a place to close their eyes and forget about their troubles for only a couple of hours. Strangers who had never even seen each other before lay all tangled together on the floorboards. We didn't know who was healthy and who was sick, where anyone came from or why they had come. Everyone was pressed together in one big mass.

During the day it was terribly noisy. People argued, cursed, fought, and stole. The screams rose up to the sky. There was a mean dog that tormented us, too. When Mother went off to work, people did whatever they wanted to us. They would hit us, take our food, or move our things to the door and take our places. At night, Mother would come home exhausted and have to fight with everyone over the way they had treated us. I found these fights to be worse than the blows I received myself. I was always afraid that people would hurt Mother, so I would stand next to her, thinking, "Hit me rather than my mother."

But this way of life didn't last long. One day, we were ordered by the authorities to go to the bathhouse. This was nothing new with the Germans; we had to obey them. That evening when we returned from the bathhouse, we found all our things outside and the synagogue locked. More than a hundred families were out on the street. There was a tremendous panic. The streets were filled with screaming, crying, and cursing. People wandered the streets, some fainted, while others scrambled about, looking for things to steal. Mother gathered a few of our things, took us by the hand, and went looking for a place to spend the night. We wandered through the streets until late at night without finding anything. Suddenly, we came upon a big, dark building. The windows were boarded up. No one had lived there for some time. We went inside and spent the night there.

The ground floor of the building, where there had been an apartment, was locked. But on the second floor there was a large anteroom that might have been a kitchen, since there was a big oven there. The doors, windows, and walls were all broken, and everything was boarded up. Having found this place, we moved in. Mother bought an old cot for us to sleep on, and we lived there.

When winter came, with its frosts and storms, streams of snow poured in through the boards. So we set up the cot beside the oven. When the oven was hot, the three of us would sit on the bed with our heads in the oven to keep us warm. When the oven was cold, we lay in bed covered by a heap of rags. Many times, as the oven was heating up, I would crawl inside. But I couldn't stay there for very long. I soon had to crawl out again, choking from the smoke and smeared with soot. We weren't cold at night, because Mother lay beside us. Then it was nice and warm.

Mother knew many people who would give her work. Her life was very hard. She washed laundry in the river even during the coldest weather. Twice she fell through the ice into the river with a sled full of laundry. She was rescued both times by a soldier, who was standing nearby on sentry duty. He pulled her out by extending his rifle to her to grab onto. As soon as she had dried off, she was back at the river, chilled to the bone, washing laundry.

We couldn't go out all winter because we had no warm clothing. So we lay in bed, nothing but our faces showing, and waited for our mother. She would relieve our hunger, our longing, and our sadness. The winter passed so slowly, each day the same as the one before.

One day after Passover, Mother ran into Father's rich uncle, who lived in a nearby town. Mother asked him if I could live with him for the summer, because I looked very pale, and she thought I'd be able to get better there. It would also be a little easier on her.

My uncle was very rich. He owned a courtyard surrounded by a brick wall, a big store, stables, and granaries. He had three sons and a daughter; the youngest was three years younger than I. No one there took any interest in my arrival on the scene. They called me for meals, but otherwise they forgot about me. I used to wander around like a lost lamb or curl up in a corner and cry for my mother. There was one thing that I did find very interesting—watching my cousin make bricks out of clay and match boxes. But he wouldn't let me watch and used to shoo me away; and when I wouldn't leave he would hit me. Then I'd walk away, humiliated, and wander around the yard with the chickens. I slept on a bench in the big kitchen. A small mattress made of hay was my only bedding, a torn black coat my only blanket. The bench stood next to the window, and when I slept my head rested on the window sill. There were no shutters on the window, and at night it would seem to me that someone was standing next to the window, demons were dancing in the yard, someone was knocking on the door, and other such childish fantasies. Many times I screamed or cried in fear, but no one heard me. Everyone else was sleeping, three or four rooms away from the kitchen. I would cry until I fell asleep.

Eventually, I became malnourished. There was no shortage of food in the house; they used to throw out things that were never even seen at my mother's house. But days would pass when no one even noticed that I hadn't eaten. I wouldn't take anything myself, and I was ashamed to ask. So there were times when I went hungry.

I didn't like the people in the household. I used to avoid them. The children teased me and called me names. They often hit me for no reason. I hated them all, but I had to be meek and polite. The worse my situation became, the more I longed for my mother. I spent four months like this, becoming even thinner and paler from not eating, from longing and crying. My skin turned yellow from the dirt and vermin. Once, when my uncle took a good look at me, he got scared. He thought I was sick, so he sent me back to my mother. I could hardly wait.

I was so happy to lay eyes on the front steps of the ruin, with its boarded-up windows. I knew that behind those blackened walls waited my beloved mother, for whom my heart longed. Once inside, I gazed at every corner lovingly. I was so thankful to see it all once again that I became completely overwhelmed. I started to cry and asked my sisters where our mother was. I didn't know where she was—yet I was sitting in her arms! Mother started to cry and pressed me to her heart. The familiar embrace cleared my mind. We both cried, and our tears spoke for us: "My dear child!" "Oh, Mama, I missed you so!"

One morning, the owners of the house in which we were living returned from abroad unexpectedly. When they saw us, they didn't say anything but let us continue to live there. They set up an apartment for themselves on the other side of the building. Unfortunately, the owner suddenly became sick with typhus. Under the German occupation, whenever someone became sick with a communicable disease the entire household was sent to a quarantine, where we were treated worse than prisoners. The building where we were held was like a prison—a tall brick wall surrounded it, and there was a barbed-wire fence, bars on the windows, and an armed guard at the door. They barely gave us enough food to hold body and soul

together. Going out on the street was prohibited; we could leave, accompanied by a soldier, only if it was absolutely necessary. The guards checked
twice a day to make sure that no "prisoner" was missing. We spent a month
and a half there. After that, they let us go and we went back to live in the
same place as before.

One day, Mother noticed someone lying on some straw at the entrance
to the building. She went over to find out who was lying like that on the
ground. It was a boy, about fourteen or fifteen years old, who was lame and
mute. His father had abandoned him, and so he just lay there. When Mother
looked him over, she burst into tears. His body was filthy and covered
with large sores. There were worms crawling around under his soiled rags.
Passersby trampled on him. He had such a pleading look on his face that it
was heartrending. Mother heated some water and washed him, gave him a
new shirt, put down some fresh straw, and left. When people in town found
out about this, they couldn't stop talking about what Mother had done.
Then the Jewish community council took an interest in the matter, and they
even offered Mother a free apartment and a little money to take care of the
boy.

Mother liked the plan very much. Within a couple of days we were in a
small second-floor apartment that had doors and windows. Mother took
better care of the boy than she did of us. We slept on the floor, while she
gave him the bed. As soon as the boy was out of their sight, the townspeople
forgot about him. They provided food for him for the first month, and after
that did nothing.

Four months passed. The boy ate what we ate; Mother didn't differentiate
between him and us. His condition improved quite a bit. His face was
brighter, he looked happier, and his sores had healed completely. Suddenly,
Mother became sick. She kept working as long as her strength held out. But
eventually, she couldn't get out of bed. Once again we suffered from hunger,
and the boy suffered along with us. Mother then took the boy in her arms
and carried him to the synagogue. She demanded that they provide him
with food or she would leave him there and they could take care of him.
(Mother never really intended to abandon him.) There was a great commotion in the synagogue. Finally, they promised Mother they would take
care of everything, and we went home with the boy. For a while the Jewish
community council did, in fact, provide food for the boy, but then they
stopped again. Mother had recovered and was able to return to work, so she
didn't care whether or not they threw something the boy's way.

The boy continued to get better day by day. He became our one interest
in life. Every day we observed carefully whether he had improved. In the
meantime, the frosts were approaching, and it became very cold in the

house. We loved the boy very much, and he loved us. He used to hug and kiss us. I remember that the word "Mama" once escaped from his mouth. That day was like a holiday for us. We thought he would soon begin to speak—but several days later, he died. It was as if something had been torn out of our hearts. Our house was empty without him. I used to spend entire days thinking about him.

When he was still alive, we often used to talk about the next world, about how his mother was there interceding for him, and so on. When he died, I had many fantasies about how his mother would come to take him and everyone would be so happy to see him. After all, he was so good, so good. And nothing would ever hurt him again. But I often thought that it would have been better if he had lived. After all, we were also fond of him. It would have been so good if he had begun to speak. He would have told us what his name was and what was hurting him. We would have told each other stories, and Mother would have brought him nice things. He loved Mother so much. Whenever I thought about these things, I always started to cry again.

In the middle of winter we got a letter from an acquaintance saying that Father had returned from the war. Mother went to see him immediately, leaving us in Lithuania for the time being. Four weeks later, she came to get us. Father had returned while the war was still raging. He had become sick and was sent home. When he arrived back in S. with quite a bit of money, he rented an apartment and went on with his life. He didn't give a thought to Mother or to us. When Mother showed up he pretended not to know that she was his wife and that he had three children; he even told his landlady not to let us in to see him.

The old battles between my parents started up once again. Our life was completely disrupted. We used to sleep in the homes of different people we knew, never staying at the same place two days in a row. When people saw how Father was letting us wander around, they continued to criticize him until he rented an apartment for us—but he did so only on condition that Mother wouldn't stay there. The place he rented for us was a small shed built onto the side of a house. The room was the size of a long, narrow crate. There was no floor. Four blocks of wood had been driven into the ground, like four feet, and several boards were laid on top of them. This was our bed. There was no oven. Only gloom peered through the small window, which was level with the ground. We arrived there for the first time at dusk. I lay on the bed and my heart ached with longing for Mother, who had just been torn away from us. Even the sky had been taken away; the window was under the bed. Lonely, hungry, and with nowhere to lay her head, Mother began to travel about the countryside, buying and selling wheat.

Mother used to come to see us every other week, sometimes even less often. My longing for her grew until it was without end or measure. My gray days were filled with wondering about her—what she was doing, where she was going, and what she was thinking. Every day I waited by the road and watched to see if she would come, but to little avail. When she did come, I couldn't tear myself away from her. I clung to her skirt and followed her every step.

With Mother gone and Father left to care for us, he rented a better apartment and we moved in with him. I didn't like living with Father. With each passing day, I hated him more and more and trembled at his glance. Father used to go to the countryside with goods and exchange them for food. When he returned with sacks full of peas, beans, flour, and potatoes, women would gather around him and buy up everything immediately. Every day my older sister and I would go with a big wooden bucket on a stick and get free food from the public kitchen. They would pour us a bucket of water with a couple of potatoes in it, and sometimes not even that. They gave out bread twice a week. But Father didn't give us any; he kept it for himself. He would go to the country for two or three days at a time and leave us a little plate of potatoes to eat along with the water from the public kitchen. We weren't allowed to ask for more. When he returned from the countryside and the bargaining began, the three of us would stand to the side, our lips trembling, and devour everything with our eyes. All this food tempted us so much that, when Father wasn't looking, we would steal a few potatoes and hide them in the bed under the mattress. Once, when Father caught us at this, he beat us so badly that we were afraid to get down from the oven for a whole week. I remember that when Father ate, we weren't allowed to sit at the table. When he left the table, my younger sister used to climb down from the oven and gather the crumbs that he had left on the table. Dirty, hungry, covered with scabs, without a mother, with no one to take care of us, we used to spend whole days lying on the oven.

When Mother visited, she wasn't allowed to come to see us. We had to meet her at someone else's house. We would surround her from all sides, cry, and tell her about our troubles. Once, when we came crying to our mother, she could no longer restrain herself and ran off to see Father in the market. He was there selling apples, which were a luxury at the time. Furious, she threw all the apples out on the street. Since we were all starving, she said, he, too, should go without food. My father responded by hitting her in the head with a heavy object. When I saw my mother with her head bandaged, I fainted. After I revived, I went berserk. I was so afraid that I ran from Mother, screaming—but my love for her brought me back. My screaming attracted attention. I was terribly afraid. But my mother was so dear to me that I was ready to die for her sake. With trembling hands and a pounding heart I unraveled the bandage around her head and saw the big, bloody wound. I started screaming even louder. But I didn't let her head be rebandaged; I just stared at the wound and screamed. Oh, how I longed to fly away with Mother and forget all our troubles.

This incident had a terrible effect on me. A fire of love and hate burned in my five-year-old heart. I pitied my mother. We were named in memory of her parents. Her brother had moved away. All that she had was a sick sister, who lived in the same town that we did and also had a mean husband. My mother toiled and cared for us. But who took care of her? Who could she depend on? Who could she cry to? My love for her was so strong that it was hard for me to live without her. And to the same degree that I loved my mother, I began to hate my father.

While her head healed, Mother didn't go anywhere, and I didn't leave her side. But when I realized that I would have to return to Father when Mother left, a shudder ran through my body. I would have to live in Father's house and see him every day. I couldn't accept this. The thought didn't let me rest. I would lie day and night, crying and thinking about what to do, until I decided not to return to Father. But I didn't tell Mother this, because I was afraid she would force me to go back to him. Also, perhaps I didn't want to cause any trouble. So I told her nothing of my plan.

When Mother's head was better, she did leave, assuming that I would stay with Father. But I stuck to my plan not to cross his threshold or look at his face. The first day after Mother left, I wandered through the streets. I didn't even think about eating or sleeping. Longing for her made me forget everything else. When it got dark, I found an unlocked hallway and spent the night there. From then on, the hallway was my bed and the streets were my friends. I don't remember exactly what I ate, or if I went begging when I was seized with hunger pangs. But it seems to me that the towns-people knew me and would call me into their houses to give me food. I do remember that I once took a big crust of bread to my father's house when he was away, shared it with my sisters, and then left again.

Once, when people found me sleeping in the hallway, they made a big fuss. They ran to Father and made his life miserable for not taking me into his house or paying attention to me. Father didn't like me either, because I was so devoted to Mother. But he did have a sense of shame. I remember that in the evening, as soon as it got dark, there would be a search for me. Together with Father, the whole town set out and chased after me, trying to catch me and bring me back to his house. I would run through the streets wildly, trying to escape their grasp. But when they finally caught me and tried to drag me off to Father's, I would scream and kick until they had to let me go. Then I would trudge through the streets once again, like a hunchback in my tattered clothing, until I flopped down somewhere and went to sleep or someone took me in. (Twelve years later, when I returned to S., I recognized the hallway where I had slept.)

Once, I learned that my mother had come to town, but it was because her sister was very sick; Mother had to care for her in the hospital and didn't even have time to see us. I went to the hospital in my rags, but I didn't know any Polish and they sent me away. However, I didn't leave. From early in the morning until evening, I waited by the door for my mother. Then she came out. When she saw me, she cried bitterly and told me to go home. (She didn't know I was sleeping on the street in those frosty winter nights.) I didn't want to go, but she begged me to because I wasn't allowed to stay there. I said nothing and left. The next day, when she found out how I was living, she sneaked me into the hospital, where we both slept in the same bed with her sister. We lay on a corner of the bed so as not to disturb her.

We spent a couple of weeks in the hospital, until my aunt recovered. When my aunt left the hospital, we stayed with her. It was a difficult time for my mother. She had spent all her money on my aunt's illness. Mother didn't have anything to bring to the market. We children also caused her plenty of sorrow. The situation couldn't go on like this. She decided to make a break with Father. Because she wasn't traveling, she took us to live with her and asked Father for a divorce. It was two weeks before Passover. They agreed to divorce after Passover.

We were so happy to be with our mother that we no longer felt the pangs of hunger. But Mother suffered just by looking at us. Her mother's heart was so deeply pained by our suffering that she neglected herself completely. She would go to Father's house, break his locks, and knock out his windows to get us some food. She even took a pot of food that was cooking on his stove and brought it to us.

A week before Passover Mother went to another town to buy some fish. I felt that I wouldn't be able to live without her. When she didn't return after two days, I couldn't stand it any longer and went looking for her.

Twelve versts away was a town where Mother often went. I set out on the road to this town, thinking she must surely be there. I was so driven by love that I didn't even look where I was going. I wandered off the road, walked through ditches, over hills and train tracks, through sand and forest, but I always found my way again. I walked quickly and fearlessly. After I had walked about eight versts I entered a dense forest. A little way into the forest, I came upon some pigs grazing. Barely six years old, I didn't know what pigs were. All I knew from children's stories was that there were bears in the woods, and that bears ate people. Thinking these were bears, I became frightened and started to scream. Luckily, there was a house nearby. Hearing my screams, everyone ran out to see what was going on. When the peasants saw me, they brought me to the house and gave me some kvass to drink. When I calmed down after resting for a while, I didn't know what to do next. I couldn't speak with the peasants. Whenever I'd start to leave, they'd stop me. I don't know how it would have ended, but just then a Jew from my town came by the house. When I told him how I'd come there, he put me in his wagon and took me to my destination. He dropped me off and went on his way. I wandered around the unfamiliar town, but I didn't find my mother. Finally I found my way to the courtyard of the synagogue. I couldn't walk any further. Exhausted, I sat down on a step and started to cry. A crowd began to gather around me; people asked me who I was, why I was crying. I had one answer to everything: "Where is my Mama?"

My young heart hadn't misled me when it sent me there and not somewhere else. Mother had in fact come to this area. She had bought the fish two miles from the town where I now was. On her way back, her heart had pulled her in my direction. She saw the crowd and went to see what was happening. Then she saw me sitting and crying. When she came toward me I couldn't believe my own eyes. We went straight home.

For Passover we ate the smelts that Mother had bought, and behind the public kitchen I found some potato peels, which we chopped up. This was our Passover feast. Our stomachs remained untouched by either bread or matzah.

After Passover, my parents started to talk about their divorce. Women came to give Mother advice about how to divide up her children. I was greatly upset. I listened each time they discussed where I should go. To my misfortune, everyone advised Mother to take my older sister and leave my younger sister and me with our father. Let him take care of us; an older child would be easier for Mother. I cried day and night. My eyes were always full of tears. I did everything I could; my tears and pleas were meant to reach all the way to heaven.

The day of the divorce approached. This day would decide my fate. I wore out Mother and everyone else by following them around and pleading, but I never grew tired. I made a fuss wherever I went; I never stopped pleading, "I want to stay with my mother." (I now wonder where I got the energy to make such an effort.) The rabbi also said that Mother should take my older sister, but I didn't let up; I didn't let go of Mother's skirt. My pleading and crying couldn't help but have an effect. Everyone talked and talked about the question, but they couldn't reach a conclusion. They all shrugged their shoulders and looked at me.

My mother didn't want to part with any of her three children, so she tried to get Father to pay her a small amount so she could keep us all. He wouldn't have to give her more than enough to keep us fed. But Father wasn't an especially generous man. Besides, what did he care if we stayed with him? He could put us to good use. My older sister saved him a lot of work.

In the end, I was "victorious." I aroused so much pity in everyone that it was decided I would remain with Mother. Everything was agreed to and arranged. The divorce could now take place. The rabbi's wife wanted to take Mother into another room and give her final instructions. But when Mother started to go in, I followed her, clinging to the hem of her dress. The rabbi's wife told me to wait, that my mother would soon return. But I refused to remain behind. I didn't trust anyone. I thought they were tricking me, only fooling when they said I would remain with my mother, and now they were going to talk behind closed doors about how I would stay with Father. I wouldn't let go of Mother's dress. Once again, there was an uproar. They threatened me and shouted at me. But I paid them no attention. I stubbornly persisted, as if an inner voice were whispering to me over and over, "Don't let up for a minute." They couldn't talk me out of this, either. I went into the room with them. My parents divorced, and I stayed with my mother. A few days later, I was with her, on our way into the wide world.

It was a warm, sunny, spring day. I went barefoot, in a light little dress, without even an undershirt. Mother left everything I had with my sisters. Oh, how good it was to take those first steps away from suffering! The sand, warmed by the sun, tickled my bare feet. The sun's rays warmed my blood, frozen by the long, cold winter. My heart felt joyous, free, and fearless. I was happy. I walked alongside Mother. Where we were going, we didn't know. But Mother had a plan. She thought only of finding work somewhere, so that she could support all three children. Then she would take my sisters away from Father, and no one would bother us anymore.

In the meantime, we wandered from one town to the next. But there was no work to be had. We spent what little money Mother had and once again went hungry. At the time the borders were open. We crossed a small river by boat and entered Lithuania. We found ourselves in a little town. There was a synagogue not far away, so we went inside to rest. We lay on a bench all day without eating. By evening, hunger began to torment us. We had no money, but we couldn't suffer any longer; we had already known enough hunger. Mother could no longer bear to look at my pale, hungry face and said to me in a tearful voice, "Go to a house, my child, and beg for food." I hesitated for a moment, and then I went.

I entered a house and said what Mother had told me to say: "I want something to eat." The people there looked at me amazed. They saw that I wasn't a local child—how could such a little girl be all alone? "Do you have a mother?" they asked. I answered that my mother also wanted something to eat. They sat me down and served me some food, and they gave me potatoes and milk for Mother.

Mother cooked the potatoes in the milk, and I sat down on the steps of the synagogue to eat. From far off a soldier saw me eating (he was standing guard at the river that we had crossed). He came over to me and put me on his lap. I gave him my spoon, and he started to eat. In a moment the bowl was empty. I went to Mother and asked for more. She gave me another bowlful, amazed that I had eaten the first one so quickly. When she came out and saw that I was holding the bowl and a soldier was eating, she stood to the side and watched, pleased with my generosity. When he finished, she served me some more.

That was the first time I begged for a meal during my four bitter years of wandering. We went from town to town. Mother never found a permanent job. Once, she worked for a few weeks in a bakery, but usually she stayed at each job for only a short time. I also made it harder for her. No one wanted to hire a woman with a child. My mother also realized that she wouldn't be able to help her children if she took a job as a servant in someone's home. So we wandered on. It was already fall. Cold winds and rain came down on our barely clothed bodies. We had no roof over our heads. On rainy nights we slept in the streets, until we caught typhus. Mother became sick one day, and I the next.

We were in a small town, where there was nothing more than a *feldsher*. For days we lay in a bathhouse. We continued to get sicker. Twenty-eight versts from the town there was a very large hospital that served the entire area. We had no choice but to pack up our things and somehow make our way to the hospital. The road was long and hard. More than once, we fell to the ground, but we managed to get up and continue on our way. To make things worse, we got lost and barely found our way back to the road. After two days of trudging, we arrived, exhausted, in the hospital courtyard. But they wouldn't admit us. Mother had to go to another town seven versts away and get a note from a committee. It didn't matter how weak or tired we were. I stayed in the courtyard with our belongings, and Mother left. She went from office to office, and each one sent her somewhere else. No one wanted to do anything for a stranger. Eventually, Mother fainted as she was leaving an office; she had a temperature of 40°C [104°F]. They were barely able to revive her and send her to the hospital.

The walking had been so harmful to us that we had to be wrapped in cold sheets to bring down our high fever. We lay there a long time. Many people died when we were there, while many others got better. I remember: there was a gentile girl near my bed. In the middle of the night she took a turn for the worse. There was no heat in the building. We rang the bell for the attendant, but no one came. We banged on the walls, we pounded and shouted. The doors were locked, so it was impossible to go and get help. In the middle of the night, the girl died. She let out a cry and fell silent. I was so scared that I ran to my mother's bed. We didn't have the strength to shout. We just lay there and trembled with fear.

From then on we got worse; in addition to typhus, we came down with something else as well. When we left the hospital—skinny, pale, weak—we could barely stand up. We didn't know where to go or what to do. We just stood there like the bags of bones we had become. Mother could no longer do heavy work. Besides being weak from her illness, she had injured herself carrying heavy sacks of wheat. The borders were closed at this time, so it was impossible to return to Poland. In any case, we had nowhere to go and no one to turn to. Our impoverished and miserable life began to decline even further. It was like a stream running downhill, sweeping us along, and we had no choice but to go with it. We were too weak and broken to resist the flow.

We became wandering beggars—Oh, how it hurts when I think of those four years of begging. When I touch this wound today, it still bleeds. I am too weak today, and there is too little time, to describe those four years in detail. For the time being, it will have to remain undisturbed deep within my soul. Maybe some day I will be able to convey it in a story. And what use would the description be? Would I be able to calculate how many dozens of miles I walked with a pack on my back? How many towns I passed through, and how many tragedies I witnessed and experienced myself? There were too many, beyond counting, for me to write about them now. Those four years had many days, but they were all the same, filled with bitter poison. How many days did I fall down exhausted in a field, with my pack on my back? How many winter days did the tears freeze on my cheeks and my body turn to wood, as I walked on snowy paths in burning frost? How many times did we sleep in the woods, the fields, or the streets? How many people raised their hands to strike us and spill our blood? How many times were we threatened with death? And there's no end to the other "how manys," which recall so much pain and make my heart ache even now. Four years passed. Four years, which led to more years that were no better. We sank ever lower into the depths of a life of begging. All means of escape were blocked for us. And yet we couldn't continue to live in misery, wandering about, a day here and a night there, mixing with the lowest underworld characters, in so much filth and degeneracy.

There was one way out, which was hard for Mother even to consider: marry a wealthy older man, so she could at least look after her children.

(We didn't hear anything from my sisters during the entire four years.) Even before she could put this plan into effect, a man who was about fifty years old took a liking to her and wouldn't leave her side. He told Mother that he had a lot of money and owned property in Poland, and that as soon as they were married they would go to Poland and open a business. Mother liked the idea that she'd be able to take back her other children. But it turned out very differently. This was the hand that dragged us deeper into the mire. After their wedding, Mother realized that this man had deceived her. He had no money to open a business. His children made their living from his property, of which he owned only a quarter share. He had no means with which to go to Poland, and there was no reason to go. When Mother found out that she was doomed forever, she beat her head against the wall, screamed, threw fits, and fainted. But it was no use—it was too late. My stepfather was a good, "educated," and refined man. He loved Mother very much. That's why he had behaved so deceitfully. Life didn't change; it continued on its cursed way. Mother gave birth to a little girl! A life of wandering became unbearable with a little baby, and we started to look for a place to settle.

Seven versts from Kaunas stood the oldest fortress in Lithuania. After the war, it was all battered and shot up. Bricks and scraps of iron lay strewn about the place, which had once stored weapons and gunpowder. Nothing remained but the walled-in underground barracks, tunnels, canals, and other secret, subterranean chambers, cisterns, and stairways that linked the entire fortress. When we arrived, there were already twenty-five refugee families living in the four large barracks. The walls in these rooms were always shiny from the water that ran down them. All the available space was already taken. People lived everywhere. Peasants even lived in huts they had built on top of the barracks.

There was a big field over the underground barracks, where people could live and even have a well and a cow grazing by the door. At the entrance to the part of the fortress occupied by Jews there was a small room where no one lived, because it was said to have once been a latrine. In fact, the walls were covered with pitch, and it had an odor that never went away. The floor was made of cement. There were two windows: one was narrow and bright and looked out onto the street; the other was big and dark—like the walls, from which dripped big, black drops of water—and looked out on a dark tunnel that seemed to be endless. It was frightening to look through this window, even during the day. Not having any alternative, we moved into these quarters, together with another family, and made this our home.

Each day, everyone left the house to look for work in the city. I stayed behind to take care of my little sister, who was still in diapers. I was ten years old at the time. I lived in this place for four years. During this time I changed from a child into a young woman, and my emotions and my reason matured. Those four years of underground life were filled with dismal, lonely, painful, despairing days.

It was winter when we first set foot in the place. There was no oven in our little room. I made food for the baby and myself on a small burner. The baby was very irritable under my care. If she was wet, she screamed. If I didn't diaper her well, she screamed again. I used to run all over the house with her, not knowing what she wanted from me. During the long winter nights, when everyone else who lived with us was still in town, I would sit in a corner with the child in my arms and tremble with fear. It seemed to me that demons were dancing in the tunnel, and whenever I accidentally looked through the dark window, an icy chill ran through my body. I was even afraid to move my own hand. I was afraid of my own shadow. Many times I wanted to cry but was afraid to make a sound.

I wasn't allowed inside the big, decaying barracks, because the people who lived there considered me a spy. Our neighbors had a son who fell in love with a girl who lived in the big barracks. His parents were against the relationship, so they sent me to spy on their son and report back to them. I also reported on other couples whom I encountered at unseemly moments. When the people who lived in the barracks found out about this, they cast me out and never let me back.

Among the twenty-five families who lived there was a quiet, forlorn couple with a small child. The three of them had a very difficult life. They had no trade, and it was hard for them to get work so far away from town, so they were always hungry. Life in the fortress didn't suit them well, either. In this cauldron, seething with more than a hundred lives, people oppressed one another. The strong dominated the weak. This family lived in constant hunger and fear. They couldn't go off to look for work, because they had nowhere to leave their child. Mother took pity on them and told them to leave the child with me. This is how I came to care for two children.

It was hard for me during those long, cheerless winter nights, when I was alone with the children. To my despair, they'd both cry at the same time. Their voices frightened me. It seemed to me that between their screams I could hear another voice. Many times I was scared even to move about the room to get something to quiet the children. I was so afraid that one cold night I took both children in my arms (one of them still asleep) and stood in the entryway. Although the darkness and the iron gates of the tunnel scared me even more, I felt better being closer to other people.

After we had lived in our little room for a year, a place opened up in the main barracks. We moved in with our few rags, boxes, and the boards that we used as beds. We had barely arranged our "furniture" in a corner near the door when our neighbor, whose space was next to ours, came in drunk and wrecked everything. He pounced on us and beat us. He needed this corner, he said, to keep his kitchen things. It was a terrible night. Everything we owned lay in pieces near the door. Our uneaten dinner had been spilled along with our belongings. It looked like a true catastrophe. We had nowhere to sleep, and we stayed up all night out of fear, sitting among our broken, scattered possessions. The next day, when the drunk sobered up, we talked him into letting us stay.

My life passed like a long, overcast day. I didn't know that there was a world with better people. I only knew that I had to care for children. Later, I also became a cook. When my mother came home from town she found dinner ready, and on Friday everything was ready for the Sabbath. At first, I had no girlfriends. I was always busy, and besides, no one interested me. And when I did occasionally feel like standing at the side and watching people play cards or jacks, they would shoo me away. I spoke little. I was always apart, always by myself. That life underground, far from the hustle and bustle, is amazing. You live simply because you aren't dead, and that is all. You know nothing else. You will do tomorrow what you did today; there is no difference between today and tomorrow. And yet time doesn't stand still. Days, months, and years fly by, just as they do in the mansions of the rich. Only there, it is more noticeable. Here, there's nothing but trouble, hunger, cold, and suffering, and it seems like one big, long day.

I became a wage earner. I carried water and took care of children, for which I was paid. Carrying water was no easy job! I had to climb up onto the roof, where there was a cistern, covered by a kind of hut with no door. The water was drawn through a wide, deep window. I had to lie down on the window ledge to pull up a pail full of water. I always had to bring a small can to fetch the water, because the pail was heavier than I was at twelve years of age.

Thursdays were especially hard for me, because then the women would go to town to shop for the Sabbath and would leave their children with me, for which I was paid. I would be surrounded by four or five children; they all had to be diapered, and I had to prepare each one a different meal. They were so much trouble! I would run from one crib to the next. As soon as one child fell asleep, another one woke up. It was really awful when they all started screaming at once. Also, sometimes a child would fall and get a scrape or a bump. Then his mother would yell at me and not want to pay me.

Summer days, when the warm sun shone, were very hard for me. From the fields and woods came the smell of raspberries, and the air was like perfume. The barracks emptied, and everyone went off into the woods: mothers with little children, boys and girls, boyfriends and girlfriends.

Smaller children who were my age used to play hopscotch and other games
near the fortress. But I remained shut behind the fortress's earthen walls,
overgrown with mushrooms, breathing the poisonous air and looking after
the children. There were moments when I sat by the window with a sleeping child in my arms and the others playing quietly on the floor around me.
I would look out the window at the children playing outdoors and cry.
My heart filled with childlike longing and sadness. The beauty of nature
beckoned and tugged at my heart. But those cursed earthen walls kept me
from everything. I loved to gather berries in the woods. When I heard
that a whole group was getting ready to go out, it upset me so much that I
couldn't go along; I'd accompany them as far as the door and then watch
with tears in my eyes as they disappeared into the hills. It was hard to tear
myself away from the door; I wanted to leap up, escape into the woods,
and never return. The cries of the children called me back into the house.
I could only go into the woods during the winter, when I tried to avoid the
watchman as I stole branches to burn for heat. Many times, I was scared by
the sight of the watchman with his rifle. I would scramble up the high hills
until I collapsed, breathless and bloody, inside the fortress. But I never complained about my fate. I never told anyone about the longing in my soul.
My heart trembled for only one thing, for my mother. My love for her continued to smolder and never cooled, despite the fact that she had grown a
little cooler toward me since my sister was born.

There were all sorts of people in the fortress: drunkards, gamblers, and
common loafers who lived from hand to mouth. Not a night went by
without fighting, quarreling, and cursing. It was especially bad for the weak,
who didn't have anyone to protect them. In addition to receiving frequent
beatings, they never had a moment's peace. Even as they lay in bed, they
were surrounded by people dancing, shouting, singing, and playing cards
until early in the morning.

Mother couldn't ignore these injustices, and she often got into fights that
came to blows. Nothing in the world was worse for me. Whenever I saw
that this was about to happen, I would run like a madwoman, first to my
mother, then to the person with whom she was fighting, and beg them to
stop. But this had little effect. They didn't pay any attention to me. When
they did start fighting, I'd run through the barracks looking for Mother's
good friends and tearfully beg them to help her. Sometimes, as I tried to
protect her, I would get beaten or trampled in the confusion myself.

Eventually, I adopted a new approach. When crying and pleading didn't
prevent a fight, I threw myself on the ground and started to bang my head
against the cement floor. There would be a big commotion, Mother would
try to calm me down, and the fight would end. I thought little about myself,

because my heart was always full of fear that my mother would be beaten. Whenever I heard a row, I would run to make sure that she wasn't in the middle of it.

On lonely Sabbaths, when I would lie in the grass and rest or wander in the woods looking for berries, I often thought about my sisters and was overcome with longing for them. Every time I thought of them, I'd see before my eyes the time I hit my younger sister. This thought gave me no rest. What wouldn't I have given to see them and beg her forgiveness? I always imagined them thin and pale like me, and I pitied them.

One evening in the fall, it was raining outside and gloomy within my heart; supper had been burned, and I stood there, full of worries. Some girls ran in and told me that one of my sisters was on her way. (Mother wasn't at home.) I couldn't believe it. I thought they were fooling me. When they convinced me it was true, I ran to meet my sister. As I ran, I imagined I would find her thin, pale, and bent like me. I imagined how we would embrace and kiss each other and cry, and tears started to flow from my eyes. But when I saw her, I stopped short, frozen to the spot. I didn't even have the courage to get close to her. There before me stood a girl with a fat, flushed face, her cheeks ruddy. She was four times as wide as I was, so fat that she even had trouble walking. She stood there and she looked at me with a cold and contemptuous gaze. An apathetic kiss reminded me that we were sisters.

From that first day, there was a distance between us. She looked down on me; I disgusted and embarrassed her. She called me nicknames like "Bent Tree" and "Skeleton."

Why did she come to visit us? This is what happened: a few weeks after Mother and I had left home following the divorce, my sister had stolen some flour from Father, sold it, and left to look for us with a family that was going to Lithuania. When she didn't find us, a teacher brought her to a small town, where she was taken care of as if she were the teacher's own child. Recently she had found out about us, and now she was here.

Coming from a better, more refined life, where children studied and didn't have to work, she always acted conceited and capricious. My sister made friends. She went to the movies and the theater and Mother was delighted with her. Mother treated me worse and worse every day; she often hit me and looked at me coldly. I would sit in a corner, alone and in rags. I saw how much Mother liked her other daughter, and I began to hate my sister.

No one could notice my hatred, because I was always quiet, gloomy, preoccupied, and grim. But suddenly it exploded over a trivial matter. Mother never made me any new clothing, nor did I make anything for myself. Whatever I earned I gave to her. She often told me that I should use the money to make some new clothes for myself, but whenever I saw that someone needed money, I gave it away. All I owned were a shawl and a colorful hat that I hardly ever wore, guarding it like a treasure. One time my sister felt like dressing up in my hat and going to the movies. This bothered me a great deal—not so much because she put it on, perhaps, as because she was going to the movies and not I. (I didn't even know what movies were then.)

I followed her, and on the way I snatched the hat from her head. But she was stronger and grabbed it back. In my agitated state, this infuriated me. All of a sudden, something erupted from me—an outcry against my silent suffering, against all the hard work I did and the way I was oppressed by everyone, culminating in my rage against my sister. But I wouldn't fight with her. With one move she could have torn me to pieces. Besides, I didn't want to fight with her at all. She was nothing more than the spark that ignited my frozen anger, which had been so patient and silent. I no longer saw my sister in front of me, but all of my futile suffering. I wanted to run off into the wide world, to wander the streets and never return to the cursed fortress. I ran off in no particular direction. Meanwhile, word of what had happened spread inside the fortress, and a crowd had gathered. The road was thick with people chasing me. I ran as if driven by some external force. No one could catch me.

When she saw that I was running away in earnest, my sister shouted, "Mother fainted and fell into a ditch." As soon as I heard this, I completely forgot where I was, what had happened to me, or what was going to happen. Immediately, I ran back, shouting, "Where's Mama?" Then they caught me, tied me up, and brought me back to the fortress. Mother hadn't fainted. They just said that to trap me. She was standing there, waiting for me with a big, heavy club. It was soft, made out of some sort of animal hide. The local toughs spent their days off trying to break it, without success. That was the club my mother was holding. They laid me out on a bench on the middle of the barracks. Everyone from the fortress gathered around, pushing and climbing on each other's shoulders. They all wanted to get a better view, as if it were a circus arena. My mother beat me, without stopping even to take a breath—now I believe she didn't realize what she was doing, and that it's possible the crowd had whipped her into a frenzy—until the club broke in two. There was an uproar, as people yelled about the destruction of the club and expressed pity for my thin, bony body and bloody mouth. I don't remember what happened after that. When I came to, I was lying in bed and Mother was sitting next to me.

The scene left no impression on me. When I saw Mother beside me, looking at me perhaps with regret and fear, I immediately forgot what had happened and felt happy that she was there. Later, I became so used to these blows that they no longer bothered me. The more Mother beat me, the more I loved her. So the days continued to pass.

My stepfather had a son who was serving in the military. Mother used to send him packages with money. At about this time he came home from the army along with a friend. Mother treated them both as if they were her own. When they came home from work, their food had to be ready. Meanwhile, my sister went to work in a coffee plant. My situation became worse day by day. I had to care for an entire household and, in addition, Mother brought home feathers for us to trim. In the morning, before she went to town, she would fill a pot with feathers and order that they be done by nightfall. In the evening, Mother wouldn't let my sisters and me leave the table. We sat and trimmed feathers until late at night.

I hated the people in the fortress very much. They were always fighting, quarreling, cursing, and insulting one another. They were frivolous and careless, always singing, dancing, engaging in lewd talk, and splitting open each other's heads. Every girl of thirteen or fourteen already had a "fiancé." Wise parents concerned about their children's future put them in a children's home, where they were taught to write and raised to be responsible people. The children's home only accepted children at an early age. When they reached thirteen or fourteen, they were sent back to their parents at the fortress. I simply idolized these children. Their refined speech, their writing skills, and their good nature enchanted me. I couldn't take my eyes off them. These were my first girlfriends. (Later they became like all the other girls there and had "fiancés" at an early age.)

I saw the city for the first time when I was twelve years old. I went with Mother to help her wash floors. The people in one house liked me and hired me as a servant. From then on I worked for others.

At the first place where I worked the people had a dry-goods store and also made tea bags at home. Once I settled in, I had three jobs: working in the store, making tea bags, and trimming feathers at night in the fortress with my mother. I felt no peace of mind at work. I could barely wait until the hour when I could go home to see what was happening there.

Two years passed like this. I was fourteen years old and my sister was seventeen. We began to realize where we were. The lewdness of life there disgusted us. We were ashamed even to say that we lived in the fortress. My sister had made some friends in town, and she nagged Mother to find an apartment somewhere and leave the fortress. When we moved out with our few boxes of belongings, I was overcome with longing for the fortress. I forgot about all the suffering I had experienced there. It suddenly became precious to me, and I didn't want to leave. I followed behind the wagon with a heavy heart.

A new life began. I found a new job in a bindery. As soon as I started to work there, I excelled at a job that no one else could do as well. I did the work of two people: at the bindery during the day, and at home until one o'clock at night. At first, my life didn't change much. I still had no girlfriends. I still worked day and night. I was always lonely; no one took an interest in me. My sister and I still had a distant relationship. She was ashamed even to admit that I was her sister. This bothered me very much. When I met her in town with her friends, she would turn away, as if she didn't even know me. I would come home crying and complain to Mother.

At fourteen, I was tall but very thin, and because of that I developed a stoop. People thought that I would remain hunchbacked for life. I was like a child who had been raised in the wild. The world seemed strange to me. Ordinary objects were foreign to me. I didn't even know the names of many things. When I learned that there were places called schools, where children were taught how to write and had books to read, it made me sad, because I had no one to teach me. If I saw someone reading, I was so resentful that I would cry. Once, when I saw a woman reading a Russian book, I went up to her and asked her to teach me to read. She laughed at me. But when I insisted, she taught me several letters. From then on, whenever I saw a piece of paper with writing on it, I looked for the familiar letters. I was happy if I found them.

The bindery had a union. I used to go with the other workers to meetings. Although I was not very worldly, they said I was smart. I began to take an interest in things that were unfamiliar to me. People gradually got closer to me. A general strike broke out in my line of work, and I became involved in a political party.

The very first lecture that I heard opened up a new world for me. I learned that humanity was divided into two classes: the hungry and the full, those who labor and those who do nothing. It was hard for me to understand everything all at once, but since I had experienced some of this in my own life, I didn't even give a thought to my lack of understanding. Passionately I plunged into the waves of my new life. With an ardent flame in my yearning heart, I devoted myself to party work. Every task I was assigned made me happy. The only thing that disturbed my happiness was the fact that I couldn't write. Late into the evening I sat with my stepfather, and he taught me the *alef-beys*, which I learned quickly. I began to write entire words. My stepfather told me what letter to write, and I would do it. For example, if I had to write *tish* [table], he would tell to me to write *tes, yud, shin*.

That's how our lessons went. I couldn't write a word on my own, and I was afraid that I would never be able to do so. So I started to do some studying on my own. I stayed up nights racking my brain, thinking. I no longer turned to my stepfather for help. It was difficult for me to figure out the correct method for writing a word on my own. But once I understood the right way, it became very easy. That's how I learned how to write. When I read over the first postcard that I wrote, I was the happiest person in the world. I started to take books out of the library, even though I couldn't read quickly yet and I didn't understand everything that I read. But I got a great deal out of this; it opened up the world for me a little, so that I could look inside it. When I got used to reading and could read quickly, I couldn't go anywhere without a book. Wherever I went I brought a book with me, so that I could read it in a free moment. My regular time for reading was from midnight until two o'clock in the morning.

Later on I found another new job, working in a large coffee plant along with my sister. My life was regulated like a machine. After work, I was busy in the city with party work from five until ten o'clock at night, from ten I knitted socks at home, from twelve until two I read. I got up at six to go to work. I slept for four hours a day; the other twenty I worked, either physically or intellectually.

My love for my mother cooled. What love I had belonged now to the party, to my ideals. Mother began to interfere with my work in the party. We began to quarrel, at first mildly; later, the battle between us raged. It wouldn't be accurate for me to say that my mother didn't love me. She did. But being a simple, over-worked woman, and living in such surroundings, she couldn't have raised me differently. Moreover, she had been abandoned by my father and had no education. She couldn't display her love tenderly, like other mothers, but kept it hidden within her heart. And that is why she didn't want me to devote my life to the party.

My external appearance changed. I gained weight, I stood up straighter and held my head higher. My gait became more certain. People even said that I didn't look any worse than my sister. The way that people related to me changed completely. In the party they had complete confidence in me. My sister also behaved differently toward me. She would now walk with me in the street. She asked me for advice and about the meaning of words she didn't know. (She had learned to write a little from a teacher before she came to live with us.)

My mother had three children, all girls, with my stepfather. Her life grew worse from day to day. She had to be both a mother to her children and a breadwinner. Her energy was exhausted at a young age, and she became weak, thin, and old. By the time she was thirty-five, she was as bent over as a woman of sixty. Her children caused her great anguish. Our political activities tormented her, but we paid her no mind. Our ideals were the most important things in the world for us, and when she got in our way we turned our backs on her.

The political organization I belonged to was the most sacred thing in my life. It made me forget what was happening around me. I devoted three quarters of my life to this inspirational work, and it even made the hard physical labor that I did seem easy. My life was like a stream of water overflowing its banks after the winter thaw, growing higher and faster by the minute. I climbed higher and higher. I occupied a respected position in the party. I was also very proficient in the factory where I worked. I could take the place of an accomplished artisan who had been working there for fifteen years, even though as I sat at work, my mind was occupied with getting ready for lectures, reading, and so forth. After work, my life was completely scheduled; every hour had its task. This lasted until twelve or one o'clock at night. When I came home, tired and hungry, Mother would greet me with a scolding and curses for coming home so late. Her screaming unnerved me so much that I would go to bed without dinner. So the days passed, one day the same as the next.

In the turmoil of my life I often thought about my other sister, who had remained with our father. I also reminded Mother about her, and eventually we wrote to her. I donated my entire savings to bring her to live with us. When she arrived she was thin, starved, and wild. I made it my task to "civilize" her. I taught her how to behave among other people, brought her books to read, and introduced her to other young people. It was hard for me to devote myself to her because I had so little time. But no one had an effect on her as I did. She would often hug and kiss me and say that she would do whatever I told her.

About three years passed like this, years about which I could say much. These were the most interesting years of my life. But I can't talk about them openly, because I don't want to reveal anything about my party activity. I was healthy, enduring the hardest work and the most difficult experiences. I walked through mud and snow up to my knees. I washed my muddy socks in the river, put them on still wet, and continued onward without even feeling how my feet were freezing. There were even times during the worst, coldest weather when Mother would hide my socks and coat, so that I wouldn't go into town. I would go anyway, wearing only my dress, and nothing bothered me. I never lacked energy and never complained. Without eating, without sleeping, I did everything calmly and with determination.

I would like to mention here just one significant detail about my party work, but I regret that I cannot describe it very clearly; there's much about which I keep silent. The party organization, in which there were hundreds more like me, chose me—-the only girl along with five men—to maintain order at an illegal demonstration. This shows how highly I was regarded in the party.

Then everything collapsed. My ability to make a living disappeared. A deep gloom gnawed at me. I always felt listless and preoccupied. I couldn't tolerate noise. People bored me. I longed for solitude and rest. I sat like a simpleton at meetings and rallies. No matter how much I strained to listen to the speakers, I couldn't do it. When they asked me something, I would jump as if awakened from sleep, not knowing what they were saying to me. I wanted to walk away from life altogether. But I couldn't, because I was too tightly bound up in it and had too many obligations.

Now, suffering and struggling with the unknown force that consumed my soul were all that remained for me. I hoped this would pass and thought that the best thing to do was ignore it. And so I threw away nine months of my life, nine months of terrible spiritual suffering from my unknown illness, nine months that seemed like nine years. I couldn't endure it any longer. Each day I sank further into the abyss. No one knew what was happening to me; I didn't understand it either. I felt as if I were carrying a heavy weight; that's all I knew. I had no close soulmates. I was in pain and a storm raged in my heart, which called out for something and wouldn't be still. I suffered silently from my cursed illness, without medicine, and life continued to pour salt on my wounds. I became so weak that I wasn't even capable of committing suicide, though I was ready to do so.

Life seemed so meaningless and empty that nothing interested me, and I had to do something to save my life. I had only one way out: to go away to a foreign land, where no one would know me; to wander the streets, greeting no one and stopping for no one; to live in a secluded spot, where no one could reach me—no parents, no sisters, no relatives, no one. This is what my ailing soul demanded.

I decided to go to Poland and live with my father, get a permit, and then move to a big city to realize my plan. And yet when I thought about this, I didn't believe that it would happen. I considered the idea no more than balm for my soul. I began to avoid going to the city. But I carried out my responsibilities to the party even better than before, because I had nothing to lose. What could I lose—my life? No one knew of my plan to leave except my mother, and she was happy about it, because she knew that I was leaving the party.

When I went with Mother to buy some little things for the trip on the day before my departure, I met a comrade whom I knew from the party. She had barely laid eyes on me before she said, "I've been looking for you for a whole week and haven't been able to find you. You're needed badly and are nowhere to be found!"

I couldn't speak to her. I felt weak and short of breath. I told her that I would come at nine o'clock. When I left her, I burst into tears in the middle of the street. I had deceived her. I had told a lie, a horrible lie. By eight o'clock I would already be on the bus. I walked through a gate, collapsed against the wall of a building, and started trembling violently. At 7:30 I was standing with my bags in the dark hallway, saying goodbye to my mother. She was so pale that her face was visible even in the darkness. Her eyes were so white and fearful that it was frightening just to look at them. We parted without words, as though we feared that even a word would ignite what was in our hearts—a kiss, and I was gone. She couldn't accompany me because I had to cross the border illegally, and the guide wouldn't allow her to come along. I heard her cries from afar. Who can put that night down on paper—the suffering of two broken people who had always been together, who had drunk the gall of life from the same glass, and who were both so desolate and broken, one physically, the other spiritually. On that night of parting, all those years of suffering together flew past my eyes, and the old feeling of love revived and burned with a mighty flame. The bus blew its horn as if to announce that it was on its way to a new life.

As I rode through the streets of Kaunas and looked out the window at acquaintances walking by, I was overwhelmed by self-loathing. "You, you are leaving," I said to myself. "What will they say about you?" And I felt so low and sinful that I wasn't worth my seat on the bus. Completely broken, I sat on the bus with my dark thoughts for a long time. Finally, exhausted from the sleeplessness of the previous night—when I had sobbed as I wrote a letter to my comrades—I fell asleep. When I woke up, I no longer had the ten dollars my mother had given me to tide me over until I found work. That was my first taste of the wide world.

The agent handed me over to a peasant, who was supposed to guide me over the border. We rode in a wagon for three bone-rattling days and nights. On the fourth night we came to within five versts of the border. I was brought to a peasant hut, together with a large number of peasants. They were all men; I was the only girl there. Sleeping was out of the question. The rascals poured water on anyone who fell asleep and played other similar peasant tricks. I was afraid to go to sleep in any case. I spent a day inside the hut. I wore a sheepskin coat, with a white kerchief over my head to make me look less foreign, and went with the peasants to cut straw.

At nine o'clock in the evening, I set out with five peasants and a Jewish young man to steal across the border. The peasants were drunk and carried packs on their backs. It wasn't a pleasant trip. We wandered around in the woods, full of darkness and fear. We fell down and got right back up. We got lost and continued on without any sense of direction. Often, we lost sight of the guide, or it was so dark in the woods that we were standing next to him and didn't even see him. And so, after nine hours of crawling with bated breath through swamps and streams, up to our knees in water and mud, we arrived on Polish territory. Our peasant guide vanished immediately, without even giving me enough for a ticket to travel to my father. (We had agreed that he was to take me to S.)

My situation was desperate. I took my basket and set off on foot. The Jewish young man who had come with me (he was from Vilna) had some extra money, so he bought me a ticket. On Friday night I arrived in the town where I was born. I didn't know where to go when I got off the train. I didn't want to ask. When I entered the town the streets seemed new to me, strange and unfamiliar. I wandered around the town for some time, until I was forced to ask for a distant relative of my mother. All I remembered was her name. I knew that she had loved us all very much, so I went straight to her home, imagining that she would be very happy to see me. But when I was brought in, I was received very coldly. When I said that I hadn't slept for several nights and would like to lie down, I was told there was no room. When her family found out who I was they took me to the home of my uncle (my father's brother), who lived on the same street. There they received me better. I fell asleep while talking with his family. The next morning, my father came and took me to his house. Later I found out that the place where I first went wasn't the home of my mother's relative at all. When she and I did meet, she was very happy. Father didn't treat me badly. Nevertheless, I felt very bad staying with him and wanted to go to Vilna as soon as possible to look for work. But I had to stay with him for two months before I saved enough money for the train fare.

In Vilna I had nowhere to go, nowhere to leave my bags. Luckily, I became acquainted with a young man who was studying there, and he found me a place to stay. I arrived with four zloty in my pocket. I found no work, but there was no shortage of trouble, nor, to be sure, of hunger. It was very hard for me to find a way to make a living, and, besides, I didn't know Polish. However, having nothing to eat, I ignored these obstacles. I found work in a pharmacy, to which I sold my twenty-four hours each day. I didn't even have a free minute. My whole life belonged to them.

It was very hard for me to accept this. It only made me more depressed.
I went around all day crying. My employers were very happy with me, especially with my skills; I quickly learned how to make up all the prescriptions.
I worked there for half a year. Then Father wrote that I should come spend
the holidays with him. Since I didn't care about the job and longed for a
little free time, I left. But I couldn't stay long with Father, either. I started
to move back and forth. After I'd had my fill of time spent with Father, I'd
go back to Vilna. And after a while in Vilna, I'd return. Then I found a job
in a workshop for ten zloty a week. I settled down in Vilna and was quite
content.

I received four letters from Mother during the first six months; after that,
not a word. No matter how many letters I wrote, I received no reply. I didn't
give too much thought to the reasons for her not writing. Perhaps this was
because I was preoccupied with myself and my mental and spiritual exhaustion. A year and a half passed, during which I heard nothing from home.
By then I had also stopped writing, because it costs a couple of zloty to send
a letter to Lithuania, and besides, I had lost hope of getting an answer.

But once, when I had the opportunity, I sent another letter and finally
got a response. Each of my sisters wrote to me about her life and about
home. There was no mention of Mother. The older girls were living on their
own. My younger sisters were living with my stepfather in a barracks (a
place similar to the fortress). This made everything clear. It was like a black
stamp on my mother's death certificate—she had been dead for a year.
Although I hadn't heard from her for a year and a half, the realization hit
me like a thunderbolt. I ran through the bright, bustling streets like a madwoman. But I saw no light. The dark, nighttime sky hung over my head. I
ran without knowing where I was headed. I wanted to escape from life, from
everyone. I went into an orchard and sat on a bench. It was a cold winter
night. No one else was in the little orchard. In the distance, I could hear the
crunching of frost underfoot. The cold ate into me. I hadn't eaten all day.
But I felt nothing; my heart was still warm, full of pain and suffering. My
tears didn't even freeze on my cheeks. Without a sigh or a groan, they
emerged from a place within my soul.

I sat for a long time in the little orchard, surrounded by skinny, twisted
young trees, which stood there alone, abandoned and covered with snow.
Was I like them? Hadn't I also lost the warm love of a mother who could
caress and fondle her child as gently as the July sun did the earth? Like them,
I, too, was frozen solid. For me, the sun had set and would never shine again.
I sat there and cried. I didn't regret my mother's death; maybe it was better
than her difficult and tortured life. But what would become of the children?
The fortunes of a whole family depended on her one life. I saw the three

little girls before my eyes. The youngest was three years old. I imagined them—skinny, dirty, hungry, tearful—lying under the feet of base, depraved people. Anyone who felt like it could beat them or spit on them. I also saw my stepfather sitting on a dirty bed, his head sinking down to his knees, his hands covering his face, mourning my mother, whom he loved so much.

I didn't think about myself and how I had lost my heart's most beloved, whom I had once loved so much. There was no one I loved more than her. But the fate that awaited her little children frightened me. They wouldn't be accepted into a children's home. I was all too familiar with life in the fortress. My sister and I were the only ones who escaped from there, where an entire generation sank under the tide of degeneracy. I took it upon myself to save the children from that maelstrom. I turned to a prominent member of the community and asked for his help in getting them into a children's home. He tried to do something, but when it didn't work out, he refused to help any further. Now I see no possibility of helping them—not in my sorry state, earning six zloty a week, which is barely enough to keep me going.

Oh, how hard it is for me not to take action, when I know that tragedy awaits these children. If I were only near them, I wouldn't rest; I would rouse the entire city. But I have to sit here with my hands tied and listen to the bleak news: The older two girls have developed serious heart and lung ailments; the youngest one suffers from headaches. The oldest of the three is thirteen years old. Instead of going to school, she has to be a mother to the two younger ones.

I have lived with this image before my eyes for three quarters of a year. Whether I'm at work or I'm alone, I can see them looking so sad, and I want so much to be with them, caress them, press them to my heart, cry with them, and be a mother to them. But this is impossible. I can't do anything. Still, my thoughts are always with them. If I worked regularly and earned more, I would bring one of them here. My helplessness weighs on me. I feel so much and can't do anything. I'm looking for other ways to help them. I've sent a letter to my father's sister in America, explaining my sisters' situation. She replied that she would send them some things. This means little to me. I know it can't save them from the immoral swamp that surrounds them. I will keep looking for other ways to help them, despite the fact that I have no prospects for finding any. But I know one thing: until I am able to take them away from there, my life has no value and I cannot rest. Their fate poisons my happiness and my joy.

Since the day I learned that Mother had died, my former love for her gradually began to be rekindled, until it blazed as it had once before. I see her in joy and in suffering. I can see her pale bony face. I can even feel her death-throes. She is always in my thoughts. It often seems to me that I see her face hovering in the air, and once I actually did see her. I'll never forget it. It was last winter, and I was sick at the time. My bed had a curtain around it. Clearly, I don't know how it actually happened, or whether I dreamed it or imagined it. When I recovered, I had no idea what had happened. I saw (and I can still see) my mother standing by the curtain, which was slightly parted. She was pale and much thinner than she had been, and she looked at me with such a loving smile that even now when I think about it I see it again, and I feel so good that I seem to see my mother once more. I often think about her at night before I go to sleep, so that I might at least see her in my dreams. Her hazy image lives again, and I'm happy to see her at least in my dreams.

Lately, my hours after work are taken up with a friend who understands my soul and knows my pain. He dispels my solitude and displaces the dear image of my mother. This friend is worth being happy with, but that sort of thing isn't for me. I have become apathetic about everything. Sometimes the bitterness of my life seems sweet to me. Solitude has an especially good effect on me. This probably shows that I'm not cured of my illness. But it weighs less heavily upon me now. I found a remedy with which to quiet the pain. I write down on paper all that oppresses me. I write poems. It doesn't matter to me whether what I write is good or bad. I write, and I feel better. That is enough for me. I care little about my own life. The fate of my sisters doesn't let me rest.

This, in sum, is the essence of my twenty years of life!

3

A. Greyno

Contest year: 1934 • Language: Yiddish
Year of birth: [1911] • Age: 23 • Sex: Male

A Few Remarks for the Researchers

Dear friends,

I am a young man, barely twenty-three years old, until now completely self-educated. I was born in P., a town near Kielce. In my manuscript I didn't mention the name of the town for various reasons. I read an assortment of journals, the daily press, and periodicals having to do with literature, art, and criticism, and I keep an eye out for contemporary political and social developments. That is how I came to notice a call to the young generation to take part in your contest for the best autobiography in Vokhnshrift *(a Bundist publication). I've never before taken part in any similar writing contest, because I've always thought that there were better talents than mine. Nevertheless, in this case I gave it a try for the first time, in order, as they say, "to test my skills." And here my age must be taken into consideration. Fearing that I was too "old" for this contest, I intended to inquire whether it mattered that I was barely a year above the age limit you set for participants. And, as you see, not only did I not inquire, but I also immediately wrote this and sent it to you, in the hope that it would not be an obstacle to my inclusion among the participants. Because, ha, ha! What difference does a mere year make in the course of a person's entire life? Also, you must accept my sincere and most heartfelt thanks for having stimulated me to recall these memories. These thoughts and images are already a part of my past, but, in the course of putting them down on paper, they shook my entire being as I experienced them once again.*

True to my memory and with the sincerest devotion, I have made every effort to elicit everything, everything that has guided me and instructed me in my life. I know that in my autobiography there might be such things that should have been avoided because of conventional or, rather, legal reasons. But how could I do so, when my still quite youthful spirit has already managed to accumulate so much repugnance, even hatred, for all of the conventions and laws which those in power have made and which do not at all suit the actual conditions of life today? Besides, in such a case would I be able to be truthful and sincere? After all, my honest intention was to write everything, freely and without shame—everything which I found inspirational and which others might as well.

Also, please forgive me for not having been able to keep within the specified—and somewhat limited—number of pages. Perhaps I am not to blame, because it's not my fault that my experiences over the course of some twenty years, which I have tried my best to abbreviate while writing down, have taken up one-hundred-and-thirty-nine pages of a regular notebook. Perhaps life itself is at fault.

Now, a couple of words regarding the technical side of what I have written: I am a laborer, busy all day at the sewing machine. My only free time for sitting down to write comes late at night. I have tried as far as possible to write clearly and to the point. To this end I first wrote a rough draft according to an outline that I thought out more or less in advance. Then I rewrote a clean final copy. In doing so, I made a few corrections, thinking that "it would be better this way." The only major defect, aside from many smaller imperfections, is that I write twice about my physical handicap. Not wanting to cross things out, and to minimize any sloppiness in the writing, I have left it to your discretion to introduce a certain order according to your own understanding.

About the entire autobiography in general: If it is even minimally worthy of being printed or of having certain sections published in a periodical, I permit changes to be made only with regard to style, chronological order (although I have made every effort in this regard), or a more precise choice of words and concepts. But in the process, the actual content is not to be changed in the least, nor is the picture to be distorted.

Trusting in your strict discretion, you may publish the names of people as they are given, with one exception. This one name I ask you to change, because while writing I found it difficult to think about someone who is so close and dear to me while using another, strange name. I believe that you will understand that I am referring to Yankl⁹.

Finally, a few words about punctuation: Do not take amiss that the periods, commas, question marks, etc., are perhaps not placed correctly. It seems that they fought a little among themselves and stormed off to places where they certainly do not belong. The blame, however, goes to the one who is not experienced in making peace among them. Leaving it to you, I remain with the hope that you will exercise your sufficiently experienced "pacifist" methods to persuade them that even in the autobiography of a young man, as in life, calm and order must prevail.

With the greatest respect,
    A. Greyno
    Kielce, 25 May 1934

P.S. Regarding your assurance that the costs will one way or another be reimbursed: A notebook: 1.20 zloty, plus the cost of postage. The exact address and my real name, together with the pseudonym, is in a separate sealed envelope enclosed with the manuscript.

AUTOBIOGRAPHY

"The past belongs to death, the future—to life."—Gorki

I remember: a long narrow room, with a single, small, four-paned window at each end. A cold autumn evening; the room grows darker and colder. My parents are away. My older brother and I climb up on the stove. We sit on the tin sheet and dangle our feet over the open burners. My older brother teaches me a song that all the children our age were singing then:

Ey, ey! Ieb tvoi mat'!	[Hey, hey! Fuck your mother!
Ty polkovnik, ia soldat,	You're a colonel, I'm a soldier,
Ieb tvoi mat',	Fuck your mother,
Ey, ey, ia soldat!	Hey, hey, I'm a soldier!]

This song may have been a sign of the times, but we sang it very merrily, raising our boyish voices and beating time on the chimney with our feet. But we kicked too hard, knocking out several tiles, and fell along with them to the ground.

At the time I may have been four or five years old. My parents—or rather, my mother, as my father was, on the whole, passive and indifferent toward the family—didn't pay very much attention to us. This was not due to lack of love for us children, but simply a lack of time. Mother, a very energetic woman, was always looking for some sort of employment in order to support our family. She was always harried and weary from working; with no extra time for the children, she was forced to shunt us aside.

I don't remember having gone to *kheyder* or public school. The latter was entirely out of the question, because in those years people in a small town didn't even dream about anything but a *kheyder*. In any case, my memory fails me. Although my parents are always trying to bring up various details to remind me that I did go to *kheyder*, I still don't remember. What I do remember is my father teaching me to read and write. We had a big alphabet chart attached to a board. Father would show me a picture of a bird, a little man, or a purse, and then teach me the letters from those shapes.

He also taught me to write on a small board with a piece of chalk. I remember that he crouched down in order to be on the same level with me, and he showed me how to draw a semi-circle next to a straight line, forming the letter *alef*—this was the first thing I ought to know. When I held the chalk in my little hand and tried several times to copy the semi-circle on the board, which lay on Father's lap, it seemed to me to be the hardest thing in the world to do. No matter how much I strained, with my tongue sticking out to the right or the left, I wasn't able to draw it as neatly or as skillfully as my father. It came out either like a "6" next to a "1" or like a little box, almost completely closed, with a little stick standing nearby, as if the two shapes had no connection whatsoever. When Father saw that I would never be a writer, he made a despairing gesture or put both of his big hands on my head, giving it a few shakes. He looked up to the ceiling and said, "Oh, some writer you are!" and pushed me away. Whenever these "exams" were done, my mother, who was always busy with some sort of work, would ask to be shown what I had written. Father showed Mother the board and laughed, mocking me even more: "Oh, don't be silly, there's nothing to see." After looking over the entire board with its circles and lines, Mother would add wryly, "Well, you know? I still have a business. He'll become a writer later." But later, when I turned to the board and chalk on my own, my father showed more interest in me. And that is how I learned, more or less, to read and write Yiddish.

The town where I was born was small. At the time it had about two to three thousand inhabitants, of whom some sixty to seventy percent were Jews. I can see before me those narrow, poorly paved little streets with their low houses, most made of wood, and Jewish stores. Here is the market with its wooden stalls, their pointed roofs decorated with faces carved on the cornices. And here is the second, smaller market, where the tavern's shabby windows display a few dark bottles with colored labels and half a roast chicken on a plate. And here is the pharmacy and the house that has a balcony. Here is the exchange, and here are the Jews, with their heavy beards and cloth coats. Their hats sit on their heads like lids, once black, now faded to a reddish brown by the sun. They stroll with pieces of straw in their mouths, waiting, as always, for the car to arrive from the big city. And here it comes, honking from the distance to announce its arrival. The Jews quickly swarm about it, like flies around a lump of sugar on a hot summer day.

I used to run around all day long, free of all cares, and when I came home I'd jump into bed, fully dressed. Mother used to sit up very late at night. Bent over an oil lamp, she would embroider all sorts of tablecloths, matzah covers, *tefillin* bags, and other items for numerous Jewish families and for brides' trousseaus. This was how she supported us. Father was either at the synagogue, reciting prayers, or in bed, asleep, snoring loudly.

I remember very little of the war years, which remain misty, as in a dream. I remember that Mother used to go about with things like mirrors, combs, pieces of soap, matches, cigarettes, sheets of paper, envelopes, picture postcards, and the like. Taking me with her, she would sell these to the hordes of soldiers who streamed in from the forest on the hill. They came by the tens of thousands, both cavalry and infantry, their swords sparkling in the sun. The neighing of the horses, their hoof beats on the cobblestones, and the endless din of the solders' voices were deafening. My mother wandered about with me, near the horses' bellies, and cried out in a loud voice: "Matches! Who wants matches?" I picked up on her words and called them out even louder. I remember that once a pair of strong soldier's hands lifted me up in the air and placed me on a horse's back. I started to tremble. I called out for help to my mother, who was standing nearby, and she calmed me: "Hush, you silly boy. He's not going to do anything to you. He's a good man." And I remember how the soldier on the horse patted me and stroked my cheeks; then he took a few coins out of his bag and gave them to me. I pressed them tightly in my little hand so as not to lose them. When he let me down from the horse, I ran to my mother and gave them to her. With tears in her eyes, my mother said anxiously, "Who knows, perhaps he was thinking of home and his own little boy there."

Something else I remember: a large cellar in the courtyard, with an iron door. It was dark. The one small window, which barely let in any light, was stuffed with a rag. Several local families had moved in there with their possessions: bedding, baskets, and pots. It was a pleasant place for us children to play. We poked around in all the corners by the light of a candle. We threw ourselves onto the piles of bedding. Then we heard the approach of cannon fire, which seemed like distant thunder on a summer's evening, and the whistling of shells getting closer and closer. They exploded right next to the walls of our cellar. The dreadful hum of their sighing, almost human voices filled us with fear, as we pressed closely to our mothers, who trembled and spoke in hushed tones. Our fathers, wearing their *gartlekh*, swayed like shadows as they quietly recited chapters from the Psalms by heart. I don't remember how long we were there. But I do remember that when we emerged it was a long time before we could open our eyes, because the bright light blinded us.

And I remember more: A temporary hospital was set up just off the courtyard, in two large rooms belonging to our wealthy neighbor, Varshavski. Those near death, moaning in agony, were brought there on stretchers—soldiers wrapped in white bandages stained with blood. Their anguished cries were heartwrenching. Dozens of corpses, men who had died in horrible agony, were carried off somewhere far away from the survivors.

The war ruined many families, but it improved the lives of others. Those who had no talent for swindling or speculating certainly suffered. But the will to live is strong, and the struggle for existence saves the individual from sinking. No matter how honest a person may be, the eternal human instinct to stay alive prevails among us all. This survival instinct is aroused most fully at these critical moments in life, and nothing can stop it. It is, in fact, the individual's fight to defend his right to exist and to thrive. And, in most cases, it succeeds.

The family in which I was raised was not talented enough to maintain its existence by dishonest means. Sinking to the level of begging or the like was also beneath Mother's dignity, as she came from a wealthy family. Father, who was very passive in these matters, left it all up to fate. There-fore, it's no wonder that poverty and misery attacked our family, in which there were now four children, one smaller than the next. I remember how Mother took the most drastic measures to save the family. She came up with a plan to move us to the big city. We needed money for this, but where it came from I do not remember. It seems to me that Mother turned to her two sisters, who were better off, for help, or something similar. When my parents had raised the necessary sum, they decided that Father should go to the city, where his sister lived, and look for a place to live.

Then one day—after Passover, I believe—Father suddenly appeared at dawn; we were all still asleep. He told us to pack up the furniture and load it onto a large freight wagon with two horses, which he had hired for the occasion and now waited for us in the courtyard. With childlike glee we dressed quickly and, with much confusion, helped pack up our belongings and bring them outside, where the Jewish driver loaded them. When the wagon was fully packed and piled high, he drove out of the courtyard and onto the street, which bore the name of the city to which we were moving. I remember how we traveled: The two smallest children sat with Father on the bedding. My older brother and I followed behind on foot. I just ached to climb up on the wagon, and I was very jealous of my little brother and sister, who had the good fortune to ride, while my brother and I had to walk, at first. But after the wagon had traveled quite far from the town, it stopped at a place where there was nothing to be seen but meadows, fields, and sky. My older brother and I happily climbed on the wagon and settled in. However, we didn't continue on our way. Father had to run back to town to find Mother. Apparently, she had not yet finished saying goodbye to neighbors and acquaintances.

The road was smooth, the day glorious, my young heart filled with a child's joy. My older brother and I crawled onto an overturned table, its legs pointing upward. We held on to the edge of the table and stamped our feet, pretending that we were driving an automobile. We blew into our fists, imitating a car horn. With boyish pluck we made fun of every cart that passed by, although our parents tried to stop us. But why pay any attention to them now, at a time of complete and uninhibited boyish glee?

Not much later our cart, piled three stories high, stopped in a small village. Peasant men, women, and children came out of all the huts and looked at us in wonder. We climbed down and went into a sort of grocery store, in which two goats strolled around, quite at home. We ate eggs, rolls, and cream. The horses also had something to eat and drink, and then we continued on our way once again.

But on the second half of the trip, something happened that took away our cheerful enthusiasm. From afar we saw a long line of carts and wagons, driven by peasants with whips and switches, coming toward us. We were scared. Would they attack us? When they were right next to us they recognized us at once as Jews and, without giving it much thought, began to lash us with their whips. The first driver started it, and it continued on down the line to the end. Each one gave us a couple of lashes. Our cart moved quickly, and we hunched over and buried our faces in the bedding. Our driver—a well-built, broad-boned Jew—struck back several times with his whip. When it was over, we looked around, and my parents thanked God that we escaped with nothing more than lashes.

We arrived in the city around evening. My mother already knew the place, as she happened to have been there several times before, and she showed us around:

"Here, you see, is the district courthouse. And there, not far away, is the town church. And right there, nearby, you see, is the jail."

"That one with the little windows, Mama?"

"Yes, yes, with the little windows and the bars."

"And is this the whole city, Mama?"

"Oh, don't be silly! This is just the beginning."

And so we had made our entrance into the big city.

My uncle, whose home we had come to, was a wealthy lumber merchant. He owned a house in the city with several acres of adjacent land, where there was a lumber yard full of boards and blocks of wood. This is where we had come with our wagon. We went into the house and stretched, tired from the hard journey. My uncle was a typical middle-aged, provincial bourgeois, with a sparse, kempt black beard. He was a born miser, who bragged whenever he performed the smallest good deed, and at every occasion he displayed his generosity—earnest on the surface, but false underneath. This type of person yearns for some small measure of honor and loves to get even the slightest chance to promote himself: "Let me! I know better! Ask me!" He isn't averse to flattery; he is a pedant, who erupts in anger and is ready to use his fists to fend off anyone who carelessly treads on his corns. He is the kind of person who hates it when others ignore him, when they fail to watch when he eats or ask him about his business. He loves to hear a friendly, smiling "Good morning, Reb Mordkhele," and he answers with the same smile, "Good morning to you, Reb Itshele," and continues on his way.

My uncle's wife (my father's sister, who is his second wife) is stout, fleshy, simple, unpretentious. She is free of any chicanery, indifferent to various changes going on about her. Although she is past her youth, she exudes a sort of childish, warm-hearted innocence. As is typical of this sort of woman, she has had many children. It was with this household—which included grown-up daughters and sons (four from the first wife), as well as several small children—that our family stayed for a few weeks, until we found a place to live on the same street, not far from my uncle. I remember how their daughter Khayele, who was my age, took me around their home, the lumber yard, and the street, showing me everything. My heart pounded, and I lowered my face, flush with shame at the first touch of a girl's hand. We walked around every day, looking at everything, until we became tired. I asked naive questions, feeling gratitude mixed with boyish respect and trust for a girl who was not only a relation but also knew everything.

Our first home, which we rented with the help of our meddling uncle, consisted of two small, low-ceilinged rooms in an attic, reached by climbing a narrow, winding, wooden staircase. At the entrance there were two converging chimneys, one on the left and one on the right, which made the place look even more like an attic. The only window in the kitchen looked out, like a tunnel, onto the roof above the courtyard. I loved to look through it at the broad fields and gardens on one side and the scattered houses, their chimneys jutting out of their roofs, on the other. The kitchen also had a pantry, which adjoined the two rooms.

Our landlord, a shoemaker, was not a Jew, and he was a nasty man. He was tall, with sharp cheekbones jutting out from his sunken cheeks. Strict and domineering, he was always in a bad mood, with an angry sneer beneath his upturned nose. At first, it was very hard for us to get used to walking quietly on the bare wooden stairs, on which our every step resounded in the front section of the building below. This was divided into two apartments, in one of which the shoemaker lived, right next to the stairs. Therefore, we had to be very careful and walk on tip-toe in order not to make any noise. And if it happened that one of us children forgot, our stern landlord would appear in the doorway, holding the sole of a shoe or a shoemaker's hammer. He would scold us loudly with such angry words that we nearly jumped out of our skin and ran upstairs, our hearts pounding and our eyes filled with tears.

I don't remember what sort of business we were in then, but it seems to me that it was not going badly. But I do remember something from a slightly later period. I was nine or ten years old, and poverty had once again entered our house. It was during the cold winter months. We had nothing with which to heat our rooms. We ate only twice a day—barley cooked in nothing but plain water. We dressed in tattered clothes made out of sacks and wore mismatched shoes that were full of holes.

My haggard mother's cursing and scolding at my ne'er-do-well father flowed all day long, like an endless deluge. This had a bad psychological effect on us children; we, too, began to curse and fight with each other. Then, I remember, Mother came up with a way to make a living, as she always did in these situations. Father took two silver candlesticks, which were family heirlooms, and pawned them. With this small sum, Mother bought some flour, sugar, and oil, and made several batches of cookies. She baked them at the baker's shop and put them in baskets for us to sell at the market. My older brother and I placed them on baking sheets in the street and sold them by the piece. My mother was so ashamed that she buried her face in her hands and was awash in her own tears. Once, when we were standing with the cookies set out on baking sheets, we were attacked by a gang of hungry Polish boys, who grabbed the cookies that our mother had worked so hard to make and trampled them. We screamed and went home, tearful, bruised, and covered with mud.

These were the postwar years. The economic life of the masses had been destroyed. Chaos and instability forced people into a wretched state of deprivation and pain. Hunger was the norm for the tens and hundreds of devastated, homeless families, who came in droves from the surrounding towns. They were packed together in compact masses, where various epidemics raged. At the time, I remember, charitable organizations established a number of public kitchens that distributed soup twice daily. We were among those who registered for this benefit. It took some time before Mother, who had a strong sense of honor and pride, agreed to accept support along with all kinds of beggars. Nevertheless, twice a day I took a jar and pushed my way into the enormous line, where I waited for hours in order to receive this little bit of food. Sometimes, when I had almost reached the window, someone else came along who was stronger than I, pushed me—small, weak and helpless—aside, and took my place. When this happened I didn't protest or scream, but, full of anguish, went to the back of the line. Often I would come home with an empty jar. Whenever I was lucky enough to bring home a little bit of food, Mother wouldn't even want to touch it. When she saw us children share the bit of soup, which had long since gone cold, she would choke on her tears, or pour out her bitter heart, cursing her miserable life and envying those who were long dead.

Time continued on its eternal way. We managed to live as best as we could. Our parents—or, more accurately, Mother—continued to devise endless new ways of making a living. As was always the case ever since I can remember, Mother was the one who took the initiative. She was the motor that made the entire machine go; Father was the wheel, and my older brother and I were the screws.

At the time we tried to manufacture candles at home. Father made the equipment we needed out of wood, and we bought a large iron pot in which to boil paraffin, which Mother bought on the black market. We poured the thin, molten paraffin into a deep, long, narrow box lined with sheets of zinc, so that the paraffin wouldn't leak out. Father stood, sweating, with two or three long sticks, from which the wicks dangled (preparing this was my job). He dipped each wick into the box and then laid it out to cool. At first, it didn't work properly. The candles came out dark and rough. But after a while it went better. Father became more skilled, and the candles came out fine—smooth and white, with a rounded point. The candles could be larger or smaller, thinner or thicker, depending on the length of the wick and the amount of dipping. After they had cooled, we sorted them out by size and put them in baskets to bring to market stands, stores, and private houses. We had to make the candles in secret, because it was against the law.

I remember one incident when we and the entire attic almost went up in flames. Father had gone out somewhere; Mother was at home with us children. The paraffin was melting in the big pot on the stove. We had forgotten to make a hole from the top layer of the paraffin down to the bottom of the pot, so that the steam could escape as the paraffin melted. As we later realized, the molten paraffin on the bottom started to boil, while at the top there was still a thick, solid layer. Suddenly, the pot exploded with such violent force that the whole attic shook as if it had been bombarded with heavy artillery. Before we could realize what had happened, thick flames engulfed both rooms; we were overcome and lost consciousness. But then Mother let out a terrible scream, and we all sprang to life. I watched as flames licked at the window panes and burst out of the windows, which we had hastily flung open. In my confusion, I wanted to jump out. I remember crouching down close to the floor, with searing flames above me. Quickly, I slid out and ran, half dead, my clothes singed, past the chimneys and down the twisting stairs. The crowds of people outside and my mother's cries made the blood curdle in my veins. I ran off somewhere, and by the time I came back the fire had been extinguished. Seeing me before her eyes, Mother smiled bitterly, as she thought that I had already been turned into a piece of charcoal. Then I found out that the landlord, who also happened to be a fireman, had immediately put out the fire by pouring a tank of water over the stove. I don't recall what happened later. But I do remember that later the landlord settled the score with us very harshly.

I don't know if Mother had always been so spiteful and provocative. I only know that the constant worrying over our family's existence, the endless preoccupation with making a living, the eternal toiling and hustling, had all made her extremely anxious. On one hand, she was devoted to her children, ready to comfort them and do everything for them; on the other hand, she was frequently ready with beatings and curses for whichever child, in her opinion, had misbehaved. She would become hysterical and moved quickly from one extreme to the other. By nature a diligent, bold, and daring woman, extraordinarily agile and energetic in her decisions, she would sit up late, weak and tired, her wizened body toiling away. I often felt sorry for her when she was in this weakened state. But when she becomes hysterical (as she still does) she is transformed into a red-hot fireball, ready to destroy and exterminate everything in her state of rage. No restraint, no attempt at persuasion can help. And when she calms down she falls into a state of depression, and a spontaneous river of tears pours from her eyes, once burning, now extinguished. At these times I no longer feel pity for her. I look for a place where I can escape her glance. For then such thoughtless words, though often justified, flow from her mouth, directed at whoever provoked the attack of madness. Father, who is accustomed to such attacks, bites his lip and remains silent. If he says a word to try to persuade her or to excuse himself, then it may very well happen all over again, but with even greater intensity.

Thoughtless, credulous, and very talkative, Mother can't be dissuaded from her misconceptions, which can last sometimes for moments, sometimes for years. Depending on the situation, she is ready either to change her mind at any moment and deliberately deny her previous opinion or to hold fast to her opinion that everyone is her enemy and is out to spite her. And as soon as she passes judgment on someone, his fate is sealed. Her hatred for him takes on a life of its own. At the slightest prompting, a whole dictionary of harsh words rains down on him, although he may well be essentially innocent. If someone tries to point out evidence to demonstrate that her verdict was incorrect, Mother is ready to assault that person with her fists, and she soon counts him as her enemy as well. Mother's psychology completely confirms Gorki's brilliant notion that "in the human heart there is much room for faith. For conviction, there is little space." Here, faith doesn't mean religious delusion; Mother has little of that. She isn't a religious or superstitious person. However, she possesses a certain dogmatism, which is related to her unique psyche. In my psychoanalytic opinion, I am inclined to describe her as a psychopath.

Compared to Mother, Father is quiet, modest, and somewhat more intelligent, someone who has the strength to withstand the worst insults with stoic calm. He is well-versed in the Bible and Talmud and has also read secular books. As a young man he received rabbinical ordination. He has traveled widely, takes great interest in reading newspapers, and has a good understanding of politics. But by nature he is very passive and lazy; he likes things to be calm and easygoing. When it comes to practical matters he is quite helpless. With an almost childlike carelessness he demands assistance with his helpless life, which is full of missteps. He is a man who loves to be pampered and is shrewd in exploiting every opportunity to attract attention as a pitiful creature in need of guidance and instruction. Whenever he isn't feeling well, Mother hovers over him and does everything possible for him with maternal care. Afterwards, however, she'll go on about it in a sharp tone and bewail her bitter fate to be married to such a ne'er-do-well.

It should be apparent that this emotional baggage didn't burden me too much. Having inherited my mother's energetic characteristics, and growing up in a family where she frequently provoked fights and scandals for trivial reasons, I developed quite a few deviant, even petty criminal, tendencies. And so I grew up to be a good-for-nothing, indulging wild, spiteful, and sadistic impulses. I would often beat up children who were smaller and weaker than I was for no reason at all, and when I saw them cry I would feel a deep satisfaction. Mother would frequently beat me with a stick until I bled and was in terrible physical pain, but afterward I would laugh through my tears. Father would come to my defense at such times if he thought that the punishment was unwarranted. Yet at Mother's urging he would beat me as well, though more mercifully and less brutally. I was an able and energetic member of a street gang and took the lead in all our boyish undertakings. I had a limp in my right leg, which I acquired as a nine-month-old baby. My mother has told the story to neighbors and friends a hundred times, with all the details and elaborations: how I lay on the operating table, how they wanted to amputate my entire leg, how in the end she beat her head and screamed that she would rather leave me dead in the Łódź hospital than raise a child with one leg, and so on.

I wasn't one to let something like this affect my ability to excel as a leader and instigator of all sorts of childish pranks, in which my gang took such pride. I was agile and fearless, enterprising and often too reckless. I used to climb up tall utility poles or onto roofs and fences and look down at all the little people. Across from our house there was a large courtyard with an orchard and a green pond in the middle, where frogs used to croak pleasantly every summer evening. We used to go boating there, on a wooden plank taken from a fence. I used to stand on the plank and steer it with a pole, proud of my "talent." When the pond froze in the winter it turned out to be the best skating rink. Here I demonstrated true wonders, wearing out the soles of my shoes or the seat of my pants, for which I really got it from my mother when I came home.

One hot summer day, my gang was practicing shooting stones at electrical wires. Just then, an elderly Christian woman passed by and was hit in the head by a small stone. She immediately raised a ruckus, and a group of Christian fellows quickly gathered, having heard that a Jewish boy had split open the head of an old Christian woman. Armed with clubs and leather straps, they chased after us in a rage. I ran home and arrived there just as my family was finishing a batch of candles. I ran straight into the pantry and crawled on my stomach up to the attic, where I hid in a corner, quietly, like a cat. I listened as several dozen men poured into our home, led by the injured woman, demanding that my parents hand me over. My parents, not knowing where I had gone, started to look for me in every corner of the pantry. For a long time the people who were looking for me tried to break into the locked attic, making wild, furious cries and harsh anti-Semitic remarks. And I? I lay huddled deep in the straw in a dark corner of the attic and held my breath, afraid that my pounding heart would give me away. Finally they left our house, issuing sharp threats that they would get even with us some other time. I heard everything. I had no desire to leave my nest until some time after things had calmed down, knowing what awaited me at home. My furious parents were running around looking for me.

Eventually, as evening approached and I could see through the small holes in the roof that it was getting dark, I began to feel afraid of "demons." I decided to place myself in my parents' hands and crawled quietly back into the house through the same opening. And the result? Ha-ha-ha! For two whole weeks, I only knew that I was still alive because I could feel pain all over my body from the lengthy beating my mother, brother, and father had given me. The pain passed, and it appears not to have influenced me for the good—and perhaps had the opposite effect.

At the time, my father used to take me with him to pray. It felt good to be in the company of a "better" class of boys. We fellows used to go into a corner of the *beys-medresh* and make a racket, disrupting the service, until the *shammes* took us by the ears and threw us out. We used to sit on the threshold of the *beys-medresh* and tell stories about demons, emperors, and princes. But I also used to take part in the service by singing, which I loved doing very much. I had a beautiful, resonant voice and could perform various fine trills (a talent that I inherited from my mother). Even at home, I got a great deal of pleasure from singing Hallel, which I knew by heart, with all of its grace notes and florid ornamentation. Mother used to enjoy hearing me sing some of the holiday Yotser, certain that I would grow up to be a good and pious cantor.

Although Mother was not pious herself and was something of a "freethinker," she would still force Father and me to study a bit of Torah and Gemara. But I shrank from this like a dog from a stick. Perhaps I didn't like it because it didn't suit my wild and dissolute spirit, or perhaps because Father didn't have a talent for explaining things to young minds. What did I care, for example, that thousands of years ago there was once someone named Abraham, who wanted to sacrifice his only son to the God in whom he believed, and other such stories? I knew that God didn't exist; this I had learned from my mother.

Often on Saturday afternoons, as she lay in one bed and Father and I were on the other, she would argue with Father that there was no God and that a human being lives only because—well, how does a lamp burn? Because there is oil in it. If the oil runs out, then the lamp also goes out. A person expires in the same way, when there is no strength left in his blood. Also, the world wasn't created by God or anyone else but is something eternal, without beginning or end—and other such secular ideas. This, she said, she had learned from a cousin of hers; he was also a freethinker and had been a fighter and a socialist in 1905.

She said that he was well educated and knew about many other things. He knew, for example, why there were poor people and rich people, slaves and exploiters, plus many other things that he had taught her, but which she no longer remembered. He also taught her a number of songs about poverty, which she often sang as she worked. These songs bemoaned the fate of the slaves and poor workers who swore to take "vengeance" on the hangmen and tyrants. He also taught her that it's not wrong to light a fire on the Sabbath. "Why not?" she would ask. "Why should I abide by all of these restrictions when 'a new day has dawned'?" Way back when, she said, you had to work very hard to make a fire, banging stones together, and so on. But today? Just strike a match, and you get fire. The Sabbath? Yes, people had chosen this day, she said, to rest after a week of work. But why shouldn't we be allowed to get a little pleasure out of the Sabbath? Why still be bound—"Don't do this," "That's forbidden," and so on.

That's how she used to talk, on and on. If Father answered her back and confronted her with a difficult question, she wouldn't be able to extricate herself and would fall back on the "knowledge" that her cousin had given her. I found these words easy to comprehend, and my spirit absorbed them. I remember well when, late one afternoon, several of us boys were sitting on the step in front of a house on our street, telling stories about how God had revived a tortured soul in hell so as to be able to punish him once more for the sins he had committed during his life, and so on. Suddenly I thundered, "No! Don't believe it! There is no God and no afterlife!" My friends looked at each other. Then some of them quickly ran away from me; others told me to pull a hair out of my right *peye* and blow it into the air (this was a boyhood remedy to make sure that a sin was immediately forgiven in heaven). Then a few of them insisted on finding out how I knew this and who taught it to me. Naturally, I didn't want to compromise my mother, who kept her secular ideas from others, so I said that I had come up with it myself. I even told them the example of the oil lamp, repeating what my mother had said, word for word, and added something of my own. From then on, the gang chased after me yelling, "Heretic! 'There's no God,' he says. *Goy, goy!*" And a few who were somewhat smarter said, "No, no. He's no *goy*, because a *goy* also believes in a God, his own God. But him? He's even worse! He'll go to hell—to hell!"

*

It often happens that a person acts against his own convictions and reasoning, which usually control his behavior, and he falls helplessly under the influence of his close contemporaries, if only so as to avoid being humiliated and ridiculed by them. And, despite his own initial, powerful impulse to resist, he is still overwhelmed by whomever possesses the power and ingenuity to influence others and win them over. Because the psyche of the average person is too complicated and becomes even more confused in such cases, he loses a sense of equilibrium. He becomes more and more caught up in the course of events that are repugnant to him, that at first seem to him to be absurd, even disgusting. And he tries not only to avoid being left behind, but to outdo the others. That is how life is, even for adults, let alone for children who haven't yet gone through the school of life and cannot foresee the consequences.

At this time my nature was quite turbulent and energetic; it knew no rest. Yet genuine emotions flowed in my blood, emotions that I got from my father. I was simple and sincere, and I avoided anyone who didn't show me the same qualities. In particular, I shrank from stealing. Nevertheless, I was dragged into a crowd that loved to steal and lusted after money. Other boys' craving for money, so that they could be independent, overcame me as well. I remember how I was taken along to stand outside and retrieve things that they stole and then make off with them. No, I couldn't do it. I wasn't made for that. My heart pounded, my hands and feet trembled. Several times, as I watched some of the boys go into a store, pretending to buy something and then making a commotion, I took the opportunity to run away.

Later I invented various excuses to tell them to cover up my cowardice. But once, I remember, we came up with a plan. It was a Polish holiday. Another boy and I entered a store through the back door. It was rather dark inside, because the shutters were closed. There were several customers in the store. The other boy went up to the counter and grabbed a handful of paper money from a basket that someone had apparently left there. He came up to me and we left as quickly and quietly as a couple of cats. As we walked away he drew me very close and showed me what he was holding close to his chest. All the while we looked around to make sure no one was coming after us. We came home and divided up the money. But that was it! I stopped hanging around with those boys. I don't know why. I couldn't do it any longer, and so I broke it off with them. One of them—in fact, it was the same one who was with me in the store—later spent a year and a half in the juvenile reformatory in Studzieniec. Today he is somewhere else, and it seems that the time he was supposed to have spent being reformed had the opposite effect.

At the time I began to mature into a young man. My erotic feelings toward the opposite sex became more serious in character. And this is where language and reason enter, those faculties with which nature endowed human beings so that they might rise above the lesser creatures of the earth and rule over them. Unfortunately, however, it appears that language has not yet been able to help humankind find the appropriate means of protecting against the harm that often occurs to children as they mature. This is because there are expressions in language that can excite and provoke a young person's immature desires to engage in degenerate acts.

I remember how some of us fellows used to hide in a corner of a courtyard and, in a quiet, mysterious tone, tell each other various secrets about intercourse between man and woman. These excited our boyish fantasies and stimulated our blind instincts. When we went our separate ways home, I would secretly follow the relations between my parents with excited curiosity—on the basis, of course, of those degenerate sexual experiences. From a hiding place, glowing with excitement and lust, I would stand for hours watching dogs and other animals copulating in the street. And if it even only seemed that an adult was following me and had noticed what I was watching, I would become red with embarrassment. A hot stream of blood would rush to my brain, and I would run away. It would take me a long time to calm down. At night I would toss and turn in bed without being able to fall asleep. I felt an urge to explode, to spill over, to overflow, so that my being would turn into nothingness. I would writhe passionately and, with a strange wildness, pinch and feel my whole body, every part of it separately, and—oh! A disgusted shudder runs through my bones just remembering those nights. And oh, how vividly I remember them!

Two or three of us boys used to meet in the loft of a stable scattered with fragrant, freshly cut hay. Two girls of the same age would also come up there, and we would lie around and touch each other with different parts of our bodies. Amidst bizarre, giddy laughter we engaged in wild, outrageous orgies. When they were over, we would lie there on our backs, exhausted. And when we came down, with dark circles under our dull, tired eyes, we would return more seriously and dutifully to the tasks that our parents assigned us. Oh, how I recall now the brilliant words of Romain Rolland, when the fifteen-year-old partisan, Christophe Krafft, heard the voice of God: "Go, go and live!" And a voice within him resounded: "But where should I go? Whatever I do and wherever I go, does it not lead to the same end, to the same results?" But God answered him sharply: "Go and die, you who must die! Go and suffer, you who must suffer! One does not live to be happy. One lives to fulfill the eternal law of life. Suffer! Die! But be what you must be. Be a man!" But I was still a bit far from being what one could call a man.

Things still weren't going well at home. I don't know why, but our candlemaking business failed and once again we took up different businesses, one more miserable than the next. I remember that we used to make whiskey in secret. My father learned how to do this from a corpulent little man with a bulging stomach. Taking a chance that a fire might break out again in our wooden attic, or that we might be arrested for "illegal manufacture," we would wait until late at night for the alcohol, which stank of rotten potatoes or soggy yeast, to start to flow through a tube sticking out of a kettle, which stood on the glowing burner, and into the vats below. This "business" didn't last very long. The fights between my parents—which had quieted down somewhat, because our family's economic situation was a little better—resumed in full force. Hysterical, my mother threw herself at my helpless father. I felt sorry for him. He would bite his blue lips and remained stubbornly silent. This further incensed my weak mother, who collapsed beneath her worries and from the obligation of supporting the family. At the time, my older brother was apprenticed to a great-uncle of ours, learning to become a hatmaker. I envied his ability to avoid getting caught up in the scenes that went on at home.

Eventually, Mother got us involved in a business once more, one in which we remain to this day. We had an old sewing machine, which Mother used to mend old, worn-out clothes for the family. We also had a pair of shiny scissors, which I had taken apart several times and turned into two swords, one for me and one for a friend. My mother had bought these scissors from an Austrian soldier for two crowns, and I was beaten severely more than once for the pleasure of having a sword hanging by my side from a string around my waist, imagining myself to be a real soldier, until the two swords were screwed back together and turned into plowshares.

Mother bought some fabric and, with additional instructions and advice from Father (who had the habit of swaying like the pendulum of a clock whenever he was involved in some sort of work), she cut out aprons and sewed them together on the machine. Then, draping several of them over our arms, we brought them to the fair on market day and sold them to peasant women for a handsome profit. Seeing that this business prospered, Mother bought some more fabric and labored away at the machine. Gradually she began to sew other things besides aprons, such as linens and skirts, which she used to cut out "by eye." The business went better and better.

I wanted to know how to do everything, so I also took to the machine. First, I learned how to sew straight seams, and I enjoyed the feeling of being an adult, working by myself at the machine. When my parents saw that I could be helpful, there suddenly appeared in our home a second sewing machine, intended for me. But soon the desire to sit all day "banging away" at the machine disappeared, and I looked for various excuses to sneak off to be with the gang outside. Every half hour Father managed to find me in a courtyard deeply involved in a soccer match, playing with a ball that I had made myself out of rags. Then I would have to go back, all sweaty, and sit down to work. And so, with the help of beatings from Mother and pleas and explanations from Father, I gradually became attached to the sewing machine at an early age (thirteen or fourteen years old). I quickly mastered the trade and even more quickly grew tired of it. But from this I earned quite a bit, enough to live on and then some.

My older brother, who already had the good fortune to earn something on his own, became more independent. At the same time, he started to bring home books from the union in which he had enrolled as a garment worker. These were books by the classic Yiddish writers: Mendele, Sholem Aleichem, Peretz, Dineson, Ansky, and others. My brother used to read some of these books aloud—mostly Sholem Aleichem—for our parents. Mother took great pleasure in hearing the different tragi-comic stories and monologues; they were so familiar and close, like a mirror held up to our own lives at the time. My brother's reading piqued my interest. As a child, I used to enjoy reading the fables in the *makhzor* and the Bible or the Yiddish translations in the prayerbooks for women. I would find these in the *beys-medresh* when Father brought me along. I also took to my brother's books with great intellectual pleasure, literally devouring them line by line. It often happened that I finished reading a book before my brother did, and I would ask him to return it early and bring home something new. I thus became acquainted with Yiddish writers, one by one, until finally my brother could no longer satisfy my passionate desire to read. Then, after working several weeks in a row without a break until bedtime, I managed to convince my mother to give me money to become a member of the town's Tarbut library. I would sit up until very late at night by the oil-lamp, immersed in completely different, new worlds, unaware of the hours flying by, until I went to bed with a loving kiss to the pages of my book. I felt as if I had acquired a fresh, brand-new skin, and, without feeling any physical fatigue, I fell asleep with a smile of intellectual satisfaction on my face.

One by one, I parted company with the friends I had then. Often they made fun of me, but a few became even closer to me. Knowing that I read books, they would insist that I tell them stories, stories from the books. This I did quite willingly, relating to them what I had read almost word for word. I remember how the older boys, who were almost fully grown, would love to inform my parents of my boyish pranks. At one time I'd had so much childish respect for these boys that I would become embarrassed in front of them until I blushed. I would lower my eyes and run away when they saw me, dirty and breathless, chasing after a goat or a dog with a handful of mud. Now these very same fellows would stop me in the street as I ran to the library with a book under my arm and quiz me on what I was reading. Was it Sholem Aleichem again? They would burst into ironic laughter and mock me, saying to each other, "What a good-for-nothing, and now he reads books."

My heart pounding with deep reverence and respect, I would slip quietly into the library, where everything was clean, neat, and pleasant. For me this

was the holiest place there was, holier than a synagogue is for someone
devoutly religious. The librarian already knew me, because I used to come
almost every evening to exchange a book. Her manner was very condescending toward me, so I suspected that she doubted whether I had actually read the thick book I had taken out only the day before. I wished that
she would ask me about it, but the librarian was a Jew who spoke only
Polish, which I didn't know at all. She never asked me anything, but continued to give me the books that I ordered according to the call numbers
that I found in the catalog. In fact, I was glad that she didn't ask me anything, because I wouldn't have been able to answer in Polish. I would have
certainly become flustered, turning red and trembling as I stammered
something. And so I would leave the aristocratic Tarbut library—happy, on
one hand, that the book I carried was in the language whose words and
ideas I understood, but unhappy, almost hurt, on the other hand, that I
didn't know Polish.

*

On the same street, not far from us, a young man lived with his parents.
Both his legs were crippled and he dragged them as he walked, leaning
heavily on a cane. This Yosele, as he was called, was one-hundred-percent
insane. A homosexual with a vain, suggestive manner, he used to dress
in a bizarre style, putting all sorts of adornments on his clothes, so that
he couldn't help but attract attention from everyone. This addle-brained
lunatic liked to gather a company of boys around himself, arrange various
entertainments and wild parties, stage "theatricals," and excite his audience
with all sorts of talk, which actually encouraged them toward sexual per-
version. At the time he used to lure boys of my age and exploit them for his
homosexual purposes. He would reward them with sweets and treat them
to delicious meals with liquor. I didn't become involved with them, mainly
because of my mother's warnings that I should have nothing to do with
those wild characters.

But once—oh, now I understand it all! It was a summer evening, after
work, and I was walking to the library, a book under my arm. He saw me
through the open window and invited me inside. At first I hesitated, but
eventually I went in. There was no one but him in the room. It was half
dark. He began by asking me where I was going, why I never came to see
him. In fact, he had been waiting a long time to draw me into his circle,
where they knew how to enjoy themselves. I looked like a "better" boy than
all those other fellows, who were fooling around with girls all night. I didn't
know what he was driving at, but somehow I was frightened. He came closer
and closer to me and began to touch my sex organ with his hand, getting

ever more aggressive and rough. I protested and quickly ran out. From then on I felt revolted by that house, and whenever I saw him on the street I would cross to the other side.

But oh, there I also met a lovely, magnificent girl. She had a small, pale face with dark, sparkling eyes; dark golden locks of hair protruded from under her small, white beret. Happy, singing, and radiant, she was the same age as I was, and we were the same height. She was a student in public school. Several boys, who were more experienced in this respect than I was, clustered around her. I got to know her as well. And, oh, now comes the poetry of life! I pursued her for a long, long time and, with bookish romanticism, sought to create a reality based on the racing fantasies that blazed in my young mind, each more beautiful than the last. My young soul glowed with a powerful fever that seized my entire being. I blazed with passionate desire to be with this girl, to spend evenings close to her for hours on end. In summer, fall, and winter I would stand by her gate with a letter for her in my hand, a letter in which I had expressed all my ardent and sincere feelings for her in literary language: "My——! I am not one of those who throng around you, no! I am different! In my heart you have long been mine, mine!" But as soon as I saw her my heart would begin to beat faster; I couldn't talk, my feet couldn't move, and I stood as if riveted to the spot, unable to do as I had planned. I went home, threw myself on my bed and wept, wept with tears from my melting heart, which loved so fervently— yes, loved. But love between two young souls is often like two drops of oil on water, which cannot meet. A wave came and separated us; the wave of life tossed each of us onto a different shore. The love that I thought I would always feel for her was cruelly shattered on the shores of life's sea and sank in my heart's deep abyss, leaving above it a place for something new, which would come soon.

This was the first blossoming of spring in my life. I felt happy with life, everything around me smiled. I began to go out into the street; I made new friends. Carefree and playful, I allowed myself to be drawn into the commotion of life. And after spending happy evenings in the street, in the park, and, during winter, on sleds or at the movies with girls, I would come home at a late hour and, without any break, turned to my books, passionately reading and reading. At the time I mainly read French novelists, Marcel Prévost, Maupassant and others, who deeply satisfied my intellectual needs then. I began to understand human psychology in various situations and to grasp human emotions and thoughts according to what these novelists showed me. I began to match everything in life to the books I read. I began to understand thoroughly every event, every act performed by one person toward another. Yet it often happened that I was disappointed by life. Immersed in the world of the characters in books, I viewed all of life through this prism. I was too credulous, too naive and impractical for real life. The trusting and ever-honest nature I was born with made me even more helpless in everyday life, which is so coarse and brutal. Not knowing any tricks or cheating ways, I was poorly equipped to deal with my surroundings. And once, I recall, I abruptly collided with sober reality.

It was a blazing hot summer day at the fair. My parents and I were standing at a booth displaying linens and various items of clothing. People were haggling, shaking hands with the farmers and their wives. Voices erupted from throats that were thirsty and dry from the heat. At around noon my parents gave me a sum of nearly one hundred zloty, from which I was to go and pay the notary public. I went there at noon and the place was closed; so, clutching the coins and bills, I went back to the booth. On the way there was a cluster of people. I stopped and pushed my short, skinny body through to the very middle of the group. There I saw a strapping, drunken gentile standing next to a chair, on which stood a small box with a glass lid. He was moving three thimbles over a black peppercorn and shouting in a coarse, drunken voice: "Well now, who can guess which one the peppercorn is under? For five zloty, I pay ten, for ten–twenty, for twenty–forty! Who can guess?"

I stood there for a few minutes and saw a number of people place their bets, and—they guessed correctly. He paid them as if mere pieces of paper, or scraps, were changing hands. Then more people guessed correctly, and again he paid them, ten zloty for five. My whole body shook, and my teeth chattered. Carefully, so that no one in the crowd would notice, I pulled five zloty from my pocket. When I believed that I had accurately noted which of the thimbles covered the black peppercorn, I handed over the five zloty with trembling hands. Certain that I had won ten zloty, I lifted up the thimble and—it was empty, hollow. A stream of seething blood rushed to my head, and I felt as if something in my heart had snapped. The light around me went out, and something danced dizzily before my eyes. My thoughts came swiftly, like lightning bolts, one upon another. My brain labored with tremendous effort to invent excuses to tell my parents about the five zloty that I no longer possessed. But—I understand it now!—the gang realized that I had more money, and once again I saw others winning. In order to save myself, I stared intently to see which thimble hid the peppercorn. I bet ten zloty and—lost again!

I completely lost all sense of reason. With blind haste I wagered one twenty-zloty note after another. I don't remember what happened next. How could I understand anything at that moment? I only came to myself under the heavy blows of my parents and my older brother, who suddenly turned up there (I don't know how). I heard the furtive laughter of various bystanders. The gamblers had long since dispersed. The police arrived and led me by the arm to find one of the players. But I was hurt, even worse than from the blows I had received, when I pointed out one of them to the policeman. He was the principal player, I clearly recognized him. I hurried after him, grabbing him by the end of his coat and loudly sobbing and yelling, with my parents behind me crying, "Help!" But then the policeman somehow disappeared without a trace. There had been several policemen, as I well recall, and they vanished together with the gamblers.

My loss of an entire hundred zloty had other consequences as well. The impression it made was indescribable. I later learned that when my parents heard about my losses and the money that had been taken from me, they quickly packed up their wares and took care of them as well as they could. During the time when the police came and then quickly disappeared, various underworld elements seized the opportunity, and they began to snatch goods at the fair. There was a huge uproar. Women's wailing and screaming filled the marketplace. The booths knocked over, their contents scattered on the ground, gave the impression of a pogrom. The police arrived late on the scene, firing their rifles into the air. Battered, confused, without a cap on my head, I ran around not knowing what to do or where to go. Night fell, and, as if in a dream, I roamed through a wealthy neighborhood that was all lit up. I didn't know what to do. Everything seemed unreal to me, as if it had happened a long time ago. I tried to remember details of the event. I grabbed hold of my pocket—maybe, maybe some of the money was left. Was it possible? Was it possible that they had taken everything from me, down to the last grosz? I searched myself thoroughly once more, but apart from pockets with holes in them, I found nothing. My battered bones began to ache. I walked past a window that had a mirror in it and saw myself, disheveled, with spots of dried blood on my face. I went into a courtyard and washed myself at a well, dried myself with the hem of my jacket, combed my hair with my fingers, and wandered on aimlessly.

A month earlier, my uncle's eldest son, a pious young man of twenty-four or twenty-five, had committed suicide by throwing himself under a train as it hurtled through the city. The reason was that he had been caught stealing from his boss at work. He was the same type of person as his father: proud and greedy. He couldn't bear the disgrace, and so he brought his life to an ugly end. And I remembered how his parents, their tears streaming, went to gather his remains and bury him. I went with them and saw the shattered body, with its intestines hanging out; there were spots of dried blood mixed with clods of dirt from alongside the railroad track. It was all gathered together and thrown onto a white sheet. I was gripped with horror, and the blood froze in my veins. Oh—brrrr! How well I recalled every detail now, as I roamed the brightly lit streets. Everything around me shone and laughed in such a bright, carefree way! I saw before my eyes the swiftly moving train, its front wheel slicing through the living person who lay waiting on the tracks. And over there is the cold grave, in which lie the gathered fragments of a body, with its protruding intestines. I could see it all so clearly. Oh, how brutal, how revolting! I wouldn't do it, no. And my parents—it turned out that they were a bit afraid that something like that might happen to me that night. As I found out later, they tried all sorts of ways to find me and bring me home. Then suddenly, as I stood before a store window, devouring all the good things displayed there with greedy eyes, my father approached me, followed by my aunt (his sister). They took me by the hand and led me away. As we walked, my aunt expressed her feelings to my father: "Look here," she said to him quietly, gesturing with her hands. "It may be that you are poorer by a hundred zloty—but was it better with my son? The main thing is that yours is alive!"

I didn't receive any more beatings at home. I was treated more compassionately. And then—yes, then—I realized that the life portrayed in books, as taught to me by French novelists, was one thing; real life, brutal and hard, was something else.

I made sure not to tell anyone my age about these events. First of all, I didn't have anyone to tell, because they were mostly boys who couldn't understand my feelings at that time. Secondly, I myself wouldn't have been able to explain to them the essence of what had happened. In addition, I was rather shy, and I knew they knew this and laughed about it behind my back.

Actually, the whole incident was no more than a minor experience. Yet as I write this, I realize how hard it is for someone who hasn't had the experience to grasp the true meaning of these words, because, when I call the experience "minor," I naturally mean this in a relative sense, in comparison with dramatic upheavals that affect the fate of whole peoples. But I also mean it in a temporal sense. Because what is a period of time not much more than half a day, when compared to the lifetime of the average person? And yet, this generally meaningless and unimportant experience had boundless significance for me, so that even today, many years later, I have to make a certain effort to control all my mental powers.

One by one, I broke with all of my friends. They seemed to me to be too common and ignorant. My life began to become monotonous. After a day of work at the sewing machine, I would slip quietly, like a shadow, into the library with a book tucked inside my jacket, then I'd read and read almost the entire night. No one gave me any guidance as to what to read. My eyes would wander through the catalog until it became late. Only when the librarian let me know that I was the last one there, and that she was waiting for me to leave so she could close, would I hastily order the number of the book whose author and title seemed to me to be the best and most interesting. Mostly I ordered translations of various European writers, because at the time Yiddish literature seemed to me to be too poor to satisfy my mind. I would mix together works by Upton Sinclair and Artsibashev, Gorki and Sienkiewicz. If I started to read an author whom I liked, I had to read all of his works that the library had in Yiddish translation.

When I went out on the street on a summer evening to get a little air, I went alone; I liked to be by myself very much. With cool indifference, I would stroll slowly through the busy streets, which pulsed and echoed with the happy, carefree laughter of painted and perfumed couples, dressed in all their finery. I know that no one paid any attention to me. Who cared that I moved alone through the carefree crowd? With almost stoic calm I would stand in the shadows near a brightly lit square and gaze intensely at the passersby. I would try to match them up with characters in the books I had recently read—that is, their experiences and their situations—from a psychological standpoint. More than once my stoicism was transformed into trembling desire—a desire to devour with greedy eyes the large, stiffly-corseted breasts and the bare, fleshy, blindingly white arms of the women, who shivered under their thin, brightly colored silks. Standing in the middle of this commotion, I felt like a weak, young creature amidst a raging sea. My young soul sensed how ridiculous and distorted were the laughing grimaces around me. I felt an ironic contempt for this vulgar uproar. And yet, though it went against my reason, I had to admit to myself that my desire was also aroused by the excitement, the violent passion, the life that thrived amid this fanaticism. What might happen to me, I wondered, if I, too, became so agitated, so passionate? What? What? I was completely torn inside. I returned home with a vision in my young mind.

Then, on one such evening, an idea suddenly burst into my mind like a bolt from the blue, an idea that made me tremble with joy: to write a diary. Yes, a diary. With every passing minute, my decision became more and more certain. And so I began. Oh, how much lighter my mood became with each page I wrote! With pen on paper, I poured out everything, everything that I had kept in my heart and soul over time. This period of loneliness didn't last long. Something new entered my life that steered me in another direction.

Everything seemed to be going well at home, according to the accepted ways of our petit-bourgeois, essentially proletarian, family lifestyle. Our

earnings sufficed for our modest daily needs and provided us with the possibility of slowly saving some money in case of a time of need. But a factor
that has its origins in the present capitalist system obstructed my family's
further normal development.

We lived in two crowded, vermin-infested rooms with low ceilings on a
back street in the outskirts of the city. Not only were we paying enough rent
to afford a comfortable apartment on the city's main street, but we also
suffered our landlord's rude, vulgar, anti-Semitic abuse. His wife, a simple
woman, low-class yet proud, found ways to express her sadistic streak at the
expense of our Jewish family. She constantly incited her husband, who was
mean and brutal enough on his own.

In the summer the gate to the house was locked at eight o'clock in the
evening, when there was still quite a bit of activity on the street. They would
open it only if told to by the police, and then they would give us children
a good beating with a leather strap. This would then excite the landlord's
vicious, shaggy dog, and it would bite us. We tried to do everything we could
through the courts, with doctors' statements confirming that our scars—
some of which I have to this day—had been the result of these beatings and
the dog's bites. But the landlord always emerged the victor with the help of
false witnesses (apprentice shoemakers who worked for him).

I remember once, when my parents were away at a fair, I went down to
get some water, and the landlord came out and started to strike me in the
face with a piece of leather. Then he let loose his dog, which tore my pants
and gave me a deep bite in the leg, drawing blood. I let loose a terrible
scream. People ran in from the street and saw what was happening to me.
They all shouted: "Go to the police!" "Bring him to court." "We will be
witnesses!" "Let's beat his head in!" Then a policeman arrived, but the
landlord immediately invited him into his house. When the policeman
came out afterwards and saw me sitting there crying, beaten, and torn, he
came over and taunted me, saying, "What's the difference? You're still alive."
He laughed derisively and left. When the people standing around (who were
Jews) tried to protest, he gave some of them citations for disturbing the
peace and for suspecting him of corruption. I remember that later several
of them were actually put in jail or given fines. This was always how such
incidents ended. It was perfectly natural for the neighbors not to want to
get involved when they heard cries from my hysterical mother or from us
children. They knew what the consequences were.

I also remember that very late one evening the landlord and some of his
assistants came to our door, which was bolted. First he knocked, and we
trembled: Why so late at night? To inspect, he said, to see if our place was
clean, because something was leaking into his apartment. And when we

assured him that there was nothing coming from our home, it wasn't long before the door was broken down and five men burst in, armed with clubs and shoemakers' hammers. We opened the window and shouted into the quiet night for help. People came running. A police inspector also came up and saw the armed men in our home. Despite my parents' protests, the landlord brought the inspector down to his apartment. It may sound like an exaggeration, but—Oh, it's the truth, the truth!

Afterwards, the inspector came upstairs and said that if this should happen again, we should report it ourselves to the station house. He asked whether anything had been stolen and then left. When Father went to the police the next day to tell them, in his broken Polish, about what had happened the previous night, they answered him, "Go home. Nothing happened to you. You're still alive." Several policemen standing nearby burst out laughing and made fun of the "damned Jew." When Father wouldn't leave, a policeman grabbed him by the collar and threw him out on the commander's order. Father came home crushed. Mother, who had been made anxious by all of this, heaped her own curses on him as well.

We suffered like this for several years. There was a housing shortage, and it was impossible to find another apartment with our small savings. We had to submit to our brutal landlord and do whatever he said, though it did little good. Eventually, he had us evicted and had my father and me sentenced to seven days in jail as well. This he accomplished with the help of the same people whom he always called on as witnesses. Even so, he didn't want to throw us out; it was a pity for him to give up such a tasty morsel. However, we realized that this would finally be the end. "Better to languish in the street or in a cellar. As long as we are out of that hell," Mother argued. But it was very hard for us to find a place to live. Oh, I remember how one day Mother went to look at a house. I went with her. She stopped by a deep river that ran through the city. It was March. The river was overflowing its banks as it hurried noisily on its way. We both stood there and looked at the rushing water. I feared for my mother. Intuitively, I sensed her thoughts, her despondent urge to put an end to her bitter life. I dragged her away. And—life, like the flowing river, went on and on. We continued on our way and breathed easier.

At this time, my mother gave birth to a baby boy. He was her sixth child and was to be the eighth member of our family—another hungry mouth to feed, more worry and trouble for my overworked mother. I remember this was a hard winter, terribly cold and stormy. Before she gave birth, Mother sat for entire days by the stove and cried bitterly. She cried rivers of tears, despite pleas from Father and from us children. Perhaps without really knowing why, she responded again and again with the same words: "I don't know why. It's just so hard for me, so heavy, as if dozens of stones were lying right here, beneath my heart. When I cry a little, it's easier for me, it's lighter." That's how she spoke, and then with a wail she wept another fresh stream of hot tears. At the time of the delivery, I was in the front room. The other room was separated by a white sheet instead of a door, which had never been there. I heard Mother's horrible agony, her terrible sighs and moans. Father kept busy, doing everything that the midwife ordered quickly and dutifully. I felt such pity for Mother, thinking every second that her strength could fail at any time and that she would be left there, lying stiff and lifeless. All of sixteen years old, I burst out crying. I wept quietly and wiped away my tears.

I was sent away. I wasn't needed here, I was told. Obediently, I went downstairs and wandered through the streets, oblivious to the cold and hunger. When I returned home it was getting late. The child had already been born, but it was dead. It had lived for several hours, and then—my parents assured me—it had been smothered in the layers of bedding, due to Mother's carelessness. There was quite a commotion. The midwife made a to-do. My father walked like a shadow among the neighbors who had assembled there, pale and lost in thought. Then suddenly, like a chill, a thought ran through my mind: Maybe. Maybe it wasn't negligence. Maybe my mother—Ah! I can't, no! No! Why? Why was I so brutally suspicious?

The next day, Father hammered together a little casket out of a few boards and laid the body inside. I caught a glimpse of it from the side. Oh, such a little thing, so tiny. It was black, bluish black. After assembling the casket, my father placed it on his shoulder and also took a piece of glass, with which he would circumcise the baby before laying it in its little grave.

The summer arrived, bringing hot weather. A cousin of mine on my mother's side came to visit us. She was from a rich family. She had joined the Zionist movement, gone with her fiancé to Palestine, and married him there. After six or seven years she came on a vacation to visit her parents, who lived in a small town. A beautiful, tall, healthy, normally developed woman, she awakened boyish feelings of love and respect in me. She conversed with an acquaintance of hers in fluent Hebrew with a Sephardic accent, of which I understood only a very few words that were from the Bible. First my brother and then I developed a strong desire to know this language. After our cousin returned to Palestine, he and I worked diligently to learn the language with the same accent. I remember, I enrolled in an evening course in Hebrew at the Jewish *gymnasium*. Within a short time I was the best student in my class. I easily grasped the difficult grammatical rules and was even chosen to help other students. I also won the teacher's respect with my modest and respectful demeanor, which has always been a natural quality of mine when it comes to learning. He put me in charge of collecting the monthly tuition. I carried out this task well and with precision, to the satisfaction of this talented teacher, who was somewhat older that I. Many of the students approached me outside of class and asked me to help them, and I was happy to oblige. But I didn't devote myself to Hebrew for very long, only about seven or eight months, after which I gave it up for various reasons.

It would not be unreasonable to think that I had become, as they say, a "civilized," "respectable" person. It's true that I valued learning and books, and that I chased after them as a drunk pursues the bottle. My interests also included sports, which I loved passionately. Because I worked at home, I also had enough time to play soccer. I have always been agile and brave, like my mother, and I excelled as a goalie. Although I limp slightly with my right leg, I was bolder and more skillful than others. The limp came about—as my mother told friends and neighbors countless times, in great detail—when I was eight months old. I was lying on the operating table, and they wanted to amputate my whole leg. Mother pounded her head and shouted that she'd rather deposit me at the Łódź cemetery than raise a one-legged child—and so on and so on. The team I played with was very proud of me, to the extent that I did play. This is because I would often give up playing soccer or spending time with the team for a while, so as to devote my free time to books, to the diary that I was keeping, to learning Hebrew, or simply to spending time by myself.

At the time, there was another soccer team against whom we played matches on Saturdays during the summer. They had a "talent" equal to me; his name was Yankl. Besides liking soccer, he was also devoted to pursuing all forms of knowledge. The two of us, Yankl and I, started to spend more time together. He was somewhat younger than I, with a sharp mind and greater skills. He had a healthy appetite for everything, a good facility for orienting himself quickly, and, above all, an exceptionally keen memory. Even though I had a reputation among the other fellows for my good memory, I was no match for him in this regard. Having gone to *kheyder*, Yankl still remembered not only the beatings he had received from his teacher, which I had never endured, but also the Bible and a little Talmud. When he heard that I was learning Hebrew we chatted a little in the language, he in the pronunciation used when studying the Bible, and I in a Sephardic accent. Later on, we got together to read the Hebrew newspapers that were published in our city. Yankl knew that I also read books and asked to borrow my library card for a while. I recommended that he read several books I had enjoyed. Then he joined the same library. As a result we became close intellectual companions.

"You know, Yankl," I once said to him, as we sat on a park bench, "at home we have a textbook that my brother got to learn a language I've never heard of, something completely foreign. But from the introduction," I added, "I learned that it's an international language that can be spoken everywhere." "And nowhere," Yankl interrupted, and laughed heartily. "But," I began again, "as far as I can tell, it's easy to learn." He told me to show him the book. I brought it over, and, oh, how quickly he took to it! It was a self-study manual for Esperanto. The book's Yiddish spelling was old-fashioned, but this wasn't much of an obstacle. Yankl quickly outpaced me, and he became my teacher. We found it easy to grasp the simple grammatical rules and also learned quite a number of words. And so we began to speak in this new foreign language, which is spoken everywhere and nowhere, as Yankl put it.

However, this didn't last long. It wasn't because we got tired of the language. On the contrary, though it was a little difficult for us to understand the nominative and accusative cases, due to the bad spelling, we still derived great intellectual satisfaction from sitting down every evening and asking, "What does this mean?" and figuring out the right answer in each case. But as Yankl was a tailor by trade, he joined the garment workers union. And because of his compulsion to be active in everything, he had to go to union meetings every evening and on Saturdays as well. Yankl also tried to convince me to join "his" union. Because I was employed in a similar trade, even though I worked at home with my parents, I did what Yankl wanted (I always did what Yankl wanted) and enrolled as a member of the union's youth division, to which he belonged. But I went to the union very rarely. I had no interest in it whatsoever and didn't think much of it. Yankl, however, was extremely involved in union matters, and so we saw each other less often.

Even though I read a great deal and didn't have a strictly religious education, I was always inclined toward a metaphysical way of thinking. I knew that there was no God who regulated the laws of life, partly from my reading, partly from my own conviction. But I was too much of an individualist, and the dialectical materialist conceptualization of the historical development of society was still foreign to me. It was no wonder, then, that I believed that human thought, intellect, and consciousness—the higher spirit, so to speak—regulate a person's actions and behavior. From this point of view, I also considered literature to be evidence that only the spirit governs the individual and stimulates him to creative action, so as to bring about certain changes in the social order. Following this line of thought, I had deep respect for the pious person who was convinced of his faith. During the High Holy Days I genuinely loved to see how people cried and beat their breasts for their sins and later, upon leaving the synagogue, felt their souls to be purified. However, I always despised and condemned hypocrisy, falsehood, the masks that people wore.

I remember: it was Yom Kippur. I stood in the synagogue among the worshippers. It was dark. The men, with *tallesim* draped over their heads, wailed, cried, and beat their breasts, as they asked their God for forgiveness for the sins they had committed during a life that was so brutal and wicked. I didn't pray, but I found intellectual pleasure in watching them and contemplating these unhappy souls, who sought redemption on this day. And suddenly, there was Yankl! He had come for me and several other fellows of our acquaintance. In his usual manner, he brusquely ordered me to go outside and wait for him. I didn't know why, but I went outside and waited. There were more than ten of us. He had some harsh words for us, especially for me, saying that we ought to be ashamed of ourselves for staying with the old folks, who didn't understand life the way we did. "We are now going," he said in his optimistic tone, "to be with our own kind."

And so we set off. The weather was bleak. He led us to the hills outside of town. A large group of young men, who were older than we were, had already gathered there. Some of them were dressed in traditional Jewish clothes. There were young women there as well. They were eating rolls and sausages, fooling around, and joking about the holiday. There were a lot of people there, about a hundred, maybe more. My older brother was among them. After we arrived the number grew even larger. Before very long the mood became somber. The older members of the group sought a place way out in the hills, in a big, deep ravine. We sat down wherever we could, filling up a large area.

In the crowd was a young woman who often spoke at union meetings. She opened the gathering on behalf of those assembled by explaining its purpose. She said that it was an anti-religious rally and indicated the necessity of enlightening the assembled workers about religion. A young man standing in the crowd came forward and addressed us. He was wearing traditional Jewish clothes. A rabbi's son, he began to explain in simple words the point of religion, which enslaves the individual and prevents him from rising to a higher level in life. This is especially the case for those workers who toil all year long. They are exploited by the very men who are now beating their breasts for their sins, in order to continue tomorrow with their exploitation of the weak and helpless, who possess nothing but their own ability to work. One speaker after another took the floor. They railed with hatred and bitterness against religion, which has become a tool that the ruling classes use to blunt the independent thought of the worker. There was much discussion of this, with examples brought from life.

Yankl also spoke. He spoke like an adult, energetically and emotionally, with passion and spirit. He exhorted and sharply admonished us. He said that it wasn't enough that we were freethinkers. We need to fight against religion as the opiate of the masses and to join the general proletarian struggle to abolish and overthrow the capitalist regime, which causes the exploitation of the working class. I was hearing such words for the first time in my life. I didn't understand everything. I wondered how Yankl, my friend, not only had grasped this so quickly, but also had become so eloquent, so capable of speaking out for his convictions.

It grew darker and darker. I stared at the nearby forest; thick with trees, it exuded a heavy mist that drifted upward to unite with the dense clouds. Heavy black rain clouds drifted slowly and lazily in the sky, as we became thoroughly soaked from the humid air. My eyes wandered over the bleak sky in the distance. My ears heard words, words, words. I thought: "Oh, there, in the synagogue the old generation cries, and their hearts' laments travel all the way to the heavy clouds." I looked around. We are so many, so many and so young. We are the new generation. We are the ones who must destroy the old, decadent way of life, filled with suffering and pain. We must build a new society, full of joy for all, in which the existence of two separate classes is no longer possible. Several slogans rang out. We shouted, "Down with religion! Long live the proletarian struggle for liberation! Hurrah! Hurrah!" The older members of the gathering distributed copies of a progressive publication, written in Yiddish. Slowly we dispersed, one by one. Night had fallen. I returned home. I felt as though a new way of life had opened up for me. I saw new paths, new paths that every class-conscious person ought to follow. That night I had quite a lot to record in my diary.

I began going to the union more often. I became acquainted with a few other fellows who were active there and was drawn into their circle. Some of them also read literature. But their approach to the books that they read was different, somewhat drier, than mine. I was always more interested in delving into the psychological condition of this or that character, into the thoughts of the individual. For instance, I loved to explore the deviant psychologies of Dostoyevsky's cast of characters. However, the others were more concerned with the conclusion that each author came to in a given work. They judged a book from a social standpoint, while I examined it from a purely individualistic point of view. From them I learned to scrutinize the socialist content of each book. Remarkably, I understood the correctness of their approach and admitted that this was how one ought to read and understand books. Because they considered themselves workers in the struggle against the present social system, the other fellows also read the daily newspapers and various periodicals, perhaps even more than books. But I observed this activity from the sidelines. I didn't read anything but short stories and poems, so I was very bad at following politics.

I was drawn into a top-secret, underground group, whose task it was to set up self-education groups for young people. Although I had no appropriate training, and therefore perhaps carried out my assignment poorly, I willingly undertook this job. This involved me more closely with the union, which I considered to be a place that offered cultural and educational opportunities for those who had been dragged out of their homes while still very young and pushed into fetid workshops. I was elected to the youth committee, then as the assistant librarian. I was still very young—seventeen or eighteen years old—and understood my duties poorly. But I loved this work very much and threw myself into it with all the passion of my young, turbulent soul. I worked fervently, with all my heart.

I began to read very different kinds of books, which taught me a great deal and from which I was able to teach others. I read nothing but sociology. I remember that I borrowed Bebel's *The Woman and Socialism* and passionately devoured every line. This was the first scholarly work that I ever read. I read through this two-volume work twice, copying out various passages that I needed for the little lectures I had to give to the young people's groups. Other works of this sort followed: Engels's *The Origin of the Family, Private Property, and the State*, Beer's *History of Class Struggles*, Cunow's *Religion and Faith*, and the like. They introduced me to new concepts of life in human society.

My life entered a new period. I was proud of the knowledge I had acquired, in contrast with the philistine who is absorbed with his personal life and is unfamiliar with the historical development of the society to which he belongs. But I related to all of this through books. I wasn't interested in newspapers or politics. I didn't appreciate the maxim that one doesn't exclude the other, that literature is political, and that politics creates new literature. As a result, I couldn't stand either the speeches of the older people or those of my own comrades. They were all so tedious, full of the same content. The words that I heard at the union meetings—"exploitation," "proletariat," "capitalism," "fascism," "revolution," and so on—didn't elicit the appropriate response from my typically bookish, intellectual spirit. I was even more shocked by the practice of one party slinging mud at another. I was completely disgusted when I happened to read the attacks that one party made against the other in the newspapers of various political orientations. I was confused and didn't know which viewpoint was right on a given matter. As a result, I picked up a newspaper only very, very rarely. While my comrades were enthusiastically engrossed in this activity and always debated heatedly among themselves, I stood on the sidelines. Thus, I gradually became part of the workers' milieu. Here, despite everything, I found it to be familiar, congenial, and friendly.

At this time my family moved to a new apartment, which we found after much difficulty. The apartment was almost in the center of town, and we were extremely happy with it. But with this came the painful conclusion of our relationship with that vile, anti-Semitic landlord.

A policeman came with a summons for us to serve our seven-day sentences in prison instead of the municipal jail. My father and I got ready. I brought a notebook and pencil with me in order to record my impressions during this time. But they were quickly confiscated in the prison office; a prisoner isn't allowed to write without permission. In the prison supply room they searched and examined us thoroughly, and they gave us each a filthy blanket, a pillow of crushed straw, a cracked bowl, and so on—all of it old, dirty, and worn-out. With this "baggage" we moved into a dimly lit hallway, where we were searched by another prison guard, and from there we went into the cell. We settled in as best we could for a week. I didn't rest. There I discovered strange, bizarre people and a life completely unfamiliar, except in books. It was hard to get used to. Still, the average person isn't basically bad or brutal. One can only be convinced of this after having come in contact with those who are being punished for their crimes. After we had become accustomed to living with our cellmates and sharing our cigarettes and food with them, each of them tried, one way or another, to prove his innocence to us and convince us of the unjust sentence he had received from a judge who hadn't tried to understand the prisoner's condition at the time in question. We understood them and empathized with them. But it was of no use! The law is the law.

I made a point of taking part in prison work outside the cell in order to become better acquainted with prison life. I went outside for exercise (my father was ashamed to do so). I went to fetch water, peel potatoes, and the like. I looked at the faces of the criminals, thinking that perhaps I would find someone I knew. Whenever I saw someone who seemed to be better off, I asked myself if he could be a political prisoner. I found out that they were held separately, on an upper level of the prison. They went out separately for their exercise, and so on. I looked up above, but saw nothing other than different kinds of other criminals. There were many who had been sentenced to quite a few years in prison. They envied me that I was only there for seven days. What are seven days compared to five years, or eight, or even more?

It was winter. Outside there were storms, snow, cold temperatures. I became acquainted with the prison life of non-political criminals, with their psychology, their unique philosophy of life. In my opinion, this taught me more than reading several books.

In the summer, my cousin Rokhtshe came to visit us. She was the sister of our cousin in Palestine. Rokhtshe was a pretty, somewhat plump girl with smooth, black, silky hair, who had come to the big city for a bit of fun. My older brother was away, working in a nearby town, so it happened that I was the only one who could play the role of escort, one to which I was little suited. I was too serious then and tried to act like an adult. Although she and I were the same age, I didn't feel that seeing me was the real reason for her visit. But, oh, what the hell! Maybe for that reason she excited me. I went to the movies with her. I told her all sorts of humorous stories. I tried as hard as possible to get her attention, and, strange as it may be, I fell in love with her.

I remember once when we came home from the movies. It was already rather late. My parents and the other children were asleep in the other room. I turned down the electric light and lit a candle. She took off her blouse. Her naked, shapely, white shoulders shone like velvet in the soft candlelight. She sat down by the table. I caressed her and kissed her downy shoulders. She didn't stop me. I became confused. I felt that I was in love, in love with my cousin Rokhtshe. I was unable to fall asleep for a very long time. Early in the morning, before sunrise, I jumped up with a strange start, washed, and dressed hurriedly. Bright stripes of light peeked through the slats of the shutters. I went quietly to her bed. She was sleeping lightly. I gave her a kiss on the lips. She slowly opened her black eyelashes. She wasn't startled. Oh, Rokhtshe! I don't know whether I will ever feel like this again in my life. I love you. Love—how small that word is; how many times people have said it. And yet it holds within itself all of the heart's red blood.

Rokhtshe stayed with us for several weeks; then she went back home. I wrote some sentiments, which I stole from poetry, in her scrapbook. Ah! How wretched life is, and yet how many beautiful and rich moments it contains. I wrote her long, long letters, the words crowded tightly together. I neatly copied excerpts from the tenth chapter of Kellermann's poetic work *Ingeborg*, and sent this to her, dedicating it to her to be remembered forever, as if it were my own creation. Ever since then, these have remained the most beautiful pages in my diary. These were the best and richest memories of my youth.

At the time, my intellectual development broadened. I worked intensively together with close comrades of like mind. I held several positions at once. I became head librarian, overseeing a collection of more than two hundred books. The readers liked me. I always spoke with them about the books they had just read and picked out works for them to read. I also joined the cultural commission, taking part in public events, "living newspapers," and group lectures for the young people's section. I performed all my duties promptly. I also had to carry out the decisions of the party leadership and, to the extent I was able, provide cultural education to illegal groups outside of the union. I had no time for myself. I had to stop keeping my diary and doing my own reading.

Thus, I was gradually transformed into a revolutionary. We were much oppressed by the authorities, in danger of being arrested at any minute. In fact, many of the older ones among us were arrested. We were beaten by the police and then, in keeping with the law, given heavy sentences, spending years in prison—something I have yet to endure. After each arrest, the number of members in the union always dropped. The best and most active ones were taken away, but it didn't take long for all our activities to resume in full force.

There was an array of personalities among my comrades, amusing people as well as serious. There were careerists who tried to make themselves more popular by giving speeches at workers' rallies. They were more full of false pathos than honest sincerity, and for this reason they failed. There were also young women who were loaded with intellectual baggage. There was also no lack of personal relations between the male and female comrades—romances and flirtations—apart from political work. This led to a variety of psychological complications, which often resulted in neglecting work at the union or elsewhere, expulsions, rehabilitations, spying, catching one another in an infraction, reprimands, and ridicule. Then this was all put in the humor section of a living newspaper in such a way that outsiders wouldn't suspect a thing and insiders would recognize themselves. This was always done by the leadership of the organization, who were in a position to do so, though they themselves were not entirely blameless in such matters. I had a great deal of trouble following the twists and turns of these boy-and-girl squabbles. I intuited more than I understood, surmised more than I knew, always observing from the sidelines. Of course, this is the preoccupation of young people who are seventeen to twenty-something years old.

But my one friend remained Yankl. I loved him very much, this clever young man, who put all these matters aside. For him, political work always came before his personal life. He was always full of enthusiasm, full of optimistic plans to organize all sorts of events. Even the older comrades were taken with the fervor of his young and turbulent spirit. When Yankl took the floor at a meeting, everyone admired him for his sparkling oratory and sharp memory. They would applaud him for a long time, both before and after he addressed the crowd. No wonder, then, that others, even those older than he was, lagged behind him. Because of his enthusiastic devotion to the cause, which inspired others as well, he quickly climbed higher and higher on the organizational ladder of this illegal organization. No, Yankl couldn't be false. With his sincere devotion, he often boldly pointed out the errors of older comrades and persuaded them to act according to his instructions. We talked with each other often. Together we read works of Marxist theory, and he would explain the difficult passages to me. I felt—and everyone agreed—that he would become a great scholar. But what does Heine say somewhere? Wherever there are people of spirit there are also the gallows, and vice versa.

A comrade of ours, Alter Hofman, died. He was a tailor, twenty-five or twenty-six years old, a healthy, tall, well-developed, fine young man. While on a mission for the party, he injured his right leg, which became swollen and infected. He was operated on several times and eventually was taken to Cracow, where they amputated his leg above the knee. Returning on a pair of crutches, he resumed party work as best he could. He became the favorite of the older comrades. Alter was a good theoretician and possessed a well-developed intellect. We younger members used to visit him in the evenings in his little room on the outskirts of town, where he would teach us and entertain us.

Eventually, the effort to walk caused him to overexert himself. He perspired and caught a cold; this developed into a lung infection, which quickly destroyed his health. With the help of money collected from among the workers, he rented a place to live, in a birch forest, from a peasant. We went there on Saturdays and savored the fragrant air, read books, and engaged in heated discussions.

In the end, Alter's cough destroyed his lungs, and he died quietly. The police visited him as he lay dying and thoroughly searched his home. We organized a funeral befitting a labor activist, and in doing so we clashed with the traditional Jewish burial society. With bare heads and carrying wreaths trimmed with red ribbons, we marched in ranks through the streets, singing labor songs as we reached the outskirts of the city. The older comrades spoke at the grave, calling for a continuation of the struggle for which the deceased had fought. Yankl also made a fiery speech on behalf of the young people's committee, and his enthusiasm inspired those assembled beside the grave. We spread the last shovelsful of dirt over the grave, laid the wreaths as we sang the "Internationale," and returned home by evening. Yankl told me to note this accurately in my diary (which he knew that I was keeping), and I did as he wished.

There were more arrests. The ranks of the union dwindled. Those of us who were left worked energetically to reestablish the cultural committee, as well as the library and the young people's section. I remember Comrade A. Klayn, the Tolstoyan, as they used to call him. He was always in a dark mood, deep in thought. Klayn opposed the revolutionary use of terror. He held himself in high regard on account of his "knowledge" and looked down on us youngsters. Klayn treated Yankl and me with a certain disdain. He always carried around with him the manuscripts of plays he had written. As he himself put it, he was a dilettante. He also used to object to the lectures I gave to the young people's section. As a result, the comrades didn't much care for Klayn; nevertheless, they loved to listen to him speak about his humanitarian, Tolstoyan approach to society. He used to give lectures on various writers and their work, and he became chairman of the cultural committee.

Once, Klayn organized a proletarian literary evening and dance. On his own initiative he also hired my brother, who at the time no longer worked in the garment trade, but had moved into quite a different line of work. Having a talent for drawing, he became a portrait artist, which is how he continues to earn a living. We organized the literary part of the program, with which we were pleased, even though it was small. I even took an active role in it. Since I had a talent for recitation, I undertook to recite Edelstadt's "A Suicide Note." I learned all seven pages by heart.

I remember: it was evening, after a day of work at the sewing machine. Nobody was at home except my parents. I started to read "A Suicide Note" out loud. These poetic, if naive, soulful words had a profound effect on Mother. At the time she was pregnant with my youngest sister. My brutal suspicion concerning the smothered child crept into my mind. I trembled and continued to read louder and louder. Father also listened attentively. And when I came to these words: "I could not bear seeing a bent, old woman washing the laundry for a healthy, young bourgeois lady. It broke my heart to see a mother seeking a way to smother the child at her breast, because she didn't have the means to nurture it." Then! Oh, then! I read it with heart and soul, and a shudder coursed through my entire being. I paused to catch my breath, and—Oh, what I saw: Mother had buried her face in her hands and was sobbing. Father became white as chalk and trembled inwardly. I couldn't go on—No! I read no more.

Feeling confused, I went out into the street. No! No! No! It's impossible, impossible! But maybe? Maybe it was so? Ah, my head was pounding, like heavy hammers on glowing, molten lead. I understood everything, my heart felt everything! I didn't go to the union. For a long time, as I wandered through the noisy streets by myself, I couldn't escape this terrible image. At home, Mother was certainly crying, beating her breast and her head. Perhaps she felt remorse. Maybe—Oh! I came home. They were already asleep. I could neither read nor write. I threw myself onto the bed and curled up. Oh, cursed life!

I wrote a great deal at the time. In addition to my diary, I also began to experiment with writing poetry. It seemed that I was writing something worthwhile, that I might become something of a poet. That was my dream, and on the wings of my emotional fantasies I saw myself as a great mature poet, whose existence is unknown, but who is suddenly discovered by accident, becomes popular, and goes on to have a literary career. As I wrote I bit my nails until they bled and, feeling no pain, tore the hair from my head. First, I worked on the subject, then the form, and as I wrote I looked for rhymes. I wrote many poems. At first, they were strictly personal: about myself, my thoughts, my outlook on life. Later came poems of struggle, proletarian poems that expressed hopes for a classless society. But—hmmm. When I read them to myself, I found them colorless, with a naive, clumsy immaturity in comparison to other poetry. I was embarrassed to show them to anyone. Still, I didn't destroy them; I put them away. Some time later, I decided to show them to some people who were more knowledgeable about literature. They selected a few of them to be recited at informal literary events. I recited them myself and found it rather satisfying. However, believing that there were greater talents than mine in this area, I never submitted them to a journal or periodical. Eventually, I gave them up altogether.

The best and dearest of our older comrades were put on trial. There were quite a few of them, and the trial lasted several days. I remember: It was winter, and the fine weather was cold, sunny, and dry. We went to visit Comrade Ferfel, who had come from out of town. He and his two sisters had sublet an apartment on a side street on the outskirts of town. We often went there to have a good time—sing, play chess, or just have fun with the girls. We held friendly drinking parties and often discussed all sorts of things. Mostly we talked about our comrades' legal defense and its methods of investigation. A short time earlier a well-known comrade, with whom we were close, had been fatally shot in prison during a demonstration demanding better treatment of inmates. We spoke about whether or not it would be just to teach his killers a lesson by carrying out a terrorist attack against one of those most responsible for the murder. We made plans to inject the man with poison when he would least expect it, while he was standing and talking; there were other similar ideas. But we hadn't gathered for an official party meeting at which such decisions could be made, and in any case it was against party principles to carry out acts of terror against individuals in such cases. Instead, we turned to enjoying ourselves. We hadn't come to have a good time, though. We had left in the middle of work to find out how our comrades' trial was going, and we trembled anxiously as we waited for the verdict.

And we did not wait in vain. Oh, how clearly I remember this! There were several of us in the room, young women and men. It was late in the afternoon. Frost covered the window panes. It grew darker and darker. We didn't turn on the electric lights. We sat on the bed, leaning back, caressing and kissing. We were waiting for Comrade Volf, who was at the courthouse. It was nearly time for his arrival. We heard footsteps on the stairs. We got up quickly, as if from a nightmare, and turned on the lights.

Comrade Volf stood in the doorway. He came in slowly and quietly, tall and thin, his cyclist's hat pulled down over his ears, the collar of his light summer jacket turned up. He was pale. His lips trembled. We surrounded him, impatiently asking, "Well?" His whole body trembled as he reported: They had been sentenced to prison terms ranging from one to eight years. He listed each of their names together with their sentences. He also described the police officers' brutal treatment of the prisoners after the verdict. They were driven back to prison in a truck and were beaten with rubber truncheons. Gradually, Comrade Volf grew more agitated. He screamed: "I don't understand! Why didn't they protest in court or in the street? Why did they submit quietly to being brutalized by the police? Why didn't they resist, for the sake of their honor?" Comrade Shvarts became angry at Volf for his accusations. She blurted out, "Just you wait, Volf! I'd like to see how you would act at such a moment."

We didn't stay long in the apartment. In a somber mood we went our separate ways. Our best comrades! Cut off from life for so long. Torn away from us for so long. Kept apart for so many years. With hopes that the revolution would set them free earlier, we each headed home.

Then our turn came. We were summoned by the police several times, and yet we continued to devote ourselves intensively to the party. My friend Yankl was more active than I was. He did technical work for the party. I managed to get away during Passover, before the workers' holiday on the first of May. I went to visit my Rokhtshe in a small town near the German border, far away from our town. I brought my diary and wrote several pages as I rode in the train. Here is what I wrote then:

26 April 192–
The train rumbles and roars as it flies through broad fields bathed in springtime sun. My heart trembles and keeps time with the hum of the rushing locomotive, which carries me to my beloved. Ah! Where is Yankl now? Where is Comrade Klayn? Where is Comrade Volf? Where are Comrades Bella and Dora? Where are all my friends now? Ah! I can't

stand it. Faster, faster! Oh, the train is moving so slowly! I can't sit still. I get up and look out the window. My head is spinning. I sit back down. An old woman—a Christian, holding her child as she sits opposite me, half asleep—irks me. I feel as if everything within me were exploding. I want to throw myself on her with all my hatred and anger, beat her savagely with my fists, and shout as loud as I can in her ear, "Ah, you old woman! What do you know? What do you know about life? What do you know about what goes on in my heart? My heart is a volcano, capable of blowing up this entire speeding train, of destroying everything, everything and everyone. It's your fault, yours, that Yankl and all of my best and closest friends are now being beaten by the police. Yours, yours!" And I am on my way to my beloved, to my Rokhtshe! Faster, faster! Let there be an end to this! Oh, how egotistical I am! No! I shouldn't have left them. I should be together with them, together!

I arrived, and all of my fantastic hopes were dashed. Rokhtshe was involved with someone else: a tall, handsome, strapping fellow from the big city, with a sense of humor and aristocratic manners, an agent for a textile firm. He spoke only Polish. I felt like an intruder. She didn't pay much attention to me. Besides, it seemed as though she'd become less attractive, more slovenly, lazy, and somewhat heavier. I spent two weeks there with my aunt (my mother's sister). I returned home empty, my soul drained. It seemed to me that everything in our town had died. The union was still open. Another comrade, Siegfried, had come to the fore. He had assumed the position of secretary and ran the union almost entirely by himself. I seldom went there. I missed my comrades: Yankl, and all of those who had become my close friends.

However, it didn't take long for something new to enter my life. I became more friendly with another member of the union, Moyshl. The other members looked down on him somewhat, because of his frequent involvement in shady activities. He was the picture of a cunning rascal, sly and sharp-witted, who nonetheless had been outsmarted by life more than once. At a young age he had been forced to support himself and to sleep wherever he could find a place to stay. He had been hardened by life, which had often treated him brutally. Moyshl almost never read books, only newspapers, and seldom even that. But he need only read through something once—a good work of literature, of course—and he understands it; moreover, he remembers much of it and learns from it. But Moyshl also has a tendency to think too highly of himself, resulting in an arrogance and, to a certain extent, an inclination to make fun of those he considers his inferiors. He loves to befriend people who are his superiors, and he is ready to push aside those closest to him the moment he feels like following his rather self-centered whims. His egotism—which is, in fact, latent in the average person—is manifest at every opportunity. Although a bit impudent and obstinate, Moyshl also has a healthy appetite for life and well-developed powers of intuition. He is sensitive and often emotional. And, in addition to all his other traits, he possesses a strong inclination to probe patiently into things he doesn't understand, and this gives him intellectual satisfaction. I became well acquainted with this fellow, who is a little taller than I am and a year older, and we became close friends.

At the time, I ran into someone with whom I had once taken evening classes in Hebrew, a fellow named Yitskhok. Something of a clown, he suddenly came up to me in the middle of the street and started speaking to me in Esperanto. I could understand only a little of what he said. We switched to Yiddish and agreed to renew our study of Esperanto. He was already somewhat fluent; in any case, he knew more than I did. And so once more I began to study this language, which I had started to learn with Yankl. Every evening we had a lesson. When Moyshl found out that I was studying a language that was easy to learn, he joined us. Yitskhok didn't last and quit, so Moyshl and I continued to study on our own. We found a better textbook and made rapid progress. We also got hold of some reading material in Esperanto. Every Saturday morning we went out to the hills, sat down in the grass, and, with the help of a dictionary, found satisfaction in reading. Esperanto is an artificially created language, logically constructed, and— more than other, natural languages—elastic and very synthetic. We found it fascinating, without even knowing that there was such an interesting field as philology or linguistics. We simply jumped for joy when we grasped the idea behind a difficult compound word, consisting only of prefixes and suffixes, or a well-constructed sentence. With unusual diligence, Moyshl would search through the book, translate, and finally explain to me the fundamentals of why one thing is correct and not the other. In this way, we not only mastered the complete grammar but also learned how to compose well-formed and logical expressions. We were completely taken with the language.

We then learned by chance of the existence of the Esperanto society, the SAT (Nationless Worldwide Association). Its main agenda was to promote the language among workers, to unite them through the organization, and to make them into internationalists in the fullest meaning of the word. The goal was to uproot people's national traditions and educate them in the humanitarian spirit, to teach them to oppose chauvinism, racial hatred, and war, and to embrace socialism. To this end, the SAT published a weekly journal called *Sennaciulo* (Nationless) and also ran an active publishing house. At the time they published many books, both translations of the best European writers and fine original works. We became acquainted with every aspect of the SAT's work, in which workers and intellectuals of all ideologies and shades of opinion were represented and took an active part. Here, it seemed to us, that the slogan, "Proletarians of all countries, unite!" was truly finding a voice and being realized. We believed in this very strongly.

Moyshl and I soon enrolled as active members. We became so involved in the proletarian Esperanto movement that we regarded it as the highest ideal, the only one capable of leading humanity out of the mire of chauvinism. We considered the SAT to be the only organization to which every intellectually developed person sympathetic to socialism should devote his life. We found it exciting to read an issue of *Sennaciulo*, which introduced us to different parts of the world that had been completely unknown to us. I also tried translating some short pieces from Yiddish into Esperanto, which I submitted to the journal and actually got published. Then we wrote some short, humorous anecdotes with a proletarian focus and submitted them to the monthly supplement to the main journal, which was aimed at beginners. We also gradually established a correspondence about various social issues with fellow Esperanto enthusiasts abroad. In this way we became part of the international Esperanto family. I also started keeping my diary in Esperanto. I felt that by doing so I had risen to a higher level intellectually.

However, my personal economic situation didn't allow for major expenses. Not being independent, and having to rely on the generosity of my parents, I had to spend less on these activities. Still, as I felt that I had mastered the language, I began to teach beginners' classes. As I had a talent for teaching, the students—several working men and women of my acquaintance—greatly enjoyed the examples that I used to explain each concept. I felt that my task was threefold: First, I was advocating for Esperanto. Second, as a worker striving to become a thorough internationalist, I was showing others the way by recruiting them as members of the SAT. And third, I regarded teaching as a way to win over others to my convictions as a revolutionary. I threw myself into this work wholeheartedly, and it gave me much mental satisfaction. However, I was completely disappointed with some of the students. Some of them only wanted to exploit the language for their own selfish reasons and to flaunt their knowledge of it. Moyshl looked askance at the whole thing and teased me about it. Nevertheless, I succeeded in winning over several of my students, and they became active members of the SAT. I felt that at least I had done something for my convictions, whereas Moyshl arrogantly flaunted his knowledge of the language while refusing to share it.

The trial of our comrades, including my best and closest friend, Yankl, took place. The trial left us feeling depressed. They had been arrested based on evidence provided by a provocateur, who then fled to another town. Also, Volf had broken under questioning by the police. He blabbed about things he should not have, which became the basis for the trial. The terror was overwhelming.

We later learned that, of all of the comrades on trial, the one who conducted himself the best and who made the strongest impression was Yankl. He had convinced his poor parents not to make any effort to save him and refused to let them hire a defense attorney. During the time between the arrest and the trial, which was almost a year, he had become fluent in Polish. When it was time to make his final statement in court, Yankl told the judges his life story. He then described the terrible tortures he had experienced as an eighteen-year-old under arrest. He explained how they had bound his hands to his feet so that he was curled up like a ball, then put a stick between his knees, lifted him up and spun him around like a carousel. He told how they had hung him up by the arms and spat in his face, stuffed a rag in his mouth and poured warm urine in his nostrils, revived him by pouring cold water in his ears, and so on.

The judges interrupted him and eventually stopped him from speaking. In protest he shouted that he knew they were going to convict him and that he didn't ask them for mercy. Then he let loose with several slogans. He was sentenced to five years in prison, Volf to six years, and others to three, four, or six years. And so the trial ended; because of the harsh sentences, it created quite a sensation in the town. We wrote a long report on it for *Sennaciulo* and kept the newspaper well hidden as a memento. From the present perspective, though, hasn't this been completely overshadowed by the trials that have recently taken place in this country?

At the time, the union moved from its cramped meeting hall to more comfortable quarters. New members, who hadn't been organized successfully until now, began to stream in. We had to increase our activities regarding industry and, even more, our cultural activities. I was involved in the latter. Comrade Siegfried was a good secretary, but he lacked what it takes to be a good organizer, much less a cultural leader. He needed a great deal of help. I was still very young and incapable of carrying out such an important mission. Nevertheless, I was somewhat familiar with the previous leadership, from which I had received as much training as possible, and so I became chairman of the cultural committee. But it wasn't long before I assumed a more serious position that involved greater responsibilities.

All of the local trade unions, together with a few intellectuals who were sympathetic to proletarian culture, established a general workers' library. Comrade Abrashek was the leader of this initiative. The town in which I live never had such an institution, although it was big enough for one and needed it very much. There were several private libraries in town, but the Jewish worker didn't have access to any of them. For one thing, the dues were too high, but the main reason was that these libraries had no respect for the proletarian reader. Their snobbish librarians, who go about their work like silent robots, look down on members of the working class. Having grown up under very particular conditions, they need direction. For this reason, when a worker does enroll in one of these libraries, he soon gives it up. I myself have known workers who walked around with books that were entirely inappropriate for them and which they never read. As a result, they acquired a contempt for books. There was a very strong need here for another library, one that would educate and, in a friendly way, provide guidance on what and how to read. To this end, the library, named after Y.L. Peretz, was established. I not only became a member immediately but, as I understood the work involved, was also active in establishing the library. We acquired over 200 books from the garment workers' union. Union members and other supporters donated more books, and there was also a book fund. The library opened with about 500 books. I was elected head librarian. I had to give up the Esperanto classes, due to a lack of time. Moyshl and I remained active Esperantists and devoted quite a bit of what little free time we had to the language.

I am reminded here of the scene in Ansky's one-act play *The Grandfather*, in which an old revolutionary, who has escaped from a prison camp, returns home and meets the intellectual children of his old friend and comrade, Yerushov. They are adrift, searching for something to grab hold of; the old man teaches them how to fill the void in their empty lives. When he finds out that they have been reading Marx, the agitator's spirit awakens within him, and he cries out with these words, more or less:

Work and study! Otherwise you will remain soulless; you will have read everything, examined everything, and you will do nothing. Then you will look around and find a greater emptiness. Your spirit will not be satisfied, so you will continue to search. You will say, "I have not yet seen the Venus de Milo." But if you *work* as you learn, then your soul will remain whole and your conscience will be at peace. And if you ever end up in prison, then you will have sufficient free time to study, plenty of free time.

At this time, I grasped the true meaning of the old man's words. My life was quite full then. I had become a useful person, working within a particular framework toward proletarian political ends. Finding myself in the library among groups of smarter and intellectually more developed people, I excelled in my task as an intermediary between intellectuals and workers. I dedicated myself thoroughly to these goals. I felt that being a librarian was my natural calling. I had to read everything. I had to become more fully acquainted with the works that I gave people to read. I selected works for readers, led discussions about the books, and offered a Marxist critique of the authors. The readers were happy with me, the directors even more so. And I was happy, too.

But that wasn't all. I also had things to do for the union and the cultural committee. I was always organizing activities at the union. I arranged excursions for the young people's section, planned events, edited the living newspapers, and, on Friday nights in the winter, sang with the young people's chorus. In the library there were others who were older and more talented than I was, and I learned a great deal from them. There, we organized more serious activities, in which I also took part. We presented evenings of readings, for example, in which it fell upon me to undertake the greater part of the recitations. I simply had no time for myself. After working all day at the sewing machine, I had to get to my post as librarian on time. I ran through the streets without having eaten dinner. When I saw people strolling calmly, I felt contempt for them, the philistines, preoccupied with what I considered to be their petty, selfish needs and goals. And yet, in a way, I envied them, envied their time. Oh, I would much rather have devoted my time to Esperanto, which gave me so much satisfaction. But I felt superior to those other people, and that in itself was my greatest satisfaction.

For "creating materially to create spiritually means: escaping from the prison of the body, which means: breaking through to the stream of life, which means: being one who *is*. Creating means overcoming death, and woe to the person who does not feel productive, who is laden with life and love, like a tree in bloom in the spring. The world may cover him with honor and fortune. It crowns a corpse." (Rolland)

My friend Abrashek was a slight, skinny fellow. Although he was over thirty years old, he seemed no older than twenty, given both his life-long interest in social issues and his personal conduct. A highly intellectual sort, Abrashek was familiar with many things, especially the law. He was a bookkeeper in the Jewish communal office. He was sharp, an experienced and skilled organizer, and an exceptional administrator. By nature a good man, he was, however, a strict fellow with regard to social matters, and was extremely stubborn when it came to his own affairs. He loved to tell humorous stories that sent him into fits of laughter, his wide-open mouth revealing several sparkling gold teeth. Whatever the occasion or the company, he would always draw attention to himself. He was a talented teacher and used to instruct me on how to do all sorts of things.

Abrashek was the founder of the library, in fact, although he never, or very rarely, admitted to this in public. But everyone knew quite well that this was the case and that he was the heart and soul of this institution. It is true that people saw me as the person in charge of the library, to whom they came with any problems or questions. However, Abrashek would come in, always in a hurry, and in a flash his sharp blue eyes would survey the situation, he would give a few short instructions, and then disappear. Although there were other intellectuals around, everyone felt that this small fellow towered over them like a giant, that he could handle any question, no matter what the subject. I have learned a great deal from this astute, intelligent man, who carried out his duties with much enthusiasm and *joie-de-vivre*, and who had an uncanny sense for life's smallest details.

In Abrashek's presence I couldn't help thinking of Yankl, who was like a copy of this enthusiastic fellow. I thought that when his five years were over and he got out of prison, Yankl would take Abrashek's place. I felt a great deal of respect for this small fellow. I always honored his wishes and did what he asked of me.

At the time, I made friends with another young man, Shloyme. A small, lively, funny fellow, he was always ready with a good joke to suit the occasion. He was a good man, often serious; he was intelligent and sharp. I got to know him through Moyshl. Shloyme was a laborer. He worked in a home for the poor. He was a practical, substantial person, who hated braggarts and was extremely strict with those with whom he disagreed. He abhorred falsehood and was a devoted friend who would give his life for those close to him. I became very fond of him, and we became quite close. I had known him earlier, when we had studied Esperanto together with several others. Because of his bad memory he found it difficult, but thanks to his intelligence he was able to master the language. He, too, became a member of the SAT. In social settings, he was a bit quieter, preferring to stay off to the side and observe.

Shloyme had read a great deal, having started to read at the age of thirteen. He preferred the classics, the great works of literature, just as I do. He knew how to summarize the plot and the author's main themes. He was quite familiar with the psychology of the common man, which he loved to probe. He was well versed in life's hardships and saw things with his eyes wide open. He never became excited and responded to new things with indifference—a quality that stayed with him throughout his quiet, modest life. Because he lived in a proletarian environment, he became completely identified with it. I always felt closer to him than to others. Moyshl easily became upset and distant; not so Shloyme. He was a true friend, a completely devoted friend. I love him very much, and am as close to him as two male friends can ever be. The three of us—Moyshl, Shloyme, and I—met and discussed all sorts of issues, both social and personal, and all in the international language of Esperanto.

We cordially shared our most intimate secrets with each other. People used to call us the "Holy Trinity." My friends, however, always had more free time than I did. And that's how things were for a long time, until Moyshl left us after getting involved with a woman. But we've remained close friends to this day.

I have now, for the third time—probably the last time—gotten involved with a young woman; I am still young, and life may have all kind of surprises in store for me, still—I'm not sure, not at all! I loved her passionately. Perhaps, as is often the case, it was all a purely physical attraction, a desire to possess her. Anyway, I've always believed in the saying, which I take to be an undisputable fact, that "When a man and a woman are in love with each other they enter into a self-deception, because each is in love with him- or herself." This girl was a laborer, a member of the proletariat. She knew a great deal and was beautiful, graceful, slender. She was exactly my height. She was lively, agile, intelligent, always happy, and full of life. Behind her thin, bright-red lips were two rows of white teeth. There were several other fellows who hovered around her.

But she made me feel different from them; I even had a fantastic dream of being in a couple with her. Previously I had taught her Esperanto, among other things. In the summer we used to take walks on Saturday evenings. We would leave the city, escaping the crowds and noise. We would walk through fields of fragrant wheat in the sunset and sing quiet songs. They were gentle, touching songs. But it became painfully clear that she didn't really love me. No, there was someone else. But then she wrote me a letter saying that she did love me, that I was the only one that she thought about. Although these words moved me at first, I didn't take them seriously. As others confirmed, the way she treated me didn't reflect what she wrote in her letter. When I confronted her with this she denied it all, and so I became the victim of her typically feminine frivolity, as she played a cruel finale on my heart-strings.

However, my brain managed to gain control over my heart, and I let her go to another. All along I suffered greatly, because she didn't want to lose me, as she sensed my true and sincere love for her was still alive within me. When she realized that I was pulling away, she asked me to come to see her, which I gladly did. We sat on a bench under a full moon. She knew I was suffering greatly because of her. I don't know if I'm selfish, or if I've begun to see her in a different light—who knows? I have no idea! To hell with it! She left me for someone else, because I pushed her away for good.

While I suffered in my personal life, I found some comfort in my professional life. I went before the military board to see if I qualified as cannon fodder. They weighed me, measured me, turned me over, looked inside my mouth, my ears—everything was fine. But finally they focused their attention on my leg, which had been operated on—a fact I stubbornly kept quiet about. They had me run across the room slowly, then jump with both legs together, and the like, for a long time. Finally came their verdict: I was free. Ha, ha, ha! One of them even said that now I could get married without any problem.

From the prison in Rawicz I received a letter from Yankl. It wasn't addressed to me directly. It was written in a clear, tiny, beautiful script and poetically phrased. In it he described his life there. He wrote that he was learning a great deal there, including Russian and Ukrainian. He also described his longing for home, his former environment, his former life. He was, he wrote, like a bird locked in a cage: peering out at the blue sky, jumping from one perch to the next, singing heartbreaking melodies that are filled with pain, and longing for his brothers and sisters who fly freely around him. In this manner Yankl jumped up onto his little table, down to his chair, and from there back to the ground, then up again, looking out through a small opening covered with bars. There he saw a bit of the blue sky and green treetops thick with leaves. However, he didn't know what to do with himself. He asked me to write back to him and to ask all of his friends to write, as this would be like a small beam of light in his gray and monotonous life. I wrote a brief reply, in which I hinted that we are now introducing the "new bookstore," as well as other things. After a while he wrote to me again, but I never wrote him back. What happened to me happens to all people who take up the mission given them by the eternal laws of history and of human society: that of fighting for a new, free life.

I worked very hard as a librarian, as secretary and member of the library's cultural committee, and as the chairman of a community council for the organization. These activities took up all my free time. After my daily physical labor was done I felt that I should devote myself to social activity that supports proletarian, revolutionary ideals.

Early one Saturday morning on a hot July day the cultural committee decided to organize a literary program, for which I served as the instructor. We worked long and hard to make this event as impressive as possible. We spent four weeks getting it ready and decorated the hall with green and red paper. The event took place on 1 August, the anniversary of the start of the Imperialist War of 1914. Although revolutionary leaders usually mark this day with an antiwar campaign, our program wasn't planned with any specific goal in mind. However, the girls in the organization, whose task was to decorate the hall, made up a banner that read "Make War on War!" and placed it right in front of the stage.

The event was scheduled to start at eight o'clock in the morning, but the performers, seven men in all, got there at six o'clock for a final rehearsal of the various readings and musical numbers. There were a considerable number of tickets for the event, and they were all sold out. After rehearsing we went outside. It was still early; elderly Jews were leaving the *mikve* still wet from their Sabbath morning immersions. I suddenly learned of an arrest that had taken place the night before. The prisoners included one of our leaders and two other young people. Apparently they were arrested for handing out leaflets at the metal factory. I was so used to frequent arrests on a regular basis that this particular one didn't make much of an impression on me. Still, we were anxious about our early-morning literary event. A protest rally would have been quite impossible, as this event had been heavily advertised and our members were looking forward to it eagerly. Besides, canceling or changing anything would make the police suspicious; they had been notified in advance of the nature of this event. Because of the previous night's arrests we were very careful to stick to the announced hours and schedule.

One by one, our members arrived. In the meantime, as we were sitting around, I decided to spend some time talking to the audience. I told them several humorous anecdotes and read aloud selections from a literary anthology. Gradually the hall filled with people. There were still ten minutes to go, and we were thinking about beginning. Suddenly, I felt a strong hand snatch the book out of my hand. Before I had time to collect my wits and figure out what was happening, I heard a loud command: "Hands up!" We stood motionless, as an army of about thirty policemen and plainclothes agents streamed into the hall. Every window was guarded by a policeman, gun in hand. For a moment I lost my sense of equilibrium, but I soon regained control of myself.

They asked for the keys and proceeded to perform a thorough search of every drawer and cabinet in the place. They also searched each one of us, including the girls. Afterwards, they divided us into groups. I ended up in one room with a few others, our faces to the wall, hands behind our backs. We were strictly warned not to utter a sound. At the slightest movement the policeman hit us in the back with his rifle. From the adjoining rooms we heard the sound of tables and chairs being turned over. We watched as the police abruptly tore the framed portraits of Marx and Engels off the walls. With raw, brute force they shattered the glass and stamped on it. They came upon the banner, which was their only evidence that this was an antiwar meeting. They shouted wildly, demanding that someone translate the slogan into Polish. When this was done we heard the heartbreaking moans of someone being beaten. They struck him and kicked him, as he cried and begged for help. All this took place in another room, but we could hear it clearly.

We shuddered; I clenched my fists. My whole body was shaking, my teeth were clenched. I moved slightly, when I felt a gun strike my back. I was shoved against the wall; my blood seethed. The others standing near me received the same treatment. Soon the chief of police arrived, and he gave an order: "If these sons-of-bitches try to scream, whack their snouts with the butt of your gun!" We were hunched over, our backs low to the ground. Unfortunately, they demolished the place in a furious rage; everything was torn apart. Though there were many of us, not one dared move. We just stood there, helpless, shaking, our teeth chattering. We all felt that we were in the clutches of the police. They ransacked the entire place, tossing every piece of paper onto the floor.

In the end they packed everything up, tying it all up in bundles with the green and red uniforms of our organization's sport club. They made several such bundles and took them outside to the courtyard. One by one we were led outside and ordered to pick up these bundles, but we flatly refused to do so. When it was my turn I, too, proudly and firmly refused. Then three policemen threw me to the ground, just as they did to those before me and those after me, and beat my head and face with rubber clubs. I gathered all my strength and shouted loudly for help, and they left me alone. They chained me securely to two others. This constricted the skin on my hands, which later became swollen. The courtyard was large. Many people were watching through windows and from balconies; they looked on and shouted protests against this brutal treatment. The police threatened them, waving their clubs at them. When this didn't help, a policeman took out his gun and threatened to shoot if they didn't go inside. The people upstairs, elderly men and women, ignored this and continued to protest. There were seven of us, bound in steel chains; we were the ones who had refused to carry the bundles.

They led us from the courtyard out to the street and arranged us in rows. There were many of us; the girls joined us and then so did those who were carrying the bundles. We moved slowly, surrounded by a chain of policemen with rubber clubs, ready to strike us.

It was a beautiful day. It was around noon, when the streets are very busy. We crossed the marketplace. Both my hands were tied to the hands of comrades on either side. I felt no shame or embarrassment. In an effort to boost my comrades' morale, I quipped that the police had helped us mark this antiwar day with a rather impressive demonstration—better than we could have done by ourselves. I looked around. At some distance from us I saw the bundles all wrapped up with our red-and-green-striped uniforms. Inside them was our organization's entire archive of "incriminating" materials, gleaming in the brilliant sunshine.

The policemen—except for those who surrounded us like a fortress—were unable to cope with the stream of curious people who poured in from all sides to see our noble demonstration. The police attacked the crowd, hitting them over the head with their rubber clubs. We heard voices of protest from some in the crowd. This only made the police more brutal. They chased after these people in a wild rage and beat them, shouting: "Run, police!" I saw how a policeman went over to an older man, a Christian, apparently a laborer. The man was standing still, not moving. The policeman struck him on the face and head with his stick. The man didn't run away, so the policeman grabbed him by the collar, hailed a horse-drawn cab, forced the man inside, and sent him off. We kept marching slowly through the main streets until we arrived at police headquarters. All this was nothing compared to how they dealt with us there.

They split us up into several groups and, as they had done earlier at the hall, had us stand facing the wall with our hands behind our back. Again they searched us thoroughly. The police stood with their rubber clubs, ready to strike. We just stood there, forbidden to make the slightest movement. Other officers were busy going in and out of rooms, repeatedly asking each of us for our names and addresses. We stood by the wall and answered them for the twentieth time: family name, parents' names, grandparents' names, etc. We began to feel nauseated, until we were on the verge of vomiting.

Then a comrade who stood near me carelessly leaned his head on my shoulder. A policeman saw this, and told another officer that we were talking to each other. The one who appeared to be the older of the two officers called me over with exaggerated politeness. The other policemen winked at each other, amused. He led me outside as if I were a small child, taking me by the hand. I had a sense of what he was about to do with me. As we walked, I hesitated; I tried to convince him that the other fellow had fallen on my shoulder unintentionally. But he dragged me brutally by the collar and, with a kick, shoved me into another room. There sat an older man with a bald head, writing. He had me sit down and, at the other man's command, struck me in the face three times with a rubber club. He warned me that if I dared let out the least sound he would put me back in chains and lock me up in a small closet for twenty-four hours. I believed that he was in earnest. My eyes went dim, my whole body felt feverish, my knees trembled.

He took me back to my spot. I felt heavy at heart. I collapsed, and when I came to, I was seated on a bench, a glass of water nearby. I only began to feel the blows I had received later, when I stood up in my spot, wobbling. I was in terrible pain. I knew that it wasn't over. I knew that there, in the "interrogation bureau," it was just the beginning. The same man didn't hesitate to say as much to me. They all burst out laughing and tried to outdo each other with stale jokes at the expense of us "red commissars." Worse than the physical pain, I felt the moral pain. The policemen spoke loudly, so that they could be overheard. One asked: "Why doesn't Moscow deal with them?" Another remarked: "We should have Hitler take care of them for a few months." A third: "They have it too good here in Poland. Don't they have it all?" And: "This gang of boys and girls, busy all day, playing politics." It went on and on, and with each joke they would snicker; I covered my ears with my hands but soon realized that I wasn't allowed to move my hands. If not, another ordeal was in store for me.

We stood there, lifting one foot at a time, wobbling as if we were drunk, swimming in our own sweat. The only good thing was the arrival of some food toward evening, which had been sent to us from home. Though none of us could swallow anything but a drink, every half hour we would take some food just so that we could move our bodies a little, even if only for a second.

The hours dragged on; they seemed endless. Night fell. A dim light illuminated the big room. Cautiously, I glanced at the people around me standing by the wall. They looked like corpses or barely moving shadows, merging with the drab walls. The guard changed every four hours, bringing fresh, healthy, well-rested policemen. With each new shift came new orders for us. They ordered us around: turn this way, that way, and back again. The slightest provocation brought a blow with a club, accompanied by cursing. We stood there in this way until midnight, when the interrogations started. They took us in, one by one. I knew already what this "interrogation" would be like. My heart beat faster as each person returned after having gone through this "examination." They were gasping and wiping their eyes with a handkerchief. With each name that they called I felt worse, because soon enough my turn would come. No one truly understands what it means to suffer unless he has counted the minutes, waiting for an unjust, cruel punishment that he is about to receive. All of us understood this, those of us there at the time and those who had gone before us.

How hard those minutes were! Is hell in the next world? Oh, it's crazy! It's an abstraction, a human fantasy. Hell is *here*, in this world! It's here, in this real, cruel world!

My turn came. I heard my name. I shivered from this nightmare, from the thoughts that occupied me endlessly and left me completely exhausted. At that moment I became firm in my resolve not to submit to my tormentors, to let them torture me to death. I would endure as much as my strength would allow. My entire body was racked with fever. I followed closely behind the agent. He led me through several rooms. Dozens of pairs of eyes, eyes filled with sadism, and faces full of hatred mocked me: "Ha, ha, ha!" "Ho, ho, ho!" "Here comes another red commissar!"

He took me a long way, until we finally entered a small room. I was greeted by a strong smell of rubbing alcohol. I could barely breathe. He quickly shut the door behind me, locked it and put the key in his pocket. In my confused state I noticed four men in front of me: strong, healthy, tall young men. They wore no jackets, and their shirt sleeves were rolled up past their elbows. They were panting, as though they had just been working hard. They all held rubber clubs in their strong, muscular hands. One of them sat near the window with the blinds drawn, papers scattered over his desk. On the opposite side of the room I saw a basin of urine. The floor was wet. There were empty bottles scattered around.

On entering the room I was greeted by a blow to the head with a hard club. I lost my balance and fell down. They shouted at me to stand up. I did so automatically. They ordered me to take off my jacket, and when I didn't do so right away they yanked it off me. The one sitting at the table signaled to me to approach: "You're a communist? Aha! You're the organizer of the antiwar rally!" I stubbornly refused to speak; I clenched my teeth. He showed me the plan I had written, listing the activities for the literary program. I recognized it. Although there was nothing suspicious in it, I said nothing. Should I try to convince them? There was no point! Then came the order: "Work him over!" One of them grabbed me, shoved me over to a second fellow, then to a third. I was tossed like a ball from one to another. "Stop!" came another order, as they let me catch my breath.

My teeth were tightly clenched, as were my fists. My determination to tell them nothing was even stronger. No! No! Nothing. Let them torture me to death! They no longer asked me anything or gave me orders. One of them grabbed me again, roughly twisted my arms behind my back, while another tied them up, using a red banner with silver letters on it. Meanwhile, others stood there pulling my ears, tweaking my nose, tickling my sides with their rough fingers. They opened the door and, singing the tune of the "Internationale," hung me from the door. I was hanging by my arms as they kept singing the tune. My limbs were cracking. They just sat there and poured themselves some whiskey. I felt weak. I barely made a sound; one of them came over and stuffed a rag in my mouth. They turned on a record player, which screeched loudly. They laughed; they told a stream of vulgar jokes. I felt that in another minute my arms would rip out of their sockets and remain hanging on the door, while my body would fall to the floor like a piece of clay. I could hardly breathe; I shut my eyes.

When I came to, I found myself sprawled out on the bench, drenched with water. They let me lie there for a few minutes; I came around and recovered my breath somewhat. Then they dragged me off the bench and forced me to run around the room quickly, back and forth. When I fell down, they picked me up by the hair, and I had to continue running. "This is gymnastics," they laughed. "Special exercises for crippled communist commissars." I don't know how much of this I did. I was mentally and physically exhausted, though my brain was still functioning well enough. One of the interrogators whispered something to another, who checked my pulse and heartbeat. He made a sign with his hand, and they stopped beating me. However, they laid me down on the bench and held my hands securely, while one of them took out my sex organ, tweaking it and handling it roughly. I have no idea why, but I burst out laughing. This upset them; they certainly didn't expect it—laughing, of all things? I watched them become enraged once again. They picked me up one last time, then they sat me back down on the bench. The order came: "A tea party!" They grabbed my head and pushed it back, then they started to pour urine from a pot down my nose. I gagged, I coughed and spat the foul liquid out of my mouth. They made this "tea party" for me three more times. I wiped my face. Along with the urine, blood came out of my nose. My handkerchief was completely soaked with blood.

The man behind the desk began talking to me. He asks if all this was worth it. Wouldn't it be better to tell him everything and avoid all this? He would arrange for me to be set free and also give me some money. But if I refused, it could cost me ten years of my life in prison. He said that he knows everything about me and my political party; that he has his people in there, and they tell him everything. I bit my tongue and said nothing in reply. When he realized that his words were pointless, he ordered me sternly and in no uncertain terms to tell him who was who and who had done what. If I didn't do so now they would throw me out the window and then shoot me, saying I tried to escape. At that point, nothing mattered to me anymore. They could do whatever they wanted to me, and I would remain silent. He told me to put on my jacket, comb my hair, and wipe the blood off my face. He took away my blood-soaked handkerchief. As he led me out of the room, he warned me sternly that if I dared tell anyone about what had happened in that room he would find out, and then things would be very bad for me. "Don't you forget, you son-of-a-bitch!"

I had to return to the same place I'd been brought to earlier. But I could no longer stay on my feet. I swallowed some water and lay down on the ground. They tortured us in this manner for two entire days. On the third day they took us in chains to the prison. We were now five men; the rest were freed after they had been photographed and fingerprinted. Our mothers were waiting for us outside. They walked along with us, crying and beating their heads. A policeman shoved one of them, and she fell on the pavement. Along the way the policemen tried to rationalize their actions. One said to another: "See how bad it is to serve in the police force? If some stupid old lady falls down, it's the policeman who gets blamed." They started recounting facts to show that in principle they're always innocent, that only the wicked tongues of instigators assign the blame to them. They talked about this in loud voices, so that we could hear them. And yes, we heard them, and we understood that, in essence, they were indeed innocent. We knew that the guilt lay only with the current regime, which maintains itself by such methods.

But we worried less about this than about our immediate future, our life in prison. We went by the district courthouse. I looked at it and thought: in the next few months I'll be there, standing before the judge, and I'll have the last word. I'll tell them everything! Everything! Oh, then I'll speak! We passed by the church, its big clock indifferently displaying the time. The crucified one looked at us sorrowfully. And—how strange! How remarkable! I remembered the day when my family first came from a small town to this city, on a wagon loaded with all our belongings. My mother pointed to these three buildings, and I naively asked: "Is this the whole city, Mama?" and she laughed: "You silly, this is just the beginning."

*

A small cell with a small, double-barred window beneath the ceiling, looking out on the city park. The door is made of several iron bars and opens onto a long, narrow corridor. There is a constant smell of tar, which comes from a nearby latrine. There are eighteen men here: ordinary thieves, members of the underworld, and, along with them, the five of us— political prisoners, Jewish boys. They make fun of us: "If you're not getting anything out of it, why are you wasting your time in prison?" We sit together in a circle on the floor, touching the painful black-and-blue marks on our bodies. We remove the bandages on our heads, which are swollen. It's hard to raise our eyebrows without it hurting. When we touch our hair we wind up with clumps of it in our hands. We report to each other on the methods of "interrogation" employed by the investigators. My throat is dry and burning, I cough, and I spit out thick traces of blood. I'm scared—could it be my lungs?

In the evening we stand "at attention" for the roll call. I ask to see a doctor; they laugh at me. At night, it's hard to sleep on the thin, filthy straw mattresses in the dense air of eighteen men. None of us feels self-conscious. From every side we are jabbed in our sore spots. In the morning, we see political prisoners pass by our door going to the latrine. We recognize them; some are old, familiar faces. Among them are a few elderly Christians, peasants with mustaches and beards. We give them a sign, and they signal us in return.

On the third day we refuse to go outside for our walk. The guard asks, "Why?" We say, "We are political prisoners and demand to be put together with our comrades!" He threatens to throw us into a dungeon and slams the door. So it goes for four days. When our comrades pass by our cell on their way to the latrine they greet us and give us a few words of advice on how to bear up. We don't have enough food, so they quickly toss us some bread, sausage, and sugar; they do this several times. On the fifth day we are transferred to another cell. We five comrades are now in a separate, whitewashed cell with a larger window that looks out on the courtyard. The door is solid, and on the window in the door many names have been scratched, among them some familiar ones. Suddenly, something is slipped through a crack in the door: a newspaper. We grab it quickly. Written on the margins, in pencil, is a message: "You're with other political prisoners." We're so happy we kiss each other. In the evening we suddenly hear tapping on the wall from a neighboring cell. We press our ears against the wall. Someone there shouts loudly; we receive a communication from our political comrades. The next day, the five of us go for a walk, alone. We get brief messages from the windows of the other political prisoners' cells, scraps of words. We communicate in this manner twice a day. Some days later we are suddenly allowed outside along with all the other political prisoners on our corridor. In the courtyard we embrace old acquaintances, and we shake hands with new ones: older Christians, tall and healthy, some of them intellectuals, teachers, academicians. There are a lot of us, as many as fifty, all different types. This was just one group of political prisoners, those from our corridor; there were two other such groups. In this way we got to know the prison community, and we became familiar with the hard collective life of political prisoners. We read newspapers, we wrote, although a limited amount, and we played chess with pieces made out of bread. One by one, our wounds slowly healed. I still spit up blood several times. The medic in the infirmary examined me and said he wished his lungs were as healthy as mine. He thought the blood came from my throat—perhaps because of the beatings, he surmised.

One day we marked the fourth anniversary of the death of one of our comrades, who was shot during a prison protest. We prepared for the occasion, as did the prison administration. At the morning roll call we all wore red ribbons on our lapels. The guards savagely tore them off of us, and we responded with passive resistance. They punished us by not allowing us to go out for a walk for two days in a row. The first day of this punishment we decided that all political prisoners in the entire prison would honor the memory of our fallen comrade with group discussions. In my cell, I spoke; I had known this comrade personally. On the third day, during our first walk since the punishment, we reported to the leaders of our group: everything was carried out as ordered. Sometimes there were petty disputes among individual comrades. In prison this is probably unavoidable, but we always resolved these matters collectively. The problem of sex is the most painful issue for healthy men who are cut off from life, forced to suppress their natural urges. I have seen men more than thirty years old, our comrades, at the risk of severe punishment, climb up to the windows and look out onto the women's section of the prison, just to get a glimpse of the girls there. One time I did so myself. The girls knew we were looking at them, so they would stick out a bare arm. Later, while lying in bed at night, full of lust, we would tell each other all sorts of pornographic stories and jokes. This didn't interfere with our studying and reading newspapers. I started to teach my cellmates Esperanto, about an hour every evening before going to bed. I taught them from memory. They learned a great deal and were pleased.

I was there for almost two months. Our discharge—mine and two of my comrades'—came unexpectedly. We were released before our other two comrades because, as I later learned, they had been accused of more serious crimes. We had been ready to serve a sentence of five years. But the charge against me as the organizer of the literary event that never actually took place wasn't enough for a conviction. And so, I walked out, once again free, free, free!

Our arrest caused a great sensation in the city, and I was seen as the central figure. Our organization remained under lock and key. Most of its almost 500 members remained active, mainly through the library, where they would go for moral support. On the same day that I was released I went to the library. My job had been filled by my friend Shloyme. He wasn't up to the task; he was too phlegmatic, so others from the administration helped him out. The members of the organization and subscribers to the library gave me a fine welcoming party. They shook my hand and said how happy they were that I would return to the post of librarian. They complained about the lack of order. Two days later I resumed my work as librarian, after reporting to a party member, who asked for a detailed account of the prison community. The library demanded a great deal of effort from me.

At home, I also felt that I had to satisfy my parents. I worked more hours at the sewing machine and took a greater interest in the family business, which at the time was doing rather well. All this, plus staying up to date on current political events in the daily newspapers, left no time for reading books. I'd work at the sewing machine from seven o'clock in the morning until half-past seven at night; from eight o'clock (exactly) until ten or half-past-ten I'd work in the library. Its membership grew constantly, reaching almost 300. Then I'd rush home and write something in my diary. And whenever I had to organize a public event with the cultural commission for a Saturday, I'd feel that it was too much for me. Still, I loved it very much. So, even if my body was shaking with fever, I'd do my best to do everything properly. I was simply exhausted from all the work I did. That's how it went for a while. Then, later, well—

Our organization suffered endless oppression by the authorities. Not a week went by without a visit from our "moral guardians." There were more arrests, involving several members of the library, including Abrashek. Fewer people came to the library; readers would come by, exchange their books, and quickly depart. The atmosphere was strained, since Abrashek was the secretary of our organization and its de facto leader. The organization was in danger of being shut down any day. But the library had to remain active, as a service to its readers. It is true that, because of the oppression, we couldn't organize any events. But the burden of managing things fell to me. I had to take on the duties of the secretary, which I was able to carry out with the help of a few others whom I recruited.

Some time later, Abrashek was released from prison on a high bail. However, he never returned to the library. Actually, he came back one last time. No one knew what his plans were, but he did wish me a very hearty farewell. Then he left, before his trial took place. For several weeks he went to various cities in Poland to arrange to emigrate, then he left to do work abroad. The cases against me and the other two comrades were dismissed.

*

Sometimes a person finds himself on top of a high mountain; he looks down at the vast horizon, which has been there since ancient times—such rolling, eternally enticing landscapes. He sees fields, forests, buildings, and among them he sees little people, wiggling little worms, from which he, too, has come. It is hard for him to believe that he actually came from there, from those swarming creatures, that he has risen up only to go back down to them. And when he does go back down and finds himself so far from the mountains, from the heights where he has recently been, he begins to doubt that he had ever been up there. All he sees are the tall mountains, but he can't see himself there anymore.

This is more or less what I am experiencing nowadays, as I feel far away from where I had once been. And when I read over what I've been through, as written down here, I begin to doubt myself: was I really there when this happened? Isn't this a figment of my imagination, a fantasy? But when I do go back a little, I do indeed find my footsteps. Yes, they are mine, I recognize them very well. I am definitely not there now, but yes, I was there once.

If every ordinary person had the ability to preserve within himself all his experiences, all the worthy and learned ideas that he has read and heard, all the good and even the bad experiences from which he has learned, which have shown him how to contemplate life, and which have proven to be for his own benefit and for that of his environment; if he could elevate himself intellectually and apply himself to this situation, then he would be able to thrive, and suffering would become something alien—such a person would be, as they say, a genius. Unfortunately, life is in reality hard and brutal; with boundless cruelty it tramples all that is decent and noble. Ah! Man, willingly or not, is placed on the anvil of life, every idea is pounded out of him, and from him is forged whatever can be kept within the bounds of painful, heartless, material life, which is so full of contradictions. Only a few individuals have the strength to elevate themselves, thanks to their secure and, to a certain extent, stubborn view of life and to their understanding of everyone and everything. Such a person decisively rejects the laws and principles of this society. He doesn't recognize them, he even fights against them. He creates his own perspectives, his own concepts, and holds them up as his own laws and principles. People like this are true geniuses, the ones who have earned the loyalty, recognition, and attention of a large segment of society. As for me—ha! I was not endowed with such power that would enable me to be one of these few people. Life has forged me into one of the many others.

I am still young, a little more than twenty-two years old. I've never ventured beyond the city where I grew up. I'm not financially independent, I still live with my parents. But my sensitive soul and I have endured much—Oh, so much!—in life. For I am a child of the people, who are expiring in the bloody struggle to maintain their existence on the face of this planet. The current epoch, through which my own modest life is roaming, is the bloodiest in human history; it is an epoch in which two classes have been engaged face-to-face in a terribly bloody, gruesome struggle. This battle is being waged by the ruling class, aided by the devices of modern technology, which human ingenuity created over time for other purposes. It stops at nothing, and will use any means against the unpropertied class. This struggle has destroyed tens of thousands of people—ordinary people, the best people, children who would be able to improve the world. They are being persecuted, brutally murdered.

I am still young, and I know that I'll experience many more things in my life. But isn't everything that I have already seen and experienced enough to enable me to draw some appropriate conclusions? After all, I have seen it all with my own eyes. For example: a well-dressed, young prostitute, who had silk pillows especially made for her cats and dogs. And this very same prostitute walks calmly and indifferently past a young man, armed to the teeth, as he uses the butt of his rifle to beat an old man, bound in chains, because he dared to raise his voice to defend the weak and helpless. I have seen this with my own eyes. I have felt the pain of dozens of people— shabby, half-naked, barefoot—men, women, and children. I saw the hunger in their eyes; I saw it eat away at their still-young bodies—emaciated, bones protruding under singed flesh, covered with dirt and grime. This mass of people, the true sign of our era, cries out in the streets. The streets are filled with the best thing for humankind—with their desperate protests against the present order, which can no longer provide them with bread and work. What do they get instead? Rubber clubs, bullets fired by healthy armed men, striking the naked bodies of the masses. And there is blood, blood on the pavement. Then is it any wonder that my hands are clenched into fists, that I want to strike my enemy with one final blow to the face, so that his blood gushes forth, blood mixed with fat? Yes, that's what I want.

I know that the world is now in the grip of a storm, a storm of the worst reactionaries, who sow hatred among people and among nations. And above it all, above the desolation and chaos, stands a tall, sturdy watchtower that illuminates the world around it with knowledge, culture, and progress. This is the Soviet Union, the only country in the world that belongs to the workers and peasants. The Soviet Union shows us, teaches us: See how people can and should live, when workers and peasants come to power! And I know that class instinct is awakening and embracing more and more people—people who are clenching their fists to deliver the final blow and who follow the example of that country which occupies one-sixth of the globe. We need to do it now!

*

Last year on 24 August the security forces shut down our library. The reason: the library disrupted the peace and public order. Again I was brought in for interrogation, again I had to endure terrible nights. I was tortured for two days straight and then released. And, well, this is how I live. Am I happy? I don't know what that is.

Diderot says: "Only someone who has a healthy stomach, a weak heart, and no conscience can be happy." But how, asks Gorki, can anyone be happy when one person wants to be higher than another? And above it all in my memory float the ingenious words of Romain Rolland:

> Go and die, you who must die!
> Go and suffer, you who must suffer!
> One does not live to be happy.
> One lives to fulfill the eternal law of life.
> Suffer! Die!
> But be what you must be—a man!

Kielce, 21 May 1934

4

Henekh

Contest year: 1934 • Language: Yiddish
Year of birth: 1913 • Age: [21] • Sex: Male

I was born in 1913, my parent's thirteenth child. If I were superstitious, I would say that the number thirteen sealed my fate.

A year later, my parents had a fourteenth child. While Father spent his days in the synagogue poring over holy books, securing himself and his family a place in the next world, Mother wore herself out running the house and the store, providing for our needs in this world—that is, seeing to it that we were fed.

Given these circumstances, it is no wonder that only five of their fourteen children survived—three boys and two girls. By the time I was four years old, Mother's strength had been sapped, like a well that had run dry. And so Father dutifully took off his *kitl* and took on the role of provider. Being honest to a fault and a poor businessman, he barely managed to put food on the table. However, he was deeply committed to our education. He taught my sisters Yiddish and Hebrew as well as arithmetic, and he instructed us boys in sacred texts and how to write correspondence in Yiddish. I was the youngest surviving child. By the age of four I was already well versed in the Torah and Rashi commentaries. Father favored me over the other children because of my strong intellect and mature manner.

I would swear that, in a psychological sense, I was never a child. As far back as I can remember, I was always serious in my thinking and manner of speaking, astounding everyone with erudition beyond my years. I never played with toys, never asked my parents for treats, and when I was given something I would share it with my older sisters and brothers. Even as a four-year-old I understood our poverty and shared the family's worries.

From earliest childhood I had a poet's temperament. My moods went hand in hand with the weather. On sunny days I was happy, cheerful, and attentive. On cloudy days my thoughts drifted off to higher spheres, and I neglected my studies, for which I was soundly thrashed. The Russian army had set fire to our town, and on each street there were more ruins than inhabitable buildings. As children we believed that demons lived in these ruins, and we didn't dare venture out on the streets after sundown.

The house we lived in at the time was no more than a burnt-out shell located at the far end of town. This house so offended my developing aesthetic sense that I spent as little time there as possible. Instead, I would spend the entire day in the *beys-medresh*, which was unusually beautiful for a small town, even by today's standards. There the older men would offer me a few coins, for which I would recite whole sections of the Bible by heart. They all loved me. Some showed their affection by pinching my cheek or whatever part of me they could grab. (Incidentally, I was an unusually handsome little boy.) All the young mothers in town wished that their children were as bright and beautiful as Henekh, Khazkl's son. When parents punished their children, they reproached them for not being more like little Henekh. Naturally, the other children hated me. In their eyes I was the cause of the physical and verbal lashings that they suffered.

When I was five years old, my life changed forever. My father, who was my teacher and my rabbi, suddenly died. Everyone at the *beys-medresh* became my father, giving me advice and telling me what to do. That's why I stopped going there and went instead to the forest, which was a half-kilometer from our town. There I wandered for hours, and in my imagination I talked to Father; together we studied the parts of the Bible that I knew by heart.

Once again, Mother was saddled with providing for the family. She apprenticed the girls to dressmakers, sent the older boys off to yeshiva, and had me do chores for a *melamed*, in exchange for which he taught me Gemara.

My older sister was exceptionally talented and served only a two-year apprenticeship before going into business on her own. She soon became known as the best dressmaker in town and earned a good living. All of sixteen years old at the time, she was physically mature and looked eighteen or nineteen. We were now able to rent a decent apartment and live "as well as everyone else." A short time later, an uncle who lived in America (a brother of my late father) sent us a considerable sum (in dollars). We used this money to rebuild our old house, which had been burned down by the Cossacks. Mother cast off the yoke of provider and placed it on my sister's shoulders. Young as she was, my sister was now the "head of the house." It was she who sent money and clothing to my brothers in yeshiva, paid for my lessons at home, and took care of household expenses. Now that she was in charge, it was little wonder that she began to lord it over everyone, including Mother. In her spare time my sister was active in a Zionist organization, the name of which escapes me. She became its chairman and, being an independent wage earner, contributed handsomely to it. She brought home books in modern Hebrew, and the two of us would stay up late into the night reading, while Mother bemoaned the waste of kerosene.

By the time I was ten, I was already a "philanthropist." I recruited a friend, and together we went around town soliciting contributions. Everyone gave generously, not even asking for what cause. I used the money to purchase Hebrew children's books, which I ordered from someone in Warsaw, and I started a children's library that exists to this day.

When I was twelve, I joined my older brother at the yeshiva in Grodno. By then I was studying Gemara and other Talmudic commentaries on my own, without a rabbi. The yeshiva opened up a new world to me. Here I became both intellectually and economically independent. I learned to manage carefully the monthly allowance I received from the yeshiva, stretching the money to cover all my expenses. Study began at eight o'clock in the morning and ended at ten at night, with breaks totaling one-and-a-half hours for breakfast and dinner. The last half hour of the day was devoted to *musar* and an accounting of one's thoughts and activities for the day; this was recited in a special wailing chant. Many a fellow student would burst into tears over his sins, which were mostly sinful thoughts, not deeds.

The yeshiva taught me to weigh and measure my every thought and deed and to be ever mindful of my place in the world. As a result, like others who attended Lithuanian yeshivas, I developed a pessimistic outlook on life. Constant, critical self-scrutiny robbed us of our courage and self-confidence and turned us into depressives, no matter how pious and full of faith we might be. The dignified bearing of the *mazhgiekh*, as well as his ethical discourses, had a profound impact on me. I became as pious as a prayerbook. I constantly thought about God and pondered the eternal vastness of His realm. I also contemplated the nature of evil in the world and concluded that it was a result of humankind's own sinfulness. In my own way, I strove to integrate religion with reason.

I remember an episode that illustrates the way we were taught to reason in yeshiva. Once, in a private conversation with the *mazhgiekh*, I asked, "If the *tanna'im* were omniscient, privy to all the secrets of nature, if they were even able to bring the dead back to life—for it is said that the Talmud contains the teachings of those who had the power to resurrect the dead—then why didn't they invent the locomotive or discover electricity?" He answered, "Do we have the moral right to sacrifice one life in order to save a thousand? Certainly not. Thus, it follows that our sages didn't wish to invent the train. True, a train does save lives in some cases, but in other cases it causes the loss of life. Granted, the probability of the latter is small—still, who has the right to exchange the life of one person for that of another? The truth is that our sages did know of trains, and so on, but they were prohibited from revealing their knowledge on moral grounds." This kind of convoluted religious philosophizing, along with relentless criticism of oneself and others (not to mention study of the Talmud itself), all informed my thinking and sensibility.

I will now digress to an earlier time, before I went off to the yeshiva. By age twelve, I had already fallen in love with my younger sister's friend Matele. My love for her was pure and platonic. To me she was the gentlest and most desirable of all God's creations. My only wish was to be near her and devote myself to her forever. Though I said nothing, everyone at home knew that I adored Matele and that she felt the same way about me. Many a joke was made at our expense. I wasn't bold and she was very shy, so we never exchanged words, only longing glances. Once, when she was ill, I hid in the woods for days and continually recited Psalms on her behalf. I couldn't do it in the *beys-medresh*, lest someone ask me for whom I was praying and discover my feelings. I was convinced that if anything were to happen to her I would cease to exist, as would the rest of the world. I had this vague notion that Matele was everything and everything was Matele; that she embodied wholeness; that if not for her, there would be nothing.

Matele recovered from her illness, and I went off to the yeshiva. My love for her wasn't extinguished. Instead, it was—to speak in Freudian terms—repressed, buried in the deepest recesses of my heart and mind. I was swept up by the current of yeshiva life and immersed in learning and *musar*. From time to time—especially before the holidays, when the tempo of study slowed—I was overcome with painful longing for Matele. I must confess that my trips home for the holidays were not so much to see my mother and sisters, but to touch Matele's hand in greeting, to behold her face and form, which to me were no less than divine.

I almost came to hate my sister for poking fun at her friend, my goddess. Often, when Matele left our house, my sister would snidely remark that during the year, while I was in Grodno, Matele insisted that my sister spend time at her house, but when I was home, Matele was always at our house and my sister was no longer invited to hers.

Every holiday that I spent at home rekindled my love for Matele, and the older I grew, the stronger grew my desire to declare my love for her. My studies at the yeshiva were not hindered by my longing. On the contrary, I had it all figured out: study hard, become a great rabbi, and this will make Matele happy.

After two years in Grodno, I moved to the yeshiva in Raduń, which was named for the Hafetz Hayyim and operated under his supervision. Here I became an instant sensation. Only fourteen years old, and looking even younger, I applied to the advanced yeshiva, where all the other students were at least eighteen. I was examined by the *rosh-yeshiva*, the renowned Rabbi Naftali Trup, of blessed memory, and passed with flying colors, being admitted to the second of the yeshiva's five levels.

In my very first week there, I suffered a series of disillusionments and unpleasant surprises. First, there was the physical appearance of the Hafetz Hayyim himself: close to one hundred years old and frail with age, his undistinguished face appeared childlike and innocent, perched above his slight, hunched body. He fell far short of my youthful expectations. Judging by his widespread celebrity, I had envisioned him as a near-divine figure, with a majestic bearing.

Actually, the Hafetz Hayyim was little more than a figurehead, and the day-to-day running of the yeshiva was in the hands of his less-than-distinguished grandsons, as is the case to this day. He limited himself to giving *musar* talks in his quarters twice a week. For the most part, his two-hour sermons were an endless reiteration: "The Messiah will certainly come, the Messiah must certainly come. And since, in the end, we must all repent, why wait? Let us all repent now. Can't you see that we are nearer to the Messiah's coming now than we were five years ago?" Far from stimulating, his rantings were murderously dull. In Grodno, I had grown accustomed to sermons illuminated by scholarly references and philosophical insights into the essence of man's being. Measuring what I heard here against what I had heard there, I began to question the greatness of the aged Hafetz Hayyim. The other students, still in awe of his glorious past, believed that his present teachings were too deep for them to grasp. To them he was the voice of the Divine Spirit. I was disenchanted and avoided his lectures by stealing away to the outskirts of town. There I wandered around, grappling with my own concept of ethics and seeking to define my own understanding of God's design.

At the time, the yeshiva's enrollment numbered 250 students. Rabbi Eliezer Kopelson, a grandson of the Hafetz Hayyim, was the *mazhgiekh*. His duty, among others, was to keep us pious, to guard the purity of our faith by weeding out heretics before they could contaminate the rest of us. To this end, he organized a network of informers within the yeshiva to spy on every student and to be especially alert for anyone reading forbidden—that is, secular—books. The *mazhgiekh* appointed someone to supervise all students' housing arrangements, granting him complete control over where and, more importantly, with whom a student could room. The housing supervisor saw to it that a student whose thinking was suspect was assigned a roommate whose faith left no room for doubt and who could be trusted to win over the skeptic.

In my time, the position was held by Hershl Kaminetser, the oldest student in the yeshiva. "Thirty years beyond bar mitzvah," was the running gag about him, to which I added: "That joke is already old enough to have had its own bar mitzvah." It was sad that health problems had prevented Hershl Kaminetser from marrying and, by then in his fifties, he was a "yeshiva invalid," incapable of functioning outside the yeshiva. He was the only student with a beard, and I am not exaggerating when I say that his beard, by then streaked with gray, reached down to his navel. He was in charge of the spy ring and reported its findings to the *mazhgiekh*.

This spy ringleader took an instant liking to me and, wishing to keep me under his influence, assigned me to room with him. I didn't take to him at all, repelled as much by his foul breath (which could be smelled half a kilometer away) as by his arrogance, corruption, and egotism, none of which I, a young man of conscience, could abide. I was also quick to recognize that he was no scholar, even though he had spent practically his entire life at the yeshiva. I explained to him that, as the oldest and the youngest students in the yeshiva, we were not a good match and asked him to place me with a more appropriate roommate. He refused. I then took my request to the *mazhgiekh*, accusing the supervisor of using his position to further his own interests and of trampling upon the needs of others. This was considered an act of heroism. After all, it was no small matter to pit oneself against the spy ringleader, whose word was enough to have one thrown out of the yeshiva. But the *mazhgiekh* granted my request and ordered Hershl Kaminetser to assign me to a more suitable roommate. This was a great blow to the aging egoist. From this moment on, he set out to persecute me, putting a brigade of informers on my trail, following my every move.

As it is written, "Seek, and ye shall find." And so it was discovered that I alone of the yeshiva's 250 students failed to attend the Hafetz Hayyim's *musar* talks. My transgression was reported, and I was called before the *mazhgiekh*. Feigning innocence, I slyly explained that the Hafetz Hayyim's lectures were above my head and were meant for the older boys, not for youngsters like me. It worked; I was cleared. I continued to excel in my studies and made great advances. The *rosh-yeshiva*, delighted with the originality and insight of my thinking, moved me up to the third level, where I displayed such fervor that I was soon acclaimed as a prodigy.

The housing supervisor, however, didn't forget his hatred of me. The higher I rose, the more he was consumed with hatred and jealousy. He wasn't above manufacturing incriminating incidents and having me summoned to the detention room, where I had to defend myself against all kinds of false accusations. Once, after chastising me for reading a newspaper, which I denied, the *mazhgiekh* declared that anyone else in my place would have been expelled for lying so brazenly. He added that, for the time being, he was making allowances in deference to my demonstrated ability and zeal. This offended my youthful sense of fair play and opened my eyes to an old truth: "Alongside justice there is wickedness." I began to view the yeshiva as a den of lies and to examine it with a critical eye. I now saw what I hadn't noticed before—that the administrators lived in luxury amidst the students' abject poverty.

To spite the *mazhgiekh* and his chief spy, Hershl Kaminetser, I began to read the newspaper *Haynt* every Friday. I did this openly, confident that my high honors in Talmud and rabbinic commentaries would save me from being expelled. At first I hadn't felt any great need to read a newspaper. But what started as a way to make honest men out of my accusers soon became one of life's necessities for me. I could hardly wait to rush out each Friday and buy the newspaper, devouring every word and thinking deeply about every article. In the process, I gained an understanding of life and a thirst for secular education. I obtained a copy of *The Book of the Covenant* (an encyclopedia of the sciences and religious philosophies) and virtually committed it to memory, reading it in the bathroom for fear of being caught and confronted with a whole new series of accusations. *The Book of the Covenant* gave me a sound foundation in anatomy, physics, geography, and the like. I had a weakness, however, for showing off my scientific learning to my friends (without telling them about its source). This led to my becoming known as a person of wide-ranging knowledge, and I was sought after by those who were drawn to the *Haskalah*.

In time, I became the center of a circle of *maskilim* who met on free days (the Sabbath, fast days, and holidays) in the Ejszyszki forest, three kilometers from town. There we discussed ideas and also mocked the yeshiva's administration and its aged chief spy, Hershl Kaminetser. Two of his former informants who joined our circle revealed that more than once Hershl ordered them to unlock their roommates' trunks and search their belongings for forbidden books, letters, or, heaven help us, photographs of girls. At Hershl's whim they were moved from one room to another to accomplish his will. Our group was careful not to be found out, and we all did well in our studies. I even received my rabbinical ordination while leading this secret group. When we were finally discovered, every member of the circle was expelled, except for me. I was spared because I was such an exceptional student and because of the yeshiva's hopes that I was destined to be an illustrious scholar.

On my own I decided to leave the yeshiva and pursue a secular education, and so I moved from Raduń to Warsaw. For three months I slept in the women's section of a synagogue, finding refuge during the day in one yeshiva or another. Later, I started to earn a modest income by giving lessons in Talmud and Bible. I also found a place to sleep in a shop where I was hired as night watchman, for which I was paid a decent wage. I began to take lessons from a university student in order to qualify for the *matura* as an extern.

While I was in Warsaw, Matele developed rheumatism, and her wealthy parents sent her to Ciechocinek to convalesce. She spent the summer there and on her way back stopped for an extended visit in Warsaw. She looked me up, and then, after seeing her for a while, I told her that I was in love with her.

Throughout her stay in Warsaw, Matele seemed so distracted as to be almost unrecognizable. I sensed that she was hiding something important from me. One day I came up to her room at the inn and, finding her asleep on the sofa, sought to pass the time by casually rummaging through the odds and ends that were lying about. Suddenly I was stunned, as if struck on the head. In her purse I found a photograph of Matele and a handsome young man, both in bathing suits, she cradled in his lap like a child. Feverishly, I emptied her purse and found the business card of a gynecologist who had an office on Leszno Street. Then I noticed several prescriptions on the window sill, issued by the same doctor. In my mind, a horrifying scenario unfolded: the seduction of Matele by a handsome young man in Ciechocinek.

Regaining control, I awakened Matele. I confronted her with the photograph, the card, and the prescriptions, and demanded an explanation. She collapsed in a faint. I didn't make the customary scene. Instead, I calmly pulled a pin from my lapel and pricked her fingertips until she revived. Then I walked out without saying goodbye.

That day I worked hard, giving longer lessons than usual and yelling at my pupils. I drove my own tutor half-mad with mathematical questions that he couldn't answer: If a point has no dimensions, how can a series of points form a line whose length can be measured? If one zero has no value, then neither do a thousand zeros. In the evening, I returned to the shop where I spent my nights. My composure during the day turned out to be the calm before the storm. Alone and locked inside the shop, I began to realize what had actually happened. Shame seared every vein and nerve in my body. I felt betrayed, as if all that was most sacred and precious to me had been trampled murderously. An indescribable anguish swept through the very core of my being, like a wave of molten steel. I was overcome with self-loathing.

There was a bottle of turpentine on the window sill, used to remove stains from clothing sold in the shop. I emptied it onto the floor and lit a match to it. It was about one o'clock at night. As flames raged around me, I hurled myself toward the window facing the courtyard, smashed my hand through the glass, and shouted with all my might: "Let the whole world burn! If she could turn out like this, the rest of you can only be worse. You're all nothing but poisonous snakes!" Then I lost consciousness.

I awoke in a hospital. I was told that I had been there quite a while and that I had been terribly ill. I regained my memory. From the hospital I was taken to the police station and from there to a magistrate's office, where I was charged with setting fire to the shop in the middle of the night. The judge conducting the investigation wanted me to confess that I had been bought off by a competitor or that the owner of the shop had set me up so that he could collect the insurance. Unwilling to make public my catastrophic love story, I improvised. I said I had been in a state of extreme isolation brought on by the many lonely nights I had spent locked up like a prisoner in the shop, which actually had seven locks. This had taken a toll on my nerves, causing the breakdown that precipitated my act. As proof, I cited the fact that I was found unconscious and ill. The judge wasn't convinced, since the owner of the shop had purchased insurance shortly before the incident, and my loss of consciousness could be attributed to shock or fear. I had a court trial and was found not guilty.

During the ordeal I lost all my tutoring jobs, not to mention my living quarters. My reputation was ruined, and I couldn't go on studying or living in Warsaw. With nowhere to go, I ended up in the *beys-medresh* of a remote town in Lithuania, where I began to study. Kind and pious people found me a place to sleep and provided me with food. I began to visit the local rabbi and impressed him with my original interpretations of sacred texts. He invited me to study with him and, in time, to share his home. Later, I also taught him Polish, of which he knew very little.

The rabbi had a daughter, about ten years my senior, with a pretty face and a fiery temperament. We soon became intimate. The rabbi, worried about his daughter's future, chose not to interfere. When she suddenly announced that, despite all appropriate precautions, she was "in a family way," I had no choice but to marry her. My dowry was the promise that I would eventually inherit the town's rabbinate from my father-in-law. My own family was thrilled that I married into a rabbinical family, and that I, too, would someday be a rabbi.

After the wedding, I learned that I had been deceived. My wife was decidedly not pregnant. I felt such repugnance that I couldn't stay with her. She didn't want a divorce, so I fled to Warsaw and resumed giving lessons in Jewish subjects while preparing myself for the *matura*. In one year of superhuman effort, I passed the *matura* as an extern and was admitted to the law school. Now, because I can't pay tuition, I'm not allowed to attend the university, and I find myself half-seriously considering—suicide.

5

Forget-me-not

Contest year: 1934 • Language: Yiddish
Year of birth: 1913 • Age: 20 • Sex: Female

I apologize for my bad style, spelling mistakes and, most of all, for not writing clearly. I wrote this under circumstances in which I was unable to pay attention to my work. I wanted to relate accurately my life's trial, which I experienced from the day of my birth to the present.

—from the author's cover letter accompanying her autobiography

*I*n my twenty-first year I look back on my life, which has been so eventful. I never would have imagined that a weak girl, as I used to be known, would be strong enough to live through so much. This has made me realize that life is stronger than everything else. When I add up my twenty years, I see that, despite my young age, I've experienced more than other people have in the course of their entire lives. I've kept all my experiences a secret from everyone who knows me. I've never been open with anyone and rarely even with myself. Even though I've spent my entire life among other people, they know very little about my private life. Everyone thinks that they know me, but my past remains a secret. Until now I have never met anyone I could trust enough to confide in. Perhaps my life has conditioned me to be this way, to see people as egotists who can't empathize with anyone else. To this day I remain locked within myself, an enigma to others. Now, for the first time in my life, I will be entirely candid. I'm sure that those who read my life story will never know me personally, so I will describe my life honestly, from my birth up to the present. It will be rather difficult to read so much; it was much more difficult to experience it.

I was born in the final days of 1913. I still don't know the exact date; apparently my birth wasn't much of an event in our home. My family never spoke about it; they never celebrated my birthday. As my father always said, I was born by accident. Such accidents were frequent in our home, resulting in the births of five sisters and one brother, who was the oldest.

I don't know how I was raised. From what I could find out later, I was always sick during my first four years. This was due to our living conditions. As my mother later told me, I didn't escape a single illness: chicken pox, measles, scarlet fever, whooping cough, every nuisance and misery. And as if that weren't enough, at the age of two and a half I had rickets. I didn't stand up until I was four years old; I just stayed in one place. I was always ninety-nine percent dead and only one percent alive. My father would have gladly let go of this part of me, too, so as to be rid of this affliction. I must have felt like an unwelcome guest in the house. Despite everything, though, my mother saw to it that I stayed alive and didn't, God forbid, become a cripple. I survived and eventually grew up to become a responsible individual.

For as long as I can remember, our home was always noisy. My father and mother fought constantly. They were opposites who couldn't get along. Father was a harsh man. He had never experienced any tenderness from his parents or heard a kind word from anyone. He hadn't ever known his mother; she died giving birth to him. As a young child, he was sent away to study at a yeshiva in another city. There, at the age of ten, he was sent every day to eat a meal at another person's house. As a result, he was incapable of living in a family. He never developed any fatherly feelings. In addition, he was very religious and miserly. He had always hated having to work. What little savings he had came from the money that my mother's relatives sent us from America. He lent this money at interest, and we lived on the income. He always taught us that saving is better than earning. Rather than work, he would always scrimp, even when it came to feeding us. We rarely had enough food to eat.

Mother was the exact opposite of Father. She was the youngest in her family and had always been surrounded with love and tenderness. Her family were fishermen, who at the time had a reputation for being well off. In fact, she got married by chance. Her father, who had loved her very much, died, and her mother feared that her daughter might remain an old maid. Barely taking her daughter's personality into account, she married her off to the first eligible young man—as long as he was pious and a scholar, as my father was then. Naturally, my mother didn't care for him. For her, their life together consisted of constant suffering and pain. Still, she never complained to anyone about her fate. She suffered quietly, knowing that all was already lost. She invested her deepest feelings in us children. Despite her difficult situation, we were the best and dearest things in her life, and she was always prepared to make sacrifices for us. We were too young to understand this at the time, but we sensed it. We detested Father, and we were also afraid of him. To this day, I remember that no matter how loud we were while playing, one shout that "Father is coming" was enough to quiet us down. We would hide under the table so that he wouldn't see us. We were less afraid of monsters or strange beasts than we were of our own father.

We children didn't get along with each other, either. The only reason for this was that we each thought Mother loved one of us more than the others. My sisters and I all disliked our brother, to whom Mother paid special attention because he was her only son. She was always giving him an extra glass of tea, saving a piece of white bread for him, and so on.

The years flew by, and we grew up. Despite Mother's opposition, my brother went to a *talmud torah*. But when the teacher gave him a severe beating, Mother took him out and enrolled him in a Polish public school. To this day, I can hear how Father screamed at the time. He didn't want to give my brother anything to eat. Mother took the blame upon herself, as usual, and shielded my brother from everything.

Mother fought with Father even harder over how I and my eldest sister (who was two years older than I) were to be educated. Father wanted a *melamed* to teach us how to sign our names and nothing more. But Mother knew better; she understood that life was a struggle. To avoid failing as she had, we had to see everything with open eyes. To do this we had to be armed with knowledge; we had to study life in order to understand it.

After a week of feuding, my parents enrolled me in a Jewish public school. I don't know why they chose this type of school. I think a neighbor, whose child went to the same school, suggested it to Mother. I started school at the age of six. Although I had once been sickly, I was physically well-developed. At first I didn't care for school. I wasn't used to being with a lot of children and had never had any girlfriends. As a rule, I disliked everyone except for my mother. When I noticed that other children at school were better dressed than I was, I became angry about our conditions at home. Other children brought a white roll for breakfast, not black bread as I always did—and sometimes I didn't even have that. I felt an inner dislike for these children, whom I referred to as "the rich." Then I began to notice that besides these few children from rich families there were many others whom I hadn't noticed before—children who came to school with tears in their eyes. Quiet as a thief, I would sneak over to one of them and whisper, "Is your father mean, too?" This was enough for her to run away and not speak to me for a long time. I especially liked those children who were dressed in rags, as I was, and who also brought plain bread for breakfast. They became my best friends.

In time I became very attached to my teachers. My greatest joy was to hear a kind word from them; a caress on my cheek was the greatest pleasure. Little by little, I began to like school more than home. The more I suffered at home, the more I valued school. The more I hated my father, the more I became attached to the teachers. I felt that they understood me much better. My teacher paid much more attention to me than Father did. When my teacher was sick, I would wait impatiently for him to return. I wasn't a bad student. After classes, when almost everyone else rushed home to eat dinner, I was completely free. Dinner was a rare thing in our home. Instead, I went to visit girlfriends after school and didn't come home until dusk, and not until it was dark in the winter. Mother rarely remembered to ask where I had been all day. That's how I spent my weekdays.

Saturdays were different. At dawn Father woke our brother up to go to synagogue. He would lecture us: we mustn't wash ourselves with soap or comb our hair, because this was forbidden on the Sabbath. He would threaten us that God sees all, knows all, and takes vengeance. I hardly knew what those words meant. One thing this did arouse in me: a strong desire for vengeance against God. If, as Father said, God sees all and knows all, then why does He let us suffer so much? I was determined to get even with Him in a bizarre way. While Father was at the synagogue, I washed myself with soap more than I did during the rest of the week. I rarely combed my hair during the rest of the week; mostly I did this on Saturdays. If this wasn't enough for the ways God wronged us, I found another means of revenge. After we'd eaten the *tsholnt*—as Father lay snoring under the quilt, and Mother and the other children were out in the yard—I would stay at home. Quietly, I'd sneak into a corner, where there were two beds—so dilapidated that only a skilled carpenter could have figured out what they were made of—as well as a half-broken cradle, which was never empty. Here I would hide on Saturdays and light matches, one after another. I knew from Father that lighting a fire on the Sabbath was the worst sin against God. In this way I would get even with Him for all that we had suffered during the week.

On Saturday nights, as Mother sat alone by the window and watched people strolling outside, I would wrap my arms around her neck and assault her with questions: Why is it quiet in other houses, but there are always fights in ours? Why do other children wear such pretty dresses, but I always wear the same rags? Most of all, why do other children have such good fathers—who sometimes come to school, where they speak to everyone and laugh—but our father always yells and sometimes, when Mother isn't looking, also pinches us? I would pester her with questions for a long time, until I'd notice her eyes were filled with tears. Then I'd feel very sorry for her. I knew that if Mother was weeping, I shouldn't say anymore. I would quickly change the subject and tell her about things that had happened at school. Sometimes, after one of these conversations, Mother would give me a kiss on my forehead. This happened very rarely.

The years continued to fly by. I was promoted from one grade to the next. Going to school was hard for me. I never had any books. Mother barely persuaded Father to pay my tuition. She often washed floors or windows and gave me the money she made to buy notebooks. Nevertheless, I did well at school. And so it went until I reached the sixth grade. I assured Mother that I was close to finishing school. Then I would be able to help her in her difficult life. But it's hard to foresee what the future has in store.

When I was in the sixth grade, on the brink of my future, the first major crisis in my life occurred. Late in 1925, when I was twelve years old, Mother had a heart attack, as a result of her constant suffering in silence. And, as if she knew that a member of our family wasn't allowed to be sick for very long, within twenty-four hours her young life was over—or, as people said, she made an end of her slow death. She was thirty-seven years old. It's hard to express in words how her death affected me. A black cloud spread over my sky, which had always been very dark to begin with.

I will never forget Mother's funeral. Many people came. All the other students in my class came. At the time I felt a strange contempt for all these people, especially my classmates. I had the impression that, though they showed me much sympathy, deep in their hearts they were glad this had happened to me and not to them. At my mother's freshly dug grave my oldest sister beat her head with her fists and strangers wept, yet I remained hard as a stone, completely unable to shed a tear. The piercing stares from all sides didn't affect me. I watched stoically as the earth swallowed the finest and dearest person in my life. I knew in my heart that on that day Mother's life had ended only for us. For her it had ended on her wedding day. Father stood near the grave. It was hard to tell what he was thinking. I felt that he was most to blame for her death.

All this affected me very strongly. I didn't imagine then that I would ever live long enough to write this autobiography. I was besieged with bad thoughts: Why go on living? For whom? If, until then, I had hated Father, as had my sisters and my brother, after those painful days I began to loathe him. I held him responsible for Mother's death. I became very apathetic about life. I wanted to make an end of it, but I was too weak. Little by little, I gained control over myself.

Our house was left like a ship without a rudder. My older sister, who by then was studying at a trade school, cried all day and night. My two younger sisters were left unsupervised. It was then that I realized that this was my first encounter with life. Having come face to face with life, I had to struggle with it and not feel lost at the first setback. I realized that this would be the first step on a long, thorny road. I spurned those people who pitied me. I decided not to grieve in front of anyone, no matter how sad I felt. This I inherited from my mother, who never confided her suffering to anyone. On my young shoulders I placed the heavy burden of running the house and raising the younger children. But I didn't want to give up school. I knew it was important for me to continue. Also, I felt that interrupting my studies would dishonor my mother. It had cost her much effort and health to bring me this far. I resolved to continue to spin the thread of learning at all costs, no matter how hard it would be. Father, as always, shouted that I was never going to become a teacher. I already knew enough, he claimed. No doubt I knew enough to cook potatoes and barley every day, but I still knew little about life.

By the time I was twelve years old I was playing a triple role: housekeeper, mother to my younger sisters, and student in the sixth grade. It was hard to work on all three fronts. My studies suffered the most. In the end I had to repeat the sixth grade. I lay the blame on my younger sisters; I had spent too much time with them. At times I loathed them. It was hard for me to play the role of mother. I still wanted to be a child. I still needed someone like my mother, to whom I could ask questions and pour out my heart. At night I always wept into my pillow, so that no one would see my tears. I especially didn't want my classmates to know that they were better off than I was. As a twelve-year-old I had assumed the seriousness and responsibilities of an adult. To my younger sisters, whom I didn't care for at first, I became a devoted mother. I tried to give them what I had demanded from our mother. Above all, I didn't stint on tenderness.

As I said, all this affected my studies, and I had to remain in the same grade the following year. It was the first time that this had happened to me, and it upset me terribly. I was in such a state; I wanted school to fly by quickly, so that my life could forge ahead. At another time, I would have blamed my teachers, as many other students do, saying they had picked on me or were angry at me and therefore wanted to keep me back a year. But I had too much confidence in my teachers to think this. They always sympathized with me. When they explained why they were keeping me back a year, I made peace with the idea and stayed in school.

I felt that if I continued to carry my triple burden any longer I wouldn't be able to continue my studies. I would have to rid myself of some responsibility. I applied to the local orphans auxiliary. Thanks to some effective intercession, they soon took the two youngest children of our family into the orphanage. This aroused an uncomfortable feeling in me. My little sisters became especially dear to me then, and I suffered greatly. I felt like a mother who had been forced to give up her own children. It was very hard for me to tear myself away from them, though I was already accustomed to much hardship. Freed from this burden, I turned to my studies very enthusiastically.

The year passed quickly. As our school had only six grades, I graduated at the end of the school year. It was a wonderful evening. I played a major role in the graduation ceremony. At the conclusion there was a dinner for the students and their parents. All the other children celebrated with their parents. I felt deeply how alone I was. At such an important occasion there was no one to say a kind word to me. I remember, as if it were today, that moment when the parents kissed their children and gave them treats. I stood in a corner, forlorn and abandoned. My brother was the only member of my family there. Grudgingly, he pulled a cookie out of his pocket and handed it to me. I was very hurt. I felt the difference between the other children and me even more. I lowered my head and silently burst into tears. The others there were too busy with themselves to pay any attention to me. My teacher was the only one who noticed my tears, and he consoled me with the fact that I had one of the best report cards.

Finished with school, I began another chapter of life. What now? I felt that I was no longer a child. Actually, I had never been one, but until now I'd had a single goal for myself: to learn. Now I faced another problem: finding something to do with myself, an aim in life. I had to make a future for myself and break free from Father, who had become unbearable. Which way should I turn? Father didn't have to think for long. He found me an easy job at once: picking over several kilos of peas every day for a restaurant. He figured it was an easy occupation that didn't require working on the Sabbath. My brother had been working for several years making quilts. He thought that I should study dressmaking. While I was learning, I could pick up a few groszy in tips, and eventually I would know a trade.

I didn't have the slightest interest in dressmaking. First of all, I knew it was monotonous. Second, I knew that since I'd gotten along for years without a dressmaker, there were obviously many others like me. Who would be my customers? Obviously, I would always be unemployed. I really wanted to work in a factory. Lots of people worked together there, and they earned good money. I hardly cared that they worked on Saturdays. But I didn't know anyone who could help me get a factory job.

Time rushed by. I didn't find any work. I saved a few of the groszy Father gave me for household expenses and used the money to enroll in the Sholem Aleichem library. After finishing the housework, I would sit by the flickering lamp and read until late at night. I didn't want any girlfriends. Books became my best friends.

One night—I happened to be reading Sinclair's *The Seeker of Truth*—a classmate who had graduated from school with me came over to visit, and he asked me a question: Are you satisfied with the system? I looked at him as though he were crazy. To begin with, I didn't understand what he meant by the last word! I asked him to speak more plainly because, as a rule, I'm not satisfied with anything. He had been waiting for this. Hearing these words from me, he got up to deliver a whole lecture. "You're not the only one," he said. "There are hundreds and thousands more, who are worse off." "Who is guilty?" I asked excitedly. "The capitalist system," he replied triumphantly. "We must organize," he went on. "When we're separate, we're nothing, but when millions of people unite, we'll become a force that will change our lives completely." Then he asked whether I wanted to help and become a member of the workers' movement. At the time I had no idea that there were so many different ideologies and parties. His talk impressed me, and I agreed to everything. And that's how I became a member of an illegal political organization.

Several days later I joined a cell. For the first time, I became interested in life. At the meetings, which took place somewhere behind a fence in the summer and on the steps in the winter, I learned that I wasn't the only unfortunate one in the world. There were hundreds more like me. My life became easier to bear. I knew that whatever happened to me was only a drop in the great sea that is life. I came to like the leader of our cell. First, I was impressed with his outward appearance. He was very handsome and physically well developed. Second, his speech impressed me. When he lashed out against the cruelty of the bourgeoisie toward the working class, I became so enraged that I clenched my fist. More than once I struck a friend on such an occasion, thinking he was a capitalist.

Little by little, our cell began to fall apart. The friend who had recruited me joined a Zionist organization to get a certificate to emigrate to Palestine. We branded him a traitor and broke off all relations with him. The other girls also began to come less frequently. They all had the same excuse: "Mother won't let us go out at night." I was free of any supervision. I devoted all my youthful energy to the movement.

When this cell fell apart, I joined another one. I was now assigned various political activities to carry out. I didn't bring much courage to the task. I knew I was doing it all for a great cause that would change my life, but I was very afraid of going to prison. It wasn't that I worried about myself, but I knew that my home would fall apart without me. Despite this, I never avoided political work and always succeeded at it. I tried to spread propaganda among those close to me. Nothing came of it, because I still knew little myself. I would come home late at night. Quietly, I would approach my younger sister, who was in the fifth grade at the Jewish public school. I told her as much as I could. I was sure she wouldn't tell the rest of the family about it. I tried to persuade her to become a member of our movement. She barely understood my trite words. A few days later she confided to me that she and a few other girls in her class had joined SKIF. I realized that I wasn't equipped to explain the difference between the two movements.

I began to read more and learn more about everything. Books had a powerful effect on me. Sometimes I would walk around distracted, lost in thought, not knowing what was happening with me. I suffered much abuse from Father when I put too many beans in the pot or peeled the potatoes too thickly. Time flew by. I completely forgot that I had to learn a trade. Father reminded me about it frequently, mostly during meals, so as to emphasize that he still had to pay my board.

As time passed, my life, which already had too many twists and turns, changed even more. In 1928 the orphans auxiliary in our city opened a new day orphanage for children who didn't have a father or mother but still had a home. Children stayed from two o'clock in the afternoon until nine in the evening and ate two meals there. I don't know who made it possible for them to take my younger sister and me into the orphanage. I was happy to be away from home for the whole day. Home was hell for me. After I'd gone to the orphanage for a few days, I officially announced that I wouldn't take care of the household anymore. "Whoever eats should cook," I shouted angrily. These words greatly upset my older sister, who would have to take over this responsibility. After a three-day struggle I was liberated from this burden.

Having become a free person, I devoted myself completely to life in the orphanage. It was a difficult adjustment at first. There were children of different temperaments, from varying backgrounds. From earliest childhood I was accustomed to having duties and chores. This was the case there, too. I volunteered to be an attendant in the dining room or the bathroom. My friends there, especially my girlfriends, didn't understand me or didn't want to. They complained that I wanted to be singled out, that I wanted the teachers at the orphanage to notice me. I had to put up with a lot because of this. Still, I couldn't be like many of the other children, who avoided any kind of work. For a while they were angry with me. The girls incited the boys, and they organized a boycott against me. I suffered a great deal and wept many tears that no one saw. But I was strong and didn't give in. I felt confident that the teachers at the orphanage, just like my teachers in school, understood me and were usually on my side. They consoled me, telling me that the group would eventually calm down and change their attitude toward me, and in fact that's what happened. During an argument between the boys and the girls (something that happened very often) the boys came to my defense. Later, the girls also accepted me. Our relations changed so much that I was chosen as a representative to the orphanage's first student council, and shortly thereafter I was elected chairman of the council.

In the orphanage I was introduced to a wide range of work and lived a full life. Eventually we even published a monthly magazine, for which I wrote constantly; my articles weren't bad. Meanwhile, my teachers realized that it wasn't good for me not to be working and, against my will, they enrolled me in a vocational school to study dressmaking. Fate, however, wouldn't let me learn this trade against my will. A short time later I developed a lung infection. At first, no one paid any attention to it, least of all anyone at home. My father would just yell that I coughed all night and kept him from sleeping. In time my illness became worse. I ran a high temperature, almost 39°C [102°F]. My teachers were the first to notice that I was sick. They took me to a doctor, who announced that I had to stop going to school and spend time at a sanatorium. I didn't tell anyone at home about this, as there wasn't really anyone to tell. After my mother's death, each of us had withdrawn into a separate world. The orphans auxiliary wasn't doing very well financially; nevertheless, they sent me to a TOZ camp in Otwock.

I was already accustomed to collective living and adapted easily to life in the camp. In particular, the camp manager won my trust. He showed me the kind of attention and tenderness that I had always longed for but rarely received. I made friends with the boys at camp. They were better than the girls, more sincere. I especially liked them because they never asked me about my life at home and my parents. This was a sore point that I always avoided. Here, too, I felt that my life was different from the others. While my friends frequently received letters and treats from home, I rarely received a letter, and when I did, it wasn't from home but from someone outside the family. This always hurt me, but I never told anyone how I felt. I always kept quiet. At night I cried my heart out into my pillow. In the morning I would go back to pretending that I was happy. In my heart I disliked everyone, because the course of my life was different from theirs. I did get along well with one boy, whose lovely singing attracted my attention. He was also very nice to me. He frequently said kind things to me and lent me money for stamps, which I rarely repaid. I don't know how to describe my feelings for him. One thing I do know: when he left I thought about him for a long time and missed him very much.

My month at the sanatorium passed quickly. My health didn't improve very much. Thanks to the manager, who had taken a liking to me, I stayed for another two months. I expressed my gratitude to him by organizing various activities. I arranged entertainments and, along with a few other friends, edited the camp's first magazine. When I left, the manager gave me a gift, a book by Y.L. Peretz with the inscription, "For your good conduct and many talents."

I returned home filled with impressions. For the first time I saw the great city of Warsaw, where I met some new people. A week later I began to study at the vocational school again. And perhaps I would have become a dress-maker if it weren't for a certain incident. My political convictions had remained the same. Secretly, I still belonged to a left-wing political group. One day a comrade of ours died in prison, and we young people organized an illegal demonstration on the day of his funeral. We waited in dark, back alleys until late at night, so that the police wouldn't notice us. A cold rain fell. My shoes, which were rarely whole, were soaked through. I caught a bad cold and once again fell seriously ill.

I kept this a secret and didn't tell anyone the reason I'd become sick again. I knew that it was my fault. Again, the doctor forbade my learning dress-making and insisted I go away to be cured. The financial situation at the orphanage was very bad. They made the greatest efforts to arrange for my cure, so that I could continue with life's struggles. After much difficulty, they sent me to a village called Dębin, near Lwów, where there was a sanatorium in the mountains.

I arrived there after a difficult journey, traveling all day and night with only a short break. I didn't care for the atmosphere at the sanatorium; it felt very assimilated. All the patients spoke Polish and wanted to go to Palestine. The teachers didn't have a good attitude toward us, but I didn't pay much attention to them. I was preoccupied with myself because of my bad health. I had a high temperature, severe pain in my back, and felt that death was near. I developed a will to live at any cost. Nothing bothered me, with one exception: the same as at Otwock, everyone here received frequent, warm letters from home—while I corresponded only with the children and teachers at the orphanage. I very rarely received a letter from home, and when I did it was so cold, almost official in tone, and seldom included any regards from my father. This had one advantage: I never felt homesick, as others did. I used to say that it was better that I had no one to miss.

Three months later I very casually received the news that I was going home. I returned in perfect health. "What now?" I thought. How much longer would I live at others' expense? Despite my good health, the doctor forbade my working as a dressmaker, because sitting bent over might be bad for my weak lungs. The orphanage looked for a different trade for me. My friends joked that the staff wanted to make me an "intellectual" and fix me up with an "intellectual" profession. After much persuasion that I was bright and honest, a pharmacist offered me a job. I've worked for him steadily to this day.

A new era in my life began. At first it was hard for me to adjust to the strict regimen. I felt insulted when—in addition to the manual labor that I did every day, like sweeping the floor and emptying the spittoon—my boss gave me other nice tasks to do, such as fetching his galoshes, brushing his coat, and so on. I felt like a tool in his hands. He could do whatever he wanted with me without any opposition. Little by little I felt more self-confident and began to refuse to wait on him. I told him that such things should be done by his wife or daughter. He shouted at me that I had a big mouth, that no one had ever spoken to him that way before. But I didn't give in. I became increasingly accomplished at work, even though I didn't care for my customers, who were either sick people coming for medication or rich gentlemen and ladies purchasing cosmetics. It was hard for me to deal with the latter, to whom I would say by rote that everyone needed this box of powder or rouge; "A woman must be pretty," I'd say. "She has to appeal to a man." This and similar tried-and-true phrases were my stock in trade. I'd think to myself that it would be much more useful if the customer would give her money to the hungry for bread rather than waste it on powder and rouge in order to fool someone. To please my boss, I had to act against my convictions and convince some not-very-bright girl or naive peasant to buy more and more make-up. The rich didn't need my speeches.

As time passed I became friends with my boss's only daughter, who was a student. I liked her very much. When her father wasn't watching, she would tell me about the heroes of the books she was reading and about her studies. I felt happy when she spoke to me. But later my attitude toward her changed. I sensed that we two were opposites, so different in our ways. She had suffered too little to understand me. In particular I avoided talking with her about family matters, although this interested her greatly. My dislike for her father grew, especially when he made his daily declaration, as he closed the store, that I should go right to sleep and get enough rest. He couldn't understand that an employee is also a human being with other interests in life besides the dull work of the store.

And so things went until 1931. That year the orphanage started to feel crowded. I'd had enough of institutional living. I talked it over with friends, a girl and two boys, and soon afterwards we left the orphanage. They held a dinner in our honor. One of the directors gave each of us a half-open rose as a memento; I've saved its petals. They remind me of our life together in the orphanage. Now I had to spend more time at home, which I'd always detested. I had no circle of friends outside the orphanage. Institutional living had isolated me from the world. My friends from the orphanage also felt lonely. There got to be quite a few of us, so we asked the teachers at the orphanage to organize a club where we could spend evenings and slowly adjust to life outside.

They honored our request. At the first general meeting we decided that our club should have a cultural focus, which would help us expand our knowledge. We also wanted the club to demonstrate that young people with different beliefs and ideologies could still get along together. We named it the Youth Club. We organized two groups, one for literature and one for political science. Our lecturers were the teachers from the orphanage. To eliminate the stigma that the club was only for orphans, we conducted a membership drive and enrolled many young people who had parents. We elected an executive committee. I was appointed the club's chairman. I found the work interesting and often very enjoyable.

It seems that I'm destined to have every new day bring changes. At this time another important event took place in my young life, a second blow to our family. One fine day, Father—who, as it was, hardly supported us financially—abandoned us altogether. He went to live somewhere in a shack where it would cost him nothing. My brother went to talk with him, but it was no use. No one was able to prevail upon Father. His heart was like a rock. He had no feelings. My brother begged him to return, pleading with him as though with a bandit: we were still so young, so helpless, we could go astray. He was too miserly to understand. To this day he has no paternal feelings. We are of no interest to him at all.

The situation at home became unbearable. I felt an even greater hatred for my father. How could someone like him have a family? In my heart I swore to get even with him at the first opportunity. My older sister felt lost as a result of this turn of events, but I became even stronger. I tried with all my might to console my sisters. They still wanted to convince Father to return or to help us out financially. But there was no way to do this amicably, and I wouldn't permit them to do it through threats or scandals. I believed that if our situation became known to others, their pity would do us more harm than anything we might receive from Father. I convinced my boss to raise my small salary of five zloty a week, and I turned over every grosz to help support my family. In order to live more economically, I took over the household accounts again. I kept all this to myself, lest anyone know of our misfortune. I didn't want to give people anything to gossip about. In front of others I remained as happy and contented as I had been before—that is, I didn't change the role I played. I was proud of being a good actor and gave no one the opportunity to learn anything about me. More than once I would come home upset from work to find my brother in a bitter mood and my older sister in tears. Instead of having supper I would wash, change my clothes, and go to the club. Despite the storm inside my heart I would be carefree when I talked about the activities at the club. I didn't tell any of my closest friends about my misfortunes.

With each day the situation at home got worse. My older sister, who was always with two girlfriends and a boy she was fond of, spoke more and more frequently about her aim in life. She would exhaust us with her questions: What would become of her? Was there a way out? Our brother began to think about emigrating somewhere and eventually bringing us over. However, that would take too long, and besides, we couldn't stay behind without him. He was the oldest and the mainstay of our home. In the past we hadn't gotten along well, but each crisis, such as when Father deserted us, brought us together. Our brother tried to take the place of parents, but he didn't succeed.

My older sister grew more and more apathetic. My brother and I looked for a way out for her and decided that she should emigrate. At the time, various trips to Palestine were being organized. The trip required a large amount of money. I thought it would have been easier to lift a mountain off the ground than to amass such a sum. At the time I possessed a great deal of energy, and with a strong will you can accomplish anything. We sold all the valuables that were left in the house after Mother's death, including our grandmother's jewelry. It still wasn't enough. I took an advance on my salary from my boss, and my brother did the same. We still needed a small amount. After we made several threats, Father contributed it.

My sister's departure moved me deeply. After she left us, I really began to care for her. I realized that we wouldn't see each other again soon. I also realized that our family was becoming fragmented, scattered all over the world—"From our town, a village remained"—and this, too, would disintegrate soon. At home, our financial situation grew worse, due to the cost of my sister's voyage. Still, I was happy I had done such a fine thing—sending off my sister, who had constantly pestered us about finding a practical aim in life. She had attained her goal. A short while later, she got married. I felt greatly relieved. I seldom thought about myself, for I have always lived for others. I devoted myself to activities at the club with greater energy. Because of my sister's trip, I had neglected my duties there for some time.

The household became easier to run. We scrimped more and more. It didn't pay to cook dinner for a family as small as we were, and instead of supper I usually attended a lecture on political science or literature at the club.

In 1933 the club decided to establish its first summer camp. We organized an interesting program of activities and a precise daily schedule. Three leaders were chosen, of whom I was the only girl. The directors of the club trusted us enough to let us run the camp. They came only as visitors, to see that everything was in order. The camp lasted for two interesting weeks. It brought us much closer to each other, though sometimes arguments broke out over politics. Almost all of us already had our own convictions, and we all tried to express our opinions on various issues. At the same time we tried to avoid politics, lest it interfere with our coexistence. I didn't enjoy taking on the role of a leader. Having always been accustomed to following orders, it was very hard for me to give them to others. To avoid this I did much of the work myself, so that I wouldn't have to order one of my friends to do it.

We all cherished the two weeks we spent together. Even today, when we meet occasionally, we talk enthusiastically about our first and last summer camp. After the camp, quarrels among members of the different parties became more frequent. The directors of the club realized that our work had reached a standstill. The club's original goal of allowing members of differing political convictions to coexist turned out to be impossible. It became more difficult to continue teaching us, as we were each set in our own views. (Many belonged to the same political group that I did.) Then, because of a political event that was unavoidable due to certain circumstances, our club was shut down. It was a blow for all of us. We loved the club. I felt the loss even more than the others. I didn't come from a warm home; the club was the only place where I found fulfillment. My girlfriends pursued other interests: some with close friends, others at home, while a few devoted themselves to the labor movement. But all this happened just as I withdrew from political activity.

The events in Germany affected me profoundly. When my friends shouted, "We were not defeated," I realized how great the defeat was, because the masses were leaving us. At the moment when everything reached a climax, fascism had triumphed and not the proletariat. I spent entire evenings poring over various books and pamphlets, looking for an answer. In my opinion, socialism had still not found the right way.

The masses aren't educated. Many still don't know the full meaning of the word "socialism." Starting with Germany, a fascist wave is now spreading over the entire world. Because of the ignorance of the masses, fascism is able to appropriate the proletariat's left-wing slogans and use them to attract the masses. The masses are blind. They have abandoned the finest ideals for a piece of bread to quiet their hunger. They will follow whoever gives them bread; this makes him a socialist. It's enough for him simply to shout that their hunger will be sated, and they believe. Another great danger is that the proletariat is splintered; their parties quarrel with each other. I also came to understand that as long as workers lack a common language, they will fight one another. Socialism will not win. Another group will prevail.

All of these internal doubts, which I discussed with no one, depressed me greatly. I completely lost my enthusiasm. I stood on the sidelines, constantly thinking about how a united workers' movement could develop. For only the power of the entire working class will be able to stop the savage appetites of fascism. I think that all the socialist parties understand this. They all speak about a united front. But I'm not smart enough to understand why it hasn't come about.

For the reasons I've mentioned, I left the political group to which I had belonged for a long time. I began to think about myself for the first time. What does life mean? Can I use this beautiful word to describe the hard and thorny road that I've traveled? Why is my life a long chain of suffering and struggle, an endless struggle to survive? For the first time I asked: Where is my home, my childhood, my youth, about which poets write so much? I came to the conclusion that I'd been born an adult; from the start I was forced to struggle with life in order not to surrender. But I couldn't dwell on such questions for long. Life was rushing along. My fate continued, as ever, to be filled with hardship.

Although my brother had been excused from the draft two years ago, he suddenly received an induction notice. As of now he has served eight months. When I asked him why this happened so suddenly, he explained that they had to save some rich boy, and so he had to take his place. I understood what he meant all too well. I felt an even stronger hatred for life, which had created such inequities and was so unfair to me. My sister and I wept bitterly until we made peace with the idea that our brother was leaving us and that, of our entire family, the two of us were to be left alone. But the state doesn't take such feelings into consideration. On a dark night, my sister and I accompanied our brother to the train. With teary eyes, he told us we mustn't lose control but must remain strong. He especially appealed to me not to break down and to continue to be the strong one, as I had been until now. In fact, that is how it turned out. I was already accustomed to every hardship. Now I remained the only one at home to see to it that we didn't go to ruin. It was a difficult task; our income was small. My sister earned very little as a dressmaker, barely enough to cover our most basic needs. It was hard to pay the rent, but in time I managed that, too. I took in a few boarders and used this money to pay for the apartment. No one knew about this, either.

I sat on my sister's bed until late at night, and we talked about our lives, how after our mother's death only we two remained out of seven. Life's waves had carried each of us off to a different place. Hardly a trace remained of what was once our home. We talked for a long time, until we burst into tears. That's how we spent almost every evening. In time I realized it wasn't good to think and speak about myself. I taught my sister my old philosophy: not to share her suffering with anyone, not to tell anyone that things were bad.

I began to look for company, for some place to spend the evenings and forget about myself a bit. I wasn't used to leading a lonely, solitary life. On 10 February 1934 I became a member of the sports club Morgnshtern. The truth is, at first I wasn't enthusiastic about joining the club. I knew that Morgnshtern was connected with the Bund. I never cared for them, but as a member I changed my opinion. I saw that the members of Morgnshtern were also working-class people. Perhaps they weren't as lonely as I was, but they were also exploited by their employers and also lived under harsh conditions. However, people don't talk about this; they want to ignore it. Both by nature and by habit, I couldn't be passive anywhere. At this club I also became a member of the activities committee and served as a monitor in the meeting hall. But the sports hardly interested me. I needed something else to make my dull days brighter.

I became active in my union and completely devoted myself to the activities there. I learned about the lives of young store clerks who worked under very hard conditions. They worked twelve, even fourteen, hours a day. I decided to campaign for a ten-hour working day. I went every night at eight o'clock with a few other friends to bring clerks out of the stores. This wasn't easy. There were several clashes with employers who didn't want to let their workers leave at eight o'clock. After many difficulties, we succeeded. The union work is very interesting. This is how I fill my time: all day in the store, in the evening at the club—but mostly I spend my evenings at the union hall.

I have hardly anything to do with romance—not because I haven't developed these feelings, but because my circumstances don't allow me to pursue them. Even if I care strongly for a young man, I am friendly with him until he begins to show an interest in my private life, my family. At this point I break off with him and avoid him, despite my feelings for him.

By now I no longer fear life. I know it all too well. I think little about the future. Life has shown me that you can't make plans. You can't swim against the tide. I am proud of myself. Despite all the difficulties I have experienced, life still hasn't succeeded in breaking me—quite the contrary. The more I've suffered, the stronger I've become. I've grown up as someone who sees everything with open eyes. I'm able to work and to adapt to society, except for one thing: I've remained locked within myself and share my experiences with no one. I'm ready and able to talk about everything except about myself. My close friends only think that they know me well. In fact, no one knows anything about me. I'm completely different when I'm with other people than when I'm by myself. Only the trained eye of a psychologist would be able to notice that I'm playing a role with people. I never laugh for my own sake but only to make others happy; I don't say what I want but what ought to be said. Others consider me happy and always content. When a bad mood overtakes me I avoid people and remain by myself. I'm sure that more than one of my friends would be disappointed in me if they were to read my autobiography. To this day, I have yet to meet the person to whom I could confide what I have experienced along this hard and thorny path, which has been given the fine name of "life."

"Forget-me-not" (my pseudonym)

6
Ludwik Stöckel[*]

Contest year: 1934 • Language: Polish
Year of birth: 1914 • Age: 20 • Sex: Male

ADVENTURES ALONG THE WAY TO MY GOAL

"*R*eports that the Russkies were approaching came with increasing frequency. We decided to hide among the thick reeds that grew around the pond. For you have to realize"—this was my mother telling me the story—"that everything looked different at Śniatynka, the estate that we were leasing, from the way it does today. This was sixteen years ago. We awaited the inevitable onslaught of the Russkies in a state of terrible anxiety. Our things had been packed away, several days earlier, just in case, as we had anticipated having to flee. You were a horrible brat then, maybe half a year old. Imagine how frightened I was when, one sunny day, I noticed that they were on horseback all around our farm, galloping toward us. I remember it was a Sunday; no one was working in the fields. We were all at home. Papa made up his mind that he wasn't going to let himself be robbed. Our horses were in the stable. As soon as the Russkies got down from their weary mares, they ordered us to show them our horses. Father objected, but when he realized that arguing was useless and dangerous, he let the squad commander into the stable.

"Meanwhile, Grandmother tried to 'get on the good side' of the soldiers by treating them to milk, bread, and whatever else was on hand. You were in the arms of your wetnurse. I saw how one of the 'chiefs' accosted Marynia (that was her name) and said something to her. A moment later I heard him shouting indignantly in Russian: 'So you're going to feed a Jewish child with your own blood?!' I realized what was going on. You were in danger! But I couldn't say a word. My heart froze when I heard Marynia start to

---

[*] author's actual name.

reply. She stammered something out of fear, and then after a moment she said: 'A Jewish baby? No! He's mine!' 'Then make the sign of the cross over him,' the soldier roared. Marynia did as she was ordered. However, that apparently didn't satisfy the brute. He pointed at her crucifix and asked why you didn't have one. Think what I was going through! I understood that I had to keep quiet, otherwise I might have been the cause of your demise. So I stood off to the side, petrified with fear, and waited. I knew that only God could save you. I neither wanted, nor was able, to give Marynia even the slightest sign. The Russkie yelled, 'Put that crucifix on him, or I'll stab him.' Marynia hesitated. The soldier put a dagger to your breast and repeated, 'I'll cut his throat.' Naturally, you were bawling your head off. Then, throwing caution to the winds, the peasant woman hung the pendant around your neck. That was how, thanks to a ruse, Marynia rescued you from the clutches of a fierce soldier. I breathed a sigh of relief.

"The Russkies took our best horses, left us their worst, and rode away. We all gave thanks to God that they had stopped at that. Now, however, we had to reconcile ourselves to the thought of leaving everything to fate. Papa didn't want to remain any longer. He said that he couldn't stand by and watch as we were being robbed. He wanted to play it safe and, besides, he was encouraged to flee by the long lines of wagons that we could see on the highway. We decided to make a run for it. Our last two pairs of horses were quickly harnessed, and the servants loaded up our belongings. In a fit of pique your father ordered that a chest filled with silver and other valuables be thrown off the cart. 'It'll be less weight!' he said. I had no desire to put up an argument. Some passing refugees told us that a new detachment of cavalry was approaching from Tłuste, so we made haste to board the wagon: Grandmother, your father and I, your aunt, Józek, you, and Marynia. We took two peasants with us. We decided to take a shortcut across the fields in the direction of Buczacz. I've already told you how we arrived in Vienna."

That is how, only four years ago, I learned from my mother's lips that I survived, thanks to the brave and resolute Marynia, with whom I am not even acquainted today. In any event, I am grateful to my protector for having been so devoted to me.

From old stories I know that we arrived in Debrecen after several weeks of arduous travel, during which I apparently howled terribly the entire time. From there we went the rest of the way to Vienna by train.

My earliest impressions are bound up with this city. I have several memories that are naturally quite fragmentary. I only managed to make sense of them after my elders filled in the missing pieces.

If I am not mistaken, the oldest image that remains in my memory is of the staircase of the apartment building in which we lived. Once, I was sitting on the stairs and crying. Then my grandfather came up to me and—what happened next, I don't recall. I only know that at the time I blubbered a lot and, as my mother says, took advantage of the situation. You see, the Viennese grumbled that the refugees "mistreated" their children, and so we were constantly to be heard shrieking. As a result, I was able to misbehave with impunity, since I was sure I wouldn't be beaten. On this occasion, however, I caught it but good, and—to prevent my wailing from being heard in the street—I was "thrown out" into the hallway. Only Grandfather was able to calm me down, after which he carried me back into the apartment.

My next recollections are connected with illness. I suffered a bout of so-called "English sickness" [rickets] and for a long time was unable to move my head. Once, my father hung cherries on both of my ears. This prompted me to move my head for the first time, a sign that my health was returning. From this period I remember lying on a pillow on top of a table, while some man patted me on my behind. This was the physician, Dr. Monti, who assured my parents that I would recover.

Beyond that, the following images have remained lodged in my memory: piles of sand in a beautiful park full of flowers, little children skipping and turning somersaults in the sand, posing for a photographer, a band crossing one of the streets (to be precise, I recall only the shiny, yellow horns). My final recollection of Vienna has to do with my brother: he was playing soccer and kicked the ball over a fence. He jumped over the fence to look for it. When my brother kicked the ball back onto the playing field, a policeman came up to him and had a talk with him. Supposedly, I also once watched an imperial procession while my father held me, but I don't remember this. Evidently, I wasn't all that interested in it. So much for my memories prior to our return to Poland.

We went back by train. I was four years old then. We stopped in Lwów, where I watched many boxcars and locomotives. While we were in the waiting room, I chased some little birds that had flown in through holes in the roof made by artillery shells. I simply had to catch these birds. I chased them all around the room, with Mama chasing me in turn. People all around us were laughing heartily. I didn't know why; I paid no attention to them. Father was the only one who could calm me down. Later on, we continued our journey.

At the farm we found everything in ruins, and so we took lodgings with a woman in a nearby village. As we didn't have much in the way of furniture, we hired a carpenter to make a few pieces for us. The carpenter was named Hrynko. I became extremely attached to him. Although he was a "retired" soldier, he wouldn't take off his uniform. I recall that he was particularly fond of his three-cornered hat. For days at a time, I used to sit next to him and "assist" him. I enjoyed myself greatly, because I got to speak German with him. I was glad to have someone I could talk to, in addition to my family. You see, at the time I liked to show off. So, when Father told me to pass on some instructions to our caretaker, I spoke to him in German. He understood what I meant, but he made fun of me. From then on, I spoke to everyone in Polish.

The other children who were my age taught me a little Russian; I tried to speak with adults in this language. I played with our servants' children. One day my brother, Józek, arrived home on vacation from *gymnasium* in Vienna. When I spotted him from a distance, I ran to Mother and told her the news. My brother brought me a little violin, but this present didn't interest me. Apparently, I've never been musical. Eventually, I broke the violin. I received a beating for this, as no one in Capowce (that was the name of the village in which we lived) was disturbed by the crying and shrieking of small children. Therefore, my mother didn't hold back and gave me what I probably deserved. In Vienna I would throw such tantrums that they couldn't refuse me anything. Now, however, I quickly realized that my extended lamentations did me no good, and so I "behaved."

After a few months we moved from the village to Tłuste, a town about a mile from our estate. I found out later that we moved because of an outbreak of disturbances among the Ukrainians. It wasn't altogether safe for us to live in the village, which was inhabited mostly by Ukrainians. In Tłuste I made friends with some boys who became my constant companions. They, too, were Jews, of course. They showed me the town's "landmarks" and streets. They took me, by way of the "Turkish" roads (I have no idea why they are called this), over and over to the same spots: the cemetery, the synagogue, a nearby ravine, the pond, etc. In exchange for this, each time I gave my new friends a toy from the ones that I had brought from Vienna. They became so accustomed to this that later on they would demand some trifle for the least favor. It got to the point that once, when I refused to give something to one of these boys, Mechel, he took my hoop during a game. My pleas to him to return it were in vain. Only after lengthy negotiations did Mechel agree to return the hoop in exchange for a pound of cheese. Thus, some cheese that my mother had made restored what I had lost.

I was now five years old. I began to study Hebrew privately, as I didn't go to *kheyder*. At the same time they began to prepare me to attend public school. Apart from my studies, I played with my friends who, despite everything, were nice and happy-go-lucky. Following the example of our elders' stories, we would organize games of war, hospital, and the like. From time to time we would climb up a nearby hill, from which we could see the entire town, half in ruins. But soon we had to give up these excursions.

Some strange soldiers in motley attire entered the town. A few of them wore what looked like Austrian three-cornered hats and threadbare uniforms; others had on colored tunics or Cossack shirts and caps, etc. They were Ukrainians. Everyone lived in constant fear; I wasn't allowed out of the house. I remember that my parents stuffed some banknotes into bottles and buried them next to the stable. We must have had a lot of these bills, because once I filled my toy wheelbarrow with them and headed toward the town. Nothing came of this escapade (although I don't know what plan I had in mind), because one of my grown-up acquaintances, an engineer named Lewin, came by and quickly escorted me home.

While the adults were constantly fretting about something, I was having a good time. I would sit at home and play with the blocks I had received as a present from this same engineer. (It's probably why I was so fond of him.) My Hebrew studies were discontinued because of the unrest in the town. I spent all my time "building." My grandmother even predicted that I would make an excellent engineer. In the evening the whole family gathered at our house. Seated at the table would be my parents, Grandmother (Grandfather had died back in Vienna), my aunt and uncle, my brother, and a cousin. To cheer up the adults, who were continually depressed, my brother and my cousin would talk me into dancing. I would perform some gyrations and skip about, after which I would deafen the whole company with my harmonica.

One day, several men arrived at our place. They spoke Russian. I thought they wanted to take someone to do roadwork, as was common at the time. But I found out that they wanted Father to give them some horses. When he refused, the men said nothing and left. They were Ukrainian bigwigs of some sort. That same night one of our horses was found missing from the stable. He was a tall, chestnut-colored horse; his partner was a gray mare with a white mane. The next day I saw that the mare was wounded. She had hurt herself on the barbed wire strung around the barnyard. The other horse had let someone lead him through the fence, but evidently the mare wouldn't allow herself to be stolen. I liked this horse very much and often fed her sugar. My father was very upset, but there wasn't anything he could do about it in the end.

A few days after the theft people began speaking in hushed tones about the approach of the Poles. I didn't understand why everyone around me had somehow become more cheerful. Everybody simply kept repeating that maybe things would soon be "better."

Unfortunately, something rather unpleasant was in store for us. While playing with my dog one day, I was startled by a strange scene. I saw two soldiers escorting Father out of the house. I skipped over to them to ask what was happening. However, I just stood there confused; I had lost my nerve. One of the soldiers shouted at me in Russian to go away. I stepped back and glanced at Mother. She was sitting on the porch, weeping. I found out that my father was under arrest. The very next day Mother went to Czortków, where Father had been put in jail. However, her first attempt to intercede was unsuccessful. Papa was accused of disloyalty to "newly arisen Ukraine." When Mother returned without Father a few days later, I burst into tears and declared that the next time I wanted to go to Czortków, too. So we set out together. My brother was already attending the *gymnasium* in Czortków. Father was ultimately set free because, in the meantime, his accuser had been hanged for embezzlement and state treason, while the chief witness for the prosecution couldn't be located. All that happened was that Father had been questioned by a military judge. Father openly stated (I was told this later on) that he had been arrested for saying that "the Ukrainian people were not yet mature enough to have their own state," but he justified this with examples drawn from the contemporary situation.

The reunion with Father upset me very much. He looked puffy and his skin had turned somewhat yellow, as a result of the conditions inside the damp, overcrowded jail. Nevertheless, I was very happy that we could go home together. Only one thing bothered me: I didn't understand how it was possible to lock up a living human being—and my father at that—within narrow confines and not let him out in the fresh air. One morning, a few days after Father's return, we heard several shots. Panic immediately set in. We all hid in the cellar; I was made to crouch in the darkest corner. I was incensed at having to sit down there, but they let me have my beloved little dog, Nera, for company, so I sat there quietly. She howled at the sound of the shooting, but when I petted her she calmed down. The rifle and artillery fire went on for several hours. Then it became still. No one budged. Only after a long pause did we move back upstairs. Defiantly I pushed my way to the windows, where all I could see were some people milling about. Soon a detachment of troops entered the town. These soldiers were dressed differently from any that we had seen previously. They came up to the house opposite ours and halted. Mother explained to me that they were Poles and pulled me away from the window.

Each morning thereafter, I would watch as the soldiers filed out of the surrounding houses, formed ranks, and set off somewhere. I think they were going off for drill instruction. I never ran after them, although many of the other boys did. Apparently, I wasn't curious about them.

At this time I returned to my studies, but I was much more interested in my building blocks. I was constantly cobbling something together out of these blocks and then demolishing it. I would build and destroy. I also played with other boys who were my own age. I was in awe of them, because I couldn't understand them; they spoke Yiddish. However, I slowly began to learn the language. The atmosphere at home helped me as well, and I soon managed to make myself understood. Every few days my parents would take me with them to the farm. I wanted to ride horseback, because I was jealous of my cousin Celek. He rode beautifully, while I could hardly ride at all; the illness that I had contracted in Vienna left me with a weakened leg. At the time they were starting to rebuild the homestead at the farm, and I enjoyed watching the masons and carpenters at work. Apparently I had a "bent" for architecture. I could watch the construction work for a long time. Once, I also tried to take the reins as we rode through the fields for our "inspection," but without success. I steered the horses so abysmally that, as we were crossing a bridge, we turned over into the ditch. Fortunately the accident passed "without casualties." However, for a long time afterward I wasn't allowed to touch the reins.

During this period I began to feel an intense attachment to my mother. She was always telling me fairytales or stories of actual events from the war. She usually concluded with words of hope for better, perhaps peaceful, times soon. To be honest, I didn't understand, but I was happy that Mother was saying these things to me. Soon, however, long troop trains began passing through town. Most of them carried cavalry. Sometimes these multi-colored horsemen were also leading camels. I was very taken with the costumes of Petliura's troops (for that is who they were). I was fascinated by their gaudy uniforms and so-called "top-knots." Perhaps this is why I wasn't afraid of them. Once I approached a huge ruffian and asked him to show me his riding whip. The soldier handed me the beautifully braided whip, and I started to run away. Of course, I didn't get far before the Cossack grabbed me, took the whip, and raised it as if to strike me. He didn't do so, but from then on I preferred to have nothing to do with soldiers.

As it happened, I was soon deprived of the opportunity. When rumors came of a possible invasion by the Bolsheviks, Father didn't want us to stay in the area. So we went to Bolechów, where we lived with the family of my uncle's fiancée. I had a fine time there. I didn't study, I had all kinds of interesting toys that my aunt gave me as presents, and I got to know several new playmates. What I enjoyed most of all, though, was the beautiful orchard that belonged to some of our relatives. While the adults would plunge into lengthy and doleful discussions (so they seemed to me, because they were interspersed with tears), we children would climb the magnificent apple and pear trees and pick the very best ones. Since I couldn't eat very many of these fruits, which weighed half a pound to a pound each, I organized an "exhibition" of them on the ledge around the stove, and I vowed that I would take a whole bushel of these beauties to Father. Unfortunately, this succulent fruit rotted quickly, so my brother and the others helped me to put them up as preserves. I also enjoyed our stay in Bolechów because sometimes I could go swimming there and go on excursions to scenic spots nearby.

After a while, I saw that troops were passing through the town. I soon learned that they were Poles. I remember asking one of the soldiers whether they had already driven out the Bolsheviks. He replied that I should "relax," because the Poles were going to take care of them. Delighted, I reported this to the whole household. I was quite surprised, therefore, to see my brother hiding a chest in the cellar. (I didn't know that just then the Poles were in retreat.) My surprise was justified, and the others' faces soon brightened. Mother assured me that it wouldn't be long before we could go back home. A few more weeks passed. Meanwhile, it had begun to rain, the weather turned wintry, and I had to stay indoors. I was bored. So I was overjoyed when Mother informed us that we would be returning home the next day. On the way back we rode in a freight car. It took us two days to reach our remote destination.

Father was waiting for us at the train station in Tłuste. Here, too, it was peaceful. Father and the others who had stayed behind told us about their experiences when the Bolsheviks were there. My cousin Isek's tales intrigued me greatly. I felt especially sorry for Isek, because my father wouldn't let him accept a gift from a little Bolshevik: a fencing foil, which was, by all accounts, beautifully decorated with crystals and sea shells.

My days of idleness were over. I resumed my Hebrew lessons. In addition, I was about to enter public school. After a few months of home study, my parents finally decided to enroll me in the second grade of primary school.

One day during the winter I went to the school with Isek. He showed me the way, told me to wait until the end of class for the director, and left. I stood in front of the Baron Hirsch building, freezing. The time began to drag and it was cold, so after a short while I went inside. It wasn't much warmer in the hallway, so naturally I entered the room where the class was taking place. Since the director (who was the sole instructor) probably knew what was going on, he didn't throw me out, but told me to wait. I took a seat at one of the desks. At the end of the lesson, the director asked me why I had come. I replied that I wanted to register for the second grade. I was given a simple exam, and I apparently satisfied the director, as he instructed me to come to class the very next day.

Thus, I began to "get an education." From the start, things didn't go well, especially in mathematics, for which it was clear from the start that I had no aptitude. Once, when our teacher asked me who did my homework for me, I answered quite calmly and candidly that it was my aunt. Although my parents praised me for my honesty, I now began to do my homework alone, without assistance.

At school I was asked about my birth, and only then was I told where and when it had occurred. Now, whenever I am asked for my vital statistics, I am obliged to report that I came into the world on 14 February 1914 in Zofjówka, near Biała Czortkowska. At the time I didn't bother to wonder where this was. Only later, when I was traveling with Józek to Czortków, did I ask him to show me the village. From the train window my brother pointed out some rather humble buildings, of which only ruins remained. This was the very same farm that my parents had leased before the war. I don't know why, but on seeing it I felt a momentary pang at the thought that I had come into the world in such an unprepossessing place, of which very likely nothing is left. However, I didn't let it upset me.

At school I made some new acquaintances. I became friends right away with two boys: Sinnek and Joe. Sinnek was a very handsome and cheerful boy, the same age as I was. Joe, on the other hand, was crippled—he was a hunchback—and was older than I. We always sat together in class. We often got into fights, including Joe; he paid no attention to his handicap. And, as far as I can remember, we never mentioned it to him. We got along famously. We studied together and played energetically. We often went on excursions to the surrounding area, and in wintertime we went sledding. In addition, we competed with one another in everything. Both of my friends were better at school work than I was, but there weren't any quarrels over this. With regard to our teachers, we strove to "collaborate" with one another. During my first year in school (that is, in the second grade), we were always respectful toward our teacher (there was only one for all subjects), who was a Jew and was very kind to us. We were never afraid of him.

It was only in the following years, in third and fourth grades, that our teachers were Catholics. They didn't spare us punishments, such as having to kneel or stand before the blackboard or behind the door, and sometimes they even struck us with a rod or a ruler. As a rule, we three tried to avoid these unpleasant occurrences; we usually succeeded, since we were prepared for class. But our fear of this system of discipline drove us to try various stunts, which were intended to prove to our classmates that we weren't cowards. We often made faces behind the teacher's back or deliberately talked a lot during class. This exasperated the others, and I recall that they often went to the teachers and told on us. We started to protect ourselves with various fibs and evasions, in order to evade the humiliation of being punished. We got along well enough with our Catholic classmates, despite their less than complete "solidarity" with us. Our school was coeducational, but there were few girls, especially Jewish ones. In any case, I was becoming more and more aware of things, and I willingly listened to—and repeated—malicious phrases uttered by the peasant children. At the time, the air was thick with gossip about one of the boys. It got so bad that he went to our teacher and begged him to stop the class from mocking him with rather unpleasant verses in praise of his "sweetheart."

I usually did my homework with my friends after playing a game or running around until we were exhausted, in defiance of our parents' advice. At the time, I was generally considered argumentative and disobedient. I wanted to show off everywhere. This didn't prevent me from still being the darling of the household, though I gave my parents nothing in return for their love. I was just decent enough that, when asked which of my parents I loved more, I placed Mother on the same level with Father, although in fact I already loved my Mama more. I even think that I was aware of this. For example, during the grownups' card games, which I enjoyed watching, I always insisted that Mother be given back whatever she had lost.

My brother was never at home. I recall that once he showed up at our house with all of his friends. They had organized an excursion to a waterfall and caves nearby. During their visit they all sat on the porch, and I had to introduce myself to each one in turn. It was tedious to have to keep repeating my name. The only time my brother and I were together in the house was during summer vacation and holidays. We both liked dogs very much. I remember that once I even took a snapshot of my favorite dog. He was gray all over. We were never apart at home, and he even accompanied me to school.

In the fourth grade I began to think about what I would do next. Some members of my family advised me to stay and complete the seventh grade in public school. But my parents weren't sure about this. For my part, I wanted to enroll in the *gymnasium*. I had little difficulty persuading my parents. They wanted to turn their sons into "people with diplomas" and therefore wished to get me into the *gymnasium*. In order to switch from the seventh grade of public school into the fourth form of the *gymnasium*, I'd have to pass a difficult examination; therefore it was eventually decided that I would transfer to the *gymnasium* straight after the fourth grade of elementary school.

I continued to study with Sinnek and Joe. Meanwhile, we moved into the home of the owner of the estate that my parents were leasing. This building was located near the school I attended and was next door to my cousin Celek's home. Celek was also my age, but because we had previously lived far apart, we didn't see each other very often. In the fourth grade something else brought us together. Although neither Sinnek nor Joe intended to enroll in the *gymnasium*, Celek's plans were the same as mine. As a result, the four of us studied together. School became very competitive, because everyone wanted to get good marks; they were especially important for those of us who were to take the qualifying exam. Yet things turned out differently. Our teacher deliberately lowered the marks on our midyear reports; he wanted to force us to take private lessons with him to prepare for the qualifying exam. For the first time, I received only "satisfactory" marks in several subjects. To tell the truth, it didn't upset me very much. I was just annoyed that I had to give in to the teacher's blackmail in order to get better marks, which I needed for admission to the *gymnasium*.

So the two of us—that is, Celek and I—began to study with our "tutor." This went on for several months. At home I did very little work. I recall that once I was reading when Mother nearly fainted while ironing clothes. Father caught her and laid her on the sofa. I know I was extremely upset, but this doesn't begin to convey the complicated emotions I felt. I didn't know how to behave. I didn't want to cry, because I was afraid of drawing attention to myself. I wasn't able to help Father keep Mother's forehead moist, because the other adults took care of this. Nor did I want to cry out or speak when I saw that Mother was conscious and had opened her eyes. I was dumbfounded and at a loss. Later, I thought about the difference between fainting and death, and thus I became convinced that nothing had happened to Mother and that the fainting spell would pass. In fact, she was soon chatting with us. Grandmother maintained that the extinguished embers had enabled my beloved mother to recover so quickly. I found this hard to believe.

When examination time came, our teacher gave us "excellent" final report cards for the fourth grade, and we finally went to Czortków. My brother, who was then in the seventh form at the *gymnasium*, reassured me, instructing me to keep completely calm during the exam. I wasn't at all afraid. It was only when the director came into the room and began assigning us topics for the Polish compositions that I became a bit nervous and dispirited.

I remember that we wrote a dictation first, and then we were asked to compose a single sentence using these words: willow, reed-pipe, meadow, and shepherd. I sat next to Celek, and during the dictation we argued over how to spell *który* [which]. Since Celek was more stubborn than I was and was able to stick to his guns, I wrote *ktury*, and that was (I found out later) my only error. As for the written assignment, Celek understood it to mean that we were to compose four sentences using the above-mentioned four words. This time, I refused to go along with him and wrote only one. After oral exams in Polish, religion, and mathematics, we were told to go home. The next day I learned that I was among the lucky ones who had passed and had been accepted into the *gymnasium*.

During vacation I went out to the farm every day. Sometimes I rode on horseback, sometimes I practiced driving the cart; my brother taught me the art of proper horseback riding and driving. At last I was able to steer without dumping passengers into the ditch, as had happened to me once previously. I would watch the field hands at work, and then I'd go play in the farm pond. I would take a board and push it along the water with a long pole. For days on end I enjoyed the shallow, dirty water and the strong, beautiful sunshine. I swam together with the dogs that we kept on the farm. It never ceased to amaze me then that even the smallest puppy could swim. Each week my brother and I organized an excursion with our cousins, both those who lived nearby and those from far away, who had come to visit our aunt and uncle in Tłuste for the first time. We would take a ride to the nearby woods or to the harvest festivals at local farms.

At the beginning of the school year I went to Czortków, where I made some new acquaintances. Józek introduced me to his friend's brother, Symek, who was my age. He didn't make a very good impression on me. He was a skinny fellow and glum as well, due to an infected vaccination on his arm. Symek introduced me to some of our classmates. In time, I came to like him much more. Symek knew how to do many more things than I did, and he also turned out to be a fine, enthusiastic playmate. Having parted company with my friends in Tłuste, I was in need of good friends. Soon I was part of a new triumvirate, together with Symek and another boy named Lonek. They showed me around Czortków and taught me all sorts of schoolyard pranks and practical jokes. We became fast friends very quickly and were nearly always together. I lived in a boarding house with Józek, where there also lived, besides the adults, a small but unattractive girl. She was a year younger than we were. I didn't care for her, but I did get along well with the girls who came to visit her.

We often invited my friends over and we all played "telephone," "monk," and the like. As I remember, we didn't feel any inhibitions. Once, for example, I chased Adzia (one of my female acquaintances) under the bed, and then during "telephone" I kissed her—this was allowed by the rules. In general I socialized with other boys. In my class there were about a dozen Jews, of whom I got along especially well with Jumek, and best of all with Symek and Lonek. I didn't do much studying, so at the evaluations I was continually flunking. During the winter I went sledding with my chums, which I enjoyed. Sometimes we organized picnics, which consisted of drinking tea, eating the bread and sweets that we all had brought along, and playing games of hide-and-seek.

I was also on good terms with Józek's friends. I liked them very much, especially one fellow named Nacek. For his name-day, Józek decided to arrange a celebration. He bought vodka, sponge cake, and so on. Nacek got wind of the fact that there was going to be something to drink and showed up before the party with one of his "propositions." He was always making "propositions." This time Nacek offered me all of the cakes in exchange for showing him where the vodka was stashed. I agreed to this arrangement, but later on I got raked over the coals by my brother, who didn't have anything to offer his other friends. On the whole, I didn't get along very well with my brother then. He was arrogant and condescending toward me, as he was about to graduate. I felt genuine respect for his ability to cram endlessly, but I wouldn't go along, for example, when he forbade any games or amusements. Nevertheless, I always heeded Józek whenever he asked me to bring him something or take care of something for him.

On the day of my brother's *matura*, I set out with him for the school, carrying an armload of books. Along the way we whistled for Nacek to come out, as was our custom; he was already a "graduate." Together, steering clear of "hazards" (e.g., nuns) and searching for pails full of water, we went along to help Józek. By then our parents had arrived in Czortków. It wasn't going terribly well for my brother; I saw him in tears during one of the breaks. Not wanting to annoy him, I didn't go up to him or ask him anything. Finally, however, we found out during the afternoon that he had passed. I raced home to give the happy news to Mother. At dinner, Father solemnly congratulated my brother and presented him with a tie-pin. Later there was a drinking party, after which all of my brother's friends went on an excursion.

Meanwhile, the school year had come to a close, and I had succeeded in advancing to the next form with quite good marks. I spent the summer vacation the same as in previous years; nothing was different. Celek and his sister, Jula, were in Tłuste; at the time I got along very well with them. We played chess and even held "tournaments," as some of my other cousins, who attended schools in Kołomyja and Lwów, were around. Some name-day parties, games, books—the days passed slowly.

I returned to the "academy" in Czortków and moved to new living quarters. Now that Józek had gone to study at the university in Lwów, I was "put up" in the boarding house that belonged to my friend Jumek's parents, Mr. and Mrs. Speiser. They lived adjacent to the *gymnasium*, so we were mere steps from school. I got along well with Jumek, but we didn't study together.

Jumek was much more diligent and devoted more time to school work, while I wasn't so scrupulous about preparing for class. I continued to get along fine with Symek and Lonek. We usually met at Jumek's orchard, where there was a beautiful pear tree. I loved its juicy fruit. We would play croquet and chess, tell each other jokes, and so on. Symek became my closest companion. We tried to get together often, just the two of us, and talk about "intimate" matters. We also became fanatics about maintaining an elegant appearance. We constantly cleaned our clothing and shoes and saw to it that every item in our wardrobe was in the best possible condition. I don't know whose approval we sought. In any case, we wasted a lot of time on these trifles. We hardly ever socialized with the girls from the *gymnasium*, but we knew a few of those who attended public school. I remember that I started to visit one of these girls on the pretext of setting up a library. This went on for some time. Once, though, we ran into Lonek and Symek's brothers in the apartment house where one of the other "managers" of the library lived. From then on, she and I were the butt of endless jokes. As a result of this constant ribbing about our rendezvous, we stopped seeing each other.

The girls in our class ignored us boys from the start. We never bowed to them; we merely greeted them with the usual "Hi." When our female classmates saw that we paid no attention to their pouting, they lashed out at us. Their reason for this, they said, was our failure to remove our caps when we met them on the street. This led to a "serious conflict." We refused to agree to such a "weighty" concession. However, since it wouldn't do to answer this "demand" with silence, we convened an "open meeting" of our classmates on the soccer field. Only Jews were invited. Although we got along fine with the Catholics, we didn't involve them in our "social life." There were about a dozen of us there. Symek led the meeting, as we considered him the most "dignified" member of the "organizing committee," which consisted of the four of us: Symek, Lonek, Jumek, and me. Symek laid out the whole matter, putting it in the proper perspective. After lengthy "deliberations," in which everyone had a say, it was "freely" decided to send a delegation to our female classmates.

The delegates' mission was to convey our "resolution," to wit—we would bow "with respect for the fair sex," but only under two conditions: the girls would all apologize, and these bows would not put us under any further obligation. The conditions were accepted, and peace ensued. While none of our foursome became any closer with the girls at school, the other boys were good-natured by disposition. Things continued in this way for some time. Soon, however, a rapprochement with these young ladies took place.

I had a peculiar attitude toward my Catholic classmates. As a rule, I conversed with them, helped them out sometimes just as anyone else would, played soccer with them, etc. At the same time, however, I tried to keep them at arm's length, and in doing so, I wasn't always on my best behavior. After all, I made a certain distinction between them and us Jews. If, for example, one of "ours" hurt my feelings or insulted me, I always tried to "have it out" and resolve the matter, and then things would be fine. Yet I remember that when one of the Catholics started to get under my skin and eventually called me a "dirty Jew," I punched him in the face. Though he didn't repay me in kind, we didn't speak to each other for a long time. Eventually he did apologize to me and admitted that I had been in the right. Having been successful on this occasion, I became aggressive toward some classmates that I disliked, and sometimes I was, perhaps, even responsible for provoking them. I calmed down, however, after I struck one of my old acquaintances from Tłuste, and he threatened to report me to the headmaster.

Once again, my academic performance was middling. I made no attempt whatsoever to be in "good standing" at the evaluations. However, my report cards were "clean." On the whole, I was indifferent toward the faculty; the only one I actively disliked was our homeroom teacher. This was because he tried to compensate for his age (he was young) and enhance his authority by giving us beatings. These blows with the rod were painful. At the time the school paid little attention to us. The pedagogical system consisted of terrorizing us, as our homeroom teacher did, or giving out a countless number of 2's. We were also frequently given detentions as punishment for our "transgressions." In this manner we often lost half of our free time on Sundays. All that the school ever did to make our lives more interesting was to organize a few magic shows and excursions to the nearby castle, which everyone already knew, as well as the other places where we went on walks: the dam on the Seret, the woods, or the hill outside of town. Sometimes they simply organized festive programs, with songs, recitations, and dramatic performances, which we liked. We went to the cinema on our own, since there were no strict rules against this at the time.

Despite the fact that school didn't provide me a great deal of satisfaction, I was in good spirits. The Speisers' home, which was where I spent perhaps the majority of my time, contributed to this. They were very kind to me. Jumek's mother showed the utmost concern for my welfare; I have much to thank her for. She always gave me instructions and comments in the form of friendly advice. She could just as calmly admonish me as acknowledge the correctness of my behavior.

Mrs. Speiser was also extremely helpful to me during the period when I began to feel homesick. During my first year in Czortków, I never thought about being away from my parents. It was only when I was about to turn twelve that I started to feel terrible pangs of homesickness. It was so overpowering that I often cried and was utterly incapable of studying. My parents came to Czortków quite often. During the first year, when I lived with Józek, I saw Father or Mother every week. My parents also visited me frequently the following year, but I found it difficult not to have Mother around all the time. I missed her the most, after all. Things got so bad that I wanted to run away from Czortków and return home in the middle of the school year. I didn't succeed in this; Jumek discovered my plan. I remained at school, but I always felt sad. This went on for several weeks; it was the only time that I saw everything in dark colors and agonized over everything. The fact that I didn't give way to despair at this time is mostly due to Mrs. Speiser. She was very adept at humoring me and explaining to me over time that, in fact, it was good to study away from home, because this way one becomes more independent. Eventually I calmed down and the feeling of homesickness dissipated.

Toward the end of the school year the professors began to examine us "for the record." I answered well and was promoted once again. I had muddled through the second year even more easily, perhaps, than the first.

The summer vacation of 1925 was more cheerful than previous ones, because two cousins I hadn't previously met came to visit. They were twins from Vienna. At first, we could barely communicate with one another. But since I had once been able to speak German and spoke Yiddish well, I conversed with them by means of a hodgepodge of the two languages. For days on end we told each other stories about ourselves. Naturally, these visitors from abroad had much more interesting things to relate, and, besides, they embellished everything with their fertile imaginations. They taught us how to play ping-pong, and we passed the time this way. We also played soccer with a few of the village boys and started to learn how to play tennis.

I played soccer (I was a goalie) with tremendous enthusiasm. I never tired of kicking the ball. I remember once I didn't come home for dinner; my aunt brought some freshly baked rolls right down to the playing field for me. First I nibbled on them, then I wolfed them down between goals. From time to time we held matches with other teams, and we almost always won. That is, we never let ourselves lose, taking advantage of any excuse whatsoever to quit the field "with honor" whenever defeat loomed.

We began playing tennis with homemade rackets. My first "racket" was the wooden lid from a milk jug. Next, we fashioned hoops from wire and "strung" them with pieces of twine. They were, of course, terribly heavy and clumsy, more like carpet-beaters. Only toward the end of summer vacation did I acquire a real racket.

I devoted considerable time to these group activities, but not so much that I couldn't read books or catch up on the news in a magazine. I wasn't all that interested in travelogues or books on natural science; I most enjoyed reading books about history. On the whole, though, I didn't read much—not even as much as was expected of a boy my age. My parents paid no attention to this.

In Czortków I again lived (as I would until graduation) with Jumek's parents. My life changed only slightly. I got along better and better with Jumek. We often took long walks together along the banks of the Seret. I don't know why, but I could never wax rhapsodic over scenic vistas, even ones I'd never seen before. Nature left me unmoved. About all I could manage to say was that something was "very pretty" or that "I like this." We usually made these walks more enjoyable by bringing along something to read.

Symek was still one of my closest friends. Lonek stopped attending the *gymnasium* after failing the second form, and so I lost contact with him. Soon, though, something happened that significantly impaired my relations with Symek. Now that we were in the third form, the older students began to take an interest in us. Symek joined Hashomer Hatsa'ir and started talking about life at the "club." He tried to persuade me to join, too, to prevent me from becoming completely assimilated, and so on, but I wouldn't go along with him. I repeated our conversation to Jumek; we both decided not to join the organization. During the winter, Symek invited me to an exhibition of drawings and paintings done by some of the *khalutsim*. Among the pictures were some by Jumek's sister, who was older than we were. I went to see the exhibition and also to observe the people there. I was put off by the dreadful noise in the club and shocked by the behavior of the older *khalutsim*. As a result, I decided that it was a good thing that I hadn't heeded Symek's requests.

I returned home with Symek and another, older friend, who began to ask me if I didn't feel isolated, if I didn't think about how the Catholics sometimes made fun of me. Finally, he called my attention to the happy times provided by the Zionist organization, with its splendid excursions, and so on. In spite of everything, however, he failed to persuade me to join the movement. To be honest, I didn't dwell on the reasons why I so stubbornly resisted these attempts to involve me in Hashomer Hatsa'ir. It was more likely a reflexive reaction. Perhaps I did need a different environment to help me give full expression to my energies, but the atmosphere at home had nurtured a different spirit in me. I had never been systematically taught the Talmud, the books that are the source of our national consciousness. I hadn't studied Hebrew since entering the *gymnasium*. Nor could Symek or the other fellow explain to me the appeal of the Zionist idea. So I remained insensible to its attractions. There were no strong bonds linking me to

Jewishness. If something did remind me that I was Jewish it was, as much as anything, the school registry, my sense of separateness at school, and the attitude of some of my more chauvinistic classmates. The fact that my life was confined to a circle of Jewish friends was merely the result of the greater number of interests we had in common. Besides, we barely sensed our exclusion at the time.

On the other hand, I didn't think that it was necessary, and I felt fine among my regular companions at Jumek's house. However, as a result of my decision, Symek and I ceased to be on good terms. To be sure, he didn't show it at school, but I sensed that he was reluctant to spend time with me outside the walls of the *gymnasium*. I felt bad about this at first; I had lost a good friend. It upset me especially because I had never been so close to anyone as I was to Symek. Jumek liked to tease me from time to time, and I took all of his jokes to heart; as a result, we were unable to come completely to terms. For a while, I had no friends.

However, this didn't prevent me from participating in regular games at the home of one of my classmates, Wilek. As a rule, we got together in the afternoon. The others who came were Janek and Kuba, Wilek's sister Lalka, her friend Adzia, and some others. Usually we played tip-cat; we often broke windows in the neighbors' houses. Next would be the traditional game of hide-and-seek, which we played inside the large house. Wilek was always the best at hiding, since he knew the house like the back of his hand. No one could ever find him. One day he paid dearly for this, though. He hid behind a laundry wringer in the cellar and covered himself up with some rags he found there. We didn't find him, but when he emerged from his hiding place, he was crawling with lice. The game ended on the spot, and the poor fellow had a devil of a time cleaning his clothes and getting rid of the "crickets" (as we later referred to the vermin).

My studies in the third form went smoothly. I didn't fail anything, and I was satisfied with this. Things went worse with Jumek. For some unknown reason, the professors had it in for him and were clearly picking on him. The final exams also didn't go well for him and, despite prodigious cramming, my friend Jumek had to repeat the year.

During vacation I went with my mother and brother to Iwonicz. I enjoyed the places we passed through on our way. The air at Iwonicz made me fall fast asleep immediately after we arrived (at five o'clock in the afternoon, if memory serves me), and I didn't wake up until dawn. I quickly became accustomed to the waters and the bathing. However, the doctor also ordered me to take mudbaths. This was a bit more unpleasant. I did bathe in the "muck," as I called it, but I loathed it.

In Iwonicz I met some new people, including a young lady from Lwów. Although she was a year older than I, we were the best of friends. We went on excursions together to the nearby woods or to Bełkotka. I played many games of chess with her and always kept her company as she did her needlework. This was the extent of our friendship. I remember that we took photographs of each other quite often, sometimes while playing tennis, which my brother and I pursued avidly. This was the first time I ever watched a tennis tournament, and I was enthralled by the skill of the "top-flight" players (or so they seemed to me).

We spent another couple of weeks in Iwonicz, which, while charming, was expensive in those days. We purchased many wood carvings and other gifts before returning home. We drove to the train station in an automobile that belonged to some people we knew, and this was my first trip in such a vehicle. We arrived in Lwów, where my brother and I amused ourselves for several hours, but I don't remember much of this, as it was in the evening. We continued on with our journey, returning to Tłuste from Czortków by auto. These car trips were something genuinely new and I enjoyed them, impressed by the high speeds more than anything else. I spent the rest of the summer vacation in Tłuste and then left for Czortków.

In the fourth form I began to "do" Latin, which I found rather easy. I wasn't as fortunate, however, with my other subjects. I was on unusually good terms with the faculty. It gave me a certain pleasure to "put one over" on a teacher. This usually involved my wriggling out of a bad mark by persistently rehashing the same point. Sometimes, however, this didn't work.

At the time the subject I liked the most was history. However, I never prepared for class. I preferred reading an historical novel, or mythology, or even another textbook than the one we were studying in school. History interested me for the sake of knowledge itself, not as a subject being taught by my instructor. I didn't see the necessity of learning dates, nor did I like it. Our teacher couldn't convince me of the importance of mastering dates and certain categories of thought as prescribed in our textbook. He plied his profession in the age-old fashion by quizzing us on dates at random, in a disconnected way. It became apparent that I wasn't going to learn them and wasn't at all able to satisfy the teacher's demands. While my answers concerning the substance of what we were studying weren't too bad, my ability to memorize dozens of dates was poor.

The other subject in which I was mediocre was mathematics, which I positively loathed. I never did the practice exercises at home. As a result I failed the course, which came as a surprise to my parents. It was hard for them to accept that I had taken a turn for the worse after my temporary improvement in the third form. Meanwhile, an odd period in my life began. I scarcely gave any thought to my studies. Although I didn't waste time on frivolous pursuits with my friends, I didn't study. I preferred playing tennis for hours at a time or riding my bicycle. I had been interested in cycling for a long time, and I was gradually starting to master it. Next, I taught myself how to carve things from wood with a little handsaw. I made a whole series of items, each one prettier than the one before—picture frames, jewelry boxes, and so on—which I then happily gave to my parents as birthday gifts. I became progressively lazier; I read less and less, and I kept having ever stranger and more outrageous ideas.

For some time, we'd had religion classes in the afternoon. At the time we were studying Bałaban's history, with excerpts from the Bible. I wasn't studying Hebrew. When I was in primary school I could converse in Hebrew rather freely and read fluently, but I had since forgotten nearly all of it. I could follow the Hebrew text only with difficulty. This, perhaps, planted in me the seed of an unfortunate idea. I considered it unjust that we had to attend religion class, during what was usually our free time, so I presented my classmates with a plan for escaping these classes. Evidently a lot of them felt as I did, and so we agreed on a "scheme"—that is, we skipped the classes. This became a more and more frequent occurrence; it wasn't long before the secret was out and a scandal ensued. At one evaluation I failed religion, but I didn't take it too hard. On the contrary, at one of the next class sessions I continued to act very arrogantly toward the instructor. However, I soon came to my senses and realized that he was entirely in the right. I apologized to him, and the "peace of God" prevailed.

I didn't improve my marks in my other subjects, partly as a result of an illness that I contracted at the time. One Sunday—I remember the day, because my parents were visiting—I had severe headaches and couldn't get out of bed. The doctor finally determined that I was coming down with scarlet fever. Mother wouldn't hear of my staying in Czortków, and I returned home with my parents. The progress of the disease was mild; my swift recovery was helped by the radical treatment applied by my uncle, who is a doctor. On the second or third day of my illness he asked me whether I'd allow myself to be "pricked in the stomach." I figured that since I probably pricked myself many times unintentionally, why not allow it once on purpose, and if it mattered so much, it could even be in my stomach. My uncle quickly prepared a potent injection and abruptly thrust a huge needle into my stomach. This lasted several seconds, during which I screamed horribly. The pain was excruciating and persisted for quite a long time afterward. Evidently, this injection helped me; I got out of bed a few days later. I still had dizzy spells, but soon I no longer had to remain bedridden. The doctor ordered me to rest for six more weeks.

Mother, who sat next to my sickbed the entire time, struck up a conversation with me during my convalescence.

"Did you have any unpleasant thoughts?" she asked.

"Yes, as a matter of fact," I replied. "I didn't like having members of the household tiptoeing up to my room and looking at me with a strange mixture of pity and fear."

"Yes, you even told me to shut the door, because you didn't like the way they were hovering about you all the time. But didn't you ever think about what might happen?"

Not knowing what Mother was getting at, I asked her.

"Why, you could have died—God forbid! Did you ever stop to think about that?"

"No."

I really hadn't thought about it. As strongly attached to life as I was, I was somehow strangely confident that I would recover. I had often been feverish, but not delirious. I was aware that all was not in order, but I had no doubt that it would pass and I would soon be better. Nevertheless, I was greatly intrigued by the question my dear mother put to me. It dawned on me that my illness was more dangerous than I had supposed. However, I couldn't bring myself to accept this possibility. I felt that death would be premature. I didn't want to die. And I was sure that I had the advantage over that skeletal figure with scythe in hand, which is how I imagined death. I was sure of my strength and not afraid that I would die.

Toward the end of my convalescence one of my ears began to ache, and soon I felt some pain in the other one. It was a serious inflammation. I tried applications of hot sand; nothing helped. I lay for a long time in constant pain. Leeches were applied to me, which I found repulsive, and this left me feeling very tired. I couldn't lie still. My nerves were frayed, and I only exhausted myself even more. These experiences had a powerful effect on me. I became extremely nervous and impatient. I didn't want to think about my illness and tormented Mother with my whims. I was unbearably petulant. Despite all the efforts made to amuse me—and my parents and the rest of the household tried their best—I was constantly bitter and ill-tempered.

This lasted for a few weeks. Finally the pain ceased, and I began to return to normal. I was exhausted and looked terrible. I was still required to sit or lie down all day. Reading helped me to relax. I found Rolland's *Jean Christophe* especially interesting. Although I didn't understand everything, I was completely engrossed in the novel, and that in itself was wonderful.

My health was returning. I spent many long hours together with Mother. We would talk; sometimes Mother told me stories about different things that I found very intriguing. She talked to me about life, and then I would talk to her about everything. I was feeling better. I was happy to have someone who listened to me and who didn't make fun of my caprices and childish outbursts. I was glad that someone understood my immature thoughts. It heartened me to have a soulmate and friend—in short, to have a mother. I loved her even more fervently and powerfully than before.

This enforced idleness went on for more than two months. I returned to school resigned to the idea that the year was lost. I studied with a tutor to prepare for a make-up examination. I did little studying. I wouldn't exert myself, and I don't know why, but it just didn't matter to me whether or not I advanced to the next form. Recalling Jumek's experience, I preferred not to work at all. I reasoned that it was better to fail without studying than to do so after cramming. My marks didn't improve. As the end of the year approached, "conscience stirred within me," and I began to work more intensively. These efforts proved to be too little, too late. I failed! Calmly, I received the "verdict": I would have to repeat the year. I was resigned to the idea; besides, I didn't consider the loss of a year to be a setback, as I was "too young" by half a year as it was. Our homeroom teacher cheered me up by observing that my age would have barred me from taking the *matura* in any event. As a result, I wasn't upset. I was sorry about the money my parents had spent, but it couldn't be helped. Only Janek "stayed" with me. From then on we went through school together until we graduated.

During the summer vacation of 1927 my Viennese cousins came to visit Tłuste again. I also invited Jumek. We all had quite a fine time together. We took up playing cards, and it quickly became an obsession. We played for money. The differences in our abilities were actually slight, but our debts mounted out of control. They attained figures that were astronomical (for us). We started to write each other IOUs. Not one of us could pay up. The adults indulged our gambling habits, so we played more and more. Our only distraction was tennis. We made ourselves a tennis court on the estate that my uncle had leased, called Różanówka, and spent our afternoons there. During the harvest season we were all busy. We supervised the reapers or those working on the threshing floor.

It wasn't all that awkward to be thrown together with my "junior" colleagues as a result of having to repeat the fourth form, since thirty percent of the class was already made up of repeaters. We soon got to know one another. The coursework was no problem for me. History became my favorite class. I knew the material and always answered the questions. Soon I was recognized as one of the best history students, because I could expound on all the general topics, which sometimes made it difficult for those unfamiliar with the material. Mathematics now came to me easily, but I was not an outstanding student. At any rate, at the evaluation I was "in the clear."

While in the fourth form, I met Fryda, one of the girls who had just been admitted to the *gymnasium*. She was a cousin of Adzia, who had caught up with me along with the others. Fryda was a pretty girl. We began seeing each other. At the time, Jumek flirted with Adzia. As the two cousins lived together, we usually got together as a foursome.

I soon discovered that Fryda loved to make things up; she was a little "con-artist." I didn't care for this at all, so our relation was confined to seeing each other at school.

During the winter Jumek and I broke off these "amours." Our girlfriends perhaps regretted this even less than we did. At the time, they were starting to learn to dance. Their partners were older students, from the seventh and eighth forms. Naturally, they were much more impressive to the girls, who had high aspirations, but this didn't bother us.

In school we were discussing Ujejski's epic poem *Marathon*. I was very taken with Miltiades's speech. I was inspired to sit down and try to capture in verse our discussion of the speech. This was my first attempt at poetry. I showed it to my friends at school, and one of them, who was good at reciting, read it aloud. They were determined to show it to our Polish teacher, but I wouldn't allow this. I believe I got the idea to write the poem because I was constantly hearing our Polish teacher's own verses. I was trying to find out whether it was all that hard to write. I began to write more and more frequently, although there were stretches when I composed scarcely anything new at all. Some, if not all, of my verses I consider to be stillborn. In this respect, at least, they resemble the works of our instructor. At the same time, I began to read a great deal. Only now did I recognize the true value of books. I realized that one's native intelligence needs to be developed and educated. I also started to read newspapers on a regular basis. Of course, I didn't understand many political issues, as I lacked any kind of preparation. An older friend who lived with me at the Speisers' helped me with this.

Gradually, I became familiar with a number of issues. I read more and more, and new problems continually interested me. I saw how little I knew and how much there was that was splendid in both literature and current events. I was especially taken with poetry. I also found newspapers to be essential for knowing what was happening in the world and observing all the changes taking place in every avenue of life.

Despite these developments, I still occasionally had strange and disturbing ideas. I enjoyed challenging my professors in class or doing something other than what I was supposed to do. I was often rude to my friends. Worst of all, I fell into the habit of consuming enormous quantities of sweets. Since I didn't always have enough money, I opened an account at a store and charged my purchases. Each month I paid off a portion of the bill I had run up. It seemed to me, however, that the shopkeeper was routinely overcharging me and telling me that I owed him more than was actually due. My suspicions inspired a terrible idea: I decided to take revenge on the shopkeeper and crassly began stealing from him. At first my thefts were "modest"; I contented myself with a few chocolates. However, when I saw that I was getting away with it, I started to swipe better and better items. I completely ignored the principles that I had been so fervently taught. It didn't occur to me that I was, to put it bluntly, committing a crime. I rationalized my behavior to my conscience, which sometimes tormented me, by saying that, after all, "as things stand, he's charging me more than I owe him." I carried on this shameless practice for some time, until I had paid off the entire balance. I was never caught in the act, so evidently I was skillful at it. From the moment I had paid back everything I owed, I began taking only as many sweets as I could afford. I could no longer argue that my behavior was somehow excusable; I refrained from stealing further. Later on, when I considered the implications of what I had done, I thought of paying the shopkeeper for his losses. But I didn't do this, because I didn't want to own up to what I had done. From then on, however, I never touched anything that didn't belong to me. The notion that such behavior was unethical had little to do with it.

I was seized with another passion: collecting stamps. This cost me a lot of money, but at least I gained something in return. I became acquainted with geography, which gave me a certain satisfaction. I had already been collecting coins for some time. Aside from this, I was on a pretty even keel.

Once I was home for a school holiday and was playing cards with the adults. Grandmother kept kibitzing over my shoulder. I won most of the hands and donated a share of my winnings to the collection box for the Jewish National Fund. I was in high spirits. I amused everyone with quips and practical jokes. Sometimes I liked to distract the company with talk and then take advantage of their lack of attention and win the hand. Grandmother enjoyed this greatly, and we would join forces to hoodwink the others. Grandmother and I were in perfect harmony. Even though she was very advanced in years she read a great deal, and we often discussed the books we had both read. Grandmother had a sound memory and would tell me stories about various incidents in the lives of the hasidic miracle workers (such as the Baal Shem Tov) and about the prankster Hershele Ostropoler. She also described how people ought to live together, what their relations with one another should be like. She often reiterated how the happy life that my mother and father shared filled her with joy. In fact, I cannot recall that my parents ever quarreled seriously. My father is a very good man, and he knew how to get along well not only with my mother but also with her relatives, some of whom lived with us permanently. Despite the fact that the members of our family weren't always the easiest people to live with, there were no heated arguments among them.

I never played cards in Czortków. Instead, I played chess and checkers. Jumek and I competed with each other. We usually devoted our evenings to chess, unless we were reading something interesting together. Certain differences between us were becoming apparent. We bickered even over trivial matters. I was especially quarrelsome. It was only later that my friend told me he had provoked me deliberately. The year passed quickly, and I was promoted to the fifth form. I was very pleased that I had finally received a gold stripe to wear on the collar of my school uniform. I spent the summer vacation cheerfully and without a care, though I devoted considerably more time to reading.

At the time, Father and I traveled everywhere together. For the first time we went to an annual fair in some remote location. I was impressed by the sea of human heads, the thousands of horses and wagons. The terrible clamor and shouting drowned out the music of the barrel-organs and calliopes that could be heard at every few paces. There were a great number of merry-go-rounds whirling hundreds of jolly villagers through the air. Peddlers with husky voices hawked their wares. They tried to outshout one another and to sell their goods for less than their competitors. A few delivered their pitches in verse, repeating them over and over. With breathtaking speed and acumen the candy merchants apportioned the chocolates; they filled glasses with seltzer, warmed by the sun and full of dust, added some syrup (made from rose paper), and took the customers' money. The toy merchants kept replenishing their stock and, in the twinkling of an eye, disposed of assorted reed-pipes, lead figurines, toy pistols, balloons, etc. Everyone was hot and dusty, and they rushed, harried and distracted, from place to place. Only on the town square, where an exhibition of farm equipment had been set up, was it peaceful. People looked over everything and negotiated transactions calmly, albeit frequently. Cracking their whips and roaring, the horse dealers drove their "steeds" and "deluxe mares" the length and breadth of the marketplace. The farmers applauded all the while and then patted the horses. They haggled and made purchases. People bustled about, and everything merged into a terrible cacophony.

In the fifth form I played quite a lot of tennis; there was no one in the *gymnasium* who could equal me. After all, the other players were all my "students." Then I trained some partners for myself, and we held regular matches. I remained "tournament champion," which gave me a certain satisfaction. At the same time we organized bicycle races. Here, too, I was among the leaders. My bad leg didn't prevent me at all from pursuing sports. Only in soccer did my left leg prove weaker than my right one, so I gave up that sport. My friends knew how to swim and wanted to teach me, but I was afraid of the water. While I did go bathing in the river, I couldn't get up the nerve to swim. I was somewhat embarrassed about this, so one time I gave it a try. I sank to the bottom and swallowed a little water, but I kept on trying. I didn't want anyone to help me in the water. I learned the strokes and then started to swim. However, I didn't get the hang of it that year. Meanwhile, the weather turned bad and we stopped going to the riverside.

Some of the girls at school organized an old-fashioned name-day party. In exchange for buying some modest presents we were treated to a luxurious spread and several hours of fun. Fryda's name-day was in November. Evidently I still "felt something" for her. I bought her a large photo album and filled it with photographs of the film stars who were popular then. The girls teased me about this and made pointed remarks about my "sweetheart." While this annoyed me—because I actually did like Fryda better than the other girls—I didn't take the bait. Indeed it seemed to me that my female friends were speaking out of envy.

That year I stopped composing verses. I wrote only a few poems. In one, written during a visit home, I described scenes of *klaberjass,* which my father, my uncle, and a cousin were always playing at our house.

Another poem was less fortunate. I wrote it on the first page of my mathematics notebook. It was composed in a light and ironic tone. As luck would have it, one time the mathematics teacher noticed this poem; he asked me what it was, and I couldn't think of anything to say in reply. This was enough to make me loathe mathematics. I behaved foolishly, and it affected my grades. Once again, I received a mark of "incomplete" in this subject.

In the fifth form the headmaster taught us Polish. I truly gained a great deal from him. He knew how to conduct class wonderfully. I enjoyed his lectures and listened with rapt attention; instead of being dry, they were presented in a jovial and engaging manner. I didn't do well at the written work, as the headmaster tended to give either very high marks or very low ones, and I wasn't able to meet his standards.

At the Speisers' I shared lodgings that year with a certain Dr. Weinfeld, who was a very witty, wise, and virtuous person. We came to like each other very much. Even though I was some ten years his junior, he would talk with me for hours on end. He always listened to my, no doubt, not very interesting tales of school life. I addressed the doctor without using his title, saying only "*proszę pana*" [sir], which I shortened still further to "*pr-pana.*" This pleased the noble gentleman, who didn't mind my easy familiarity. Only once did he upbraid me, when I committed a breach of etiquette by saying, "You'd have busted a gut laughing." But this didn't prevent us from living together in complete harmony. I became so close and comfortable with him that once, for example, when he lay down on his bed (after a bath) at four o'clock in the afternoon, I also stretched out on my own bed. We slept in the same room. I even recall that on this occasion we talked about the Yellow Peril.

Dr. Weinfeld advised me to write about whatever came into my head for my school assignments. I thought that surely this would result in some terribly stupid things. But to my surprise, when I once complied with his advice, I received a good mark. So I continued to follow this recommendation and wrote better and better compositions.

I studied with two friends who belonged to the recently founded Betar. Symek, meanwhile, had quit Hashomer Hatsa'ir and became one of the founders of Betar. I found it astonishing but didn't dwell on how it was possible to change one's convictions so easily. Hersch and Milo (they were the friends with whom I studied) told me about the new organization's scouting activities and urged me to join. I wanted to be consistent, so I told them "no," as I had done in the past. They asked me whether I was a Zionist. Of course I was, I replied, but I didn't want to join the group. The real reason I wouldn't join any organizations in those days was that it was against the "regulations." Later on, I became somewhat annoyed by the school's regulations. Eventually, I resolved to become active in a political movement once I had my own convictions.

At the age of fifteen, however, I chafed under the various prohibitions that restricted our private lives, such as the one just mentioned, or the ban on going to the cinema and the theater, and so on. The main reason that I didn't join any political organization at the time was because I considered the possible consequences, and I didn't want to cause any unpleasantness for my parents. Another reason was that my friends' arguments were unpersuasive. I became particularly incensed when they told me that it was fun to be in the organization, because there were girls there. I thought that if I joined a group, it wouldn't be for the girls or the amusements, but so that I might attend a lecture or do some political work of my own.

I said as much to my friends. They tried to think of a response and wound up making fun of me. But I had the great satisfaction of knowing that two of my friends, Dr. Weinfeld and Jumek, thought I was right. The doctor advised us not to be in any hurry to sign up anywhere at all. Instead, he recommended various books to us and encouraged us to educate ourselves.

In spite of everything, I sensed that something was missing from my life. I didn't realize that the very thing I needed was some sort of educational organization. I was embarrassed that I wasn't well-versed in Jewish literature. I didn't know how to write in Yiddish. I would gladly have expressed my thoughts in Yiddish, or even in Hebrew. But what of it? After all, I could speak and read Yiddish fluently—I just couldn't set my thoughts down on paper. To this day I write Yiddish with difficulty. (This is also why I am writing my autobiography in Polish.) Moreover, I had no intellectual discipline; I lacked the mental rigor that Talmudic scholarship provides. This, perhaps, is the source of certain difficulties that I had, especially when I was younger, in mastering some subjects, such as mathematics.

At this time there was a whole array of clubs in our *gymnasium*. I joined the history club. The activities were enjoyable: there were frequent lectures, and I learned a great deal from them. Once I gave a talk myself, after which there was a lively discussion. I spoke about the significance of geographical discoveries. During the discussion, the older students filled in some of the gaps in my report, and then our sponsor, the history professor, brought everything together and provided a proper analysis. These meetings took place weekly, and they broadened our knowledge.

Then there was the sculpture and painting club. I participated in this, too, but only in the sculpture section. I didn't know how to paint, and drawing no longer held any interest for me. In the third form I had been quite fond of drawing but had no talent for it, so I gave it up and now only made things with a fretsaw.

Our headmaster proposed that we elect a student council this year. The elections took place in an atmosphere of great excitement and resulted in the establishment of the *gymnasium*'s first student council. The other classes followed our example, but, on the whole, this student government enjoyed very limited powers and didn't function very effectively. Toward the end of the year, during a slide-show about ancient Rome and Greece, our homeroom teacher, the Latin instructor, asked me whether I'd like to orga-nize an excursion. I was surprised that he asked me, but naturally I agreed. Later on I realized that I had been asked because the route of the trip went across our farm. I got my parents to agree to this and, after obtaining the headmaster's approval, helped put the plan into effect. One group of boys, I among them, set out on bicycles; the others went on foot. The *gymnasium* was still "segregated"; the girls attended separate classes. As I knew the farm roads, I wanted to take the cyclists by a shortcut. However, I couldn't orient myself properly, and we got a little bit lost, but we reached our destination by evening.

Father had sent some wagons to meet my friends. Even so, our instructor showed up with all the "underclassmen" only late in the evening. My mother plied everyone (some thirty boys) with excellent beverages: cold borsht, sour milk, and regular milk, plus a great variety of other things. We refreshed ourselves, and then we devoured huge quantities of bread, meat, and the like. It was a warm, beautiful night, so we sauntered about on the roads and fields and didn't turn in until midnight. We slept in the barn. After a few hours' sleep and an ample breakfast, we traveled by wagon to Czerwonogród. It was quite fine and jolly. Gales of laughter roared from one wagon to another. The jokes, all more or less crude, went on nonstop; there was continuous singing almost the whole way. We felt free, even in the presence of our instructor. At Czerwonogród we pitched camp in a meadow next to a waterfall, the highest (at sixteen meters) in Małopolska. We bathed in the frigid water that cascaded down. After fooling around a bit we headed to nearby Uścieczko. We visited the grotto of a hermit who had carved a bed for himself out of rock in the middle of the forest. The hermit had died long ago, but the bed still remained. After a few hours we went back to the farm. Worn out by the day's activities, we were in no condition to fool around and went straight to bed. The next day, after taking a group photograph with my parents on the farm, we caught the train back to Czortków.

This excursion left me with very fond memories. The atmosphere was excellent, and all of my friends thanked me later. I believe they also appreciated the spread my mother had provided. The student council composed a letter of thanks and sent it to my parents; to this day it remains a cherished memento for me. A few days after the excursion our final grades were distributed.

I spent the first month of summer vacation in nearby Zaleszczyki, which at the time had become a well-promoted, if not famous, summer resort. Once, it had been a real backwater, not much bigger than Tłuste. However, the Dniester flows through Zaleszczyki, and this was the main reason, I believe, that the town was touted as the "Polish Riviera." It is true that the summers are warmer here than they are, say, in Warsaw, because Zaleszczyki is situated in a gorge on the Dniester.

I was in fine spirits. I went to the beach every day and basked in the sun until I was bronze. I made great progress with my swimming. Meanwhile I made several new acquaintances. However, I had one failing, or, rather, deficiency: I couldn't dance. Still, I always accompanied my "girlfriend" when she went dancing. She was a charming young blonde, rather intelligent and thoughtful. We were constantly in each other's company, having met in the guest house where we were both staying. After a few days we got along famously. Although I was fond of her, I regarded this "relationship" casually, as a summer romance. We played tennis, went swimming together—in short, we were inseparable. This young lady wanted to teach me to dance, but I demurred, because I had no faith in my ability to master this art, what with my weak leg. So I limited myself to observing her exceedingly graceful movements. Then, after spending time at the dance, we returned home together.

It was a marvelous summer night. A starry sky, and the full moon seemed to be smiling at us (at such times a person becomes a romantic). We snuggled together and walked along the riverbank. Barely making a sound, our feet sank in the sand. The Dniester reflected the moonlit night in its waves. We remained silent. All we could hear was the soft murmur of the peaceful water. I was "happy"—that is, very contented. So, I imagine, was my companion. She threw her arms around me; we kissed as we never had done before. When we got back to the boarding house I escorted her to her door. I wanted to leave—but I didn't, couldn't. I felt a strange thrill. My alluring girl held onto my hand as I was saying goodbye—and I entered her room. Then I learned what sensuality is, what "love" is. The next day we felt awkward at first, but fresh, passionate kisses repaired our mood. Life went on cheerfully. She was beautiful and exquisite. At this time I experienced many pleasurable and "intoxicating" moments.

I spent the final weeks of summer vacation immersed in books. I couldn't stand the company of my cousins with their endless card games. I was in somewhat of a reverie, although the correspondence with my summer "sweetheart" didn't last long. All the same, I felt a little lonely and dwelt on my memories. These were splendid, and the actual experiences I recalled even more so. My summertime friends were surprised when I kept my distance from them. They teased me—I must be in love. I didn't deny it, even though I assumed, or had an inkling, that I wouldn't see my "seductress" again and that this wasn't true love.

At the beginning of the sixth form I took part in an excursion, organized by our *gymnasium*, to the Universal National Exposition in Poznań. The first stop on the trip was Lwów. We visited several museums, took snapshots in front of some monuments, and continued on our way by the evening train.

While we were still in "our" Galicia, we had the coaches to ourselves. After Lwów, though, our quarters were more cramped, and so we got little sleep. The next day we toured the monuments of Cracow: the Wawel, St. Mary's Church, the Sukiennice, more museums, collections, paintings—we saw new paintings all the time. In the afternoon we took an excursion to Wieliczka. I liked the salt mine there very much, especially the lake that is illuminated from within, the Chapel of St. Kinga, etc. I was just as interested in the technique for extracting the salt. The atmosphere there was pleasant and somewhat solemn. People spoke in hushed tones. It was impressive to be some 300 meters below the earth's surface, where I lived, and to become acquainted with the marvelous riches inside the earth.

In the evening we continued on our way. It was crowded and rather chilly in the unheated "Prussian" cars. We traveled through Silesia. We couldn't even stretch out, due to the lack of space. We formed "mixed doubles": groups of two girls and two boys. Taking turns leaning against each other, we dozed or talked. One girl sang. The cozy, delightful mood was broken only by frequent stops along the dense string of stations in Silesia. The ever-present lights of the towns reflected our high spirits. Glimmering in the night, they harmonized with our sentimental songs. We didn't sleep but simply reclined against each other, lost in reveries. It was a lovely, wonderful moment in our lives. Young as we were, we were transported by bright and lofty hopes. We believed that the world was not evil.

Finally we arrived in Poznań. The cleanliness of the city impressed me right away. We became so engrossed in the exposition that we ate almost nothing the entire day. That night we stayed in a school along with another excursion group. At five o'clock in the morning I heard a shriek from one of my friends. I jumped up. A thief had crept in among us. The culprit got away. I began checking to see whether anything of mine was missing. I had my money. No one had lost anything. The only thing stolen was my brand-new coat. I was furious and upset because it was a very expensive trench coat, only recently purchased. I didn't carry on about it, though—I knew it wouldn't do me any good. We continued on with our tour of the fair. We went on many of the rides at the amusement park. The roller coaster made the greatest impression on me. I deliberately sat in the front seat. I wanted to experience the full gamut of emotions. The steepest plunges took my breath away. I had the sensation that I was flying into an abyss. I went on the ride several times, until I lost the thrill of the colossal speed and the sensation of the bottom falling out as we plunged downward.

I greatly enjoyed the horticultural hall, the pavilions of machinery, air travel, railways, automobiles, etc. After staying three days in Poznań, we left for Warsaw. We saw Łazienki Park, the Castle (I saw Branicki's tapestry, which the government had just acquired), the Poniatowski and Kierbedź Bridges. I was staggered by the traffic, for example, on the Marszałkowska. Fatigued from walking and the constant lack of sleep, I was glad to be able to rest a bit in Saski Park. However, I was cold and couldn't sleep. Later, leaning up against Janek and wrapped in his coat, I dozed as we walked. That was the only time I ever experienced first-hand the ability to sleep on one's feet. After a quarter of an hour I felt significantly better. I was reinvigorated.

In the evening we crammed into the sleeping compartments two hours before our departure. Our money was almost all gone, thanks to our group leader's careless management. We gradually became tormented by hunger. Exhausted, we fell asleep and only woke up in Lwów, where we spent our last groszy on a few rolls. This was all we had to eat until we reached Czortków. After a week of travel I would have gladly gone even further, despite the fatigue, the cold, and the lack of food.

During the excursion I didn't dwell on anything in particular; I looked and marveled at everything. I took stock of previously unfamiliar cities, museums, natural resources, and manufactured goods, and I enjoyed everything thoroughly. Only on later reflection did I come to the conclusion that I had very little to show for this excursion. I got confused about what I had seen where. We made the mistake of visiting so many museums in such a short time that I couldn't remember the details. Only a few things stuck in my memory: "The Battle of Racławice" in Lwów, the salt mine, and the exposition itself. The buildings and bridges didn't count, since I was already familiar with them from pictures. I felt that the tour was conducted in an unplanned and senseless manner. To be sure, I had many pleasant impressions and memories, but I derived little actual benefit.

I got through the sixth form without a hitch. At this time, relations with our Catholic classmates began to sour, echoing what was taking place in the universities. The fact is, we avoided the Catholics. Though the two groups were on speaking terms with each other and kept up appearances, the atmosphere was tense. Our mutual dislike was obvious; on the Catholics' side, it was further reinforced by the anti-Semitism of the priests who taught classes in religion. It was clear that any improvement in our relations with the rest of society would require a rational program of education, starting in the earliest years. Now it was, perhaps, already too late. After all, education (even when it is provided) is no substitute for culture, for building something from the ground up. Assimilation cannot be the solution to the problem, since there are certain essential differences in the way that we and the Catholics live, which make assimilation impossible. In this case, it would be a diminution of one's own worth. On the other hand, this doesn't preclude peaceful coexistence in the schools. It is entirely possible that the two sides could come to an understanding. All that is required is to take little things into account, beginning in childhood. This is important, because from such little things it is possible, over time, to establish good relations between Jew and Catholic. Indeed, it is the teachers' task to direct young people toward the path of genuine mutual understanding, the path of coexistence, in the spirit of concord and tolerance. Yet this is what we lacked. Thus, I wasn't surprised when at times things escalated to the point of malicious conflicts and dissension, as this was the consequence of our educational system.

That year our *gymnasium* became a coeducational school. Thirteen girls joined our class, and among them were only two Catholics. The proportion of Jews rose to fifty percent, which may also have annoyed the Aryans.

Even though this new element entered our lives, little changed. We merely became more circumspect in our choice of words and profanities. Otherwise, we treated our female colleagues as regular classmates. I was on friendly terms with most of them and paid "due respect" to the rest. But after a short time there were only three that I still addressed formally. As far as studies were concerned, although many of the girls were "honor-roll students" and some of the others were also highly regarded, their answers in class were far from the best. In contrast, the boys displayed greater intelligence, reasoned more easily, and were quicker than the girls. When it came to memorization, however, the girls usually did better, as they were considerably more diligent than we were.

There was no rivalry; in this respect, the boys exhibited little ambition. And if it is universally believed that coeducation is beneficial, because the girls' industriousness somehow stimulates the boys to redouble their efforts, then I must beg to differ. I am not generalizing; I base this on the example of our class. It seems to me that, under our influence, the girls started to work less. We were more cunning. By means of lies, evasions, and tom-foolery, we usually managed to bluff the teachers. We dissembled so skill-fully that often our instructors didn't catch on. This impressed the girls and encouraged them to behave similarly. More than once they told us quite openly that it wasn't worth their while to study, since without doing a thing we could answer in class all the same. But the path of the con-artist is a slippery one. It requires a lot of skill and self-control to be able to wriggle out of working hard without slipping up. And practice was just what our female classmates lacked, so they didn't always succeed in faking their way through class. Thus, they were constantly obliged to fall back on tedious and exhausting study. At any rate, the professors complained that the girls had been influenced by us, and that the level of the whole class had fallen as a result. No one took this too hard, though, and I couldn't have cared less. I studied just enough to keep from constantly falling flat on my face, doing whatever was most urgent. Mathematics was the only subject that I neglected. I cribbed the assignments from my friends and never was any good at this demanding subject, which I found repulsive.

My relations with girls outside of school were limited to playing tennis on occasion with Adzia and Lalka, and sometimes visiting Lalka at her home. Once again, it was a place where boys and girls got together. We had a pretty good time. We would talk about the movies or the theater, which we attended despite the ban in our school and its curfew rules. Politics had no appeal at all for our female classmates, so we avoided it, unless there were only boys present. At this time the girls all quit the Revisionist Zionist organization, after having been members for just under a year. I never knew their reason for doing so. I was only glad that I had never let myself be dragged into Betar, especially since I had slowly begun to work out my own political views. At the time I felt more and more that I ought to join a suitable youth movement, one that provided its members with an appropriate setting. However, I had been compelled at an early age to choose my own companions, guided by intuition. Perhaps this is why I was better able to get my bearings—in this respect, I created my own independence—in choosing the friends and associates I have lived with and live with now. By not belonging to any youth movement I may have developed on my own a kind of instinct for picking friends, and my individuality may have taken shape more naturally. As a result, however, I came to loathe strict forms of social organization—or, rather, strict obedience in society, conformity. This isn't always healthy in the life of a group, for it must be based on organization and discipline. While society requires people who are free, it shouldn't tolerate complete individualism. A certain degree of discipline is necessary for the masses. And who knows, perhaps the curfew rules in our school served, in part, to curb this very exuberance in the development of our personalities. Still, the system had its defects. I simply couldn't stand it. Many times I felt like a criminal or, at the very least, like the victim of senseless and cruel rules. Since the professors couldn't control us by themselves, they enlisted the help of the older students. An odious network of spies and informers developed (whose identities were so well concealed that I was never sure who performed this function). They repeatedly pried into our personal affairs, and this came as a shock to me. After all, you can't go around spying on young people. On one hand, I found this very depressing, and it induced a kind of persecution mania in some of the students. On the other hand, I was intrigued and attracted by whatever was forbidden. For example, I took up smoking for a while because I found it enjoyable, but when I graduated and didn't have to do it on the sly, I gave it up completely. Smoking lost all its appeal for me, and I don't miss it at all now.

When I was in the sixth form, our *gymnasium* organized a public program, to which other schools were invited. Students from nearby Trembowla paid us the honor of a visit. I got to know the young people from there who were our age, but they didn't make a very good impression on me. We performed *Antigone*, which everyone enjoyed.

Professor Ryszard Ganszyniec, of the University of Lwów, was also present, and he expressed genuine admiration for the acting of our amateur performers, as well as for the music and our chorus. (I didn't participate, even in the orchestra, though sometimes I played the side-drum. I have no talent as a performer.)

A short time later the *gymnasium* in Trembowla organized a jubilee celebration in honor of Kochanowski, and we paid them a visit in return. It was a very pleasant trip. Everyone went by train except Wilo and me, who rode our bicycles. In Trembowla I met several very attractive girls. We returned home with our hearts in thrall; Jumek, who also came with us, was struck by the "arrow" of one winsome girl his own age, while I had "captured the affections" of one of the older girls. She and I started to correspond, and that was the extent of our acquaintance. But as I was unable to content myself with this, I became friendly with Marysia, a Catholic girl in Czortków, who was two years younger than me. She was a very pretty and well-developed girl.

At this time I was moved once again to write poetry. Marysia was the first to read these "works" of mine. During the winter we went ice-skating and on sleigh rides. While she was an excellent student, she wasn't long on brains. I also realized that going out with her made no sense, since sooner or later people would start to talk. Then Marysia would express some unflattering opinion of me in front of her friends, because it wouldn't be to her advantage to have a Jew for a close friend. And so, although I never felt that there was anything peculiar or coarse about the way she treated me, I was ill at ease in her company. I wasn't free in my choice of topics of conversation, and I often had to watch what I said. So I decided it was better to give up these encounters (which were quite innocent, by the way). By the end of the year this close friendship had completely faded away.

During the summer vacation of 1930 a sports club, Maccabi, was established in Tłuste. They announced a bicycle race. As I was proficient at middle distances, I decided to take part in the competition. I trained together with my neighbor, Munio; it was cycling that had brought us together. Munio had been riding longer than I and was one of the people who had shown me the tricks of riding. I soon surpassed my mentor, and we now trained together. I adhered to a very regular routine, tackling several kilometers a day with Munio.

There were about a dozen entrants in the race, which covered a twenty-five-kilometer route from Tłuste to Zaleszczyki. While we both had a chance to come in first, anything could happen. During training, I usually had better times than Munio. Two days before the race, I arranged to have my heavy iron bicycle overhauled. The mechanic, however, returned it the next day with a completely unusable wheel. It so happened that I saw one of my competitors in his shop; I suspected a "fix." I started to disassemble the bike, but I was so upset that I couldn't get it back together again, even with my brother's help. I gave up and went to bed. On the day of the race I woke up an hour before the starting time and told my brother that I wanted to ride after all. Józek tried to talk me out of it. My parents had no idea what was happening. I went downtown to a shop that belonged to a friend of mine and borrowed a complete rear wheel. I assembled the bike as fast as I could and rode to the starting line. Our pair was fourth. When I was supposed to go, I noticed that one tire was flat; my inner-tube was punctured. I requested a ten-minute delay of the start. I quickly had the tube replaced; I was unable to help mount the wheel or inflate the tire. Fuming with exasperation, I just stood there and watched.

Finally I was ready, and we set off eight minutes behind the last pair. Munio immediately moved ahead of me. Soon he had left me far behind. Eventually, I could no longer see him. He was two or three kilometers in front of me. At the half-way point, I was ready to turn around. Then I heard an auto horn. I realized that in the dust Munio would have to slow down, because he didn't have any eyeglasses. I put on my glasses, and then it was as if I got a second wind. I began to go all out. The wind slowed me down somewhat, but in spite of that I spotted the silhouettes of several cyclists. I caught up with Munio and together we started to pass the others. At last: the finish line. I knew that one of us would come in first; since we passed the cyclists who had started before us, we had made up quite a lot of time. It was only a question of who was going to be the actual winner.

The final stretch ran downhill and then around a curve. I streaked along with dizzying speed for a bicycle. I was even with Munio and just about to pass him, when he cut me off at the curve, and I had to brake to keep from falling. With this not very sporting maneuver, my rival took first place. All the same, I wasn't angry with him; after the trouble I'd had before the race, I was content with second place. The race gave me a great deal of satisfaction; it convinced me that persistence is important not only in sports, but in life in general. From then on, I never let myself be discouraged by momentary setbacks.

After a summer vacation like the others, the new school year commenced. I resolved to make a "good name" for myself at school. I was determined to study and read more. To tell the truth, I wasn't interested so much in my reputation as I was in making good progress academically. I had heard that in order to get into the university one's final marks for the seventh and eighth forms were taken into consideration along with one's diploma.

Moreover, I had a mixed reputation. During all my years at the *gymnasium* I had been free and easy and cheerful. While I couldn't be counted among the so-called polite and respectable students, I was, nevertheless, clever and cool-headed enough to keep the faculty from catching on to me.

It wasn't hard to achieve a good ranking. We were taught French by an elderly priest. He was an inveterate drunkard, but a good man. He taught us hardly anything in six whole years. His course not only required no preparation on our part but even made it possible for us to do some of the work for our other courses during the class session. Our written assignments in French consisted of taking home the topics and then rewriting what we had prepared in class.

Latin was a different story. I was better at it than I was at French, but we copied the written assignments from crib sheets. Thanks to the excursion I had organized with the Latin teacher, I was somewhat in his good graces. And since Janek sat next to me, this "royal favor" was extended to him as well. Although we were called on frequently, we always recited with ease. Our professor didn't ask us to recite from memory, though, because he knew that we could never do this. Thus, I was in "good standing" in these subjects.

Mathematics, as usual, was my downfall. Even so, I found physics intriguing (thanks to the professor, who was a gifted and skillful lecturer), and I had no trouble acquiring a good record. In several other subjects I maintained my tradition of good grades.

History was worse. The previous instructor had left the school and "bequeathed" me a good mark. His replacement was, in comparison, an ignoramus, and this put me off from the subject. The new teacher couldn't lecture at all or lectured the same way we answered in class: he "faked it." In addition, he was extremely conceited and loud, incapable of impressing us with his knowledge of life, much less his erudition. He had only two merits: he was handsome and extremely loyal. All the other professors sized him up right away. At every opportunity he demonstrated his loyalty to the current regime in Poland with bombastic speeches full of lofty but vacuous phrases. Aside from this, I have the impression that his memory was exceedingly short. One time, for example, at a conference with my parents, he said that I was doing very well, but then he gave me a mark of "satisfactory." So I wasn't in such good standing in history. However, this didn't worry me much, and I kept on working as usual at the meetings of the history club.

While I was in the seventh form I gave my first lessons. There was a great demand at the time for tutors, so I could take on students without competing with my friends. With the money I earned (which I found immensely gratifying), I bought myself some shoes. It was very satisfying not to have to borrow money from my parents, and I was pleased to be able to earn something on my own as well.

My social life was confined increasingly to a circle of Jewish boys and girls, together with a select few Catholics. My friends and I met frequently at Janek's home. We talked about different things, often about our political convictions. We never quarreled, however, since no one had any fixed opinions. On one such occasion I told Jumek that I was a Zionist and a socialist. This surprised him; he scoffed and told me he couldn't imagine me as a socialist. I tried to prove to him that although my parents were rather well off and I had some money and wanted a lot of things, it still didn't mean that I was completely happy. Besides, I don't believe that only poor people should be socialists. Although, to be sure, I haven't experienced what a truly destitute and hungry person must feel, I understand it nonetheless. This is why it is my duty help the "downtrodden." Since this can be brought about only by transforming the general way of thinking and living, I will help indirectly, and perhaps directly, by working together with other like-minded persons. Moreover, I think that people have a duty to strive to create better forms of social life. I believe that the socialist agenda will ultimately lead to the birth of a new way of life, based on justice, freeing all social groups from oppression. This is why I am a socialist. Now, socialism in no way conflicts with Zionism, but I was still too unsure of myself in these matters to be able to convince Jumek. I noticed at the time that the boys who didn't attend school were a lot more astute about certain political questions, particularly those concerning Zionism, than were those of us who were getting an education. I perceived this as the politicization of young people, but I didn't see what was healthy and valuable about this development.

Two friends, Kuba and Charlie, always entertained us with their impressions of Lopek Krukowski and Charlie Chaplin, or with their own improvisations and jokes. We often smoked at Janek's. I didn't inhale, so I couldn't get used to it and smoked only to be "sociable." This bothered my friends, who said I was just wasting cigarettes. My friends also started drinking at every occasion, real or invented. Evidently this fad started with the Catholics, but a certain number of my Jewish friends didn't want to lag behind them.

In the winter, I started to take dancing lessons. I decided that I would finally learn how to cut a rug, and so I took my first steps on the parquet. At the dancing classes I was attracted to a certain girl. She was very good-looking, although she had red hair. I was teased about my Titianesque taste, but it didn't bother me. Besides, our friendship began and ended with the dancing classes and my escorting her home. At the end of the course, the class put on an impressive ensemble performance. We had a terrific time. I received my first cotillion favors on this occasion, and though I was neither impressed nor flattered, I kept them as souvenirs.

Both Charlie's name-day and mine fell in February. We decided to hold a drinking party, which took place in secret, because this was against the rules. We celebrated with an intimate group of friends for several hours. This was the first time I ever tried to get drunk. I consumed an enormous amount of liqueur and a little vodka, and still I was totally alert—just extremely pale. I learned that alcohol neither warms you nor raises your spirits. Since then I haven't drunk at all, except for wine and beer on occasion. I consider it pointless to get drunk. That party left me only with a distaste for drinking.

During this "merry carnival" I began to feel something. My subconscious told me that it was love. Despite the fact that I made translations, for example, from Virgil, wrote parodies of Mickiewicz, and occasionally proclaimed skeptical opinions, I found myself "in love."

I had always liked Adzia. Yet as long as I had known her, I had never really gotten to know her. She was very kind and rather clever but—when you get right down to it—not an intellectual. She was cheerful but on the noisy side. She had many charms as well as faults. I didn't see them but fell head over heels for "the whole person." At first I kept this to myself. I didn't say anything to Adzia, and she didn't suspect anything, either. Then I wrote some poems with her in mind. I was evidently over-sensitive. I would turn her most innocuous remark into a tragedy, despite the fact that Adzia couldn't have an inkling of my state of mind. On her name-day I gave her a poem. Later, when I had my first date with her, she intimated that she was fond of me, too. I was in a daze.

My first real love affair had begun. I lived in a world of constant daydreams. I ran wild with her slightest remark and fretted about everything that didn't fit in with my fantastic plans. During this year's school excursion (to my parents' farm again) girls came along as well, including Adzia. She was completely at ease, while I behaved very stupidly, to be sure. I didn't speak with her very much. It was as though I was afraid to go up to her and touch her, lest she vanish like an apparition. At the end of the year the whole school went on another excursion to the forest near Czortków. Some alumni also came along, including Wilo, who was regularly on the school grounds.

Apparently he, too, was in love with Adzia, but not the way I was. During the games Adzia paid more attention to him than to me, which upset me terribly. On the way back to Czortków I walked with Fryda, with whom I always got on well. We talked the whole time. As I reflect on this more soberly, my behavior seems more incomprehensible. I took it into my head that no one understood me, and I felt sad. Later, when I spoke to Adzia, she reproached me for walking with Fryda. Once again, I was in despair.

Then the time came for us to part. Until now it had been enough for me to see Adzia each day. During vacation I was far away from her. This only made my love for her grow more intense. I became engrossed in reading the works of lyric poets. I thought of her with a capital L (for Love) and wrote more and more poetry. I read a great deal, met some new people, and had a splendid time, yet I daydreamed about Adzia constantly. The longer I was away from her the more I missed her, and at the same time the more I felt in my bones that this love was not mutual. As a result, I was glum and miserable.

Of all the people around me, only Mother realized I was going through something that was bothering me and making me depressed. After all, I looked terrible and was quieter than usual. (I am a talkative person.) Despite these symptoms, Mother never asked me any questions; she intuited what was going on and perhaps didn't want to pry into my love affairs, knowing that I wouldn't divulge my feelings. At the time I cared more deeply than ever for Mother. On the whole my love for her became even stronger during the period of my love for Adzia. I also rewarded Mother with a poem for her name-day. At any event, I was more certain that my feelings were reciprocated where Mother was concerned, and affection also had a lot to do with it.

I didn't correspond with Adzia, so I was all the happier to see her again. We began to see each other quite often. And yet, when I talked with Adzia, I changed, I grew timid. I felt happy, but at the same time I wasn't entirely at ease. With all the other girls I had been attracted to up to now, I had behaved otherwise. But I simply adored Adzia. I held her in such high esteem that she seemed to me to embody an ideal, and everything she did was beautiful and good. I treated this love affair with utter seriousness. I didn't keep anything back. I was sincere and open. This attitude quickly degenerated into a sickly, romantic love that held me in its relentless thrall.

Seeing that my love went unrequited, however, I began to let go of her, despite my initial ardor. By the same token, I waxed lugubrious over my dashed hopes. I had moments of tranquility, but also moments of turbulence. Yet I didn't cease to believe in the "kinship of souls" or the idea that our souls were inseparable. I constantly deluded myself with the hope that nothing could undo our love. My feeling didn't grow cold, it merely changed into one of friendship, which I confided to Adzia in a flush of sentimentalism. At the same time, my love was bound up with a whole complex of beliefs and aspirations. I loved Adzia so much it was hard for me to accept that I had to remain simply her friend. I couldn't imagine life without her.

It seemed to me I would never again be able to care for any other woman, and that was why I kept experiencing this powerful feeling of love, which wouldn't allow me to share my beloved with anyone. I felt that I had the right to expect Adzia, as my future life-companion, to care only for me.

I knew that Adzia was close to Wilo—only in a platonic sense, of course—and so I was assailed by continual doubts. Eventually, I resolved to settle the matter once and for all. I told Adzia everything that was on my mind, to which she replied—quite sensibly, I should add—that we were still too young to take love so seriously. I felt that this was actually the case, and that I myself couldn't really sort things out for the time being.

I decided to ask Mother what she thought about this and went to Tłuste. At home I pretended to be sick, and the following day I revealed everything to the person who understood me best in all the world. Mother was sympathetic and said that while she didn't want to hinder me in anything, she thought that I shouldn't commit myself forever to anyone just yet. Although she realized that first love was powerful and—so it seemed—eternal, she advised me to get to know the world and life first. My mother's understanding of me and her calm advice filled my heart with such immense gratitude and affection that she became even more precious to me than before. I loved and respected her more than anyone else on earth.

I went back to Czortków. I continued to see Adzia, until one day she told me that she didn't want me wasting so much time on her; I should get down to my studies, because graduation was imminent (this was two months before the examination). And, in fact, we stopped seeing each other. I soon went home for the Easter break, anyway. There were still many times when I felt pangs of bitterness. When I returned, Adzia suggested that she would be neither mine nor his (that is, Wilo's), since she didn't know which one she loved more. From then on we didn't see each other at all outside of school.

I set down to work with determination. I had begun the eighth form with the firm intention of passing the *matura*. My love affair had taken up a lot of time; my literary "output" had grown as a result of it, but this had nothing to do with my studies. Jumek became my friend. Hitherto we had lived alongside each other; now we lived with each other. I told him everything, and the poor fellow had to listen to all of my trials and tribulations. He advised me how to act, but I never listened to him and followed the dictates of my irrational emotions. I also got along well with Milo, who was a versifier, like me.

Immediately after my first evaluation I decided on the subjects in which I would be examined. It would be Latin, Polish, and physics for the written exam; I intended to take a oral exam only in history and—in the event that my written exam wasn't successful—in another one of the natural sciences. Meanwhile, I worked hard enough to maintain the "good progress" I had already achieved in the seventh form. We got a new French professor, a woman. The Doctor (she had an advanced degree) wanted to get tough with us, but at the very first class she broke down. Our class was a bit bewildered, so we held a meeting to figure out what to do. I proposed that we tell our new instructor quite candidly that we didn't know anything. My suggestion was adopted, but no one was willing to do the honors. This being the case, I mustered up the requisite courage and, when Madame Doctor began speaking to us in French and we sat there mute, I stood up and suggested to her that we talk in Polish, otherwise "a major misunderstanding would likely ensue." Compelled to play my part to the end, I stated that we wouldn't write compositions, since we hadn't done so previously. The instructor was furious, but she was at a loss. My classmates giggled quietly to themselves, as this conversation was very comical.

A war broke out between our class and the French teacher (who was, by the way, a very pretty young woman). We emerged victorious, because the headmaster was very fond of our class. The French lessons were trimmed down so that it was mainly the Jewish students who were called on, as we were the only ones capable of saying much of anything. We also got a new professor for Polish, a dignified and even-tempered man. As for his views, we had the feeling that he was an Endek, although he never disclosed anything about himself to us.

By now our Catholic classmates had all but openly adopted the ideology of the rightwing hoodlums who were on the loose in Lwów at the time. However, they treated us with the same civility that we showed them. Then, an explosion occurred during one of our discussions of a report. We were discussing the Jewish question. The author of the paper and the discussion panelists, most of whom were Jews, emphasized that assimilation of the Jews was impossible and offered no solution to the Jewish problem. However, they argued, as Poles and Jews lived side by side, they should at least get to know each other better. The Poles were under a special obligation to take an interest in us, as this hadn't been the case so far. While the Jews were acquainted with the majority national culture from many angles, because of their circumstances, the Poles were indifferent to our problems and to our spiritual, cultural, and political life. To overcome this, the Polish community ought to take the initiative by getting to know the Jews and demonstrating an interest in us. During the discussion, one of the "greens," as we called the Endeks, openly stated that the only way to deal with us was to wield a club. This provoked a series of protests from us and from the one Ukrainian in the class. The discussion grew more and more intense and heated. If it hadn't been for the recess bell, I don't know whether it would have stopped at words.

During the recess, the argument continued in small groups. I was in one of these groups. When I saw that I couldn't hope to get through to our Polish classmates, thanks to their obstinacy and utterly non-intellectual narrow-mindedness, I shouted sarcastically, "Go ahead and beat the Jews, then." This upset our youthful heroes; it hit home and silenced them. We broke off the discussion, even though we had proved our absolute superiority to these poorly educated and, when it came to some matters, ignorant *goyim*. From then on, personal relations with our Polish classmates grew much cooler and even more formal. There were only a few first-rate fellows—and they were "free-thinkers" or socialists, after all—with whom we continued to be on good terms.

A few weeks before the *matura* I had a confrontation with the history teacher. During a review of the material, he accused me of trying to "snow" him. This infuriated me, especially because our teacher had a reputation for "snowing" himself. I sharply denied the charge, replying that I had said what I knew and wasn't trying to bluff. The upshot was that when I asked the professor in private why he had insulted me, he told me not to take it so hard.

At long last the days of feverish excitement were at hand. We didn't organize any pre-graduation parties. Almost everyone was sure of passing, since the chairman of the examination committee was (as he was every year, for that matter) our headmaster, and we were his favorites in the *gymnasium*. Besides, we were well prepared. On the first day of the written exams I loaded myself up with crib sheets and summaries for the Polish exam. However, the topics for the essays were quite easy. We all took advantage of exam-time strategies, even as we sat for the written exams upstairs. One of my classmates tossed copies of the topics, with false names on them, out the window. Then, during lunch, the janitor or our classmates who went out brought the completed compositions, forged on the outside, into the classroom. I, too, had one of these compositions in my possession.

However, I didn't crib a single word because, in the first place, one of the teachers watched me like a hawk and, in the second place, the essay I got was weak and poorly worded. I chose to write on the free topic that was the "most suitable" for me. I discussed "the significance of physical education and military training for the state in the present era."

The Latin text was also very easy. It was a passage from Cicero. Once again I wrote my exam and then compared notes with Jumek, who sat nearby. On this day, a classmate sitting by the window set up a kind of pulley, with which he could lower the topics and haul up the written exercises. The next assignments, in Polish and Latin, I wrote with total ease. The essays in physics were harder. We were given four difficult topics. After several hours of agony (in this case, combined with "communicating" and cribbing) I finally turned in my examination papers. The written exams were over. The tension was enormous, of course, but I wasn't at all afraid. I was just as calm as I was when I did my regular written assignments. I simply tried to do a better job of developing and composing my responses to the assigned topics. After the written exam, I began to review history intensively. I expected to take an oral exam in this subject only. I didn't prepare for an oral exam in physics, for although I didn't excel in solving problems, I knew that they had turned out well. But then I learned that I had to do an oral exam in physics, too. Meanwhile, several of our classmates were taking their written exams in the men's seminary, so we "sent over" the cribbed essay. I succeeded in salvaging the exam for one fellow, which made me (and him) very happy.

Our oral examinations began on 23 May 1932. On the first two days everyone passed. My classmates got hold of the questions in history. The Catholic students had already had them for some time. 25 May was the day of my "graduation" exam. That morning Jumek, Adzia, and my cousin Mala passed. In the morning group there were two weak students (both Catholics), who gave almost no answers at all. The headmaster became annoyed with them, and they were "rescued" (by the Polish teacher and our homeroom teacher) only with difficulty. After hearing the news of their misfortune I was beside myself all morning, especially as the history teacher hadn't given me the questions, while the other students already knew them. Three hours before the exam, however, I obtained a question. I rushed home and prepared for the exam. I spoke only a few words to my mother, who had arrived in the meantime.

We entered the room. The green table produced a disagreeable impression on me. The solemn instructors struck me as comical. I was asked the questions in physics. They weren't very hard; I answered them well. In history: two questions. I talked for a long time. I could feel my heart pounding. I knew the material and kept up a steady stream of talk. My lips were parched. I was dying to take a drink of water, but I didn't want to get up from the table, knowing that this would make a bad impression on the committee. Finally, the chairman thanked me on behalf of his colleagues. I walked down the stairs and happily ran home. Only now did I have time to eat lunch. I went back up the hill to the school and listened calmly to the answers given by my classmates. The result: a handshake from the headmaster, a speech by the girl representing the graduates, and the chairman's reply.

The end. I was a "graduate." Our group was the last to go. No one failed from our class. Forty-three seniors left the school with no casualties. This was the first such instance at our *gymnasium* in years.

I quickly gave Mother the happy news and said goodbye to her. Mother went back to Tłuste, while I stayed behind in Czortków. My friends and I lazed about for a while.

I didn't feel the least bit awkward after graduating, as people had told me I would. I was glad to be leaving this backwater at last and drew a certain satisfaction from having attained my goal. For the time being, I didn't think about the distant future. I was still much too wrapped up in my feelings for Adzia to accept the idea of having to part company with her. When I distanced myself from her by going to Tłuste, I began to miss her terribly. I tried to explain to myself that I would still be able to fall in love many more times, that I couldn't be with Adzia all the time, and that I should stop thinking about her—and, finally, that she had treated me unfairly, by allowing others to read the verses I had dedicated to her (despite my request that she not do so) and letting them make fun of me. But it was all to no avail.

My anguish was truly painful and quite intense. Shortly after our diplomas were distributed, I organized a party for my Jewish friends. Adzia was there, together with some of the other girls. Everyone ate a great deal of food and had a good time, but I was depressed. I decided to have one more talk with Adzia. During the game of "monk" I wanted to kiss her, but she wouldn't let me. I knew that I looked ridiculous and humiliated. The only thing I could do now was write to Adzia. I was obviously still "head over heels in love," for despite her plainly revolting behavior toward me I still wrote to her and about her—albeit in a somewhat different strain.

In order to forget about everything, I turned to reading, devouring a large number of books indiscriminately. I was a different person when I read.

At this time I invited my cousin Mala to visit over the summer vacation. I talked to her a great deal about my love affair, and it fell to her to play the role of comforter to my wounded soul and pride. I didn't tell Mother anything. When she asked me once why I was so downcast, I asked her to leave me alone. Time allowed me to forget about Adzia, and after a little while I was quite serene and composed. I ceased believing in love; I went from one extreme to the other. While formerly I thought that real love had been all mine, now I stopped thinking this way. In spite of this, however, I regard my love affair as the most powerful emotional experience of my life, as it has exerted the greatest influence on me thus far. However, I am unable to assess how my views on this eventually took shape, because I still hold these views. Though they bring me happiness and they have had a major influence on my entire life, I can't be sure that the effect is permanent. This love affair had an impact on me that has not yet completely subsided—or so it seems, at least, for now. As far as these opinions are concerned, I believe that they are liable to fluctuate to a certain extent. Furthermore, I can't designate this as my most important emotional experience, because to do so would require a certain perspective of time. I still don't have this, as I have yet to make any change in my ideology. Finally, I can't describe political consciousness as my most important sentiment; to do so would be insincere.

I started to correspond with Mala and her friend, Masza, who was also a friend of mine, and at the same time began to think seriously about two issues: what to do with myself, and what political organization to join.

What to do? I examined this question from two perspectives, individual and social, combining the two. I have always known myself, it seems. I have been able to weigh my abilities without overestimating them. I considered it my duty, given the opportunity, to take up a career in which I could be of service not only to myself but also to society. Here again there were two possibilities: Palestine and the diaspora. I have never had, nor do I now have, any intention of remaining in the diaspora. However, as my emigrating to Palestine wasn't likely in the near future, I didn't want to "fritter the years away." I wanted to study at university. I considered two disciplines: pharmacology and law. I knew that there was no need for lawyers in Palestine. Pharmacology, on the other hand, was a profession that might come in handy even there, but the fact remains that it didn't quite appeal to me. I was drawn more to law. I liked history, which has much in common with law, after all; besides, I wanted to get better acquainted with such subjects as politics, the law of nations, the theory and philosophy of law, and so on. Therefore, despite its being an "unproductive" profession, I decided to embark on the study of the law. Another factor that influenced this decision was a desire to acquaint myself with "student life" in a big city. However, I never had any intention of practicing law, nor do I today. I thought only about how I would enjoy exploring this branch of knowledge. Moreover, I believed that the more educated people a nation has, although not necessarily university educated, the stronger it is morally and spiritually. A healthy dose of learning is indispensable, especially for us Jews. Of course, this doesn't prevent me from giving serious consideration to living and working on a farm as my ultimate goal. After all, this is in accordance with my political views. Our people need farmers, so I will be a cultured and civilized farmer!

I discussed my views at length with Masza whenever we saw each other. Masza was a member of Hashomer Hatsa'ir. While she never pressured me to join their ranks, she did, however, advise me not to join the Revisionist party, even though there wasn't any likelihood of that. Then she suggested that I stay out of any and all organizations and just work for the Jewish National Fund.

I continued with my law studies in Lwów. University life didn't hold my interest for long, particularly as there were clashes almost from the start with the Endeks, which I found extremely troublesome. I was contemptuous of the "green-brains" and afraid of them at the same time, because of their lunatic behavior. The brutality of the student toughs filled me with disgust. I felt immeasurably superior to them. Yet it grieved and oppressed me that, despite our intrinsic superiority, or precisely because of it, they beat us or wanted to attack us (or get rid of us "culturally"). In my soul these two feelings merged: I felt an intellectual and moral superiority, as well as scorn for the Jew-baiters who wanted to brand us as second-class citizens or pariahs.

I felt myself a Jew more than ever before. The rage of impotence seethed in my heart. When all is said and done, I have no use for brawling, and I felt (as did many who thought like me) all the more powerless for the very reason that I had to be more responsible toward the nation as a whole, humankind, and myself. My anger swelled when gangs of reckless "nationalists" began attacking individuals on the street.

I was at the university on the first day of the disturbances. We were not admitted into the lecture hall. It was only when the dean (Gerstmann) arrived that we were let in. In a "reassuring" speech and in private conversations he made it clear that he cared only about maintaining peace within the university's walls, while what happened in the street was "of no concern" to him. Taking the hint, the Endeks started to run riot in the streets.

As I was leaving the assembly hall in the company of some women from my class, I heard the following behind my back: "Hey, is that a Jew?" "Looks like it to me," somebody replied. "Well, what are you waiting for—let him have it!" Naturally, I didn't try to run away, to avoid being "provocative." Yet I wasn't hit. When we got to the sidewalk I saw that several of my classmates had been attacked. I quickly sent the women on their way home and left the scene with my male friends.

That same day I watched from the window of another building as police standing in front of a dormitory were pelted with spittoons, water, pots and pans, and so on. All the while a crowd of several hundred "students" were "peacefully demonstrating." All the shops were closed, and people were running away from the student roughnecks, only a few hundred meters ahead of them. There were cases reported of people being slashed with razor blades, a weapon that was just then coming into use for the first time. The following evening I was riding the tram. I spotted a group of about thirty thugs on the sidewalk. A moment later I heard a shriek. They were chasing a man, who just then boarded the tram with a wound to his head.

The newspapers were already full of blank spaces, and the *Kurier Lwówski* reported "minor incidents." The city looked as if it was under siege: hordes of police wearing helmets on patrol, broken windows, subdued conversations. People slunk past each other; it seemed that no one dared look his neighbor in the eye.

On the fourth day of the riots there was a "lull." I was walking with some classmates. We stopped by chance in front of a gate. A policeman approached us and "requested" that we not "assemble"—there were four of us. When we asked him why he didn't disperse a large group of fraternity members who were gathered not far away, he replied that that was not his "sector." A moment later I saw eight people coming toward us (I was walking with Celek). We were calm, since they didn't have any sticks. Suddenly, right in front of our noses, one of the fellows in front pulled out a club from under his coat. Without waiting, I gave him a shove in the stomach and elbowed the others aside, dragging Celek after me. We escaped the attack, but it seems that the hooligan wasn't after us, because I could hear the sound of blows, and I saw him start to beat an old man. The guardian of order and public safety appeared to be deaf and blind to this.

I bore witness to these scenes and heard accounts of other, more gruesome incidents. In addition, the exploits of the cutthroats were later reported in the newspapers.

The rioting by the Endeks utterly destroyed any desire on my part to study. Attending classes, or simply being at the university in such a charged atmosphere, was hardly a pleasant experience. Meanwhile, however, I had passed my midterm exams and stayed in Lwów. I occupied my evenings with movies, theater, and dancing. During the day I studied (very little) and read new books and magazines that were impossible to come by in our backward province.

In Lwów I allowed myself to be "seduced" by a succession of new girl-friends and stopped thinking about Adzia completely. Because I am rather passionate, I've had a fairly intense sex life, although I don't go beyond my physiological needs. I greatly enjoy sexual intercourse; only rarely have I ever felt disgusted afterward. All that remained of what I call my "paper" love affair with Adzia (on account of the huge amount of paper I filled with writing) was a silly memory. I considered her a friend with whom I once had a lot in common.

I lived in Lwów with Janek, who was in business school. Janek decided he wanted to join a fraternity. As the majority of my acquaintances in Lwów belonged to various fraternities, they wanted to enlist me as well, but I declined to join.

Soon I went back to Tłuste, because I neither needed nor wanted to stay in Lwów for the second trimester. At home I read a lot. In addition, I played ping-pong. This gave me an opportunity to meet the local Zionist "leaders." They all tried to get me to join their organizations. Each of them pulled me in his own direction. I talked the most with one of the younger fellows, Herman, who had been my classmate back in public school. He belonged to the Gordonia movement and understood the range of Zionist factions. Since I held rather extreme views for some time, I wanted to become more familiar with the ideology and activities of the Zionist-Socialist party, as well as with this movement's work in Palestine.

I would talk with Herman for hours on end about the principles of the movement, the ideological differences among the various subgroups, the diaspora and the land of rebirth, etc. We discussed a whole array of practical problems of the present and the future. I was struck by Herman's intelligence and grasp of the situation; again and again, he knew more than I did. At the same time I talked things over with Celek and his sister Jula. Celek was a Revisionist, so I had a hard time agreeing with him. Jula had very liberal views, it is true, but since she grew up in an assimilated atmosphere (as we all did)—and, what's more, among people with indifferent attitudes toward politics—her progressivism drove her to an extreme position having nothing to do with being Jewish. Later, she "returned to the fold."

I gave a lot of thought to all these political problems and to the relation of the individual to the community. These days, it seems, this relationship is in a state of crisis. The individual isn't taken completely into account by the leaders of the world—hence, the vogue for "total" states. But I don't believe that it has to be this way. There ought to be a close connection between individual and community. I realize that the individual shouldn't withdraw into himself but should work for the common good. At the same time, the community ought to foster the well-being of individuals. A person's worth should be measured according to his work for society, but also according to his own qualities and the independence he displays in life. Otherwise, a person would be reduced to a lifeless coefficient of the development of the group; this would lead to the elimination of distinctions among people and, furthermore, to the decline of all original thought and creativity, to spiritual and moral degradation, and to the mechanization and automatization of life.

No! It cannot be so. The nation should serve as the basis both for people to channel their energies in the social bond and for the individual to develop independently. For it is just as inconceivable that the individual can develop without a basis in society as it is for society to develop without energetic and creative individuals who can think for themselves.

As far as I am concerned, while I should acquire knowledge (not necessarily at a university), I should also work to improve myself by striving to educate others (and, of course, fulfilling this goal). I have to realize my own happiness, yet secure the possibility of self-fulfillment for the nation and humankind. And it is just this sort of happiness and opportunity that I could have on a kibbutz. Therefore, I have formulated a plan for the rest of my life.

Several other factors at this time were not without influence on the ultimate shape of my views: the reading that I absorbed; my contacts with the people in Gordonia and my observations of their life; and also, finally, the behavior of Hitler (who had then come to power) toward Jews, pacifists, leftists—toward humanity! Hence, for several months I had been, for all intents and purposes, a committed Zionist and socialist, even though I hadn't declared my entry into any organization.

Two months before my first-year final examination, I left for Lwów. I realized that I wasn't ready, since my friends knew the material far better than I did and, more to the point, had reviewed all of it. So I decided to put my exam off until the fall.

In Lwów I joined the student association affiliated with the United Hitahdut Po'alei Zion Party. The life that I encountered there, filled with work and thought, appealed to me enormously. I quickly became thoroughly familiar with my new social milieu. The ongoing collection of money for the Jewish National Fund, the reports, the informal talks, the meetings and educational work in the popular associations—I found all this congenial, and I was very pleased to know, at long last, people who thought the way I did.

Since it turned out that I couldn't take the exam before summer vacation, I went back home. I was unable to study. The material was terribly dull; Roman law in particular held no interest for me. I informed my parents that I didn't want to attend the university. We started quarreling at home. In the first place, Father was opposed to my political convictions. This formed the backdrop for a number of disputes. My father couldn't reconcile himself to the idea that I—the son of a "capitalist"—could turn into a "garden-variety Bolshevik" and associate with "riff-raff."

To no avail were my explanations that socialism was something completely different from Bolshevik communism, that the "riff-raff" was none other than ninety percent of the Jewish people, that my views were what they were because that was how Palestine ought to be built—that, finally, no one can impose his views on anyone else, because this is a personal matter for each individual. None of this did any good. Father was dead-set against me. On top of this, the strained atmosphere of the town's election campaign (for the Zionist Congress) tarnished me in Father's eyes; it left our movement exposed to accusations that were often completely unfounded, which made Father even more depressed.

In sum, we lived in "great dissension." Mother was more lenient, chiefly because I talked a lot with her about the issues that mattered to me. All the same, Mother, too, opposed my ideas. My rebellion against my parents' power and authority provoked misunderstandings, ill will, and quarrels among us. For ten years I had been out from under their supervision. I now felt that my parents shouldn't restrict my development according to their own views.

Following the disappointment in love that I had endured alone, without moral support from anyone else, I didn't (as writers often put it) tumble into a void. No, I had my goal clearly in view and wanted to develop myself in this direction. And I felt that if my life was to be happy and productive—because I am, after all, an egoist—then I would have to strive for independence in the atmosphere of a new life outside the narrow confines of home. I am very attached to my parents and love them dearly, but my desire to be free to develop is essential and proper, and perhaps even stronger.

They tried to persuade me to study, despite my attempts to prove that there was no future in the law, especially for me. I told them in no uncertain terms that sooner or later I would emigrate to Palestine. My parents, however, worshipped the diploma. This prewar tradition hadn't died out in my family. The crisis of the intelligentsia and the unemployment in their ranks could not assail this anachronism, nor could the current reevaluation of the idea that one should value a person not according to his doctoral degrees but according to his actual worth. During this stormy period I was quite worn out by the constant, pointless conversations, the ordeals that tormented my spirit even as they tempered it, and the moral suffering.

In the end I made a kind of pact with my father: he would leave my opinions alone, and I would refrain from associating with my comrades in Tłuste, since this was what irritated him the most, even though there were a number of intellectuals among them. I knew that it would be difficult to stick to this agreement, but I entered into it for a very important reason. During one of our arguments Father got so carried away that, seeing how threats and shouting were of no use, he started to beg me to give in. Then he burst into tears. I was so moved by this that I could no longer maintain

my composure and continue to resist. I decided to make the concession—
and did so, blubbering like a child.

Things were peaceful for a few weeks. My parents absolutely refused to
let me go on *hakhsharah*, so with Mother's consent I applied for admission
to the Hebrew University in Jerusalem and the Institute of Technology in
Haifa. I still thought constantly about emigrating at the earliest possible
opportunity. At the same time, I worked on my Hebrew. Mastering the
language came easily to me, and I made rapid progress. No reply had come
from either institution. In the meantime, I immersed myself intensively in
Hebrew and soon was able to read simple books.

Summer vacation was upon us. Many of my friends had gathered in
Tłuste. The crowd from Vienna arrived straight from their first exams in
medical school: my cousins, including Celek, who brought a friend along,
and Jula with her girlfriends, among many others. The round of excursions,
amusements, and so on, began.

Aside from this, I read and thought a great deal. Contemplation became
one of my greatest pleasures. While sunbathing, or whenever the occasion
presented itself, I had the capacity to think for long stretches of time. I experienced the sensation of opening larger and larger gates leading to vaster
and vaster spaces, where the horizon appeared ever clearer and more joyful.

During that summer my brother, Jula, and I organized a wagon trip to
the sub-Carpathians. However, the weather was bad, and we had to turn
back along with some Hutzuls (this was before the harvest). While the field-
work was in progress, I often rode out to the farm and did some physical
labor. This preliminary *hakhsharah* did me little good, though, for I worked
in the knowledge that I could quit at any moment. Moreover, this was not
work "to earn my bread," and I lacked both companions who shared my
ideology and the proper atmosphere that a *hakhsharah* creates.

In this way summer vacation passed. I received no response from
Palestine. My father, who had in the meantime found out about my
intentions, decided that I should re-enroll in the first year of law school.
Seeing that I had no alternative, and knowing that there would be a renewed
outbreak of hostilities with my parents should I stay at home, I decided to
give the examination a try, despite my total lack of preparation.

I went to Lwów. My exam was scheduled for 4 October; I had only four
weeks to prepare. I returned home with law manuals and began studying
furiously. I assured everyone in advance that I would fail. I didn't work on
Roman law at all. I "condensed" all of the material from 2,500 pages to 700
pages. I did everything I could and, finally, after another postponement, I
took the exam on 6 October. I was quite calm, expecting the worst. I gave

answers in legal theory, Western law, and Polish law. In Roman law, though, I couldn't think of a thing to say on a single topic. However, to my surprise and that of everyone else, I passed without even having to sit for a reexamination. I was pleased; the year hadn't gone to waste.

Right after the exam, Celek handed me a letter from the Hebrew University informing me that I could be admitted for the following year. So there was nothing else for me to do but to continue my legal studies. All of my hopes were dashed. I resigned myself to the situation and stayed in Lwów. My exam was a sensation and gave my parents cause for great celebration. I registered for the second year in law school and prepared for my courses in political law.

I would drop by the headquarters of my political organization and devote much effort to improving my mind. However, my nerves were badly frayed. I began to feel indifferent toward everything. The organization appealed to me, but I didn't have the necessary peace of mind or equilibrium, so I didn't partake in the general gaiety and enthusiasm. I was depressed. I began "running wild," on the theory that this might help. I met many women: dates, dancing, amusements, etc. I had a lot of fun, but this wasn't enough to lift my spirits. I had enough money, but this in itself was perhaps a bad thing. Not having to earn it, I became extravagant. I spent my money unwisely and got no benefit from it. I didn't feel at all happy, and many times I thought that I wasn't "behaving like a socialist," inasmuch as I was indulging myself while so many people lacked the means to buy bread. Though it was clear to me that I could accomplish nothing with philanthropy (which, in my case, would have been on an exceedingly modest scale), these thoughts gave rise to bitter reflections and further dissatisfaction with myself. I continued to be of the same mind as before—if anything, I was becoming more rooted in my convictions.

Meanwhile, I got to know Tema, a friendly and attractive woman. I began to see her often; we became attached to each other. Tema was intelligent. She understood me and had the ability to listen to me for hours. She displayed common sense about everything. We were very close—for all of three weeks. We grew accustomed to each other, and I greatly regretted it when we had to part company. Tema interrupted her studies and left Lwów. From then on our relations, which had been close and down to earth, were limited to exchanging letters.

After Tema's departure, I became close to Fryda. But nothing remained of our former mutual attraction. Over the years Fryda had changed for the better. During the previous year we had shared textbooks. This brought us closer together, as we had to see each other frequently. We talked with each other often. Fryda knew me better than anyone else did. She knew that I am difficult by nature and more than once was able to bring herself to forgive me. She became my best friend. We aren't the least bit awkward around each other and often point out each other's faults and mistakes. I am grateful to Fryda, because thanks to her I have become more self-critical. Our friendship doesn't stop there, however. We often argue about our general views as well as our particular opinions (which are similar). The main thing lacking in our friendship is that I don't see the woman in Fryda, and for this reason she sometimes fails to understand me. But this has no bearing on the sincerity and strength of our relationship, which is one of profound comradeship. Although it is not an "amorous" friendship, as the French author Henri Bordeaux defines a certain intimate type of friendship, it is nevertheless durable. When we aren't in Lwów together, we correspond.

Thanks to Fryda and Tema I completely regained my composure. I began to read a great deal, often reading aloud with Celek, who rooms with me. In this way I helped conserve his weak eyesight. During the winter I was elected, along with two other comrades from the Union of Zionist-Socialist Students, to the chapter of the Society of Jewish Lawyers. The Society's work didn't appeal to me; most of its members belonged to Revisionist organizations and paid no attention whatsoever to our legitimate demands.

I much preferred the more congenial and stimulating atmosphere of my organization (the UZSS), where I could give full range to my intellectual self-expression. Being a member of the Zionist-Socialist movement enlarged the circle of my interests, my mental horizons, and my outlook on the world. For although the centrist Zionist parties (in particular) rail about partisan fanaticism, in reality this is not the case among us. We, the young, are quite critical in our thinking. We have our sights set on an unassailable goal: a wholesome and productive life, for the benefit of the common good, in a free Jewish homeland. We are strong, and we possess new and powerful ideas. We think for ourselves, and in the event that the "brass" are in danger of making a mistake, we won't be "blind and mute." Granted, obedience and discipline—discipline properly understood, not the kind that is so fashionable and extolled of late, even among us—are important, but still more important are critical thinking and perspicacity. And the diversity of minds is more valuable than the subordination to one individual or the leveling of opinions and consciences.

I am also getting to know the other men and women who belong to the organization better all the time. Our lives are constantly becoming more tightly linked, more intimate, sincere, and fraternal. This connection remains unbroken even after the departure of some members for kibbutzim in Palestine. Although there are many young women in the association, none of them is quite my type. Apart from this, I believe that sexual and cultural self-expression should be kept separate. (I am not speaking of *hakhsharah* or the kibbutz here.) Therefore I have met all of my "girlfriends" outside of the organization.

Ever since things ended with Adzia, my attitude toward women has been extremely different. I have become a realist; I see women just as they are. I weigh all the good with the bad and react accordingly. I will be able to care deeply for some young women I find attractive, but I don't know whether I could indulge in the platonic fantasy of "falling in love." Nevertheless, I need the companionship of women from time to time, and I like them (in general, at any rate)—although my disillusionment with love during my adolescent days could have permanently alienated me from the fair sex.

I was in Lwów for two trimesters; this was as long as my proseminars at the university lasted. The second-year material in law is interesting, especially political and international law. I also enjoy studying economics. Canon law, on the other hand, reminds me of Roman law from last year. I will postpone the second-year examination until after the summer vacation, because the aforementioned reading and political work have taken up much of my time during the year. I should also mention that the Warsaw *Opinia* recently published two of my articles (albeit in the "World of Youth" section, in issues 22 and 24). I was happy about this, but my parents were positively thrilled.

Today I am pleased that my parents have come around to accepting my outlook. They were persuaded because I informed them that I wouldn't renounce my ideals as long as I believed in them. And now I have a specific plan. I don't intend to continue my study of the law. There is a possibility that I might enroll in one of the institutions in Palestine, since I also received an offer of admission from the Technical Institute in Haifa not too long ago. But, as I intend to join a kibbutz, I have no desire to carry out these plans. Moreover it isn't beyond the realm of possibility that my parents will resettle permanently in Palestine, and then I'll have to see what course my life takes. Regardless of this, however, I have decided to follow the path of productive labor and go on *hakhsharah* after the exam (which I am taking for the sole reason that I have paid the fee). My parents have even given me their approval, and I believe that I shall no longer encounter any obstacles to the realization of my plan.

I know that life on a kibbutz is hard, but I see it as imbued with a noble charm, and I look forward to finding peace and happiness there. Living according to socialist principles and working as a pioneer in one's own country, for the good of the nation and of humankind, is harder than pro-claiming even the most revolutionary slogans while failing to live up to them in one's daily life.

And yet it is the very difficulty of life that exalts it.

7

Hanzi

Contest year: 1934 • Language: Hebrew
Year of birth: 1917 • Age: 17 • Sex: Female

I opened my eyes and found myself in a large, empty room. Here and there, snatches of conversation from people in the house reached my ear. A soft voice spoke, hesitant in tone: "He was captured and now is in the torturers' hands. It's too bad that he left behind a little girl." I was three years old then. The voice continued: "She's already pregnant with her second child and will give birth again very soon." (Incidentally: these same words appear in my journal, written when I was twelve.) In the evening an elderly woman, about sixty years old, approached me and told me to call her "Grandmother."

Those were days of panic and confusion in the town, days of bombing and screaming and frequent fires, as the Russians entered the region around Vilna: It was 1917, the same year that I was born, on 15 Shevat [7 February]. In those days, I would lie all day in an empty room. I didn't see anyone. From time to time the same elderly woman would come in, feed me, and occasionally say something appropriate for someone my age, in order to amuse me. Later, when I was five or six years old, Grandmother would talk to me in the evenings about my mother and father. Only in this way did I learn that I, too, had parents.

I learned about many things from what she told me; her words were a rich source of information, and I sometimes reflect on them even now. My father was of humble origins. His father was a *shammes* in the local synagogue and was a devout and intelligent man. Father spent many years in Petrograd, where he pursued his studies. To Grandmother, this was amazing: he spoke perfect Russian, and he also knew Hebrew—the holy language in which prayerbooks are written, as Grandmother would say. Then, only in passing, she would add with her usual sigh that she once saw Father eating without covering his head. By this time I knew all the Jewish customs and religious laws. Grandmother had taught them to me, as she was extremely devout.

Mother was the exact opposite of Father: a young woman of means, petit bourgeois in all her desires. However, she had never attended school and could only read and write with difficulty. Grandmother was happy that her daughter was married to an educated man. Several times she mentioned that he was a member of the intelligentsia. I knew a lot about my parents, but I still wasn't allowed to see them.

During the long, empty days of summer I would invent beautiful fantasies. Images of my parents formed in my imagination: once, I envisioned my father as an outstanding student returning from the university with a large book in his hand; once, I imagined him as a drunkard, walking down the road and tossing money around. I even saw him in such scenes in my dreams. I recall my father's appearance when I saw him for the first time, that same year. He bent half-way down over my crib and fixed his eyes on me. The tension in his face was evident. I was quiet and only saw that his eyes were slightly red and moist from crying. I didn't see him again for a long time.

The next day Grandmother told me that the same night Father had come to visit me, Mother had given birth to their third daughter. I was their first daughter, and the second one had died. She was very beautiful, and God took her away because of her beauty. God hates beauty, because it leads to sin. This is how Grandmother explained it to me, and I replied that under no circumstances would I want to be beautiful.

As it happened, I saw Father another time and Mother, too. In the other room there was a long table. On one side Father sat drinking soda water from a white bottle. On the other side sat Mother. She was thirty-five years old then, and Father was only thirty. Mother was short and her very long hair was unkempt. Her head was turned toward the window. She didn't move her eyes but, steeped in sorrow, stared the whole time at a fixed point.

I didn't see Mother and Father again for a long time. Grandmother once told me that Mother was very sick, and I seized on the idea that perhaps she had "acquired" another daughter. Then one day, during winter, the door opened wide and my aunt entered with Father. They were carrying lots of packages. My aunt was returning from being in quarantine after a bout of typhus.

I was seven years old when my parents asked whether I was being raised in a sensible, appropriate environment at Grandmother's. I was almost always alone. Occasionally I stole out into the yard to play in the sand. At night I slept well, because I was awake through the long evenings, when I almost always heard people talking about Father and Mother in the other room.

A strong religious feeling and a love of God began to take hold of me, as this is what Grandmother taught me.

At this time I came to know more about Father: Mother had given him a lot of money as her dowry. He didn't invest it in a business or a store but distributed half of the money among his poor relatives out of the goodness of his heart. He spent the other half on drinking brandy and playing cards at night in a stranger's house. He would return home at dawn, completely drunk; then he would shout at Mother. Sometimes, he also hit her. She would cry all night long, her head buried in her pillow. People said that days, even weeks passed without Father speaking to her. All day he read books written in a foreign language. I felt both fear and respect for Father. I considered him to be a man of great knowledge. While I lived with Grandmother, my parents lived in another house. Grandmother loved me very much, and, as I didn't really understand the matter then, I had no objection to this arrangement.

I will always recall an important event in Mother's life: one Saturday she came to Grandmother's house to take me for a walk outside the city, she said. On the way, Mother explained to me that soon we would meet Father, who was walking with two women. Mother told me that I was to go over to him, calling, "Father," and I was not to stop, even if he turned away from me. Later the situation became clear to me. We met Father, and I saw two women with him, both about his age. They gave me some sweets. I stood there for a few minutes, as they talked to each other in a language that I didn't know—it wasn't Yiddish—and smiled at one another. I left them and returned to Mother, who was standing beside a bush, her eyes wet.

Almost three months later, mother gave birth to her fourth daughter. When she was a little older, the four of us were brought to the rabbi's house. Grandmother came with us and asked the rabbi to lay down the law with Father. Perhaps, she thought, this would have an effect on him and encourage him to change for the better. It seemed that the rabbi's words did influence Father. He tried to go to a big city to buy some merchandise to sell. Two weeks passed, and he hadn't returned. We received a letter from the hospital, informing us that he was ill with pneumonia, after having drunk brandy and then sleeping outside all night (it was winter).

When Father returned home, Grandmother took me to Mother's house for the first time. I saw my sisters; it was strange to meet them. My youngest sister was beautiful, much prettier than I was. She had black curls and big blue eyes. Father loved her very much, it seemed: he caressed and kissed her again and again. I resented this terribly. Then I heard Father say that he would rather have a son, as he already had enough daughters. It seemed that he absolutely loathed me, while I loved him with all my soul—perhaps a love that wasn't conscious, but one with feeling and heart.

After he had recuperated, Father occasionally came to visit me at Grandmother's house. Sometimes he even cried and said that he loved me very much. But Grandmother didn't believe him and said that he was pretending. When I was eight years old I went to school for the first time. It was a Hebrew-language school, consisting of five classes. I wanted to learn very much and thought that studying would be a source of consolation for me—or so, at least, I hoped. That evening I went to tell Mother that I was now a student. I found her standing by Father's clothes, looking for something, and while she was doing this she began to cry.

When she saw me she said that Father wasn't there. The previous day he had gone to a nearby village to sell cakes to workers who were building a road. In the other room there was a small, cast-iron stove burning, as it was freezing inside the house. Instinctively, I sat down on the floor beside the stove. Mother followed me and sat on a chair not far from the hearth. The fire illuminated her cheeks, which were moist with tears. Mother said to me that there was nothing in the house but emptiness and desolation. Father didn't bring home the money he earned selling the cakes; instead, he lost it at cards. I moved from where I was sitting, because I wanted to see Mother's face. I saw that it was distorted and that her eyes stared off at one point. I thought that her stare could have crushed an army; it could have paralyzed someone's nerves. From then on, I always saw her in this state.

My sisters lived with my parents in terrible poverty. The house needed repairs, it was cold, and there was no wood for heat. There were days when they didn't even have a piece of bread. As a rule, the children were quiet and never asked Mother for anything. Still, there were times when they drove her to despair. My youngest sister was especially demanding, as she was by nature more difficult than the others.

In this respect, I was fortunate to be living with Grandmother. She never begrudged me anything. It is interesting that I had a good relationship with all the children in my class. I could give them anything; sometimes I even took things without Grandmother's knowledge and gave them to the poor children. But my relationship with my mother and sisters was different. Of course, I understood how serious their situation was and their bitter circumstances caused me pain. However, the fact is that I didn't behave toward them as I ought to have.

In school I studied diligently, especially mathematics, for which I displayed a talent. On market days in our town, I would walk along the streets all day and help the poor women figure out their bills for the potatoes, carrots, beets, and the like that they were buying from the farmers. The women would invoke God's blessing upon me. They knew just what to say to touch my soul. Indeed, I dreamed about God a great deal. Sometimes, Father would sit me on his lap and talk to me about such things, despite the fact that he wasn't religious—he absolutely did not believe in God. Nevertheless, he tried to explain to me what was most important without touching on divine secrets. He always knew how to lift my spirits rather than discourage me.

In my class I stood out only because of my extreme feelings about religion. I could be swayed on any other matter except this. My faith gave me the patience to endure my current situation, since I hoped for a better tomorrow. When I read a chapter of the Psalms (which I did very frequently) I felt complete satisfaction. My peers made fun of me. In our town, people—including children—were generally divided into two groups: on one hand, there were the children of wealthy families, who had every book and nice satchels, dressed well, never went barefoot, and, if they were pious, went for strolls on Saturday evenings with their parents and not with their friends. On the other hand, there were the children of the poor, who were more devout and humble, who always bowed to the will of the wealthy. I understood this, because I was often in their company and observed these phenomena with a critical eye. I was not counted among either of these groups. However, though I was apart from them, they always treated me with respect: first of all, on account of my many talents. I always asked my teacher questions, and he took an interest in me and invited me to his house. Second, I was treated with respect because of Father, about whom the entire town spoke a great deal, although no one knew him. To them he was a figure of mystery.

Father obtained a teaching position in the next town. From then on he visited us only twice a year. Rumors circulated in our town that Father would never return and that he would make any excuse in order to be free of us. Mother was always depressed and angry. I heard Grandmother say that Mother was still ill from her last pregnancy, and from then on her stomach grew bigger, as if she were always pregnant. I saw her almost every day when she came to take potatoes from Grandmother's garden.

During this time I devoted myself thoroughly to my studies, especially to the Bible. The teachers were fond of me, which perhaps attracted me to school even more. I remember in particular one young teacher from those years, who had just graduated from a Hebrew *gymnasium*. He had blond curls, bright blue eyes, and the face of a happy child. It was said that he strolled through the streets with girls until midnight and smoked cigars on the Sabbath. This teacher also directed our Purim play, in which I had the

role of Mordechai. I was proud to be the noble Mordechai and was glad not
to play the wicked Haman.

This is how I spent the days between Purim and Passover, which was a
very exciting time: Grandmother promised to give me money for candy as
soon as Passover was over. But then Father suddenly burst into the house.
Although it had been half a year since he had last seen me, he didn't even
kiss me. Instead, he whispered something in Grandmother's ear, and she
left the house quickly, with a large bowl in her hands. I followed her and
slipped into Mother's house. It was dark in the front room. Only a few rays
of light shone in from the next room. My youngest sister, who was three
years old at the time, stood in the corner playing in the dust. Father stood
at the doorway, with one hand on his head. This entire scene upset me, and
I started to cry. Father paid no attention to me, and from time to time he
looked out the window. I tried to stop crying and sat down to read a chapter
from the Second Book of Kings, but I wasn't able to calm down. Soon,
Grandmother entered and told me that Mother had given birth to her fifth
child, this time a boy. Father, who had been waiting for a son, was pleased.
From that day on, I visited Mother regularly. When the doctor arrived they
would take me out of the room, but I never left right away; I always waited,
in case I might see something through a crack in the door. They only
showed me the baby once, and that was when he was sleeping. Once I heard
Father say in a soft, pleasant voice that the baby would grow up to be like
Professor Weizmann or Sokolov. When I asked Father who those two men
were, he told me all about them. Sometimes, when I had the opportunity,
I thought about Weizmann and Sokolov. I imagined them to be great
experts in the Bible, who no doubt knew it by heart.

Father didn't remain at home for long. Before he returned to his teaching post he promised to send Mother more money, and, as usual, no one
believed him. Grandmother was busy with Mother and paid no attention
at all to me. I spent all day roaming about the streets. This was a dangerous time, as there was a scarlet fever epidemic in town. I didn't escape it; a
week later I came down with the disease. I became so ill that the doctor said
at first that it would be impossible to cure me completely. I would be left
with some handicap. Our situation at home was grim: Mother, still recov-
ering from giving birth, spent half the time lying down and half the time
pacing. I, of course, stayed at Mother's house, not with Grandmother. The
other children were sent to Grandmother's house, while the baby remained
with Mother and me.

For six weeks my temperature never fell below 40°C [104°F]. I lost
consciousness during the second week, and at the time they thought I was
either confused or deranged. They tied me to the bed with towels so that I
couldn't jump out. It was hardest for Mother, as she was still nursing the

baby. Our local doctor was greedy, and when he wasn't paid properly he would take back my medicine. He would visit me twice a week, but he didn't make any real effort to help me. During the first days of my illness, when I was still conscious, he wouldn't even remove his gloves. He did everything superficially, to little effect.

The only treatments I received during my illness were applications of ice. They were changed frequently, and this helped lower my temperature somewhat. I almost always rested on my right side, so the ice was less effective there. The high fever caused my right eye to weep endlessly, day and night. There was no money to bring an eye specialist from the city. My doctor knew hardly anything about eyes; he only raised my eyelid casually and babbled something in Polish.

Mother didn't come in to see me often, as she suffered from a weak heart and didn't want to upset herself and start crying. (Her tears told everything!) Only Grandmother never left my room. Day and night she sat by my side and discussed our common misfortune. One morning my fever had dropped enough so that I could understand when someone spoke to me. Then Mother came in with a radiant face (I had never seen her in such a state) and told me that Father was coming to see me, just me, and for no other reason. It seemed strange that Father was coming to visit me, it was like a paradox. Grandmother constantly told me how they always found Father by the window of my room, his head bowed. I didn't understand and perhaps didn't want to understand what was happening around me. I didn't really believe Grandmother, and I told her to her face.

The condition of my eye deteriorated. The tears didn't stop, and my eye shrank a great deal, until it almost "disappeared." For six weeks the tears continued, day and night. When my health improved slightly, they began to think about having me see an eye doctor, a good ophthalmologist. Bringing one to our town depended on many things, especially money. Then a strange thing happened. One evening, my mother's sister approached my bed as I was in a semi-conscious state. She placed a bundle of money beside me; it was a considerable sum. I soon realized that all this money hadn't come from one source. Apparently, it had been donated from many people, so that I would be able to go to see the doctor. This thought caused me to blush terribly, and for the first time I felt what it was like to be humbled. That same evening everyone gathered around my bed; they were quiet for the most part and only glanced at me with a concerned eye. Father sat at the edge of the room, his head turned toward the window and his eyes red (when Father was upset, his eyes became red).

During my illness I developed sexually. I matured physically and began to become attracted to boys who were slightly older than I was. I remembered, though, that I was very poor and that the town had taken up a collection for me. For the first time I felt depressed about my eye. As much as I sought a way out of my situation, I found only one: education. This would enable me to overcome my degrading circumstances. And so I began to think about studying at a *gymnasium* for the first time. This inspired me to take action with great enthusiasm. It may have also given me the strength to look into the eyes of my dreaded future, when the doctor would determine the course of my life: I would have either two eyes or only one.

That night a relative came to visit me from abroad. Father brought her into the room without saying a word. She kissed me a few times, and when she gave Father her hand in greeting I sensed that he was greatly embarrassed. The young woman asked me a number of questions as Father paced about the room. It was obvious that Mother didn't care for this guest and glared at her. That night I wasn't able to sleep and heard a commotion from the next room, but I dismissed this as a side-effect of my illness.

The following day I was taken by carriage to Vilna. Father traveled with me, not Mother. When I asked him why, he replied that Mother had had a miscarriage the previous night, but her condition was improving and she would be well in the near future. On the way Father told me about Shifra, the young woman I had met the previous day. Her father was a tailor in a small town, where he sewed cloaks for peasants. Her mother was ill and almost always in bed. Shifra had several brothers and sisters. Her eldest brother was very talented. He went to Berlin to study law, but because of his poor financial situation he fell ill and went mad. He returned home and still lived there. He suffered from depression: weeks passed and he didn't say a word; he remained alone and ate very little. Shifra's second brother was a communist (it was difficult for Father to explain to me what this meant). He had been in prison for a long time, and they didn't know anything about him. One of Shifra's sisters contracted a bone disease and walks with a limp. That was the situation. Shifra herself had a talent for music; however, she couldn't afford to study. At the time she was about forty years old and still not married. Later, Mother told me that Shifra had once been in love with Father and perhaps still was. Father had sent her almost half of her dowry. Mother told me this later. Father always knew how to arouse all kinds of feelings in me, but at this moment I saw him as a miserable wretch. He knew how to provoke my emotions and my heart.

In order to prevent me from succumbing to horrible thoughts, Father took out a lovely Hebrew book and read aloud a section on Palestine, describing Jewish workers who were building a road. (To this day I consider this book to be sacred.) Then Father wanted to discuss the question of religion. When I realized this I became upset, because Jews must protect their faith, otherwise they will become gentiles. Father loved Hebrew and

Palestine much more than religion and God. This upset me, and several times I said something inappropriate to him.

My first glimpse of the great city of Vilna was of its high walls, the likes of which I had never seen in my town, of course. Next to the gigantic buildings I felt smaller, closer to the ground. But soon I realized that perhaps one doesn't see as well with only one eye (at this point I couldn't see anything out of my diseased eye). This last thought truly crushed my spirit. At the doctor's office I took the opportunity to look at everything around me. It was the first time I had ever seen such a nice building and furniture. Father didn't sit with me but waited in the doctor's room. The doctor didn't say a word in front of me, and this frightened me. I understood that the matter was very complicated. The doctor told Father that this was the first time in his life he had ever seen a case like this one (and he was an old doctor by then. He died two years ago; his name was Gurfayn).

Father never kept anything from me, and so after we left he told me what the doctor had said. There was a small hole in my eye through which tears dripped endlessly, and they wouldn't stop until the hole was closed. But the hole would be difficult to close, because there was a danger of harming my other eye. It might be necessary to remove my bad eye completely. All of this made quite an impression on me; still, I didn't feel like dwelling on it. I reassured myself by thinking that even with one eye I could continue my education in a *gymnasium* and then become a pioneer in Palestine. At night I thought more about the latter idea.

Father left, and Mother's sister stayed in his place. I will always remember her; she was a wonderful person. For four months she put up with me, becoming tense and exhausted, but she withstood the ordeal. Slowly, the hole in my eye began to close. But my every mood, whether cheerful or angry, brought a new flood of tears. Then a white crust began to grow on my eye, covering it over. When the hole closed up completely, I returned home and went back to school. My eye always had a bandage on it, as I couldn't see with it; this also prevented the eye from becoming cold or inflamed. When I resumed my studies I almost forgot about the recent past. But whenever I left the house, my aunt always reminded me to be careful. When I went for walks with my girlfriends, people would constantly either insult me or pity me. More than once I told them to stop worrying over me, because it was insulting. Yet, to this day, they still say the same things to me.

I found my sole comfort in religion, and I prayed and read Psalms almost every day. I spent my evenings at the home of one of my girlfriends. She was a talented girl who understood me well. I told her about everything. The one drawback was that she was the daughter of wealthy parents and was very spoiled. All the girls would gather at her house to hold races. I wasn't allowed to run because of my eye, so I always stood to the side, feeling depressed. Everywhere, people upset me. Women would stop me as I walked down the street and ask me about my eye. This upset me, too. However, there was much opportunity for my psychological development.

At the time, a striking event made a deep impression on me, one that I will always remember. It was the end of winter and the start of spring. One Saturday morning I saw a kitten lying outside, dying from cold and hunger. I stole some bread from the cupboard and, in the middle of the street, I broke it into pieces for the cat. A Polish shoemaker approached me from behind. He kissed me on the forehead and said that Poland didn't deserve a girl like me. I didn't understand what he meant. There was much talk about this shoemaker in our town. Everyone was afraid of him, and there were rumors that he had come here from Russia in order to organize the workers. They even said that he had once set a house ablaze, which then caused an enormous fire in the town. I knew nothing about this, but I was very interested in him and listened to every word I heard about him.

So the days passed. I went to visit Mother almost every day. My sisters didn't like me—on the contrary, they considered me an enemy and sometimes called me "the blind girl." At first I cried, but I soon got used to everything.

When I was twelve, I registered at the library. No one else my age thought of reading books. I would borrow books twice a week. The first book I read was Zitron's *Herzl, His Life and Work*. I almost filled a notebook with notes on it. In particular, I lingered over the poem at the end of the book, which I memorized, especially the first verses: "He is dead! Is there a God in the world? Is there a world, and do we live in it?" Once, as I was going to sleep, I told Grandmother that I wanted to be like Herzl. At first, Grandmother was alarmed. She gave me a sharp look and warned me to go to sleep quickly, as it was already quite late. The next morning Mother woke me up. In a torrent of words she accused me of becoming a socialist and told me that in no case was I allowed to join those people, who denied the existence of God. I tried to explain to her that Herzl was the opposite of a socialist, but she didn't listen to me and burst into tears.

Near us was the town where the Hafetz Hayyim, of blessed memory, lived. Many people went to see him to receive his blessing. Mother also took me to be blessed by him. The Hafetz Hayyim had a great influence on me, and after I left his house I became even more fanatically devout. The blessing of this sage reassured Mother. When we returned from his house Mother went to bed, and during the night she gave birth to her sixth child.

It was a boy, thank God; Father would be pleased. The next day Father left us to look for a teaching position. He said goodbye and left. I went out after him; I didn't want to cry in front of Mother, who was very weak. I caught up with Father and asked him what we children would eat and how the midwife would be paid. When I looked up at him I saw an arrogant man. He kissed me and promised to send us a lot of money. I controlled myself and didn't cry. I have never been free to cry. When I was very young I didn't understand much, and Grandmother satisfied my needs. Now I was forbidden to cry on account of my eye. The doctor had warned me that the hole in it might reopen. I was able to control myself only thanks to my strong character.

Mother recovered after a week. We became impoverished. Days passed without a piece of bread in the house. Mother sat hunched over in the corner, the baby in her lap. She nursed him all day, and her face bore an expression of shock and bitterness. Her large eyes, with heavy bags underneath them, were especially depressing. My younger sister was eleven years old and had yet to attend school, because there was no money to pay her tuition.

I was still living with Grandmother. I finished four years of school, and then the school was closed. What was I to do? I read and studied the Bible. It was the one companion that I never tired of. The Bible was always at hand, and, as a rule, I started to read it at the crack of dawn. In the evenings Grandmother didn't let me read because it was bad for my eye. The crust covered more of the surface of my eye, and I couldn't see anything out of it. But I saw very well out of my other eye, even from great distances.

My passage into adulthood began. Physically, I was very well developed. But I was always standoffish around boys. Occasionally I felt like talking to a boy, but I would start to blush immediately. It occurred to me that boys and girls studied together in the *gymnasium*, and my thoughts turned in this direction. I began to threaten Grandmother that if she didn't send me to a *gymnasium* I would cry and my eye would be ruined. Grandmother all but promised me that she would do so, and in order to mollify me she began to plan for my future as I listened attentively. Without asking anyone I decided to take lessons from a local boy, who had graduated from the Hebrew *gymnasium* that year. He demanded a lot of money, twenty zloty a month, which was an enormous sum in our town. I told Grandmother that it would cost only ten zloty. Where would I find the rest of the money? I struggled within: On one hand, I could choose not to pay the teacher; on the other hand, I could take the money secretly from Grandmother. During the major fairs that were held in our town Grandmother handled a great

deal of money. With a trembling heart I took several zloty every week
without her knowledge. At the time it felt as though I were running a temperature of 39°C [102°F]. But I was forced to do it; I had no other choice.
For three months, this was my life.

Meanwhile, summer vacation ended, and on 1 September the municipal
attorney was to travel to Vilna with his wife and son in a private carriage.
I made quite a fuss at home, announcing that I was going at once to study
in Vilna. I packed my bag and prepared for the trip. Grandmother feared
that I might become upset, to the detriment of my health, so she went to
ask permission for us to travel in the carriage. The attorney was a very pleasant man and allowed us to ride with him. Before leaving, I went to see
Mother to bid her farewell. I will always remember how she looked at that
moment. The baby was shivering from the cold and crying silently, as if he
didn't want to upset her. Mother's eyes widened, as if she was straining to
see. But I was sure that even then she couldn't see, for her eyes were filled
with tears.

She kissed me weakly, and as I was standing in the doorway she shouted
after me: "Remember what the saintly Hafetz Hayyim said." Her letters to
me were also full of such questions: "Are you washing your hands before
eating? Are you saying your prayers before going to sleep? Remember that
the saintly Hafetz Hayyim commanded you to be devout, otherwise your
eye won't heal." Most of her letters were full of words like this. My family
never let me forget my great misfortune for a moment! I rarely looked in
the mirror, because my reflection depressed me greatly. It was so strange:
one eye dark and the other one white. Everyone looked at me as if I were a
freak. I was accepted into the third form of the Tarbut Hebrew *gymnasium*
in Vilna. I did well in every subject except Polish and German. My classmates were cold to me, and even among the "reactionaries" I found no allies.
They mocked me when they discovered I was religious. On top of this,
I didn't know how to speak to boys in order to attract them. Of course I
had a good relationship with teachers. The Hebrew and Bible teacher was
especially fond of me, as I had a deep knowledge of those subjects.

I roomed in the house of some people Grandmother knew. They were
hasidim but were very poor, and their house reminded me of my family's
own poverty. I didn't have nice clothes; they weren't even clean. The class
tutor told me several times that I ought to comb my hair, clean my shoes,
and so on, but I paid no attention to this. I only devoted myself further to
study and reading. To this day, I still have my notebooks from that year.
They contain book reviews and, especially, my notes. At the time I read *The
Last Day of a Condemned Man*. When I was in the fourth form, I read *Good
Is Man* by Frank. The psychological passages in each book made a strong

impression on me, and I reread them two or three times. In the fourth form I delved most deeply into the works of Georg Fink. From them I learned that dogs hate the poor and love the bourgeoisie.

The poor came into our classroom to beg every Wednesday. I would run after each one and make some effort to help, whether it was appreciated or not. For a long time I had hated the bourgeoisie and sympathized with everyone who suffered. I often went hungry. Grandmother didn't send me money regularly. Of course, she had to help Mother as well. Yet at just those moments of suffering I felt enormously ambitious and energetic, independent in every sense of the word. After I had been in Vilna for half a year I received my first letter from Father. He wrote that it would make him happy if I wrote back to him. He also promised to send me some money. I reread this letter almost every day. My financial situation worsened, and I stopped reading. At first I felt a great emptiness within me, like a hole in my heart. In time I became accustomed to spending many hours making up stories about different sorts of heroes, which I found very satisfying.

The girls in my class once called me over to a corner; they warned me that if I didn't wash properly and change my clothes, they would throw me out because I smelled so bad. At any rate, this is what the class tutor told them to say. I blushed and didn't say a word. During the days that followed everyone avoided me. I sat by myself on a bench. Later on, when we were taught anatomy and hygiene, I sat there as though I had been nailed down. I felt like running away from it all and disappearing.

During breaks the monitors would open the windows in order to air out the classroom, and it seemed to me as if they were looking askance at me, as if all the bad air was on account of me. Those moments were very difficult to bear. I was weary and no longer wanted to live, but God didn't heed my call. My financial situation grew even worse, and I became more desperate. It occurred to me that I could steal books from my classmates, sell them, and use the money to buy some food. I tried to think of some way to justify this to myself, but I never succeeded. These were difficult moments, and they forced me to take stock of my life.

Several times, I did steal books and sell them; twice when I was at one girl's house. I went there, and when she left the room I tucked a book inside my coat. On the way home, my heart was pounding and my eyes were filled with tears. I never cried; my character was too strong for that. Still, I enjoyed doing this sort of thing, because I believed that my strong character would always be able to overcome these evil deeds, and I wasn't afraid of this becoming a habit.

After this period of hardship Mother came to visit me. She was very thin, and the bones in her face protruded so much that she was almost unrecognizable. Mother treated me like an adult and talked to me about everything. I didn't want to listen, because she quickly became upset and vomited. This frightened me at first; I thought that she was very ill and wondered what the other children would do without her. She couldn't say much, as she was choking on her tears, especially when she spoke about Father. From what little she said it became clear to me that Father hadn't sent her any money for three months. However, Mother said it was because he was sending it all to someone else, since he was a teacher and was getting paid, of course.

Mother begged me to visit Father for the holidays, at least to see him. The trip wouldn't cost anything; a carriage loaded with merchandise was going there, and although the driver was a Christian, I agreed to go. I reached the town where Father lived at 6:30 in the morning. The streets were quiet, with someone appearing only occasionally. I ran into Father's landlord, who led me to his house. I entered the kitchen but didn't expect to find him there. He was sleeping on a bench, covered with a filthy sheet. I tried to wake him up, but I was frightened. At first, he stared at my face and then went back to sleep. I thought he would give me a piece of his mind and then throw me out. But I quickly found myself making excuses for him: he had gone to sleep at a very late hour, he was tired, he led a busy life. I realized that Father would never be happy, because he hated his wife and his children. I just stood there for an entire hour. After Father woke up, he kissed me on the head (as was his custom) and, in a forced manner, inquired about the situation at home. I didn't respond, and he didn't wait for answers. While he was in school I sat alone, thinking about all the things that I had seen on the way.

After Father returned he took me to the home of some people he knew. At first I only saw an old woman moving about. Later, a woman who was about thirty years old entered and spoke with Father. From time to time she gestured toward me with her eyes and smiled. At first I was confused. Only a little later did I remember that, before my trip, Mother had told me about a woman to whom Father was giving all of his money. I was seized with a feeling of contempt for her. I tried to speak to her sharply. For instance, I fiercely criticized a picture hanging on the wall across from me, arguing that it was hardly a work of art. She and Father smiled, as if they both understood what I meant. I urged Father to leave. He got up, but it was evident that he intended to stay. He had brought some food for dinner. At first, I insisted that we return to his home. Then I realized that if she was to eat with us, I would be able to watch her interactions with Father, and from this I could determine the nature of their relationship. From the start she tried to take Father's hat off his head. I didn't react, but on the sly I wrote everything down, so that I wouldn't forget any details.

The next day Father spoke to me as though to a friend. Indirectly, he brought up the question of whether I was in love with a boy. Our discussion added a new dimension to my self-understanding, because until that moment I had been unable to arrive at any decisions myself. Instead, I always tried to erase this subject from my heart, even though it was terribly difficult to do so completely. I said nothing for about ten minutes. Father understood that I was thinking and didn't interrupt. I didn't keep anything from him and gave him a brief survey of my life: The fourth form at the *gymnasium* was a period of transition from childhood to adulthood for us. The boys treated the girls with a total lack of manners, and during the breaks it was difficult even to walk across the room. After class the boys would get in the way of the prettiest girls, closing the door until the class tutor arrived and opened it. The teachers never discussed this matter with us in a serious way; they only tried to preach morality and nothing more. The boys never got in my way or touched me. I wasn't surprised; I knew that I was ugly because of my eye. The boys' indifferent attitude toward me caused me to dismiss any thoughts of love. While the other girls sat together and told each other stories, I sat on the other side of the room deep in my thoughts, which were almost always serious. On one hand, I felt depressed and inferior; but on the other hand, I felt invigorated and independent. As a result of my situation, I didn't fall in love with any one boy. At times, when I couldn't control my feelings, I would fall in love with boys in general—as they were the opposite sex—rather than individually. Sometimes I didn't pay attention to the lesson but stared at the boys who sat across from me. I made sure that no one caught me, God forbid.

Father was satisfied with my explanations and didn't ask to hear more. He also wanted to tell me something about his personal life, so that our exchange would be mutual. But at the moment he couldn't concentrate. I let it pass, because I didn't want him to get angry. In the end, he kissed me and said that he loved me very much. I never believed that he loved me, though I was careful not to tell him that I thought he was lying. But at the time those thoughts vanished, and I saw that he was filled with compassion. His pale face seemed to be blushing slightly. I said nothing to him about Mother the entire time. I knew that this would only make him angry. When I left he gave me fifty zloty. I sent the money to Mother.

After I returned to Vilna, I felt terribly exhausted. I didn't pay attention in class. At night I didn't sleep. I felt as though a coat of armor had been glued to my body, weighing on me during the day and even more so at night. I suffered like this for two weeks until the first signs of a disease appeared on my skin. Apparently, this happened because of the filthy conditions in which I had been living for three years, and perhaps because of the strain on my nerves as well. White pustules appeared all over my body, many of them on my fingers.

My situation was very difficult. I had to be wary of my teachers and the other students, lest they discover my illness, because then I would be expelled from the *gymnasium*. I couldn't afford to see a private doctor. And as for physical education, several times I didn't go. The class tutor shouted at me every day and threatened to give me a 3 for conduct. My landlady also began to suspect something, and I was forced to move to different lodgings. Naturally, I looked for a filthy house and, most importantly, busy people, who wouldn't pay attention to me. Of course, everything turned out just the opposite. As it happened, I found myself in a very intellectual household. My landlord, a very decent man, was the editor of the newspaper *Di tsayt*. His father, Mr. Yehudah Aryeh Apl, lived in Palestine, having gone there with the Biluim. My landlord also had a brother in Moscow, who was an engineer; I always heard about the content of his letters. They were very interesting, and I learned a great deal from them about the situation in Russia.

My landlady was quite lovely but near-sighted (to my satisfaction). Incidentally, in this house I had a good opportunity to get to know different kinds of people in various circumstances. For instance, my landlord often visited a neighbor who taught in a Jewish school. She was much prettier than my landlady, who would get angry at her husband. During their arguments, which were, supposedly, intellectual, I developed an understanding of life and of human desires. My landlady had a friend who would occasionally come to visit. Raised in a wealthy family, she was spoiled. She knew how to play the piano beautifully and had a law degree from the university. This woman suffered terribly. She had married at a young age and in a short time gave birth to three children. Then her husband died of tuberculosis, which also claimed the lives of their children. Together with her elderly mother, she moved from a spacious home to the confines of a narrow room. Her financial situation compelled her to behave improperly. In our house she would sometimes dance and sing at the top of her lungs. My landlord would smile at her, and my landlady would show her compassion. This woman lived far away, and on her way over to visit, she said, various people had harassed her. Once, I took her home, and on the way she told me the interesting details of her life.

I had all sorts of wonderful opportunities, but my difficult physical condition (the skin disease) made it impossible for me to become involved in any other activities. I was always playing comedy, but I felt my tragedy all the more forcefully, because I was so different from the rest of my peers. In my reading I lingered increasingly over the descriptions of the heroes. The authors would describe the details of their external appearance and, in particular, their eyes, which were so expressive. Their eyes, their eyes! What were their eyes to them or to me? At such moments I felt a terrible contempt for myself and for everything around me, and in the mirror I saw my misfortune—ah!

Until this time, my religious convictions remained strong. But now the first signs of rebellion appeared. A proletarian consciousness awakened within me, and I chastised myself for my lack of action. Why was I so calm, why didn't I do anything? I waged a quixotic internal war over religion—the same war that Lilienblum fought in his day. But I was unable to join a group whose members didn't already know me, because they would immediately turn their eyes toward me. This has been my problem with starting any task. I felt oppressed and looked everywhere for work, in order to escape the people who stare at me, whom I call "those who wallow in my blood." I suffered terribly from this. It wounds my spirit no end to feel constantly that people might be staring at me.

I became close with members of my class who belonged to Betar. Of course, they wanted to recruit me, and the idea of Jewish national politics interested me greatly. When I asked that they assign me some task, I was given the responsibility of organizing the Betar youth movement. When members of the chapter greeted me on the street with the cry of "Tel Hai," I would feel very self-conscious. It was the first time in my life that anyone paid attention to me.

Once, when I was strolling with the leader of my group, she asked me if I had ever been in love with a boy. I answered that I had not. With a coy smile she said that all the girls in our group had already experienced the pangs of love, except for me. (To hell with that, I thought, from now until I'm ninety-nine.) Although I laughed silently, traces of this conversation remained in my heart. I despised myself—why was I different from everyone else? I was always confronted by this question. Instinctively, I made excuses for myself: All this will pass quickly, and then there will be another task for me to carry out for the cause. I was definitely being selfish.

I went to Betar only on days when there were meetings, in order to take care of my organizational responsibilities. I loathed every moment that I spent there. Whenever I returned from a meeting I experienced an internal struggle. On one hand, I felt strong national religious feelings; on the other hand, I thought about the workers, the poor, the victims of war. I still felt the strong impression made on me by the book *Good Is Man*, which I had read in the fourth form. In Betar I found no suitable peer group. Among the girls in my group I remember two in particular. The first was very beautiful, a brunette with dark eyes and curly hair (like a boy's). All the boys were taken with her beauty. I felt a special pride whenever I walked with her in our group. Occasionally, I saw a boy approach her and watched how they behaved. She was essentially a decent girl and of good character. But sometimes I noticed that she became annoyed if I disturbed her while she was talking to boys. Despite this, she never distanced herself from me and sometimes sought me out. She loved to talk to me about different problems. We devoted a great deal of time to the question of the Jewish worker (together we read *The Jewish State*). Occasionally she smiled and stammered, "You're a born proletarian." We were too young to understand the glory in those words. Sometimes I feared them and would shake my head in disagreement. But for this reason I never ceased to think about them, and I spent many nights awake, immersed in such thoughts.

The other girl from my group whom I remember well was neither talented nor mature. She hurried home every day at six o'clock in order to put on the kettle; this was her only duty at home. She was always organized and strong-willed. She could walk around with ten groszy in her pocket for months and not spend a single one. Consequently, she was our treasurer. We were always short of funds. The girls suggested to me that I take some newspapers from my landlord and sell them. For the group's sake I did this, though I trembled slightly at the time.

After almost a year in Betar I still didn't fit in socially. Everyone there was quite different from me. Most had attended a state *gymnasium*; they were bourgeois, always well-dressed, and spoke Polish like members of the intelligentsia. I thoroughly despised them. I had only one dress that I was forced to wash every day. It was usually dirty and torn in several places. I had an even worse impression of the revisionist academics, who were prepared only to march in the P.B. unit of Betar, in processions of Polish celebrants. I never went along with them but scorned and mocked them. I often received a demerit from the group leader. I would then have to report to him, like a soldier facing his superior officer. I never paid any attention to these reports, nor was I ever told to do so. The group thought that I was an ideal member of Betar who was very mature, and that once I had made a number of improvements, I could contribute much to the movement. For this reason everyone was pleasant and respectful toward me, but underneath I felt slighted. I felt that no one sympathized with me.

Rumors circulated in our chapter that Jabotinsky had been in Vilna but hadn't visited us. This upset me. On Saturday there was a regular chapter meeting, as if everything was fine. Everyone was standing in rows, laughing happily, full of the joy of life. I was the only one whose heart felt empty. I knew that the leader of our chapter had had a private meeting with Jabotinsky. I was extremely jealous. I decided to step forward and ask him to tell us at least what Jabotinsky said. I felt very embarrassed and wanted to change my mind. Everyone will turn toward me, I thought, and laugh at me. None of them will understand how I feel. But I was so agitated that I wasn't able to stop, and instinctively I did what I had mind. I blushed. Everyone whispered something to his neighbor, but I didn't hear what they said. The girl standing beside me also blushed. Our chapter leader agreed to give only a limited account. He said that Jabotinsky is getting older, that he is sick and weak, and that we could help him only if we listened and followed his lead. As he spoke, everyone else in the room was silent. My heart froze, and only afterwards I realized that my eyes were wet. The girl standing beside me led me out of the assembly room and sat with me for a long time in another room. Stories circulated about this incident. From then on, I had a reputation as a messenger of death.

In the meantime, I went home for the holidays. The situation there remained as it had been. Father was nowhere to be found, and Mother worked hard to provide for her six little children. The look on her face was frightening. Occasionally, she would tell me that she had cancer. She would immediately get upset and cry. It would fall to me to raise the youngest child and look after the others. At those moments I found the pain overwhelming, but I didn't cry. Grandmother would approach me, her face thin and her eyes reddened, and ask, "Are you still praying as you used to?" I would always answer, "Yes," because I didn't want to upset her. That would satisfy her, and she would mutter something to herself. Mother said that Grandmother's condition was also deteriorating, and that she might be starving while she sent me all her money. A few days later we received a card from Father. He had lost his position and was going to look for work elsewhere. Finally, he asked after his two sons, his future professors.

Before I left town I organized a general meeting for Betar. Even some older boys, who were about twenty years old, attended. Though I wore a serious expression on my face, I was trembling within. For the first time in my life, I had to give a speech before so many people (the chapter had 120 members). But once I began, I forgot that I was in front of an audience. It felt as though I were reading out loud from a book. I spoke for more than an hour and a half, and everyone listened. It seemed that people found the talk interesting. My first such effort was a success, and I felt that I had an inner strength.

After the talk, as I left with the chapter leader, I saw Mother standing by the window with the baby in her arms, together with Grandmother. I

immediately felt depressed and very embarrassed. Mother and Grandmother looked pleased. They said something to me that I didn't even hear
because I was so angry. At that moment, I wanted to be free. For the first
time in my life, I came home at a very late hour. Mother didn't hear me
come in, as she was already long asleep.

I returned to Vilna the next morning. How did I pay for the journey? No
one told me what to do, but in fact, for some time I had been giving private
lessons and used the money to pay my expenses. A week later I found
another student. As a result, I was very busy and was forced to curtail my
reading. I also spent less time studying for my own lessons.

One day the door opened and Father entered. At first I was alarmed. I
shook his hand but didn't have courage to kiss him, nor did he kiss me.
First he asked whether I had eaten that day, and in the midst of our conversation he took a zloty from his pocket and gave it to me. He didn't have
any more money. I said almost nothing the entire time. My heart beat
rapidly, and I looked straight into his eyes, which were somewhat red and
irritated. His clothes were threadbare, and he looked rather like a beggar.
People stared at him. There was much one could understand by looking at
him. Father's face looked strangely noble. He spoke to my landlady in
Russian and to me in Hebrew. He spoke the language fluently, with popular
literary idioms—it was a pure, proletarian Hebrew.

After a few hours had passed, my landlady scolded me for not giving
Father something to eat, so I bought some pickled herring for him. As he
ate, I asked him to tell me something about his recent experiences and his
plans for the future. At first, my questions angered him, but when I blushed,
his heart softened, and he promised to tell me. I looked forward to the
evening. At least there would be something to listen to, as Father always
expressed himself so thoughtfully.

He remained in Vilna for four days, coming and going during the entire
time and always returning to my place. I had no idea what was going on
inside his heart. At first, I felt certain that he was devising ways to rid himself
of us. Then images of Mother appeared in my mind, carrying the baby in
her arms, while around her the rest of the children begged for food. They
rarely had more to eat than black bread, and they never saw beet or onion
soup. We were all miserable, and my misfortune was the greatest.

I was afraid to bring up questions about home in Father's presence, lest
it make him angry. When I was with him I felt both at one with him and
also remote from him. On one hand, he was completely closed; a solid wall
separated us, as he understood much more than I did. On the other hand,
I felt a personal closeness with him that was unmediated, instinctive, since
both of us were suffering. An internal war raged in his heart, and the same

fire burned continually in mine. There was much more that we had in common.

When Father left he said "goodbye" to me and nothing more. The evening before his departure he kissed me several times. Then he told me in confidence, his face glowing, that I had many of his emotional traits. He spoke to me as to a friend. Even his tone was youthful. I felt enormous sympathy from him.

Casually, Father steered our conversation toward the subject of religion. From the beginning, I sensed his intent and blushed. He raised a subject that was extremely precious to me, not only for religious but also for personal, intellectual reasons. I turned to God with all of my personal troubles. Even at moments of doubt I still had the same essential belief, which was so precious to me, and without which I could explode at moments of crisis. The fact is that faith in a supreme being helped sustain me spiritually. But life robbed me even of this last spark! And cruel people rejoiced at my distress.

Vacation was approaching. I was promoted to the seventh form. Then I learned that Father was at home, and I hurried back there. Why? I couldn't explain. I learned that Mother would give birth to a seventh child. I sensed this from the first moment I saw her. Sometimes I scoffed at her and spoke disrespectfully to her. This pained me greatly, and I felt terrible remorse.

During the day Father spoke very little with Mother and glared at her fiercely. But at night he became affectionate with her. I was aware of this, even though I was sleeping in the next room. Without a doubt, this was a loveless couple. From everything I had read about sex and biology I was aware that no normal children could come from such a couple. I also came to similar conclusions about the Jewish people as a whole. This vacation was a very emotional time for me. First, I was still suffering from the skin disease. And that summer, for the first time in my life, I let myself fall in love with a boy.

He was the cantor's son. Like me, he didn't stay in town all year but went off to study in a *gymnasium*. When I met him I had Nemilov's book *The Biological Tragedy of Women* in my hand. Together we read sections of it and afterwards discussed each section individually. He was very mature and gifted, and I loved him more for his talents than for his looks. I looked for opportunities to run into him. He knew nothing of this, and I certainly didn't interest him. I was so lowly in my eyes that I couldn't imagine anyone falling in love with me.

I had tremendous energy then, but I didn't use it as I should have, because if anyone looked at me it would reduce me to dust. My one true companion was my tough character, which helped me through every crisis. My torments taught me a great deal.

Slowly the days of summer passed, and I was forced to consider how I would manage during the coming school year. I was certain that my family would send me nothing from home. Sometimes they didn't even have bread. I thought of the three steady private students I had, and I had no other choice, damn it!

However, I was able to achieve what I had hoped to do. One of my students was in the fourth form. He was a tall and healthy boy. I agreed with his mother to tutor him for two hours a day, but he and I almost always spent some time chatting. His father was a prominent capitalist. The boy told me in passing, dropping various hints, that his two uncles, his father's brothers, had abandoned their property in Poland and fled to Russia. One of them had spent a number of years in prison. Now they both had important positions in the Soviet government. From what the boy told me, I gathered that his father had also been a socialist once, but under the influence of the wealth he had accumulated he had betrayed his ideology. This boy had no great talent for study, but he was mature, and I liked to talk with him. He was also somewhat sympathetic toward socialism, though this was perhaps still unconscious. He was still an adolescent, so these lessons gave me much opportunity for psychological insight. This year made my mind weary, but its place in my life is fixed. I felt my place in society was more secure and better grounded.

Father actually sent me money a few times—small sums, to be sure, but they generally sufficed. I always had money for library dues and would read at night. During the day I had no free time. At night I was afraid that my landlady might appear and get angry that I was wasting so much electricity. But this was never really an obstacle for me. At the time I was reading Kautsky, Bebel, and—very occasionally—Jabotinsky as well, though I found him rather boring. I also read Russian literature: the works of Romanov, the diary of Kustiya Ribodov, and so on.

Although I studied less for my classes in *gymnasium*, it didn't have an adverse effect on how much I knew. On the contrary, my reading gave me a deeper comprehension of every subject. I did especially well in foreign languages. I hated mathematics; it all seemed useless to me. I loved history most of all, because our history teacher was a very fine man. First of all, he was a man of profound intellect. His perspective was one-hundred-percent Marxist. In class he approached everything in a concrete way. His examples were very simple and occasionally naive. He used popular, rather crude expressions. We also respected him as a person. He knew how to behave in every social setting, and although he was a Yiddishist he never criticized others' choice of language or their opinions. Perhaps we liked him because he always treated us like adults. His relations with students were entirely different from those of the rest of our teachers, who were reactionaries.

My classmates got to know me better, and their sense of me improved. One girl, who was religious, became very close to me. Although her economic circumstances were good, she was a born socialist. She was able to reach into another person's soul and form a close bond with it. She was a very bright girl with a broad intellectual scope. I could discuss everything with her, and when we spent time together the hours flew by. What did we talk about? We discussed different types of people, the society of the future—in short, everything under the sun. Once we even thought of writing a book together, but we put this off. Together, we had an influence on our classmates. It seemed that we created a new atmosphere around us. We were quite successful, in fact, and at first it seemed to relieve me somewhat of all sorts of difficulties and troubles. But those days of tranquility didn't last. Quite unexpectedly, I experienced an ideological crisis. On one hand, I felt a sense of national pride, while on the other hand I felt enormous sympathy for the world proletariat and for Russia and its revolution. I had great respect for those who marched on May Day, holding the red flag of the workers. I wanted to be like them and add my voice to the song of their uprising.

When I was in the seventh form my health worsened and, consequently, so did my eyesight. Until then I had seen very well out of my healthy eye, even from great distances. But I read a lot in the evenings, which harmed my vision. Now I am no longer able see things that are far away. Occasionally, I even find it difficult to recognize someone who is several meters away or to read small print at night.

If the wind blows bits of dirt into my eyes when I'm walking outside, I shut my good eye, and then I can't see a thing. When this happens on streets with heavy traffic, I am as helpless as a blind person. Sometimes I walk with my classmates from the *gymnasium*, and, although I find this unpleasant, I have no alternative. If I had enough money I could consult doctors, but it has been three years since I last saw a doctor.

My religious feelings continued to decline, and now I feel myself free from religion. I have only some distant memories of God.

Half a year ago I developed a severe infection on my leg. At first, it was just a mild inflammation; the doctor at the *gymnasium* determined that it was contagious, and so I had to be quarantined. I didn't let Mother know, as she had no means of coming to see me, so why cause her further pain? My illness alarmed my landlady, and she insisted that the class tutor bring me to the hospital. I was in no condition to determine this, as my temperature had risen to 40°C [104°F]. I was put in a room next to the typhus patients. At night they would burst into my room and wake me up; I got almost no sleep. The infection spread across a large part of my leg, and the doctor did nothing to treat me. On the contrary, several times she said that this was a difficult disease that could drag on for months. This upset me only more, just when I needed to be calm. After a week, Mother came to see me. They didn't let her inside the hospital, and I saw her only a few times through the window. Thanks to the considerable efforts of the principal of the *gymnasium*, I was able to leave the hospital. The hospital wanted to keep me there, so that I could participate in medical experiments.

Mother didn't believe what the doctors said and was certain that only a woman's touch could help me. She decided not to ask for any further advice from the doctors. By the time I arrived home my condition was serious. My leg was very red, completely swollen, and it hurt above the knee. Our town had a public hospital and a fairly decent doctor, who was called in after a few days. I won his favor at once, and so he didn't mind the meager payment we gave him. He determined that there was an inflammation of the muscles that ran from the top of my leg to the knee. There was an open wound in the middle of my leg; this had to be operated on immediately, because it was responsible for my fever and could possibly lead to gangrene.

Everyone in town knew about my illness. There were even rumors that I had come home to die, as the doctors had rejected all chances of my recovery. Every day dozens of women would come to Mother and cry over my fate. My poor mother fainted, and after that it was almost impossible to communicate with her. Every time she looked at me it would rob her of years of life.

Only one thing upset me: Father was not at my bedside. My brothers and sisters also hated me. They intentionally made noise when I had a headache, which was caused by my constant fever. They even smashed a few windowpanes in the house. I now think that perhaps it was because they wanted to eat. I remained in this state, lying in a bed of dirty pillows, for four days. On the fifth day the doctor came with his instruments and, without asking Mother, operated on my leg. Where were Mother and Grandmother at the time? I didn't know. Only during my moans did I feel that they cried along with me. I felt their pain as well as my own. Two days later, three new sores appeared on my leg, one near the knee and two at the very top of the thigh. There was no choice but to operate immediately, because I had already developed gangrene.

They brought me to the hospital (which was a kilometer outside the town), because my prospects for recovery were better there. I remember that moment, when three people carried me and placed me in a cart standing beside our house. My eyes were closed, but I was later told that the whole town had surrounded our house, and everyone was crying over my misfortune. I didn't see Mother. She hadn't been in to see me since the first operation. On the way to the hospital, I began to fear that perhaps she had taken her own life. But the extraordinary pain erased any thought of Mother from my heart. After three hours they operated on my three sores, without giving me any anesthesia. I was convinced of only one thing: a human being is stronger than steel.

Two hours after the operation Mother came in, her face white as chalk and her eyes bulging. The very sight of her almost frightened me. She didn't speak to me, and I was incapable of responding in any case. After a few moments, a nurse entered and sent her out. I didn't sleep all night. At five o'clock in the morning Mother appeared by the window next to my bed, looking at me. Behind her, I could see Grandmother's shadow.

While in the hospital I had the opportunity to meet some priests, who came to hear the confessions of the dying (there were only Christian patients there). Twice a priest spoke to me for more than half an hour. We talked about everything, especially about Hitler; the priest hated him as much as I did. A nurse named Maria became especially close to me. To this day, she sends me very long letters. Sometimes they contain brilliant ideas, which I read over and over. In the evenings, in her spare time after work, she sat by my bed and told me about what she had done during the day. She also told me a great deal about her past. She's an interesting character, and it's worth devoting some time to her here. Maria was born in Siberia. Her parents were aristocrats. When revolutionaries attacked their estate, her parents were killed. Maria, who was then six years old, survived, along with her twelve-year-old brother. He disappeared about four years ago, and to this day she has no idea where he is. In the meantime, some neighbors took care of her and brought her to relatives in Poland. From then on she lived in Warsaw, in the home of a deputy to the Sejm.

At the time she had yet to adopt any religion. Her father had been a Catholic and her mother an Orthodox Christian. Her foster parents had given her complete freedom until she was older, when she could do as she pleased. Maria had no religious beliefs at all. She always denied the existence of God and of any superhuman power. When she lived with her guardian she showed her rebellious side, which challenged all forms of bureaucracy and sympathized with the revolution. She also ran away from the *gymnasium* where she studied. She had tremendous energy and a brilliant mind. When she was eighteen years old, her guardian left for Brazil and arranged for her to study nursing with the Red Cross. She had a natural aptitude for this and had always truly loved caring for invalids.

Maria had a very weak constitution. Her lungs were not at all healthy, and she often suffered from terrible heart palpitations. She once told me in passing that all the women in her family had died at the age of thirty-three from heart disease. Her mother also expected to die of it, but she was murdered about one year earlier. Maria recognized her own tragic destiny, but her energy and enthusiasm for life erased all these troubles from her heart. Only on rare occasions could I see a silent wave of sorrow in her bright eyes. Gradually, as she talked to me almost every evening, she told me more about herself. Occasionally she would mention her love for a sailor who drowned at sea. But she never lingered on this topic and would quickly begin to sing in a forced manner.

Maria helped me greatly and relieved some of my pain. For six weeks I lay in the hospital, and, despite all the obstacles I faced, I recuperated. To a great extent this was due to the doctor, who devoted his great ability to my recovery. After I left the hospital, I remained at home for another three weeks, as I still could walk only with difficulty. Maria visited me twice a week. Now she told me about more personal matters: though she didn't believe in God, her membership in the Red Cross forced her to play the role of a believer. She also told me a great deal about the priests' private lives, about irregularities in the Catholic Church, and about the reactionary masses.

Maria was sympathetic to the idea of a Jewish state. From time to time she asked me naive questions about this, for example, "Why don't the Jewish people send a representative to the League of Nations to ask for Palestine?" and so on. I explained to her as much as I could. I told her about the Jewish agricultural settlements in Palestine and their collective way of life, which would be the basis of their future society. Although she listened and understood, the idea of Palestine became clearer to her when I talked about Tel Aviv. At the time, the editor of *Słowo* was visiting Palestine, and the paper published articles about it. I got hold of the paper and read these articles to her. Sometimes we had interesting conversations afterward. I waited with great impatience for those two days of the week when Maria visited me.

Meanwhile, the first half of the school year had passed. After the winter vacation, I was stronger and returned to Vilna. My leg would swell after a day of walking on it. In addition, my eyes were tired. I decided to give up reading entirely for several months. I also decided to study a great deal and devote myself to school with all my heart. The reason for this was that I was still in the seventh form and had to advance to the eighth.

I had only just begun my school work, when once again something upset my plans. Nathan Bistritski, a Hebrew writer from Palestine, came to Vilna. I had heard of him before and had read his book, *Days and Nights*. I even knew several passages from it by heart. On the day of his arrival I ran from school and went to the rally for him. His first glance caused my face to turn quite red, and I felt as if a great weight had fallen on my heart. I realized that something was bound to come from my being in such a highly excited state. Bistritski arrived in the morning and gave his first lecture that evening. The tickets were very expensive, and I had no money. But I knew that I wouldn't sleep that night. That day I was quite furious at everyone. I tried to borrow some money from my classmates, but they all wanted to avail themselves of the opportunity to hear his lecture. There wasn't one among them who was willing to make a sacrifice on my account. Perhaps none of them understood how I felt.

I walked around the hall where Bistritski's lecture took place numerous times, only to go home after I was frozen from the cold weather (it was already midnight). My leg was very swollen. "Damn it," I shouted over and over, I had walked too much. At first, I was especially furious at Father. But suddenly a new idea flashed into my mind: Perhaps he was worse off than I was? Perhaps he wasn't sleeping tonight, either? We are two of a kind. He had also once said that we have psychological characteristics in common. Perhaps we were similar in this case as well. Everything was hard for me; even a few tears from my heart came only with a struggle. During the eight days that Bistritski was in Vilna, I was on Mars. I can't describe what feeling I had for him. Perhaps it was love? No! This was more than love.

I saw in him the man of the future, who devoted his efforts to the task of human liberation (my national chauvinism had weakened). What I felt was perhaps a synthesis of love, respect, and something else. After I learned of his next lecture, "Moscow and Jerusalem," I sold my Latin textbook, the only one I had, and bought a ticket. My classmates realized that something was not right with me. Several of them wanted to go with me to the lecture. I objected forcefully: I wanted to enjoy the full pleasure of staring straight into his eyes alone, for hours, looking neither to the right nor to the left.

The hall was packed. I stood far from the stage. I leaned against other people, and they also leaned against me. I stood like this for more than two hours, so that afterwards I suffered enormous pain. During the lecture I knew of no possible distraction: I only felt that I absorbed every word that came out of Bistritski's mouth. As I returned from the lecture, I felt empty and dull inside.

I attended the *gymnasium* once every three days, and even then I sat through the lessons day-dreaming. The teachers shouted at me, sometimes frequently. The mathematics teacher threatened me all the time, and once he said that instead of giving me a 5 he would now give me just a 2. I paid even less attention to mathematics. There were teachers who picked on me because I didn't pay any tuition. In particular, the Bible teacher sent me to the principal's office almost every week and reminded me that I had to do as I was told. I felt embarrassed before the principal; he was a decent man, who understood everything. Inside I felt like letting loose a torrent of words against all existing authority, but I stopped myself. It is difficult to be poor in today's society.

Just as my teachers caused me to suffer, so, too, at times, did my fellow students—the children of the bourgeoisie, who had never tasted the bitterness of life. But, of course, such difficulties only strengthened my powers of observation. I learned to judge people from different perspectives, and I saw many different types. Ultimately, school proved to be a setting in which reactionaries and revolutionaries, different individuals from different classes, encountered one another. That is what I gained from school. But school also took a lot from me, showing me a lack of social justice, which was a consequence of the old society. The school's approach to education wasn't right at all: they didn't teach economics (even the study of geography wasn't linked to economics); they didn't spend any time on the role of the worker in society, and so on. Though it was laughable to make such demands, I always felt like doing so, even during my period of ardent nationalist activity.

It wasn't true that they evaluated a student according to his degree of intelligence, understanding, and development, in relation to his class and background. Instead, they evaluated him by the number of pages of a book he knew, how many years of history he had memorized, and so on. Bad students are always at the mercy of good students. The latter ask the former to speak less to the teachers; they always take the good students at their word. This causes the good students, who lack any trace of humanity, to influence the bad students, who are superior human beings. I reached this conclusion in almost every situation that I saw. To understand this but not to help matters was difficult for me, too.

After I got caught up in all my classes at the *gymnasium*, I turned my attention to the Betar organization and my involvement in it. I had always experienced ideological doubts and contradictions, but now they became increasingly pronounced. I decided to turn to the leader of my Betar unit and reveal everything to him in a private discussion. He was an intelligent young man who had graduated from a Polish *gymnasium* and didn't know any Hebrew. He came from the petit bourgeoisie, and his political inclinations were fascist. I spoke with him at length. But how could he help me if he didn't understand me, because he didn't have the same class background that I had?

I turned seventeen and advanced to the eighth form.

I no longer had the same ideological foundation. I held myself in contempt. Did I even have the right to walk on this earth?

After more than a year Father sent me a letter with ten zloty for some shirts. How did he know that I didn't have any shirts? He closed the letter by encouraging me to "be strong," and someday I would find happiness.

A month ago I left Betar and severed all ties with the revisionist movement. I hated them and all their aims. To hell with them, I proclaimed loudly. I have since attended two meetings of Hashomer Hatsa'ir. Here I feel that I have found myself a home and can breathe freely for the first time in my life. But the younger *shomrim* stare at me and whisper about my eye. I want to burst into tears, but I then remember the final words of Father's letter.

8

The Stormer

Contest year: 1939 • Language: Yiddish
Year of birth: 1917 • Age: 22 • Sex: Male

J'm called the Stormer. I was born in the town of A. in the small house where my family still lives today. This event—a happy one for my parents and a not particularly happy one for me—occurred in 1917.

My father's name was Alter Khosid. He was a pious and learned young man. I have a large bookcase full of valuable holy books that I inherited from him. He was a considerate man, he never preached to anyone, and always got along well with other people. Yes, I remember my father. I remember his refined face, his short, black beard, and his sonorous voice. Other people have told me about all of my father's virtues, because I barely knew him.

He was descended from a very wealthy family, who owned all of their town's quarries and sandpits. I've heard that they used to eat with silver spoons, and that their house was completely open to the poor. My grandmother lived in A., dealing in leather and drawing money from her inheritance. She was a tall, heavy woman, goodhearted and generous. She had lived through much, surviving three husbands. Her name was Frimet, and she gave birth to my father.

My dear mother's name is Rokhl Miriam. On her father's side she is descended from a very scholarly but poor family. On her mother's side she is descended from the rabbi of A., who was also quite poor, as I recall. I don't know how the match between my mother and my father was made. She once told me that my grandfather, the rabbi, selected the young man. My mother's father was a great *melamed*, who taught older boys. He was also always quite poor. This is the kind of family from which I come. Now there are three of us in the house: my mother, myself, and my sister Hinde, who is four years younger than I. Since my earliest years, and for as long as

I can remember, we have lived in poverty. I'm not ashamed of this now; it's no cause for shame. My father was a quilter, and he used to work hard, day and night, in order to eke out a living.

Once, I remember, I was sitting on the table—this was a long, long time ago—and crying for food. My father paced up and down the room, absorbed in thought. My mother stood there, holding me as she looked into Father's eyes and at my mouth. Suddenly, Father ran out and a while later returned with a pound of bread, which he gave to Mother. Those were bad times. I had a little sister who was sick in bed. She was teething and having a difficult time of it. All of Father's earnings were being spent on doctors. We went all day without food more than once, because Father didn't want to go to his mother, my grandmother, to ask for something to eat. He felt it was beneath him. My father was a proud man.

I also remember, as if through a fog, that I was once standing in front of the gate, playing in the sand, when I saw a lot of people pass by in a very, very long procession. Then Father ran over to me, grabbed me by the hand and dragged me into the house, shouting, "Hurry, hurry. The Bolsheviks are coming. They're kidnapping little children, they're massacring people." It was 1920, and my father didn't have an especially high opinion of the Bolsheviks.

My sister who was sick because of her teeth soon died, and our spirits were very low. Mother would cry all day, and Father would walk around depressed. I remember that my little sister had lain in bed, sleeping for a long time, and then an old man came and carried her out of our house on a board—nothing more. Very shortly afterwards, though, I got another sister, and she grew up healthy and full of life.

As I recall, my father and mother got along well together. They always spoke pleasantly to each other. This is what I remember from the years before I went to school. Then, not long after the birth of my second sister, I was sent to *kheyder*. I was a good student and wanted to learn. I wasn't like my friends, who raced home from *kheyder*. Instead, I was always the first to arrive and walked home together with everybody else. I soon began to study the Bible and went on to a more advanced teacher. At this time my father contracted an illness; I believe that it was typhus. He lay in bed for a long time, and finally went to the spa at Szczawnica. I don't know how we supported ourselves then. In addition, I scalded both my legs by being careless with a teakettle full of boiling water, and I had to lie in bed for a long time. By the time Father came home from the spa, he was healthy and happy.

But our happiness didn't last long. One evening before Passover, I came home from *kheyder*. Our neighbor Yankl Zeygermakher came in and, after exchanging a few words with him, pounced on my father. When I saw this I started to scream for my mother, who wasn't in the house at the time. Eventually, I ran over to my father's attacker and bit him on the thigh. In the meantime another neighbor, Yoyel Shnayder, came in and broke up the fight. Soon afterward, Father began to spit up blood. When Mother found out about this, she became very upset and cried all the time. This was the first time that I ever saw a person spit up blood. Father became seriously ill, and the following winter it was very sad at home. He couldn't work, and Mother stopped singing me to sleep with her pretty songs.

Father would always call me over to his bedside and stroke my head and face, kiss me on the forehead, and say to me, "Do well in your studies, my son, and you'll grow up to be a wise and great man." Then I would lower my eyes and run off to the *kheyder*, to be with the other boys and forget about all this: our sad house, my sick father, and my good and beautiful mother, may she live. My father's illness became ever more serious; he was less and less able to sleep at night. He coughed and spat up blood. Late one evening, around Passover, I came home from *kheyder*. In the winter Father kept saying, "If I only survive until summer, then I'll be all right." But that evening there were more people at our house than there had ever been before. My grandmother; Uncle Hershl, Father's brother; and Uncle Ben-Tsien, Father's half-brother, were all there. There was a different mood than usual. And after I had eaten and said grace, my mother turned to me and said, "Take the Psalms and pray that your father gets well." I did so, reciting Psalms with great devotion until late at night. When I went to bed, Mother said tearfully and sorrowfully, "Pray that your father gets well, my child, because it looks very bad." She moved my young heart. I had never experienced anything like it. I lay down in bed, turned toward the wall and began to cry bitterly, soaking the whole pillow. With a heavy heart and a child's uncertainty on my lips, I fell into a heavy sleep. When I woke up early in the morning, the house was already full of people. Strangers quickly dressed my sister and me and sent us to a neighbor, who stuffed bagels into our mouths. Suddenly, we heard a shout, mixed with cries from my mother and grandmother. I remember that I threw away the bagel and began to scream and cry terribly. My little sister did the same. I did this because I sensed something bad. The situation alarmed me very much. When the neighbor heard the shouting from our house, she raised her hands to the sky and said, "Merciful God, You are righteous and Your judgment is righteous." I stayed in her house for a long time. Then my grandmother came, took me by the hand, and led me into our house, saying, "Go and grieve over your father for the last time."

Someone opened the door for me and closed it behind me. I saw a pair of thin, bony, blue feet stretched out on the floor, stiff and motionless. Their soles were yellow. There were lines etched into the clay floor (there was no wooden floor), and on top of them lay the long figure of my father, covered with his silken Sabbath coat. At his head stood two candles burning sorrowfully. Uncle Hershl was sitting on a stool, wailing and wringing his hands. Mother sat and sobbed hoarsely; she no longer had the strength to cry. The mood in our house was sad and melancholy. I began to cry bitterly, holding my hands in front of my eyes. But soon, the same hand that had pushed me into the room pulled me back out and sent me out to the street to play with the other children.

There were many people at Father's funeral. I stood at the open grave of my young father—he was only thirty-two years old—and cried. I remember that Crazy Yankl, the one who had beaten my father (that's what they called him, Crazy Yankl), stood next to me and spoke softly into the grave. And when they covered my father's body with boards, my grandfather, the rabbi of A., came over to me. Pale, with two large, sad eyes and a white beard, he took my hands in his trembling hands and called out with a deep, quivering voice, "May you have a long life, Tsvi-Khayem, for your whole family." Then he started to say the first Kaddish with me.

At home, people ate bagels and eggs, which really astonished me; I didn't eat anything. It was 3 Nisan 5683 [20 March 1923]. My father's death made a strong impression on me, and even today, as I write these words, I cannot keep from crying.

For thirty days, services were held at our house, attended by the most important men in town. And for thirty days my mother, holding my little sister, Hindele, in her arms, sat with my grandmother on a small stool in a corner. Both of them mourned the death of my father—my mother as a husband, and my grandmother as her favorite son (although she had three other sons, he was her favorite). On the last of the thirty days of mourning, my grandfather came to our house and, after the services, sat down to discuss what we should do next. He advised my mother to go into some kind of business. But she wouldn't hear of it, because she could no longer bear staying here. Every corner seemed sad and dead to her, and the whole city was like a vast cemetery. She stuck to her position: She wouldn't give up the house but would go to Łódź with my father's sewing machine. There she would live with her parents and make a living sewing linens, a trade that she knew. She also insisted on taking my sister and me with her, because during this period Mother had become even more devoted to us than before. She imbued both of us with her goodness and love. At night she would lie in bed with us and teach us all kinds of sad songs—one about a king of Siberia, and another about a mother's love for her children. She played with us and caressed us, crying and laughing as she did. This period affected me so deeply that to this day I remember those songs, and I can still see my mother in all of her majestic greatness. After the tragedy that we had all suffered, Mother didn't want to abandon either one of us. We decided—that is, Mother did—to move to Łódź, and so we went. Later, however, she regretted it, for, if my grandfather the rabbi had said to go into business, as she used to say later, "I should have done that and not taken up this cursed occupation."

We lived in Łódź at 13 Kamienna Street, on the second floor of a very large building. In those days, it seemed to me that all the buildings in Łódź were the largest in the world. For a long time, my mother didn't allow me outside. I had to sit at home on a small stool next to her, while she sat at the machine and sewed linens for other people. I would get up with her very early, and she sewed until late at night. As she worked she sang beautiful, sad songs, which have remained in my memory to this day. There were five beds in the room where we lived, because, in addition to the three of us and my grandmother and grandfather, there were also my Uncle Mendl, who was a bookbinder, and my Aunt Tsiporele, who was still in school. Every morning my mother had to make all of the beds and clean the apartment. I don't know why; we had enough to eat and even used to play with money.

The apartment had two windows. When no one else was at home, I used to sit at one of the windows, my sister sat at the other, and we used to look outside. We could see our dirty courtyard, with its bin full of garbage. Opposite was a large courtyard where there were always people tossing bricks. A large building was going up there, which eventually blocked the light from our windows. Off to the side I could see boys, somewhat bigger than I was, running around, playing, jumping over boxes, and gesturing with their arms. I wanted to play with them very much, but my Uncle Mendl once told me that they were rich children, who attended a private school nearby. I was silent and never said anything else about this. Further off I could see tall smokestacks from which smoke poured day and night, both when it was cold and when it was hot. And I saw people running—tall, healthy, and lively. I felt fine then. I had no sense of what I had and what I ought to have.

After a long time, I was allowed to go outside. Now I saw a different Łódź. I was sent to *kheyder*, where I studied very diligently. The tall houses, the dirty, suffocating streets, the sky thick with smoke, a group of friends, all kinds of games, races, and dirty tricks—all of this excited and fascinated me. This was my world, my all. Something else in particular stuck in my memory. An old man, carrying a box that stood on one leg, often used to come to our courtyard, which always full of children. We would pay him five groszy, and he'd let us look into the box, where we saw all sorts of pictures. He would take advantage of our interest by swiping rolls, bread, and sometimes money from our bags. I got along well with my friends, because I was agile and good at climbing fences.

Our good fortune didn't last long, however, because my Uncle Mendl had an attack of appendicitis, and we were left with one less breadwinner. Then my mother, after sewing linens during the day, worked at night at a *mikve*, cleaning the bathtubs for rich women. Mother became pale and, in addition, came down with the measles, which we children also contracted. Night and day I lay in bed with my eyes shut, and my mother and the rest of the household felt very sorry for me. I even ruined the first Passover seder for them, because they had to call first-aid workers to care for me. I don't remember how long my illness lasted, but I did recover. Once, while I was sick, I saw my father in my sleep. I saw him standing by my bed, dressed in a black suit buttoned up to his neck. I became very scared and began to scream terribly. Only after they put on the lights did I go to sleep.

Mother began to realize that nothing would come of us staying at my grandfather's place, because she had to contribute money to the household, and after working a whole year there was nothing left over for us. She then turned to her five brothers, who were all wealthy, and asked them to give her enough money for an apartment, so that she could remain in Łódź. They refused. Mother then turned to her other rich relatives. Even this didn't help, but we stayed a little while longer in Łódź. By now I was studying Gemara with my grandfather. I sat with him in the *beys-medresh* all day long and studied. My heart nearly burst when I saw that other boys could play outside, while I had to sit there and study. When my grandfather and I were studying about some rabbis, such as Akiba or Hillel and Shammai, I envisioned them as men with big, gray beards and sad eyes like my great-grandfather, the rabbi of A. I saw them debating fine points, studying, and arguing with one another. As my grandfather continued to study, I would just sit there like that, until he happened to look at me and wake me from my dream.

My grandfather was a good man, a hasid, who was always on the alert against sinning. When he got angry, his eyes sank deeper into his head, he grew pale and trembled all over. He wouldn't hit or shout, but he would go without eating or speaking to anyone. I saw him several times like this: Once, when my Uncle Mendl lit a match on Friday evening, and a second time, when Tsiporele read a secular book on the Sabbath. I was terribly scared then, and I even burst out crying, because my grandfather looked so terrible. At the end of my stay in Łódź I served as an errand-boy in the *beys-medrash*. After all, I had said Kaddish there for almost a whole year for free. The least I could do was some service to the community. I used to light the gas lamps, and at the end of the Sabbath I would turn on the lights and fetch beer and herring. I suppose that if I had stayed longer in Łódź I could have grown up to be a respectable *shammes*. It's good that things didn't turn out that way. My mother thought it over, packed up the sewing machine and our meager belongings, and returned to our former home.

When we returned home the first thing I noticed was that some books Father had left us were missing from the bookcase. Later, we found out that my Uncle H. had taken some of the books. He said that he wanted to have a memento of my father. Our house was neglected and looked like a stable. With all her maternal energy, Mother began to rebuild a nest for us. Soon the house became a refuge where the three of us felt at home, and I felt good under the protection of my mother's wing. As an act of kindness Mother took in old women as boarders. These women were as lonely as she was, and they were childless. They made a very bad impression on me. I couldn't stand them. They were dirty and full of lice—that's how Mrs. Y. and Mrs. M. seemed to me. Both have since passed away.

I started to go to *kheyder* again, now with an advanced *melamed*. I did different kinds of things with my friends. We used to wage entire wars, "capture cities," and so on. In the evening I enjoyed crawling into an empty brick cellar to sit down and dream about things that I'd never seen but only heard about. Mostly I thought about the other side of the River Sambatyon and the resurrection of the dead. And I had a vision of my father rising out of his grave and coming to me, leaning on a cane. Then I would weep and wail. My friends never found me, because they were afraid to go there.

I thought about another problem: the Earth. I heard an old man say that the Earth rested on the Leviathan, which held its tail firmly in its mouth. And if, God forbid, it let its tail out of its mouth, it would mean the end of the world. After talking this over with my friend A., we decided nothing less than that God Himself kept watch over the Leviathan to keep it from harming the world.

Some time later I had a friend, S., whose father sold fine foods and delicacies, such as candies and imported fruit. This friend of mine was a real sport. Every evening he used to bring us different delicacies, which were quite a treat. This fellow also began to teach me how to steal, but my mother noticed this early on and kept me away from him. Still, my mother couldn't follow me everywhere. So S. and I started to keep our surplus goods in a cellar under the synagogue courtyard. No one discovered us there for a long time. But then it happened that a friend of my father's was walking by and caught us sneaking into the cellar. He followed us and found the cellar empty, because some other friends from *kheyder* had already discovered everything and removed it as a favor to us.

S. and his parents moved to Łódź, and I remained in our home town. After talking it over with her family, my mother decided to send me to public school. I was a good student, even very good. But one time my teacher, Mr. Majewski, twisted a girl's ear until he tore it. All of the children, including me, became angry and started to stamp our feet noisily. The teacher took me—I don't know why he picked me—and stood me in the corner. I started making various rude gestures behind his back, until he noticed. From then on he kept an eye on me. In the end he kept me back in the first grade for "not knowing" gymnastics and singing.

My mother soon took me out of this school and put me in the *kheyder* Yesod Hatorah, where they also taught Polish. I went there for two years. I started to study "difficult" subjects and was promoted each year to the next grade. The director of the yeshiva (as it was later called) was a refined, God-fearing man, very learned in the Torah. In addition, he was a man of insight and for this reason barely made a living. At the time, we used to go to school at seven o'clock in the morning and return home at nine in the evening. We worked hard there. But I was happy, because every Saturday I was sent to different wealthy members of the Jewish community who would test me on the Gemara, which I knew very well. They would give me a piece of fruit as a treat for the Sabbath and a pinch on the cheek. But the yeshiva folded, despite the director's dedication, because it lacked financial support.

I had to return to the Polish school, and after taking an examination I was immediately placed in the third grade. At first I was very shy, because I had very long *peyes*. I was ashamed to look at the girls who sat near me. But after a while I got used to everything and got along well with my schoolmates.

That year, I remember, we suffered many losses. My great-grandfather, the town rabbi, died in a hospital in Warsaw. My grandfather and grandmother from Łódź also died. My mother spent most of the year in Warsaw and Łódź. My sister and I stayed at home with our other grandmother, who was a leather merchant. She wasn't a bad person, but after we had stayed with her for more than two weeks, she began saying bad things about Mother and us. Some things made me happy during this period: my Uncle H. got married, and my Uncle D. emigrated to Palestine. I remember that Uncle D. was a very handsome young man who always paid attention to me. I was very sorry when he went away. But my heart told me then that I shouldn't be sad, because my uncle wasn't doing anything wrong. He was going to a land that I longed to see with my own eyes and tread upon with my own feet. My uncle wrote to me many times, and I answered him as well.

Other than this, my life was ordinary. I got along quite well with my schoolmates, even though there was a big difference in our economic situations. My mother, though, worked hard to erase this difference. She wouldn't let me eat the bread at school, though she couldn't provide me even with that. Instead, during the breaks she would bring me rolls and slip them to me off in a corner—just to see to it that I was equal with everyone else. But I wasn't that close to all of my schoolmates. How could I compare myself to someone like S., the son of a rich lumber merchant, who had all the books and school supplies, or to someone like A., the son of a miller in a nearby village, or to L., H., and M., who were the sons of prosperous merchants? I was the son of a poor widow, a pale boy who wore a long Jewish coat and a Jewish cap. There were only two friends with whom I was very close. The first was E., the son of a driver who rode through the streets with his horse and wagon and transported goods. The second was Y., who was a neighbor of mine. His father, a tailor, was a former revolutionary who had spent time in prison. I usually did my homework with them. I also had many friends who were girls; they used to copy my work, because I was a good student then. But I was shy in front of girls, and didn't want to deal with them. During the time I went to school, I didn't neglect my studies at the *beys-medresh*. Every day from three o'clock in the afternoon until nine at night I used to sit with others at the yeshiva table and study Gemara, *tosafoth*, and other subjects. I also remember that at this time there was an examination at the yeshiva, during which I recited ten pages of Gemara by heart before the Radoshitser Rebbe. He gave me a pinch on the cheek, presented me with a book, and expressed his hope that I would grow up to become a great scholar. Other yeshiva students also demonstrated their acumen and received gifts. At the time I was also invited to join the Gordonia youth movement. But I was such a religious fanatic that whenever they approached me I would run away and hide.

Poverty and want reigned in our house. I remember times when I would come home from school and find our apartment clean and airy. But the stove would be cold and covered with sheets of paper. My mother would turn her head, and, with sorrow in her beautiful, dark eyes, she would say: "You must be hungry, my son. Wait, Mother will go and buy some food." Then she would sit down at the sewing machine and work faster with her hands and feet, as rivers of tears flowed from her eyes. I cried along with her then, though I didn't know the source of our troubles. We had nothing to eat, while there were other children at school who threw away their food.

Why they, and not I? My mother once told me that the sewing machine didn't want to make a living.

At times when my stomach called for food, I would run to my grand-mother and ask her for food. She would grumble quietly and hand me two slices of bread and butter. I made sure that the slices were as thick as possible, because I had to give some to my younger sister, who was also hungry. Mother, however, was so stubborn, despite her hunger, that when we offered her a piece of bread she wouldn't take it. Saying that she was full, she would continue working quickly with her hands and feet in order to bring in some money to buy food. There were many days when we bought no bread, cooked no lunch, and went to bed without dinner. But our neigh-bors weren't supposed to know this, because Mother taught us to keep quiet and bite our lips. Later, when I was in the seventh grade, I was ashamed to go to my grandmother for bread. Instead, I would send my sister and wait for her at the nearest corner. I would grab the two pieces of bread, hold them tightly in both hands, hide them under my coat, and run home so quickly that my sister could barely keep up with me. At home we had a feast, satisfying our hunger for a short time.

This is how I passed my youngest years, my years at school, and half of my years at yeshiva. Poverty and hardship were my companions. I saw before me a finer world, about which I dreamed but which I couldn't reach. People were amazed at how thin and pale I was. But how would they know anything about hunger, when they were all so well-stuffed, with fat bellies and snouts? I would actually turn away from them. I couldn't look at fat people. I lived a modest life with my friends, my youth forgotten and gone forever, never to return. The synagogue of the Gerer hasidim, where I used to pray every Friday evening and Saturday, is deeply etched in my memory. My friends and I used to accompany the cantor there. I would forget about all the troubles and worries of the whole week, even about food. I felt so happy then, as if I were in another world, one of dreams and visions, the world of the future and the resurrection of the dead, the world of my father and my grandfather.

At the time I cried a great deal over my fate, which I felt instinctively, though I understood it but little. When I went to bed at night, while Mother still sat at the sewing machine, I would think, "Why does it have to be my mother working so hard, when millions of other mothers in the world are sleeping now?" And as I would fall asleep, I would feel my mother's lips on my warm forehead. She would tuck me in, lest I, God forbid, be cold and something bad happen to me. This is how I spent my mostly carefree years—years of learning and playing, years of poverty and foolish dreams. I turned fourteen years old and finished both the Polish public school and the last grade at our yeshiva. Then a new period in my life began, a period of worrying about making a living, about my existence, about my further possibilities. My struggle to live had begun.

School had given me a great deal, and it served as the basis of my subsequent self-education. In school I had also made many friends, who left indelible impressions on my psyche. Some of them have remained loyal friends of mine to this day. From my school years I also recall a whole gallery of teachers of various types. One teacher, Mr. Fachalczyk, sticks in my memory. He caused me a great deal of trouble and used to make fun of my *peyes* and my long coat. He taught history and Polish. Today he is the leader of the Endek Party in our area and is known to be very anti-Semitic. I was very fond of the director of the school, Mr. Kowalski, who in his time had gained a reputation as a great humanist.

I had wonderful conversations with him (in the seventh grade) about the Bible and the Talmud, which pleased him quite a bit. On the whole, I remember him as a very refined person with great pedagogical abilities. However, he, too, has now moved over to the anti-Semitic camp, although he still holds the same post. Among the female teachers, I still remember Miss R., a Jewish woman who was an outstanding teacher of mathematics and physics. Yet her conduct toward us wasn't very admirable either, as she was completely assimilated and couldn't even bear to look at a Jew. Today, however, she belongs to the Zionist camp and has renounced assimilationism.

From the yeshiva, I recall, in addition to the teachers—highly intelligent men with pale faces and high foreheads—some very important episodes concerning my friends. I invited them to stay at our home, as they had come to study from different places. Mother didn't object to this; she considered it an important obligation. These young men would sleep with me; sometimes, there were two or three of us in bed together. Before going to sleep we felt very comfortable together. Once asleep, I sensed that my bedmates were still awake. One time I caught them having sexual relations. They were very embarrassed then, and tried to calm me down by inviting me to do the same. I refused, because I was still young and had little understanding of these things. But they continued to try to persuade me, and who knows what I would have done had it not been just before Passover and they hadn't gone home. They never came to stay at our home again, no doubt because of this, and so I was saved from their homosexual madness. This is what I got from my friends at yeshiva.

Right after I finished school, my mother sent me to a yeshiva in Łódź. She sincerely wanted me to become a rabbi. I grew my *peyes* even longer, became even more God-fearing, and prayed with the devotion of an adult.

I used to shake so much when I prayed that I would become dizzy and fall down. At the time, I literally went crazy with my religious fanaticism. So I left for Łódź and the yeshiva. My uncle, who was the representative of the town rabbi, traveled with me to the Radoshitser Yeshiva in Łódź. I soon found a number of people who would provide me with regular meals, but I had to sleep at the yeshiva on a bench, because there was nowhere else to go. I studied diligently. From five o'clock in the morning until late at night, my voice would resound among the others standing at the lecterns. My voice would echo from one end of the room to the other and disappear into space. Oh! Those were bitter, albeit interesting, times. The *rosh-yeshiva* took notice of me. But what could come of it when I had nothing to eat and didn't want to depend on my family? Sleeping was even worse. I lay on a cold, hard bench near the oven and shivered from the cold. We even moved all the benches together so that all six of us who stayed at the yeshiva could sleep together to keep warm. I slept like this for three-and-a-half months, without ever getting undressed. Within a short time I contracted scabies, and it became impossible for me to stay there. Night and day I cried over my fallen state and looked forward to the minute when the holidays would come and I would be able to go home. My mother came to Łódź before Rosh Hashanah and, when she saw me half dead and covered with scabs, immediately took me home, swearing that she would never again send me to a yeshiva. At home I was ashamed to show my hands to my friends from school, and I suffered terribly as a result. Still, I enjoyed studying a page of Gemara and other subjects on my own.

Gradually I recovered and began to think about my life. My family was very poor, and, on the advice of friends, I started to learn carpentry. But at the time there was little work, so I often spent the entire day reading news-papers and books that my friends foisted on me. These were Labor Zionist publications with a revolutionary perspective, and they had a very great influence on me. Sometimes when there was work, my boss would give me planes or other tools to sharpen. Eventually I got into a fight with him, because he insisted that I go with him to the cemetery to repair his father's tombstone. This made me angry, and I threw aside the basket of tools and ran home. I had a good cry and finally realized that my mother couldn't support me while I studied, a fact that she herself confirmed. So I asked her if I could go back to Łódź to work in a business. From the start, my mother had objected to my becoming an artisan and had advised me to find work in a business. How could a young man right out of the yeshiva become a carpenter? It didn't make sense.

So that's what happened. In fact, my mother went to Łódź to look for a position for me. Several weeks later she wrote to me. I took a bundle of underwear, my *tefillin*, and a prayerbook and went to Łódź in search of a means of supporting myself, my mother, and my sister. I was hired by a certain P.K., who ran a shoe accessory business at 10 Nowomiejska Street. My employer was a blond young man with a beard. His wife was fat and dark. They had married not long before and were just beginning to get established. He was a hard-working merchant and she was a refined woman. My pay was six zloty a week, with lunch. My job was to sweep out the store in the morning, pack merchandise, deliver packages, and run various errands. I was busy all day long from eight o'clock in the morning until ten at night. Later, I also had to sort, straighten, and stack the merchandise so that the store had an attractive appearance. The rest of the time, I ran all over Łódź. In short, my boss exploited me to the last breath. I slept at the home of my Uncle H., who had once been rich, but since losing his job had become quite poor. He had a broken-down sofa that was at least forty years old, as he had bought it already used at the time of his wedding, and this is where I slept. I covered myself with my uncle's overcoat and a few sacks. I couldn't turn from one side to the other because the springs poked my body and left me with many wounds. I remember that once during my time there my uncle came home from work, threw off his coat, washed, and sat down, looking terribly preoccupied. When my Aunt R. asked him why, he answered: "Today I heard my boss tell his son that I should be fired." My uncle's son, A.—who was, I later learned, a friend of P.K.—stood there and listened sympathetically.

"You see," he said to my aunt, "as long as I was young, as long as I had the strength and energy, I made a good workhorse for them. I used all my energy lifting pieces of iron a meter long and loading them onto the wagons. Then they spoke nicely to me. But now that I have grown gray working for them and they have sucked all the strength out of me, I am too old and useless to earn my bread."

My aunt's paralyzed hands began to tremble. She began to cry and mumbled over and over with her invalid's lips, "Who will feed us? What will we do?" A. stood there, gnashing his teeth and biting his lips, and could say only one thing: "We'll settle accounts with them." And he walked out of the house. This scene made a tremendous impression on me. I trembled and couldn't sit still, as if I were responsible for all of this. I cried along with my aunt, not knowing why. A short time later, my uncle was fired from his job, with 200 zloty in severance pay for thirty-five years of loyalty and hard work.

From then on I began to think and to see things differently. At this time the era of my stormy youth began, inconspicuously. The world began to seem distorted, as if seen in the twisted mirror of hypercriticism. My environment became the target of my rebellious awakening; nature seemed dull and indifferent to the suffering of humanity. This was a period of great exertion and suffering. Then my cousin came along. One quiet evening he sat down next to me and told me a great deal about the suffering of humanity, about the proletariat, about the bad conditions we all shared, and—this interested me most of all—about people who were taking a stand against all of this, people who wanted to create a new order and a new world. I was not at all used to this way of thinking. Nevertheless, I began to understand.

Over time, my cousin brought me many newspapers in Yiddish and Polish with very simple articles and revolutionary verses. Later, he brought lots of books to our house for me to read. After a hard day at work I would crawl into a corner with my cousin, and we would study various books by candlelight. I never stopped reading; I devoured everything. My uncle used to yell at us, but I was so absorbed that I didn't even hear him. My cousin brought his friends to our house and introduced them to me, one at a time. They were twenty to twenty-five years old, much older than I was, but they admired the sincerity with which I expressed my ideas in conversation. Later we formed a cell, and our work proceeded in an orderly fashion.

I don't want to say much about this time in my life, because very few people know about it, and I want it to remain a secret. But I can say that the work in my cell, which consisted of three students, one laborer, and me, was very absorbing. I lived a very stormy life then. Although I didn't have much free time, I spent every Saturday and Sunday evening with my comrades. Gradually, our cell distinguished itself and became one of the best at the time. This is how I spent my years working at Mr. K.'s shoe accessory business. At the time I regarded anyone who had a fat belly with contempt and sympathized with every worker. I realized that any tattered beggar could become a respectable person, were it not for the conditions—the conditions.

I went home for Passover. I wanted to scrape together a couple of zloty, because it's not nice, after all, to arrive empty-handed. So I started to save, grosz by grosz, and my circumstances became even more difficult. Sometimes I went to bed without dinner, woke up the next morning with a dry mouth, and once again swallowed nothing but my own saliva. I never lacked for books or newspapers, but always for bread. This was my life in Łódź. I realized that this was not a viable existence. When I asked my friends what I should do, they told me I should go home, learn some sort of trade, and come back to Łódź to work, because without a trade a person isn't worth much. At the same time, I ought not forget what I needed to do in my home town: organize political groups that would learn the same lessons we were learning here. Eventually, these groups would link up with those in Łódź for instructions. I even met with a regional leader, who told me the same thing. He added that we should not be afraid of anything but should proceed bravely with our work, until we achieve the victory that will transform the world and infuse it with a different meaning. His words and his face made an impression on me that I will never forget as long as I live. He also gave me a lot of propaganda to distribute to the young people in my home town. I packed it into a bag along with a bottle of kosher wine for Passover.

When I arrived home, I fully believed that I would succeed in carrying out what the regional leader had told me to do. In fact, I never went anywhere during the entire holiday. But when friends came to my house, I showed them the propaganda, on the pretext that I had found it in Łódź. Then I began to talk with them about the world, about labor, capital, and so on, until we had discussed these matters thoroughly. When I saw that they agreed with me, I proposed that we create a group in order to further our knowledge of socialism. Most of my friends rejected my suggestion; they told me that they already belonged to a youth movement called Gordonia. But one of them, my friend Y., agreed with me. He also distributed the propaganda to other young people, who took it but didn't commit to doing any work. Then my friend Y. found out that this was illegal and that he could go to prison for it. So he told me that he could no longer continue, as his other friends had warned him that he could get into trouble. And indeed, he, too, joined Gordonia.

Right after Passover, I went to work at the "meadow," which was located at the eastern end of town. There were about twenty buildings there, where sheepskins were processed. I worked in one of those buildings. My job consisted of soaking the skins in the water that flowed past the factory, washing them out, and bringing them back into the building. From six o'clock in the morning until seven in the evening (we had to work for twelve hours), I stood in the water holding a knife and scraping dirt off the wool. As for where the sheepskins came from, I was told they came from Romania, Germany, and other countries. It was my miserable task to do this work, and quickly, because there were other workers waiting for me. The work made the small of my back throb with pain, because it's hard for a seventeen-year-old boy to lift waterlogged sheepskins. And I had to carry the wet skins for about forty meters through the sandy water. At the end of the day, I collapsed on my bed, exhausted, and quickly fell asleep, only to get up the next morning for another day of the same hard work.

Eventually, I told my boss to give me a different job, because my feet hurt from being in the water. He smirked and gave me a job as a water carrier.

Now my task was to carry water all day to a vat and to see that there was always a fire going there. This work was much easier. I went about in a light shirt with my pants rolled up above the knees, sweating and red in the face from the heat. My daily wages were 1.65 zloty. More than once when my mother brought me my lunch she burst out crying and begged me to come home with her. She said she didn't raise me so that someone else might destroy me or that I should waste my young life here. I cried along with her, clenched my fists, and thought about doing something unspeakable.

At home, after work, I continued to read books and newspapers that my friends gave me, which advocated a Jewish state in Palestine with a socialist character, with kibbutzim, *kvutsot*, and collectives. I recalled the discussions in the cell in Łódź about *kolkhozi* and soviets, and saw that this material was very similar. But here it also dealt with nationalist interests, while in Łódź it was purely internationalist in character. Here it concerned the Jews; there, all of humanity. I missed being able to discuss this issue in detail with my comrades in Łódź. Unfortunately, we were far apart.

I saw that I was becoming independent and isolated. After long consideration, I joined the Gordonia youth movement, with instructions from a comrade in Łódź to carry out a certain mission. My ideals, however, remained the same. I kept to myself and never spoke to everyone all at once. Instead, I would take walks separately with individual comrades and discuss things. They would advocate for their approach, and I would advocate for mine. They put the Jews first, and I—humankind; they—Palestine, and I—the world. Nevertheless, I succeeded in forming a group within the Gordonia organization to study the writings of Bogdanov, Luxemburg, and Liebknecht. We also talked about the kibbutz and the *kvutsah*, about the Zionist pioneer movement, and so on.

After a while, I thought it over and realized that they had influenced me as much as I had them. I didn't know what to do, so I wrote a letter to my comrades in Łódź. I didn't receive a reply to this letter or any new material from the cell. Today I know that two of my comrades are in the Soviet Union, one has died, and one is a merchant in Łódź.

My work, however, became harder every day, and my employers didn't want to give me an easier job. My legs began to hurt, and one day in the summer I could no longer go to work. But then it was my good fortune that the local leader of the Maccabi sports club offered to send me to the mountains for a month-long course in teaching physical education. I eagerly accepted the offer. Finally, I could relax in the fresh air. I became a member of the sports club straightaway. To this day, I don't know what prompted Maccabi to send me. That same month, an instructor came from Łódź to run a three-day preparatory program for the whole club. At the end I was chosen, along with four other boys and one girl, to go the camp at Skała. The club paid for half of my expenses, and I had to earn the other half. Except for S. and me, the others came from wealthy families. We made all of the necessary preparations together, and we looked forward to the day of our departure as if it were a great holiday.

I will never forget the last night before we left. The club arranged a special evening in our honor. All of the members were present as well as invited guests. It was very pleasant, but, being shy, I sat off to the side. They wished me much success. One man even wished me to become a star like Vayngortn. The people there didn't amuse me, nor I them. I thought of my mother, sitting at home with nothing to eat; my younger sister, who went to bed hungry; and my poor Uncle H. in Łódź, who couldn't make ends meet. And I imagined my dear cousin A. and my comrades in the cell looking at me with pity and saying, "You have betrayed us. You are return- ing to the synagogue." All I had in mind was the chance to rest, because I was so weak and exhausted. I felt terrible inside, I seethed and trembled all over. I cannot express what was going on inside of me then.

Like everything else, this evening also came to an end. The guests said goodbye and left; then we went to the train and departed at dawn. In Lwów we changed trains for Skała.

The mountains made an indescribable impression on me—a wonderful natural phenomenon. Enchanting little places. Tall, old, majestic, dark- green forests. There's fog in the morning, and it's very hot during the day. Mist rises from the valleys after a rain as if something were cooking. And the air. And the place. The natural environment had a healing effect on me. I fell in love with the mountains at first sight, just like an inexperienced youth with a——.

I learned a great deal there about physical education and related subjects. But in my free time I put my blanket over my shoulder and wandered deep, deep into the woods in order to get away from the people and the chaos and to be closer to nature, to the silence and solitude, to the moon and the stars. I sat there for hours and thought about my current situation and my immediate future. As a result of all my thinking, I came to the conclusion that I had to find productive work, which would make it possible to support myself and my household.

Being on night-watch duty—when I walked alone among the canvas tents, protecting my comrades who were fast asleep, a staff in one hand and a lamp in the other—made an unforgettable impression on me. More than once I had a scare, because every shadow, every grazing horse, every suspi- cious thump startled me, and I thought it was something coming at me.

We also went on many excursions, both short and long. Once we went to a *moshavah* run by Hashomer Hatsa'ir. I met many of its members, who explained their ideology to me. I thought about it quite a bit afterwards and came to the conclusion that labor, freedom, the kibbutz, and Palestine could all become part of my aspirations, which I would realize in the near future.

The days flew by. And I—once a yeshiva student, then a laborer, and eventually a socialist—was now in a setting in which I couldn't open my mouth about my belief in a great revolution. This idea became duller in my mind, but its spirit grew stronger.

When camp ended and I had my diploma in hand, I recited Tuwim's poem "To the Common Man" at the campfire that was held on the last evening. My recitation was successful, and it was well received by everyone except the camp directors. My first camp experience came to an end, and I returned home as an instructor in physical education. Back home they wanted me to work for the Maccabi club and for Gordonia. I was even given a group to lead. But I refused to do any such work and started to look for employment. I sent applications to various Jewish-owned factories but unfortunately wasn't hired anywhere.

Then, a card arrived for me from my Uncle H., saying that I should come quickly to Łódź because he had a job for me. I didn't deliberate for very long and hitched a ride in a truck full of geese. The next day I was at my uncle's house. His son A. had been arrested, and all of the books that he had once shown me had been seized. My mother arrived in Łódź the next day, and together we went to see a clothing manufacturer, Mr. Z. We entered a low building that was full of machines. Fan belts led from one machine to the next. An old man with a red beard stood next to the machines with a dark young boy. My mother went up to the man and spoke with him, then she came over to me and said, "He's offering you eight zloty a week and board on the Sabbath." I realized that he wouldn't give me any more than this, and since the machines held a certain appeal for me, I accepted and started working at the factory straightaway.

At first I served as an errand-boy. I was sent to the store to buy butter, eggs, and rolls. When I had become acquainted with how things worked, I was given the task of carrying garments from the factory to the manufacturer's house, which stood in the same courtyard, and packing them. Later I was taught how to sew on the buttonhole machine. Then I sat for days cutting holes in underwear. The factory produced finished fabric out of cotton thread that the manufacturer bought. I transported the fabric, sometimes carrying it on my back, to a mill, where it was scraped until it acquired a grain like that on winter stockings. Then I brought the fabric back to the factory, where it was cut into jackets, underpants, etc. These were also sewn in my boss's factory. I sewed buttonholes, packed the garments, and shipped them to different cities in Poland, mostly in Galicia. I was also the shipping clerk.

Friday afternoon they piled a wagon high with packages, and I rode to the different shipping agencies, making sure that, God forbid, no one stole a package.

I worked from 7:00 in the morning until 10:30 at night. And if the courtyard gate was already locked by then, I would sleep at the house of the manufacturer, who would wake me at five o'clock in the morning.

The situation was tolerable as long as I had a place to sleep. My uncle no longer had his couch, so I slept at the home of my uncle's son-in-law, where there was an empty bed. But he was an anxious person, and when I came home late from work, he would complain that I was disrupting his sleep. Eventually, he kicked me out and my Uncle H. took me back in. He never did me any wrong; on the contrary, he always wanted to help me. He now made a living selling junk. The house was always filled with things, each of which had its own "appeal." My uncle would stay up until midnight, sorting them and stirring up the dust. My aunt lay in bed and cried that she couldn't sleep. But what could the old man do when this was his fate? I slept on top of the sacks of junk. After a hard day's work I had to go to bed in a virtual garbage can. The situation was unbearable. I became angry easily. I began to feel weak and worn out.

After a long time, I was allowed to sleep at the factory. The reason for this was that there had been several robberies there. For almost half a year I slept on a chair and couldn't straighten my legs. This was during the coldest days of winter, when the windowpanes cracked from the frost outside. By then I was more familiar with the machines, and so I became a more valuable and important person in the factory. Everything was my responsibility and I took care of it all, from buying cotton cloth to paying the bills.

One winter evening a machine for sewing elastic worth 1,500 zloty was stolen from the factory. The boss's wife ranted and raved, but in vain—the machine was gone. Then I was sent to see Y., the employee who had worked at the missing machine. This fellow had once been a notorious thief, who stole gold and jewels, and he had served four years in prison. Late at night I went with him to several seedy houses of gambling and prostitution. Eventually, I recall, we went to Radogoszcz, where he visited a man, treated him to a drink, and conferred with him quietly. The man said to me, "You can tell your boss's wife that we have the machine, and that she can have it for 500 zloty. If not, it will be destroyed next week." I related that to my boss's wife, and she burst into tears. But several days later the machine was back in her house. I am certain that Y. was involved in the robbery, because

1) after one conversation with me he knew where the machine was, and
2) after the ransom was paid he bought me a treat.

Shortly thereafter, I had a fight with my boss, because he didn't want to
pay me two weeks' wages, and I quit. Afterwards, he wanted to rehire me,
but I was foolish and didn't go back. As a result, I lost my best chance to
become a tradesman and a useful member of society. Some of the fault lies
with the cutter, L., who egged me on. He didn't care at all about his or my
class struggle. As it later became clear, he was just playing a "comradely"
diplomatic game, because his younger brother wanted my job. The major
factor in my decision to quit the factory was my extremely bad situation:
the lack of food and of sleep, my uncle's poverty, plus having to sleep on
piles of rags soaked with oil from the machines and the spit of workers,
some of whom were sick. In addition, my mother wrote to me that she had
little work and was in dire straits. People around me, even my boss, used
to say: "See what a fine and proper young man we have in our factory.
Someday he'll be a respectable person," and then they would smirk. I would
become completely enraged and felt as if I were on fire. My anger coursed
through my entire being. Did my mother give birth to me only so that
others might make fun of me, so that others' laughter and ridicule might
feed on me, so that my mother ought not to be proud of me, and that I
ought to forget who I am? Yes! I must work like a slave for someone else,
not think of myself, and let my family starve and be assaulted by poverty
and petit-bourgeois morals. Something within me shouted, "No! I must free
myself from all of this, and soon."

I never left my thoughts unanswered. I quit the factory and went out
onto the street. For two weeks I wandered around Łódź looking for employment, but everywhere I went people shook their heads: "No." My situation
became increasingly hopeless with each day. I was left without a livelihood.
Sometimes I went a whole day without eating, and at night I would beg my
poor uncle for a piece of bread and some tea.

It was before Passover, the season for baking matzah. So I went to several
bakeries where I had often been a customer. But when I mentioned that I
was looking for work baking matzah, they immediately shook their heads,
"No". Why? "We have our own to take care of." I looked like a beggar asking
for work. Everywhere I went it seemed that they considered a job to be a
handout granted to someone who had been humiliated and rejected by
bourgeois morality. I often started to argue, but then I seemed to have too
sharp a tongue and they threatened to call the police. It didn't matter to me,
but when I thought of my mother and sister, I left.

At the time I often met with members of Hashomer Hatsa'ir, who gave
me a lot of material to read. I didn't need their socialist publications,
because I knew more than any of them. Instead, I read Brenner, Gordon,

and other writers. I never had the slightest doubt that the revolution could liberate all of humanity. But I had changed in one respect. Until then I had looked for socialism; now I began to look for the socialist. In my short young life I had already seen many people, both young and old, who thought about socialism in the prettiest phrases and finest sermons. But I had met very few people who actually put socialism into effect. The realities of diaspora, together with the individual himself, his thoughts and education, were certainly to blame for this.

I began to abandon political communism, but I stood by its economic component. I began to think about the kibbutz, which could become a reality, albeit with new people and in Palestine. I made up my mind that, no matter how I did it, I must go to Palestine, in order to get away from my current debilitating circumstances. Łódź had been a bitter chain of failures for me. I never found any work, and so a couple of days before Passover I went home empty-handed. My situation was very bad. I didn't know what to do.

Right after Passover 1935, my mother and I went to the Vulcan glass factory to get me a job. There, a young man looked me over carefully and finally said, "Come back tomorrow." I went to work early Monday morning. They called my name at exactly seven o'clock, when the factory whistle blew. Together with another Jew and six peasants, I was taken to a pile of oak logs, which we were to load onto a wagon that day. Everyone took a pole and began to pry the logs from their place. I was not yet used to such work, but I did whatever the others did.

Several hours later, my legs began to buckle, and the pole slipped out of my hands several times. The peasants saw this and began to laugh and look askance at me. Seeing that they were making fun of me, I became even more resolved not to give in and to continue working. The stack in the wagon grew higher and the number of logs on the ground shrank. When I didn't think that I could hold out any longer, I heard the factory whistle blow. I threw down my pole and sat down for a while on the ground. The whole world was spinning around me. My mother brought me lunch. I wanted to run home, but my ambitions didn't let me.

They began lifting up the logs with a rope because the pile was getting too high. Now my job was to pass them along, using my shoulders and arms. After work, tired and weak, I looked at myself. My hands were black from the bark. My shirt was torn at the shoulders, and my body was scratched up. I went home, threw myself on the bed, and went right to sleep.

But the next morning I was at the place once again, waiting for work. A man came out of the office and told all of us who had worked on the wagon the day before that there was no work for us that day. However, we should come the next day. To tell the truth, I was happy because after that first day of work I was extremely worn out.

I worked at similar jobs for a while, until I went to the office and asked that they give me steady work in the glass factory. I remember as if it were today how the director hemmed and hawed and finally told me to come to work Sunday at midnight. I came.

The work was fast. I forgot that it was night. I ran like the devil. In the morning I found out that I had passed the test. I was the first Jew to be hired to do what is known as "hardening the bottles." A year at this job flew by as quick as the wind. My daily wage was 1.80 zloty. I couldn't help out my family very much with wages like this. But it was better than nothing, because until then, poverty had its way with us. But now we banished poverty with bread and potatoes, which we hadn't had before.

That year I also experienced the death of my grandmother, the leather merchant. When it came to dividing up her possessions, my uncles treated me very unjustly. They took the best things and, as heirs on our father's side, tossed us the old rags and broken dishes. My mother quarreled a little with them. I didn't get involved, because I knew that it wouldn't accomplish anything to argue with my uncles. That year I was busy with Gordonia. I only worked in their cultural activities; I didn't get involved in their politics. I even refused to go on *hakhsharah*. But for a whole year I was assigned to a group to which I presented lectures on various subjects. I also wrote articles for the "living newspapers."

That year one notion took shape in my mind. I realized that my current existence was no way to live, sitting and wasting away for 1.80 zloty a day. I made a firm decision to go to Palestine in order to escape two exiles: that of the diaspora and that of the Jewish manufacturer. I worked out a detailed plan. I studied the map several times and waited for the month of May. In the meantime, I acquired various identity cards and papers and made myself a book for registering at each town hall. My preparations were secret. Only during the last week did I tell my mother. She didn't believe it, but after I had made all of my preparations and my departure seemed a foregone conclusion, it hurt her very much.

I remember that on the day of my departure I got up around ten o'clock. I sat down outside in the yard to read, but I couldn't. My head was buzzing. A shudder coursed through my entire body. Everything upset me. My head was spinning. I was feeling melancholy. I sat with the book in my hand and stared into space. I didn't see my surroundings: the yard, the fence, the children from the Tarbut school. I felt as if I had reached a turning point in my life. I was breaking away from the present; it was as if I could already see the future. Light flashed before my eyes. I saw nothing. Everything was dark. I didn't know where I was. I was dreaming in a convulsive state, yet it seemed that I wasn't dreaming at all. I heard nothing and saw nothing. That was my state of mind just before I left. Is it any wonder—after all, was I embarking on anything certain?

I took leave of my bed, and I looked at everything with one final, sad glance. I felt as if I were being torn apart. Mother looked at me sadly with downcast eyes, stealing a very woeful glance at me from time to time. My heart was breaking, but I didn't show it. Mother was paler than she had ever been. However, I no longer thought about whether or not I should go, because it had already been decided. I felt my mother's weak heart crying, and I knew that she had shed millions of unseen tears. But what could I do? I couldn't turn back. It was too late.

My sister didn't have the courage to look at me, either—my sister, always so excited and sometimes as good as a dove. She was very close to Mother and they were both in the same mood that day, because it was 17 May 1936, and I was going off into the world without any money, so that I might eventually arrive in Palestine.

All day long, my friends brought me presents. The worst moment came when I said goodbye. I took Mother's hand in mine. She was trembling all over, certainly out of fear for my fate and for her own existence. She held my hand and said, crying hysterically, "How can you leave me like this now?" I cried terribly and explained everything to her. My friends who were there cried along with us. But I broke away from Mother with an egotistical animal will, without any thought to how she had sacrificed her life for us.

Quite a few people accompanied me to the train. I never would have expected it. Other than my ticket to Końskie, all I had in my purse were two zloty. Mr. R. called me over and gave me five zloty, which I gave at once to my sister.

The locomotive chugged into the station. Quietly, I bade everyone farewell. The train carried me away. My friends continued to wave to me with their handkerchiefs. They grew further and further and further away, until I couldn't see them at all. I stood at the window looking out into the distance, where I saw peasants walking. The earth raced by, and I was on the way to my future, to my fate, to my dream—ever farther from home and nearer to another town.

In Końskie I met an acquaintance, Comrade R., a student. He suggested that I organize a Maccabi club in return for the money I needed to continue on my way. At about eight o'clock in the evening I found myself among many young people. I spoke about the importance of physical education for the individual as a human being, as a Jew, and as a worker. They were convinced. I helped them choose an executive committee and promised to correspond with them. I slept over with one of them.

The next day, I visited Końskie and saw everything there was to see. I was there for three days, spending one day with acquaintances and the other two at the Hekhaluts kibbutz. I met many people there, who encouraged me to continue on my journey. They were all good people. There I also planned my subsequent route, to which I kept until the end. A *khaluts*, who came from the places I had to pass through in order to reach my destination, helped me draw up the plan. The *khalutsim* asked me to stay, but nothing could hold me back. And so on a rainy day three other *khalutsim* and I hitched a ride to Skarżysko Kamienna on a truck hauling whiskey.

I arrived soaked from the rain, but my knapsack was dry. I said goodbye to the *khalutsim* and left. This town was still in the process of being built. I went to someone I knew from this town, a student in the eighth form of *gymnasium*. We spoke at length about our situation. He found me a cheap hotel in which to stay. There were no youth movements here, so there was nothing for me to visit. The next day I left for Wierzbnik. There I spent time with some young people in a political organization. We sang and danced. I sang several workers' songs for them. They liked me and invited me to a meeting of their executive committee; I don't know why. They didn't receive me like a tourist but like an official visitor. They treated me very cordially and made a very good impression on me.

Late at night one of them took me to sleep in a barn, because there was no place in anyone's house. A little boy led me into the barn quietly, stealthily, and then left. It was pitch black. Little by little, I made my way to a wall, walking on straw. Suddenly I fell into a deep hole, but luckily it only went up to my legs. I finally came to a corner and fell down on some straw, exhausted. But I couldn't fall asleep, because I was shivering from the cold, and something was scratching my face. I lay with my knapsack under my head. Soon, gray light began to seep through the cracks. The straw stank. The roosters began to crow, and I was so sleepy. But I opened my eyes and saw that I was lying not far from some horse manure. I jumped up, revolted, and began to clean off my clothes.

That day I visited the local Bundist group and spoke with its members. On Saturday I went off into the woods with a group of girls. That evening I went with a few comrades, all girls, to the nearest station and boarded a train. I hadn't bought a ticket because I didn't have the money. So I had to play hide-and-seek with the conductor all over the train until I reached Ostrowiec. As soon as I arrived in town I went in search of food. All of the

Jewish businesses were closed because it was Saturday. I could only imagine what my mother's reaction would have been if she had seen how her only son was traveling and buying food on the Sabbath! Having no other choice, I went to a Polish restaurant. People sitting near me were talking a lot about Jews, but apparently nobody recognized me as one. I finished my meal in peace, but I was left without a penny in my pocket. I also happened to see the Jewish proprietor of the hotel where I was staying get beaten up. Eventually a man, a Christian, was arrested, but they soon released him because he was, after all, a Polish freedom fighter.

For a whole day I had nothing to eat but water and a few stale pieces of bread that I still had in my knapsack. I wanted to move on. I didn't know what to do. Maybe it would be even worse in the next town. I went out into the street and met some people I knew. I told them about my situation, and a little while later they gave me 1.20 zloty. Around dusk I spoke with a Christian fellow who told me he would see that I got to Sandomierz for one zloty, because he knew a conductor. I breathed easier; I wouldn't have to stay here any longer. At ten o'clock at night I boarded the train. The Christian fellow went with me and handed me over to the conductor. I paid the zloty and continued on my way. There were other Jews in the car. I told them everything. A fat man took out a zloty and gave it to me.

The route into Sandomierz was long and dark. I arrived at about one o'clock in the morning. There was a young woman wandering around on the street. I asked her where I could find a place to sleep. She led me to the home of a Jew. I paid a whole zloty to spend the night there, and still I had nothing to swallow but my own saliva. I racked my brains thinking of where I would get money to buy food and continue my journey. Then I ran into some people whom I was able to coerce into giving me some money, and once again I had some plain bread and travel money.

I rode to Rozwadów in a peasant's cart. It was Shavuoth, and I was reminded of home. More than once I crept off someplace where no one could see me and had a good cry. But afterwards I felt free and that my situation was good. Here I sang and recited poems at the Hashomer Hatsa'ir hall. The members gave me a few groszy and something to eat. The young people liked me because I could make them a little happier. I found this surprising myself. I don't know where I am. I have nothing to eat and no money. Nevertheless, I'm happy. I laugh and sing.

I put the few groszy they gave me into my purse and set off on foot for Nisko, twelve kilometers away. I remember a young man whom I met on the street there. I told him my story and he gave me a zloty. He told me that there weren't many young people in town, so I picked up my knapsack and walked another twelve kilometers to Rudnik.

I didn't have the strength to walk any further, so I spent the night here. The next day I went to Leżajsk. My feet ached. My stomach was empty. I got up the courage to approach a peasant. I told him that I was making a trip around Poland. He gave me two whole pieces of black bread and a cup of fresh milk, which I enjoyed greatly. My feet carried me differently. I breathed easier. The peasant gave me another piece of bread for the road. I was saved. I rejoiced, singing a marching song as I continued walking with a confident gait. I didn't give a damn about the world. I was happy, because I was going where I wanted to go and doing what I wanted to do. No one controlled me. I answered to no one. I was on my own, all by myself. This is what I wanted. I was now free as a bird in the woods. No one was chasing after me, but still I walked fast. I didn't need permission from anyone. The world was mine. Nature enchanted me. I walked through meadows and forests fearlessly, bravely forward. I was certain to reach my goal. Only the thought of my mother saddened me a little. Then, even better, I met another cart on the road, and the peasant gave me a ride for a while. I was over-joyed. This is what my life was like then, and I was happy even though sometimes I wept hot and bitter tears at being exhausted and hungry. But I gritted my teeth and laughed at the world. I was on the way toward my goal, which I loved more than any girl.

I hiked through Leżajsk, Tryncza, Sieniawa, and Jarosław, where I watched a peasant festival in which 50,000 people took part. Then I went to Przemyśl and from there hitched a ride to Lwów. There is much that I could tell about the important things I saw in these towns and what happened to me along the way, but I'm afraid that the gentleman who reads my biography will get bored and throw it away, and then I won't win first prize. However, if you insist, I will write about this.

I must dwell a little upon Lwów, because, first of all, the largest city in eastern Galicia made a deep impression on me, and, second, I stopped there to rest and gather the strength to continue on my journey. The entire time I stayed at a *hakhsharah* run by Gordonia. Its members were very good to me and treated me just like one of their own comrades. At first I had nothing to do, so the group had me run errands and peel potatoes. After lunch I went with the *hakhsharah* members to visit the city.

I went to different neighborhoods, rich and poor, Jewish and Christian. Along the way I chatted with various people whenever I had the opportunity. They were all workers and were all entrenched against the present order. They told me about recent events in Lwów. There had been a spontaneous uprising of the masses in which people performed truly heroic deeds. I was shown the shattered windowpanes and broken signs of the different businesses. I found everything extremely interesting.

While I was there I visited all of Lwów several times, for a variety of reasons: to pass the time, to carry out assorted tasks for the *hakhsharah*, to raise money from the Jewish community council and various societies to continue my journey, to collect insignias from various youth movements and sports clubs, and to find work, because I wanted to earn something with my own hands.

I was successful in many of these efforts, but the last was the hardest. I couldn't find any work the entire time I was in Lwów. However, I had the same room and board as the other *khalutsim* at the *hakhsharah*. There I shared the group's quiet way of life from 3 to 17 June 1936. They tried to convince me to stay with them, but I refused categorically. And so once more I continued on my way, which was sacred to me. During the time that I spent with the group, I worked packing waste paper into large bales, which were sent who knows where, and I also worked at the Pazet candy factory.

My departure from Lwów didn't go smoothly. I had only a couple of groszy in my pocket, so I decided to steal a ride. I sneaked into the Zamarstynów train station and ran on board the train, which I had selected beforehand. After the train had begun to move, I asked where it was going. A passenger told me that it was going to Brzeżany. Quickly, I opened the door, stepped out, and wound up sprawled out on the next track, with my things scattered all over. Apparently, the train was already well under way. I got up quickly, straightened myself out, and walked away unnoticed. I wandered around for a long time, looking for a way to get to Przemyślany. Finally, as the sun descended behind the trees, I put my knapsack on my back, and set out with a heavy heart on the road toward Przemyślany, forty-two kilometers from Lwów. I walked for a long time. My feet ached terribly, and the night was dark, like my future. I sat down to rest. I was awakened by the revving of a motor. I decided to stick out my hand. It was a motorcyclist. When he stopped, I asked him to give me a lift to wherever he was going. I showed him my tourist book with the stamps of various cities. He agreed, and by six o'clock in the morning I was in Przemyślany. I found a barn outside of town, dropped onto the straw, and went to sleep.

My stomach woke me up. This happened more than once on my journey, because I frequently suffered from hunger and want. I was like an outcast. People completely ignored me, as if a heart didn't beat beneath my skin. I had to find whomever I could and ask for something to eat. I had to bow my head to everyone. But I didn't want to abandon my goal. Sometimes I received support from rich Zionists, who took pleasure in giving it to me. But when I left their houses I spat on them, thinking that my mother hadn't given birth to me for their amusement, nor had I chosen my path for their smiles. In my eyes, the rich seemed to be useless parasites. They filled my nostrils with the odor of an outhouse. I was happy only when I was with the young people in a town. Only for them did I sing and dance; only for them did I recite poems with enthusiasm. They gave me the strength and courage to continue on the road, because they understood me and I them. Our hearts were lifted and our souls communed. They were as poor as I was and just as lacking in opportunity. Like me, they had no future. More than one member of this legion of Jewish youth envied the life I was leading and wanted to go with me—but none succeeded in doing so. I didn't want to take anyone with me. They looked upon me as if I was a hero. Their lives were completely without prospects, without a sturdy foundation. Most of them were unemployed, with no means to make a living. More than once I cried along with the many young people I met as they told me about their fate, which was so similar to mine. Most of the time I met with the poor— after all, would the fair-haired children of the rich even look at a tramp like me?

These were my thoughts as I passed through the towns of eastern Galicia, such as Brzeżany and Potutory, where I spent the night in the sawmill of a certain Mr. Dovid G., who helped me continue on my difficult way. I walked through Soronczeky, a Ukrainian village with a single Jewish inhabitant, until I reached the town of Podhajce, where I stayed for a long time at a branch of Hashomer Hatsa'ir. I bound several books for their library. They gave me food, a place to sleep fit for a human being, and a couple of zloty in exchange for a literary evening that I presented, and then I went on my way. I was getting closer and closer to the Romanian border, so I visited the towns of Monasterzyska and Buczacz, each for a very short time, and spent a several days with the *hakhsharah* unit of Gordonia in Czortków. Afterwards, a Jewish driver gave me a ride in his cart to Tłuste. The very next day I went by bus to the famous Polish spa at Zaleszczyki, which is also the last town on the Polish border.

During my first days there I tried to find a place to sleep instead of having to spend the night on the public beach along the Dniester, which was open to all. Later, I befriended a young man named Hersh N., who became my best friend in this town. I told him everything that was in my heart and revealed my secret plan to him. He tried to dissuade me, but of course I didn't listen to him. He also found me a job guarding a tomato field that a Jew had leased from a Ukrainian. This job was a big responsibility, but I took it for forty-five zloty a month. I said goodbye to my friend and went out to the field.

The field was no more than about twenty-five meters from the Dniester, which separates Poland from Romania. I always had the Romanian side before my eyes, both during the day, when the sun burned brightly, and at night, when the moon clearly lit the entire area. I was entranced by this scene and longed to reach the other side. At night, when all was still, I walked around with a staff in my hand, wearing a shirt and long, thick pants. When I came to the edge of "my" field, I could hear the flow of the Dniester.

I had a single task: to cross the Dniester and go to Constanța. This was the most difficult task yet. I began to ask the Ukrainians where the water was shallow enough to cross to the other side. A peasant showed me. Then, one dark night I tied my knapsack atop my head and walked into the water. I went perhaps 100 meters, but the further I went, the deeper the water got. It was already up to my mouth, and I was still quite a distance from the other side. With great difficulty I started to swim, and a while later I arrived back at my hut. The hut was so small that when I went to sleep, my feet stuck outside. I lay on a bit of straw with no cover. And there were worms that used to bite me all night; it was so bad that more than once I found it preferable to get up and walk around rather than sleep. Oh, those worms— they were everywhere, all over my body, in my ears and nostrils. When I think about them now, my bones shudder. During the day, when I had nothing to do, I pulled up weeds; sometimes I read or wrote.

The month ended, and I had saved up twenty zloty. My friend Hersh helped me find another job, taking me with him to pack tomatoes in boxes. This job paid well. I ate and slept with the other workers, paying for board, but not for bed. A long time passed, then the rainy season arrived, and the tomato season came to an end. My friend and I started to look for someone who could smuggle me over the border. We found a well-known Ukrainian, a professional bandit and ex-convict by the name of Mishko Klitshuk. When we spoke with him (in the meantime I had learned to speak Ukrainian), he told me that he would take me to the village of Veritshan on the Romanian side. There, he would hand me over there to a Jew named Gotesman, who would take me to Cernăuți. We planned to steal across the border on a Wednesday, as I recall. But that day he came to me and said that the moon would be too bright and there was a strong wind that could tip over the canoe. He postponed our trip until Thursday at ten o'clock at night.

That night Mishko arrived on time, and I was ready to go with him. I quickly said goodbye to my employees and went with my friend to the Dniester. The three of us moved in silence. Not far from the river I said goodbye to my friend. My guide and I walked quickly along back roads and hunched over as we walked through fields. We stopped at a place where there were some canoes. Mishko went down to the water, apparently to see what the situation was. A few minutes later, he returned and told me to hand over the money. I gave him twenty-five zloty, as we had agreed. We took a canoe and a small paddle for each of us and approached the water. We went a little deeper into the water and got into a canoe, I facing toward Poland and Mishko facing toward Romania. He stroked the water with the paddle, and my heart beat like that of a thief: thump-thump, thump-thump. We moved further and further from the Polish shore and approached the hilly banks of the other side.

I didn't know what to do when the canoe came to a stop on the Romanian side. I thought that I had made it past all the obstacles and had reached my goal. But then I heard Mishko's voice saying that I should get out quickly. As I stood on the Romanian side of the river, where there was a tall hill about 500 meters high, my guide turned the canoe around and started to head back. I went into the water, which was quite deep, and scrambled into the boat, dripping wet. But Mishko took me back to the bank and shoved me out of the canoe, saying that this was not a game and that we could both be killed. I stood there like a fool. A minute later I began to climb the clay hill. When I heard footsteps below, I fell to the ground and held my breath. Sometime later I was at the top. I ran through damp fields, across streams, and through small thickets. I didn't see a soul. I was so scared that my hair stood on end. Every few minutes I stopped to wring the water out of my pants. There was also a breeze, so they dried quickly. I can't describe how I felt. My entire life passed before my eyes.

At dawn I reached a highway and headed to the left. A while later I met a man driving a cart, and, to my great joy, I saw that he was a Jew. I told him everything that was in my bitter heart, everything that I had lived through that night. He informed me that I was already thirty-three kilometers from the border. He also showed me which direction to go to reach Cernăuţi. At about eight o'clock in the morning I found myself in a town called Cosman. I went to the home of a Jew to get something to eat and then went to sleep. It was Friday. I woke up on Sunday, having slept without interruption. I was told that I had been talking in my sleep.

Early Sunday morning I arrived in Cernăuti. I looked for some acquaintances and found them. For two nights I stayed at the home of a fellow named Shekhter, a member of Hashomer Hatsa'ir. He exchanged my forty zloty for lei and bought me a ticket for Constanţa. Tuesday evening I boarded the train, and Wednesday at about two o'clock in the afternoon, I found myself in the Black Sea port of Constanţa, at the Hotel Tel Aviv.

I tried to get information about ships going to Palestine and learned from a young man, a German refugee, that one was leaving the next day. He also took me into his home and gave me some food and a place to sleep. His window looked out on the sea. It was the first time in my life that I had seen it, and I was entranced. When this fellow found out that I didn't have much money he no longer wanted to speak with me, and he threw me out. In low spirits, I wandered around like a dog that had been kicked out onto the street, walking past buildings and along the seashore. I tried to think of a way out of here, jumping from one idea to the other. Eventually, I decided what to do. I went to the port. Determined and defiant, I strode past the first check-point at the gate. Continuing to walk the exact same way, I boarded the ship carrying someone else's valise. I knew that the ship was bound for Palestine. I was dizzy and my head was spinning. I raced to one end of the ship, where there was a pile of baggage, and burrowed as deep inside the pile as I could. I hid there for a long time—I don't know how long it was—until I was trapped by a beam of light and then taken by the collar and lifted up. I was addressed in an unfamiliar language; I didn't reply. As I was taken away I saw two sailors sorting through the baggage.

I was put in a narrow little room. I was stripped completely naked, and a man with a beard examined me with a light. A minute later the first blow struck me, and it seemed as though the lights went out. Everything went black before my eyes, and I could feel them beating me hard.

I awoke in a lonely cell, on a plank cot covered with a black blanket. My head ached, my shirt was bloody, and my face was swollen. I lay there for twelve days, taking very little food. A while later I smuggled out a note to the German refugee and waited. The days I spent waiting were difficult ones for me. Gruesome thoughts overcame me. My head was bursting with pain, and I spent entire days pacing back and forth in my cell without growing tired. The days and weeks were hard, and it was hard to bear my troubles.

One afternoon I was summoned from my cell and brought before a group of several judges seated at a table. Through an interpreter, I answered their questions in Yiddish. It was very unpleasant; I was even accused of being a spy. I explained everything as it had happened. Only after a long while did a man take me by the arm and lead me out to the street. I couldn't believe that I was free; I didn't want to move from that spot. Upon release I had been given a shirt, a pair of pants, and a pair of shoes with worn-out soles. The German refugee took me home, bandaged my body, and repaired the shoes. He also gave me a ticket to Bucharest and told me to go there. Feeling defeated, I did as I was told. But where could I find someone with a friendly Jewish face, from whom I could ask advice and to whom I could unburden my heart? I could see people with a lot of baggage on their way to Palestine. My heart was breaking with grief. Everything within me was crying, and I was shaking. I had to leave this port, which had taken me so long to reach and cost me so much.

I met a woman who was going to Bucharest. She gave me a place to sleep and told me that a couple of months earlier she had put up another young man like me with similar goals. I stayed with the family of Yosef Balter on Halfon Street in the part of town called Cala Vacarest. He was an Egyptian Jew and knew eight languages perfectly. His wife was from Bessarabia. They also had a child. I lived together with them in a basement apartment.

I found odd jobs in Bucharest. I was a tobacco worker, an errand boy in a tavern, a tomato vendor, and finally a newsboy. Early every morning I would get up, dash to the main newsstand, get an assortment of newspapers, and run around with them, shouting "Dimineaţa" [The Morning], "Zorile" [The Dawn], "Tempo." Yiddish newspapers weren't sold there openly. My spirits were low. My shoes wore out quickly. I lived together with other newsboys. My earnings were meager; sometimes I didn't even have enough to buy some plain bread. And the people around me, with their double chins and fat bellies, didn't even hear me, as though they were deaf as posts, though I shouted the names of my newspapers and ended with a loud whistle. After a day of running around I collapsed on my bed and slept like a log.

Eventually I found out where some Polish Jews lived and went to ask them for money. After a long time, they started to give some to me. These were all rich Jews, and a hundred lei meant nothing to them. However, they did invite me to a first-class hotel, where I had to tell them about my entire journey.

One day an acquaintance of mine, a homeless tramp, came up to me and told me we should go to Palestine via Bulgaria and Turkey. I have much to write about this fellow, and he told me many stories. This is not the place, but I will write about him if you ask me to. I had quite a few lei in my purse, and I went with him. We crossed the border by train without incident. We arrived in Sofia, the capital of Bulgaria, and hadn't been there more than a day when the police conducted a massive raid. Together with my friend, who was a deserter from the Turkish military, I fled back to Romania. He always acted with precision and forethought. Crossing the border was easy for him, and two days after we had left Sofia we were already back in Bucharest. I went to the Polish Jews that I knew there and insisted that they either send me back home or give me money to continue on to Palestine. I knew at the time that this was too brazen a thing to do, but I had no other choice. I had no work, no bread, and even these people, who owned factories, didn't want to hire me because they were afraid of the authorities.

After a month in Bucharest, I received a ticket to Cernăuţi and 750 lei in cash. My landlord brought me to the train, and as we parted he swiped my

quill pen. I already knew people in Cernăuţi. I visited a Polish Jew, a certain
Mr. Rozen, to ask for his help. He didn't give me any money, but he sent
me to an estate that he owned right on the Polish border with instructions
to his manager to see that I was transported over the border. And so it was
that the next day, late in the afternoon on the eve of Sukkoth, I was at his
estate. I ate and slept there for two days, and on the third day a Ukrainian
transported me across the Czeremosz River, which lies on the border
between Poland and Romania. I crawled on my stomach up to the Prut and
crossed it on a large ferry. My second guide, Dmitro Kapivka, was waiting
for me on the other side under a tall tree. He led me to the home of a Jew.
There I ate, and then I went into the town.

On the way I was stopped by a border guard, who recognized me as
someone who had crossed the border illegally that morning. He had a piece
of paper with my description: light pants, a dark jacket, and black shoes. I
went with him to the border post. After an exacting examination, during
which the guards stripped me naked and even inspected my hair; after
shouting at me several times, "You're a spy, you're a smuggler!" and finally,
after they put together an official report, which took about an hour, they
sent me to the police in Zalucze, who locked me up in a cell until morning.
My guide, Dmitro Kapivka, had it worse. He was given a beating at the
border post.

The next day a policeman came, handcuffed us, and we went to Śniatyn.
We were still handcuffed as we were led through the streets. I felt terribly
ashamed whenever someone looked at me. A short time later I was handed
over to the court, which sentenced me to fourteen days in jail; this was
reduced by seven days because I had no previous record. My money,
700 lei, was confiscated; I don't know why.

The cell was dark; there was a small window in the wall. There were only
three beds, and I was the cell's fourth occupant. The first couple of days,
I slept with a Ukrainian, a first-class smuggler, which wasn't so bad. But
during the last days, I was forced to sleep with a German traveler who, like
me, had returned from Romania. The bed was full of lice. This didn't bother
my cellmates, but I had to get out of bed several times each night and shake
out my shirt. If the days were hell for me, then the nights were hell's lowest
depths, when I felt the greatest sorrow. During the last nights of my sentence I slept on a bench. My cellmates treated me like a Jew.

I was given little food here—water instead of soup. I received some food
from town, and this sustained me. When I got out of this living hell,
an organization gave me expense money, and that same day I went to
Kołomyja. From there I went to Stanisławów, where I was stopped by a
policeman as I was on my way to meet a friend whom I had learned about

while still in Kołomyja, and I was put in jail. I was held there for twenty-four hours and then he let me out with apologies. In despair, I went to the office of the Jewish community council to ask for money to travel to Lwów. After lengthy conversations, I succeeded in getting the expense money.

In Lwów I was left without any means to live or to travel. I even spent one night under a bridge. The next night I managed, with great difficulty, to board an international express train, and I made my way into the first-class compartment where nobody was sitting. I never felt such pleasure as I did then. I was awakened by a light shining in my eyes, then I was dragged off at some station and put in jail. It made no difference to me because there I might get something to eat. I didn't know what time it was. When I was put in the cell, I became very worried. I had been in prison before, but I had never seen this—ten people. Ten pairs of curious eyes fixed on me as if they were trying to swallow me. The others started to make jokes at my expense, but eventually I managed to get along with them. I lacked for nothing there, except for freedom—but that is, after all, the most precious thing. I fell into the lowest moods at dusk, when the cell became gray and melancholy, and our eleven pairs of eyes looked out through the bars on the window at the setting sun. After a while I learned that I was in Rozwadów. My situation was bad. I was held there for one week, then another. My life was miserable, and I sent a card home.

On Friday of the second week, a lawyer came in response to the card and got me out of jail. Saturday evening I left for home, and by Sunday I was already there. I received a joyous welcome. My mother and sister cried with excitement, and so did my friends. Our house was packed with people, as if some celebrity had arrived.

Several weeks later, I returned to the Vulcan glass works. After all I had been through I acquired a new appetite for work, and I soon won praise for being a good worker in my department. But my wages, one way or another, were not raised.

Due to various developments at the factory, all of the Jewish workers joined the trade union affiliated with the Polish Socialist Party, as there was no other union. I was elected to represent all of the others. I was always there when it came to defending the workers' interests. I would run to the office even for the non-Jewish workers and take care of their grievances. To my shock, however, my comrades betrayed me. When I was thrown out of the factory for no reason whatsoever, they did nothing in response. The union and my faith in my fellow workers had become a part of my sense of self, but after their disloyalty nothing but deep wounds occupied that space in me. At first I simply couldn't believe that my comrades had done this to me. As a result, I resigned from the union, realizing that my comrades, both

Christians and Jews, were great egotists. It was a serious blow. I was left without the means to make a living and with no prospects. Hunger hovered before my eyes like a phantom. I didn't cease believing that there were good, loyal workers in other cities. In my town the workers are unenlightened and unaware of their situation. I have met many interesting working-class people during this time and lived through much with them. I would gladly write about them if I had the time, in a more appropriate place than here. I also met many interesting characters during my journey. I should also write about them; the Jewish reader should know about them as well. But I don't have the time, which I use to earn a piece of plain bread for myself and my family. Thus, both the beautiful and the ugly people I have known are hidden from public view. There are also the many young people I have met, who are my sole interest. They are my life, and I am their living mirror. But what can one do? Time is often a murderer, and, regrettably, it has unleashed its fury at me. I believe, however, that all is not yet lost. I believe in something better, because I know that those who believe are better off. I know that people are good, that true humanity will awaken within them, and then it will also be better for me. If it's not good now, at least it is not forever.

Yes, two years after returning from my unsuccessful journey, I am working in the glass works. I don't regret my travels, because I learned much from them. After all, life is the greatest teacher, and for me it was the universal teacher.

My work here is divided into three areas. It is my fate to work day and night along with many other oppressed and exploited people. We work hard, very hard. Life is sometimes unpleasant, because I am not happy with my job. I earn two zloty a day and the work is very difficult. My task is hardening the bottles, which is menial labor. Lately, my health, which I considered my most precious gift in life, has started to deteriorate. Sometimes I think about whether I, a young man barely twenty-two years old, have accomplished anything in life. After going through so much, have I reached a goal of any kind? Have I made a life for myself? In response to all of these questions, I can only stand with my wheelbarrow in hand and view myself as degraded and rejected. What does it matter if all the people in town have great affection for me, if the young people here love and respect me, if I am successful with girls—if I am still without a true life, with no foundation for my meager existence?

I devote all of my time after work to reading Yiddish books, which I consider precious. I literally devour them, day and night. I also occupy a responsible position in the town's communal life. When I am called upon to speak in public, I ask the following: There are so many fields of study these days. There is psychology, sociology, economics. Why don't these fields strive to create a better life for the individual? Why don't they give clear answers regarding life, which is so bitter and full of suffering? I have read a great deal of sociology and economics, but neither has changed my life at all.

I see that in these times one must seize a life by any means necessary, even with brutality. Ancient people knew this well, and I know it, too. What good does it do me, the plain working man, that someone has found this order or that system of government doesn't work, when my situation hasn't changed either way? They come to psychological or sociological conclusions and seek to ground them in facts—but I remain as ever, an ordinary, menial worker, who doesn't even earn enough to live day to day. If I work five days a week, or even less, I am left with an average of nine zloty a week. Let the greatest economist in the world figure out how this can be enough to feed, house, and clothe my mother, my little sister, and me.

My job is tolerable in the winter when it's cold outside. But as the summer heat waves approach, and the sun burns us on one side and the ovens on the other, then the situation is unbearable. Each worker drinks an average of one large pail of water every eight hours. The sweat runs off us like rain off a roof. More than once one of us has fainted on the job. And for this I receive two zloty a day. I have asked many people to try to find me a more bearable job, but they all shrug their shoulders. What do they care if someone else is suffering? Still, I have not yet lost hope, and I believe that someday the sun will shine in our windows and give us light.

Memories of my experiences often come back to me, but I don't feel like writing them down. Writing my biography has also cost me much effort. I hope that it's not the worst. I am convinced that something compels me to write. But how does one get the frame of mind and the means? I am writing my biography only because I am convinced of YIVO's good intentions, and because I would like those young people who are now awakening from childhood to know what path to take in their lives, so that they may be better situated than I am when they reach my age. I know that the situation of Jewish youth is very grim, and we need good advice. May my life, such as it is, serve others as a guide.

My journey left a greater impression on my life than anything else, and I bear its imprint to this day. I'm now looking for a way to emigrate from Poland. But all of my efforts run into a brick wall. I'd like to emigrate to America and if not there, then to Palestine to live on a kibbutz. That way of life appeals to me very much, and I'd be able to adapt to it because I have long since discarded any egotistical illusions. This is not to say that I have withdrawn from my own sense of self. On the contrary, I am convinced that my life would serve the interests of the society in which I have lived.

Lately, all of us at work have been laid off, and my situation has become even worse. Once again I must take my pack on my back and my staff in hand and wander on. I think that I will go to Łódź, the Polish Manchester, in order to find food there. The city where I was a yeshiva student may now become the city where I am a worker.

My future is as dark as a moonless night. I can't see anything. My situation has begun to grow bitter. Without work, without bread, without support for my family, I now go naked into the world. I am liable to be drafted into the army, and in the present situation, my time does not belong to me. But I leave here with great hopes that the situation of all humanity will take another direction and that my own situation will change for the better along with it. I believe that within today's human being humanity will awaken.

9
G.S.

Contest year: 1939 • Language: Polish
Year of birth: 1918 • Age: 21 • Sex: Female

J was born in 1918 in M., the second daughter of H. and H. S. My father works as a manager of rural estates. My arrival into the world wasn't a happy one. My parents had wanted a son very much. When they were expecting their first child, they had hoped for a boy, and when it turned out that their second child was also a girl my mother took an instant dislike to me, which I have felt all my life.

When I was just a few months old I contracted measles, and, having been carelessly exposed to the cold, I developed a problem with my eyes. This lasted about five years, and, although I was very young, I still remember quite a few details from this time. Throughout my illness I was completely blind. I've been told that even before I was three years old I realized I wasn't like other children, and I very much wanted to be able to see. My parents did everything they could to cure me. They sold several household items, spent my mother's dowry, and took me to see several doctors. I do remember one visit to a specialist in Cracow, who stated explicitly that nothing could be done and that I would remain blind for the rest of my life. I heard his merciless words, and I remember how painfully they struck my young mind—how they hurt the heart of a little girl, who should have had a childhood of fun and games but was already experiencing life's disappointment and hopelessness.

We returned home. My sister and other girls played with their dolls, ran in the yard, invented all kinds of games and pastimes. And I? I sat on a bench by the stove and thought. I don't exactly recall what I thought about. I remember wondering what chickens and cows looked like, because I could tell them apart by the sounds they made.

My mother fed me and dressed me. When she needed to go somewhere and had to take me along she carried me on her back. I often wondered why she didn't lead me by the hand, but apparently she was ashamed of having a child who was blind.

Still my parents didn't lose hope, and my treatments continued. Gradually I started getting better, and because they didn't know which of the latest medications had actually helped me, they made me take several at once. Finally, I was completely cured and regained my sight. I don't recall exactly how it happened. I was too overwhelmed with the abundance of impressions.

Soon afterwards, I went to school. Considering the experiences of my childhood years, it will come as no surprise that intellectually I was the most advanced among my peers. I stood out among them in terms of my intellect and abilities. I was an excellent student; I performed in school productions, recited, sang, and soon I was declared a prodigy. In later years, I came to realize that this did me harm. Until then I'd had an inferiority complex, due to my physical affliction. The sudden change in my life led me to believe that somehow I was above average and better than other children. I became proud and conceited, and it wasn't until later that failure and poverty taught me that life wouldn't treat me any better, and I was just like many other poor girls.

My parents each had a distinctly different attitude toward me in those days. Father, who loved me very much, was proud of me and began planning what I would be when I grew up. Mother was completely indifferent to me and has remained so to this day. This was rather difficult for me, because Father's love wasn't enough. I constantly longed for affection and love.

In the meantime, my parents' long-awaited and much-desired son was born, but, sadly, he died after a few weeks. Two years later, another brother—whom I love very much to this day—was born. My parents' love focused on him at once, as did my sister's and mine.

This is how I spent my school years. All my report cards were filled with excellent grades. At school I was well liked by teachers and classmates. Adults began to ask me what I wanted to be when I grew up. After some consideration, I decided I was interested in becoming a doctor.

Meanwhile, as always, things were not going well at home. Father often changed jobs. We led a truly nomadic life, staying in one place for three or four years at most, then moving on—like real wandering Jews. As to my family's Jewishness, it was rather weak in those days. Both Mother and Father were brought up in extremely religious households. They felt liberated when they left their childhood homes, away from this pressure, and—as often happens in such cases—they became completely secular. In addition to their lack of religiosity, my parents developed a desire to assimilate. We children didn't really know who we were, because of the way we were raised. At Christmas we put up Christmas trees; we had Christmas Eve suppers, and we broke wafers. The main reason for this was that we lived on country estates. These celebrations were held for the servants, so we took part as well.

From 1925 to 1927, Father had a job near Nowy Sącz. It was the first job he liked, and, moreover, he made enough money to support us and even to save what was for us a substantial sum. Unfortunately, the estate was leased, and after four years at this job, Father had to search for another position once again. It was then that Mother had the misguided idea of opening a store. Father agreed; as usual, he gave in to Mother in order to avoid arguments and fights. Once again, we moved to W. We had lived there before. Father was born in W. and we had many relatives there.

Mother opened a grocery store, which soon used up all our savings and went into debt. We had a hard time then. After much effort, Father landed a modest position, this time as a superintendent of a warehouse, but his salary wasn't enough to make ends meet. Money problems led to frequent arguments and quarrels at home. Mother fell into bad moods, which lasted for weeks. She kept arguing with Father and, in the end, we children bore the brunt of it. I was particularly affected, as the child whom Mother liked least.

Life became extremely difficult, even unbearable. In the afternoons, after school, I tried to help Mother. I cleaned the house, did the mending, polished the shoes, but none of this improved her bad mood. Vacations and school holidays were horrible. The constant arguments and shouting would upset even the calmest person.

Once, during my summer vacation following the sixth grade, I could stand it no longer and ran away from home. I moved in with my aunt, who also lived in W., but on another street. With my cousins' help I found a job with a tailor, where I worked as a finisher of trousers. I was earning six to eight zloty a week, and I gave all the money to my aunt in exchange for room and board. My aunt didn't want to accept it, but I insisted. She finally agreed, and from time to time she would use some of the money to buy me something to wear. I felt comfortable at the tailor's shop and even grew to like my job, but there were moments when I was gripped by feelings of regret about not going to school and about my unfulfilled dreams of studying medicine.

After several months at this job, I ran into my teacher in the street. When she asked me why I wasn't attending school, I told her that I couldn't because I had to work. She became indignant and insisted that I absolutely had to return to school, and she assured me that a student would be found for me to tutor in the afternoons. I had to agree. I went back home, quickly studied the material I had missed, and in the second semester I returned to school.

My teacher kept her word and found a girl from my class for me to tutor. At the time I was twelve years old. During summer vacation, I worked as a salesgirl in the grocery store. In this way, with much effort, I managed to complete seventh grade. I didn't know what to do next. My teachers and relatives talked me into enrolling in a teachers' seminary, where I could graduate in less time than at other schools. They also believed that this degree would make it easier for me to find a job. I took their advice and enrolled in the seminary. I attended classes and tutored in the afternoons. Mother thought this was foolish and claimed my studies would be of no use to me. My sister, having graduated from elementary school, was learning to sew, and this pleased Mother much more.

After a long search, and after we had endured much poverty, Father finally found a job in the village of Poczapy, near Złoczów, in the region of Eastern Małopolska. The job was quite good for these times. We had a nice apartment and a decent income. A silent feud developed between my parents and me. They both now thought that I should drop out of school, stay at home, and help Mother. But I was stubborn and prevailed, enrolling in the seminary in Złoczów. However, I attended the school only for a few months until the end of the school year. During summer vacation, Father managed to convince me that attending the seminary was a waste of money, and that as a Jew I would never get a teaching job. Besides, the program at the seminary lasted five years, and tuition was so high! However, since I desperately wanted to study and become accomplished, Father and I decided that at the beginning of the school year I would enroll in a commercial school. Despite the openly anti-Semitic attitudes that increasingly prevailed, we firmly believed that I would end up working in an office.

During that summer vacation I was depressed. Although I didn't work outside the house, as I had the two previous summers, my thoughts were unhappy. It was so sad to abandon my dreams and start something else again. Once before, I'd gotten over the disappointment that I wasn't going to study medicine; I had consoled myself that I would be a teacher, and I liked this idea. Now I was leaving it behind to take up something else again.

That year my brother passed the *gymnasium* entrance examination, and both of us went to school in Złoczów. We rented a room there; our sister kept house for us, our parents paid for my brother, and I earned my keep by tutoring. I had promised to do this, and on this condition I was given permission to go to school. It wasn't hard for me to find students to tutor, because I earned a reputation as a bright student very quickly, and my professors liked me. I had about five or six tutorials, which paid enough to cover my tuition payments as well as my room and board. Clothing was always a problem.

The best of my private students was a classmate of mine, who later became my best friend. She was a Catholic, the daughter of a well-to-do engineer. She was staying in Złoczów with her grandmother, who was the wife of a court councilor. For tutoring her I received thirty-five and later forty zloty a month; her grandmother also invited me for a snack every afternoon. We became very close friends, this girl and I, and this friendship—despite the difference of religion, ideology, and now the distance between us—has lasted to this very day.

The letters my friend has sent me lately are quite interesting. She refers to me in them as her sister and asks me not to take to heart certain Catholics' attitudes toward the Jews, because—in her view—these Catholics constitute a small minority, while the rest recognize the equality of all. I told her about my latest wishes and dreams, which involved going to Palestine. I joined the Betar youth movement. Many of my friends also joined, but we did so secretly, so that no one at school would know, as it was strictly forbidden.

I remember fondly those evenings, when, after exhausting tutorials, I would drop by the Betar headquarters, at least for a short while. It was always noisy and cheerful there, and when I left I always felt refreshed. Whenever time allowed, I also tried to be involved and help out. Unfortunately, I always had very little time. In addition to my studies and tutorials, I also signed up for classes in French and Hebrew, but later I had to drop them due to lack of time.

I myself don't exactly know how it happened that, despite my upbringing, such a strong feeling of Jewishness awoke in me, but the strongest influence was the anti-Semitism that flourished in schools then. My sister and brother also became ardent Zionists at the time, and this had an influence on our parents. To the extent that they could, they began to contribute to Jewish causes, shop in Jewish stores, and socialize in Jewish circles. Today, a portrait of Herzl and a map of Palestine hang over Father's desk.

My first and second year at the commercial school passed uneventfully. I was the best student in class, and for this reason I was liked and respected. As I had in elementary school, I performed, recited, and so on. I spent my vacations with the friend I mentioned earlier, at her parents' invitation. My vacations with them, following my first and second years at the commercial school, were extraordinary. They lived in a beautiful villa in the woods of Wołyń. I really rested there. I spent the entire vacation lying in the woods or bathing in the river. Also, as I ate more than I ever had at home, I gained

seven to eight kilograms during each vacation, and I acquired new strength
and eagerness to work. Yet even there I had some unpleasant experiences.
For instance, my friend's mother persuaded me to have my dirty underwear
washed along with everyone else's. I agreed, and then, walking through the
yard, I inadvertently heard the washer-woman and a servant laugh at my
underwear. Indeed, my garments—which were made out of ordinary cloth
and were full of patches—made a poor impression next to my friend's
elegant batiste lingerie. Today I wouldn't feel ashamed of such things, but
then it hurt me deeply. I ran to my room and cried for two hours, feeling
ashamed. But because everyone was nice and kind to me, I was soon
consoled.

That's how two years of school went by. The third and final year was the
worst. Although I still had my tutorials, I was getting paid less and less, and
my expenses increased. I started to economize as much as I could. I told my
sister that at one student's house I was served dinners three times a week,
and at another one's house I ate lunch three times a week. This way I paid
less for my board. I had lunch every other day and on the days I had lunch,
I would skip dinner.

The condition of my shoes was rather tragic in those days. Instead of
getting new soles, I stuffed my shoes with pieces of cardboard and rags all
winter long. There was no way to tell from looking at my shoes from above.
Always beautifully polished and shiny, they concealed the holes underneath.
The constant smile on my face offered no hint that my stomach was empty
and my head was buzzing from studying and tutoring. I usually returned
home after ten o'clock at night, wrapped myself in a blanket to keep warm,
and sat down to study. I'd place a glass of water in front of me; whenever I
began to fall asleep I'd wipe my eyes with some water, and this helped. I
didn't worry too much about obstacles in those days. I overcame them
easily, and I waited impatiently for my graduation. In those days I was
convinced that as soon as I graduated I would find a job, and this belief
sustained me and gave me the desire to work.

Midway through the school year I experienced a major blow. Once again,
the estate that my father managed was sold suddenly (due to the owner's
death), and my father was left without a job. As if this were not enough of
a disaster, our family grew with the birth of another little boy. It was a terrible time for us. Because Father couldn't find a job, despite his strenuous
efforts, my parents rented a small apartment in Złoczów and settled there.
As they hadn't saved a penny, my parents literally had nothing to live on.
Although Father received some support from the state unemployment
agency, it was barely enough to pay the rent and heating bills. My brother
was taken out of *gymnasium*. He wandered aimlessly around the apartment

with nothing to do and nothing to eat. My sister took in sewing, and I picked up two more tutorials, giving almost all the money I made to my parents.

I turned to the president of the trade school association for help. He personally asked my school to reduce my tuition. Then, with the money I earned from one tutorial, I paid for my expenses, and I gave the rest of my earnings to my parents. Skimping and struggling, I somehow made it to the end of the school year. In May, despite everything, I passed my final exams with excellent grades.

That same month, Father accepted a meager job that barely kept us afloat; the estate on which he now worked was being leased and was very small, so there was no money to pay him more. But he had no other choice, because I lost my tutorials during the summer and had to start looking for a job of my own. My parents thanked God that the job had turned up and moved to Zarwanica. I started to seek work right away. I stayed in Złoczów and decided to look for a job energetically and with determination. After my other unfulfilled dreams, the time had to come to realize new ones.

My dreams were now more or less as follows: to find an office job, work there until I saved enough money to go to Palestine, buy some decent clothing, and leave for Palestine. There I would work on a farm, then buy a little house with a small garden, a cow—in a word, I'd have a small place of my own, where I could bustle about, a homeowner and homemaker. Alas, these, too, remained merely dreams. I kept reading ads in all the newspapers and sending in applications, I pursued connections through my friends, but all in vain.

The greatest obstacle to getting a job was my religion. I came to realize this when there were two job openings, one at an insurance company, the other in the town hall. I approached the president of the trade school association, who liked me very much. He was also the mayor of Złoczów. He knew me from school; I was always sent as the commercial school's representative to wish him all the best on his name-day, and he had always promised to help me. Now he said to me, "I could help you if you weren't Jewish." This was very painful for me. Was it my fault that I was born Jewish? Did anyone ask my opinion about whom I wanted as parents, or who I wanted to be? Despite being Jewish, hadn't I always participated in every patriotic event? I was the best student in school, and my Polish compositions were read aloud in class as models of good writing. And how much devotion and love for the country in which I was born and raised was contained in them!

Days passed and summer vacation was coming to an end, but I still had no job. It was one more great disappointment in my life, but it wasn't the last one. The Betar movement was a great solace to me at the time. As I had more free time, I became more involved. I was a member of the command and a leader of a *kvutsah*. This was all well and good, but it didn't bring in any money, and I had nothing to live on.

If I am to write an honest autobiography, I must also mention that I experienced emotional "upheavals" at the time. As soon as I joined the movement, a Betar commander began to follow me around constantly. At first, I paid no attention to him—just as I had ignored my schoolmates in this respect—simply because I never had time even to engage in casual conversation with anyone. I noticed him only when my girlfriends started teasing me, and when our names were mentioned together more and more often. I liked him. Although he was short and not particularly handsome, there was something about him that I found attractive. He was exceptionally intelligent, and he was so engaging that it was impossible to be bored in his company. At first he only walked me home from our meetings, but later, after I graduated from school, we went everywhere together. He also tried to help me find a job, although without success. He loved me; I knew it, and I also got used to him and fell very much in love with him.

When summer vacation was over and I had nothing to do, he suggested that we both go on *hakhsharah*, and then we would certainly manage to get certificates to emigrate to Palestine. This was more likely because he was a commander and had greater influence; in fact, he had already earned a certificate. Once again, I had a dream: we would complete *hakhsharah* and leave together for Palestine.

We went to work on a farm in Kalinka. A new life began for me, doing physical labor that I hadn't tried before. Although at first my body ached, I was in rather good spirits. I raked hay, dug up potatoes, milked cows, and so on. Hanging over all this like dark clouds were the arguments between my boyfriend and me. He was tremendously jealous and made a fuss over every word I said to another man. Unfortunately, I was so conceited and stubborn that I didn't want to offer him any excuses or explanations. I knew I wasn't doing anything for which he should reprimand me; I just wanted to be friendly with everybody in the unit. After all, this was what life in the movement called for. Besides, our misunderstandings didn't last long.

A few weeks after my departure for Kalinka, I found out that our organization was starting an instructors' course in W. The Złoczów branch of Betar wanted to send me there as their delegate, paying all my expenses. I considered it an honor and wanted to go. My boyfriend was opposed to it, but I went, against his wishes. We were angry with each other over this for a long time. I suffered a great deal; I was sad and missed him so much that

I almost became ill. I was sorry to have gone and knew that I was to blame; still, I waited for him to apologize.

When I returned from W., my former unit was no longer in Kalinka; it had been disbanded. I was sent to complete my *hakhsharah* in Zbaraż. There I chopped wood at first, then I did laundry, and in the end I kept house and cooked for the unit. The organized activities were very enjoyable. In the evenings, after work, we studied Hebrew and attended lectures on the geography of Palestine, Jewish history, and so on.

Of course, some unpleasant conflicts were unavoidable. There was a girl in the unit who—I don't know why—disliked me. She conspired with a few other girls, and they began to make fun of me. Their reason was that I couldn't speak Yiddish. Was it my fault that I never heard a word of Yiddish spoken at home? And where was I to learn it—at school? The other girls didn't know it, but I have a contrary nature; when someone annoys me or yells at me without justification, I will sooner pretend that I don't care rather than explain or make excuses for myself. I would have explained, but only if they had asked me politely, without accusations and shouting. This squabbling led to arguments in the unit, and as a result I acquired the nickname of "*shikse*." Later, after that nasty girl left, we all got along. I had one other small quarrel with the head of the *hakhsharah*, because I went sledding without permission. As a result, I was confined to the barracks for a weekend and made to stand duty there.

I spent the whole winter in Zbaraż, and in the spring, after I completed the *hakhsharah*, I came home. I couldn't leave for Palestine. Not only had the fighting there not stopped, it had intensified. In addition, it was very hard to get an emigration certificate. I saw no possibilities for my departure. Besides, I had no funds; I hadn't made any money while on *hakhsharah*. Nor could I stay at home. Father earned so little money that it wasn't even enough to support my parents and the other children.

My sister earned a little as a seamstress, but it didn't help much. My brother wandered about aimlessly, without a job. There was no money to feed my baby brother properly. It was back to this misery and trouble that I returned. I understood perfectly well that I couldn't and shouldn't sit at home idly and become a burden to my parents. I was nineteen years old; I had ceased being a child a long time ago. But the situation got worse, because on the very day that I returned home, my mother started haranguing me terribly. She berated me, accusing me of not having looked for a job, since I hadn't found one. She claimed that I'd only had *hakhsharah* on my mind, that I shouldn't have gone on *hakhsharah* but should have stayed at home and earned money and helped my parents. I listened to these complaints and accusations for days, until I, too, started to believe that I was the worst child and the greatest failure in the world.

My father and brother defended me as much as they could, but this only made Mother more aggressive. Still, I offered her no excuses or explanations. I only said that I wanted to work and would work, that my unemployment was only temporary. But Mother wouldn't listen to me. Therefore, I decided to leave it all behind, trust fate, and go to some other place and look for any kind of job. I chose Lwów, because it was the nearest city.

So as not to upset Father, I told him—this was just a week after my return from *hakhsharah*—that a friend of mine had found me a job in Lwów, and this was why I was leaving. Father lent me some money for the trip, behind Mother's back. I packed some of my belongings and left for Lwów. This was the most daring move I had made in my life. Before my departure my boyfriend contacted me, and we made up with each other. We came to realize that we truly loved each other and that our quarrels were silly. He was leaving for Palestine. He couldn't take me along because he wasn't traveling legally, but he promised that in a short time he would bring me over. We promised to love and be loyal to each other, and he left for Palestine on the same day that I left for Lwów.

I found it very difficult to part from him. Although I trusted him completely and he assured me that we would see each other in a few months, I had some terrible premonition that I would never see him again. Four months later he was killed by Arabs, and with him my youth and my pleasure in living ended forever. I will never be able to love another, nor will I ever forget the shock of that experience.

As soon as I arrived in Lwów, I went to the headquarters of Betar to request that they accept me into a *hakhsharah*. Otherwise, as I was penniless, I would have no place to live. They agreed, providing I found an outside job and contributed money to the unit. I had no choice but to accept. I moved in with them, and, just as I had done a year earlier, I began to look for a job.

Someone who has never experienced it certainly will not understand what it means to hunt for a job in a big and completely unfamiliar city. I simply went from store to store, from office to office, and asked for a job. Some sent me off politely, but with nothing; others snapped at me rudely. Some made promises they had no intention of keeping; still others made unpleasant remarks or indecent proposals. I walked along streets that I didn't know and looked jealously at people who were employed. How I envied the salesgirls I saw bustling about in the stores! It seemed to me that, as I was told I wasn't needed everywhere I had asked for a job, I really wasn't needed in this world. In the meantime, the members of the unit hadn't asked me for money. To make sure that they wouldn't notice I wasn't working, I didn't eat lunch there, but ate only breakfast and supper, which consisted of terrible coffee and a piece of bread. This couldn't satisfy my hunger, of course; I was starving. Quite often I found myself standing in front of restaurants and pastry shops, greedily looking at food. In order to feel less hungry, I tried to upset my stomach. One day I ate a pickle on an empty stomach and then an apple, and with my last pennies I bought some buttermilk. If I had been the closely watched child of affluent parents, I am sure I would have caught typhus, but since I was very poor and nobody cared about me, all I got was a mild case of diarrhea and a much bigger appetite. After almost two weeks of suffering and searching I shared my sorrows with one of my girlfriends in the unit, who had been very kind to me. She suggested that I go to an employment agency affiliated with Dr. Klaften's trade school.

The manager of this agency, a very decent and dignified woman, took an interest in me. The very same day she sent me to a woman who hired me as governess for a six-year-old boy. I worked there only in the afternoons. I was given lunch, an afternoon snack, and ten zloty a month. I lasted at this job for just two months. I continued to live in the Betar unit and, since I couldn't pay them much, I had to clean and cook in the mornings in addition to working in the afternoons. The distance between Balonowa Street, where the Betar dormitory was located, and Bajki Street, where I worked, was about five kilometers. Although I was quite strong and healthy, I did not have the energy to walk so many kilometers after working so hard in the morning. Then I had to patiently care for the boy, tutor him, talk to him, and take him for walks. It was too much, and I definitely couldn't handle it. In the evening my whole body ached, and I had a constant ringing in my head. Now that I had food, I couldn't eat because I was so exhausted. Just as I had once dreamed about food, now I dreamed about sleeping at least one day or simply lying with my eyes closed. I knew this couldn't go on, or I would get sick from exhaustion. So I went back to the office manager and asked her if it was at all possible to find me a full-time job with better pay. I obtained a job as a governess, this time for a whole day, with room and board.

So I said goodbye to the Betar unit and moved here, where I have been to this day—that is, for two years. I am in charge of two boys. The older one is seven years old, so I have to tutor him; the younger boy is two years old, and I take him for walks in the stroller. At first I felt very uneasy and embarrassed, but now I've gotten used to it. I receive room and board plus twenty-five zloty a month (at first I was paid only twenty). Of this I send ten zloty every month to my parents and use the remaining fifteen zloty to buy clothing and to save. I haven't as yet completely resigned myself to fate, and I don't want to spend my entire life doing this kind of work. Despite everything, I intend to leave for Palestine and work there. I have persuaded my employer to let me have two free evenings a week to study Hebrew. Perhaps I will go to Palestine, so this will be useful. I would gladly learn other languages as well, but unfortunately I have no time. Also, I no longer attend Betar meetings; I have neither the time nor the drive. Jobs such as this one are very exhausting; the children are annoying and mischievous. The mothers have whims and "moods," and one has to endure it all patiently. If I had the money, I would emigrate illegally, but I don't. I hope God will give me strength and endurance so that I can stay here long enough to save money for the trip. Then I'll leave for Palestine and start a new life. I hope that its description will be more pleasant and cheerful than this one.

10

EM.TEPA

Contest year: 1939 • Language: Polish
Year of birth: 1919 • Age: 20 • Sex: Male

J was born in 1919, in a home where the music of each day consisted of the blows of a hammer, the rumble of a leather-stitching machine, the constant oh's and ah's of my father as he bemoaned his hard life, and the eternal complaints of my ailing mother. Everything was in one room: kitchen, bedroom, dining room, and workshop. For this reason I can boldly assert that I was raised in an atmosphere suffused with the struggle to earn a living. As a small child I did not yet understand, with my fledgling mind, the environment in which I was being raised. No doubt, I looked at everything around me with a child's inquisitive eyes. Even so, despite the haphazard way almost every child has of recalling the facts of his life, a few episodes from this tender age have, for better or worse, lodged in my memory.

As I recollect, it was evening. Something terrible was happening at home. Mother was screaming at the top of her lungs and gesticulating wildly. My two older brothers, it seems, were crying, as Father sat glumly at a table while working, no doubt. His head rested on one hand, and his eyes stared mournfully. I don't know what power resided in this scene to fix it in my memory. I remember it to this day, and quite often in moments of depression it appears before my eyes.

I don't recall that my brothers paid much attention to me. From a remark that Father made—"You used to hang about the dingy streets in town, like a little urchin"—I gather that even then I was a "member" of the fraternity of street children. I spent the better part of the day out on the streets and played there as well. What sort of games these were, I no longer recall. Once, Father came back from Warsaw. He had brought me a small, light-blue suit. I longed for Friday to come, so that I could show off my new outfit to my playmates. The happy day arrived; Mother bathed and combed me and dressed me in Father's gift. My transformed appearance was all the justification Father needed to take me by the hand and accompany me out on the street. Bursting with pride, I strutted alongside my father. Whenever we ran into some of my friends I averted my eyes, because I didn't want to look at them. My new outfit completely clashed with their worn-out trousers and threadbare jackets; besides, I wanted to let Father know that I would repay him for his splendid present by having nothing more to do with those ragamuffins. This decision did not last long, however. After that Saturday, as soon as I was back in my old jacket, I felt like part of the old gang once more, and things picked up right where they had left off, as if nothing had happened.

I was six or seven years old at the time. Like all the other Jewish boys, I attended *kheyder*. As I later learned, my father, who was a man of progressive views, hadn't intended that my education would proceed this way. Here, however, my grandfather intervened and did everything in his power to keep me from turning into a "*goy*." I don't recall that my new surroundings made much of an impression on me. I quickly got used to my new friends and to the Jewish teacher, who initially lavished attention on me for two reasons: first of all, because he received every new pupil warmly, and second, because I was the son of a town councilman. I didn't know exactly what a councilman was, but I deduced my father's status from the fact that he sat on the council with the director of the Polish school.

As I stated previously, my new surroundings made little impression on me. I find it surprising that the squalid conditions in the *kheyder* didn't provoke any protest on my part. I didn't rebel against the arbitrariness shown by the teacher, who simply patted some of his pupils while beating others for the very same "infractions." However, this apathy was short-lived. As soon as I started attending public school my passivity vanished, and I resorted to protesting by the most readily available means: running away from that kennel they called a *kheyder*. Whereas my response to the *kheyder* was (*at first*) neither pleasant nor unpleasant, the public school struck some inner chord from the moment I crossed its threshold. Even the way I was prepared for my first day of public school was different and had nothing in common with the *kheyder*. As I put on a clean shirt and my Sabbath outfit, I felt as though a warm, summer breeze wafted over me. I felt a warm and caressing hand in these preparations, quite unlike the one the *kheyder* teacher offered me the first time he came to escort me to his "school." It was the sharp contrast between the first "school" and the second, real one that roused me from my passivity. When I saw how clean the public school was, I became disgusted with the filthy, smoky room of the *kheyder*. The public-school teacher's dignified appearance reminded me of my father, who dressed in European style, and made me despise the other "teacher" in his dirty, long, black coat, who always had a cap on his head and particles of food in his unruly, black beard.

It's interesting that the *kheyder* didn't bother me until I was introduced to the other school. Only after I found myself in a classroom where, for the first time, I sat on a nice, smooth bench, did I experience a wave of repulsion and contempt for the *kheyder*, with its long tables and grimy benches. From then on I began to run away from *kheyder* as often as I could. I would spend the whole morning in public school, after which I was supposed to go to *kheyder* for the afternoon. My whole being recoiled at such a multitude of obligations, and so I resolved to put a stop to the afternoon classes at any cost. This decision led me down the path of deceit. At home I would say that I was going to *kheyder*, but instead I whiled away many an afternoon on the town square playing soccer with the other boys. One time, Father found out about my chicanery and became terribly angry, and as a result I was beaten with a leather strap. However, this didn't succeed in breaking my resolve. I persisted in my childish obstinacy and—I prevailed. At the age of eight (I was then in the second grade) I stopped going to *kheyder*. I felt like a free person. Mother, who didn't get too involved in these matters, tried to persuade me to go back with pleas and admonitions—"It's not nice for a boy not even to know how to pray"—but this didn't work, either. Father, as I have already mentioned, was no devotee of this sort of education, so he all but approved of my quitting *kheyder*.

At public school I did well in my studies. While my brother made a fuss about going to school, I set a good example. The second grade ended triumphantly for me; I passed with good marks. I set about preparing for the third grade very seriously. I made a solemn vow to study hard, especially as I had heard from my friends that getting promoted to the fourth grade virtually guaranteed that you would never be "held back" in any class. We all regarded the third grade as the most difficult one.

The final months of this school year are bound up with a fond memory. Our class instructor was supposed to put together a skit for the school show. She selected the little "actors" and, thank God, I was among those she picked. At the time, I was beside myself with joy. It was the same old story once again: I felt just a bit superior to my friends. The last time, it had been on account of my blue suit and the walk I took with my father; now it was the role I was to play in the skit. I recall that I spent the whole morning before the show and the distribution of our grades getting ready. Finally the eagerly awaited moment arrived. Along with the other "actors" I got up on the stage and gave a fine rendition of my part. This same day was distinguished by a second triumph: I got promoted to the next grade, once again with good marks. The one thing that disappointed me was the response to the skit. After the performance I had expected to hear my name on the lips of my classmates. I thought they would be talking about me, but it was as if I hadn't participated at all. This hurt me deeply, but there was nothing I could do about it.

My eldest brother could recite beautifully. He always took part in the annual celebrations that were held at the "cultural union." After these performances, he was invariably praised in front of our parents. It wasn't so much that this made me feel bad as that I was envious of my brother. Motivated by the desire to show off my own declamatory skill, I asked Father to bring me a volume of Yiddish poetry. I set myself to memorizing it. Soon I found an opportunity to put my talents on display. There was a banquet for my father's sister, who was emigrating to Canada. On this occasion, I managed to recite flawlessly a poem entitled "Hope and Believe." This performance made me a celebrity and demonstrated that I had a little spark of my brother's talent. Soon after this first "triumph," a friend of Father's took me with him to the Zionist association, where I was given a poem to recite at a ceremony in memory of Herzl. I had no idea that this gathering would bring me not the laurels I expected, but sorrow and anguish. When I got on stage I was overcome with stage fright. I recited the first few stanzas, but (contrary to the way I had imagined it) when I got near the end I became tongue-tied and stopped, unable to continue. Dr. B., one of the presiding officers, took pity on me and prompted me, so that I was somehow able to stagger, in halting Yiddish, to the end. I took a bow and, in place of the bravos I had anticipated (in my dreams), I heard only the feeble applause of one lone, kind-hearted person. All through the rest of the ceremony I sat backstage, crying, and I could hardly wait to slink away unnoticed. I barely slept all night. Crying ceaselessly, I decided to run away from home and from town.

I thought of walking to another town to look for work and to live on my own, away from all those who had "done me wrong." This childish scheme, so vivid in the gloom of night, vanished with the dawn. Instead of getting up the next day quite early, as I usually did, I stayed in bed until noon. I was too ashamed to face my father or my brother or anyone else. While pretending to be asleep, I overheard them talking about my failure. Finally I got up. The more I tried to appear calm, the more obvious was my dejection, and the clearer it became just how much of a calamity had befallen me. My oldest brother was clearly itching for an excuse to start in on me. When Mother asked me why I wasn't eating and I replied that I didn't want to, my brother butted in, saying, "What difference does it make, now that the worst has happened?" This really hit home, and I started to cry again. However, this sorry episode gradually faded, although for a long time thereafter I would still turn bright red whenever poetry or recitations were discussed in my presence. Thus, the "career" of a public speaker came to a painful end.

My father—I can't write about him without stating at once that, from my earliest years, I felt great sympathy and sincere love for him. His figure, always bent over his workbench, evoked my respect. From the time I was old enough to understand, my ears were filled with praise for my father. I instinctively felt that I, too, basked in his reflected glory. It made me proud to see how his acquaintances would come to ask him to write something for them or to inquire what was going on in the world. My father divided up his workday according to a kind of schedule. In the morning he always sat down to read the newspaper. Each day he would spread open the enormous pages of *Der moment* (and, later, *Di naye folkstsaytung*, which he still reads), devouring the print with his eyes. After this he would start to work in his customary fashion. Knife in hand, he would "torment" the different-colored pieces of leather. When his work was finished he would often open a book and read for quite a long time. Sometimes he would engage his father in conversations that made no sense to me. Grandfather would bring in some oversized books, point to certain passages on the enormous pages, and command my father to read. As a rule these conversations between father and son came to a stormy end. Grandfather would shout, and Father would respond in kind, raising his voice somewhat.

Father's outward appearance in itself made me love him. It wasn't just the way he lived his life or his interests that set him apart from the other artisans of our town; he was distinguished even in the way he dressed: always—even in the shop—in clean clothes, always in a tie. Somehow he was different from the Jewish men I saw in long, dirty coats and tall, unpolished boots, who spoke in a coarse manner so unlike his. Often Father became despondent. On these occasions he would sit at the table, his head resting on one hand, and his sad, expressive eyes seemingly fixed on some unseen point. Concealed in their depths were things I couldn't fathom, mysteries of some sort, swathed in a sad and plaintive melody. I knew he was suffering; I knew even then that he was married to a woman who was not his equal in any respect.

Mother cared nothing for his interests. She constantly reproached him for being too preoccupied with public affairs. She provoked scenes with him over his participation in the town council, over his "supervisory" role in the Jewish community. The root of this incessant discord lay in their different, even opposite, natures. Father was a progressive man, inclined to get swept up in the current of life. A man of the widest intellectual horizons, he was forced to live with a backward and narrow-minded woman, who was imbued with the cult of domesticity and most unfortunately afflicted with a nervous disorder—a manic disorder, according to the doctor.

Gradually, I myself became aware of the tragedy of Mother's illness. I realized that the melancholy look in Father's eyes, the gentle sighs that welled up from the depths of his being, had their source in the misfortune that had overtaken Mother and affected all of us. From the very moment I first began to understand, I looked on Father as a man bearing a cross. I couldn't, of course, ease his burden, much less shoulder it myself. However, in my own childish way I tried to show my solidarity with Father; whenever I saw his brow grow overcast, whenever I saw the pupils of his eyes fill with profound sadness, I tried to rein in my childish mirth. I would become downcast at such times and weep quietly somewhere in a corner. There was nothing feigned or artificial about this weeping. Hot tears trickled down my cheeks and left their salty taste on my lips. By crying I wanted to convince myself that I wasn't indifferent to what was happening in our house. I saw my tears as a kind of gift to my tormented father.

Mother was difficult to get to know. Her personality was distorted by her illness, and so it took a greater effort to understand her character. To this day I still find it somewhat impenetrable and confusing. As far back as I can remember, there was never a time when Father and Mother lived together amicably. They were always quarreling over something. There was never any harmony; their life together always contained false notes; the dissonance often grew terribly shrill. It was in this atmosphere that I grew up along with my brothers and my younger sister. While I always looked at Father, trying to discern something in his face or his gaze, I treated Mother as if she were an older sister. All I wanted was for her to take care of my requests; but it never occurred to me to scrutinize her in the way that I regularly looked at Father. Perhaps this was because Father always seemed more worthy of attention than Mother, who, both in her intellect and in her appearance, was a typical provincial woman.

Later on, I did get to know Mother; only then did I begin to gain some insight into her character and her soul. I saw in her a type that was Father's exact opposite. Her restlessness contrasted with his tranquil nature; her ideas and piety were the opposite of his progressive, secular outlook. As a result, Mother's views—on people, the world, and the problems of daily life—were constantly at odds with Father's. I don't know what made me love Father more than Mother, unless it was the intuition (even in my youngest years) of the superiority of his character and intelligence compared to her commonplace and narrow world-view.

I had very little in common with my brothers. Since the older ones didn't tyrannize me, as sometimes happens, we got along quite well, contrary to what one might expect, but we lived in separate worlds. My brothers liked to give themselves airs and treated me like a little brat. Not surprisingly, we had almost nothing to do with one another outside the house.

Life went along as it usually did for a working-class household in a small town. Our financial situation was shaky. There was almost never any money when we needed it. I heard Father constantly complain that, as bad as things were on ordinary weekdays, Friday was a nightmare. It was true—we could make ends meet on a workday, but when Friday rolled around we needed more money; it was obvious that Father was right. Among my two brothers and I, only the eldest had a coat, owing to the fact that he had a job. The next oldest didn't have any warm clothes, even though he worked at home in the shop, and as for me—the free-loader—a coat was out of the question. During the winter I went to school in summer clothes; later on, I was given Mother's warm, sleeveless jacket to wear. I was embarrassed to have to go around in women's clothing, but the cold won out over my shame.

I think that, despite our less-than-ideal financial circumstances, a more harmonious atmosphere could have prevailed in our home were it not for Mother's illness, which gave us no peace at all, day or night. I don't know whether anyone unfamiliar with this terrible affliction realizes the emotional and physical suffering it entails. As a child I felt ashamed when my friends would say, in the middle of an argument, that my mother was crazy. Later, however—many years later—I realized that the real tragedy wasn't the "unsightliness" of the disease. For a long time, though, I was still sensitive to those childish taunts. I used to shy away from quarrels and let my friends have their way—anything to avoid having to hear the word "crazy." However, this isn't what I intended to discuss. I want to describe how this illness tore apart our home life. I want to record how it turned Father into an old man before his time and deprived the rest of us of the radiance of our youth.

During the most beautiful, sun-drenched months of summer, when others were enjoying the bounty of the season, an air of despondency pervaded our home. We didn't sleep at night, because that was when Mother would take to screaming at the top of her lungs and singing songs with incomprehensible, disjointed lyrics that sprang from her afflicted imagination. She often became belligerent and would react to some innocuous remark by breaking everything she could lay her hands on. When, as quite often happened, her wrath spared the dishes, it would be her clothing that suffered. These weeks seemed like years, they wore all of us down physically and morally and also undermined our household economy. We didn't get enough to eat, because at these times our income shrank drastically, for the simple reason that the workshop stood idle.

And yet there were also pleasant moments during these weeks of sadness, when we would all sit down at the table to have some soup that Father had prepared. We would feel such a bond of closeness at these times. Each of us could feel the others' warm glances. The squabbling and complaints ceased, and we were all bound together by our life of misfortune. Even more pleasant and cheering were those times when one of us would say to the other, "You know? Mother is a little better." At such moments a strange sort of joy would pervade the soul. Deliverance was sure to come, after all; the days of warm dinners and a little peace would return.

Father had a sincere love of music. He was infatuated with the sound of the violin, with its plangent tones. He used to tell me how he had studied this instrument when he was young, and how he would have become proficient if it hadn't been for his father, who preferred—demanded—that he devote his free time after work to gleaning wisdom from holy books instead of playing the violin. Yet Father didn't renounce his aspirations without a struggle. He bought himself a violin and started taking lessons from a local musician. Father's great desire clashed with the incomprehension of my grandfather, who, enraged by his son's "tomfoolery," smashed the violin and gave the would-be violinist a thorough beating.

Father would say to me, "I wanted to play, but unfortunately I was knocking my head against a wall. But if you ever have a serious desire to learn, nothing will stand in your way." I sensed a challenge in these words, but at first I didn't pick up the "gauntlet" that he had metaphorically thrown down. I didn't want to make such a commitment, because I dreaded the strenuous work Father had described to me. "In order to play," he would say, paraphrasing Napoleon's dictum, "one has to practice, practice, and practice some more." Even more than this incessant practicing, the tedious scales and exercises in Father's accounts alarmed me. I had the feeling that, by passing on all these details, Father was giving me fair warning, in case I came to him one fine day and said, "Father, I want to learn to play." He had good reason to proceed in this manner, having been burnt once before, when my oldest brother's enthusiasm to study music turned out to be short-lived. Afterward, Father confided to me: "It wasn't so much the money spent on lessons that upset me, but the letdown I felt—that's what hurt. I wanted him to have the right conditions and my genuine support, so that he could learn what I had once set my heart on so much. But, unfortunately . . ."

After these talks with Father, I would daydream about being able to play the violin well, to coax such sounds from the strings that his eyes would light up and his face would come to life. At the same time, I was full of apprehension that, instead of cheering him up, my playing might have just the opposite effect and make him sad. I dreaded causing Father a second such disappointment, and so I hesitated. There were times when the prospect of Father's delight written all over his face would prompt me to go and tell him that I had decided to learn to play. But before long this "resolution" was undone by other ideas that took hold of me. Then, as fate would have it, an event took place that brought me to a firm decision.

The cinema in our town was showing a film based on the story *Janko the Musician* by Sienkiewicz. I was so enthralled by this film—or, should I say, it held me so tightly in its grip—that I remained under its spell for a long time. Janko's exquisite playing stimulated my enthusiasm for Father's violin to new levels. Janko's path strewn with obstacles, his ultimate triumph, and his fame convinced me that it was worth it to practice the boring scales and exercises if only to become a Janko—not the Janko who was beaten for breaking into the palace, but the Janko of the stage, who filled people's hearts with enchantment and delight. Making up my mind once and for all, I went to Father one day and delivered a speech that I had prepared in advance. Father looked at my eyes filled with tears and replied, "Starting tomorrow, then." Apparently he could see from my eyes that I really meant what I said. The very same day he repaired my brother's violin and on a sheet of music paper wrote out the scales, which he still remembered from his own lessons. The next day, as he had promised, he gave me an introduction to the secrets of music.

My father was my first music teacher, but only for a single day. After this first lesson he sent for the town's music teacher and placed my musical education in his hands. From then on I was visited three times a week by my teacher, who simultaneously worshipped at both the altar of the muse of melody and that of Hephaestus, for he worked as a locksmith. This musician, who combined delicate strains with the less dainty rasping of a file, taught me to read the "angelic" script, as my father called musical notation. Father had done the right thing by telling me earlier about the tedium of scales and exercises. The only way to cope with them was to arm myself with patience. Mindful of my commitment to Father, I practiced daily and prepared for my lessons thoroughly. In this way I earned Father's acknowledgment of my diligence, but was that enough of a reward? No—I wanted to win Father's praise not with my hard work, but with my tone; I wanted to gain his approval with a beautifully played composition.

But such was not the case at the time. The notes I brought forth from the strings sounded like geese cackling or crows cawing. Meanwhile, my teacher would get Father's attention with his splendid renditions of the "Solfeggio Song" and other works. Were it not for Father, I would have abandoned my plans for becoming a "Janko of the stage." I didn't want to let him down, so I worked even harder and spent even more time grinding out the exercises: "Practice makes perfect."

And so it was. My work had its effect; not only did I get better and better at playing scales, but in the meantime I mastered some of my teacher's compositions and began to rival my mentor. The results surpassed my expectations. One evening when I had finished playing and put aside my violin, Father came up to me and said, "You know? That teacher is of no help to you anymore." I myself knew that I was practically on a par with him. That same evening I took the violin out of its case, and I simply kissed it and thanked it for helping me to achieve my first victory.

On Father's advice I stopped taking lessons from the music-teacher-*cum*-locksmith and switched to another instructor. It so happened that just then the only Jew in our town who had ever graduated from a *gymnasium* had returned home. People said that he played the violin superbly. It was even rumored that he had studied at the conservatory. This small-town gossip rendered my second teacher that much more mysterious. Just the fact that, at his insistence, I went to see him rather than vice versa placed him a few rungs above his predecessor. Apart from all the qualities that he possessed or that were erroneously attributed to him, he did, in any event, have that diploma. As I saw it at the time, a diploma was proof positive that one commanded all the secrets of the universe. A graduate from the *gymnasium*—it sounded fantastic. It was also rumored that he studied by the light of the moon, because he had no lamps in his house. At the time I was taken in by these tall tales. Add to all of this his quite solid knowledge of music, and it's no surprise that the comparison between my first teacher and the second one put me in mind of David and Goliath.

My second teacher guided me onto the true path of music. Every lesson with him propelled me forward, and I could tell that I was making headway. My new instructor not only knew how to teach but also had a knack for making the subject interesting, so that it was a pleasure to play as well. All the same, I can't say that our sessions were altogether peaceful. As I had in the past, I once again perceived a vast gap separating my playing from my teacher's. From the moment I began to study with him, I regarded myself as mediocre. Gone was the belief that I had accomplished something in the field of music. Yet this wasn't the cause of my dissatisfaction. From time to time my teacher paid a visit to our home. Usually, he passed the time by playing the violin. To be frank, I wasn't overjoyed to see him in our house, because next to his playing I sounded like an amateur. He had only to play a single piece, and all my musical accomplishments would be eclipsed, both in my own eyes and in my father's. On such occasions I would retreat into a corner and sob. I don't know whether this was an expression of jealousy so much as an acknowledgment of my own lack of ability. I renewed my vow to practice in order to make further advances. I told Father and my brothers that I wanted—that I was determined—to reach the same level as my teacher, but to myself I said, "You're just tilting at windmills."

While making progress in my music studies, I was also advancing each year at school, until I finally reached the uppermost rung of the ladder: I found myself in the seventh grade and on the verge of graduating. It was high time to think about what course to follow next. I fantasized about enrolling in the conservatory. This wasn't based on any sense of calling; rather, it was tied to dreams of fame and greatness. My imagination teemed with visions of the careers of celebrated violinists that Father had told me about or that I had read about on my own. In my reveries I strode down this path boldly; boldly I crossed the threshold of the conservatory and with equal dispatch received my diploma as a virtuoso. Yet had I been given the opportunity, I wouldn't have had the nerve to travel down this road. With such thoughts, my "ambitions" faded more and more until they had just about vanished, leaving behind only insignificant traces.

Meanwhile, Father toyed with the idea of sending me to the *gymnasium*. The first time I heard about this it seemed improbable, because I simply couldn't believe that our financial situation would allow it. I thought such a plan bordered on the impossible, but I didn't have to wait long for the first indication that it would be carried out. Father discussed terms with my music teacher (who was, as I mentioned, a graduate of the *gymnasium*), and one day I had my first tutorial. This was the beginning of hours of slaving over books—hours when, on more than one occasion, my thoughts would escape from an algebra problem or a history map and wander about somewhere in the future: the school uniform with its epaulets; living in a big and unfamiliar city; coming home for the holidays—all of this filled these moments of reverie. The idea of leaving home and starting life on my own was enticing, but other thoughts disturbed the picture: I would be cut off from home; weeks would go by when I wouldn't get to see my loved ones. However, I resolved to sacrifice the latter for the sake of the former—a choice that an innocent, childhood love affair helped me to make.

Up until the fifth grade, I attended school with the daughter of the local physician. I fell head over heels in love with this rosy-cheeked member of the female sex; it was a child's infatuation. I always felt that the difference in our social status got in the way; I was plagued by fears that someone might spirit away from me her tender looks and words brimming with ingenuous love. In the sixth grade, my "heart's choice" no longer sat with me in the same classroom. I stayed behind in the red-and-white building of the public school, while she entered the *gymnasium*. She would come home to visit from time to time, and we would see each other then. She told me stories about her new school and new classmates. I would make a few remarks here and there, but deep inside I would be thinking about the gulf that had widened between us. I was the son of an artisan and a student in public school; she was a doctor's daughter who attended the *gymnasium*—what a colossal difference. This was yet another reason why, when the chance came to undo one of the inequalities between us, I pursued it with all my will. I threw myself into my studies in order to do well on the entrance examination for the state *gymnasium*.

One day in June 1933 Father saw me off as I boarded the bus for the city of S. From the moment I set foot on unfamiliar territory, I felt a terrible desolation all around me. The cousin who was supposed to take care of me had no idea how to cheer me up. The next day I found myself within the school walls, from which I felt a distinct chill. Moving from the care of my "ordinary" teachers in public school to the tutelage of the "extraordinary" professors here magnified my sense of self-worth. The anti-Semitic remarks that some of the professors made right in the middle of the examination, as well as other insults from my potential classmates, produced a rather negative picture of my future life in school. In an atmosphere charged with anticipation, the moment finally arrived when the results of the exam were announced; I learned that I had been accepted into the fourth form at the *gymnasium*. I could barely wait to stop by the nearest store, where I bought my school cap, and then I caught the first train home.

Everyone greeted me warmly. At home the question of where to find a place for me to stay became the subject of extensive discussion. It was bound to be expensive to stay with strangers, so they began to cast about for a relative, some forgotten cousin, and one was found. The choice fell on one of Mother's cousins, who was recalled after years of oblivion. Two weeks before the start of the term, the "negotiations" were launched. They were brought to a satisfactory conclusion, for my brother (who served as the emissary in this affair) reported in a letter that I could come on ahead.

Here begins the most important period in my life. As soon as I was left alone in this strange city, I had to assume responsibility for myself. While I had felt that I was a link in the family chain at home, here I began to regard myself as an independent individual, living on my own. As a result, I set aside the anxieties and emotional upheavals I had gone through at home, as they were inextricably bound up with the situation there. Here, on unfamiliar ground, my concerns and day-to-day aspirations began to take on a shape of their own, which, over the course of five years, centered around life in the *gymnasium*.

My first encounter with the horde of boys in uniform was less than encouraging. At first, the other Jewish students seemed to treat me cordially enough, but I had the feeling that to them I was nothing more than a laboratory specimen. They gave me oddly facetious looks; there was more irony than comradeship in their expression. To be sure, I was different from them. To begin with, my knickers and provincial jacket contrasted with their handsome, full-dress school uniforms. These were superficial differences to be sure, but there was likewise no shortage of differences between our views and aspirations.

My schoolmates (I speak of the Jewish ones) led a happy existence. After school they played volleyball, socialized together, and went to the cinema and the theater, while I sat doing Latin and mathematics. It wasn't that I found their amusements repugnant—on the contrary, I was drawn to them. However, as I was unable to take part, I came to detest them. I began to put the scholarly thoroughness of my studies on a higher plane than their gracefulness at volleyball or their knowledge of film actors. I came up with the justification (and eventually persuaded myself to believe it) that my well-done homework meant more than their escapades, which they took such delight in describing.

This outlook didn't come naturally but sprang from my involuntary isolation. I had never been a recluse—quite the contrary. I enjoyed sharing the company of friends, both boys and girls, and I liked to play and laugh, to daydream and swap stories just like any other adolescent. There were aspects of my character that would have flourished, had my classmates welcomed me with open arms, or had they displayed a genuine desire to accept me into their company. Their coldness toward me—and, even more so, their aloofness—drove me to choose another path in life, utterly different from theirs.

After failing to make friends with my coreligionists, I tried to strike up acquaintances with the Catholic students. Among them were some that it was possible to get along with, but these few individuals were forced—under pressure from the majority, who were rabid anti-Semites—to keep a Jew at arm's length. When these efforts proved a fiasco, I had no choice but to withdraw from the society of my classmates and was fettered to my books more than ever.

I didn't find complete peace of mind in this "surrogate" labor. My nature, which was not at all inclined toward the cloistered life, was constantly at odds with necessity. Sometimes, while holding a book in my hands but not reading, I looked on as two ideas competed with each other. The instinct for sociability wrestled with the desire, born of necessity, to read and learn. Although the first had all the stronger arguments, it yielded to the second.

Spurning isolation, my instinct for companionship cried out that this was unacceptable, that a young man was supposed to have friends. Puny desire had only one argument to make: this was the way it had to be. You have to sit at home; you have to cut yourself off from everyone, since there was no other way out; you can't butt in where you aren't wanted.

This argument carried the day. I began to skip classes, and I opened my books with growing satisfaction. What's more, I came to place even more value on my drudgery as opposed to my schoolmates' rushing around. I regarded the time they spent having fun as wasted, while my own long hours sitting at home were the way to achieve a goal of the utmost importance, to accomplish something more permanent. These truisms became more and more embedded with each passing day, but they could never completely eliminate the envy and longing that tugged me in the direction of my class-mates. As a result, a string somewhere within me was constantly stretched to the breaking point; it was the source of a nearly indelible shadow of discontent.

In addition, there was another issue that prevented me from joining that clique of merry schoolboys. For most of my schoolmates their "burden" consisted of doing their homework and attending classes regularly. In addi-tion to these obligations, I had another one: that of earning money. Just before I left, Father explained to me that giving private lessons was the main source of income for a student. He made it quite clear that I would have to earn money while at school in order to help him bear the cost of my attend-ing *gymnasium*. I obeyed this instruction, and during my first year I secured some tutorials, so that I might contribute from my own meager earnings to the huge sacrifice that Father made. This extra obligation, no less sacred to me than my commitment to study diligently, once again created a barrier between me—the student who worked for a living—and them—the boys who were not thus encumbered.

My school days were rather dismal. After a short time, the buttons on my student jacket had lost their luster. I no longer put on my school cap with the same feeling of reverence, and I had begun to regard the school badge with its embroidered number as utterly commonplace. In a word, it took only a short time to destroy the aura of glory in which the freshman schoolboy had seen himself during the first few months. In my new "status" I saw myself stripped completely of anything exceptional, and I realized that I was harnessed to the chariot of intense work: an eternal round of books, compositions, translating Latin, memorizing poetry, tutoring in one part of town, giving lessons in another, running from pillar to post—drudgery and more drudgery.

As I hurried down the street to a private lesson, I would think of how they lived, those fashionable schoolboys who sported around on their bicycles during the summer and strutted proudly, carrying their skis, in the winter. Then I thought of how I lived—I, who had to earn money and lived in fear of losing my sole source of income, tutoring. In the midst of these reflections I sought refuge in an explanation of what my way of life meant versus theirs. I became convinced that I was accomplishing something, that I was wresting something away from a harsh existence, while they gadded about. Yet this accurate assessment did nothing to allay my discontent. Even when I seemed to have convinced myself that I was on the correct path, I couldn't quite extinguish the flames that they had fueled. The other boys in school (that is, the Jewish students) knew that I gave lessons to earn a living; their attitude toward me wasn't what it should have been, and this was what hurt. I would rather have heard nothing at all than to have to put up with their cheap and humiliating expressions of "friendly" concern.

This is why, whenever the opportunity arose to get away from the city of S., from those detested surroundings, I would go home. There I could talk to my father, my brother, and my acquaintances as equals. There I had no fear of being laughed at behind my back, or of having someone dare to take an unfair swipe at me. The holidays were always too short, and I always became depressed on the eve of departing. Once, as I said goodbye to my family, I wasn't even able to hold back my tears. I never revealed the reason for my sadness to anyone.

I wouldn't be telling the truth if I were to claim that the holidays I spent at home were idyllic. No, almost always during a holiday (by what combination of circumstances, I don't know) Mother would be sick. On one hand, it felt good to help bear the burden of suffering, but on the other hand, I endured some painful moments. Among Mother's medley of complaints was the notion that I was to blame for her worsening health and for the family's increasingly precarious financial situation. Perhaps there was even a kernel of truth in this. The money spent on my education was undermining the household finances. More and more often I overheard family "conferences": was there really a need for such a luxury—attending *gymnasium*? Increasingly there were scenes involving my brother, who, as he put it, didn't want to work for someone else's benefit. I realized how burdensome my education was. The anxiety made my father stoop-shouldered and whitened his already gray hair. For my part, I fought off the reproaches of my conscience: Why had I done this? Why had I agreed, knowing what it would cost, to put on the school uniform? Knowing—no, I didn't know this; I had approached the decision more from a child's perspective. Moreover, in making this choice I had been guided by a silly "love affair" and not by any genuine inclination for study.

As there was no one to whom I could pour out my troubles, I turned to pen and paper. Once I wrote:

> Ah, harsh life, stern and malicious,
> Why are you so merciless?
> Why do you bestow smiles on one,
> Deal painful blows to another?
>
> Some you love and coddle,
> Others you trample with heavy tread;
> For some you are all thunderbolts,
> Others you caress with whispers.
>
> Ah, harsh life, stern and malicious,
> Why are you so merciless?
> You, so liberal with your fatal shafts,
> Answer! Why is it thus?

I wrote these words at a time when Mother had dozed off after a nervous attack, and I could hear the muffled sighs that escaped from Father's breast.

A few days later I went back to S. My experiment with verse back at home prompted me to take pen in hand repeatedly and commit my thoughts to silent paper. Again I was swept up in the daily routine of school life; again I would return exhausted from giving private lessons. Filled with fresh dissatisfaction, I wrote:

> Strange is life's monotony,
> The grayness commonplace and strange—
> A chain of identical rings,
> A large canvas, but bereft of light and shade.
>
> Engraved in an endless sequence—
> The common days and lifeless months,
> The chain of years, years lost and with no echo
> Filled with constant striving and toil.

My picture of student life was composed of such hues, more or less. After completing the sixth form and receiving the *mała matura*, I went home for vacation, as usual. Here, too, there was nothing new in store for me. When my oldest brother and I talked, we often came to the subject of school. During one of these conversations, he told me that Father was sending me to the *gymnasium* out of a desire to realize his own aspirations through me, to turn me into what he might have become, if only his father had shown any understanding. In another conversation, my brother informed me in so many words that my education was putting the whole family in a bind, that it was draining the resources of our household. I sensed an ulterior motive behind these words: perhaps I might be satisfied with just the *mała matura*?

Thereafter, this idea began to contend with my genuine desire to study, a desire born of years of attending school. Sometimes these two ideas gave me no peace; my nerves were shattered. I sensed that the idea of abandoning my studies—an idea that had been thrust upon me—was starting to gain the upper hand. It put forward strong arguments, in the face of which my desire to learn began to yield. Silently, it said to me: You shouldn't drive the whole family deeper into poverty for the sake of finishing the *gymnasium*; don't be self-centered, let them breathe—let them, let them.

Meanwhile, vacation was drawing to a close, though I made no preparations whatsoever to leave. I hadn't yet reached any decision; I was still wrestling within. The other students were already back at school, while I still hadn't even considered my departure. When Father asked, "When are you going to leave?" I would reply each time with a later date. Strangely, my desire to continue my studies grew by leaps and bounds with each passing day. Father's face bore an unusually sad expression. It occurred to me that this was my fault, that by not leaving I was causing his sadness.

Stricken with such pangs of conscience, I decided to leave after the following Saturday. About two days before the appointed time, a card arrived from the *gymnasium*, informing Father that I had been expelled for not showing up on time. (It was almost a month after the start of the term.) I ignored this and left. I laid out the whole story from A to Z before the teacher who was in charge of our class, and, thanks to his intercession, I was readmitted. Once more the work got underway; books lured me into their snares again and held me fast with bonds of genuine desire. I felt a sincere interest, especially for literature. Many times I was taken with some work, some poem; I would read it over several times at home, imitating the gestures and the voice of our professor, who recited magnificently. I studied well and was promoted from the seventh to the eighth form with good marks, as one of the best students in the class.

One more year of hard work, one more year of exerting myself, and the goal would be attained. I did well on the *matura*, and in 1938 I received the "title" of graduate from the state *gymnasium*.

The heady feeling that came with getting my diploma didn't last long. It quickly vanished, and, sooner than I had expected, I found myself face to face with the difficult question: What now? As long as I was in school, I still had plans; I wanted to continue my education. It seemed to me that if I made my motto, "When there's a will, there's a way," I would manage with a little effort to forge ahead.

I had calculated all wrong. After reading the newspapers I came to the realization that people were offering the work of their hands for a pittance, yet there were no "customers" who would put a hammer, a saw, a pair of pliers, or a pen into these hands. My ears, which prior to this had reverberated with Ciceronian periods, the laws of mechanics, and the words of Żeromski and Prus, had not accurately registered the pulse of the street. I had deluded myself into seeing a field of endeavor in the labor market, which called out to me: "Finish as fast as you can, we're waiting for you." When I was a cog in the daily workings of the school machinery, I had no time to direct my gaze at those who were idle against their will. It was only when I began to consider going to Warsaw to look for work and, at the same time, to follow my chosen path (of continuing my studies) that I came into contact with "true reality," with its minimum of possibilities and maximum of impossibilities. Only then did my own hands cheapen and lose their value, for I saw thousands of other hands in search of work.

My enthusiasm for my former aspirations cooled. Once, when I was weighed down by depression, I wrote:

> Youthful dreams,
> Sailing by light of day or in the shades of night,
> How much greater and more occult the powers,
> How vividly they float before our eyes—
> Then, it seems, that besides them
> There is nothing else.
>
> The years go by,
> Life rushes ever onward at a gallop,
> And with it, its real outline looms forth,
> The tender childish dreams abate,
> And somewhere vanishes that Fata Morgana
> From the days of reverie.

When I compared my possibilities with my plans, I saw that the thought of continuing my education was, for the time being, a pipe dream. I resigned myself to deadening the pain for a year with an anesthetic bearing the label "postgraduate sabbatical" (taken involuntarily, I might add).

The Year Off: A Kaleidoscope

A whole year has elapsed from the time that I graduated until now, when I am writing this autobiography. Day after day has gone by, month after month, and it is always the same. I haven't budged from the spot where I came to a dead halt a year ago. Thousands of ideas, mountains of projects have come and gone during this time, and all of them have been dashed to pieces against the same cliff: my material circumstances.

Initial Reflections

I couldn't remain indifferent for long to my existence as a parasite in a house of toil. After all, what other name is there for my inactivity in the midst of ceaseless work and constant straining of muscles? I was fully aware of this, but despite everything I failed to make any change in the situation. Was it, perhaps, because my attempts were too feeble? Quite often I accused myself of being a "leech" and asked myself: How much longer will you have to stay here? Various schemes for leaving occurred to me. More than one idea for taking some radical step arose, but on the following day these ideas would strike me as typically escapist fantasies. In my mind everything went smoothly, everything fell into place with the best possible results, but when it came to putting the plan into action and building on a foundation of money, I saw once again the helplessness of my position.

I didn't dare ask my parents for any money. Even if I'd had the nerve, they wouldn't have been able to fulfill my request, despite having the best of intentions. In the midst of these difficulties a question gradually arose: What if, in the final analysis, I'd made a mistake? What if I'd made a mistake in choosing to pursue an education, instead of taking my place at the machine and upholding the tradition of family craftsmanship? No: I can say that, whichever way my life goes, I am content with what has happened. This is a profound conviction, one that comes from the satisfaction of having forced life to yield up something, of having triumphed over certain obstacles by dint of effort and toil.

Art for Hire

During the entire period of my musical training, it never occurred to me that I might someday turn my instrument into a source of income. Of course, I was intrigued by the prospect of giving concerts on the stage, but never with the aim of making money. In the space of a few years circumstances forced out my philosophy of *ars pro arte* and replaced it with "art for hire." This change was dictated by the need for a decent pair of shoes and presentable trousers. In spite of my aversion for earning money with my violin, I started down this road. For, like it or not, daily life made a host of pressing demands and was more than equal to the task of crushing my resistance.

The entire time that I made the circuit of villages and small towns, performing at parties, I never reconciled myself to the world of the bandstand. I wasn't like those "professional entertainers" who had been at it for years and had no concept of honor. They were always bowing and scraping to gentlemen in tuxedos.

There was bound to be a parting of the ways between us. It took place at a ball held in my home town. The carnival-like show attracted a large crowd of guests, among them a social "giant," the senior official at the local excise bureau. When it came time for him to leave, together with his entourage, the entire orchestra headed for the door to send off "His Most Excellent Excellency" with a march. I stayed in my seat, which later led to a dispute between the bandleader and me. I have promised myself to quit playing for these local band concerts, but it remains to be seen whether life will permit me to withstand the consequences.

Advice

"Find yourself a rich girl and smooth your path with her help"—such (or something similar) is the advice I get from my "nearest and dearest." I am quite disgusted with this advice and with those who give it. Such tremendous revulsion wells up inside me at the very thought of putting myself on sale for a price. A simple business transaction: sell yourself in exchange for getting rid of certain impediments. To strive after happiness on these terms reminds me of the slave trader, with the sole difference being that in this case I would be both the one for sale and the one selling him.

Final Thoughts

It goes against my nature to divulge my personal secrets, to recount the details of certain experiences (about which those closest to me are ignorant) to total strangers. Even now, as I bring the story of my life to a close, I can feel resistance to what I am doing smoldering within me. At times I stop writing and think: "Shouldn't I put an end to this? Wouldn't it be better to take what I have written and consign it to the flames, rather than have it become an object of scrutiny?" I'm aware how much easier it would be for me to leave my own secrets undisturbed rather than pass them on to all and sundry—and yet I will submit this. I will do so because reality is once again winning the battle with my thoughts. After all, which is preferable: to continue to live off the charity of others, or to go out and make something of myself? So, for the price of betraying my own innermost experiences, I am acquiring the hope that maybe, just maybe, fortune will smile on me and I will win a prize that would enable me to leave home and search for work. This reason alone prevails; this and no other reason compels me to fling open a window onto my own experiences for the benefit of strangers.

11
G.W.

Contest year: 1939 • Language: Yiddish
Year of birth: 1919 • Age: [20] • Sex: Male

I am sure that you will find my work very useful, although the language is perhaps not very good. But this isn't my fault, as I never attended a Yiddish school, and therefore my writing is full of mistakes—please take this into account. If you can, please send me some material that will teach me how to write Yiddish well. That would be a great thing for me to have, and I would be forever grateful to you.

—from the author's cover letter accompanying his autobiography

MY AUTOBIOGRAPHY

Chapter I
My Earliest Youth

I was born in D., a very small town near Siedlce. There, in 1919, I came into the world in my parents' home, located on narrow Notavizne Street. Our house was made of brick. There was a big yard in front, which belonged to my mother's family. My mother's parents died not long after I was born, as did my father's parents. I never knew any of my grandparents. The first people that I got to know during my earliest years were my mother's sisters and brothers. I felt closest to my mother's older brother, Khayem; he would sit with me for hours at a time telling me all kinds of stories. I really enjoyed them, even though they were all about religion. They had a powerful impact on my childlike imagination. I showed him my appreciation as often as I could by fetching things for him and doing other small favors.

To the right of our house, closer to the road, stood a small *beys-medresh* called Khaye-Odem. To the left stood a big brick house, and Zalmen-Shimen the Baker's house was in the middle.

My mother tells me that on the day I started to learn to walk the Bolsheviks arrived. It was a beautiful day, and I was taking my first steps, chasing a rooster around the yard. Just then a hail of shrapnel and bullets rained down on our town, striking all the roofs with a great crash. We went into our house and boarded up the windows and doors. And so the first pleasure that my mother had from my accomplishments was ruined. I will never forget this incident. Then my grandmother died and, eight days later, my grandfather died, too. The war years had exhausted him and drained the last ounce of life from him. My mother, who had just given birth to my second brother, became ill as a result of all these troubles and was bedridden for several weeks. After that, she got up and had my little brother put in a cradle. I used to play with him and rock him to sleep. Sitting there, I would get tired and fall asleep, leaning against the cradle. That's how I spent my very early childhood years.

Chapter II
Life in the Area Surrounding My Home Town

First, I will describe the way my town looked. Notavizne Street led straight to a wide marketplace paved with cobblestones and surrounded with buildings on all four sides. Some were low, one-story brick houses, but most were wooden buildings. On the other side of this not-very-large marketplace, to the right, was the Polish Catholic church, the first building on the street to Niemojki. Not far from the church were the town hall and, opposite that, the post office. Next to the town hall there was also a small building, which was a public school. This neighborhood was almost completely Christian. On the same side of the marketplace, on the left-hand corner, was the synagogue and, right next to it, the *beys-medresh*. The road to Międzyrzec began there. Walking to the *beys-medresh* on the Sabbath with my father, I would point to all these buildings and ask him about them. He would answer me very patiently, teaching me the names of everything, and thus they were engraved in my mind. Even though I haven't been in my home town for many years, I can still see it vividly today.

*

One fine summer day during Shavuoth, we all set out early in the
morning on the road to Siedlce—my mother, my mother's younger sister,
and I—for a picnic. We took some food to eat and a bottle of milk to drink
on the way. From the very first glance I saw how beautiful it was there:
meadows, fields of grain, gardens, orchards, small low houses with thatched
roofs, a well in almost every yard—these were the charms of the peasants'
home life. A Christian man whom we knew had a swing in his yard. I played
with the children there, swinging with them for a long time. At noon
Mother could barely tear me away, and we went home.

Another time we walked through the fields and meadows to the river.
We lived close by. The river was quite narrow, barely a few meters wide.
The water was very clean, because the ground was sandy. The river got
gradually deeper the farther downstream we went. We managed to find a
very shallow spot where we often went swimming. The sun shone down on
us—it was delightful. I felt so good during the summer, when I could run
around in the lush outdoors, without a care. I would say this was one of the
most beautiful chapters of my life.

Chapter III
My Friends When I Was Three to Five Years Old

At the time, there were four of us—Yosl, Hershl, my younger brother, and
I—who were friends. We all played together on Notavizne Street. We had
already started going to *kheyder* but weren't that keen on it. Being children,
we would get distracted. We would meet in the yard after breakfast, before
our mothers had finished cleaning up and could take us to *kheyder*. The
four of us would run off somewhere and get caught up in our games, and
our mothers would spend a long time looking before they found us.

We boys didn't fight with each other much. One of us had only to suggest
something, and the others agreed to it right away. Behind our house there
was an empty lot where goats used to graze. I don't know who owned it.
We used to wriggle through a hole in the fence to get to this lot. In the
middle of it were several piles of logs. Some were big, some small, some
round and some square. Apparently, something was going to be built there,
but in the meantime we took advantage of the opportunity to make a
see-saw. Lots of children came there and played on the logs. Together we
took one of the smaller logs and placed it across a pile of logs. We would
sit on either end of it and would play see-saw for hours. Once, we met in
the morning to play in the street as usual, but then we got lost and wound
up in a Christian woman's garden. The woman was digging up beets, and

she motioned to us to gather them together into piles. We stayed there for a few hours until the work was done. Then she gave each of us two beets as payment, and we ran home happily. As I approached my house Mother was running toward me. She gave me a good spanking, because she hadn't been able to find me when it was time to go to *kheyder*.

Chapter IV
My *Kheyder*; the *Melamed*

When I was three years old my mother took me to *kheyder*. To get to the *melamed*, who lived not far from us on Siedlecka Street, we went through a small passageway between two brick buildings, behind which were several very low, crooked, old houses surrounded by a wire fence. We entered one of these houses. I stood on the doorstep with my head hung low, my finger in my mouth, angry, as if I somehow understood that I was being robbed of part of my childhood freedom. The teacher was a short man with a long red beard. He wore a traditional Jewish cap and a long coat tied with a sash. The teacher called me over to the table, where about ten children were sitting, and introduced me to the first letters of the *alef-beys*. He told my mother to leave me at the *kheyder*, and she went home. I sat there silently, looking around to see where I was. It was a small, low room. On the right, near the window, was a cot, and near that was the table where the children studied. On the other side was a long bench, and at the narrow side of the table was the teacher's chair. Opposite this, near the wall and in the very middle of the house, was a small chest with an iron band all around it. Near that was a door leading to an alcove. In the corner, opposite the door through which we entered, was the fireplace, which also served as a cooking stove. It was nice and warm in there, and it reminded me of the song that my mother used to sing: "On the hearth a fire burns, and it's hot in the house." The teacher recited a blessing with the children. I already knew it, because my mother had taught it to me, and I said it along with them. I went to this *kheyder* for two months and learned the *alef-beys*.

From the first day I went to *kheyder* I felt at home with the other children. We all played together, jumping up from the ground onto the top of the chest and back down again. On one of those jumps I smashed into the corner of the chest and cut my forehead, right in the middle. I started bleeding, and the teacher's wife applied cold water to my head. In the meantime the teacher sent for my mother, and I was taken to the *feldsher*, who stitched me up and bandaged me. It really hurt, and every day I went to be rebandaged. I didn't go back to this *kheyder* anymore, and the cut left a permanent scar in the middle of my forehead. That's why this *kheyder* has remained so vivid in my memory.

Chapter V
My Second *Kheyder*

After my head had healed my mother took me to another *kheyder*, with a better *melamed*, where I learned how to recite prayers. He was an older man with a gray beard, and he was very strict. He maintained authority with a leather whip that lay on the table. His face looked severe and angry, and all the children trembled at his glance. In addition, he had a particular practice of keeping delinquents after class. We had lessons together twice a day: first, in the morning, and then, after he finished working with each one of us separately, we would have a second lesson together. This meant that we had to be in *kheyder* almost the entire day. But because we weren't used to this we would run outside, and for this the teacher often struck us with his whip. Once, I got into a lot of trouble by talking a few children into going outside and, one by one, we sneaked out of the *kheyder*. We ran off somewhere far away to play. As usual, the teacher ran around looking for us and couldn't find us. When we returned later he gave each of us a beating and asked who had told us to run away. One of the children unintentionally let it slip that I had put them up to it, and the teacher punished me by keeping me after school. It was a summer evening and already quite dark, and I had to sit there alone in the *kheyder*. I was getting very hungry, and the teacher still hadn't said I could go home. I started crying, and he came over to me and told me never to do that again, and then he let me go.

Chapter VI
My Father and His Occupation in Our Town

My father was a shoemaker, and he worked in our house with his partner, Hershl. They also employed two less experienced journeymen, and the four of them made shoes. My father used to travel to Warsaw all the time with crates full of all kinds of shoes, both large and small, for sale. He would return with bundles of fresh leather. The shop was in our house for a couple of years. At the time, taxes were rising like yeast dough. The burden of paying taxes was becoming more difficult, as was the means of collecting them—such as "Grabski's hearse," which would come and confiscate everything in the house. This made things harder and ruined the business. My father and his partner were forced to sell off all the shoes and go look for other work. To this day I remember the scene when we heard that the tax collector was coming; we would scurry around, in a frenzy, hiding the featherbeds and pillows; this happened often. If you kept up with your taxes, you couldn't stay in business. Our business was pitifully small compared to others, which had to pay the same amount of taxes and so could operate with more capital.

Ours was a town of shoemakers, with factories of different sizes. But my father wasn't able to get a job in a factory, for all sorts of reasons having to do both with him and with the factory owners. Doing piecework at home had not yet become a common practice. Given all this, he had no other choice but to seek his fortune in another city.

Chapter VII
My Father Left Our Home Town for Włodzimierz

At the beginning of 1925 my father, his partner, Hershl, and a few other shoe-makers from our town went to investigate the market in the area around the town of Włodzimierz. There they rented an apartment and opened a shop, where they made shoes and sold them. This lasted until the end of the summer, when they split up due to a whole host of reasons that I don't know much about and don't interest me at all. Then my father and Hershl rented a shop in the arcade of the city's market, and they continued making and selling the same kinds of shoes. They hired two journeymen, and they continued to work just as they had in our town. All the while they lived in very poor conditions, without either a decent bed or regular meals. Most of the time they ate dry food, because they didn't make enough to pay for both room and board, and they certainly couldn't afford to eat in restau-rants. They slept in their shop on a loft above where they worked in filthy conditions. It was also quite chilly where they were, and they stayed there through autumn, until the bitter cold weather started. Then they decided to bring their families to live with them in Włodzimierz.

Chapter VIII
My Home Town and How It Looked Before We Left

After my father had left, summer seemed to race by with incredible speed. The weeks and months seemed like days. From time to time a letter would arrive with ten zloty, or sometimes twenty, for us to spend. Very little changed in our town. The only thing that I found interesting were the three big gas lamps in each corner of the marketplace, which were lit at dusk. Walking home from *kheyder* at night I would stop and wait eagerly for the night watchman to come and lower the lamps with a crowbar. He would putter around for a few minutes, then pour in kerosene from his jar and light it. He waited until the lamp started burning, then he lifted it up again, and it glowed with light. I watched this closely; it seemed so amazing to me. Some new buildings were also going up rapidly. They filled my young imagination with questions. I would stand for a long time watching the bricklayers placing brick upon brick, mixing the cement, and carrying the bricks up higher and higher as the wall grew. I saw all this for the first time, and it aroused my creative instincts. It seemed to me that I, too, could learn how to build. I had already concocted an entire scheme in my imagination. I just didn't know what bricks were made of or how they were made, so when I saw my Uncle Khayem, this was the first thing I asked him—childish dreams and a fantasy world.

Chapter IX
Before Leaving My Home Town

The summer was over, and a cold, damp autumn was setting in. While my father wasn't having the easiest of times, we were also experiencing difficulties. We had been living in a big house that was very cold. My mother didn't want to heat it, because we didn't really need such a big house just for her and us children. Soon we rented a place from Hershl's wife; it was in a small, warm house behind the synagogue. My mother installed a bed and a cradle for the baby, and we lived there. In a few days we got the measles—my little brothers and I, as well as Hershl's children. We all lay in bed, burning with fever and not knowing what was happening to us. My mother gave us lots of water and milk to drink. I drank eagerly, but my little brothers and the other children didn't want to. I laughed at them because I was feeling better, while they were lying there feeling very ill. Then the doctor came and examined all of us, wrote some prescriptions, and said that we should be fed honey, so that we would eat more. This remedy actually helped, and the others started drinking, too. Seven days passed, and we all began to get better. In the meantime, a letter arrived saying that we should pack up and move to Włodzimierz, and a few days later money arrived to cover all our expenses. We lay in bed for another week. My mother and Hershl's wife prepared for the trip and got everything packed. In my imagination I pictured the train, which the other children and I always used to talk about. Mother described how it looked and the iron tracks on which it ran. In my dreams I saw it as if it were alive, whistling and billowing clouds of smoke. We traveled on and on, riding off into the distance for a long time, until we arrived at our destination.

Chapter X
We Left Our Home Town and Moved to Włodzimierz

At the end of 1925 we all left our home town together: my mother, my two little brothers, and I, with Hershl's wife and her two children. It was freezing outside and a fine snow was falling. The wind was blowing fiercely. We all sat in the sleigh together. We children were covered with pillows, because we were still weak from the measles and could barely breathe. The train station was four kilometers away. The coachman drove the horses quickly, and in an hour we were at the station in Niemojko. It was a small, low, wooden building, not far from the tracks. We raced inside the station to a big empty room with several long benches on the sides along the walls. Not far from the ticket window there was a warm stove. We ran over to it to warm ourselves. My mother and Hershl's wife went to the ticket window to buy tickets. There was still half an hour until the train left and we sat and waited patiently. My mother's younger brother had come to the train station with us. He said goodbye to us and gave candies to all of us children. My mother and Hershl's wife bought the tickets and came back to wait with us. Many people stood at the ticket window buying tickets. The train whistle blew; it was coming. Soon it whistled again and stopped. My uncle helped us get on board. He said goodbye to all of us once more and dashed off the train.

Soon the train whistled again and moved. It was dark all around. It was nighttime; I looked out the window and saw nothing. We were moving. The other children and I went to sleep. My little brother slept in my mother's arms. I lay on a bench. In my sleep I imagined that I was with my father, and we were all laughing and happy together. In the middle of the night we arrived in Brześć nad Bugiem, where we had to switch to another train. We went into the station to wait. It was a large, beautiful station with many doors and rooms, brightly lit with electric lights. It was the first time I had ever seen them, and the brightness was blinding. We waited for about a quarter of an hour until our train came. Taking all our belongings, we boarded the train, which went directly to Włodzimierz. As we traveled it grew light. I sat and looked out the window, watching as we quickly passed through regions I had never seen before: snowy fields, villages, towns that couldn't be distinguished from each other. Finally we arrived at the station in Kowel, where the train stopped for a quarter of an hour. From there it was only five more hours to Włodzimierz. We traveled on, the train puffing hard, as if it were exhausted from the long journey that took almost a full day.

Chapter XI
We Arrived in Włodzimierz for the Winter

It was a dreary day and was snowing. Thick, damp snow lay like a downy featherbed all along the way from Kowel to Włodzimierz. At about three o'clock in the afternoon we began to approach the city. We rode past the first crossing and then another. The train whistled, it finally stopped at the station in Włodzimierz, and we got out. The station wasn't very big, nor was it as tall as the other stations. This building still stands to this very day. We walked through the station and came out on the other side, by the road leading into town. My father and Hershl were waiting for us there. We hugged and kissed and were overjoyed to see each other. My father hired a sleigh, and we all rode into town together, talking on the way. My father and Hershl asked us how the trip was. They felt bad that we had had a difficult time and had to switch trains, because we could have gone at another time and avoided that. The first person we visited was one of my aunts from Międzyrzec. She lived on Piłsudski Street near the German church. We slept at her place for a few nights. It was crowded and stuffy. My aunt was so happy to see us, because we had just seen each other in Międzyrzec quite recently, and now we were together again and everyone was well.

Chapter XII
Our First Home; I Continued Going to *Kheyder*

My father and Hershl rented a place to live. It had two rooms and a kitchen, and we all lived there together. We settled in as best we could. The building wasn't very nice—it was low and crooked and looked like a hovel from the outside—but it was warm enough, and we lived there for more than a year. Together with Hershl's older son, Khone, who had bad eyes, I was sent to a *kheyder* not far from our home to continue my education. I got to know new children, we played together, and so the weeks and months flew by. My mother got used to baking every Friday, which was the custom in Włodzimierz; we weren't used to doing our own baking.

Winter passed quickly and Passover arrived. On the first morning of the
holiday my father took me with him to the synagogue to pray. I looked at
the synagogue inside and outside, and I liked it very much. It was quite
large, extremely wide, and taller than almost all the other buildings in the
town. The raised platform where the Torah is read was in the middle of the
building. The platform was surrounded by four large pillars, which supported the ceiling. But on the outside the synagogue was crumbling and
peeling, as were all the other buildings then. After the service we went home.
On the way I looked at the store windows for the first time, because I hadn't
ever been on that street before. After Passover my mother's younger sister
arrived from Warsaw. She brought me lots of nice things and was very
happy to see us. After spending a few weeks with us she went back, and she
later returned during the summer. A match was arranged for her here, and
a few months later she got married, so she's stayed with us in Włodzimierz
to this very day.

Chapter XIII
How Włodzimierz Looked When I Arrived

At the time, the town looked as though it had just been burnt or destroyed.
I couldn't quite appreciate how big it was, but I certainly knew that it was
big. Most of the houses were made of wood with mossy, shingled roofs.
Here and there on the streets were many ruined buildings, which had been
destroyed during the war. Looking at them you could clearly imagine the
war in all its horror. This didn't add to the town's charm. It was clear that
the destruction had been extensive. All of the large buildings were in ruins,
making the scourge of war so visible. But let's go back to our neighborhood
and to the other areas where poor Jews live, which were closest to me at the
time. I would walk to the synagogue with my father on Saturday mornings,
and while he was praying I would go outside behind the synagogue. Many
of the other children who came with their fathers used to play there. Whenever I met one of my friends from *kheyder* I would ask him to take a walk
with me down the little streets that run behind the synagogue and the big
beys-medresh nearby, and he would gladly go with me. We would walk along
the first street next to the synagogue, and I'd see houses that looked just like
ours, bent with age; they surely remember the ghetto. This is the oldest
Jewish neighborhood in town. The narrow streets are muddy and filthy.
There are wooden foot bridges in front of the houses, without which people
can't get to their homes. People live in extremely cramped quarters, so there
are many women, both young and old, sitting on the steps with their little
children, dressed up for the Sabbath, and gossiping. At first glance it seems

to me that that's how Jews are supposed to look. At the time, when I was a child, I couldn't imagine that it could be different, given that the house where we lived and the homes of the poor working people nearby weren't much better. When I thought about it all, I certainly had reason enough to accept my surroundings.

Chapter XIV

The Next Year We Lived Closer to the Center of Town in a Store

A year passed. In the fall of 1926 my father and Hershl split up, because their business started to decline. The market was flooded with shoes from big factories in other cities, which provided all kinds of shoes that were better made, more stylish, and much cheaper. My father and Hershl had to sell off their stock. After they split up, our family moved to a big store located on Sienkiewicza Street, not far from the synagogue and the *beys-medresh*. My father took up repairing shoes, which he had done when he was younger, and gradually he built up a clientele.

Hershl, however, wasn't much of an expert in this line of work. After living for a few months in cramped quarters and poverty in the store on the marketplace, he went back to our home town with his whole family. And that's how it has been to this very day. I continued going to *kheyder* with a *melamed* who taught in a small school located next to the synagogue. I started studying Torah. I found it very interesting and understood it easily. I was full of energy then and still in good health. A little while later I developed a lung ailment, from which I suffered for a long time. I was treated at a TOZ medical center. The following summer, after I recovered, I was enrolled in a summer camp run by TOZ. The camp was located outside the town in a fruit orchard. We would spend the day there and go home to sleep at night. Most of the time I lay under the trees and rested, as I was very weak physically. I was also weak intellectually, because I had forgotten much of what I had learned.

Chapter XV

My Tutor; I Prepared for the First Grade of Public School

After summer camp my father found me a tutor, an acquaintance of his who often brought him work. I went to the tutor's house every day to study Polish and arithmetic in preparation for going to public school. He didn't teach me himself but turned me over to his children, who were *gymnasium* students. He was always busy working as a bookkeeper for a brewery. I went to their home for a lesson every day at two o'clock.

There was one incident that I can't ever forget. It made me despise the tutor and his deputies, the *gymnasium* students, and made me realize what frauds they were as teachers. This is what happened: One day I arrived for my lesson, and my tutor's younger son sat with me in the back room, teaching me to read Polish. After I finished reading he assigned me some arithmetic problems in Polish and left me alone in the room, bolting the door behind him. Then he completely forgot about me and went outside. I finished doing everything, so I went to the door to tell him that I was done, but it was locked. I knocked but nobody responded, so I sat and waited for an hour and knocked again, only harder, and once more, nobody responded. I wondered if they had all died, and I kept on sitting and waiting. Eventually I got very hungry in my unexpected prison, and I began to cry bitterly. Then I started to look for a way to get out. Finally, I went over to the window, opened it, and threw all of my school supplies out onto the grass. Although the window was rather high, I crawled out to the other side and jumped down. In the process I hurt myself slightly, but it was nothing serious. I gathered up my things and went in through the kitchen door to see if anyone was there. Their mother, who was a little deaf, was in the kitchen. She hadn't heard my knocking, and that's why she hadn't let me out. She felt very sorry about it. I went home, and on the way I decided that I wasn't going to go back there for lessons anymore. My father was angry about it, too, and I never went back.

Chapter XVI

Because of my illness, I didn't start going to public school until I was eight years old. When the school year started after summer vacation, my father enrolled me in public school on Ostrowiecka Street. To this day, the street where the school stands looks the same as it did years ago. Most of the people who live there are Christians. The school is a low, wooden building surrounded by gardens and trees. The air there is very healthy and pure. Because of my illness I was a whole year behind for my age. I was both emotionally and physically too weak to take the entrance exam for the second grade. I had recently had diseases, such as the measles, which left me in a weakened condition, and then the lung ailment made things even worse. Although I was now attending school, I was still weak, and for the next three years I often suffered a relapse of my illness.

Now I'll get back to the school. The warm weather was soon over, and winter came. I dressed warmly and went to school every day throughout the winter with very few interruptions. Our teacher was a cheerful fellow, although he used to mumble. He used to teach all his classes in a sing-song, so we called him "the silent singer." He was a good man, very friendly, and his students would literally climb all over him.

I, however, was very quiet by nature, and for this reason the teacher liked me and had me sit on the bench closest to him. I did very well in school, as I'd already had some advance preparation, which made it easier. From my very first minute at school I showed great aptitude in painting and pasting—that is, arts and crafts. I put so much effort into everything I made that the teacher simply marveled at my work. I used to paint all sorts of birds and flowers and other things, too. This talent has remained with me to this day. Even though I'm out of practice, I still pick up my pencil from time to time and draw something. (That's how I was able to copy a picture of Bronisław Grosser that hangs in our meeting hall.) So I've never really lost this ability.

But let's talk some more about my school. We had this teacher for only one year, in the first grade. He was devoted to us, and we got along very well. Our class was the nicest and had the fewest problems. We got a lot of attention, because there were only twenty-five of us. We also had a smaller room. There were sixty children in the other first-grade class, and it was impossible to give them enough attention. We were our teacher's pride and joy.

Winter passed and spring came. All around the school everything had turned green, and it looked so nice that it was simply a pleasure to go to school. For Constitution Day on 3 May, our teacher organized a choir of children in the upper grades, and they put on a very fine concert for the school. There were also some recitations, and at the end they performed a scene from a play. This was the first public performance I had ever seen, and I liked it very much. The school year was at its end. There were eight days left to distribute exam papers and grades. There was a lot of commotion at school, and we weren't learning much because our teachers were busy with grading and writing reports. We played outside for hours at a time, happy because our two-month vacation was about to begin. Report cards were handed out on 20 June. I got very good grades and ran home, happily looking forward to the vacation. At home, as always, I found my father working at his cobbler's bench and my mother preparing lunch. When I gave them the results of my first-grade report card—and especially when I told them that I had been promoted to the second grade—everyone in our house was happy. Even the younger children were happy, although they didn't really understand what was happening. My father promised to have a new suit made for me, and he kept his word. In a few weeks he actually had suits made for me and my younger brother. Then I went back to the TOZ summer camp for a month. We used to go at eight o'clock in the morning and stay until six in the evening. This enabled me to recuperate.

Chapter XVII
The Following Year Our School Moved into a Big Building
Closer to the Center of Town

In the middle of vacation we learned that our school was moving to the center of town. It would be on the street where we lived, Sienkiewicza Street, but at the other end, near the town hall. The vacation passed quickly, and soon we were back at school. The new school building was very comfortable and had every convenience, including a splendid gym for physical education during the winter. Our classroom was one flight up, on the side facing the highway. In the second grade we had a woman teacher who wasn't as good as our first-grade teacher. She had a stern face, was always angry at the whole world, and she never laughed, not even a chuckle. I trembled before her as if she were a murderer. I wasn't doing as well in school as I had before, so my father hired a tutor to teach me at home and help me with my homework. My younger brother also started going to school that year as well, and he had the same tutor. She also began teaching us to read and write Yiddish. As she didn't know it very well, we acquired an inadequate knowledge of Yiddish, which is still the case to this very day.

That year we had to move, because our landlord needed the shop, and we moved down to the basement in the same building. Even though the basement was large, it wasn't comfortable. It was dark and had a damp wall, and one by one we all got sick. It became hard for me to breathe, and I was always coughing. Still, we had to live there for several years. Even then, I asked why we had to live in such a damp cellar, while other people lived in beautiful houses—I couldn't understand this.

During the second winter that we lived there, a typhus epidemic broke out in Włodzimierz before Purim, and all of us children came down with typhus; naturally, I was the first. I was taken to the hospital, while the others lay ill at home. As a result of a fever my second brother's lung collapsed, and after I came home from the hospital he still had to lie in bed for a few weeks. He lost his appetite and became seriously ill. But he was cured with the help of a young doctor, who had just completed his training and moved to Włodzimierz. He used to make a free house call every day because he wanted the experience, and he understood our situation. He was a very kind man, and he really did make my brother well. Thanks to him and to our devoted mother—who stayed up all night, caring for my brother just like a nurse, if not more—my brother recovered. During the vacation he went to the local TOZ camp, where I had gone the year before, and I was sent to a bigger camp in a village thirteen kilometers from the town of Nowy Ośrodek. There were many forests and fields there, and I spent a month free as a bird, luxuriating in the lap of nature. I felt refreshed; after all, there we had everything we needed. But then I returned home and approached our house. The worst was when I headed downstairs into the basement and walked into a black cloud that covered my eyes. This was probably caused by our stove, which used to smoke whenever the air was abnormal, and I felt overwhelmed, because—this issue remains unresolved for now.

Chapter XVIII
The School, My Friends There, and Other Schoolmates

At school I came in contact with all kinds of children, both rich and poor. I could tell them apart by their appearance and dress. We used to study and play together; we spent time with each other and became friends. In the lower grades the gap between rich and poor was very small. But as we got into the upper grades—say, fifth or sixth grade—there were fewer and fewer poor children. At the time, I looked at who my friends were and who attended school with me. At first I couldn't accept the idea that there was a divide between the working class and the middle class. The children of wealthy families and even of the lower middle class were more friendly with the other "big shots" than with us. When I was in the fifth grade there was still a group of eight to ten children from working-class homes, but by the sixth grade there were only three of us left, because the rest got left back in the fifth grade. Only then did I see clearly the line that divided me and my two friends, Yudl and Moyshe, from our other classmates.

What were the factors that deepened this rift? Very simply, my friend Yudl and I didn't have textbooks, and it was hard for us to learn. We studied together; he had one book and I had another one, but we didn't have any of the other books we needed. We tried to borrow them from our class-mates, but our requests fell on deaf ears. Yudl's father was a bookbinder, and we both studied in his workshop. He was a class-conscious worker. As he worked he would explain to us why something was the way it was or why it was different, and Yudl and I would stand there and listen. We began to understand what separated us from them. The school year was over, and we were both left back in the sixth grade. I wasn't surprised that this happened. I didn't register to repeat the sixth grade, because even repeating the year would have interfered in my pursuit of a trade. So that was the end of my public school education.

Chapter XIX
My Six Years at School and What I Got from Them

As I start to put together an answer to the question of what I got from my school years, I would have to say an elementary education, such as reading and writing Polish. This is extremely important in the life of every young person, and it's something every citizen ought to know. In addition, I was taught other subjects; we studied natural science, geography, the history of our country, world history, physics, and chemistry. All of this was very useful to me. But when I look around today, as I read and search for what is considered knowledge, I see how weak was the history that we were taught, and how little education we actually received. I feel impoverished— just as I am poor in daily life, I am also poor in knowledge. My mind is thirsty; I search and grasp at everything that comes to hand. For me, the struggle for existence is tied to the great drive for knowledge. And as I strive for a better life, I also strive to exist on a higher cultural level. I would never deny that school introduced me to the great treasures of knowledge and culture, toward which every working person must strive.

Chapter XX
My Aspirations While at School

When I was in the fourth and fifth grades I began to have aspirations for my future. I knew that there was such a thing as *gymnasium*, a more advanced school where you continued your studies, and that then you went to university and became an educated person—a doctor or a lawyer—and there were many other things to study as well. It never occurred to me that I wouldn't study and realize my aspirations. My dream was so bright, so full of desire for something loftier, something grand and beautiful. In a word, I was filled with a great desire to become an educated person. The turning point came unexpectedly. In the sixth grade I felt instinctively that this road was somehow closed for me. When I saw that I didn't always have enough money to buy a book or a notebook, I began to wonder why this was the case and what would happen in the future. Gradually I became more resigned to my fate. Life's harsh realities put an end to my dream all at once. I was very upset when I finished the sixth grade with poor marks, even though I had been expecting this for a long time. Now came the turning point in my young life. When I came home my father explained that I wouldn't be going to school any more and that I would start to learn a trade. I finally realized that higher education wasn't for me, that having to live on my father's income didn't afford me the possibility of going to school. I had to make peace with reality and abandon my dream.

Chapter XXI
We Moved Outside the City and into Our Own Apartment

During my last year at school, after the autumn holidays, we received a letter from our home town. The letter was from my mother's brother, who wrote that they were about to sell the house, and that my mother and her younger sister should come and get their inheritance. They left right away and stayed for a couple of weeks until the house was sold (this was at the beginning of winter), then they came back before Hanukkah. My mother's share was 700 zloty, and my family began to think about buying a small apartment. After Passover we were offered an apartment outside the city on Szpitalna Street. My father went to look at it with a broker and liked it. Then on Saturday we all went to look at it together, and we liked it, too. During the next two weeks the broker and my father settled on a price, and we bought it. We moved in after Shavuoth. Finally, we could breathe freely, because the air there was very good. The place was actually not all that large—one room and a small kitchen. However, we felt lucky to be out of the damp, dingy basement that had caused us so many problems. My father rented a small shop for his work, and our life became easier. My health improved, and, on the whole, so did everyone else's.

Chapter XXII
I Looked for Work and Enrolled in a Vocational School

The year after I left school dragged on slowly. I went about with nothing to do; I looked for work and couldn't find anything. I really didn't know what kind of work I should pursue. It was difficult to find a place to learn a trade, as many positions had been filled the previous year when I was in the sixth grade. While I was looking for a place to work, I also enrolled in a vocational school. These days this is very important for any trade. I used to go there every evening from six o'clock until ten. There I met many young people I had known well during my years in school, which was where I had last seen them, who were now studying to be tailors. I found out that they had left school quite early, one in the third grade and another in the fourth grade. I got along well with them, and some of them have remained my friends to this day. I spent part of each day in my father's workshop, helping him out with whatever I could do. And so a year passed with nothing happening. In the meantime, I entered the second level of the vocational school.

Chapter XXIII
I Decided to Learn to Be a Tailor and, After Much Searching, I Entered a Small Tailor's Workshop, Where I Was the Only Journeyman

Eventually, I decided to learn to become a tailor. After Passover, during my second year out of school, I entered a small tailor's workshop and started to learn the trade. I bought a thimble and some needles and sat poking at a scrap of cloth until I learned how to stitch. It was very hard for me at first, because I had to get used to sitting in one spot all day. During the first weeks I was bored and tired. My shoulders felt as though they were breaking from sitting hunched over a needle thirteen hours a day, but I felt that I had to do this, that I had no alternative. Somehow, I persevered and got through this period.

My boss was a short, fat man. He was so stingy that he would save the basting threads and reuse them. Gradually, after I had become somewhat used to things, he had me do various odd jobs. He made me wash the floor of the workshop, and he would have me carry packages to his home. When it came to teaching me, he was no expert, so I decided to look for another workshop, and, after only two months, I left him.

Chapter XXIV
My Second Tailor's Workshop and My Three Years' Experience under Contract

After Tisha B'Av I entered another, larger shop, where they mostly made military clothes. There were four journeymen employed there, and I was the fifth employee. At first, the work went quite well; as soon as I arrived they showed me how to do various kinds of hand work. They didn't use me to do any odd jobs, because the other workers didn't allow it. One of them was the shop steward; he was a class-conscious worker, so I felt quite good about the new shop. After two months had passed I had to sign a contract, which the union required my boss to offer me, to work for three years. Half a year later the workers in the shop changed, and the shop steward also left. Knowing that the contract required me to stay until my time was up, the boss started to use me for all sorts of odd jobs. Tailoring was still quite a good trade, because at the time there was no anti-Semitism in Włodzimierz. The boss was a good craftsman, and he got a lot of orders from the three regiments stationed in town. Gradually, he had me go to the barracks and do all sorts of other things. As a result the days just slipped away, and my training was neglected. At the barracks I often got a tip—fifty groszy and sometimes a zloty—but still I wasn't happy about it, because I knew very well that I wasn't being taught the trade. Sometimes I would remind my boss that time doesn't stand still and that I wasn't learning anything. He would brush me aside without a reply, telling me that he still had plenty of time and that eventually I would know something. I would tell my father all about this, and he quarreled with the boss several times. This had some effect, and after every argument with my father the boss would teach me something.

Almost a year had passed since 2 November 1934, the day that we had made the agreement. The weeks and months went by routinely. I was already a little more hardened and had gotten used to the trade. I also had made my peace with going to the barracks, because that's the way it had to be; I had to serve my employer and his clients. But this wasn't the end of it.

Chapter XXV
The Workshop and the Journeymen; My Boss and His Wife

The shop was in my boss's home, and this didn't do me much good. As I describe the people in the shop, its virtues and faults will become clear. The workshop was in a small room with one window hidden from the sun. There were two sewing machines, an ironing board, an upholstered couch, several chairs, and a narrow tailor's workbench. It was very crowded. In front of this room was a smaller kitchen, and beyond that was another large room, which served as both a dining room and a bedroom. Some of the journeymen stayed on after two other workers had left. One of these two, the shop steward, was a class-conscious worker, and the other, an older man, a traditionally observant Jew, wasn't a bad person, either. Of the other workers, one was a tall, young fellow who did piece work; he was foolish and ignorant, always laughing and making fun of everybody. The other was a short man, who was married; he only made trousers. He was dark and sly, not a very good person. Then another worker came on, a very handsome young fellow, who was not yet very aware of workers' issues, and then there was me. I worked with them until I finished my training. They didn't have the slightest desire to stand up for me, because they were ignorant, coarse, and uneducated, like people living in the Dark Ages. Although they were union members, they showed no closeness or friendliness toward me. The short fellow who only made trousers deliberately gave me only simple hand-work to do and wouldn't let me do anything more substantial, because he was very afraid that if I learned the trade well enough I would put him out of a job. This was especially the case because the more senior workers always made fun of him and led him on, saying that I would take his place. I saw that I was in for it.

The boss was a short man and not very heavy. He was very coarse and not overly smart. He had absolutely no education, and this made it very difficult for me to discuss with him the things that bothered me. His wife was a skinny woman with a sallow complexion. She was anxious and nasty and harangued everyone, including her husband and children. She actually managed the workshop and interfered in everything that had to do with money or work. Whether or not she knew what she was doing, she would butt in and cause an uproar. She didn't spare me, either. In fact, I consider her my one enemy in life, as I don't think I've had any other enemies and perhaps won't have any others. She took revenge on me at every turn, for every little thing. Sometimes she would pick on me so much that I actually cried. It was worse than getting a beating. When I thought about how I was being exploited for no good reason, that I wasn't being taught the trade, and, in addition, that she was constantly tormenting me—then I felt that I could not forgive her.

The three years were nearly over. Gradually, I had begun to master the trade, but this had happened only because the other workers went on strike over money that the boss owed them. As I was an apprentice and didn't get any wages, they didn't ask me to strike. The boss was angry with them and wanted to spite them, so he said that he would work just with me. I took advantage of the opportunity, and he started to teach me how to do some things, giving me one piece of work after another. During the two weeks that the strike lasted I learned how to make many things, including a pair of trousers. The boss still owed me seventy-five zloty, according to our contract. He didn't want to pay me, but I decided that I had to get the money, come what may. Seeing that our agreement was soon up, my father came and talked things over with the boss and his wife. Though she had to pay me, she screamed that she wouldn't. When they realized that they couldn't do anything about it and that I had the right to demand payment, she gradually paid me thirty zloty. When my father went to demand the remaining forty-five zloty, they explained to him that he wouldn't get the money, and that if he forced them to pay through a union arbitrator, then the boss wouldn't sign my apprentice's certificate. The boss wasn't aware that the trade union office could force him to comply, but my father didn't want to go that far. He summoned the boss to appear before a union court, which ruled that he had to pay me what I was owed. He wrote out an IOU in court, because he had no choice; he had to pay what he owed me. This was my only revenge. I used the money to have a new suit made.

Chapter XXVI
My First Entry into a Youth Movement and What It Gave Me

Of course, I didn't join the movement by accident. For a long time I had been looking to become involved in an organization that represented my interests. When I was still in school I learned of the existence of these organizations, because many of my friends there belonged to various Zionist groups. Even then I wondered what these organizations were doing, as the people in them were always feuding. When my friends invited me to join one of the four different Zionist groups that were around at the time, I replied that I didn't see eye-to-eye with organized movements that all strive toward the same goal and yet aren't united but are divided and fight among themselves. Therefore, I couldn't join them. At the time it didn't even occur to me that there was an organization that was opposed to all forms of Zionism. Later I took night classes, where I met friends from my childhood who had become tailors or carpenters or were employed in other trades, and who had already joined Tsukunft, the Bund's youth movement. They began to recruit me, informing me about the principles of socialism, and I realized that this was the cause that all workers must take up. I decided that after I finished night school I would become a member of Tsukunft. I had started taking night courses before I began learning a trade. I finished the three levels of night school during the second year of my vocational training. In fact, I joined the movement right away; it was still in its early days. Here I discovered a new life, a life full of belief in the future. It prompted me to think about describing the evil that I'd had to endure in the workshop, about denouncing everything that is dark and bleak, bloodthirsty and exploitative. I thought that if I had someone to tell all this to, I would describe it and fix it in my memory forever. I hate how I have suffered, I hate the people who have exploited me; even now, when I think about them, I feel a surge of anger, and I can't forget—my hatred for them continues to grow.

Chapter XXVII
The Youth Movement Opened up Another World for Me; I Got a New Outlook on Life

The youth movement drew me in, and I became a part of it. I felt at home there. I started to understand my world and how best to live in it. I began to devote my free time to the organization and became an active member. I started to think independently about everything around me, my material existence, my poor living conditions, both private and communal. I had to think about whether things had to stay the way they were or whether they might be different. I had to think about my station in life, which I had only partially attained, and about why I didn't even have the possibility of living better and enjoying life, nature, and everything created by humankind. In today's hard times it's very difficult for me to find answers. One person lives at the expense of another, and that person lives at the expense of a third; the world trudges on in its crooked old way, and we can't attain our goals. This is why I had to start looking at life differently than I had previously.

I gave serious thought to my social relationships with my friends, both male and female. I'll try to explain my personal views on young people, both within the youth movement and outside it. There are different kinds of young men and women in the organization. Some are class-conscious and others aren't, but each one is full of energy and possesses a spirit that demands this energy be expended somehow. At this time, young people are full of aspirations. They are seeking their way in all areas of life, both social and personal. Young men and women meet in the youth movement, and they start to feel comfortable with each other. They are attracted to one another, and when their passions erupt they find themselves, I would say, in a very bad situation. As it will take years until they have the means to live independently, their spirits reach the breaking point. This causes them to withdraw from social and sometimes even cultural activities, which harms both them and the organization. They suffer physically and emotionally, because it is clear that not every young person is mature enough in the early stage of puberty to engage in intimate activities. They possess neither the material nor the emotional resources to solve the difficult problems that they face. This is the crux of the question that all young people ask of themselves.

I'll try to give my answer to all this: It's my opinion that in today's capitalist system it's difficult to solve the problem in a way that's favorable to young people, male or female, and conforms with their desires, which is how it is today in communal organizations. Because the way things are today can be considered a crime. True maturity is first and foremost emotional maturity, and this comes when one's actions are governed not by blind desires and instincts but rather by a clear, goal-oriented will and the acceptance of full responsibility. For this reason young people today need to pay more attention to communal, organizational activities and less to the intimate affairs of each individual, male or female, so that they can help build the future of the labor movement. Indeed, while young people are not yet adults they should avoid intimacy as much as possible, so as to avoid stimulating their feelings. You may think that I am against free love, although thousands of young members of the proletariat dream of it. It's not true that a socialist can't be for free love; indeed, the opposite is true, and, in fact, I am a proponent of it. But this will only be attainable when the social order becomes what we envision. Then no one will be a burden on anyone else; everyone will work equally, create equally, and live equally, both male and female, with no difference as to sex. In the meantime, young people have to wait until they grow older, mature, and can afford to live with someone independently. Only then can they act on their natural desires and urges. I say this in all sincerity. This is the reality, and this is how it has to be. (P.S.: As friends of youth, I ask you, especially the scholars who will study these materials, to please send me your opinions on this matter. You'll be doing me and many others a great service.)

Chapter XXVIII
More about Myself and My Family

More than a year and a half have passed since I finished my training. During this time I've already been through a great deal. I've worked in several shops, where I've acquired some on-the-job training, and I've learned a lot of the things that I didn't know until now, but I'm still far from being fully qualified in my trade. I've been unemployed for many months, but I haven't been sitting around idly. I've used the time for my intellectual education. I read a lot and studied Dubnow's history of the Jews, then Graetz's. From these I learned many facts about the Jewish people. I read Sholem Aleichem and Peretz, the shining stars of Yiddish literature. I read many things about the Jewish labor movement, so full of vitality and struggle, and about our great, devoted freedom fighters. I've come to believe in the workers' cause, and although I am far from reaching the highest level of class-consciousness, I am certain that I will. My ambition is youthful and idealistic, but it rests on a good foundation.

I got my younger brother involved in the youth movement, and he, too, is now an active member. He also has the same views as I do. At first, he was in the Zionist movement Hashomer Hatsa'ir, and then he became convinced that it wasn't for him and joined Tsukunft. Our next brother in age belongs to SKIF, the Bund's children's movement, so we're all part of the organization. This brother is still very young but he's quite lively. I sometimes get to look after him, and I'm sure that he won't turn out any worse than the other two of us. The other children are still small and go to school. My father is somewhat class-conscious. He was once an active member of his union. For a long time he was part of the union administration, and although he's moved far from that today and has become somewhat religious, he still thinks highly of the labor movement, and he understands that there is no better way for us. So I don't have any obstacles or conflicts in this regard today. Several years ago, when I was the only member of my family in a youth movement, I had some minor conflicts with my mother, because she didn't want me coming home late at night. But that's behind us now. My father has seen to it that his children receive quite a good education. Our home life is normal. Although our economic situation is often very poor and we struggle to survive, I've never seen the kind of fighting or cursing in our home that I've seen elsewhere. It almost never happens with my mother and father. My younger brother is also a tailor, and he's been able to find some work. We don't earn much, because the union is no longer functioning and the trade isn't regulated. While experienced tailors earn from twenty-five to thirty zloty a week (they snatched up the positions when the union was active), young workers who only make trousers and vests earn somewhere between six and seven zloty a week, and that's why our situation is so bad. Meanwhile, nothing can be done about it. If we succeed in reviving the union maybe things will improve for my brother and me and for all the other young people in the trade.

I'd like to return to the subject of my family. We live and run our household economically, within our means. When my brother and I aren't unemployed—there are bad times during the year when we don't have work—we share our earnings with the family, and my mother takes care of everything. If one of us needs an article of clothing and we can afford it, it's taken care of, and if not, none of us will say "I have to have it," because we share the responsibility for our household jointly with our parents. Our life goes on normally, though we often have to struggle to make ends meet. If we have our health, we will be able to live like this for years, continuing a normal life.

Chapter XXIX
How My Future Looks in Light of My Great Ideal

A person's life must have substance—that is to say, support from society. Like every other young person, I had to seek out this society from among the many options that currently exist. As a member of the proletariat, I had to come to the labor movement, to the Jewish working-class youth, to the Bund's youth movement, to socialism. I became deeply imbued with a genuine belief in the workers' cause. I am deeply convinced that thanks to the Bund, which is now more than forty years old, Jewish life has emerged from the dark alleys of the medieval ghetto. Thanks to the Bund, we have Yiddish schools and a school organization responsible for establishing them. Thanks to the Bund, we have the YIVO Institute for Jewish Research, which elevated Yiddish culture to a high level, placed it on an equal footing with other world cultures, and is concerned with its continued existence. Young people live with hope and faith in a bright future. Those who are deeply convinced, believe. But there is a question as to when that day will come. When do we stop hoping? No one has determined this yet. I have set a limit, you might say, on my hope. I think that the old ways will persist until the 1950s, certainly no longer. And then the day of true brotherhood among nations will come, the day of our ultimate belief in a completely classless society will arrive, and people throughout the world will be free— they will be free.

12
Esther

Contest year: 1939 • Language: Yiddish
Year of birth: 1920 • Age: 19 • Sex: Female

I was born in 1920 into a strict hasidic family. My father was a Gerer hasid. As far back as I can remember, I was steeped in hasidic traditions. At the age of five I remember feeling lucky that I was a Jew. I felt sorry for people who weren't Jewish and didn't have such good fortune. According to my childish reasoning, they were unhappy because they lived the wrong way.

When I was five, my father hired a *melamed* for me. I don't remember much of what he taught me, for at this time my field of vision was widened, revealing new horizons that made me forget everything else. A woman named Sara Schenirer came to L. Her arrival caused an upheaval in our house. I had heard amazing stories about this extraordinary woman. People said that she was establishing schools for Jewish girls.

The word "school" was magic to me. I was full of questions. How would it look? I imagined countless benches. For some reason, I pictured the teacher as a tall, large woman with a ruler in her hand. With extraordinary impatience, I awaited the founding of a school in our town—and, what was more, a Jewish school. I envisioned a paradise. Imagine! To be able to learn. Knowledge! I kept asking whether they would teach us writing and arithmetic. Father answered: "First you will learn to pray, to write Yiddish, and to translate the prayers." And when he told me that we would also study the Bible, it took my breath away. I asked him if we would be able to study Rashi commentaries, too. His answer was: "Girls don't study Rashi and Gemara." Well, that meant "no"—but it still left the Bible. As if I were intoxicated, I ran out to the shed in the courtyard where we children played. I told anyone who would listen that there would soon be a school for girls in L., where we would learn Yiddish and how to pray and, I concluded triumphantly, study the Bible.

Then I went to hear Mrs. Schenirer lecture. I can remember how she spoke. Everyone applauded—and I clapped the loudest. To make a long story short, a Beys Yaakov school was founded. My father worked actively on behalf of the school, often giving public lectures. It didn't take long for the school to be opened. I was an excellent student. In the school I experienced my happiest moments as a child. Finally, I was able to study. Of course, we didn't study the Bible, but we did learn the *alef-beys* and singing as well.

After two years in Beys Yaakov, I started to think about public school. My older friends were already going there. The topic was barely mentioned at home. Father didn't like the idea of my going to a school where Yiddish wasn't spoken and where boys and girls studied together. Knowing this, I didn't insist but meekly requested that I be sent to public school. Father answered that there was no rush. He tried to comfort me by saying that I already had a school. I burst out crying and pleaded with him, but again I didn't dare to demand. Finally, Father promised me that I could go to public school, but on one condition only: the Beys Yaakov school was to come first. Perish the thought that I would neglect the Beys Yaakov school for the Polish school! Meanwhile the registration period was over, and I missed a year. I regretted this but made use of the time to study on my own.

To this day I can't recall who taught me the Polish alphabet. But I do remember reading the signs on our haberdashery and a placard carried by someone on the street. It seems that I was able to do this because I had already learned how to combine letters to make words. I longed for my first day in public school, and finally it came. No child was happier than I was; yet at home my first day of school passed almost unnoticed.

When I arrived at the school, they wanted to put me in a preparatory class. I tried to figure out what to do; I knew that my parents wouldn't come to school to intercede on my behalf. In my broken Polish I insisted that I was ready to enter the first grade. After being tested, I was placed there at once. From then on I never parted with my primer. I finished it and in a short time knew it by heart.

Naturally, I cherished the Beys Yaakov school more than ever. I didn't consider the public school to be "ours," even though we were taught by Jewish men and women. Since they didn't observe the Sabbath and always spoke Polish, as far as I was concerned they were "unfortunate people." I also felt that the way that they taught religion was wrong. More than once I found myself in tears outside the classroom door as a consequence of challenging my teacher. I had no intention of making myself important; I only wanted to point out where the teacher had erred. I would explain that this or that in the school's teaching of history didn't conform with what we were taught in Beys Yaakov and therefore was wrong. For this I got paddled liberally. While I continued to protest at every opportunity, this didn't prevent me from getting straight 5's on my report card. Father was very pleased and stopped talking about my becoming a "*shikse*." He was glad that I opposed the lessons in religion.

Still, my freedom during those school days was limited. Father didn't let me go to the movies. This was forbidden because indecent and sacrilegious things were being shown there. But I had a strong desire to go, so I saved up my money and went. My heart throbbed with joy and excitement. What I actually saw was marvelous! I cried and laughed with heroes and heroines on the screen. When I came home I was terrified that Father might find out. Quietly, I sneaked off to bed. After a few days passed without my being scolded, I was overjoyed. When the whole school was being photographed, I wasn't allowed to take part. I didn't understand why, but I had to comply.

I was an outstanding student, promoted to the next grade every year. There was a library at school. What treasures I imagined behind the glass panels of the bookcases! When I came home and said that the teacher had given me permission to sign up for the library, Father stopped eating his dinner and declared that under no circumstances was I to read any Polish books. Once again I swallowed tears of sincere regret. I simply couldn't understand why Father would not allow me to read them. I looked for someone to help me. This time, Mother came to my aid. Together we decided that I would sign up for the library without Father's knowledge. And that is what I did.

I devoted myself to reading with a passion. Within the red and blue covers of the library's books I found an enchanted world, filled with regal characters involved in wondrous tales that completely captivated my young mind. I read in secret, so as to escape my father's notice. It hurt me that he wouldn't allow me to read. I was tormented by the thought that I was deceiving him, but I lacked the courage to tell him, because I feared that he would categorically forbid me to read. Then—one time I fell asleep while reading. I woke up distraught from a dream and forgot to hide my book. By the time I remembered, it was too late. Father happened to walk into the kitchen where I had been reading and saw the book; an interrogation followed, and if Mother hadn't intervened I would have suffered considerably.

When he realized that I had been reading despite his prohibition, Father settled on a compromise. He would allow me to continue reading on the condition that my Beys Yaakov teacher monitored my selections. The teacher I had at the time turned out to be very lenient. She let me read whatever I wanted and even praised my enthusiasm for reading. This continued through the third grade of public school, and in this way I was able to achieve my great aspiration.

Although I read a great deal, this didn't keep me from becoming active in a youth organization. In addition to the classes at Beys Yaakov the school had a youth organization, called Basya. I was one of its first and most active members. I was ready to make any sacrifice to help develop this organization. I recruited members and also served as secretary. I often did my school work late at night because I had so little time. As important as school was to me, the organization rated a hundred times higher. I remember that I began neglecting the public school. My teacher there was angry when I missed school once because of a performance at Basya. I bore this anger bravely and was happy that I was being punished for a principle. I was proud of my convictions. I read books that gave me issues to debate with the Zionist girls, among whom we recruited.

I participated in every spiritual aspect of Jewish life, both at home and in the Beys Yaakov school. I found spiritual pleasure in the poetry of the Sabbath and holiday table, the melody of my father studying Gemara; these inspired me with reverence for all that is beautiful and uplifting in the Jewish tradition. In addition, the lessons of the youth organization had an influence on me. The noble call to "love your neighbor as yourself," proclaimed on the wall of the Beys Yaakov school, lived within me. I understood what it meant to live in a community. And at the age of thirteen, I was elected leader of our group. Those were years of faith—faith in the success of all that we were doing with enthusiasm and in a spirit of humanness and mutual love.

I was so busy with community life that I forgot my private life at home. The latter wasn't as successful as the former. At home we were beginning to feel the impact of the unfolding economic crisis. The haberdashery we owned became smaller and smaller. My father had to find other means of supporting us. He became a *melamed*. He taught older boys, but it was still a big blow to him, as he was used to wealth. His parents had owned an iron foundry on their own estate. That is why he suffered so much from this humiliation. The hasidic aristocrat in him also suffered. Father often mentioned his great lineage. He was a grandson of the Alexander Rebbe.

All this had very little impact on me. I had my youth organization, public school, books. However, it isn't true that these changes made no impression on me. While I was affected by Father's situation and felt sympathy for him, I consoled myself with the thought that his dignity wasn't diminished. So I continued to live an active and happy life. I was always cheerful in the company of my friends. My sense of humor helped me forget unpleasant things. I laughed, joked, sang, and danced until I was exhausted. I did everything to the point of exhaustion.

My reading was no longer monitored. Father believed me when I told him that I wasn't reading any harmful books. I was reading the historical novels of Sienkiewicz, Prus, Orzeszkowa, and others. At the same time I read Yiddish books from the Beys Yaakov library, especially those by Lehmann and Schachnowitz. The Polish books gave me much to think about. I saw life from a different perspective. For the first time I saw another kind of existence. I learned about the extraordinary heroism of historical figures, and I also saw their private lives.

I discovered the existence of a new feeling—the feeling of love. This raised another problem for me: whether or not to read books on this topic. My Orthodox upbringing dictated that I shouldn't. I sensed that love was something people didn't discuss. Hadn't my father told me not to talk to the boys in school? They were boys, and I was a pious girl. In fact, I felt that way myself. What should I do now—read about love? From within, another, bolder voice sounded: "It's no sin! Read!" So I read. And the more I read, the more I kept my thoughts a secret. During this time I worked less enthusiastically for Basya. I became a world unto myself. Thoughts tortured me and didn't let me rest. I wanted to find out everything, understand everything, and I sought this only in books. This didn't please my parents. Although they were preoccupied with making a living, they noticed how distraught I had become. They advised me to stop reading.

My father reproached me for no longer being so devout. I myself didn't know the reason for this. I read about the early Christian martyrs and was alarmed at my reaction. The thought that they impressed me was upsetting, and I pushed it away. I was afraid of myself. Often I didn't want to be alone. I was afraid of my thoughts. In addition, my friends grew distant from me. Actually it was I who withdrew from them. Still, I felt the need to confide in someone, to pour out my heart. My public school friends were childish and empty and couldn't understand me. I had no intimate girlfriends. Then the thought of writing a diary occurred to me.

At the time a friend of mine from Basya died. Her death made a deep impression on me. I don't know where this came from, but I was obsessed by dark thoughts. No spark remained of my former cheerfulness. I began keeping a diary. At first I wrote in Yiddish, but I had no place to hide the diary. My older brother found it and read it aloud to everybody. I was deeply embarrassed and stopped writing. But I didn't feel better. I constantly felt stifled and troubled. Finally, I realized what was wrong with me: I was in love. Well, what of it? Such things are not unheard of among sixth graders in public school. But I had felt so remote from love. Could this be happening to me? It was forbidden. I wasn't even allowed to talk to "him." And the boy who was the object of my feelings didn't even have the slightest suspicion. After all, I was a Beys Yaakov girl. I suffered, but it was easier for me because I suffered in silence. Now that I knew why I was suffering, the inner conflict vanished. I was no longer as unsure of myself or as gloomy as before. I considered it an affliction that had to be overcome, if I wanted to remain true to my ideals. My sense of humor returned.

I studied diligently. Public school now occupied all my thoughts. I still attended the Beys Yaakov school, but without my former devotion. A public school teacher played a decisive role in this. Unlike the other teachers, she would speak with me outside of school. She loved me for being a gifted student, above all in Polish and in history. As I've said, this teacher had a great influence on me. She organized a student council for our class. I was chosen as an officer and a judge in our school court. I arranged independent study programs, and the teacher and I constantly planned social evenings and amateur performances. Amateur theater was my life. I was never too tired to act in plays, and I especially liked to direct them. In Beys Yaakov I had performed since I was six or seven years old, and I continued to do so in public school. I passionately loved all the preparations, the rehearsals that led up to performances. My imagination carried me to a far-away place, a dream world. I immersed myself in the roles I played with complete devotion. This made me forget the suffering at home, where things had taken a turn for the worse.

We had to sell the store. This was a painful period to endure. As far back as I could remember, we'd had our own store. It was hard to get used to the idea that we wouldn't have one anymore. We had become one with the store, and parting with it seemed like saying goodbye to a piece of my life. But I had to be strong. I was mature enough to understand that this was an unavoidable step. I understood that keeping the store was impossible; there wasn't enough money to stay in business. We had to move to another apartment. Mother started selling goods from our home, and Father continued teaching boys.

I was then in the seventh grade of public school. I kept a diary in Polish. I was becoming more and more immersed in the Polish language. I especially loved Polish literature. I idolized the Polish Romantic poets Mickiewicz and Słowacki. Polish history was also a subject I loved and learned easily. I was enthralled by everything connected with Polish history. I was consumed with the great martyrdom of Polish heroes in their struggle for Poland's independence. I venerated Marshal Józef Piłsudski. I experienced a great deal on account of this.

On 11 November our school, together with all Poles, celebrated Poland's Independence Day. I wrote a speech about Marshal Piłsudski. I read the speech in the municipal auditorium before a large crowd, including the mayor. Whether it was my speaking ability (which I had developed in the youth organization) or the impassioned sincerity pulsing in the words of my speech, it was sufficient to have pleased the mayor greatly. He, too, is a devotee of Piłsudski. He applauded me loudly and personally thanked me. Afterwards, the school director told me that the mayor had expressed interest in me and wanted to be helpful to me. However, as this happened in the middle of the school year, it wasn't possible to talk about reduced tuition for *gymnasium*. Apparently, the mayor wanted to do something to help me to continue to study.

Soon thereafter, the school celebrated Hanukkah with another performance. It was about the Maccabees, and I played a leading role. I also gave a speech on Hanukkah and the Maccabees. On 19 March, the Marshal's name-day, I gave another speech on his life and work at a celebration, and again the mayor was present. He thanked me sincerely and asked me to give him a copy of my speech. Then he asked me what book I would like to choose as a token of his thanks and as a remembrance of him. I chose the complete works of Mickiewicz. He promised it to me but didn't keep his word. But this wasn't his fault; the school director failed to take care of it. That was in 1935. Just then, Marshal Piłsudski died. Because of this, the school year ended on a completely different note, and my book was forgotten.

I completed public school and was faced with the question: What next? The teachers at school advised me to go to the mayor. They said he would surely help me, given the interest he had already shown in me. I made every effort to continue studying. I had an enormous thirst for knowledge. I was convinced that I had no talent for learning a trade. But I was all alone; no one helped me.

I knew that I would have to take care of myself. I had planned to go to the mayor and ask for his help, so that I could study in the *gymnasium*. But my father intervened. He said categorically "No! Enough of the 'others'!" He said that if I spoke about it again he would disown me. It pained me to see how miserable my desire to study made him. Still, I wouldn't have given up on my plan if Father hadn't told me that he was sending me to study at the Beys Yaakov teachers' seminary in Cracow. With this prospect ahead of me, I no longer thought about the *gymnasium*.

From the time I was a very young girl, everyone at home had always said that I would become a Beys Yaakov teacher. I didn't know how this would come to pass. I was fifteen years old and couldn't go to the seminary until I was sixteen. The idea of being a teacher excited me. I was happy that I would be studying again and pleased at the prospect of earning some money. I began to imagine what it would be like to be on my own. I saw myself somewhere in a distant city, a dedicated pioneer of Jewish education. I dreamed of trips to far-away places, of glorious impressions. But dreams alone accomplish little. I had to begin earning money. The public school teachers referred several children to me for tutoring. I didn't want to do this, but I had no choice. I came to school with tears in my eyes. Everything there was so caring and friendly. I wanted to stay in school so much.

And so I became a tutor. I enjoyed every new thing I taught them. However, while it is a pleasure to teach bright children, the ones I taught were very limited. Learning new things didn't give them any pleasure at all, and I had to use all kinds of methods to motivate them. It is impossible to describe fully what I endured at the time. It was a tragedy. I was such a good student, learning came so easily to me, and now I had to wear myself out to teach the simplest thing. It was a struggle. I was very conscientious and devoted. I wanted to teach them. Even though I was often barely paid anything, I worked hard. I regarded the lessons as my responsibility, and if I wasn't conscientious about them, then as far as I was concerned I had failed to fulfill my obligation.

I began to write again. I had no one to tell my thoughts and feelings, so I kept a diary. This time I wrote in Polish. Actually, it wasn't a diary in the true sense of the word; it consisted of scattered images of my life, a reflection of my feelings and ideas.

At this time we were promoted from the youth organization Basya into Bnos Agudas Yisroel. We participated in a solemn induction ceremony, at which the speakers repeatedly stressed the exalted nature and significance of our duties. Although their speeches impressed me and made me think, my enthusiasm had waned. I had done a lot of reading, and sparks of protest had ignited my youthful soul. I couldn't abide the organization's extreme restrictions. Bnos had rules that forbade a great deal, preferring restrictions to fresh experiences. For example, I loved going to the theater and longed to see real actors, but I wasn't even supposed to think about this. Doing so would have resulted in unpleasant consequences for me in Bnos. I found such narrowness oppressive.

I had begun to see people differently. Until then I hadn't believed in human malevolence. I thought everyone was good, that everyone had a heart. My ordeals became difficult to endure once I was convinced of the error of my thinking. I realized this when I became involved in situations where I had to suffer other people's capriciousness. I often had to grit my teeth as I catered to the whims of some of my students' mothers. These women were very limited. They didn't appreciate my efforts. All they saw was that their children were making very little progress. I was held responsible if a child didn't remember something. This made teaching loathsome. My only consolation was the hope that this was temporary.

My father said I would soon be going to the seminary. He went to Ger to see the *rebbe*, hoping to arrange a reduction in my tuition, but accomplished very little. Nevertheless, I began to study and prepare. Every group that had some influence wrote a letter on my behalf. I studied with a friend, the daughter of a wealthy merchant. She had barely attended Beys Yaakov and had already earned the *mała matura*, so we were both supposed to go. We studied nine hours a day to prepare for the examination. She was generous to the extent that she wanted to benefit from my knowledge. There was little I needed to learn from her, but I wrote out the required exercises for her. Yet when the time came to go to the seminary, I was the one who remained at home. The reason for this was simple, but so tragic! "Why? Why?" a voice within me cried. "Why do I have to suffer like this, when I have such a drive to learn? Why must I suffer within the narrow confines of my limited duties, when everything in me longs for broad horizons? Why must I content myself with conforming, when I know that, given the opportunity, I can accomplish great things?" These thoughts tormented me. I began to understand the enormous power of money, but this didn't make me worship it. A curse erupted from my heart. It wasn't only that I regretted losing the opportunity of entering the teachers' seminary in Cracow. My thoughts were full of hate for money, which dulled every feeling of human kindness and made people deaf to the cries of unfortunate souls.

In addition, I was swept by a wave of regret at the thought that I had lost my chance to go to the *gymnasium* because of the prospect of attending the teachers' seminary. I could no longer think about obtaining a reduction in tuition for the *gymnasium*. Relations between Jews and Poles had deteriorated significantly. This, too, had a powerful impact on me. The loyal Polish patriot in me suffered. Now I, whose soul was so bound to Poland, had to give up my cherished dream of Poles and Jews living together in harmony. I had drawn such a pretty picture of it. The impassioned patriotic thoughts expressed in my youthful speeches were genuine. And now all of this had vanished. Every day the newspapers brought fresh, grim news of the persecution of Jews. My faith in Poland's "heart" was tarnished. I no longer saw a nation with brotherly feelings for all of its citizens, as Poland had been in her prewar dreams.

The situation for Jews in general upset me, especially as I had experienced it personally when I lost the opportunity to study in a *gymnasium*.

Now I began to look for a home in a Jewish milieu. I realized that in the present situation Jews must fortify themselves. To do this, I felt it was necessary to learn the history of the Jews, acquaint myself with the Jewish poetry of the prophets, and study ancient Jewish law. This gave me the strength to endure my painful memories. I countered the disparaging attitude of others with our own spiritual values. The magnificent voices of the prophets made me aware of our feeling for righteousness, and the vision of the "end of days" (in Isaiah, Chapter 2) hovered before my eyes.

The sparks of excitement, dimmed by disappointment over the way my schooling ended, were ignited once again. Only one thing remained unclear: I couldn't understand why Jews had so many political parties, which were constantly at war with each other. I didn't realize that people have different ideas and passions and therefore have to organize different parties. And where would you find a wider range of viewpoints and concepts of good and evil than among Jews? I didn't understand any of this. To me, people were first of all people, and if others belittled us and despised us, then we ought to stick together in order to prevail. However, I saw something different. I saw how one organization opposed another. I heard the leaders of Bnos declare that we had to protect ourselves from "strangers" on the street. They talked about "nets spread to entrap our souls." Evidently, it wasn't enough that we hadn't become like "those Jews," but we also had to continue to protect ourselves from them. I had my doubts. It seemed crazy to me to be afraid of the same Jewish girls who had gone to public school with me. Why should I be afraid? Was this the way to carry out what I was taught, or did I not understand the meaning of "to study and to teach"? Wouldn't I accomplish a great deal more if I brought our ideas to these allegedly alien circles? It certainly wouldn't do me any harm, and perhaps it would even prove useful to the Jewish people.

What are we, then, as a separate group? What courage does it take to be good and pious when this is all one knows, and everyone breathes the same air? Questions flickered through my mind as quickly as shapes in a kaleidoscope, but I didn't dare speak openly. When I did speak out once, people let me know that they were displeased, and they misinterpreted my motives. They accused me of yearning for the "free world" and for gentile pleasures. Perhaps there was some truth in what they said. But one thing is certain: what they understood as my craving for the freedom of a cheerful life I regarded as a compulsion to move toward broader horizons, a desire not to become frozen in the narrow confines of their ideas. I still wished to live my life among others and to spread our spiritual values among the many young Jews who were unacquainted with them. But my voice was stifled by their shallow precepts of "keeping the treasures at home," of adhering to the chosen nature of our calling to continue the traditions of the Jewish woman of the past.

And, as always, I had to comply. My protest against all of this remained unspoken. I thought that they would cast me out as a "destructive element," out of fear for all the principles that they had instilled in us. I realized what the consequences were and felt that I would lose more than I would gain. First of all, my situation at home would become intolerable. But that wasn't important. I loved Bnos despite its faults. I didn't want to lose the opportunity to study, so I was silent. I was silent only with other people; on my own—I wrote. No one knew what lay hidden in the pages of my notebook. Perhaps only the trees could have revealed this, but they were silent witnesses, and for this I loved them. Under their gentle, maternal shade I poured out my heart, my feelings, and the thoughts that tormented me. I loved nature, and she inspired warm and trusting feelings in me. She wouldn't reveal my secrets. How magnificent she is! When I walked out to the open fields, or the forest, I was so happy. I felt far from human evil. Here everything was so gentle, clear, open, full of vital joy, with unquenchable lust for everlasting life, always moving, pulsing with blood—Life.

At the time I was reading Lindsey's *The Revolt of Modern Youth*, and I admired the author for his understanding of all that tormented young people. What he presented was the opposite of what we had been taught. It would have caused an uproar at Bnos. On the whole they looked askance at my excessive reading and predicted that no good would come of it. Outwardly I laughed at this, but inwardly I was hurt that they had so little understanding of the pain that young people experience. I couldn't bear the pretense, the false faces they put on when they dealt with important issues. I wanted all to say what they thought, and then perhaps something substantial might be accomplished. I wasn't a renegade but I had a passionate love of the truth. I strove to see the truth about our lives lead us to a sound understanding of all eternal truths. At the time I had no doubt that these truths existed.

I was still an observant, pious young woman, full of trust in the Almighty and reverence for tradition. But living a spiritual life alone was not enough. Only those who were financially secure could afford to do so. I had to be practical. Even though I was quite young, I understood that without some means of earning a living I would be lost. Although I made some money tutoring, I knew that wasn't providing me with a living. The only possibility for me in our town was teaching in a public school, and I hoped to leave this place. I wanted to see other worlds and other people and to experience a different kind of life. I wanted to test my strengths and to see how successful I could be in becoming economically and intellectually independent. I wanted to prove to myself that I could live by my own convictions. I wanted to see how they would hold up under new experiences. My convictions, it seemed to me, were influenced by my orthodox upbringing, and I didn't question it. I just wanted to take a chance and see to what extent the powerful dreams of my youth could be realized. I realized that to accomplish this I had to know how to do something. I wasn't good at working with my hands, nor did this interest me. Whenever I sewed or knitted something I became very impatient. This wasn't a solution. There was very little I could do with my seven years of public school and six years at Beys Yaakov.

I went to my father and asked, "What next?" His only answer was, "You won't have to sew for a living, and you won't have to join a trade union." I think he was more afraid of the latter than the former. And since I didn't want to learn a trade, I agreed. "But what next?" I asked. "You'll be a teacher, a Beys Yaakov teacher," he answered. When I replied that this seemed impossible, he said that he would definitely make it happen. "Just continue to be pious, and with God's help," he concluded, "everything will work out." But the uncompromising nature of life extinguished every spark of optimism in me. Despite the fact that Father had promised me so much, things continued to get worse. Unable to bear this situation calmly, I looked for another way out.

I don't know how it happened, but my thoughts began to take shape in rhyme. While I was jotting down thoughts in my diary at the end of the day, without any effort I would write in verse. These were poems of hope for a better life. They expressed my own pain and the suffering of the Jewish people in general. I wrote everything in Polish. Because I read Polish books and thought in Polish, I wrote in Polish. Once, while visiting a girlfriend's house, I wrote "The Jew, the Eternal Wanderer," "The Jewish Merchant," and some other poems. This was a revelation for me. I didn't know whether to be happy or worried—happy at the fact that I had succeeded in writing poetry or worried that I wouldn't have the opportunity to develop this further.

In public school I had written programs for various events and, according to my teachers, some of them were very good. Since these were for school productions, I didn't think too much of them. But this was a different matter. Naturally, I didn't tell anyone about my poems. I read several to my Beys Yaakov teacher and she liked them very much, but I didn't tell her who the author was. I didn't consider myself a poet, but I enjoyed writing. I rarely knew when I would feel like writing. I might be walking down the street, or I might notice a shining star deep within the dark blue sky or a human sigh echoing in the stillness. Then I would feel such a rush of warmth in my heart that I'd drop everything and rush off to write.

Father was surprised that I spoke so little about going to the Beys Yaakov teachers' seminary. Not knowing the real reason for my silence, he interpreted it in his own way. He though I was no longer a pious Jew, no longer committed to Beys Yaakov, and no longer eager to go to Cracow. As a result, he redoubled his efforts to send me there. He had finally succeeded in getting a considerable reduction in my tuition, and I was preparing to go to the teachers' seminary, when grim fate intervened. Apparently fate shows no consideration for the intensity of people's plans. A calamity befell us! My father died suddenly. He passed away in the prime of life, at the age of forty-nine. What a blow! I felt as if I had been struck in the head. Never again to—how horrible! I ran through the house aimlessly, collapsed, bewildered, before his body, and screamed. I screamed until I choked, until I had no more strength, until I forced my screams back down my throat and into the depths of my heart. Two years have passed, but it is still impossible for me to forget and for my burning wounds to heal. Although this is no place for clichés, I can't suppress my sighs as I write these words.

Yes, it is true that he was a strict father, but he never meant to harm me, nor was it his fault that he didn't understand me. He didn't see the contradiction between his desire for me to be happy and his desire for me to be like him. I was left an orphan. My sadness was great. I experienced it with my entire being. But there was no time to contemplate this—life was making its own demands. Father had been the family provider. In losing him we also lost our means of support. Mother, my sister, and I faced a difficult task. How would we make a living? I had an older brother, but he got married just after Father died. Meanwhile, I continued tutoring, but this brought in very little money. My mother started a business, but she did poorly because of the boycott. Once again came the grim question: "What next?"

Now I had an abundance of "sponsors" among my family and friends. (How did Sholem Aleichem put it? " 'I'm doing fine, I'm an orphan,' says Motl, the cantor's son.") During all the time that we had been struggling, unable to manage on my father's meager earnings, they were unconcerned. Now, suddenly, it dawned on them that I didn't have a trade or a job so as to help support my mother and sister.

It pained me to realize that there was no longer any question of realizing my dreams. As I said, I had "providers." They, too, sent letters to Cracow to convince the school to reduce my tuition fees, but to no avail. Even a personal intervention with the seminary director by the chairman of Beys Yaakov in L. didn't help. Without money, nothing could be done. I could always continue tutoring, but now this work offered no hope that my situation would ever be different.

This was the beginning of a difficult existence, a struggle to stay afloat on the crest of life's waves. It was a two-fold struggle: first, a struggle to find a means of financial support; second, a struggle within myself not to sink into apathy or be overwhelmed by pessimism. This was how far things had come. I had suffered too much to still have the strength to be an optimist. However, I realized that if I wanted to survive, I would have to become stronger—perhaps not so much for my own needs and satisfaction as to be able to help my mother. As the oldest daughter in the house (barely seventeen years old), I felt that I had responsibilities, and this made it possible for me to keep up my energy. I listened to my mother's reassuring words, unable to reveal to her that my faith in a better tomorrow had grown rather weak. Still, I knew that she was trying to assuage her own sad resignation with faith. I wrote little at the time; my diary lay forgotten somewhere. Whenever I tried to write I started to cry, because I had to write about Father. Otherwise, my mind felt empty.

And then I made a friend. She was the morning star after a dark night. I had many friends whom I had known earlier, who sympathized with me and even tried to help me. But she was entirely different. Even though they were intelligent, the other girls didn't understand me and couldn't tolerate the satisfaction I found in books. They criticized me for not conforming to fashion. But this young woman whom I had just met was different; she possessed an endless source of enthusiasm.

We began by reading a book together, and before long she knew my innermost thoughts. It was a marvelous summer. Every hour I spent with her my spirit exulted. I read my verses and a portion of my diary to her. She liked my poems very much. Although she never actually asked me anything, she said she discovered who I was in my poetry.

My friend wasn't a member of Bnos and had left the Beys Yaakov school while still a student. This caused the leaders of Bnos to denounce our friendship. My older brother, who was secretary of the Beys Yaakov committee, demanded categorically that I break up with my friend. I tried to persuade them, to explain what she meant to me, but they didn't want to accept the idea that she was a source of vitality, that she was a breath of air from another, freer world. To say this would have meant confessing my desire for freedom, for something different, which was "forbidden." So I had to give in, outwardly. I promised not to meet with her anymore. But we still met in secret, taking long walks on the outskirts of town. We met either early in the morning or late in the evening. She knew about everything that had happened, and our attachment to each other grew even stronger. I had to endure a great deal because of our friendship, but it was worth the price. My own mother criticized me severely, although she had nothing against my friend. Nevertheless, she said that I had to conform.

This friendship might have resulted in my being expelled from Bnos had I not left L. and gone to G. to see my brother. While I was there, I received a letter offering me a position as a Beys Yaakov teacher in a small town. Although I hadn't graduated from the seminary, I had so many skills that they considered me capable of starting a school. I knew this to be true. When I was in L. I could have held such a position. Still, I wasn't pleased at this prospect for a number of reasons: To begin with, I didn't want to teach without certification. Moreover, and this was the most important reason, the idea of being a Beys Yaakov teacher was now far from my thoughts. I had suffered too much to feel that I could preach what I myself thought cramped people's lives. I was too conscientious. But when I received a letter saying there was no work to be had at home, I reconsidered. Given the general situation, I began to look for the positive—"Seek, and ye shall find." First of all, I tried to convince myself that I wouldn't start a Bnos group there; therefore, things wouldn't be so difficult. Teaching young children to write, pray, and study the Bible is not that terrible, after all. It wouldn't go against my convictions. I won't start a Bnos group, I thought, and in that way I could avoid any conflict with my conscience. And so I went.

At seventeen years of age, I set out on my journey all alone. I didn't even know where this little town was located. Getting there was an ordeal. It was somewhere on the Vistula River. Transportation was possible only along the river. It seems I chose the wrong road. I was traveling all alone somewhere along the river and I didn't know where I was, but I braced myself. There on the banks of the Vistula I felt a surge of independence within me. I had only one thought: to keep going! I could never give up. I had to accomplish what I had set out to do. This made it possible for me to spend a whole night waiting for a boat. I had my strong will to thank for being able to wait until the boat finally appeared.

I arrived in a very small town: a sleepy country community, a few squat houses, a marketplace strewn with sand, where all sorts of animals lazed about, and a church tower. This was the town at first glance. As if that weren't enough, I had to put up with a long line of children, who had come out to look over the new arrival in town. Apparently strangers were a rarity for them. This scene didn't inspire courage or arouse very cheerful thoughts in me. However, I was so used to extraordinary twists of fate that I smiled.

When I arrived at the rabbi's house, I learned that the Beys Yaakov school had yet to be established. What they had written to me was purely imaginary. It turned out that nothing was ready. It was too late to quit. I felt that there was no turning back, and I made peace with my fate. After all, here I would be able to work and help my mother.

I got down to work. I formed a men's committee from among the children's parents. On Saturday I delivered a lecture. It was quite a draw. The small synagogue was packed with men and women. I didn't have time to reflect. I was swept up in a whirl of work and responsibilities.

Registration began and I had to be everywhere. When I had a chance to be alone, I was amazed at what I was doing. I had no idea where this ability to get things done came from. All by myself, I assigned sixty children to classes, scheduled lessons, and even went along to rent space for the school. I had to write appeals, post announcements, give lectures. I had to accomplish all this and quietly, too, because the school was still unofficial. The men's committee did very little. Finally, regular work began. It was a very difficult assignment. I was dealing with children who had never learned to read or write Yiddish. I had to start at the very beginning. It is impossible to imagine how limited these children were.

By late fall, after Sukkoth, the school was running smoothly, and I was busy ten hours a day. When I found myself alone, the energy of the day evaporated, and I was overcome with longing and regret. I ached to be home. More than anything else, I missed my books and my friend. But these were only momentary yearnings, and I considered them a weakness. I knew that I had to be strong and must struggle against anything that would distract me from my work. I worked very diligently, and this gave me a certain pleasure that nourished me.

What I taught my young students filled me with joy, and I had the satisfaction of knowing that there were talented children among them who could be educated. Indeed, they had to be disciplined before they could be taught. They were exceptionally wild. They didn't have the slightest idea of how to get along with each other. They were provincial egotists. They tattled on one another. It wasn't easy to have a conversation with them. They were very suspicious and always looked for an opportunity to make mischief and to laugh. I had never encountered anything like this. It took me several weeks to convince them of the need for community.

All of this would have been bearable were it not for the interference of the parents. They expected their children to learn everything in one month. When the first mother came to me after I had been teaching for a month, wanting to know why her daughter still hadn't learned how to pray, I laughed in astonishment. My laughter turned sour when I realized that she wasn't the only one, that almost all the parents had the same complaint: why didn't their child know what others knew? I tried to argue, explain, but I realized it was no use. It was simply the custom to complain. Apparently this was a way of passing the time. Whatever the reason, it bothered me. I took it to heart that these people were so limited. Their lack of appreciation for someone else's efforts upset me. Didn't they see that I had made a revolution in their children's small world? The children themselves were truly pleased and came to school eagerly. The parents were at fault for measuring everything according to its usefulness to them. Here, too, as with everything else in their little world, they wanted to "get the most for their money." It irked me, but I couldn't talk to anyone about it. I controlled my temper and continued teaching the children.

The only light in this darkness was the mail that I received from home, especially the letters I received from my friend. These letters came from the bottom of her heart; they were written with the intent of bolstering my courage and were imbued with the power of faith. They managed to curb my rebelliousness. No one understood me as she did; she knew how to divert my thoughts from all that was unpleasant. I hardly read any books at the time, so she also wrote to me about books she had read. But what was most important was the way her letters revealed the complexities of life. These weren't superficial thoughts from a girl's narrow little world, but a reflection of human struggle, joy, and suffering.

Suddenly, something happened that altered the course of our future correspondence. The chairman of the school board, in whose home I lived, found part of a letter that I had misplaced. After going through it, he asked me why I was corresponding with a socialist. (He actually called her something stronger.) He said he was afraid of the police. It just so happened that on the page he saw she had quoted a passage from a book by Karl Kautsky. He simply didn't want to understand it, calling it "pure agitation," "compromising," and so on. I had to find a solution. As always, I promised not to write to her anymore. But I did write to her at another friend's address. It was risky. She wrote to me without signing her letters, interspersing them between pages of my mother's letters. In this way, defying restrictions, we once again continued our correspondence.

Meanwhile, I put on a play. I was the director, and, because of the lack of material, I wrote the play myself. The children had never before appeared in any type of performance. My work was crowned with success. The day after the performance everyone in town slept late.

Then the cold weather began. The poorer children stopped coming to school. This was a disastrous blow; there were days when only half the children attended. The school board's ineptitude was responsible for this crisis. Nevertheless, they decided to wait it out and not close the school, since when the warm weather returned there would surely be more students. Their optimism didn't reassure me. I saw the situation in all its starkness. Now, with meager earnings, I thought of home with even greater longing.

My letters to my friend were filled with outbursts of doubt and rebellion against the cruelty of life. Life, which I had once imagined to be so fine, so grand, now forced me to stagnate among heartless people, to wander along thorny paths, through gray and lonely days. As long as I earned money and was able to help my mother, I felt that at least I was fulfilling my obligation to her. But now I no longer felt this satisfaction, I felt that I was suffocating.

At the time I wrote a great deal. In addition to writing letters, which were from ten to twelve pages long, I kept a diary, in which I expressed all my moments of boundless despair, passionate protest, and longing to escape from this morass. I felt I would never escape, that all roads were closed, and so I became lonelier. While I was there I also wrote several poems and two novels in Polish. The first novel was called "Why?" All the voices of my suffering—the cruelty of fate toward the weak and innocent—were expressed through the mouth of my heroine. Her only weapon was the single word "Why?" The other novel depicted a young hasid struggling between two forces: a waning hasidic force and a powerful social force. He flees from the first and finds refuge in the second. But when a fire breaks out in the beys-medresh, he sacrifices himself against his will on the altar of his past convictions, the call of his hasidic origins. This novel was called "A Blood Sacrifice."

But all this didn't comfort me. I had to struggle within not to lose my balance. I was suffocating and yearning, but my yearning was mixed with something else. While I wanted to go home, I also knew I would be unable to accomplish anything there. I might not even be able to give any private lessons. Then what was next? Again, there was no way out. Perhaps I was better off here. But that, too, seemed impossible.

The anti-Semitism in this little town increased. It could be seen in the shrinking non-Jewish clientele in Jewish-owned shops. It could be heard in the smashing of a windowpane on a dark night. It could be seen in the black eye of a Jewish peddler. Naturally, I felt it at the school as well.

The police began to show interest in the school, which still wasn't licensed because it hadn't met the state's financial requirements. Several times they asked me who I was, what I was doing here, and so on. Evidently, whatever they had been told didn't satisfy them. The police followed me, observing my every move. I was aware of this. Every time I saw a policeman I thought he would stop me and ask about the school. During class I was uneasy and nervous.

Every Sunday, peasants from the surrounding villages would gather outside the school window, look in and make fun of the "Jewish school." I got used to this; I was only afraid they'd tell a policeman. Work turned into a vigil. I had to struggle to be strong. I suffered inwardly, but I continued to teach. Then once, during class, a policeman walked in. The children were petrified. For a moment I looked into an abyss, and shining from its depths was a face with two green eyes, over which hovered a mother's tears. But I quickly took hold of myself. With my last ounce of strength I firmly and matter-of-factly explained that I was a relative of a merchant, whose children I was teaching Yiddish. Because there were other children who wanted to learn, I was teaching them as well. Apparently he believed me, but his face glowed with malice. On behalf of the village mayor, he declared that schools weren't allowed unless they were licensed in distant Kielce by the provincial school superintendent. The chairman of our school board was afraid of being fined and recommended closing the school immediately. I didn't see any other way out, especially as it was winter, before Passover. And so I had to close the school—another disappointment. It's true I felt stifled here. But how characteristic! Eternal wandering. No rest anywhere.

I no longer thought that a dire fate hung over me. I stopped thinking I was being punished. For what reason? Was it a sin to try to sustain myself and my family? No, I had people to thank for all this! I sensed their cruelty. By then, even if I had been very naive, I would no longer have been able to believe in justice after what I had experienced. Was it only the Beys Yaakov seminary director's extreme caution that kept me from achieving anything? Was it because he was deaf to all my pleas? At the time I hadn't considered whether my soul could survive as a Beys Yaakov teacher. I simply felt the ground falling away beneath my feet.

Again I had nothing, again I was searching. I returned home. As depressed as I was, I had to put on a cheerful face. My mother's beseeching eyes compelled me to do so. She didn't yet know what I had been through. Why tell her? She was heartened by my being a teacher. But when I talked to my friend, I removed my mask. I told her everything. I confessed my suffering, recounted endless inner misery. I told her stories of the boundless struggles of my pure heart with immeasurable human indecency, and I expressed my total disgust with how cruel the world was.

Had it not been for my friend, I would surely have collapsed emotionally. She was a socialist, and she gave me some political pamphlets. I seized them with a passion. I devoured them, and at the same time I became calm—but not quiet. I merely subdued my most extreme feelings. I took myself more firmly in hand, and a new world opened up before me. That is, it seemed to be a new world, but in reality it was an old story living within me. What was new was the fact that now I was aware of it. I recognized the naked truth. I raised the backdrop and looked behind the scenes at charity and the philanthropist. I saw people differently. I didn't regard them as bad or guilty. They weren't born either evil or good. Their motives depended on the material and social conditions under which they had developed. Then was the policeman who had made me lose my job simply fulfilling his duties as dictated from above? Was the director of the seminary completely innocent? It wasn't that he wanted to harm me. The successful development of the movement demanded that he do it. Well, yes. But the question remains: Is this good? Is it right that one person suffer and another live happily without even appreciating it? An eternal question. It's a difficult problem: "Why do the wicked prosper and the righteous suffer?" Can I justify suffering in this world with a reward in the "next world"? I had suffered too much from people—who were, after all, made "in the image of God"—for my beliefs not to have weakened. I was too young to think of my share in the "next world." Nor was I interested in going there.

This world was calling to me. What was I to do? Now that I perceived the truth, I stopped idealizing everything. I understood life without my former fantasy. I merely looked for a way to maintain myself, so as to avoid being crushed by the brutal wheels of daily life. Moreover, I didn't feel alone. The whole world felt closer. The millions of brothers and sisters, proletarians like myself, felt closer. I saw myself among their ranks, among all those who have suffered. I observed them. Even though they may have been hardened by work and weren't used to thinking about themselves, I understood them. The threads of our common fate bound us together. The one thing that pained me was that the young people of our town, especially those among the proletariat, were very shallow. With few exceptions, they did little more than amuse themselves. But I wasn't angry at them. They did this in order to survive. And youth demands what it is due.

I became a silent admirer of socialism. Its truths eased my life. I stopped searching for a position. With a feeling of indifference, I began to tutor again. I knew I wouldn't accomplish anything with my modest strength. My mother had no idea what was happening with me. She was only surprised that I was so unconcerned about the position I had lost. She didn't realize how far I was from the idea of being a teacher.

Only one thing was amiss: The people at Beys Yaakov began to harass me again about my relationship with my friend. I didn't leave Bnos; I couldn't. The town was small, and my leaving the organization would have caused all kinds of comments. First and foremost, I would have been accused of longing for "a life" (a way of putting it that was peculiar to L.). My mother and our whole family would have suffered terribly. All that was left for Mother was the belief that she and I would be happy together. What would have been the use of disappointing her so soon? So it was impossible for me to quit. Perhaps I would have, but there was no other organization to join.

I returned to Bnos, but they weren't happy with me. First of all, I opposed what was being said there too frequently. We had a certain "freedom" to speak out, but this wasn't what they had in mind. Rather, they envisioned the Talmudic argumentation of the good old days in the yeshivas, when even a certain number of questions regarding the "outside world" were discussed. But all of this was used as a means of showing that "our way" was everlasting, that "our way" was correct, that we were God's chosen people. So it was no wonder that they found my outspokenness a hindrance.

I was often summoned for questioning. They had problems with me, but they weren't entirely sure what they were. They were displeased that I had signed up at the public library. Apparently, they considered it terrible to read books. They didn't mind Polish books as much as Yiddish books. The latter, to their way of thinking, were dangerous. Polish books, they argued, didn't have the direct power to make a Jew less pious, but Yiddish books, written by godless heretics, were filled with made-up stories that cast aspersions on innocent, pious Jews.

Despite all this, I read. A new world opened up for me. Until this time, I hadn't shown any interest in Yiddish books; I didn't know they existed. Now I was delighted with every page of Yiddish. I discovered a new basis for my thinking. I hadn't understood Jews from the perspective I now encountered in the works of Mendele Mokher Seforim, Sholem Asch, Sholem Aleichem, and others. I realized my hypocrisy in previously showing so little interest in Yiddish literature.

Bnos had already begun to think seriously about expelling me. Their only deterrent had been the memory of my father. They had considered it a good deed to be my spiritual mentors. But now they were ready to expel me. Their main accusation against me was that I associated with outsiders. I knew very well whom they meant by this. Still, I wouldn't, couldn't give in to them.

Then something happened that overshadowed all the efforts of Bnos: I became ill. I was giving lessons on the outskirts of town. Every day I walked the two kilometers, regardless of the weather. During the summer, this wasn't a problem. But when the rainy autumn began, I caught a cold and became very ill. There was talk of my needing an operation. My illness lasted two months. During this I endured so much! I thought I wouldn't recover. I had moments of extreme anguish, but never resignation. I wanted to be well, to live! No matter how, as long as I could live. I suffered for weeks. During sleepless nights, my conscience gave a terrible account of my life, amounting to a collection of unfulfilled desires, a constant quest for something uplifting, a little forbidden joy. That's all there was. I was riven with spasms. Bizarre images raced through my feverish brain. And above everything hovered a tragic "Why?" My desire for life cried out. The vision of paradise vanished.

My young body conquered the illness without any need for surgery. I got well. With youthful vigor, I rejoiced in my recovery, especially since the board of Bnos no longer held anything against my girlfriend. They were moved by how much devotion she had shown during my illness and how much she had sacrificed for me. There was little time for me to convalesce. I went back to work. It was difficult, but I had no choice. Throughout the winter I divided my time between working and lying in bed. As a result of failing to get enough rest after my illness, I had a continuous cold.

I took up writing again, but this time only in my diary. After all, I have no ambition to become a poet or a writer. My friend tried to persuade me to send one of my manuscripts to a publisher. I didn't do it for fear of being ridiculed. All my writing was precious to me, and I had invested too much of myself in it to be able to endure that. Nor was there any place to send my manuscripts. I had written everything in Polish. Although there were Jewish periodicals in Polish, I wouldn't have sent my writings to any of them. I doubted they would accepted my work because of the subject matter.

Lately, however, one question began to trouble me: Why didn't I write in Yiddish? Since I was a Jew, why did I have to write in a foreign language? The answer was quite simple: Until recently I hadn't read any Yiddish books, other than those that had been translated from Hebrew. They were just Beys Yaakov textbooks; they weren't literary in character. I promised my diary that I would write in Yiddish, although this would entail certain difficulties. But despite my promise, I continued to write in Polish, until I read an announcement from YIVO in the public library. My heart skipped a beat. I knew that I would write my autobiography. It would be my first work in Yiddish.

This wasn't my only cause for rejoicing. At last! I would write candidly. It would be an interesting experiment, solely for myself. Until now, if I had occasion to write something of this sort, it was usually in a specific context. But now I'd be able to speak freely, without any obligation to comply with specific requirements. It would be an account of my own life, in the light of my own feelings and thoughts. Still, I had certain qualms because of my home and Beys Yaakov.

Yes, I still belonged to Bnos. I've stressed the reason for this previously. I have nowhere else to go; it's my milieu. My mother would suffer a great deal if I quit. Even so, I might quit, but there's no other organization that offers anything other than frivolous pleasures. I'm not an active member of Bnos. I seldom go there. My excuse is a lack of time, which is actually the case. I am busy twelve hours a day. Yet I'm unable to live in more than a single room that I sublet along with my mother and sister. After a whole day of running around giving lessons, it's hard to read a book. Fortunately, at least, summer is coming, and when my students are on vacation I can read outdoors.

Even now, as I write these lines, I'm exhausted. But the fatigue doesn't bother me much. As I see it, since I am writing for someone far away, what's close by becomes easier to describe. I know very little about the YIVO Institute. But the bulletins from YIVO reflect such an implicit understanding of young people, such rapport, that I am writing this despite the considerable risk. The slightest suspicion that I am writing an autobiography would provoke an extremely strong response in Bnos. They would certainly not tolerate it. Only the assurance that those to whom I write will abide by my wishes that nothing be revealed publicly has given me the courage to write. No one at home knows what I'm writing. My notebook is well hidden. Only my friend knows about this.

Who knows? Perhaps this autobiography will change the course of my life. This is something new for me. I have never before examined my life seriously. In any case, it's been a difficult life to this very day. There seems no possibility of improving it. My financial conditions are oppressive. The ambiguity of my situation is agonizing; the need for duplicity, the way that I am misunderstood is unnerving. I can't speak out because I'm not understood, while those who do understand me can scarcely help. My soul aspires to distant horizons, yet I remain in this little world of narrow duties. It's impossible for me to break away because this would mean losing the basis of my life. Therefore my protest is silenced by the voice of reason. Reading books substitutes for reality, and life goes on. And when a sigh escapes from the depths of my heart, when sparks of rebellion and protest ignite in my tired but youthful eyes, they vanish in the turbulence of life, which casts off the weak and battles the rebellious. Still, from my lips comes an eternal "Why?" Then my shoulders straighten and brace themselves, ready to endure anything, never to surrender, but with faith—onward!

Through my neighbor's thin, wooden walls I hear the whirring of a sewing machine. The sound clatters in my head and interferes with my work. At the same time I think: How limited my aspirations are! I desire nothing more than to have a room of my own. For me this is typical: a great, beautiful, idealistic thought runs into a material obstacle. But this, in turn, provokes fresh ideas.

"Esther"
7 May 1939

13

J. Harefuler

Contest year: 1939 • Language: Polish
Year of birth: 1921 • Age: [18] • Sex: Male

MEMOIR OF A JEWISH YOUTH

A Few Introductory Words

*H*umanity is great—but it is only a particle lost in space. Nations are great—but they are lost in humanity. Individuals number in the billions—but they are lost in nations.

Who takes note of the individual?

The individual makes his way unnoticed through crowded streets, lives in apartments and workshops, traverses lands and seas—but rarely does one remember that individuals form the nation, humanity, the world.

Looking at sand, one forgets that it is formed from billions of tiny grains. And this is bad.

For within a nation, each person propagates his tradition, psychology, and culture through his family, which in later generations multiplies and merges. This contributes to the shaping of the culture and tradition of his nation.

We should study individuals.

We will learn much less truth about a nation and its internal psychology from its dances and customs, its folkways and ceremonies, than we will learn by studying the individual.

Interesting—what would someone doing such a study think of cosmopolitanism?

I am not doing this study, yet I believe that a Jew, for example, is different from a Pole, not only superficially, but also internally.

I am a Jew! This I feel today.

Once I believed deeply in this. Then, I called myself a citizen of the world and did not believe at all in nationality; more recently, I "was" a Pole.

But today I know that I am a Jew and that I am far from calling myself a Pole. I've become convinced, by being somewhat assimilated—I write and read Polish, I know Polish history, and so on—that I characterize myself as a true, twentieth-century Jew of the diaspora.

Forgive me for writing in Polish instead of Yiddish—this is not my fault. Everywhere I am surrounded by Poland, and I have fallen under its influence.

However, I want to feel closer to my Jewishness, so that Polishness will eventually be something with which I am familiar but not a part of my psyche.

My Family and I

I was born on 15 March 1921. My name is Jakub°; I am the oldest child in my family; I also have two brothers and two sisters. The next oldest is sixteen years old; his name is Boruch°. After him are Gitl°, who is fourteen years old; Mirl°, who is twelve years old; and finally, the youngest, Menachem°, who is ten years old. We live in a dark room, where the filth makes me cringe, although there's nothing I can do about it. Boruch and I work at home with our father; we earn our living by sitting at machines, making baby shoes.

My father is a wretched, overworked man. He's suffered a great deal during his life, from his childhood to the present. He endured all the horrors of the World War as a soldier in the Russian army. He was held prisoner by the Germans, doing hard labor in a coal mine. He seems to know nothing but the struggle to make a living. He works until midnight, and he's glad when we, his children, do so, too. In particular, he can't stand my reading and studying. When it comes to learning, he has the feelings of inferiority of a simple man, and he would prefer that I just pursue making a living. It's no wonder, because his life lacks a goal, and everyone needs to have a goal, even if it is nothing more than earning a living. He works simply as other people "pass the time." But I'm an enlightened person, and I can't imagine that work, the means of our existence, is also its end. Mankind is meant for higher things.

And so I study, although my father disapproves. But beyond the misunderstandings and conflicts that arise from the things I do against my father's will, he and I are of two separate worlds. Aside from a sentimental, filial attachment, nothing ties me to him. He doesn't understand me; he knows nothing about me. Our "talks," such as they are, don't do anything to bring us closer or help either one of us understand the other. I can't share my thoughts with him or ask his advice (the way I can with my best friend, Josek). My father has never had a real conversation with me, and if we exchange words, they only have to do with work, the family, and so on. If he weren't my father, there would be nothing to tie me to him.

Much the same can be said of my younger brother Boruch. If he weren't my brother, there would be nothing to tie me to him. He is very empty. In his whole life, he's read perhaps one or two books. He went to school for only four years. He's unhappy and has little to say; everything he does is dictated by instinct rather than logic and reason. He does only what is convenient and pleasant for him. He has no understanding of education, since he doesn't find any satisfaction in it. He's overly familiar with me, and I wouldn't put it past him to raise a hand against me. He doesn't care that I could explain things he doesn't understand. He would have more respect for me if I were an actor, or at least a famous boxer, soccer player, or the like. For this is what Boruch has made his aim in life: to pass the time he plays soccer in the courtyard, even with ten-year-old children. Lately, when he can't play in the courtyard he turns to playing cards. Also, despite our limited financial situation, he is addicted to the movies.

As for Gitl, I won't say she's bad, but I won't say she's all good, either. She's a decent fourteen-year-old girl. More than with anyone else in the family, I'm somewhat friendly with her. But sometimes she, too, gets to me. It's rather strange; she always seems sad and overly serious, compared to her cheerful girlfriends. Her sadness and seriousness suggest some deeper cause connected with an inferiority complex, which is something all of us have in common—even me.

Gitl is unkempt and frail; she slouches, but she has noble features and makes an attractive impression. On the whole she's intelligent, quick, and sees things rather clearly. She likes to read, but she reads only stupid thrillers and bestsellers. This year she's graduating from elementary school. Sometimes I think someone should take an interest in her, and I reproach myself for not doing so. At least someone should point her in the right direction with regard to reading—go with her to the library, pick out books, develop her interest in them, and explain literature to her. Someone should explain what sex is to her, being a young woman, recommend the proper books and discuss them with her. But all this takes time, and I don't have enough for my own needs. All we do is talk, when I sit at the machine working and she stands next to me, but these conversations aren't enough to bring us closer together.

I don't understand Mirl at all. She's spoiled, becoming most petulant when told that she's pretty—and yet she's shy. She's quite brazen with me, however, and attacks me with her nails and feet. Then, immediately after such a scene, she can ask me something without a trace of childish arrogance, with an obsequious look on her little face. I don't understand her; sometimes what she says is clever, sometimes it's silly. Sometimes she giggles, and sometimes she weeps endlessly.

Menachem is the most unfortunate child in our family. He's fallen under Boruch's influence. He's the least physically and mentally developed of us all, the loneliest, shyest, and most dejected. His troubled mind is full of silly, disjointed fantasies. Several times I've noticed that when he's alone in a room he'll make strange gestures. With a flourish he'll mount a chair that's probably supposed to be a horse and shoot an imaginary gun, shouting, "Bang-bang." Other times he'll say such crazy things that you can't help laughing. He's already in the third grade, but he has no interest in studying. Like Boruch, he's better at cards and ball. Menachem stutters, but his teacher ignores this. Even at home, instead of giving him some treatment or medicine, we mimic him and tease him, thinking that this will shame him into getting over it.

What's worse, the man who lives in the rooms adjacent to our apartment recently became the building manager, and he has a son the same age as Menachem. But Moniek, the manager's son, looks two years older and is better developed physically and mentally. He gets everything his heart desires. He's almost always eating: cookies, oranges, apples, chocolate, and so on. And he eats all this in front of Menachem, who practically drools as he looks on sadly and meekly. Moniek contributes a great deal to Menachem's inferiority complex.

*

So, that's my family. I don't have a mother; she died when I was fourteen. Soon after that, my father married my aunt (my mother's younger sister). I once thought a stepmother was something awful, but now I see that it's something sad. She wants to replace our mother; what is sad is that she wants to feel within herself something that can only be felt for one's own children. Motherhood comes of itself; one can't make it exist. And while she's not a mother, she's no "fairy-tale stepmother" either. If we might find fault with her, it's not because she's a stepmother but is a matter of her character. Take, for example, her constant complaining about her fate and about us. It's true, children are disobedient by nature, but our aunt doesn't understand this. And she can go on all day, saying that if she were our mother, we would behave and be respectful. She yells and threatens us, making our lives miserable. Even when she is at her most cheerful, she has never spoken to us with a smile, although she harbors no bad feelings toward us. I can imagine how bad it would be if she weren't here—for now, the shirts get laundered, there's food on the table, the fire's lit when it's cold. It could be that shirts wouldn't be laundered, we'd have to leave the machines and get our food by ourselves, and the house would be cold. But aside from this she doesn't do anything for me.

That's the way I feel about the whole family; aside from the material side of things, nothing ties me to them. And yet I've known them the longest and the best; I was raised here and grew up to be the kind of person I am. It's strange, then, that in my mind and soul I outgrew my family. I can't bear what unfortunate people they are, and I feel both compassion and contempt for them. Knowing them now, I feel sorry for them. I'm unhappy and my soul is torn. Sometimes it upsets me that I'm not as frivolous and empty as they are, or that they aren't as educated as I am. All we have in common is our struggle to have a roof over our heads, food, clothing, and so on—and in this respect I love my father, my aunt, and my brothers and sisters.

When I'm hungry, I eat; when I'm cold, I go home to get warm; when my shoes have holes in them, my aunt takes them to the shoemaker's—this is when I am aware of what my family is to me.

I pity them, I feel contempt for them, and yet—I love them.

Childhood

I think that I felt then what everyone experiences as they come to know the world, life, and people. The sun's light was brighter then, more fiery and golden. The air felt sweetly cool in my lungs, and the wind was more pleasant as it caressed and wafted across my face. I experienced the feeling of becoming acquainted with the foreign, the unknown. A child with a new toy has the same feeling; he wonders at it, is enchanted by it, and examines it until it becomes familiar. As for me, that new toy—life—has since become ordinary. Those joyous, sunny feelings were stifled, first in a crowded garret and then in a dark basement.

*

During the first period of my life we lived in a garret over my grandmother's kitchen. That's where I was born, as were Boruch and Gitl. It was a cozy room that used to be my grandmother's kitchen. This was on Niska Street, a street inhabited by poor, simple people and by the dregs of society. This street was the first to leave its mark on me, and it formed my earliest impressions of life. It was there that I first learned the difference between boys and girls. I also remember my first "love," when I was about four years old. I remember that I liked to play with one little girl from my neighborhood more than with the other children, and I liked her very much.

At this time I still had my mother's attentive care and guidance. I didn't yet have any intellectual needs, for which my mother couldn't provide, as I would in later years. All I needed were the various toys my mother whittled out of wood and the ones my Uncle David made by gluing together pictures from caramel candy wrappers with soap. In those days my mother was the center of my thoughts. I was happy, and she was happy.

*

When I turned five, we moved to a basement apartment on Muranowska Street. My childhood impressions became more varied, less ordinary or monotonous. I have more memories from this place than I have from Niska Street. I remember my fascination with a faucet, which had a knob in the shape of an "X." When we moved into the apartment—I had seen the faucet earlier, when my parents took me with them to look over the place—I moved a chair up to it and spent hours turning the faucet on and off until it became familiar. I'm amazed that I remember such a silly thing so vividly.

This is where my courtyard childhood began. On Niska Street I knew only our cozy apartment, our quiet, clean, gray front hall, and the piece of blue sky that I could see though the window, in which the golden sun appeared every day. In my child's eyes, this was a fresh, healthy, bright symbol of the world around me. In the basement apartment I no longer experienced nature's charms; here I came to know people and life. I stopped being a lonely child and left the exclusive care of my mother for the world of playmates. Now, in addition to my home, I lived in the courtyard and the street. My first friend, whom I remember very well, was Moszek. He lived in the garret. His mother was a little crazy, and his father was an old, overworked man—he was both a stove maker and a *shammes*—who didn't care at all for his only son. I played with Moszek all day long. I remember quite well how intensely we collected cigarette boxes. Moszek would even buy six boxes for five groszy from the tobacconist. Every one of these boxes was a prized possession. We later did the same with the silver wrappers from chocolates. This childish habit made me happy.

There were two empty lots on our street, where in the summer we played with marbles and chestnuts, ran around, and played "cat and mouse." In the winter we spent time skating, making snowmen, and having snowball fights.

I remember that once Moszek took a five-zloty bill from his mother's purse (I wasn't there when he did this). We went to a store and bought a flashlight, and then Moszek decided he wanted a toy tin gun, too. This made the storekeeper suspicious. He took the money and told us to go get our father before he'd give the money back. We cried for a long time, but it didn't do any good. That evening Moszek's mother came crying to us about those five zloty.

Another friend of mine had a lot of stolen money. He lived at 6 Gęsia Street; he was the son of a rabbi. Together with Moszek we spent his money. We rode the tram, bought sausages, and went to the *mikve*. I never stole. Whether I was afraid to do it or didn't have the opportunity, the fact is that I didn't steal. But when I was sent to the store, I'd bring home less change if I managed to haggle the price down or if my mother didn't know the price.

Lately I often see Moszek on the street. We look at each other but act as if we don't recognize each other or aren't on speaking terms with each other. Only time has separated us and made us strangers. Moszek's a poor man; he wears rags and apparently works as a porter. His father died before my mother did.

*

The place where we went during the summer marks a separate period in my childhood—my rural childhood. There, close to nature, my soul was uplifted and my mind developed. There were so many impressions and so many things to wonder about. The blowing of the wind, the aroma of the plants, the coolness of the air, the heat of the sun, the dry, hot sand, freedom, and unlimited space—a city child takes none of this for granted. It all gives him an unforgettable feeling, awakens in him the most wonderful impulses and instincts, develops his imagination. What impressed me most was the free, unlimited space, so different from the city's maze of tight and narrow streets. I came to love this freedom. I felt so happy in the spacious fields and forests, without the restriction of my mother's attention.

*

When I was three I went to a *kheyder*, but I don't remember it. I do remember going to the *kheyder* of Hersz-Judel, may he rest in peace; by then we lived on Muranowska Street. It was in a bright, spacious room on the ground floor, with windows looking out onto a quiet, sunny street. Hersz-Judel would sit at a table covered with green paper, which stood near the first student's bench. On this table were books, a pen with an ink stand, and a ruler—we called it the "paw"—with which our teacher used to punish guilty students by hitting them a few times on the palm of the hand.

I will never forget Hersz-Judel's breakfast. On the green table, I remember, he piled a stack of slices of black bread liberally spread with butter. He would cut the bread into portions and eat them slowly, savoring them as he listened to us chant the Bible. (I still remember this monotonous melody, even though thirteen years have passed.) While peacefully chewing his bread and sipping coffee, he would make comments to the students and correct their mistakes. On the wall behind our teacher were colorful portraits of Aaron and Moses; a little further to the right, closer to the door, hung a large, white piece of cardboard printed with the blessing recited at the beginning of a new month. Every month the teacher would slip a long piece of paper with the name of the month on it into a special slot in this piece of cardboard, and he would recite the blessing with us.

At Hersz-Judel's I studied the Bible and Rashi commentaries. I think I had learned how to read Hebrew with him, too, but I don't remember.

The Bible was my first intellectual and spiritual source of inspiration. Studying it prompted vivid fantasies and awoke a strong sense of Jewishness in me. I saw Adam and Eve, the sunny land of Palestine; I saw Jacob sleeping in a hut made of stones and the ladder with angels on it stretching to heaven; I saw Joseph and his brothers, Egypt, slavery, Moses, the desert, and manna dropping from heaven. In my vivid imagination I saw everything. I believed in it and took it to heart. This instilled in me a faith in my existence and in God's existence, a faith in everything that religion proclaimed.

Passover, Purim, Sukkoth, Hanukkah, Shavuoth—the holidays inspired my most heartfelt feelings. How can I describe them? Memories of sitting at the Passover seder in my new clothes; of putting on a mask and looking at a temple made out of cakes; of playing with a *dreydl*, getting Hanukkah money from my grandmother, eating sweets and playing with colorful candles; of decorating the *sukkah* with colorful paper chains, baskets, and cut-outs, and watching my father dance with the Torah scroll as I held a little flag in my hand on Simchath Torah; of the fresh smell of green reeds and how they made a shrill bird-call when I put one against my mouth. I remember all this as part of a completely different time, one that was happy, more serene, joyful. These memories evoke a completely different feeling than even my liveliest memories of ordinary days.

Whenever I remember these things today, I become furious with the so-called "Enlightenment." I would give a great deal to be able to experience this celebratory feeling, this mood, this cheerfulness, once again. Education opened my eyes, awoke me from a religious dream, from the wonderful, age-old poetry of my people, and converted me to realism.

I'd had a beautiful dream and it was—Jewish.

I was lulled to sleep by Hersz-Judel, and I was awakened by the Pioneers. But the dream was more beautiful than the awakening.

*

Sometime later I stopped going to Hersz-Judel's and was sent to another *kheyder*. The teacher here didn't inspire any emotional memories for me. I remember him as dull, gray, and ordinary. We children called him "Royter Borek" [Yiddish for "red beet"], because his face was dark red like a beet. He always had a switch in his hand and was quick to scold us.

My religious education dragged on. The room here was dark and not very spacious. Instead of benches, there was a long table on trestles, with children sitting on both sides. The teacher didn't have a separate desk; instead he sat at the end of the table near the window. Any student who made even the tiniest mistake was hit across the back with the switch. And I should make it clear that there wasn't a single student who didn't make mistakes. So it was no wonder that a day spent playing hooky was a happy one. School became an ordeal.

*

After that, I didn't go to *kheyder* anymore. When I now recall my childhood in *kheyder*, I realize what an unusual direction my life has taken. I had always lived in a Jewish neighborhood; I mostly saw Jews and rarely saw a gentile on the street. Therefore, I thought there were more Jews than non-Jews. Since the gentiles were a janitor, a maid, a gardener, or had other similar, demeaning jobs, I thought them to be beneath me. What could they know? The gentile knows nothing; he doesn't think, he just beats Jews. And while I thought that Christian boys were wanton savages, I was terribly afraid of them. I divided the world into Jews and gentiles.

I thoroughly despised heretics. I included among their ranks every Jew who was elegantly dressed in modern clothing, every child who didn't go to a *kheyder*, and every Zionist. The word "communism" frightened me. In my imagination, this was worse than stealing. A communist wasn't even a heretic, but something worse than a gentile.

I myself was very devout. I never went to bed without wearing a *yarmulke*, for example. But I did this more because I was afraid of demons than because of the ritual itself. All in all, religion made me afraid of things I had never seen. My faith was blind in every way. I was afraid to be alone, and I was afraid of the dark and of every unexpected shadow. I think that this fright is the seed of my cowardice, with which I wage constant inner battles to this day. Religion wasn't the only thing that taught me fear; my parents also introduced me to the bogey man. I remember as far back as Niska Street lying in bed with Boruch and crying for some unknown reason. Then Father moved Boruch to Mother's bed and got into bed with me. This apparently didn't help, because I remember someone banging on the door—probably my grandmother—and my father, terrified, whispered in my ear: "Hush, or else the bogey man—"

*

In 1930 we moved to Nalewki Street, where we live to this day. When we lived in the basement I was ashamed of it and kept it a secret whenever I could. I always judged people according to wealth, so I was very proud when we moved out of the basement.

Again, new impressions: the courtyard, the "palace," the "king."

The courtyard was always noisy and lively. There were two partitions there, made of boards that had been used to mix cement when a floor was added to our building. When I moved in, they were empty and had been sitting there for a long time. These two partitions were the "palace," and Motek, whom I fortunately knew from Royter Borek's *kheyder*, was the "king."

I was swept up in the life of the courtyard immediately. Compared to Muranowska Street, it was all new to me. When Motek asked me whether I wanted to join them, I agreed, and he made me an "officer." Moniek and Aron were "presidents," Saul was a "marshal" and the most dedicated "subject of the king," and the rest were soldiers. We often waged wars with weapons, which we made from long strips of metal that came from packing crates. Our enemy was the neighboring courtyard, from which I still know some people to this day.

I assumed a distinguished position in the "state" right away. I was recognized as the strongest, because I beat everyone in wrestling, and I quickly advanced to be a "president." Even the "king" needed my protection. Once, Szmulek, who later became my best friend, picked on the "king," and Motek ordered me to take revenge on him. I locked Szmulek in a hold, dug my chin into him, and flattened him out. All the boys, and even the girls, roared with loud shouts of joy and admiration. This brought me great distinction and satisfaction, although later Szmulek threw a piece of wood at me, hitting me hard on the leg. Szmulek didn't take part much in the "state." He played with us because he didn't have any other friends. He was the only boy in the courtyard who was serious and reserved. I became best friends with him, which lasted until I started working and he started going to trade school. We didn't swear eternal friendship the way others did. Our friendship came about by itself. Why he took a liking to me I don't know, but I appreciated his decisiveness, his seriousness, and his knowledge, as I was always asking him about things. We went everywhere together and told each other everything. The very fact that we were friends for so long—four years—meant something to us. Now, one of us passes by the other in the courtyard indifferently, as if we were strangers. I think that this is someone different; that the Szmulek from my childhood, whom I loved as much as myself, doesn't exist any more—and I mourn this bygone time of my childhood.

Our friendship began to dissolve as soon as Szmulek started going to trade school. His school cap brought him no small honor. Not only was I not going to a vocational school, but I had stopped going to school altogether and began working. We started to see less of each other, and finally, as we entered adolescence, our childhood friendship disappeared altogether. Now that we are grown-up young men, we don't acknowledge one another; it's just the same as with Moszek.

*

After we had been living in our new apartment for a few months, I was sent to the Jewish Community Denominational School. This school took an enlightened and progressive approach to Jewish education. I was expected to enter the second grade, but I qualified for the third grade, because when I was in *kheyder* I had learned how to read Polish fluently, and I could write decently. The woman who taught Polish in Hersz-Judel's *kheyder* always praised me as her best student. I remember that when I first began to learn Polish I didn't pass a single shop sign or poster without sounding out the syllables. It's not surprising, then, that I went straight into the third grade. The school, classes, studying, lessons, recess—all this was new for me. Right away I found the school overwhelming and alienating. I didn't feel as comfortable here as I had at Hersz-Judel's or Borek's. The teachers were so unapproachable. I didn't like them, except for one: the Bible and Hebrew teacher, Mr. Bromberg, who taught in Yiddish. He didn't torment us with our lessons but talked openly with us and aroused our interest with his stories. He also told jokes all the time. Everyone liked him, because his class was easy-going and cheerful. Nobody was embarrassed to speak up in class. He didn't really seem to be a teacher but rather a friend, even though he was demanding.

I went to this school for two years. Bromberg wasn't our teacher during the first year. Instead, the principal of the school taught the class. Principal Łabędź wasn't a bad instructor, but for some reason he didn't take an interest in all of his students, discriminating between those with whom he was familiar and those whom he treated as "gray," anonymous. No doubt, if the gray students had taken as much part in the life of the school as the ones that he recognized, then they, too, would have done well in their studies.

But there was a hierarchy in Łabędź's class. He had the same rapport with his favorite students that Bromberg had with the entire class. Łabędź smiled and joked only with them, and he dealt with them exclusively when taking care of class business. I was one of the gray, unknown students, and like all of them I was intimidated. I was rarely asked a question or answered one, but I smiled during the playful chats the principal had with the "good" students. The gray students sat in the back of the room, I among them. We would have been very happy if we, too, had some importance in the school, if someone had taken an interest in us. Oh, then school wouldn't have felt like a chore, an obligation. We were almost never chosen to be class monitor, class steward, class chairman, librarian, or given any function at all.

I got the chance to find out how valuable it would have been if all the students were equal. For some reason, Łabędź appointed me the class treasurer when we collected money to buy school caps and other items. Everyone looked at me, which made me uncomfortable, and I blushed. It was such an unexpected honor—in short, it was a happy day. I was given the key to the cash box, which hung from a silk string around my neck, like a whistle. That day I ran home, flaunting the key and my function. I felt important, and school was no longer an ordeal. It was like becoming an active member of an organization. I was eager to go to school. I had a responsibility and was proud of it, especially when I wrote in my notebook the names of the students and the amounts they paid.

I was treasurer for barely a month; then everything went back to its usual course. Once again, I felt put down and undistinguished—an inferiority complex. In addition, I wasn't promoted to the next grade.

Although I didn't study in school, my head wasn't empty. I was preoccupied with thoughts and observations, contemplating everything that I encountered. I became a loner, withdrawn, or, as my father says, "His wisdom dies inside of him." I remain like this to this day. I look, I understand, and I am silent—but someday I will speak.

If I had found school to be interesting, I wouldn't have been drawn to the courtyard. I wouldn't have rejoiced whenever I was free from school and could spend the day in the courtyard. Every day unusual things happened there, every day there were some changes. During the year that I repeated the third grade, the courtyard was where we established the "fellowship alliance," with clauses, laws, stamps, and ID cards.

By then the "state" had long since ceased to exist. Szmulek and I had been the first to ridicule that stupid game. We were called the "revolutionaries." The "fellowship alliance" held a meeting every day, and each time there were new laws concerning fellowship and loyalty. Almost every day we went to the "trenches," where the school vegetable gardens are now, and there we played soccer. We also had a separate sports club, called Yehuda, in which I was the goalie.

The life of the courtyard absorbed me completely. Also, once again I "fell in love." Genia once stopped me in the front hall, tripping me. Another time she was standing with her friend Roza, who told me that my fiancée was standing next to her. Although Genia was annoyed at her and called her "snotty," I felt good in my heart. From that time on I played only with Genia, and I "dreamed" about her. We spent whatever free time we had together. But eventually she got mad at me, and that's how things have stayed. It's the same as with Moszek and Szmulek—it's as if we'd never known each other.

It's strange—those with whom I was once closest are now like strangers, while I'm still in touch with those I've known only casually, and I talk to them whenever we meet.

*

I didn't do any better in my second year at school; on the contrary, I felt discouraged and neglected my studies. Bromberg suggested that if I got down to studying I could still pass, but it was a "sure thing" that I wouldn't pass this time, either. As it turned out, I didn't finish the school year; I was expelled. This is what happened:

Once, I came to school and went to hang up my coat. Accidentally, I knocked down Feld's coat; he was sitting nearby, putting on his shoes. Seeing that I had knocked down his coat, he jumped up and called me a second-year lazy-pants. If he hadn't made such a fuss I would have picked up his coat, but when he started ordering me to pick it up right this minute or else, I became stubborn. Then he started a fight. I was stronger than he was and easily pushed him away. Maybe he would have backed off and gone away, but all the other students there were looking at me contemptuously and laughing. When I pushed him away he spat at me. I couldn't forgive him for that, so I slapped him lightly and somewhat apprehensively. Then it started. The others laughed some more and winked at each other, amused at my daring. One of them, who stood behind me, tweaked my ear. When I turned around to see who had done it, someone else kicked me in the pants. I received more and more shoves, kicks, and smacks on the ear, from the sides and behind. I wanted to cry, but I froze and tried to back out, humiliated, as if nothing had happened. But then Feld, who was still holding his cheek, suddenly and unexpectedly hit me right in the eyes with all his might. I snapped. Bursting into tears, I threw myself at Feld like a wild, mad dog and, almost without knowing it, bit him. Feld started screaming, and the teacher came running. She heard out his story, grabbed me by the collar, and took me to the principal, Łabędź, who was giving a lesson to the fourth grade. Łabędź called me abnormal and retarded. He started to ridicule me and make jokes at my expense, while the whole class looked at me and laughed.

Then Łabędź sent me to see a psychologist. I went to see her with my father. She asked me a lot of questions, which I thought were riddles, such as, "What happens when a candle goes out?" to which I replied, "It gets dark." Then she told me to listen carefully and said, "One friend was going to see another. He walked across a field, then through the woods, then across a bridge, then again across a field, and again through the woods, and then he was at his friend's house." And she asked me to tell her what areas he went through going back. When I answered correctly, she told me to draw a circle, which she said was a garden. Then she said that boys were playing ball in this garden and they lost the ball. Where did they look for it? She told me to mark the spot with my pencil. I thought there was something very intelligent behind all this, so I answered tentatively. She asked me a lot of other similar questions, most of which I answered correctly. Then she asked me a second time about the details of the fight, which surprised me. I lied, just as I had when she had asked me about this before. I told her in detail all about how Feld and the other boys started picking on me until everything went dark in front of my eyes, and that's when I bit Feld.

Afterwards, she reassured my father that everything was all right, and she asked me to bring her my report card at the end of the year. In her report to Łabędź she wrote that I was completely normal. Then, I suppose, there was some qualification in there that I couldn't read, because after this positive statement she wrote the word "but—." That evening my father was exceptionally nice to me and was so thrilled at my answers that he bought me anything I wanted. All this comforted me and lifted my spirits.

Although the psychologist's ruling obligated Łabędź not to expel me, it didn't have much of an effect. Some time later, he simply told my mother that I wasn't to come to school any more, because it was a waste of time. He added that I was a hopeless oaf and that he had never seen such a sluggard. Later, my mother cried for a long time to my father, but she didn't say anything to me. She just pitied me, kissed me, and ran her hand over my head with a sigh. I was upset and didn't sleep most of the night, thinking and crying.

I never went back to that school again.

*

A new change entered my life: the school Khinukh Yeladim, which had been founded by Dr. Nisenson. This school was recommended to my mother, and, not having much choice, she sent Boruch and me there. I took the entrance exam and was placed in the fourth grade. This was because my parents had hired a tutor (a high-school student) for me when I stopped going to the community school. He prepared me for the exam and was also the one who recommended Khinukh Yeladim.

Khinukh Yeladim is almost as pleasant a memory for me as Hersz-Judel's *kheyder*. Hersz-Judel evokes sweet feelings and sentiment, but my memory of Khinukh Yeladim is of a vibrant happiness that I still feel.

My first contact with this school was unusual and made a memorable impression on me. My mother and I went in through the front entrance (marked "For Teachers and Parents"). The principal greeted us very politely. When everything concerning me was settled, I went out of the office and waited for my mother in a square lobby that had four doors, one in each wall. There was the entrance door in front, to the left of which was the office door, and then there were doors to two classrooms. Across from the entrance, over the door to the third-grade classroom, was written "Welcome" in Hebrew. Suddenly a bell sounded for recess. First the door of the third-grade classroom, next to which I was standing, opened. Mr. Ajzenkowicz (I would later learn his name) appeared in the doorway with the class roster in his hand, and before I knew it a whole group of boys surrounded him like some sort of entourage. Each one was craning his neck upward and asking the teacher something or telling him something. Surrounded by this disorderly circle of children, he turned his smiling face to one child and then another, answering questions with humor and wit, just like a big child himself. The children didn't leave him alone for a long time. They kept asking an endless number of questions on a subject that must have come up in the lesson. Finally the door to the other classroom opened. Mr. Amsterdam came out and took Ajzenkowicz with him into the office. He was still answering questions, with his head turned back toward the children, as he was pulled into the office.

This evidence of the casual relationship between the students and teachers and of their respect for each other went straight to my heart. When my mother and I left the school, I was excited and full of expectation for the next day. For the first time I would go to a school that was so relaxed and happy, where there were no unapproachable, intimidating teachers, and where the children were my equals. My mother was satisfied. No doubt, she expected better results from her offspring than she'd had so far.

The entire school consisted of an office, three classrooms, a cloakroom with a kitchen, and two lobbies: one by the front entrance for the parents and teachers, and another by the cloakroom for the students. The setting was just right for this cozy, intimate school. What good was the spaciousness of the community school, where I felt uncomfortable, like an outsider? I have no particular memories of what I studied in the fourth grade. Perhaps the one important thing was that at the end of the year I had a report card with all 4's and a 5 for behavior. The reason for such a radical change in my performance lies in the school's approach to learning, development, and teaching.

My last year at this school, when I was in the fifth grade, is etched in my memory. The fifth grade was the school's highest. When I entered the school there wasn't a fifth grade yet, and before that there were only three. I was lucky to be attending the school when it was being systematically expanded. I always benefited from being in the highest grade, which was always the most important. The fifth grade had only seventeen students. It was small and intimate, and we all knew each other as if we were brothers. (In the community school my class had been huge, with thirty students.)

During recess, we sat on the benches like a close group of friends, eating and talking about all kinds of interesting things. No one was left out, unless it was someone "cramming" for a class for which he wasn't quite prepared.

Except for the "dunce," which is an inevitable part of every school, each one of us would have studied here for the rest of his life, as we said when we bade a final farewell to the school. I sincerely sympathized with the "dunce," Zymelman, because I understood his plight very well. The fifth grade, being the highest, was taught by the principal herself. Her youth, energy, and especially her good pedagogical skills motivated us to study and nurtured our good relationship with the school and teachers. She taught us Polish language, history, geography, and botany, so she was with us more than the other teachers. She taught us well and got through to us. One thing about her that I think everyone valued was that she didn't make distinctions among us. She treated each student with the same sincerity and, when necessary, with rigor. She understood each one of us equally, and we felt the same confidence and sincerity in dealing with her. Sometimes at the beginning of class she resolved an argument that had come up during recess. These were childish disputes, such as which game is better: checkers or dominos? We were never embarrassed to ask the principal for her opinion, and she would offer it without irony, but usually with a smile, as if pleased to be asked. That's what she was like, and all the other teachers were just as accomplished educators as she—or even more so, as was Ajzenkowicz.

Mr. Glanc, the math teacher, was too strict and anxious. He couldn't control his temper because, as usual, children are impossible, and he couldn't be as understanding of us as he should have been, because he was too nervous. Therefore we were somewhat afraid of him and weren't as sincere with him, although more than once he convinced us how much he cared for us. No one would dare whisper a word to his neighbor in Glanc's class, because when he explained something even a deaf person would have paid attention. Glanc would have found some way to compel even an indifferent student to listen. As a result, everyone listened to him and did well in math. However, no one got the grade he deserved from him.

Ajzenkowicz taught us modern Hebrew: grammar, reciting from memory, reading, and translation. Pieczennik sometimes substituted for Ajzenkowicz, teaching us Hebrew spelling and the Bible. More precisely, these two teachers taught us Jewish studies.

Everyone liked Ajzenkowicz, who was a young, agreeable, and very pleasant man. He was always gentle, smiling, and cheerful; I don't remember him ever having a sour face. His disposition influenced us, too, and we were very devoted to him. While Glanc taught us to be disciplined, and we responded to him like soldiers to their superior officer, Ajzenkowicz didn't have much authority over us children and we didn't listen to him. We listened to Glanc and appeared to respect him (although behind his back we said things about him that were at sometimes rather vulgar). Ajzenkowicz probably thought that Glanc was more of an authority figure for us than he was—but still, he's the one who remained in our hearts as a friendly teacher. We spoke of him as though he were one of us. He always took the children's side, and he even stood up for us when we weren't exactly right and asked for us to be forgiven.

Mr. Pieczennik was somewhat like Ajzenkowicz, somewhat like Glanc. Even though he might smile at us, we felt that this smile came down to us from on high. He wanted to gain our respect through his dignity, rigor, and friendship. And even though Ajzenkowicz made no effort to gain our respect, in reality he had more of it than anyone else, although it wasn't obvious. He never acted superior toward us; on the contrary, he made every effort to treat us as equals. But Pieczennik always seemed stiff and unapproachable. We showed respect for him, but in our hearts we had more affection for Ajzenkowicz, although Pieczennik was more enterprising in various school events and was more visible. The arts and crafts teacher (I've forgotten his name) didn't take an active part in the life of the school. He was a smart, quiet, practical man who always spoke slowly and with ease. When he explained to a student how to cut something, for example, he usually approached him calmly and quietly, because he especially liked things to be calm and quiet. He didn't associate with the students individually and didn't know who they were. He only knew which class it was and often forgot students' names. He was a kind person, and we neither loved him nor disliked him. I don't remember any other teachers, because, although there were two others in the school, they never taught me.

Aside from their own methods, all these teachers had a common approach. Except for Glanc, I remember each teacher with a smile. Together, they took us in hand and led us toward what was good.

We looked forward most of all to the holidays of Hanukkah and Purim, because then we put on a show for the members of the society that supported our school. Pieczennik helped us prepare the Yiddish part of the show and the principal helped us with the Polish part. We made a stage out of boards in the largest classroom and put up scenery, which the art teacher painted for us. In one of these shows I sang in the choir, and in the last show in which I took part another student and I recited Tuwim's poem "Silesia Is Singing." Preparations and rehearsals started a month in advance. The show itself was attended by many guests and all the "members" (that's what we called the people who supported our school). Everything was so beautiful and so full of feeling. At the end of the show we were served pastry, wine, candy, and chocolate. Everyone was pleased with us and praised us.

That was the most wonderful time of my childhood. The freedom and friendship I enjoyed there was something I never experienced again. I got a great deal out of it. Most of all, I really learned something there, whereas in the community school I didn't understand anything. Even more important, the school developed my sense of being a Polish Jew. I hadn't been an old-fashioned, zealously religious Jew for a long time but had become rather casual about my Jewishness. I came to love Poland and the Polish language more than Yiddish. Modern Hebrew and the various stories about the history of Israel that I learned furthered the Jewish feelings I'd had in Hersz-Judel's *kheyder*, only now these feelings were more developed, more emotional, and took on a Zionist orientation. And the Bible reinforced this sense of my background with its heroes and beauty.

But the influence of Polish culture, which I got to know here, was no less important. I understood it immediately, even though I still didn't know how to read or write Yiddish at the time.

The one thing that wasn't good about Khinukh Yeladim was that there were only three classrooms in the school. Because of this, I had to go to school in the afternoon and got in the habit of getting up late.

Leaving the school was very sad. Since I wrote compositions well, I wrote one about what I got out of the school and how I felt about leaving it. On the last day of school, when the diplomas were being handed out, I read this composition aloud. The children and their parents sat on the benches and the main "members" sat at the table. Some of the students had tears in their eyes as I read my composition, and some looked lost in thought. At the end, the president of the society gave out our diplomas, shook each student's hand, and wished him success in life. After vacation all of us who were in the fifth grade gathered on Nowolipki Street, where the school was, and asked, "What now?" We deluded ourselves with the false hope that maybe the school would add another grade, as it had done before. But in the end we were transferred to the public school. When I came home, no one was there, and I burst into tears. I was ready to swear that I'd study forever if only it was at this school. I missed my classroom, my friends, the shows, Ajzenkowicz, the principal, Pieczennik, the art teacher, and Glanc.

*

I began attending Public School No. 174 on Bonifraterska Street. This school was the complete opposite of the late Dr. Nisenson's school. First of all, there were sixty students in the class. I felt like a complete stranger there. If I had attended this school from first grade, maybe it would have been all right, but as it was I couldn't get used to the atmosphere there. None of the teachers knew my name, or worse, knew anything about me. They just saw my name on their class rosters. If they hadn't had roll call every day, my presence or absence wouldn't have interested anyone; it was as if I weren't there. Also, I wasn't used to being in a class together with girls, and so I felt ill at ease.

In Khinukh Yeladim the whole class was like a single group of friends; as a result I had sixteen schoolmates, whom I know to this day. But in the public school I didn't have a single friend. I wasn't fortunate enough to finish all seven grades of public school, because in the midst of my studies my mother died. This was an enormous shock to my spirit. My mother was the closest person in the world to me. Often in moments of sadness I remember her and how she cared for me. Her death will always be a loss for me. She was the dearest person in the world, because she was everything to me. Will I ever love anyone with the love and attachment I felt for her?

After her death I stopped going to school and started working.

Youth

When I started to work I completely broke my ties with the courtyard. I no longer had time for it.

I started working at home with my father. I remember that when I was still going to school my mother was worried about which trade I should enter. She used to say that she wanted me to be a mechanic, because I liked to tinker with everything: the sewing machine, the clock, and so on. And yet she objected to her own idea, because I was too weak for such work. My father said that if a trade was too difficult for me, it would be better if I went to work in a store.

But neither plan came to pass, even though I had a real passion for mechanical things. Because of my family's situation, all such prospects and plans were in vain. Now I'm buried in work that I've never cared for from the start; every day free from work brings me great relief and pleasure.

Since I started working I've become somewhat more serious and have started reading again. I started to enjoy reading when I was still at Khinukh Yeladim. All seventeen students in our class borrowed books from the free library, to which the school sent us. At the time I read books by Karl May, Jules Verne, Maine Reed, and other such authors. I remember in particularly how avidly I read *Uncle Tom's Cabin* and *Robinson Crusoe*, which made a big impression on me.

I read these books with a passionate and free sprit. They developed my imagination, brought me closer to the vastness of life around the world, and acquainted me with things I've never seen. Also, they ennobled my heart and made it more sensitive, developing my sense of justice.

These books were the foundation of my intellect. When I started attending public school I no longer had the opportunity to read, and so I had nothing to do with books until I started to work. This was a long interruption.

When I started working I didn't get my books from a library, because at the time I felt completely cut off from the outside world, society, and community life. It all seemed alien to me, sometimes even hostile. As a result, I became somewhat antisocial, and so it's no wonder that rather than enrolling at a library I simply bought books. I didn't even dare to think of joining a library, but I had to read books.

*

At this time I found an outlet for all my feelings and opinions in the emotional poems and prose that I wrote. My literary talent had first emerged when I was still at Khinukh Yeladim, and it now gained new emphasis and form. In solitude I contemplated the world, life, and all things and ideas. I developed my own worldview and became immersed in philosophical thoughts. And all these ideas, linked by my feelings and my vivid imagination, became literary material. The first poem I wrote during this period was inspired by my sad fate as a recluse. In this poem I depicted a young man alone on the open sea, where the sky touched the water all

around. I described the beauty of nature: schools of fish and the flight of
seagulls, the setting of the sun, the quiet murmur of the waves. The young
man would give up all these charms of nature for just one traveling companion. In the endless sea I depicted life, and in the young man, myself. I
gave it the title "Alone among the Waves." At the time I was filled with beautiful dreams, and their sad, monotonous, but beautiful images brought tears
to my eyes, tears of inspiration. I was able to direct my thoughts everywhere,
engaging everything from the limitless universe to my own life—my misery,
misfortune, and aimlessness.

Despite their gloomy mood, these thoughts were elevated and beautiful,
and they prompted the "opus" that I started to write. Inspired by bright,
unusual, and beautiful visions in unheard-of hues, I set out to write "The
History of the Eternal Nation." Egyptian slavery, Moses, the desert, and
Moses' death on Mount Nebo—all of this I intended to paint in imagina-
tive and heroic tones, writing in verse and prose. I know that Shakespeare,
too, wrote imaginatively in such a form. Like him, I made the moon, the
sun, and all of nature move; I even represented dreams as the moon's squire,
who imagined the night above the beautiful Egypt I depicted. But I didn't
get very far with this and stopped writing, discouraged because I lacked
broader knowledge of the history of Egypt.

I didn't stop writing poems, though. Yet here, too, I'd start a poem and,
discouraged, abandon it, unfinished. That's almost always what happened.
I had many ideas and inspirations, but I could never finish anything,
because I had more ideas than time. Also, I always lacked some information or word to express my thoughts. This continued until I joined the
Pioneers. Until then I wrote only for my own pleasure and needs. But in
the Pioneers I wrote for everyone, and so I had to finish my poems.

Most of what I wrote was in Polish; my ability to read and write
Yiddish was poor and acquired with difficulty. Using my knowledge of the
Hebrew alphabet, I pored over Yiddish newspapers on my own, guided by
intuition and the knowledge that the letter *ayin* made the sound "e" and
vov was "u."

*

Whenever Chaskiel met me on the street he'd ask me why I no longer
came to meetings of the Pioneers. When I had attended the community
school, Chaskiel got me to join the Pioneers, the communist youth organization. But then I became afraid and stopped going to the meetings without
giving the others any explanation. Chaskiel kept asking why I was "blowing
it off" and not coming; this went on for almost four years. I always simply

said that I was going to come, so as to get out of an uncomfortable situation. But once, Chaskiel ran into me during my "Alone among the Waves" period, and joining the organization seemed like a natural thing for me to do. This was after my mother had died. I didn't have any friends at all, but, more importantly, I was reading and had acquired some knowledge and a sense of justice. Although it still frightened me somewhat, the word "communism" meant to me (although not complete consciously) a consistent, continuous, and fearless struggle for justice. Communism was an authority that I held in esteem as being forceful and just. These two motives—the appeal of communism's authority and the need for a community—propelled me to join the Pioneers, rather than any intellectual conviction.

The Pioneers roused me from my intellectual stagnation by appealing to my ambition to learn, which was one of the organization's many virtues. In the Pioneers I came to know the vast life of the street and society.

I also enrolled in the workers' library and the newspaper reading room; I went to lectures and on group walks, and I talked with my comrades. In a word, I was drawn into the whirl of group activities. The Pioneers transformed me from a solitary person into a comrade. However, I still had a bad habit of blushing, even long after I had joined the organization. I'd blush for any reason and in front of any person of authority who spoke to me. This usually happened when I came in contact with "*yentes*" (girls), whom I couldn't relate to at all. I felt completely lost around them and didn't know what to do with myself; my legs trembled and I blushed.

There was nothing unusual about this. I'd been friends with girls when I played in the courtyard, and I'd fooled around with them and been in love with them. But I had become remote not only from girls but also from boys, and I couldn't help feeling anxious. However, I got over it when I advanced to the KZM (the Communist Youth League) at the age of sixteen, and my attitude toward girls and authority figures changed. But I'll describe that later, because it doesn't belong to the Pioneer period, but to the KZM period.

*

When they found out that I wrote poetry, the Pioneers became interested. But they all turned up their noses when they looked over my poems, because they weren't revolutionary; they weren't in the spirit of the Pioneers. Over time, though, I changed from an inexperienced petit bourgeois to a member of the collective, and I began to write different poems with a socialist perspective. These poems won the Pioneers' respect. Some of them were recited at our celebrations. When our Pioneer group had a party in honor of our graduation into the KZM, I recited a poem called "To Youth." Another time Chaskiel recited my poem "New Year" at the New Year's party. I compiled a notebook of some other poems, and almost everyone read them. Now my poems were no longer left unfinished. I was nicknamed "the Poet" or "Jakub the Poet."

When I was sixteen I advanced to the KZM. This was the most important period in my life. In the KZM I found enlightenment. The gathering places, cell meetings, distributing of leaflets, hanging of posters, flags, mass assemblies—all this shaped my intellect. Every occasion gave me pleasure and satisfaction, because I knew that I wasn't simply an onlooker at even the most simple discussion and that I had my own independent view of things. I must emphasize that this was not solely because of the KZM, its ideals, organizational work, and heroics. My enlightenment was primarily the result of my close association with people: instructors and members of the KZM of both sexes. They boosted my self-confidence; they were kind and always eager to explain and advise. I remember that once there was a discussion on the subject of sex. I didn't know the scientific terminology and didn't understand anything. The instructor saw that I was only listening and not saying anything, and he realized that I didn't know what they were talking about. When everyone left, he walked with me for a long time, talking about sex. I was unhappy that I didn't know anything and that he had to explain it all to me. I felt like a child and was ashamed that everyone except me was informed and could take part in the discussion.

That same day I went to the library and took out books by Klinger, Van de Velde, and others on the subject. And that's how it always was—I was inspired to become more ambitious, even when it wasn't intended. (I was reading more books—not the ones that were recommended to me, but those someone or other had read. I became the puppet of my pride, which was my weakness.)

I was most influenced by Josek, who has remained my best friend. He and I were in the same cell when I met him. At the time, he was so far above me mentally that I couldn't even carry on a conversation with him. But that was when I was lonely and somewhat confused. When we advanced from the Pioneers to the KZM, Josek and I were in different cells, but this didn't keep us from continuing to meet and be friends.

Josek is smart and really understands what's happening. The reason for this is strictly physical. While my senses (vision, hearing, smell, taste) are very weak, his are healthy and well-developed. I have intimate conversations with him that sometimes last well into the night. But he doesn't always understand me. While I'm an idealist, with a mind that is lofty and refined, he's a realist and has a practical mind. We often find ourselves disagreeing.

*

At my uncle's place I met Moniek. He had come from the provinces and got a job working for my uncle. Moniek was a beggar's son. He was a smart fellow, unusually mature for his age. We went on walks together. I wanted him to join the Pioneers, which is why I always spent time with him instead of with Josek. Moniek was amazed by my knowledge, and I was taken with his intelligence and sincerity. He hungered for knowledge. I explained everything to him patiently, and he understood it all.

I soon noticed that he had surpassed me intellectually, and I felt insignificant next to him. He had great gifts as a performer. He imitated everyone with such talent and feeling that he simply won you over. And he knew how to tell stories so well that his listeners were captivated by his words and his beautiful diction. His sole aim in life was to become an actor. Even though this was an unrealistic dream, he seemed to live only for this goal. Once Moniek told me that either he'd become an actor or he would stop living.

In spite of the sorrow within his soul, he was always cheerful and full of jokes. He described himself to me as a "cheerful pessimist."

Moniek badly wanted a girlfriend. Once he even fell in love with the cashier at a soda bar. His love for her was great, honest, and earnest. But he had fallen in love with her without knowing her personally, only from watching her at the cash register. Nevertheless, he acted boldly. As she was heading home from the soda bar he walked straight over to her, shook her hand, and introduced himself. He spoke to her using words that I had composed earlier, because he didn't know many expressions in Polish. I listened as he introduced himself and started up a conversation. But she wasn't keen on him. She told him that she had her own set of friends. He didn't give up at first and followed after her every evening. But eventually he saw that nothing would come of it, and he was overcome by an even greater sadness. On top of this, he never had enough to eat, because he didn't always have work. I admired him. I saw in him the misfortune of a bright and intelligent young Jew, who is idle, resigned, and disheartened.

Finally, Moniek made a wild stab at realizing his goal. He tried to get to France by hiding under the wheels of a train. However, he was caught in Zbąszyń, and the court sentenced him to a month in jail, which was suspended. He didn't give up, though, and soon he tried again. This time they caught him in Germany. He spent two months in jail, and then he came back. He now seemed an unusual fellow—gloomy, serious, and intense. He didn't try to go to France again.

Moniek drowned in the Vistula right in front of his friend Berek, who brought his clothes home. I remember my last conversation with Moniek. It was like something out of a novel. "Life's not worth living," he said. "What's the use? I'm not going to spend my life operating a sewing machine. I'm weak and ruined by masturbation. I now see that nothing will come of me. Getting to France and then going from there to Hollywood is a childish fantasy. There's only one way out for me, to work until midnight. But I can't do that, I won't be able to take it, I'll go crazy. No, I don't know why I'm still alive."

That's what he said to me, and that's why I assume that his death was a suicide. But Berek, who was there when he died, told me that he drowned because of a girl. He wanted to show off in front of her, and he jumped from the public beach into the open river and drowned.

*

When Moniek returned from his first unsuccessful "trip," Josek and two comrades from my cell also set off on a similar "trip," albeit with a different goal. They simply wanted to go to France to better their lives, and if they couldn't stay in France, they were going to fight for the Spanish Republic. Icek and I went with them to the main train station. We even had our picture taken on the way, since we were sure that this was our final farewell. But it didn't work. Beniek had already crawled under the train, but he hadn't found the "pipe" he was supposed to lie on, and he barely made it out from under the train before it started moving.

They quit after their first foiled attempt. "Too bad," Josek told me, "we'll have to stay in Poland."

*

I can't describe the feelings I've had on camping trips and outings. My first time camping left an indelible impression on me and will always be a touching vision of the past. This was a winter camping trip that took place six months after I joined the KZM. There were five people in our group, all of whom except Josek belonged to our cell. We stayed at a cottage owned by Leon's father.

We traveled with a large group from the Pioneers, who were going to a camp somewhere not far from our cottage. We spent almost the entire day with them. They weren't much younger than we were. (Some of them were even the same age as we were, and they were supposed to advance to the KZM after returning from the camp.) Because we were already in the KZM, they looked up to us. When we walked over to their place we could hear them shouting from a distance, "The metalworkers are coming." (Since Chaskiel was a metalworker, he got me into the metalworkers' unit of the Pioneers. Later, they wanted to move me into the leatherworkers' group, but I didn't want to go. When we joined the KZM, once again they wanted to move me into "leather," but I still didn't want to go.) It was nice and cheerful, but I'm sure that it wouldn't have been so much fun if there hadn't been some older girls among the Pioneers. When we danced and played games it was so enjoyable, because there were boys and girls there. This wasn't a big deal, but a boy isn't a girl and a girl isn't a boy.

We also took part in discussions with the Pioneer children, and all in all we felt as though we were at their camp, because we spent the whole day there, only eating and sleeping separately from them.

All this had a positive effect on me. In particular, the way I related to other people, especially girls, changed radically. At one time, other people made me uncomfortable. I wasn't sociable and didn't have any manners. (Until this particular camping trip, *yentes* made me uncomfortable. When I was in both the Pioneers and the KZM, there weren't any girls in either group that I belonged to, by the way.)

Now, all at once, I had clearly changed. I didn't even notice how comfortable I now felt with the *yentes*. Also, it's strange that I didn't fall in love with any of them, even though each one was very alluring and I genuinely liked them.

On this occasion my nickname, "The Poet," spread beyond my own cell, and I became rather popular after demonstrating my talent by writing a parody of the camp. On the last day, when a few more day-campers arrived from a different branch of the Warsaw KZM, we had a closing ceremony to mark the end of the camp. Altogether there were about 150 people. At the beginning of the ceremony the camp commander gave a speech, then there was a debate, and to conclude there were dramatic performances and recitations. Among others, I recited a few of my poems. They were well received, not only because they were good but also because they were recited by the "author" himself.

This camp seemed to be a completely self-contained period in my life. When I returned to Warsaw, I was constantly amazed by how things appeared. I now saw the dark, narrow streets with different eyes. A person who is used to darkness doesn't recognize the gloom he lives in until he returns there after being in the light. I didn't realize what a teeming maze of narrow streets my youth had been crammed into until I returned from broad, unlimited spaces. Now my apartment, which I'd forgotten about, also looked strange. I saw what I'd never noticed while living there: dirt, stale air, darkness, peeling walls. Only now I saw my great poverty, which I hadn't noticed out of habit. I'm ashamed to say that I burst into tears as I sat on Menachem's bed. He woke up, cheerily called out my name, put his little arms around my head and pressed against me, happy to see me. I had to cry. His skinny arms embracing me, his pale, haggard, sleepy face lit up, the dirty sheets, the peeling walls, the unpleasant smell, and the still-vivid impression of the freedom I had experienced moved me to tears. With my head on my pillow I cried and whispered to myself, "I'm crying over the living grave of this child, over the grave of an awakening life."

That was the first camp I went to in my life. I've since been on a few similar camping trips and outings, and they've all had the same effect on me. I returned satisfied from each one, and each one left me with a wealth of memories.

*

After the first radical change in my attitude toward girls at camp, I continued to change constantly and systematically. I was engulfed by even more organizational work. Girls and boys, everyone together. Joy, merriment, camps, trips, walks, the beach, sports—everything was embraced by laughter and the collective spirit of the KZM. But the nature of the KZM affected me the way it did everyone. I knew when to joke and when to be serious. And, while before I couldn't talk to girls, now I carried on conversations with them. I noticed that there was something strange in my new relationship with girls. In the past, when I felt awkward in their company, I would fall in love with almost every girl. But during the period when I enjoyed good relations with them, I wouldn't fall in love with any of them. It was just pleasant to be around them.

A few days after we returned from a winter camping trip, our instructor proposed that we merge our group with a group of older Pioneer girls who had entered the KZM, with whom we'd gotten along well on the trip. His suggestion was approved. We had a party with the girls and began working together.

Until this camping trip, my life as a member of a political movement didn't extend beyond the limits of our cell. Then it expanded, until my life was almost totally subsumed by organizational work. Although Josek didn't belong to our cell, he also joined us for group walks and discussions. Josek and I were on particularly good terms with two girls from the KZM. One of them fell in love with me, although I didn't even realize it until Josek pointed it out to me. However, I didn't love her; I was sorry, but I didn't reciprocate her feelings. She never dared confess her love to me, but it was apparent from the way she behaved toward me. Eventually the course of events intervened, because soon Comintern dissolved the Communist Party in Poland. Everything fell apart—the cell, our comradeship—everything. Only those who had been friends beforehand stayed friends; all that remained for the rest was a casual acquaintance.

Nothing was left of the artificial togetherness that had joined me to these people, and we drifted apart. Josek and I are still friends. Icek is also our friend. We three stick together, forming a group, a community. We are often joined by one person or another. One drops out, others come along, and so it goes.

*

Much has changed now that we no longer have the organization. Our group consists only of boys, and that in itself is sad. I know how to hold my tongue, but my friends can go on, openly and shamelessly—and somewhat dogmatically—talking about what ails them. I have come to the conclusion that young people of both sexes need to spend time together, not only to satisfy the libido, but also for balance and peace of mind. A young man who sees a girl only on the street and has no relationship with her thinks about her more than the one who flirts, romances, and so on. When we spent time with girls in the organization we didn't think of them as anything special; only when we lost the organization did we notice that we needed them. I'm afraid that I'm an erotomaniac, because sex occupies a considerable part of my brain and can't be driven out. Books, movies, games, and thinking don't help; daydreams of some ideal love give me no peace. I can't read, work, or sleep because my thoughts almost always lead to masturbation, which I had stopped after joining the Pioneers. All this is more or less true of my friends—everything they think and everything they do is intertwined with "that" (*cherchez la femme*). Sheer erotomania.

*

It often happens that the person who studies is not the one who wants to but the one who has the opportunity. Some of us have a genuine, boundless desire to learn, but we're not the ones to go to school. For those who are in school, learning means a school badge on their shoulders and navy-blue uniforms with blue stripes on their pants. Most of us who want to learn are wasting our time looking for an education. When we had the organization, we studied and didn't see it as anything special. But then we lost the organization and, along with it, the workers' education committee, which assigned members of the KZM to self-education groups. Then learning became our fervent desire, which it still is and will continue to be. And no one, I think, longs for education more than I do. I would renounce everything for knowledge; I would sacrifice my life for it. Because learning is essential nutrition for my mind, and my mind's appetite is as big as my stomach's.

Every bit of information that one learns is like raw material for creating energy. This runs the entire mechanism of my brain. The smallest novelty enlivens my mind. I move quickly from the details and delve deeply into a subject. This brings me the kind of bliss that a drug addict experiences when he satisfies his addiction. The better I come to know everything that my eyes see, my ears hear, my nose smells, and my mind comprehends, the more curious I am to know. But when my mind doesn't get this nourishment, it gradually falls asleep, cools, becomes anesthetized, and finally dies. Now I look upon all matters of life indifferently, not in a lofty way. Sadly, I remember that once I had such beautiful and profound thoughts, and everything inspired me—the smallest changes, objects, observations made me wonder and moved me to philosophical, sentimental reflections. Now I see and hear everything without becoming absorbed in it; I perceive everything indifferently.

I still needed to learn. Having no other options, I proposed the idea of self-instruction. Josek, Icek, Beniek, Mietek, and I got together every Friday night at my place. We started going through Bogdanov's *Political Economy*. At first it went well, but then, one after another, we stopped taking it seriously and, instead of studying, started joking and fooling around, until finally the group fell apart.

*

Leon told me he belonged to a study group. It was conducted by a student named Lena, who belonged to the student education committee in our former organization. She was a communist, and she taught us after the organization had dissolved its education committee, because this was her *idée-fixe*. I willingly took advantage of this opportunity to study, although at the time I had better prospects. Josek and I decided to join the Friends of the YIVO Institute. Together with Izaak we went to 2 Chłodna Street. There was no sign on the door for the society. We searched for a long time and finally went to ask where it was. We peered in the windows, but it was dark. We began to doubt that this was the right place. We waited by the door again. The apartment belonged to a doctor, and there were two doorbells. I got up the courage to ring the first doorbell. We waited a while, then from behind the closed door a voice told us that the society closes at eight. We went home with nothing.

We would have gone again, but Josek's cousin, who was a member of YIVO, brought us applications to fill out. He said he'd be back to pick them up, but he didn't come. Seeing that nothing was going to come of this, I joined Leon's group, and Izaak, Beniek, Josek, and Mietek followed my example. It so happened that some of the other students had stopped coming to the lessons, so the group wasn't overcrowded. We studied world history. In spite of having a great deal of knowledge, Lena wasn't a good teacher, because she hadn't mastered the art of public speaking. She often lost her train of thought and became confused. We got almost nothing out of these studies. The circle stayed together only because it provided what the organization had given us—company. Until Lena would arrive, there would be plenty of playing and joking. Of the girls who were in the group, it could easily be said that their primary interests weren't intellectual. And so it went, until Lena insulted Josek's and Izaak's sense of honor. This is what happened: Once, they came a little early, and as no one had arrived yet they waited by the front door. After a while Josek saw Lena coming, so he stepped forward and greeted her, but she kept her head up and didn't even look at Josek, who froze with shame and indignation. Izaak and Josek decided not to go inside. Meanwhile, we were waiting for them upstairs, because Lena said she'd seen them by the front door and that they would probably come up soon.

When Izaak and Josek told us about this, we decided to stand by them and stopped going to the lessons. Only Leon remained loyal to Lena. He said that, because he needed to learn from her, he wasn't going to put on airs.

*

At the textile workers' union someone approached the sister of Regina, one of our former comrades, and introduced himself as an agent of the Joint Distribution Committee. He struck up a conversation with Regina's sister and told her that his assignment was to help solve the problems facing young Jews. He told her he didn't want to be formal about it, so he had approached her instead of the union secretary. He asked her if she could put him in touch with a larger group of young people, and so she sent him to Regina, whom she knew had many acquaintances. That's how we got involved. Regina managed to assemble a fairly large number of former comrades, young men and women, and made an appointment with the agent from the "Joint." No one in our group was involved yet, except for Leon. Then he told us that there'd been some kind of meeting, and the agent had promised them mountains of gold. He said that the "Joint" wanted to improve the situation of young people once and for all. To do this, he planned to set up workshops for unemployed young people in various trades. He asked them what workshops they wanted and how much money would be needed. Finally he handed out questionnaires, saying that they would provide important information about our problems. We looked at the questionnaires, which immediately aroused our suspicions. First of all, they were handwritten on pieces of plain paper. Second, they asked the sort of questions that, had our political organization still been in existence, would have left no doubt but that the agent was with the police. Regina told us that the agent from the "Joint" wanted to meet with older fellows, not the youngsters who had attended the meeting. We decided to take advantage of this and act. We arranged to meet with him again, just the members of our group. But he didn't come, and we grew even more suspicious. We decided that Beniek and Josek would go to the "Joint" in order to clarify the matter.

It turned out that the "Joint" had sent the agent, but his task was only to investigate our situation and not to recruit us for workshops. "If he said anything about workshops," the director of the "Joint" told Josek and Beniek, "then he did so in order to get young people interested and to gather information more easily." Josek started quarreling with the director: "What's the 'Joint' doing, anyway? What's it doing for young Jews in Poland, if it's studying the situation so intensely? It only gathers questionnaires and information and gives reports on the life of young Jews, but does it do anything? No." In defense of the "Joint" the director said, among other things, that it had agricultural colonies in various countries, where young people were learning to farm. The "Joint" made an agreement with them that, after three years, they would get a piece of land to work, so as to support themselves.

When Josek told me about this I fairly jumped; such an opportunity happens only once. It sounded like a dream: walking behind a plow under the open sky and breathing fresh air. I compared this to the work I did in a stuffy kitchen, where I sit in one spot all day. It's strange that even though it matters and isn't difficult, this work exhausts me more than hard physical labor. I'd like to work hard to develop my muscles and become strong. Instead, I fall asleep as I pore over my job, and I keep having to straighten my back and stretch, because I feel such a strange fatigue in my arms and legs.

If working at a sewing machine is authentic Jewish work, then work in the fields is something totally alien to the urban worker, for whom agriculture is an unattainable ideal. And I, a Jewish worker, sincerely want to become a farmer working in the fields.

At first, Josek claimed that this wasn't for us, but eventually, after others expressed their interest, he went back to the "Joint." The director met with Josek, but when he heard why Josek had come, he became embarrassed and evasive. Finally, the director called in a woman, explained the matter to her, and told her to settle things with Josek; then he left. This woman knew exactly what she had to do. Josek said that, before he knew it, she had smoothly justified and explained away everything, so that in the end the "Joint" was completely vindicated. Josek came back with nothing. Our hopes and visions of a better future, which were filled with fervent anticipation, were dashed. Our visions of what we would do there were so foolish! I had even blurted out that once you were familiar with farming you could study to be an agronomist, and that's how I got the nickname "Agronomist." They laughed at me for having such fantasies. But I thought to myself, it's sad that being an agronomist is unattainable for us, because someone who is one is no different than any of us.

Oh, we are so far from having a real life, from the broad life of society, from its living pulse! We are estranged from mankind's conquest of the world! We know only that there are authorities who rule over us, but we don't know them. We know only those who do their bidding. We know that on the street we have to walk straight and not falter. We can't sing or laugh or walk in a group and move about freely. We live in constant fear that this or that deed is a transgression. We stand, humbled and intimidated, before the authorities, who block our way toward freedom and the sun. Not only do we suffer because we're workers; on top of that, because we're Jews, we're even less able to stand up to the authorities. We're put down, treated like some ignorant, savage people who have to be supervised by that "culture" and "civilization." We're treated like cattle, whose backs are beaten with rubber clubs, for almost no reason at all—only because we dare ask, "Why?"

Things I Forgot to Include and Entries from My Notebook

After returning from the film *Young Forest*, filled with enthusiasm, I wrote the following: I'm a poor, assimilated fellow. I'm a Jew and a Pole, or rather, I was a Jew, but, under the influence of the environment, language, culture, and literature, I evolved into a Pole—I love Poland. Most of all, its liberation and the heroism of its battles for independence thrill my heart. But I don't love the Poland that hates me for no reason, that tears at my soul, that pushes me into apathy, melancholy, and dark aimlessness. I hate the Poland that doesn't want me as a Pole and sees me only as a Jew, that wants to chase me out of the country in which I was born and raised. That Poland I hate— I hate its anti-Semitism. You anti-Semites, I blame you for my inferiority complex and for the fact that I don't know what I am: a Jew or a Pole.

Poland has made me unhappy. It has made me into a dog, who shamelessly begs not to be left alone in the wilderness but to be led along the path
of Poland's cultural life. Poland raised me to be a Pole but brands me a Jew
who must be chased out. I want to be a Pole, but you won't let me. I want
to be a Jew, but I can't; I've moved away from Jewishness. I don't like myself
as a Jew.

I'm already lost.

But when I think of my generation, oh, then I suffer. What will they grow
up to be, Jews or Poles? I know that if they grow up as Jews, they won't be
able to become a nation, but if they grow up as Poles, history will repeat
itself. My ailing soul is lost, in any case, but this will never end; our generation will stay the same. Unless Poland's leaders change—as well as most
Poles—then this sad process, which produces culturally disoriented souls,
will not change for the better. The only alternative is the emergence not
merely of a Jewish national identity, but of a Jewish country, a state.

While I might not heal spiritually and develop a clear sense of belonging to a culture, my generation will return to a bright and healthy life as a
nation. I must strive to realize one of these two alternatives and choose the
one that has better, wider, and more realistic prospects. This is my life's
calling, more than the class problem, more than the problem of economic
issues.

*

Today, sitting at the sewing machine, the melody of the Song of Songs
reminded me of Hersz-Judel's *kheyder*. I like music; it expresses beauty and
my heart. There are many kinds of songs and melodies. There are pretty
songs, even prettier songs, and then those that tower above all the others.
Songs of my soul, songs of my heart, and songs that have merged with my
being—you tower over all the others. When I sing to you, I feel you within
me. You dwell in my heart, you are part of my heart, my soul, my being.
You are the history of my life, you are my memory, you are me. Each of
these songs is a different memory, and each one recalls a different feeling.
When I hum the Song of Songs, I am reminded of Hersz-Judel. When I hum
the Akdamuth, I remember Royter Borek. When I sing "She Had a Red
Apple," I am reminded of the courtyard on Muranowska Street. When I sing
"Mother Sleeps, Father Sleeps," I remember the basement on Muranowska
Street. When I sing "The Happy Sailor's Note," I remember the boat on
which we took a trip to Kazimierz—and on and on. I would have to write
a great deal more to describe all these songs. They evoke not just memories but also their mood and feelings, because each period in life had its
feelings and its perspective on the world. The song that is most beautiful is

the Song of Songs. The words and melody evoke feelings that no one can describe: Hersz-Judel; a sunny, peaceful sensation; health, and the joy of a newly awakening life.

Sometimes I stand at the window, torn away from reality. I don't know what I want. The cool morning air strokes my face, and a stifled joy catches in my throat and thrills my heart. I don't know the source of this joy. Is it the thought of a girl? of freedom? of an idyll? No, it has nothing to do with these. It's something different. It's the secret passion of writing, the desire to write.

Something of beauty and ethics floats in my subconscious; its conscious side is, perhaps, the beauty of the word. This is what gives me joy when I stand lost in thought at the window and feel within me the impulse to create heroism, beauty, and ethics. I feel within me the whirl of scattered, individual elements, which I can arrange into a beautiful and moving opus. And I feel joy.

*

The fate of young Jews is sad—torn away from society and deprived of equal rights. But the life of the group of young people to which I belong is even sadder. Once, the whirl of activity of our political organization kept us going and kept us from dwelling on our sad situation. Now we no longer have the organization, we no longer have something to do, and we live without a goal. Where to go? What to do? What to think? What to read? Nothing: There's nowhere to go, nothing to do, nothing to think, nothing to read. This stagnation and paralysis of our youth is like a spiritual death. It is the enemy of the most beautiful period in one's life—youth. And what are we to do? What will enliven us? What will awaken us to life, to the sun, to youth?

In these sad circumstances, we see the true face of our life more and more clearly. Increasingly, I see that I am a Jew. This is not simply because I have some familiarity with Jewish culture; everything leads me to this conclusion. My Polish environment is alien to me. Poland rejects me as a Jew and only a Jew, treating me like a foreigner. Indeed, I have started feeling foreign here. Someone told me the truth—that as an internationalist I cared about all of humanity, but I forgot about my own people and didn't see my own misfortune. Now that the organization has been disbanded and my enthusiasm for its ideas has cooled, I look around and see that Poland isn't mine, and I can't be free here. The gardens, boulevards, and other public places also aren't mine. Moreover, I can't even show my face here as a guest, because I'm not wanted, and it's dangerous. Here, the most empty and ignorant lout—who doesn't possess even a fraction of my knowledge of Polish culture, but who's a Pole and a "defender of Polish culture"—can wound my human dignity with impunity and with pleasure. He can degrade me horribly, taunt me and punch me in the face, disfiguring me—simply because I was born a Jew in Poland. Isn't this why I feel humiliated as a Jew? Isn't this the source of my inferiority complex?

This lout, this simpleton, this illiterate, looks at me with contempt, his head held high. I am nothing next to him; he is a man and I am not—simply because I'm a Jew, someone any Antek or Wojtek can lord over. Just try making a peep, and right away you'll be charged with insulting the nation. And yet you can be insulted, called a "filthy Jew," because you don't have courts, you don't have jails to punish those who insulted you and beat you for nothing, literally for nothing.

How can you find healthy, productive social fulfillment in such an environment? Once Lazor told me he'd like to join the navy. It's his dream, because there life is different, better, peaceful. At the very least he'd like to join the labor battalions, because he's bored with everything here. "But, unfortunately," he said, "neither of them take Jews. All of society's roads are closed to Jews." He, too, has taken a hard look at the world around us. I responded that he could easily get into one of these forces if he were in Birobidzhan or Palestine, and as a joke I suggested that he go to these places.

What Next?

The turning point has already come. I don't know when it was. I only know that I used to be different. And yet this period has not passed entirely. My soul has not yet completely crystallized from the nightmare. Things are not yet entirely clear in my mind. I still look at some things with doubt and uncertainty. I still don't have a fixed view of things. My soul is constantly taking shape. Clearer ideas are emerging from the tangle of thoughts.

I started taking an interest in the Zionist movement. Recently I had a conversation with Josek about the Jewish question and told him my views. I didn't come out categorically and tell him what I want to—that not everything's right with our view of this issue. I didn't tell him that, in a sense, I'm already a Zionist. But I did tell him that if a new organization arose with a new idea of the Jewish nation, I would be the first one in its ranks. I wasn't honest and didn't tell him—because I couldn't—that what I have in mind is Palestine, which I understand better than he does. Josek had been a hasid before he became a member of our organization, and so he can't understand Palestine the way I can, because I went to the Jewish community school and to Khinukh Yeladim. Josek laughed at my conclusions and suggested sarcastically that I create "a new idea of a Jewish nation."

With this conversation I noticed once again the difference between us: His practical and rigid way of thinking, vs. my refined striving for beauty, for the sun, for desires redolent with fantasy. Indeed, what I believe in seems like a beautiful and unattainable fantasy. I can imagine the "new life"—life with a goal, with a future. I can imagine the journey to the land of my dreams. I can see myself torn away from the stagnation of life and pulled into the whirlwind of pulsating life, a life of diverse experiences. I can see myself walking behind a plow with a rifle on my shoulder, with a free heart, a free gait, and a proud, peaceful gaze. And yet I lack faith in this distant, wonderful dream. However, I will strive toward this fantasy, to make it real—the airplane, telephone, radio, and television were also fantasies once—and then I will have faith.

I have resolved to tell all this to my friends. I have resolved to join an organization and sacrifice my youth and strength for the good of future generations. I have resolved to study more, to gain more knowledge, even if no one helps me or notices. If I must, I will study completely on my own, because I want to renew my being.

Enough stagnation. Enough sadness. Enough idling about without a goal. Enough emptiness. Enough nightmares, chaos, wasteland. I want renewal—the sun—a future. To live and know for whom and what I live. I don't want to waste my youth.

Yet I'm in no condition to defend my views, and so I don't want to discuss this with anyone. I feel this, and my intuition tells me it's good and beautiful and ethical. Later, I'll come to believe. For now, although I don't know how to swim, I plunge into the churning waves. I'll move my arms and legs, and I'll have to stay above the water so that I can swim with the current toward my goal. I'll tell everyone that I am returning to my goal, not with the slogans of the proletariat, but as a Jew and a worker.

14

Eter

Contest year: 1939 • Language: Polish
Year of birth: 1921 • Age: 18 • Sex: Female

*A*lthough what I am writing is not in the least like a novel, I will start with a prologue.

During the World War my father was the rabbi of the town of Kuzmin, in Russia. He lived with my mother and my older sister, who was still a very small child then. In 1918, my parents came to Poland because of religious persecution in Russia and decided never to return. For a while they lived with my mother's parents in the village of Z. in the province of Stanisławów. The nearest town to Z. is K. The rabbi of K. had left for Vienna during the World War, and, as he was over sixty years old, he did not return afterward.

When the Jews of K. learned that my father was in Z., they invited him to serve as their town rabbi. At first my father lived in K. by himself. Because the town's official rabbi was still in Vienna, my father was given a provisional appointment, which was fine with him and with the townspeople.

I was born in my grandfather's house in Z. on 27 November 1921, when my older sister was six years old. My mother moved to K. a few months after my birth. Almost two years later, my youngest sister was born. My parents like to tell the story that I burst into tears and screamed that I wanted her thrown into the chicken coop.

At this time our situation in K. changed. My father got along well with the leaders of the Jewish community, but he considered it to be a casual sort of friendship. Apparently, though, they were expecting to get something out of it, and when they didn't, they started to plot against Papa. First, they talked the old rabbi into returning from Vienna, which rendered my father's provisional certification invalid. But this enraged people, because my father was generally well liked and the old rabbi was not. After a while the conspirators—Majer Haller was the central figure—had a falling out with the old rabbi, who had started to take my father's side. The old rabbi felt that he had committed an injustice and said that he regretted returning to K. Not many people had taken up his cause; most of the town was on our side. On all the holidays people would come to our home for a celebratory drink.

To earn a living, Papa taught Talmud to a few students. (Some of these students remain our very good friends to this day.) Whatever our income may have been in those days, I was not aware that we lacked anything. I had lots of toys, and all the girls my age came to play with me. I was good at every game, especially at playing ball, and all of my girlfriends admired me for it.

When I was five years old, Papa started to teach me the *alef-beys*. I made good progress, and within a year I started to study the Torah. At the same time I began to study Polish and arithmetic. Our friends said that I had "a good head on my shoulders."

We went to L. for vacation. I liked the countryside so much; I felt better there than at home. Picking berries and gathering flowers made me very happy. I think I was happier than any of the other children then. Wherever I went, everyone was delighted with me. I had a pretty little face, I knew how to read and do arithmetic, and I understood the Torah. When we left for K. at the end of vacation I wanted to cry.

The day after returning home, my sister and I went to the director of the local elementary school, and she told him that I wanted to be admitted to the second grade. The director said that it would cost fifteen zloty. He advised that I would do better in the first grade, because I was so young. The next day I started to attend first grade. At home I was taught to write out the year, 1928, on my school notebook covers, and from then on I was able to recognize dates.

As soon as I walked into the first-grade classroom I felt at home, because I saw so many familiar faces. Everything came easily to me, except that I didn't know how to speak Polish. But I quickly learned the language, and school was fun for me. I became close with Nusia Zussman, the pharmacist's daughter. I would pick her up every day on the way to school, and after school she would walk me home. I learned to speak Polish from her, because although she is Jewish she didn't know Yiddish. I liked going over to her house because they always had lots of company. Her aunt, Dr. Kanarienstein's wife, would visit with her son Julek, who was younger than we were. Miss Reich, a teacher, would come with her pupil Ignasz, who was older than we were, and Dr. Topf's wife would also come over with her daughter Felicia, who went to school with us. The only problem was that I had to go home before tea-time, because I didn't want to eat non-kosher food. Although there was not much room at our house, Nusia also liked to come over to play.

I went to Z. again for vacation. At this time our family celebrated an event that I've witnessed only once in my life. Grandfather had commissioned a scribe to write a Torah scroll, and it was completed just at this time. Many guests gathered for the dedication ceremony. In the evening there was a supper, and the celebration lasted until very late into the night. The procession that carried the Torah scroll from Grandfather's house to the synagogue was beautiful. Distinguished guests accompanied the Torah under a canopy. Alongside them, people carried candles and lit sparklers. The peasants kept their distance; none of them dared come close. For a long time afterward I dreamt every night about the dedication of the Torah.

Some time later my father's parents died, and he inherited over 1,000 zloty. Until then we had lived in a rented house; now Father wanted to use his inheritance to build our own home. All of the money was spent on the first stages of construction, but it wasn't possible to quit in the middle, so the work continued. Debts began to pile higher day by day. Father couldn't sleep at night. We started cutting back on everything at home, but I didn't mind as long as we could reduce our debts. Time passed, and the unfinished house became something of a laughingstock. Children from all over town gathered at our house to play. They pulled its bricks apart and sawed away at the porch. Birds nested in the fireplaces. Among ourselves we kept repeating, "From where will my help come?" This expression has stayed with me, and today, whenever I am uncertain about something, I repeat it.

Toward the end of the school year we went on a school outing to the village of Maniawa. Near the famous Maniawa "Skit," someone stole about ten groszy from my coat. It was then that I understood, for the first time, that someone could do something as hurtful as taking someone else's property. It was the first time that I experienced human malice.

Later, whenever one of my girlfriends at school hurt me in some way, I felt a pain in my heart; I could only wonder if adults were malicious like this, too. My relationship with my friends at school was peculiar. It seemed that all my schoolmates were friendly to me. But in reality they liked to say bad things about me, and they delighted in even the smallest of my misfortunes. That's why I didn't trust any of them except Nusia. I don't know how she felt about me, but she could call me a true friend. When we walked together we were so carefree, always laughing. Meanwhile, we were getting closer to the sixth grade. It was already decided that after Nusia finished sixth grade she would go away to *gymnasium*. She only regretted that I wouldn't be able to do the same but would have to stay in K. Her mother (whom I liked very much) often told me that I should continue my education.

I went to Z. for the last time during the summer vacation before sixth grade. As we drove away at the end of the vacation, Grandmother was completely healthy; at least that's how she seemed to us. But soon afterward she got sick and came to stay with us. The doctor who examined her said she had cancer. We were very upset, but there was nothing to be done. We tried to convince ourselves that she might be able to live for a few more years. It turned out otherwise. During the fourth week after she came to our house, she died.

Friday, in the middle of the night, Mama's crying woke me. I realized right away that Grandmother was dying. I felt the greatest pain I had ever known. I wanted to see Grandmother one last time, but I was afraid to enter the room. I also thought to myself that there was no use going in, because she wouldn't know I was standing next to her, as her ability to understand things had already left her. It seemed to me that Grandmother's spirit had left the room and was circling above the house. I experienced an awful night, full of terrible dreams and even more terrible moments of being half awake. Grandmother lay there all day Saturday, because the funeral was not until Sunday. For several weeks afterward, I avoided listening to any musical instrument and I didn't sing in school.

Before the end of the year all of my well-to-do girlfriends began to prepare for the entrance exam for *gymnasium*. I consoled myself with the thought that, for the time being at least, I would continue my education in the seventh grade. All of my girlfriends who took the entrance exams passed. Nusia Zussman was accepted to the Jewish *gymnasium* in Stanisławów. When she returned from taking the exam, she came over to my house and told me about the questions she had been asked. We spent the vacation together. At the beginning of the next school year she left for Stanisławów. From then on, I had no friends in my class. I became close with a girl who was my neighbor and spent all of my recesses with her. She was my class partner. It turned out to be to her advantage, because she could always copy something from me or trace one of my drawings. Our homeroom teacher sometimes commented that our maps seemed to have come from "the same workshop." In the lower grades, there had been a few good students with whom I vied to be the best. Now there wasn't even anyone to compete with. On the President's name-day I delivered a speech, which I had been assigned to prepare only the day before. Even so,

I knew it completely by heart. At the end of the school year I also gave
a valedictory address. I was a little sad to be leaving elementary school,
but curiosity about what I would do next helped me overcome my
sadness.

The following autumn, dark clouds gathered over the Jewish community
of K. A short time later, the storm burst. The old rabbi became ill and left
for Vienna. A few weeks later, K. learned that he had died.

The head of the Jewish community leadership placed an advertisement
in the newspapers for a new rabbi. Papa published a notice in the papers
that he had been living in K. and acting as rabbi for over ten years, and he
asked that no one apply for the position here. He also sent all of his certi-
fications to the Jewish community leaders and submitted his candidacy. It
was rejected immediately.

Two distinct factions formed in our town: one was "the Rabbi's party,"
the other was "Haller's party." Elections were held at the end of winter.
Meanwhile, various legal actions were initiated. Members of each party
complained of the abuses and offenses they had suffered. Papa was also
named in several law suits, and denunciations were lodged in as many
administrative offices as possible. Every evening people would come to our
house to plan legal strategies. Our house became known as the headquarters. I devoted all my attention and energy to these cases, about which I
became very knowledgeable. I knew when and how to call for appeals,
repeals, and retractions, how to lodge complaints and to prepare applications and petitions. I had even memorized some of the statutes. Meanwhile,
I finished elementary school. One of the many people who were always
at our house began to give me violin lessons. There was another student,
a boy one year older than I, who also came over every day. At this time
I tutored the tavern keeper's two children: a boy in the sixth grade and
a little girl in the second grade. The boy was a real dunce, and at midyear
he received a very bad report card. His family hired a *gymnasium* student
to tutor him, and from then on we both taught him; either I worked
with him first and then the *gymnasium* student did, or the other way
around. Even so, the boy didn't do well. At about this time I lost interest in
teaching. I didn't want to have to teach someone else; I wanted to have
someone teach me. But at the time I was engrossed in books; most were
good books that taught me much. Thanks to them I developed my own
style of writing. I was still taking classes and did well on all my school
assignments.

Because of all the local politics going on, I learned to write various
official documents, which we needed on more than one occasion. But

although this consumed a great sum of money, it all came to naught. In the spring of 1936, Dr. Kanarienstein—one of the most important local political figures, whom we had looked to with great hope—became ill. He was taken to the hospital in Nadworna and died there on 30 April. The town went into mourning. At almost the same moment that Dr. Kanarienstein's body was brought back to town, the newly elected rabbi arrived from the other side of town. That day it seemed to me that I would go mad with anguish. I was drowning in tears.

The opposing party had triumphed. There was no hope left. Papa tried to make amends with the Jewish community leaders, but this didn't work. Then the last round was fired. About two weeks after Shavuoth, Papa went to his home town of Ottynia to learn the rules of kosher slaughtering from an elderly *shoykhet* whom he knew. The day that Papa went away, my younger sister took the only money left in the house to a school carnival. My older sister worked in a store, and her wages supported the household. Our situation attracted attention. Young people, who in general aren't much attached to religion or are even anti-religious, became very friendly and helpful. Even some Catholics took an interest in us. One night the new rabbi had his windows broken. When he tried to go for a walk in the evening, he was pelted with stones.

Meanwhile, vacation was approaching. Nusia Zussman came home. We were always thinking of ways for me to continue my education. Then I got an idea. In secret—only the two of us knew about this—I wrote a letter to the President of Poland. I asked that he help me attend a commercial school. I knew that general *gymnasia* were overcrowded, and articles in the newspapers were encouraging young people to enter commercial and trade schools.

In the meantime, Papa sent word that he would return to K. the day after Tisha B'Av. Almost the entire town waited for his bus to arrive. When Papa got off the bus people crowded around to greet him, and then they all escorted him home. Someone told me that two young women who were visiting K. at the time assumed that a great *rebbe* had come to town. Soon people began bringing their poultry to Father to have them slaughtered. This gave them as much satisfaction as pious people once got when they brought sacrificial offerings to the ancient Temple.

Vacation ended. A few days later, I received a response from the office of the President, by way of the provincial administration, that my letter of request had been forwarded to the school district in Lwów.

My father's work as a *shoykhet* hurt the interests of the Jewish community leaders. They pressed the sheriff in Nadworna to harass my father. (The man who was sheriff at the time was later sentenced to several years in prison for fraud.) Once a policeman came and demanded to see Father's slaughtering knife. When it was shown to him, the policeman took it away. A second time, the policeman began searching for the knives himself.

It was almost Rosh Hashanah, a time when many animals are slaughtered, but this year the slaughtering had to be done in hidden locations. The sheriff issued fines to my father, and we appealed them in court. Before Yom Kippur there was also much slaughtering to do. We assumed the Jewish community leaders would pressure the police to interfere, and apparently they agreed to do so. Papa would slaughter in secret locations, which he changed often, because they were repeatedly discovered. A full-fledged chase began, involving the entire police force. I stood on the street in front of our house and watched the movements of the police. Then one of them came up to me and ordered me to the police station, because I was "spying" on him. I went. It was 7:30 in the morning. Meanwhile, Papa was being followed more and more. He fled to a nearby village, Monasterczany, and then walked to another village, Dzwiniacz, where he received wagonloads of poultry from town. I was kept at the police station until noon. They probably expected that Papa would come to get me, and then they could detain him; I gathered this from some words I overheard from an adjoining room. When I was released, people came forward to meet me. For the first time, people were overjoyed to see me. Papa returned home at ten o'clock at night.

At this critical moment, when we were suffering the worst of the harassment, our house was nearing completion. In mid-October I received a letter from the school district in Lwów, instructing me to apply to the commercial *gymnasium* in Stanisławów. I wrote to Nusia Zussman and she went to the director of the *gymnasium*. At first he was angry: "Why did she have to go and write to the President?" But what was done is done. I would have to wait for the next year to begin school, right after summer vacation.

As I waited, I was constantly busy with family matters. First of all, we moved into our new house. Throughout the winter we had to take care of various matters in the administrative offices in Stanisławów and Nadworna. I was only fifteen years old, but I would brazenly go to the sheriff or the tax collector's office as if I were an adult.

At the end of winter my grandfather became ill. One day he came to stay with us and died the very same night. As a rule I'm very fearful. I never leave the house alone in the evening. But this time, when I saw that Grandfather was dying, I ran to get the doctor, even though it was already past midnight. Later, I stood at Grandfather's bedside after he had died and felt no fear at all. Just a few years before, when Grandmother died, I was afraid to go near her.

Two weeks after Grandfather's death a family friend, who was a partner in a wholesale flour business, offered me a job as his bookkeeper. I had to record the daily receipts in the account books. I worked two or three, sometimes four, hours a day. He paid me twelve zloty a month. Sometimes, when I got to my desk at the office and there was nothing for me to do, I composed little poems. I worked there for only a few months.

In July I wrote to the director of the commercial *gymnasium* to say that I would like to be admitted to the first-year class. When about twelve days passed without a reply, I very nearly gave up hope of taking the entrance exam. Then, on the first of September I received a card notifying me that the exam would take place the following day. At this point, several problems arose.

My parents realized that I would have to go to school on Saturdays and that, in addition to tuition (which would probably be waived), there would be room and board to pay. *My* greatest worry was that I would fail the exam, because I hadn't prepared for it. Nevertheless, I went to take the exam. I had a few books with me on the bus, but instead of reviewing anything I asked God to let me pass. And, in fact, I did pass. Right after the exam I went home, so that I could return to school five days later, just after Rosh Hashanah.

Now that it was actually about to happen, my parents told me that I could go to school only if I could be excused on Saturdays. I would give private lessons to deal with the problem of money, and I would also receive some food from home.

On the first day of classes I submitted a request to be excused from attending school on Saturdays. Three days later, during one of the recesses, a teacher informed me that the director would not grant my request, because "the regulations of the school required all students to attend on Saturdays." Despite this, I went to the director, but he told me the same thing in person. When I went to the office to collect my old report cards, the secretary tried to talk me into staying at the school, because once I left I would never be allowed to return. But I didn't hesitate even for a moment. By evening I was back home.

I began to give lessons again to the tavern keeper's children, now to the younger ones. The oldest boy was being tutored in the first-year *gymnasium* curriculum by his teacher. He was never able to solve his math problems and would give them to me to do. They were easy for me. I looked through all his books, and it occurred to me that I could teach myself—even Latin, because the textbook had a glossary at the back. I was uncertain only about German. At about this time a very intelligent young woman began to give lessons in English and German. I talked three other girls into joining me, and we made up a German class. Of the three, I liked Rachel Langer best.

I bought the textbooks for the first year of *gymnasium* and studied on my own. By vacation-time I had completed the first-year material. I decided not to take the first-year exam, but to begin working on the second- and third-year material right away.

At the beginning of the school year I bought myself the second-year books, but it was very hard for me to settle down and study. Although there are no exceptionally interesting diversions in K., somehow I found things to do that were more appealing than slaving over Latin grammar. My one bit of good fortune is that I don't belong to any youth organizations, otherwise I'd surely have no time left for my studies. I should say something here about why I don't belong to any of these organizations. For about ten years we've had Gordonia, Hitahdut, and Freiheit in K. My girlfriends from school had become members of these organizations when they were about eleven or twelve years old. I didn't join any of them, because I knew my parents would be against it. As I grew older and learned more about various Jewish ideologies, I began to lean toward the Revisionists. The Gordonists knew that I didn't agree with them, but that didn't prevent me from being the best of friends with my schoolmates who were in Gordonia. When Rachel Langer and I became friends, she left Gordonia. My girlfriends all said she did this due to my influence. It's true that she defers to me; that's because she has an exaggerated opinion of me. She believes that I know a great deal and that she will never be my equal. All my girlfriends seem to feel the same way, and this makes me very uncomfortable. Sometimes, when we go for a long walk to the outskirts of town, they ask me to tell them a story. What sort of story can I tell them? I summarize a novel or tell them about some event from ancient history. What I enjoy most is trying to "convert" them. Although they all believe in the existence of God, they don't think it's necessary to observe all the commandments of Jewish law. On the whole, I like to "convert" people.

That autumn a bookkeeping teacher came to K. He was Edmund P., a *gymnasium* graduate from Stanisławów. My parents wanted me to study bookkeeping. I had no one to take the course with me, so I talked Rachel Langer into it. We took lessons at the same time and did our homework together. The teacher was an agnostic, and I worked on converting him, too. I was always having discussions with him about religious observance, and we reached the point that when he committed a sin, he would rationalize it to me. My opinions mattered a great deal to him, and he tried to convince me that he led an exemplary life in Stanisławów. I knew that wasn't true, and for this reason he reminded me of Horski, a character in Helena Mniszek's novel, *Gehenna*. A sign that I had influenced him at least a little was his promise that if I would write him a letter before Yom Kippur to remind him of the date, he would fast for the first time in his life. I told him I definitely would not write the letter.

My girlfriends teased me and said that this teacher had a crush on me and that I definitely had one on him. Not only did I not like him, I hated him. How could I stand a person who says that he doesn't like Jews, when he is one himself? Still, he wanted to be on good terms with me. Once, when the local amateur theater presented *King Lear*, he tried to get me to go with him, but I turned him down. Another time he came to take me on a sleigh ride, but I told him that I go on sleigh rides only in the daytime. The only things I never refused from him were books. I always accepted books, however many he wanted to give me—three, four, sometimes even five a week.

Learning bookkeeping was not at all difficult, but the homework assignments took up a lot of time. Because of this I fell behind in my own studies and gave up trying to work through all of the third-year *gymnasium* curriculum. The bookkeeping course ended on the first of April; then I could really concentrate on my *gymnasium* studies. But by the end of the school year, I wasn't sufficiently prepared for the examination. And even if I had been ready, there was no possibility of my taking it. (My father was still involved in legal actions in the district court, although he had already won an appeal before the Supreme Tribunal. In addition, he pays a tax that is almost equal to our income.)

A few weeks ago, my sister opened a small clothing shop, and now she'll be able to help me. I promised myself that however much I manage to learn for the examination during this vacation, I will go and take it. And if I pass, I'll stay in Stanisławów and attend school. I'll stay even if I have to support myself by giving lessons. After all, it's high time, at the age of seventeen, for me to be in the third year of *gymnasium*. If I ever do graduate, I'll be able to make the bold proclamation that I made it to the North Pole at a snail's pace. I've never had a vacation as horrible as the one this year, because it seems to me that uncertainty is the worst possible misery. All day long the same thought pounds inside my head: Will I pass? Many times a day I recite to myself Julian Tuwim's poem, "If only . . ." I call it "Hope." It goes like this:

And if nothing? And if no?
I was poisoned by delusion
O you brightness, O you wonder,
And poisoned now dream on:
And if not?
Then . . . too bad.

But if something? But if yes?
Dawn on doves' wings
Sets the world ablaze
Poppy-red,
For if yes,
Then . . . my God?

15
Yudl

Contest year: 1939 • Language: Yiddish
Year of birth: 1921 • Age: [18] • Sex: Male

I was born in 1921. My parents weren't well-off. You can easily imagine what my childhood was like. My mother told me that I was raised without a cradle, without even a pillow under my head. My father was a teacher's assistant in a *kheyder*. My mother also worked at various jobs. We children were neglected at home. My mother didn't have any time to enjoy being with her children, and we didn't have time to play with her. That's how I was raised. When I was six years old, I already knew what it meant to be poor. I ran around barefoot with cuts on my feet. No one paid any attention to me or noticed my feet. Maybe no one knew? It doesn't seem very likely.

I had a grandmother who sold milk. Many times I tagged along on her delivery route. After a while, she saw that I was able to do the job. The first time, she gave me one milk can to carry. When she saw that I could manage it and could make my way back home, it wasn't long before she gave me a second milk can to carry. I was a tall, skinny boy. Given what I had to eat, I didn't have the strength for the job. But when there's a will, there's a way. People were worried I'd get a hernia from the strain, because I was so thin, but nothing happened to me. I've always believed that where there's life, there's hope.

I got used to this hard work. I remember my grandmother waking me up, yelling, "Yudl! Get up! It's five o'clock. It's already late. Come on." As I got dressed, I cried inside. Everyone else was still sleeping, and I had to walk such a long way out of town in the early morning, when the ground was still wet with dew. It was cold. More than once I caught a chill, but still I went out. More than once I went out without eating. I'd come home at nine or ten o'clock in the morning. I wouldn't let myself take even a sip of the milk. There wasn't any for me, but there wasn't anything missing from the accounts, either.

Once, when I was carrying the milk I ran into a fierce dog. I was scared. The dog approached me, and I ran as far as my legs could take me, forgetting all about the milk cans. When I came back I found the cans had tipped over and the milk had spilled out. I was still afraid to go near the cans. Someone passing by laughed at me: "Afraid of a dog?" I had no choice but to go back for the cans. I picked up the empty cans and went home. I was miserable. On the way, people asked me when I would deliver the milk. I said that there would be no milk that day. They asked, why not? This time I didn't answer but ran away. When I got home I was given a sound beating. I was owed a few groszy, but they didn't give them to me. Because of the beating and not getting the money I was owed, I didn't want to deliver the milk anymore. Besides, now I was afraid to walk on that road.

By then I was seven years old. I wanted to go to public school, but no one would hear of it. My father said, "Your older brothers don't go to school, and neither do your sisters. So why do you want to go?" I begged him: "Why do all the other children go and not me?" He said he didn't want a child of his to sit with his head bare next to a crucifix. I didn't know what to do. Since I wasn't delivering milk anymore and wasn't going to school, I became a real street urchin. I had nothing to do until late in the evening, when I had to study sections of the Torah, Rashi commentaries, and Gemara with my father. While we studied together, I complained, "Papa, why can't I go to school?" This time he gave me a different answer: "You know very well I don't have the money for books or notebooks." I told him I'd find the money. The next day I ran to see my uncle. I earned a few groszy from him and immediately bought two notebooks.

My father saw how much I wanted to go to school. He told my older sister to enroll me in the school the very next day. When I heard this, I jumped for joy. I didn't sleep all night. I kept thinking about what it would be like in school the next day. I got dressed even earlier than I used to when I delivered milk. I washed up and combed my hair. I could hardly wait until my sister took me by the hand and walked me to the school. They asked my name, and I answered, gleefully.

When I entered the first grade I didn't know the difference between a "1" and a "2." But I could speak Polish well; I'd learned how to during the year that I picked up the milk from the peasants. Just as it hadn't been hard for me to learn to deliver milk, it wasn't hard for me to learn to write. I learned how and knew as much as the other students. I could speak Polish better than all the other Jewish students in my class. At the start of the next school year I went into the second grade. I couldn't have asked for anything better.

That year my father stopped working as a teacher's assistant and started selling animal hides. Life at home improved somewhat. My parents bought me a pair of shoes for the winter. As soon as I put them on, I fell downstairs and banged my head. They laid me on the bed to take the shoes off. Then they noticed that I'd put the left shoe on the right foot and the right shoe on the left foot. It was all because I was so happy that they'd bought me new shoes; this was no small matter.

During summer vacation I earned some money to buy books for the second grade. My job was driving animals to the slaughterhouse. For every goat or calf I got twenty groszy. I earned up to sixty groszy a day. The rest of the time I played ball with the boys on our street. We had a lot of fun. I got hurt only once. I was twisting a piece of wire on the wheel of the pulley on the well, and my finger got caught. It hurt badly. The worst thing was that I had to go have the bandage changed every other day. When it was time to go to the *feldsher*, I hid. Eventually, though, I had to come home. The school term had already started, and my finger still hurt. I told the teacher that I'd hit myself with a hammer. For several days I didn't write, I just listened in class. But I finally got better. My hand stopped hurting, and I didn't have to go have the bandage changed any more.

Once again, I found myself in a new world, though it didn't last long. My brother, who worked in a dye shop, found me a job there. I've never turned down a chance to earn money. I got started in the dyeing business the same way I began to deliver milk. I kept going to see my brother there, until I began to make myself useful. I was able to do everything. As soon as I came home from school, I went straight to the dye shop. I was given work that kept me there until late at night, and soon I began to be paid. As a result, I neglected school. At school they started scolding me for not being the same student I'd been before. Before long the teacher found out that I was working in a dye shop. I didn't do any of my homework. My classmates told me I wouldn't finish the year. But I didn't care; now that I was earning money, I didn't need school any longer.

Winter came. There was less to do at the dye shop, and I wasn't needed there anymore. But I still earned a few groszy, enough to join in a game of dominoes. I was the best dominoes player in our neighborhood. I started going to school again and made up for all the time I'd missed. At the end of the year I was promoted. I was now nine years old, and I entered the third grade. I spent my vacation with all the biggest trouble-makers. I stole some wheat for a young hoodlum. More than once I was beat up for stealing.

I lived near the town's Jewish institutions: a synagogue, a *beys-medresh*, a *mikve*. I liked to play soccer there. I was pretty good at it; I knocked out more than one windowpane trying to score goals. The caretaker of the *mikve* would come out and start to chase after us. He could catch other boys, but not Yudl. Once, I bought a new ball, which he immediately snatched away from me and destroyed. I pretended to ignore it, but then I picked up some rocks and started throwing them at the windows, and that kicked up a lot of dust.

Before Sukkoth, I was asked to work at the dye shop again; I wound up staying there until I was fourteen years old. My brother approached me and said, "Come work here. We'll give you a permanent job and pay you a weekly wage." It seemed clear and straightforward to me. My father also approved. He thought I would learn something there. People would stop hounding him, saying he had a son who breaks windows in the *mikve*. I was hired for two zloty a week, plus room and board. My father came every week to collect the two zloty.

I forgot all about school. I would go to school for a day and then not go for three days. The teacher wouldn't look for me because everyone said I smelled of chemicals. I didn't think the teacher cared anymore whether or not I came to school. So I went every day and did very well. However, I was upset about one thing: my hands were stained by the aniline dyes. It bothered me a lot that the stains wouldn't come off after one washing. More than once the teacher sent for my parents. He wanted to ask them why they let me work at my age, let alone work with dyes. I went home and didn't even mention that the teacher had sent me home. The next day I went back to school with the same stained hands but without my parents. The teacher sent me to the janitor to see if he could clean my hands. This janitor was an anti-Semite. He scrubbed my hands with a hard brush until they bled. I ran home, crying inside, my hands on fire. I never returned and haven't been back to this day. I could read and write a little, so that was the end of my school days.

I began working full days with no breaks, along with my brother and another man. They showed me all the rooms in the shop and all the different kinds of work I would have to do. By then I was ten years old and worked more than some who were older than I was. When it was time for lunch, they put out a spread on the table the likes of which I'd only seen at a wedding. There were traces of dye in the food, though. There wasn't anything that didn't have dye in it. I liked it anyway. I sat down and so did the others. After eating they said grace. On my first day there, I couldn't understand why they'd serve such a feast for an ordinary meal. But I learned later that the owners would feed us well and then give us even more work.

My job consisted of making putty, milling and pounding chalk, chopping wood, sometimes stoking the fire, and sometimes peeling potatoes. I did all this every day. My brother was given better, more important work. At first it was kept a secret from me; I wasn't supposed to know about it. But eventually I found out. The dye shop made litmus [a purple dye] and carmine [a red dye], which the peasants used to dye their clothes. On market days, whenever I had nothing to do for a few minutes, it was my job to take some boxes of carmine and go out among the wagons in the marketplace, where I sold the boxes for five groszy each. If I could get more than five groszy, it went straight into a separate pocket.

When I had a few groszy in this pocket I ran off, boxes in hand, to play cards with the biggest low-lifes in town. I didn't know what was going on and soon was out of the game, so I needed more money right away. I went back to the shop and told them that I'd lost the money, even though that was a lame excuse. I was short more than a zloty. The boss wanted to take it out of my wages, but I wouldn't let him. If I had, it would have shown that I hadn't really lost the money. He didn't take the money out of my wages, but he said he would if I ever lost money again. At night, when I got into bed, I thought it over, and my conscience tormented me. "Why was I doing this? Why did I need to play cards?" I asked myself. Was I short of money? I had everything I wanted: good food, a good place to sleep, plus money for treats. Why did I need to steal? I promised myself that from that day on, I would never touch a groszy that wasn't mine. Otherwise they might catch me and throw me out. Then I'd lose my room and board, plus my income. I swore an oath and have never touched a grosz to this day.

Because I never took anything, people always said I was an honest fellow and that you would have to search far and wide to find someone as honest as me. These words reassured me and made me feel better. There was only one problem: I always worked very hard and was always dirty. The other workers made fun of me. I looked filthy, in a long coat, with long *peyes* and a traditional Jewish cap. I laughed at it all. I was happy. It was better to be on the path toward honesty than the path toward a life of crime. I had so much money I didn't know what to do with it. I gave my little brothers five groszy each and still had a lot left over for myself.

The others at the dye shop stopped trying to hide their secret work from me. This work was very secret. Today I realize that people wind up in jail for such underhanded business practices. There was an ultramarine [a blue dye] factory in Riga that had an agent in Warsaw. Our dye shop bought 100 kilos of ultramarine from Warsaw. It came in forty small packages, each weighing two-and-a-half kilos. In the dyeing business, the labels and packages all looked the same; our dye shop also bought them from the agent, who had a share in the scheme. Every month I sent him 100 zloty by mail; no one was supposed to know about it. We took one kilo of the dye from each package and replaced it with ultramarine that we made ourselves. It was hard to tell the difference. No one knew about it except us workers and the members of the boss's family.

We did this work at night. We took a wash tub, poured everything into it and mixed it thoroughly. We sifted it through a coarse sieve. Every night I had the difficult job of raking and kneading the mixture, which made my arms ache.

The boss had no children. People live differently when they have no children and no family life. The boss and his wife quarreled constantly. Eventually, she betrayed him and gave all their money to her sisters. But at first the boss and his family made a lot of money from the scheme. Even an engineer doesn't earn as much as they did. The boss undersold all the other merchants in B. People came from nearby towns to buy dye from him. One package of ultramarine cost 12.5 zloty at the factory price. After we had taken out one kilo and put in our substitute, we could charge one zloty less than all the other merchants in town. These merchants came to see my boss and complained that he was taking all their customers away. He answered that he charged less, so everyone came to him. They asked: "How can you charge less?" He said that he had bought a lot of ultramarine all at once, directly from the factory, so it cost him less.

The other merchants didn't know where the factory was. They bought their supply from the agent. They tried buying up a lot of the product at once, and it went moldy on them. It hadn't cost them less either, because there was only one price, which was set by the factory. Every day they came crying to my boss: "Have pity on us. After all, we're Jews, too. Tell us, how can you charge less than we do?" He could never tell them. He would shout back that they should also buy directly from the factory at the same price that he paid. He gave them the address of the factory and told them, "Stop pestering me." They wrote to the factory, and the company answered that it had an agent in Warsaw: "You can buy the product from him in any way you want." This answer had to satisfy them. They had no alternative but to go begging.

Meanwhile, we worked day and night without rest, as people snapped up the merchandise. The boss ignored his other products and sold off what was left of them. The business grew even bigger. The merchants in town got together and sent for the agent from Warsaw, so that he could explain how my boss could afford to charge a lower price than everyone else. He told them that it wasn't his business, since my boss didn't even buy through him but through someone in the factory.

This didn't satisfy them. The other merchants wrote to the company again. This time the factory sent someone to go with the Warsaw agent to

B. and see what was going on. They arrived and went straight to my boss and looked everywhere, but they didn't find anything. The Warsaw agent had warned us a week earlier that there would be an inspection. That whole week we cleaned up and washed the floors three times a day. I took a pack of labels and a lot of other things back to my attic, but I kept calm and said nothing to anyone. The inspectors went away without finding anything. The man from the factory even apologized and asked that no one take offense; he was just doing his job. He shook everyone's hand and went home, but the Warsaw agent kept winking at us. A week or two went by and all was calm again, so we went back to the same work.

A little while later we got a letter from the Warsaw agent telling us he had been fired. My boss and his wife were in shock. They were already out of labels and packing materials. The place was in turmoil. We tried to copy the labels, but it didn't work. Things started to go downhill for my boss. He and his wife didn't have any other business, and now they had to pay for living recklessly. There was no money left from the whole scheme.

They started quarreling. She screamed that he had given away all the money, and he screamed that she had. More than once they hit each other. The truth came out that she had given all the money to her sisters. It got to where they wanted a divorce. People tried to patch things up between them, but he screamed that they had nothing to live on and that he didn't need her. He threw her out. She went to Działoszyce, not far from Cracow, and stayed there for four weeks.

During those four weeks my brother was laid off, so I was left at the factory by myself. It was so quiet, it felt eerie. The electric bill hadn't been paid and the power was cut off. During the daytime, the boss and I would sit reading the Bible. Every other minute he'd roll his eyes heavenward; it was scary. We ate nothing but bread and drank tea without sugar. Once in a while he sent for his sister, who would reluctantly give him some warm food. She was angry because when he'd had money he hadn't given any of it to his family.

Soon the whole town knew what had been going on and how the boss had been able to undersell everyone else. He got sick from his troubles. His wife returned from Działoszyce and called a doctor, who cured the boss. He then borrowed some money and they went back into business, but they didn't do as well as before. The electricity was turned on and the roof was fixed. Eventually, things went back to normal. They made putty for other businesses and earned a lot of money. One thing they no longer sold was ultramarine, which used to be their best seller. If they needed a kilo of ultramarine they had to order it through someone else, because the factory would no longer send it to them.

But then the boss and his wife found out that the Warsaw agent had been sent to prison. They were in a state of shock, convinced that someone would come to get them. The boss didn't want to so much as lift a finger. He screamed at his wife, "You brought me bad luck, so that I have to work in my old age." He lay in bed all the time, groaning and sighing: "Where will I get money, now that I'm getting old? Who will support me? She gave the money away, so let her work. I don't want to work anymore." His wife worked like a horse. She wanted to have money again. But she didn't live to see any, not even enough to take care of herself. As a result of her troubles, she got it into her head that she was sick and that there was no way to save her. Doctors came from Warsaw to see her. They discovered that her gallbladder had ruptured as a result of working non-stop and from all the stress. That's what did her in. A lot of people came to her funeral and said nice things about her. Yet she had never given anything to anyone—a fine Jew she was! After she was buried, her worries lived on in the house. Her husband wrung his hands: "Who knows, maybe I tortured her to death? Who knows if I will ever have a proper Jewish burial?" He swore on his *talles* that he would save the first groszy he earned that week to pay for a *melave malke*. Maybe God would forgive him and maybe she would, too.

A new life began for me, with new problems. During the first week after the boss's wife died, my father told me to stay in the shop, and he would try to find me something new to do. But I didn't go back, not even after that first week. Instead, I stayed home. I was owed a lot of money, several weeks' worth. I didn't have the courage to mention this to the boss. He tried to atone for his sins and asked me to come back to work for him. When he said this, my hair stood on end. I shouted that I was afraid and wouldn't come back to work, not for any amount of money. For once, when I insisted on this to my father, he understood. I spent four years of my life there; I will remember those years until I die. The quarrels, the tensions, and the dirty, heavy work!

When I left the dye shop I was thirteen years old. I began to pray with *tefillin*. As I walked down the street I felt proud of myself. It was no small thing to be putting on *tefillin*. But I didn't remain proud for long. I soon got tired of it. I started hanging out on the streets, just like everyone else. Then one day my father came back from the synagogue and told me that he'd found me a job working for a friend of his. Right away I asked him what kind of business it was. "You'll be making fly-paper." "Whatever!" I shouted. "I'll build stone walls, as long as it means not working in the dye business, especially back there."

I was hired for five zloty a week. During the first week I couldn't wait to get to work. The week after that, they had to find me first before I would go to work. I only made a total of ten zloty. Like the other youngsters on the street, I was more interested in enjoying the summer. I went around barefoot and lazed around by the water all day. I had never known how to swim, but it wasn't long before I learned how. I'd spend the whole day kicking a ball around; that's what I liked best.

Since I'd left the dye shop I'd become a real trouble-maker. I had quite a reputation: In one place I was responsible for breaking a window, in another for putting a hole in some boy's head. I got into fights with everyone. I was covered with scratches from head to foot. The best place to play ball was next to where the caretaker of the *mikve* lived on the square. When we went there to play we used to have two fellows serve as lookouts to warn us if he came. If he did, we moved the ball to the other side. We broke windows more often than we kicked the ball. The caretaker knew very well who I was. He went to my father and shouted: "Whoever heard of boys breaking the windows of a *mikve*?" I came into the house and my father chased after me. Even though he was an adult, it wasn't easy to catch a street urchin like me. When I came home at night, my father didn't let me in the house. But I was proud and wouldn't beg: I slept in an attic with one of my friends. There were other fellows who had been fighting with their families sleeping there, too.

One morning a woman came and shouted at her son: "Wake up! What's going to become of you? You just want to run around. You won't learn a trade, you'll never amount to anything." I pretended to be asleep but I listened carefully to what she said. The woman yelled, "You're already fourteen years old, and you don't know how to earn a grosz. Tell me what's going to become of you. Who's going to care about you? Come with me. Get something to eat and come with me to the tailor. You'll go to work there." This fellow's mother brushed him off, picked the bits of straw off of him, took him by the hand, and led him to work. When he heard that he was going to become a tailor, he ran to work faster than to a soccer match.

In 1935 a trade union had just been established in B. I'd also like to be a tailor, I thought, because otherwise I couldn't become a member of the union. Every Saturday all the union members went to the woods and sang labor songs. On May Day they held a demonstration in the street. That's why everyone wanted to join the union.

That woman's words had a great effect on me. I quickly got dressed, went straight home, and told my father, "Believe it or not, I want to go to work." When he heard this, he jumped for joy. If I hadn't come home within the next five minutes, he would have gone to get me. He said, "Eat and come downstairs. I've already apprenticed you to Blisko, a bootmaker." Before he had said that, I'd thought I might work for the tailor who lived downstairs.

I didn't agree to Blisko right away. However, I was apprenticed to him for a whole year without pay.

That was the hardest year of my life, because I had been used to having a lot of money and then I didn't have anything. But I consoled myself with the thought that after a year I'd be making money. I really took to the work and learned the trade very well. There wasn't a single shoemaker's last that I couldn't identify. The boss was always surprised that my mind was so sharp I could keep the shape of every last in my head. There were three hundred of them in the workshop, and whenever someone needed one I knew where to find it. The boss wasn't a bad fellow, but he had a son who had a very hard time learning the trade, and I was supposed to work with him. Where there's life, there's hope.

The year passed, a difficult year. I worked until one or two o'clock in the morning. I slept in the shop. At home there was no place for me to sleep; my family was sleeping four to a bed. A house with eleven children, *keyn ayn-hore*, and all living at home. The worst thing was having to work until late at night. When the boss woke me early in the morning, I washed and went straight to work. My lunch break was no longer than fifteen minutes. If I took any longer someone would yell: "Yudl, come down here. Let's get to the machine." I didn't try to finish eating; I went right down. This was my destiny—to work hard.

In 1936 there was a train trip for students up to fourteen years old. Although I was a year older and not in school, I went with all the other children. The trip cost twenty groszy. My boss gave me one zloty and my father gave me another. I went to the station by myself, put my bag on the train to Łódź, and set out. I arrived in Łódź, where I had an address to go to. I asked around and found my way to the home of one of my mother's sisters. They welcomed me and showed me all the parks, all the big buildings of Łódź, and all the movie theaters—that, I thought, was the best of all. I spent seven days there and went home feeling happy. While riding on the train, I remembered that soon I would be earning money. My life would be the way it had been two years earlier. When I came home I had stories to tell about the wonders of the world. Everyone was eager to listen, and I was the storyteller! It was no small thing.

I was now earning three zloty a week. I could afford to dress better. I spent my free time out in the street with my friends. One day I was approached on the street by two members of Betar, who gave me an invitation to a recruitment meeting. I couldn't read the leaflet. Although it was written in Yiddish, I couldn't understand what it was about. The contents made no sense to me. I gave it to my father to read. He tore it up and said it was all a joke. But the same day a friend told me that he had received an invitation to a Betar meeting and showed it to me. It was the same as the one I'd been given. I went straight to the meeting and joined. When I became a member they asked me my father's name, my mother's name, and where I lived. This was my first involvement with a political organization. I went to meetings for two months and didn't like it at all. They talked about nothing but gold buttons and brown uniforms—Hitler's color. It wasn't for me. I saw how immoral their leaders were. They were nothing more than corrupters, criminals, in fact—blackmailers, Jewish Hitlerites, Jewish fascists! I left; I didn't even want to tell anyone that I had crossed the threshold of the Betar inquisition, which exists today in Palestine, too.

By then I was borrowing books from my friends. I began to read parts of the newspaper until I got used to reading. At first I was a very poor reader. My friends could read a lot better than I could. Whenever they went off somewhere to read I wouldn't go along, because I couldn't read as well outside as I could at home. I read pamphlets from the *Groshn-biblyotek*, and the like, until I reached a certain level.

When I was sixteen years old my friends and I joined the Bund. The Bund was very good for me. It had a big influence on me. I read Bundist publications: *Yugntveker*, and the like. In the Bund no one talked down to me the way they had in Betar. I was regarded as the equal of everyone else. By then I was earning six zloty a week. I kept one zloty for myself and gave the rest to my family. I had to survive a whole week on that one zloty. I needed fifteen groszy for party dues and twenty-five groszy for the movies—these were the most important things for me—plus ten groszy for a copy of *Yugntveker*. With the rest I bought myself some herring to go with my plain bread. I lived like a real proletarian on that one zloty a week.

My boss was a sick man. He suffered from hardening of the arteries. In a short time he died, at the age of forty-six. The boss's widow took over the workshop with her darling son, who was a Jewish fascist. While the boss was alive there was no need to go out on strike. He gave everyone a raise when the time came; but his widow didn't believe in this. And I knew she could afford to give us a raise, because she made a pretty good income. It couldn't hurt to talk to her. The other workers and I agreed that we would work until Friday at the current wages and then go out on strike the following week. We made very modest demands, because there was no bootmakers' union in B. The boss's widow swore she wouldn't give us a raise; anyone who didn't want to work for the same wages could leave. After this, we became really determined: "No, we won't give in! We'll stay on strike until we win!" She brought in a scab from Opatów, but he didn't work there for long. There was one coward among us who got frightened and wanted to give in, but I put a lot of pressure on him to hold out.

After the first day of the strike we went into the shop. It was nine o'clock at night. The scab was still sewing. We told him what was going on. He made excuses for himself, saying that his job in Opatów had been taken away. I asked him bluntly, "Are you going to leave or not?" Meanwhile, the boss's widow went to my father and asked him to come and see what I was doing. She shouted that she was giving me a raise but not the others. My father shook his finger at me, as if to say, "What does it matter to you? You're getting a raise, what more do you want? Let them go on strike, and if they're needed they'll also get a raise." It wasn't a matter of what my father wanted, though, but what I wanted. The scab got up and walked out. We put him on a bus and sent him home.

The strike continued. When the boss's widow found out that the scab went back to Opatów, she came up to me the next morning and said, "Come back to work, but without Yankev." He was our apprentice. It seemed she was very upset that this youngster had also gone out on strike. She swore she wouldn't be a mother to her own children if she let him back into the house. She kept her promise the way Hitler and Chamberlain stuck to the Munich Agreement. On the second day she approached me again: "Come back to work." She made herself cry in front of my parents, as if she were being attacked on all sides: "They talk at work and waste time." In other words, she was paying money for nothing. We stayed out on strike for another week and came back one-hundred-percent victorious. Even though I was not the oldest worker in the shop, I had organized the strike and led it to victory. When I walked down the street, people patted me on the back: "You're a good guy, a fine member of the proletariat."

I was earning twelve zloty a week. Things were better. I learned to write Yiddish, though not according to the new spelling. I taught myself completely on my own, and I've learned to read more quickly and with better understanding. I spent more time going out to do things: helping comrades who are sick, taking part in discussions, going to lectures, and working for the Bundist program. For various reasons I left the Bund, but I stick firmly to my principles. Although I work twelve hours a day, I also read a great deal. I go out a lot, and I am a fully politically conscious Jewish worker. Thanks to Comrade Blankman of B., I'm learning to write Yiddish with the new spelling. I don't know it very well yet, because I've only been studying it for a month. I hope that he will teach me proper Yiddish and Polish.

I now earn fifteen zloty a week. It's still not enough. I have two older brothers; the three of us support the household. We've been through good and bad, but times are changing. My father won 1,600 zloty in the forty-fourth lottery. We've started to think about plans for our oldest sister's future. I myself have gone through good times and bad times, but I have come through it all. The main thing is that I am healthy. I have a job. I get up at five o'clock in the morning to take part in YIVO's international competition. I, a simple Jewish worker, send greetings to YIVO for taking an interest in Jewish youth. I thank you for building up Jewish culture.

EPILOGUE

As they finished writing their autobiographies, each of these fifteen authors stood at a threshold of both personal and historical importance. Not only were they at the beginning of their lives as adults; soon they and all Polish Jews would abruptly confront an unprecedented struggle for their very existence. The great majority of them did not survive the Nazi-led genocide. At the same time, though, Polish Jews who were in their mid-teens to mid-twenties during World War II—the generation represented by these autobiographies—proved to have the best chance of surviving persecution. As we finish reading these life histories it is almost impossible not to wonder, what happened next to these young men and women? Did any of them survive the war, and what did they do then? Are any of them still alive?

With regard to most of the authors of the life histories in this volume, we are unable to answer these questions. In some instances, we do not know their actual names in full, nor do we have enough other information—date and place of birth, last place of residence before the war—to search the extensive records that document the life and death of millions of European Jews during the Holocaust. In a few instances, though, there is evidence that indicates some of these autobiographers did not survive the war. The last word heard from the author known to us as "EM.TEPA" was a letter sent from his home town in 1943. Relatives of "Eter," who now live in Israel, report that they do not know what happened to her during the war; they never heard from her after 1939. In other cases, we are certain that authors did not survive the war. The death of the author known as "G.W." is listed in the *yisker-bukh* (communal memorial book) for his home town.

Quite remarkably, two of the authors whose autobiographies appear in this volume did survive the war and lived to witness the arrival of the twenty-first century. The author known to us as "J. Harefuler" survived the Holocaust by escaping to the Soviet Union. After the end of World War II he returned to Poland, but soon thereafter he decided to emigrate to Palestine, arriving in early 1948. As this volume goes to press he still lives in

Israel. In 2000 Ludwik (now Eliezer) Stöckel reported to YIVO from his home in Netanyah, Israel, that in 1935 he fulfilled his dream of settling in Palestine. There he joined Kibbutz Kfar-Hachoresh in the lower Galilee, where most of the settlers were, like him, Jews from Galicia. At the kibbutz he met his future wife, Tirza, who came from Vienna, and they married in 1939. They left the kibbutz in 1942 and settled in Netanyah, where Stöckel opened a business selling building materials and took part in communal affairs. In his letter to YIVO he wrote that he is retired, and he and his wife have two daughters, five granddaughters, and one great-grandson.

ENDNOTES

1. S. ETONIS

Translator: Fruma Mohrer
Inventory no.: 3845; notebook, 40 pp.

R. = an anonymous town (author's own term).

"Hatikvah" ("The Hope"). Official anthem of the Zionist movement. The Hebrew lyrics were composed by Naphtali Herz Imber ca. 1878. The music, by Samuel Cohen, was based on an East European folk melody.

Ha-lashon **. . . the tongue.** In Hebrew, *ha-lashon* can mean either "the language" or "the tongue" (that is, a part of the mouth). In this context, only the former meaning is the correct one. The author, responding in Yiddish, answered *di tsung* (the tongue) rather than *di shprakh* (the language).

"Cast your burden upon the Lord and He will sustain you." Psalms 55:23.

reciting psalms, giving rubles . . . to the poor. Reciting psalms and giving charity are traditionally believed to intercede on behalf of someone seriously ill.

The Selling of Joseph. East European Jews traditionally staged amateur productions of plays in Yiddish for the late winter holiday of Purim. Some Purim plays dramatize the Book of Esther, the Biblical text that is read aloud in synagogues on the holiday; some are based on other episodes of the Bible, especially *The Selling of Joseph* (*Mekhires Yoysef*), the story of Joseph being sold as a slave by his brothers.

communist meeting. Poland's Communist Party, established in December 1918, was declared illegal by the Polish government in January 1919.

Treaty of Brest-Litovsk. The author has confused the Treaty of Brest-Litovsk (a peace agreement between Germany and the new state of Soviet Russia) with the Treaty of Riga. The latter agreement, signed on 18 March 1921, ended the Polish-Soviet War, which had begun in 1919. The Treaty of Riga established the border between Poland and the Soviet Union, which remained in effect until 1939.

A new smugglers' language developed. The author gives a few examples in his text, including *lokshn* (noodles) = money; *farfl* (egg barley) = gold.

yeshiva in Baranowicze. The Yeshiva Ohel Torah was founded ca. 1917–18 by Rabbi Yosef Yudl Hurovitz of Nowogródek, a disciple of the *musar* movement.

Ramayles Yeshiva. Renowned rabbinical academy in Vilna, established in 1831. Among its directors was Rabbi Israel Lipkin Salanter (1810–1883), founder of the *musar* movement.

study partner. Traditional Talmudic study in yeshiva involves the review of texts with a partner, rather than studying on one's own.

The Examination of the World (*Beḥinat ha-ʿolam*). Lyrical, ethical monograph in Hebrew by poet and philosopher Jedaiah ben Abraham Bedersi (also known as Ha-Penini, ca. 1270–1340), dealing with the themes of the futility and vanity of worldly existence and the benefits of religious pursuits.

Duties of the Heart (*Ḥovot ha-levavot*). Treatise by moral philosopher Bahya ben Joseph Ibn Paquda (ca. second half of the eleventh century) addressing the social and spiritual obligations of a religious life. Originally written in Arabic in 1080, this work was translated into Hebrew in 1161.

"Eight Chapters" by Maimonides (*Shemonah peraḳim leha-Rambam*). An introduction to the medieval Jewish philosopher's commentary on Avot, a tractate of the Mishnah. In this ethical treatise, Maimonides (1135–1204) harmonizes Aristotle's ethics with rabbinical teachings.

Sins of My Youth (*Ḥaṭ'ot neʿurim*). Hebrew-language autobiography of Moses Leib Lilienblum, written in 1873–76, in which he describes his personal struggles against religious tradition and the development of his beliefs as a *maskil*.

Hebrew teachers' seminary. The Hebrew teachers' seminary in interwar Vilna was run by the Tarbut school system.

Raduń yeshiva. Rabbinical academy founded in 1869 by Rabbi Israel Meir Kahan (known as the Hafetz Hayyim), a renowned center for the study of *musar*.

Yoreh Deʿah (*Teacher of Knowledge*). The second of four sections of the *Shulhan Arukh* (*The Prepared Table*), the late medieval code of rabbinic law written by Joseph Caro and first published in Venice in 1565. This section deals with laws concerning diet, interest, purity, charity, and mourning, which were of special relevance for routine rabbinical adjudication.

"a spade with which to dig." A reference to Mishnah Avot 4:7. "Rabbi Zadok said: . . . do not make of the Torah a crown with which to aggrandize yourself, nor a spade with which to dig."

economic crisis. In the early 1930s the economic situation in Poland, as in other European countries, worsened significantly as a consequence of the Great Depression. Tariffs rose all over Europe, and as a result Polish agricultural exports to Western Europe declined. Unemployment grew in the industrial sector, which could not absorb Poland's beleaguered rural population.

2. KHANE

Translator: Daniel Soyer
Inventory no.: 3610; notebooks, 71 pp.; letter; Yiddish journal in separate notebook
(22 pp., plus 2 separate sheets)

*In addition to her autobiography, the author submitted to YIVO a journal, also written in
Yiddish, with entries dated April–July 1928.*

I didn't want to reveal secret things about the party. See **S. Etonis,** "communist meeting."

lying on the oven. Large ovens, used for both cooking and heating, were prominent fixtures
of East European domestic life. Sometimes these ovens were built with a shelf on top, which
was large enough to be covered with a mattress and provide a place for an adult, or one or
more children, to sleep. The interiors of these ovens sometimes had compartments for
baking or heating water.

S. = an anonymous town (author's own term).

At the time the borders were open. This took place prior to the onset of hostilities between
the new Polish and Lithuanian republics in July 1919. In October 1920 the city of Vilna and
adjacent territory were proclaimed an independent Republic of Central Lithuania. In 1922
its parliament voted to incorporate the region into Poland. This decision, and the ensuing
border change, was accepted by the League of Nations in 1923 but was rejected by
Lithuania.

oldest fortress in Lithuania. A number of stone fortresses were built in Lithuania during
the late Middle Ages. Over time the function of these sites changed or they simply fell into
disuse. The Kaunas Castle, for example, built in the late fourteenth century, was used as an
army barracks by Russian forces beginning in 1847, and civilians were allowed to build
dwellings around the fortress. During the 1930s, a number of these fortresses were restored,
and any people who had established residence in or around them were expelled.

3. A. GREYNO

Translators: Daniel Soyer, Elinor Robinson, and Michael Taub
Inventory no.: 3690; notebook and loose sheets (folded), 139 pp.; letter

P. = a town in Kielce province. In 1921 its Jewish population was almost 6,000, approximately seventy percent of the total population.

Vokhnshrift (*Weekly Publication*). A weekly cultural journal published by the Bund, 1931–35.

should have been avoided because of . . . *legal* reasons. This is probably a reference to
the author's involvement in illegal activity in the Communist Party. See **S. Etonis,** "communist meeting."

fire forbidden on Sabbath. Traditional Jewish law forbids performing a wide range of
activities on the Sabbath, in keeping with the basic injunction against doing any form of
work. These activities include lighting fires, smoking, traveling, washing with soap, handling

money, and writing. Some pious Jews refrain from other activities on the Sabbath as well, such as reading works of secular literature.

Christophe Krafft. Protagonist of the novel *Jean Christophe* by French author Romain Rolland (1866–1944), which traces the life of Jean Christophe Krafft, a talented musician and German expatriate living in France. The ten-volume work was published between 1904 and 1912. In the tradition of the European *Bildungsroman*, or coming-of-age novel, the protagonist undergoes a spiritual crisis but finds his soul in music and in the universal divine spirit. Popular throughout Europe, the novel had a special appeal for adolescent readers. A Polish translation of *Jean Christophe* appeared in 1925–27; a Yiddish translation was published in New York, 1918–21.

turned into plowshares. A reference to Isaiah 2:4: "And they shall beat their swords into plowshares. . . . They shall never again know war."

Yiddish translations in the prayerbooks for women. Many Hebrew prayerbooks published in Yiddish-speaking communities feature Yiddish translations, and sometimes commentaries as well, alongside the original prayers. These prayerbooks were sometimes described as being especially for women, whose knowledge of Hebrew was often less than that of men.

circumcising dead baby. According to Jewish tradition, a male infant who dies before he is eight days old is circumcised and named at the cemetery.

Hebrew with a Sephardic accent. Believing it to be more authentic to the pronunciation of ancient Hebrew, the leaders of the movement to revive Hebrew as a modern vernacular promoted the Sephardic pronunciation of the language, as opposed to the Ashkenazic variant used by Yiddish speakers when reciting prayers and reading sacred texts. The two variants differ over how certain vowel and consonant sounds are produced, as well as where the accent usually falls in words with more than one syllable.

Esperanto. Philologist Lejzer (Ludwig) Zamenhof (1859–1917), a Polish Jew, laid the foundations of this planned international language with the publication in 1887 of a basic grammar and vocabulary. Zamenhof hoped that the adoption of Esperanto would improve relations among peoples and pave the way for international accord. During the interwar years Esperanto classes, societies, and publications flourished throughout Europe. Esperanto textbooks in Yiddish were published in New York, 1909, and in Warsaw, 1930.

The book's Yiddish spelling was old-fashioned. Standards for modern Yiddish orthography were widely debated during the 1920s and '30s in Europe, the Soviet Union, and the Americas. The YIVO Institute's rules for standard spelling, issued in Vilna in 1936, were followed by secular Yiddish schools and some publications in Poland but were not universally adopted.

traditional Jewish clothes. The daily dress of traditionally observant Jewish men in interwar Poland might include a long coat, a cap or other headcovering, and an *arbe-kanfes* (an open-sided vest worn under the shirt, with ritual fringes, like those on a *talles*, on each of its four corners).

The Woman and Socialism (*Die Frau und der Sozialismus*). August Bebel's enormously popular 1883 treatise was widely accepted as an authoritative statement on Social Democratic theory and goals. A Yiddish translation was published in New York, 1911.

The Origin of the Family, Private Property, and the State (*Ursprung der Familie, des Privateigentums und des Staates*). This 1884 study by Friedrich Engels was the Marxist theorist's effort to develop a materialist anthropology. A Yiddish translation was published in New York, 1918.

Beer's *History of Class Struggles*. The author probably refers to *Allgemeine Geschichte des Socialismus und der sozialen Kämpfe* (*General History of Socialism and Social Struggle*) by Max Beer, published in 1924. A Yiddish translation (*Geshikhte fun sotsyalizm*) was published in Warsaw, 1926–29.

Cunow's *Religion and Faith* (*Ursprung der Religion und des Gottesglaubens [The Origin of Religion and Belief in God]*). 1913 study by German social scientist and folklorist Heinreich Cunow (1862–1936). A Yiddish translation was published in Warsaw, 1930.

Kellermann's *Ingeborg*. This 1906 novel by Bernhard Kellermann (1879–1951), written in an impressionistic, neo-Romantic manner, was translated into Polish (1909), Hebrew (Warsaw, 1918/19), and Yiddish (Warsaw, 1924).

living newspapers. Documentary form of theater, in which actors present fact-based reports and statistics in live performance.

we clashed with the traditional Jewish burial society. The revolutionaries' practices—marching bareheaded, singing labor songs, carrying wreaths, making political speeches at the grave—are all in defiance of traditional Jewish burial practice.

"Internationale." A revolutionary socialist hymn, sung by communists and other left-wing political groups, written in 1871 by Eugene Pottier with music by Adolphe Degeyter.

"A Suicide Note" (*"A briv fun a zelbstmerder"*). An undated Yiddish short story by David Edelstadt about a man who is about to kill himself as a protest against human injustice and suffering.

26 April 192–. Year omitted by the author.

Sennaciulo (*Nationless*). Weekly journal in Esperanto issued by the Sennacieca Asocio Tutmundo (SAT), first published in 1921.

trials that have recently taken place in this country. The author may be referring to the most famous political trial held in Poland during the early 1930s, known as the Brzeski trial (or trial of Brześć), a trial of the Center-Left Coalition in the Polish parliament that opposed the Piłsudski regime. Leaders of the coalition, who were prominent Polish politicians, were jailed in Brześć. The trial, which took place in 1931–32, provoked widespread resentment and many public protests throughout the entire country.

Ansky's one-act play *The Grandfather* (*Der zeyde*). This undated comedy appears in volume 3 of Ansky's *Collected Works* (*Gezamlte shriftn*), published in Vilna/Warsaw/New York in 1925.

4. HENEKH

Translator: Rena Borow
Inventory no.: 3582; notebook, 36 pp.

started a children's library. During the interwar years many East European Jewish youth movements and other organizations set up local, private lending libraries. Often these were named after a famous Jewish writer, such as Sholem Aleichem or Yitskhok Leybush Peretz.

yeshiva in Grodno. The renowned yeshiva Sha'arei Torah was founded under the German occupation during World War I by yeshiva students themselves. Between 1920 and 1939, under the leadership of Rabbi Shimon Shkop, it was transformed into one of the leading yeshivas in Eastern Europe, attracting hundreds of students from near and far.

of blessed memory. It is common in Yiddish and Hebrew, after mentioning the name of someone deceased, to say or write *zikhroyne levrokhe* (of blessed memory) or *olev/ole hasholem* (may he/she rest in peace).

"Seek, and ye shall find." Matthew 7:7, Luke 11:9.

"Alongside justice there is wickedness." Ecclesiastes 3:16.

Haynt (*Today*). Daily Yiddish newspaper, published in Warsaw, 1908–39. One of the most widely-read and influential Jewish newspapers in Europe, *Haynt* was Zionist in its political orientation.

Book of the Covenant (*Sefer ha-berit*). First published in Bruenn, 1797, and reprinted several times, this book presents the general sciences from the perspective of Jewish tradition. It was written by Phinehas Elijah ben Meir Horowitz, a pupil of the Gaon of Vilna, the eighteenth-century leader of the rabbinical opposition to hasidism, who expressed a limited interest in the study of natural sciences, while giving Talmudic studies preeminence.

extern. A student who is not enrolled in a *gymnasium* or university but prepares independently for the diploma.

5. FORGET-ME-NOT

Translator: Chana Mlotek
Inventory no.: 3539; notebook, 42 pp.; letter

he was sent every day to eat a meal at another person's house. This widespread practice, known in Yiddish as *esn teg* (literally, "eating days"), provided poor yeshiva students living away from home with regular meals. Offering *esn teg* to these students was considered an important good deed, because it supported traditional Jewish scholarship.

Jewish public school. During the interwar years, Polish public schools reflected the sensibility of the republic's Catholic majority. A number of common practices—holding classes on Saturdays, displaying crucifixes and other religious images in classrooms, seating boys and girls together, requiring boys to remove hats indoors—proved troubling, if not untenable, for many Jews who wished to attend these schools. Some Jewish children attended special public schools, known as *Szabasówka* (Saturday) schools, which did not hold classes on Saturdays. The author may be referring here to a *Szabasówka* school.

this was forbidden on the Sabbath. See **A. Greyno**, "fire forbidden on Sabbath."

Sholem Aleichem library. See **Henekh**, "started a children's library."

Sinclair's *The Seeker of Truth*. Upton Sinclair's 1910 novel *Samuel the Seeker*, the story of a man who tries various religious and ideological identities before settling on socialism, was translated into Yiddish as *Der zukher fun emes* (Warsaw, 1927).

illegal political organization. A reference to Poland's Communist Party. See **S. Etonis,** "communist meeting."

certificate to emigrate to Palestine. The British mandatory government issued certificates for legal immigration to Palestine beginning in 1920. The Jewish Agency in Palestine was responsible for choosing which of those Jews who wished to settle in Palestine would receive these certificates. The British issued a series of immigration restrictions during the interwar years, which were designed to limit the number of new Jewish settlers in proportion to Palestine's Arab population. Because of these restrictions, many European Jews attempted illegal immigration to Palestine during this period.

because the masses were leaving us. During the early 1930s many German workers left the Social Democratic Party for the Nazi Party.

united front. The political agenda of a united front—i.e., the joining of all left-wing parties in opposition to Fascism—was supported by the Soviet Union beginning in 1934.

induction into the Polish army. Throughout the interwar years military service was obligatory for all male citizens of the Polish Republic. However, during this period the Ministry of Military Affairs issued a number of orders regulating the draft policy with regard to ethnic minorities. In 1934 a directive specified general quotas restricting the induction of ethnic minorities into different branches of the military: none of the "foreign nationalities" (i.e., those who were not ethnic Poles) could serve in armored units, communications units, military police, or the navy. In other branches of the military the percentage of minorities that could be admitted varied.

6. LUDWIK STÖCKEL

Translator: John Weeks
Inventory no.: 3675; loose sheets (folded), 64 pp. (plus "Annotations," 42 pp.); letter

The author's autobiography was accompanied by an extensive selection of poems and other "annotations," which he keyed to his main text.

Russkies. The author uses the term *Moskale*, Polish slang for Russians.

We must have had a lot of these bills. . . . Uncontrolled inflation began in Poland during World War I and accelerated considerably after the war. In 1918, one U.S. dollar was worth 9.8 zloty; in 1922, one dollar was worth 17,808.3 zloty.

extinguished embers. The author probably refers to the embers that heated the iron his mother was using to press clothes. Such irons either rested on a bed of coals or contained a chamber in which hot coals were placed in order to heat the iron's smooth bottom surface.

avoiding nuns, searching for pails of water. These are understood as, respectively, bad and good omens in Polish folklore.

giving out a countless number of 2's. Grades in Polish schools ranged from "5" (very good) to "2" (unsatisfactory).

Bałaban's history. The author probably refers to *Historia i Literatura Żydowska* (*Jewish History and Literature*) by Jewish historian Meir Bałaban, published in three volumes in 1925.

Jean Christophe. See **A. Greyno,** "Christophe Krafft."

Ujejski's *Marathon*; Miltiades. An epic poem by Kornel Ujejski that portrays the battle of Marathon (490 BCE) between the ancient Greeks and the invading Persians. When the Spartans are defeated, the hero Miltiades urges them to come to the aid of the Athenians. At the climax of the poem, Miltiades exhorts his troops to fight against their foes.

Wawel. Royal castle compound, including a cathedral, armory, treasury, and royal crypts, dating back to medieval times. Built on top of a hill, the Wawel is situated on the highest point in Cracow, overlooking the Vistula River. In modern times it has been a popular tourist attraction.

St. Mary's (Mariacki) Church. Largest church in Cracow, located on its main square. The current Gothic brick structure, the third to stand on the site, was erected in the fourteenth century.

Sukiennice. A large, ornate, public hall in the middle of Cracow's main square, originally built to house cloth merchants. The present building was erected in the sixteenth century.

salt mine in Wieliczka. Located fifteen kilometers southeast of Cracow, this vast underground mine with a series of rooms and figures, all sculpted out of rock salt, has been a popular tourist attraction since the eighteenth century.

Castle. Former home of Poland's royal family, located in the Old City of Warsaw.

Branicki's tapestry. Branicki is a well-known Polish noble family.

Marszałkowska. A major commercial street in central Warsaw.

"The Battle of Racławice" by Jan Matejko (1838–1893), a popular painter of Polish historical subjects, whose works shaped the Polish national iconography. This panoramic painting depicts the 1794 battle between Russian invaders and a Polish peasant army lead by Tadeusz Kósciusko. This battle came to symbolize Poles' national valor in the years following their defeat at the hands of the Russians in 1863. Matejko completed the work around 1880 for the newly established National Gallery in Cracow.

echoing what was taking place in the universities. National Democratic (Endek) students frequently attacked their Jewish colleagues or restricted them to back benches in classrooms (so-called "bench ghettos"); though these actions did not have official government or university administration support, they did have tacit approval. Throughout the 1920s and '30s right-wing nationalist parties called for an introduction of a *numerus clausus*, a quota that would restrict the number of Jews enrolled in universities.

addressed formally. Like most other European languages, Polish distinguishes between familiar (*ty, wy*) and formal (*pan, pani, panowie, panie, państwo*) forms of the pronoun "you."

"greens," as we called the Endeks. The author uses the term "green" (Polish: *zielony*) and later "green-brains" (*zielono-mózgi*), which are Polish slang for an ignoramus.

green table. Tables for formal examinations and conferences were typically covered in green baize.

"green-brains." See the note on "greens" above.

the newspapers were already full of blank spaces. This was a sign that their contents had been censored.

Kurier Lwówski (*Lwów Courier*). An influential Polish daily newspaper, liberal-democratic in its political orientation, published 1883–1926.

Zionist Congress. Members of the Zionist movement met at annual or biennial congresses in various European cities, beginning with the first Zionist Congress, convened by Theodor Herzl in Basle in August 1897. The eighteenth Zionist Congress was held in Prague on 21 August–4 September 1933.

Hebrew University. Following a mandate from the Zionist Congress of 1913, Chaim Weizmann initiated the establishment of the university in 1914. The university officially opened in Jerusalem in 1925, with Hebrew as the language of instruction, and granted its first degree in 1931.

Institute of Technology. Also known as the Technion, this engineering university was built in Haifa by members of the German Jewish community beginning in 1912. World War I and a conflict over the language of instruction delayed its opening. The Zionist Organization subsequently acquired the building, and classes began in Hebrew in 1924.

Hutzuls. Also known as Carpatho-Rusyns, an ethnic minority living in Transcarpathia, mostly in the borderlands of Ukraine, Poland, and Slovakia.

Opinia (*Opinion*). Polish-language Jewish political weekly published in Warsaw, Cracow, Lwów, and Vilna, 1934–36. Focusing on the social and political situation of Jews in Poland and in Palestine, it was mostly read by moderate Zionist intellectuals.

7. HANZI

Translator: Alex Molot
Inventory no.: 3618; notebook, 46 pp.

Petrograd: St. Petersburg was known as Petrograd from 1914 to 1924. It was then named Leningrad and renamed St. Petersburg after the fall of communism in 1991.

Father eating without covering his head. Traditionally observant Jewish males keep their heads covered during most activities while awake. It is considered especially important to do so during prayer, while studying sacred texts, and while eating meals (before and after which blessings and prayers are recited).

smoking cigars on the Sabbath. See **A. Greyno**, "fire forbidden on Sabbath."

Purim play. See **S. Etonis**, "*The Selling of Joseph.*"

Zitron's *Herzl, His Life and Work* (*Hertsl: ḥayav u-fe'ulotav*). A Hebrew-language biography of Theodor Herzl by journalist Samuel Leib Zitron (1860–1930), published in Vilna, 1921.

of blessed memory. See **Henekh.**

The Last Day of a Condemned Man. Victor Hugo's 1829 novel *Le Dernier Jour d'un Condamné* was translated into Hebrew in Warsaw, 1898.

Good Is Man (*Der Mentsch is Gut*). A 1917 novel about World War I by German author Leonhard Frank (1882–1961). Hebrew translation published in Warsaw, 1920.

disease appeared on my skin. The author refers to her illness as "leprosy" (Hebrew: *tsara'at*); however, the symptoms she describes are clearly that of some other skin disease.

3 for conduct. See **Ludwik Stöckel,** "giving out a countless number of 2's."

Di tsayt (*The Time*). A Yiddish daily published in Vilna, 1921–39.

"those who wallow in my blood." A reference to Ezekiel 16:6: "When I passed by you and saw you wallowing in your blood. . . ."

Tel Hai. This Jewish settlement, established in the northeastern Galilee in 1918, was attacked by Arabs in 1920. Six Jewish settlers, including Zionist leader Joseph Trumpeldor, were killed. The attack at Tel Hai became a powerful symbol for Zionist movements, especially for Betar, which was named in Trumpeldor's memory.

The Jewish State (*Der Judenstaat*). Theodor Herzl's widely influential treatise, which advocates for the establishment of a modern Jewish state as the only solution to the economic and social plight of European Jews, was first published in Vienna in 1896. Herzl's text was translated into Hebrew (Warsaw, 1896), Yiddish (several undated editions from the early 1900s, as well as those published in New York, 1927, and Warsaw, 1936) and other languages.

P.B. unit of Betar. It is unclear what the author refers to here. (The letters "P.B." are written in the Roman alphabet in her text.) It may possibly be a reference to "Pierwsza Brygada" (First Brigade), the legendary Polish unit that fought for independence during World War I. Betar's members were great admirers of Polish military valor.

Nemilov's *The Biological Tragedy of Woman* (*Biologicheskaia tragediia zhenshchiny*). A study of women's health and sexuality by Soviet histologist Anton Vitalievich Nemilov (1879–1942), published in 1930. Yiddish translation published in 1933.

Słowo (*Word*). A conservative Polish daily published in Vilna, 1922–39.

Bistritski's *Days and Nights* (*Yamim ye-lelot*). Hebrew novel about kibbutz life in Palestine published in Jerusalem, 1926.

8. THE STORMER

Translator: Daniel Soyer
Inventory no.: 3707; notebook, 94 pp.

The cover of the author's manuscript is dated 11 February 1939, and the last page is dated 13 April 1939, suggesting that it took him two months to write the text.

A. = a town in Kielce province. In 1930 its Jewish population was about 3,000, approximately forty-five percent of the total population.

may she live. When referring to someone who is still alive right after mentioning someone who is dead, it is customary in Yiddish to say *zol zi/er lebn* (may she/he live).

Kamienna Street. Located in the middle of Łódź, this street, largely populated by Jews, was known for its poverty and street gangs.

lighting a match on Friday evening, reading a secular book on the Sabbath. See **A. Greyno**, "fire forbidden on Sabbath."

Uncle H., etc. These and all subsequent initials for personal names were supplied by the author.

River Sambatyon. Legendary river across which, according to Jewish lore, some of the Ten Lost Tribes of Israel were exiled by the Assyrians following their conquest of the Northern Kingdom of Israel.

Leviathan. Legendary giant fish which, according to Jewish lore, will be eaten at a great feast following the arrival of the Messiah.

Gerer hasidim. Followers of one of the most influential hasidic dynasties in Poland, centered in the small town of Góra Kalwaria, near Warsaw. The founder, Rabbi Yitzhak Meir Alter (1789–1866), was the great-grandfather of the third Gerer Rebbe, Rabbi Abraham Mordecai Alter, who played an influential role in supporting Orthodox Jewish political activism and educational institutions, including Beys Yaakov schools, during the interwar years.

people who would provide me with regular meals. See **Forget-me-not**, "he was sent every day to eat a meal. . . ."

My friend Y. found out this was illegal. See **S. Etonis**, "community meeting."

"To the Common Man" ("Do Prostego Człowieka"). Popular poem by Julian Tuwim, first published in 1929, which denounces capitalist exploitation of the masses, especially by sending them to war.

living newspapers. See **A. Greyno**.

recent events in Lwów. Beginning in 1934 the number of workers on strike in Poland increased dramatically. In 1936 some 675,000 workers were on strike in all major industrial centers. The most violent and bloody protests took place in Lwów in mid-April that year, when riots lasting several days left several protesters dead and hundreds wounded. These events captured the attention of the entire country.

9. G.S.

Translator: Regina Grol-Prokopczyk
Inventory no.: 3739; loose sheets (folded), 15 pp.; two letters.

The author originally submitted a short, four-page autobiography to the YIVO contest. One month later she wrote back to YIVO, apparently in response to a letter from the institute, with a longer version of her life story, which is the version translated in this volume.

M. = a small town in Małopolska. On the eve of World War II there were 37 Jews living in M.

breaking wafers. Breaking and sharing wafers is a part of a traditional Polish Christmas Eve dinner and signifies a close bond with family members.

W. = a town in Cracow province. In 1931 its Jewish population was 19,300, approximately sixty percent of the total population.

certificates to emigrate to Palestine. See **Forget-me-not.**

10. EM.TEPA

Translator: John Weeks
Inventory no.: 3792; loose sheets, 52 pp.

I longed for Friday to come, so that I could show off my new outfit. It is a common custom among observant Jews to wear one's best clothes for the Sabbath, which begins Friday at sundown.

"Hope and Believe" (*"Hof un gloyb"*). Yiddish poem by Yitskhok Leybush Peretz. Written in 1891, it appeals for the renewal of Jewish peoplehood, employing images of nature's reawakening in spring.

Dr. B. The author's own abbreviation.

Der moment. Yiddish daily newspaper published in Warsaw, 1910–39, one of the most influential Jewish dailies in Poland, with a circulation of ca. 30,000, which sometimes escalated during moments of crisis to 150,000. During World War I *Der moment* backed the Folkspartei, a populist autonomist Jewish political movement. In the late 1930s the newspaper supported the Revisionist Zionist movement.

Di naye folkstsaytung (*The New People's Paper*). Daily Yiddish newspaper associated with the Bund, published in Warsaw, 1921–39.

Janko the Musician (*Janko Muzykant*). 1930 Polish film directed by Ryszard Ordyński, based on a novel of the same name by Henryk Sienkiewicz. Janko is an illiterate peasant shepherd boy with a natural love of music. He discovers his talent for the violin when he sees Jewish musicians performing in a tavern and eventually meets a tragic end.

city of S. = an anonymous location (author's own term).

Fata Morgana: legendary evil sorceress in the medieval story of England's King Arthur. Here she appears as an illusory figure, a phantasm.

11. G.W.

Translator: Sheva Zucker
Inventory no.: 3713; notebook, 60 pp.; letter

Chapter I. A distinctive feature of this autobiography is the author's division of his text into twenty-nine short chapters, each of which he gave a title. This provides some sense of how the author conceptualized his life story, and it suggests that he may have prepared an outline before beginning to write.

D. = a town in Lublin province. In 1930 its Jewish population numbered 2,800, approximately seventy percent of the total population.

the Bolsheviks arrived. The author probably refers to fighting following the second Polish offensive of the Polish-Soviet War, which began in the spring of 1920. The ensuing months were the most intensive period of this conflict, when ended the following year.

"On the hearth" (*"Afn pripetshik"*). This widely popular Yiddish song was written ca. 1900 by Mark M. Warshawsky (1840–1907). Originally entitled *"Der alef-beys,"* it describes a *melamed* instilling his young pupils in *kheyder* with a love of traditional Hebrew and of Jewry as they learn the *alef-beys*.

"Grabski's hearse." This was the nickname for the tax collector's wagon in interwar Poland, when Władysław Grabski (1873–1938) was secretary of the treasury. The tax collector often confiscated private property from people who didn't pay their taxes.

they surely remember the ghetto. Before the period of Nazi occupation, East European cities and towns did not have ghettos—i.e., streets or neighborhoods, bounded by walls or gates, where Jews were required to live by law—as had often been the case in Western and Central Europe from the early modern period until the emancipation of Jews during the nineteenth century. Here, the author may be using the term *ghetto* to invoke more generally the premodern, unenlightened Jewish world, as he does at the end of his autobiography.

Chapter XVI. The author provided no title for this chapter.

Constitution Day. Celebrated on 3 May, this holiday marks the anniversary of the Great Sejm's adoption of Poland's constitution (the first in modern Europe, and the second after that of the United States) on that date in 1791.

at the time there was no anti-Semitism in Włodzimierz. Boycotts of Jewish businesses and other discriminatory practices became increasingly frequent in Poland following the death of Józef Piłsudski in 1935.

Dubnow's history of the Jews, then Graetz's. Simon Dubnow's two-volume *World History of the Jewish People* (*Vsemirnaia istoriia evreiskogo naroda*) originally appeared in Russian in 1924–25; a Yiddish-language edition was published in Vilna, 1933. Several Yiddish-language editions of Heinrich Graetz's *History of the Jews from Ancient Times to the Present* (*Geschichte der Juden von den ältesten Zeiten bis zur Gegenwart*) were published in Europe and the United States before World War II.

the Bund and YIVO. Although YIVO had no official ties to the Bund, as the author suggests, the research institute and the political party shared a commitment to promoting secular Yiddish culture and championing the rights of Jews to live in the diaspora.

12. ESTHER

Translator: Rosaline Schwartz
Inventory no.: 3559; 2 notebooks, 57 pp.

Gerer hasid. See **The Stormer.**

L. = a town in Warsaw province. In 1930 its Jewish population was over 5,000, approximately sixty percent of the total population.

5's on my report card. See **Ludwik Stöckel**, "giving out a countless number of 2's."

When the whole school was being photographed, I wasn't allowed to take part. Some traditionally observant Jews avoid or restrict being photographed. There are several reasons offered for this, from concerns about image-making (in keeping with the second of the Ten Commandments) to concerns about protecting the modesty of observant Jews, especially women, in public.

"love your neighbor as yourself." Leviticus 19:18.

the unfolding economic crisis. See **S. Etonis**, "economic crisis."

11 November. Poland's Independence Day, which marks the reestablishment of an independent Polish state at the end of World War I.

Relations between Jews and Poles had deteriorated. Following Piłsudski's death in 1935, his political successors adopted anti-Jewish measures, which included sanctioning the boycott of Jewish businesses, encouraging increased Jewish emigration from Poland, and, eventually, limiting Jews' access to university education.

"end of days." From Isaiah 2:2: "And it shall come to pass, in the end of days. . . ."

"to study and to teach." This phrase appears in Ahavah Rabbah (Hebrew: great love), a prayer recited during morning worship services immediately before the Shema, the central declaration of Jewish faith in one God.

Lindsey's *The Revolt of Modern Youth*. A study of juvenile delinquency and sexual ethics in Denver by Benjamin Barr Lindsey (1869–1943) in 1925. A Yiddish translation was published in Warsaw, 1930.

boycott of Jewish stores in Poland. During the mid-1930s, the right-wing Endek Party called on Poles not to do business with Jews. This effort received some support from the Polish Catholic press and trade associations.

Motl. The protagonist of *Motl Peysi dem khazns* (*Motl, Peysi the Cantor's Son*), one of Sholem Aleichem's last works. At the start of this serialized novel, begun in 1907 and left unfinished at the time of the author's death in 1916, Motl's father dies, leaving him an orphan. He is the subject of so much attention and sympathy that he proclaims, "I'm doing fine, I'm an orphan."

G. = an anonymous town (author's own term).

"Seek, and ye shall find." See **Henekh**.

"Why do the wicked prosper and the righteous suffer?" Babylonian Talmud, Berakhot 7a.

13. J. HAREFULER

Translator: Dobrochna Dyrcz-Freeman
Inventory no.: 3598; 2 notebooks, 121 pp.

Niska Street. This and the other streets mentioned in this section were in Muranów, the neighborhood of Warsaw with the highest concentration of Jews during the interwar years.

Jacob sleeping in a hut made of stones. According to Rashi's commentary on Genesis 28:11, Jacob took stones and built a structure with them to protect himself from wild beasts as he slept.

putting on a mask, cakes. Masquerades and amateur theatricals were a popular Purim custom in Eastern Europe, especially for children attending Jewish schools. (See also **S. Etonis**, "*The Selling of Joseph*.") Exchanging cakes and other treats and holding a special festive meal are other widely observed Purim traditions.

green reeds. It was customary in Eastern Europe to gather greenery in late spring to use as decorations for the late-spring holiday of Shavuoth.

Khinukh Yeladim. This school was the first Yiddish elementary school in Poland. Originally founded as a Hebrew-Russian school, it was taken over in 1912 by Yiddishists, who changed the school's educational policy and made Yiddish the language of instruction.

Tuwim's poem "Silesia Is Singing" ("Śląsk śpiewe"). This undated poem celebrates coal mining in Silesia, a region in southwestern Poland.

***Uncle Tom's Cabin*, *Robinson Crusoe*.** Translations of Harriet Beecher Stowe's 1852 abolitionist novel were published in Polish (1901) and in Yiddish (New York, 1911). Translations of Daniel Defoe's 1719 novel were published in Polish (1911) and Yiddish (Kiev, 1935; Warsaw, 1937).

***ayin* made the sound "e" and *vov* was "u."** Although Yiddish and Hebrew use the same alphabet, they use the letters of the *alef-beys* differently, especially when indicating vowel sounds. These two letters, which function as consonants in Hebrew, serve as vowels in Yiddish.

to fight for the Spanish Republic. Some 5,000 Polish volunteers, including some Polish Jews, fought in the Spanish Civil War in the years 1936–39. Most were Communists; in many cases they were deprived of Polish citizenship and refused the possibility of legal return to Poland.

Comintern dissolved the Communist Party in Poland. In the late 1930s, Poland's Communist Party worked to establish a united front with the Polish Socialist Party. In 1938 the executive of Comintern accused the Polish Communists of anti-revolutionary espionage and dissolved the party.

Bogdanov's *Political Economy*. The author may be referring to *Vvedenie politicheskuiu ekonomiiu* (*Introduction to Political Economy*) by Aleksandr Bogdanov (1873–1928), first published in 1914; Yiddish translation published in New York, 1920. The author may also be referring to Bogdanov's *Kurs politicheskii ekonomii* (*Course in Political Economy*), a two-volume work published in 1910–19, which was translated into several languages.

Young Forest (*Młody Las*). A 1934 Polish-language film directed by Józef Lejtes, based on a drama by A. Hertz. Set in 1905, the film depicts a strike organized by Polish students against the Russian government's efforts to impose Russification in their school.

"She Had a Red Apple" . . . **"Mother Sleeps, Father Sleeps"** . . . **"The Happy Sailor's Note."** The first and third are Polish songs; the second is a Yiddish song.

Jews barred from labor battalions and navy. See **Forget-me-not**, "induction into the Polish army." Labor battalions were voluntary groups of civilians, mostly unemployed, who were used for building public works such as roads and bridges.

Birobidzhan. The Jewish Autonomous Region, located in the Soviet Far East on the Manchurian border, inaugurated in 1928 by the Soviet government. During the 1920s and '30s, some 40,000 Jews moved to this territory of 13,900 square miles, mostly to work on agricultural collectives; many, however, chose not to settle there permanently. As an alternative to the Zionist plan to establish a Jewish state in Palestine, Birobidzhan attracted much attention from Jewish communists and secular Yiddishists outside of the USSR.

14. ETER

Translator: Andrej Tumowski
Inventory no.: 3764; notebook, 34 pp.

Z. = a village in Stanisławów province.

K. = a town in Stanisławów province. In 1921 some 600 Jews lived there, almost thirty percent of the total population.

dedication of a Torah scroll. Jewish law requires that a Torah scroll be handwritten on parchment with a special quill pen and ink by a qualified scribe. The completion of a Torah scroll, which usually takes from several months up to a year, is traditionally marked by a public ceremony, in which those present are invited to fill in the outlines of letters in the first and last passages of the scroll, thereby playing a symbolic role in its creation.

"From where will my help come?" From Psalms 121:1–2: "I turn my eyes to the mountains; from where will my help come? My help comes from the Lord, maker of heaven and earth."

Maniawa "Skit." The ruins of a seventeenth-century monastery, which was a popular local attraction.

funeral was not until Sunday. Jewish tradition calls for burial within twenty-four hours of the time of death. However, funerals cannot be held on the Sabbath or a holiday; in these instances, burial takes place the following day.

I avoided listening to any musical instrument, and I didn't sing in school. It is customary for Jews to refrain from musical performances or other entertainments during the year following the death of an immediate family member, as part of the mourning process.

Gehenna. Polish novel first published in 1914 by Helena Mniszek (1878–1943), author of numerous popular books and short stories. *Gehenna* is a sentimental story of an aristocratic Polish woman's tragic life and unhappy love. After two men who are in love with her die (due to circumstances for which she is partly responsible), she marries Horski, a Polish-English aristocrat, who is attracted only to her wealth.

Tuwim's poem, "If only . . ." ("Jeżeli . . ."). This love poem is dated August 1915.

15. YUDL

Translator: Elinor Robinson
Inventory no.: 3514; notebook, 40 pp.

to sit with his head bare next to a crucifix. See **Forget-me-not**, "Jewish public school."

B. = a town in Kielce province. In 1921 its Jewish community numbered over 10,000, approximately fifty percent of the total population.

Groshn-biblyotek (*Penny Library*). A series of Yiddish books published in Warsaw during the interwar years. Aimed at a working-class readership, the series familiarized its audience with classics of world literature, history, music, and science, all in a popular form.

Yugntveker (*Awaker of Youth*). A Yiddish-language socialist newspaper for young adults, published in association with the Bund. It appeared as a monthly in 1922–26 and as a daily in 1926–39.

Munich Agreement. Pact signed by leaders of Germany, Britain, and France in late September 1938, which sanctioned Germany's occupation of the Sudetenland (western Czechoslovakia).

new Yiddish spelling. See **A. Greyno**, "The book's Yiddish spelling . . ."

APPENDIX I: PERSONALITIES

Ahad Ha-Am (pen-name of Asher Hirsch Ginsberg, 1856–1927), prominent essayist and Zionist leader. Ahad Ha-Am was a pioneer of the intellectual discourse of Zionism and championed the notion of cultural Zionism, centered around the revival of Hebrew as a modern Jewish vernacular.

Rabbi Akiba (ca. 50–135), major rabbinic scholar in Jerusalem during the time of the Roman conquest of Judea. Akiba's teachings had a formative influence on the development and codification of rabbinic law.

Alexander Rebbe. Rabbi Isaac Menachem (1880–1943), the last leader of an influential hasidic dynasty in Poland, with a court in Aleksandrów Łódzki, active from the second half of the nineteenth century. The last Alexander Rebbe established a network of Aleksandrów yeshivas in Eastern Europe.

S. Ansky (penname of Solomon Zanvl Rapaport, 1863–1920), author, folklorist, and activist. Ansky drew on Jewish folklore collected during a pioneering ethnographic expedition that he organized (1911–14) to write his best-known work, *The Dybbuk* (1912–17), which became the most famous modern Jewish drama, performed frequently in Yiddish and Hebrew. During World War I, Ansky played a leading role in Russian Jewish politics and organized relief committees for devastated Jewish communities in Eastern Europe.

Mikhail Petrovich Artsibashev (1878–1927), Russian prose writer, whose works were noted for their extreme pessimism, violence, and eroticism.

Sholem Asch (1880–1957), Yiddish novelist and dramatist, one of the first Yiddish writers to become famous beyond the Yiddish-speaking audience. Asch is best known for historical novels on East European Jewish life and on immigrant Jewish life in America.

Rabbi Avia, fourth-century Babylonian rabbinical scholar, whose teachings on Jewish law are recorded in many passages in the Talmud.

Baal Shem Tov (popular name of Israel ben Eliezer, ca. 1700–1760), charismatic Jewish mystic and preacher, the founding figure of hasidism. The Baal Shem Tov's teachings and legends about his life are fundamental sources for hasidic belief and lore.

Meir Bałaban (1877–1942), Jewish historian, author of several landmark studies of the history of Polish Jewry. During the interwar years Bałaban served as director of the Instityt Nauk Judaistycznych (Institute of Jewish Studies) in Warsaw and was a professor of history at Warsaw University.

Otto Bauer (1881–1938), Austrian socialist leader. The first foreign minister of the Austrian Republic (1918–19), he was a prolific writer on socialist problems. Although he represented the Marxist left wing within the Socialist International, Bauer was an opponent of Communism.

August Bebel (1840–1913), German socialist thinker, whose work had a major influence on the labor movement in late nineteenth to early twentieth century.

Micha Josef Berdyczewski (1865–1921), Hebrew writer of essays, fiction, folklore, and scholarship. Berdyczewski railed against older Hebraists and defended the claims of individual freedom and creativity against the stifling demands of traditional religion, majority will, and ideology.

Hayyim Nahman Bialik (1873–1934), Hebrew and Yiddish poet, essayist, translator, and editor. The premier Hebrew poet of his generation, Bialik played a central role in forging a modern poetic idiom in Hebrew.

Nathan Bistritski (also known as Nathan Agmon, 1896–1980), Hebrew dramatist, critic, and publicist, who began his literary career in Russia before emigrating to Palestine in 1920. His early writings described life in collective agricultural settlements in Palestine, and he was one of the first original Hebrew dramatists to be presented on the Palestinian stage.

Aleksandr Aleksandrovich Bogdanov (pseudonym of Aleksandr Aleksandrovich Malinovskii, 1873–1928), politician, economist, sociologist, and philosopher. A prominent founding member of the Bolshevik Party, Bogdanov's theories on proletarian culture remained highly influential after he left the party in 1917.

Henri Bordeaux (1873–1963), French novelist, essayist, and critic. Bordeaux's novels and criticism described the life of provincial families firmly rooted in Catholic tradition.

Joseph Hayyim Brenner (1881–1921), Hebrew writer and journalist. Brenner advocated a psychological approach to modern Hebrew literature in his novels, stories, and criticism.

Jacob Dineson (1856–1919), Yiddish novelist, who wrote several very popular sentimental novels in the late nineteenth century. A disciple and close friend of Yitskhok Leybush Peretz, Dineson also played a leading role in establishing secular Jewish elementary schools in Poland, some of which were named after him.

Simon Dubnow (1860–1941), prominent Jewish historian and ideologist. In addition to his pioneering work as a Jewish historian, Dubnow was active in East European Jewish politics, organizing the Folkspartey (Jewish People's Party) in St. Petersburg in 1906. In his ideological writings Dubnow championed secular Jewish diaspora nationalism, while supporting a pluralistic approach to modern Jewish culture.

David Edelstadt (1866–1892), Yiddish poet, who began writing revolutionary verses in Russian before emigrating to America in 1882 and joining the anarchist movement. Edelstadt's poetry addressed the struggles of immigrant Jewish workers. Following his death from tuberculosis, he became a legendary figure in the Jewish labor movement.

Mordecai Ze'ev Feierberg (1874–1899), Hebrew author, whose stories express the spiritual and cultural conflict between adherence to traditional Jewish life and aspiring toward a secular, modern, cultural existence in Europe.

Georg Fink (pseudonym of Kurt Münzer, 1879–1944), German-language prose writer and playwright. His most successful novel, *Mich Hungert* (*I Am Hungry*, 1929), was translated into Yiddish and Hebrew.

A.D. (Aharon David) Gordon (1856–1922), Hebrew writer and spiritual mentor of the Zionist labor movement. Through his writings and by personal example, Gordon emphasized self-realization through settlement on the land.

Heinrich Graetz (1817–1891), pioneering modern Jewish historian. His multivolume *Geschichte der Juden von den ältste Zeiten bis zur Gegenwart* (*History of the Jews from Ancient Times to the Present*, published in 1853–76) is regarded as the first attempt to write a comprehensive history of the Jewish people from a Jewish perspective.

Bronisław Grosser (1883–1912), a leading activist in the Bund during the early twentieth century, renowned for his power as a writer and speaker.

Hafetz Hayyim (Rabbi Israel Meir Kahan, 183?-1933), Talmudic scholar, moralist, and author, one of the most influential leaders of Orthodox Jewry in Poland. Founder of a yeshiva in Raduń named after him, he was best known for his book *Hafetz Hayyim*, after which he came to be known. First published in Vilna 1873, the book is an ethical discourse on the laws against gossip and slander.

Theodor Herzl (1860–1904), author and founder of political Zionism. Beginning in 1895, Herzl worked tirelessly for the cause of establishing a Jewish state, through his writing (most famously, *Der Judenstaat*, 1896), meeting with world leaders, convening the first Zionist Congress (Basle, 1897), and inaugurating funds to support Zionist activity. Herzl's portrait was a familiar icon in many Jewish homes and organizations.

Rabbi Hillel (first century BCE–first century CE), leading rabbi of the Second Temple period. Hillel played a formative role in defining Talmudic law and rabbinic interpretation of scripture and was very influential in establishing hermeneutical laws for the exposition of Torah. A major figure in the Talmud, he and his disciples were the chief adversaries of Rabbi Shammai.

Baron Maurice de Hirsch (1831–1896), German Jewish financier and philanthropist. As the originator of the Jewish Colonization Association, he was the first benefactor to plan the large-scale resettlement of European Jews. The Baron de Hirsch Foundation (est. 1888) and Jewish Colonization Association (1891) promoted Jewish educational institutions, immigrant aid associations, and agricultural colonies in Eastern Europe and the Americas.

Vladimir Ze'ev Jabotinsky (1880–1940), right-wing Zionist leader and author. During World War I Jabotinsky helped establish the Jewish Legion, which fought to liberate Palestine from Ottoman rule. In 1925 he established and led the World Union of Zionist-Revisionists. Throughout his career Jabotinsky championed Jewish self-defense, adopting Hebrew as a modern Jewish vernacular, and large-scale Jewish emigration to Palestine.

Karl Johann Kautsky (1854–1938), German-Austrian political theorist, whose writings had an extensive influence on left-wing politics in Europe. A devoted Marxist, Kautsky was an opponent of Lenin and of Bolshevism.

Aleksandr Kerenskii (1881–1970), leader of Russia's provisional government between the February and October Revolutions of 1917. Following the Bolshevik takeover of the government in 1918, he fled to England.

Jan Kochanowski (1530–1584), Poland's leading poet during the Renaissance. He was the first Polish writer to attempt both satirical poetry and classical tragedy in the vernacular.

Peter Kropotkin (1842–1921), Russian revolutionary, the foremost leader and theorist of the Anarchist movement. Fleeing imprisonment for his revolutionary activities in 1876,

Kropotkin lived in Western Europe until 1917. While in exile he wrote his most influential works, which include memoirs, historical and literary studies, as well as revolutionary theory.

Kazimierz (Lopek) Krukowski (1902–?), Polish actor and entertainer, who performed in theaters and cabarets in interwar Warsaw.

Marcus Lehmann (1831–1890), German Orthodox rabbi, scholar, and author. An opponent of Reform Judaism, Lehmann was the founder of *Der Israelit*, a leading Orthodox German weekly periodical. He wrote numerous historical novels and short stories for young readers with religious themes, some of which were translated into Yiddish.

Karl Liebknecht (1871–1919), German revolutionary, first active in the left wing of the German Social Democratic Party. Shortly after helping found Germany's Communist Party, he was arrested and was later murdered, along with his collaborator, Rosa Luxemburg.

Moshe Leib Lilienblum (1843–1910), Hebrew writer, journalist, and leader of early Zionist movements. After championing religious reform among Russian Jews as a young man, he advocated reforming Jewish economic life through agricultural work and promoted Jewish nationalism.

Rosa Luxemburg (1871–1919), economist and revolutionary. Luxemburg helped found the Social Democratic Party of Poland and Lithuania before emigrating to Germany in 1898, where she became a leading figure in the revolutionary left wing of the German Socialist Movement. German army officers murdered Luxemburg in Berlin.

Abraham Mapu (1808–1867), creator of the modern Hebrew novel. A leading exponent of the *Haskalah* in Eastern Europe, he is best known for his first and most successful novel, *Ahavat Ziyyon* (*Love of Zion*, 1853).

Karl May (penname of Karl Hohenthal, 1842–1912), German author of popular stories for young readers, typically romantic adventures set in remote, exotic locales.

Adam Mickiewicz (1798–1855), Polish Romantic poet and author, one of Poland's most popular and beloved literary figures. In his epic poem *Pan Tadeusz* (1833), the character of the musician and innkeeper Jankiel offers the most famous image in nineteenth-century Polish literature of Jews as a fixture of Polish society.

Mendele Mokher Seforim (Mendele the Bookseller, penname of novelist Sholem Yankev Abramovitch, 1835–1917), novelist and playwright, widely regarded as the father of modern Yiddish and Hebrew prose. Abramovitch's fiction satirized the traditional small-town life of East European Jews and advocated for modern social and intellectual reforms. Abramovitch used the fictional character of Mendele the Bookseller as his public persona, through whom the author presented his novels and plays to the public.

Neumann, Yeheskel Moshe (1893–1956). Yiddish writer, based in Łódź. The literary editor of *Haynt*, Neumann also wrote theater and film reviews.

Eliza Orzeszkowa (1841–1910), Polish writer, journalist, and novelist. One of the very first acclaimed women writers in Poland, she championed women's emancipation and the assimilation of Polish Jews. Several of her works advocate for amity between Poles and Jews.

Hershele Ostropoler (late 1700s), famous Yiddish prankster in Poland. Collections of his jokes and anecdotes about his cleverness were published after his death and continued to be reprinted into the twentieth century.

Yitskhok Leybush Peretz (1852–1915), Yiddish and Hebrew author of fiction, drama, memoirs, and essays. A pioneering voice of modernist Yiddish literature, Peretz was best known for his short stories, which typically offered pointed social critiques of traditional Jewish life, sometimes with ironic, iconoclastic twists on traditional hasidic or folk-tale motifs. Peretz also championed Yiddish as a Jewish national language and played a leading role in nurturing young Yiddish writers in early twentieth-century Poland. A widely admired figure among secular Jews in interwar Poland, Peretz was memorialized in a number of schools, libraries, and other local institutions bearing his name.

Symon Petliura (1879–1926), military leader of independent Ukraine in the early 1920s. Petliura's troops perpetrated violent anti-Semitic pogroms during Russia's civil war. He was later assassinated in Paris by a Jewish watchmaker, who was subsequently acquitted.

Marshal Józef Piłsudski (1867–1935), military hero and political leader of interwar Poland. Beginning in the 1890s, Piłsudski was one of the leaders of the Polish Socialist Party. During the 1905 Russian revolution, he organized Polish military units, and he later served as commander of the First Brigade of Polish Legions during World War I. Piłsudski played a leading role in establishing the Second Polish Republic and served as commander in chief during the Polish-Soviet war of 1920–21. He was elected to the Sejm in 1923 and led a military *coup d'état* in 1926, after which he served as minister and prime minister. An advocate of the rights of ethnic minorities in the Polish Republic, Piłsudski was widely admired by Polish Jews.

Georgy Valentinovich Plekhanov (1856–1918), Marxist theorist, the founder and for many years leading exponent of the Marxist movement in Russia. A Menshevik, he opposed the Bolshevik seizure of power in Russia in 1917.

Marcel Prévost (1862–1941), French writer, who rejected naturalism in his novels, most of which explored the mysteries of the female soul.

Bolesław Prus (penname of Aleksander Głowacki, 1847–1912), Polish writer and journalist. In addition to writing numerous essays for the Polish press in Warsaw, Prus was famous for his realist short fiction.

Radoshitser Rebbe (Rabbi Osher Anshul Gutschal, 18??–19??). Although not a descendant of the main line of the Radoshitser hasidim, Gutschal was a popular *rebbe* in Łódź during the first decades of the twentieth century, attracting many followers with his message of asceticism.

Pantelemon Romanov (1885–1938), Russian writer and journalist. Romanov wrote short stories, poems, and satires, as well as autobiographical works.

Selig Schachnowitz (1874–1952), a leader of the Orthodox movement Agudas Yisroel, as well as a journalist and author. He wrote many popular articles on Jewish history, thought, and literature that promoted traditional religiosity. Although Schachnowitz wrote in German, his works were translated into Yiddish and used in Orthodox Jewish schools in Poland.

Sara Schenirer (1883–1935), teacher and pedagogue of Orthodox Jewish girls and young women in Poland. Schenirer pioneered efforts to provide a traditional alternative to Polish public schools and secular Jewish schools by initiating the Beys Yaakov schools in 1917. She subsequently oversaw the spread of these schools throughout Poland and beyond.

Rabbi Shammai (ca. 50 BCE–30 CE), rabbinic leader and scholar, the adversary of Rabbi Hillel as depicted in the Talmud. In the laws transmitted in Shammai's name, he adopted more stringent views than Hillel, particularly in areas of ritual purity.

Sholem Aleichem (pen-name of Sholem Rabinowitz, 1859–1916), enormously popular Yiddish author and a leading champion of modern Yiddish literature and culture. Sholem Aleichem was best known for his affectionately satirical portraits of traditional East European Jewry, living in small towns and villages, as it confronted the challenges of modernity. While most of the author's works originally appeared in the Russian Yiddish press, they were frequently republished in book form after his death. One sign of his posthumous popularity in Eastern Europe was the naming of local Jewish libraries in his memory.

Henryk Sienkiewicz (1846–1916), Polish novelist, playwright, and short-story writer. Widely recognized as one of the greatest Polish nationalist writers of the modern era, Sienkiewicz crafted powerful, panoramic, romantic novels, which were widely popular with generations of Polish readers. He was a proponent of the Positivist literary movement, which championed Polish national pride in the wake of Poland's unsuccessful uprising against Russia in the 1860s.

Juliusz Słowacki (1809–1849), romantic Polish poet and dramatist, who spent most of his adult years as an émigré in Paris. Słowacki's patriotic poems were extremely popular among nineteenth-century Polish nationalists.

Perets Smolenskin (ca. 1840–1885), Hebrew novelist, editor, and journalist. A leading exponent of the *Haskalah* in Eastern Europe and an early advocate of Jewish nationalism, Smolenskin is best known for founding the Hebrew journal *Hashakhar* in 1868 and working as its editor until his death.

Nahum Sokolov (1859–1936), Hebrew journalist and publisher, prolific author, and Zionist leader. Sokolov became one of the principal spokespersons for the Zionist movement in Eastern Europe and served as a leader of the World Zionist Organization and the Zionist Executive.

Joseph Trumpeldor (1880–1920), Zionist pioneer and soldier. After serving as an officer in the Russian army during its war with Japan, Trumpeldor went to Palestine and helped Vladimir Jabotinsky form the Jewish Legion during World War I. He died while defending Tel Hai, a Jewish settlement in Palestine, against Arab attack.

Rabbi Naftali Trup (1871–1928), *rosh-yeshiva* of the yeshiva of the Hafetz Hayyim in Raduń for twenty-five years, during which time he trained thousands of rabbinical students.

Julian Tuwim (1894–1953), a leading modernist Polish poet, renowned for his stylistic innovations in Polish verse, as well as the explosive energy and great emotional tension in his work. An assimilated Jew, Tuwim addressed the theme of the plight of the common man in some of his work. He first wrote about Polish Jewry after World War II in a poem entitled "My Żydzi Polscy" ("We, Polish Jews").

Kornel Ujejski (1823–1897), romantic Polish nationalist poet, whose work combines folk motifs with patriotic sentiments.

Theodoor Hendrik van de Velde (1873–1937), Dutch gynecologist and author on sex and the psychology of marriage.

Chaim Weizmann (1874–1953), Zionist leader and the first president of Israel. Weizmann emerged as an important Zionist leader during World War I and led the Jewish delegation to the 1919 peace conference in Versailles, where he campaigned for international recognition of the Balfour Declaration. He served as president of the World Zionist Organization in 1920–31 and 1935–46.

Stefan Żeromski (1864–1925), novelist, short-story writer, and dramatist, the foremost prose writer of the neo-Romantic "Young Poland" literary movement.

APPENDIX II: ORGANIZATIONS

Agudas Yisroel (Hebrew: Society of Israel), international Orthodox Jewish political organization, founded in Poland in 1912. Anti-Zionist in its orientation, Agudas Yisroel also opposed the use of Hebrew as a modern vernacular.

Basya, a junior division of Bnos Agudas Yisroel, which ran after-school and Sabbath programs for students in Beys Yaakov schools.

Betar (Hebrew acronym for Brit [Covenant of] Trumpeldor), right-wing Zionist youth movement associated with the Zionist Revisionist party, founded in 1923 in Riga, Latvia. Betar promoted modern Hebrew language and culture, learning methods of self-defense, and emigration to Palestine by both legal and illegal means. The movement fused the Revisionist leader Vladimir Jabotinsky's militarism with the ideal of Zionist pioneering exemplified in the life and death of Joseph Trumpeldor.

Beys Yaakov (Hebrew: House of Jacob), a system of schools for Orthodox Jewish girls, founded by Sara Schenirer in Cracow in 1917. The schools were endorsed and partially funded by Agudas Yisroel. By 1937 there were about 250 Beys Yaakov schools in Poland, including both full-day schools and supplementary afternoon/Sunday schools, with 38,000 students. Beys Yaakov schools were also established in other countries and continue to function in Orthodox Jewish communities in Europe, the Americas, and Israel. The Beys Yaakov teachers seminary was established in Cracow in 1925. Under the personal supervision of Schenirer, the seminary trained hundreds of young women in secular and Jewish subjects as well as in pedagogy and psychology.

Bilu (Hebrew acronym for "House of Jacob, let us go up" [Isaiah 2:5]), Russian Jewish organization, founded in response to the anti-Semitic pogroms of 1881, which pioneered Jewish settlement in Palestine. The first group of Biluim, as the settlers were known, arrived in Palestine in July 1882 and established a settlement at Gederah in 1884.

Bnos (known in full as Bnos [Hebrew: Daughters of] Agudas Yisroel), a young women's organization founded in Łódź by Agudas Yisroel in 1925. Bnos provided cultural and educational programming in a religious atmosphere for young women who had graduated from Beys Yaakov schools. In the mid-1930s Bnos had over 14,000 members. As part of its anti-assimilationist agenda, Bnos discouraged the use of Polish and encouraged its members to speak Yiddish.

Bund (known in full as Algemeyner yidisher arbeter-bund in Lite, Poyln un Rusland [Yiddish: General Jewish Workers' Union in Lithuania, Poland, and Russia]), Jewish socialist political party, founded in Vilna in 1897. The first workers' mass movement organized in Russia, the Bund played a pioneering role in radical politics in the Russian empire at the beginning of the twentieth century. In interwar Poland, the Bund was an important political and cultural presence, running candidates in local and national elections, sponsoring Yiddish periodicals (e.g., *Di folkstsaytung*), youth movements (Tsukunft, SKIF), secular Yiddish schools, and children's camps. Bundists supported the international workers' movement while also championing a secular Jewish diaspora nationalism, in which Yiddish language and culture played a central role. In contrast to Zionists and other Jewish political movements that advocated Jewish emigration from Eastern Europe, the Bund fought for the rights of Jews to live in Poland.

Endek Party (Polish acronym for Narodowa Demokracja [National Democracy]), right-wing political party in Poland, which became a leading force in organized Polish anti-Semitism during the interwar years. As it championed Polish nationalism, the party opposed both Jews and liberals and frequently called for anti-Jewish economic boycotts.

Freiheit (Yiddish: Freedom), Zionist youth movement affiliated with the Zionist-Socialist Party. Like other Zionist youth movements, Freiheit organized scouting and pioneer educational activities, but it was ideologically more oriented toward the diaspora and promoted the use of Yiddish, rather than Hebrew or Polish.

Gordonia, pioneering Zionist youth movement, affiliated with the Hitahdut party, founded in Galicia in 1923. Following the teachings of Zionist pioneer A. D. Gordon, after whom the movement was named, Gordonia advocated Jewish settlement in Palestine and promoted secular education and the creation of a modern Hebrew culture.

Hashomer Hatsa'ir (Hebrew: The Young Guard), international Zionist socialist youth movement, founded in 1916. Based on the model of British scouting and German youth movements, Hashomer Hatsa'ir had roots in earlier European Zionist youth movements. Its aim was to prepare Jewish youth to live in Palestine and work as colonists. Hashomer Hatsa'ir advocated the use of Hebrew as a vernacular and promoted socialist ideals of collectivized living. Following the military model of the scouting movement, local groups were organized into troops called *kvutsot*, which, in turn, became part of larger units, known as *plugot*. The movement sponsored *hakhsharot*, agricultural training camps, in interwar Poland, where young Jews learned skills in anticipation of emigrating to Palestine.

Hekhaluts (Hebrew: The Pioneer), organization dedicated to promoting Jewish agricultural colonies in Palestine. Hekhaluts sponsored several model kibbutzim in interwar Poland, where young Jews trained to settle and farm in Palestine, as well as an industrial collective near Łódź.

Histadrut Haovdim (Histadrut Haovdim Hale'ummit [Hebrew: National Labor Federation]), Zionist workers' organization founded in 1934 in Jerusalem by Revisionist workers who decided to leave Histadrut, the mainstream Labor Zionist organization. Histadrut Haovdim emphasized the national rather than the class interests of workers.

Hitahdut: see United Hitahdut Po'alei Zion Party.

Jewish National Fund. International organization that raised money for the purchase and development of land in Palestine for Jewish settlement. The JNF was established by the Zionist Organization at the Fifth Zionist Congress at Basle, Switzerland, in 1901.

Joint Distribution Committee (full name, American Jewish Joint Distribution Committee, also known as the "Joint" or the JDC). American Jewish philanthropy, established in 1914 to provide economic relief to East European Jews. During the interwar years the JDC provided extensive support for vocational training, medical care, and financial aid for Jews throughout Eastern Europe and helped establish Jewish agricultural settlements in the Soviet Union.

KZM (initials of Komunistyczny Związek Młodzieży [Polish: Communist Youth League]), an illegal communist youth organization, established by young Polish communist activists in 1922. Like other youth movements, the KZM sponsored outings and educational activities, and it also promoted political activism among its members. The several thousand members of the KZM were also connected with left-wing student organizations in Poland. When the Polish Communist Party was dissolved in 1938, the KZM ceased to exist.

Maccabi, sports organization for Jewish youth, formed in the late 1890s; the first Polish club opened in Lemberg (Lwów) in 1901. Maccabi sponsored athletic training and sports competitions. Named after the ancient Jewish revolutionaries in the books of the Maccabees, the organization was Zionist in orientation and had clubs in Palestine as well as throughout Europe during the years before World War II.

Morgnshtern (Yiddish: Morning Star), sports organization of the Bund, founded in Poland in 1926. By 1927, Morgnshtern counted 31 member groups throughout Poland. In addition to sponsoring general physical education, Morgnshtern held local and national athletic tournaments. It conducted activities in Yiddish, in contrast to the use of Polish or Hebrew by Zionist sports clubs in Poland.

Pioneers, international communist junior youth organization for children and young teenagers; see KZM.

Po'alei Zion (Hebrew: Workers of Zion), Labor Zionist Party, which linked a commitment to international socialism with political Zionism. Several groups called Po'alei Zion, organized around the beginning of the twentieth century, merged in 1907 to form the World Union of Po'alei Zion. In 1920 the movement split over differences on international socialism and communism and on Zionist political activities into Po'alei Zion (right) and Left Po'alei Zion. The latter, more outspokenly Marxist, initially sought unconditional affiliation with the Third Communist International but later reorganized itself independently while maintaining a positive stance toward the Soviet Union. In 1926, Po'alei Zion (right) merged with the Zionist-Socialist Party.

Polish Socialist Party (also known as the PPS, or Polska Partia Socjalistyczna), founded in Paris in 1892. The governments of tsarist Russia and Austria-Hungary often suppressed the PPS, until the newly independent Polish Republic officially sanctioned it in 1919. Jews played a prominent role in the party, particularly in its left wing. The PPS distributed some of its propaganda in Yiddish.

Revisionist Party (Union of Zionist-Revisionists), right-wing Zionist political organization, founded by Vladimir Jabotinsky in 1925. Revisionists called for mass immigration of European Jews to Palestine and for creating a Jewish state on both sides of the Jordan River. They advocated private capital investment in Jewish settlements, intensive agricultural cultivation, and the compulsory arbitration of labor conflicts.

SAT (initials of Sennacieca Asocio Tutmundo [Esperanto: Nationless Worldwide Association]), international organization, founded in Paris in 1921, to popularize the Esperanto language among workers and to develop international solidarity and accord through the promotion of Esperanto.

SKIF (Yiddish acronym for Sotsialistisher kinder-farband [Socialist Children's Union]), the children's organization of the Bund, founded in Poland in 1926. SKIF organizers appealed to children in secular Yiddish schools as well as to child laborers and street children. SKIF sponsored scouting activities, social clubs, and a weekly children's page in the Bund's newspaper, *Di folkstsaytung.*

Tarbut (Hebrew: Culture), Hebrew-language educational and cultural organization, affiliated with the United Hitahdut Po'alei Zion Party. Tarbut maintained schools throughout interwar Eastern Europe, especially in Poland. Its educational programs were pro-Zionist and promoted pioneer settlement in Palestine.

TOZ (Polish acronym for Towarzystwo Ochrony Zdrowia Ludności Żydowskiej [Society for Safeguarding the Health of the Jewish Population]), Jewish public health organization founded in Poland in 1921. TOZ sponsored clinics, pharmacies, convalescent homes, sanatoria, and public health periodicals for Jewish communities throughout Poland. In 1939 TOZ oversaw over 400 medical and sanitary institutions in 50 towns, with some 1,000 employees.

Tsukunft (Yiddish: Future), youth wing of the Bund in interwar Poland, founded in 1919. Led by young adults themselves, Tsukunft addressed problems specific to young workers, especially unemployment and long working days. Members organized lectures, libraries, dramatic clubs, choirs, conferences, and summer camps. Membership in Tsukunft numbered 15,000 on the eve of World War II.

United Hitahdut Po'alei Zion Party, Labor Zionist organization, politically to the right of Po'alei Zion. Hitahdut (Hebrew: Federation) was established in 1920, the result of a merger between Jewish labor organizations in Palestine and in Europe. Hitahdut advocated for establishing a Jewish labor commonwealth in Palestine, fostered productive vocations among the Jewish masses in the diaspora, and promoted the use of Hebrew as a modern vernacular.

YIVO (Yiddish acronym for Yidisher visnshaftlekher institut [Institute for Jewish Research]), secular research institute dedicated to the study of East European Jewish life and the culture of Yiddish-speaking Jewry around the world. Founded in Vilna in 1925, YIVO had branches in cities throughout Eastern Europe and in the Americas during the interwar years. YIVO pioneered applying modern social-science methodology to the study of contemporary Jewish life and frequently appealed to the general Jewish community to support and collaborate in the institute's efforts to collect folklore, statistics, and other materials. Among its many research efforts were youth autobiography contests conducted in the 1930s. YIVO's main headquarters have been in New York since 1940.

Zionist-Socialist Party, Labor Zionist organization, formed in 1921 by activists to the left of the groups that formed the United Hitahdut Po'alei Zion Party. In 1926, Po'alei Zion (right) merged with the Zionist-Socialist Party.

GLOSSARY

Akdamuth. Liturgical poem written in Aramaic, sung on Shavuoth by Ashkenazic Jews, for whom its melody has become a central characteristic of the celebration of this holiday.

alef. First letter of the Jewish alphabet. The *alef* is itself silent, its sound determined by an adjacent vowel sign.

alef-beys. The Jewish alphabet, used to write Hebrew, Yiddish, and other Jewish languages.

ayin. Sixteenth letter of the Jewish alphabet. Usually a silent consonant in Hebrew (in the Ashkenazic tradition), it functions as a vowel (*e* as in *bet*) in Yiddish.

beys-medresh. Room or building for traditional Jewish study and prayer, especially by adult men. A *beys-medresh* is often part of a synagogue, and the term is also sometimes used to refer to a small synagogue.

dreydl. Small, four-sided top, inscribed with letters of the *alef-beys*, traditionally used in playing games of chance during the holiday of Chanukkah.

Elul. Late summer month (August/September) according to the Jewish calendar.

feldsher. Traditional healer, who uses folk remedies instead of modern medical treatments.

gartl(ekh). Sash worn around the waist during prayer by some traditionally observant Jewish males, as a symbolic separation of the upper and lower halves of the body.

Gemara. Compendium of rabbinic commentaries, codified by scholars in Jerusalem and Babylon during the second through sixth centuries CE, which comment on and supplement the Mishnah, the core of the Talmud. The Mishnah and Gemara together make up the Talmud; the term "Gemara" is also sometimes used to refer to the Talmud as a whole.

goy(im). Gentile. When used by Yiddish-speakers to describe a fellow Jew, the term has a derogatory connotation, akin to calling that person a heretic.

grosz(y). Polish currency. One hundred groszy equal one zloty.

gymnasium (gymnasia). Secondary school in Central and Eastern Europe with an academic curriculum for students preparing to enter university. Class levels of *gymnasium* are identified in these translations as "forms," to distinguish them from the grades of public school.

hakhsharah (hakhsharot). Zionist training farms, which typically prepared trainees for life on a kibbutz or other agricultural collective.

Hallel. Psalms 113–18, chanted in part or in full during various Jewish worship services.

Haskalah. The Jewish Enlightenment. This intellectual movement advocated that Jews abandon many traditional practices—including language, worship, and dress—and integrate as modern Jews into mainstream Western culture. The *Haskalah* was initiated among German Jews during the late eighteenth century and subsequently spread eastward.

hora. Circle dance, traditional to East European Jews and also popular with Zionist youth movements.

Kaddish. Prayer praising God, recited during synagogue worship and by Jewish mourners. It is a traditional obligation for a Jewish male to recite Kaddish when mourning the death of his parents, wife, siblings, or children.

keyn ayn-hore. Literally, "no evil eye," this Yiddish folk expression is uttered to ward off potential misfortune. It is said, for example, when mentioning the number of people in one's family, lest they come to harm, or when mentioning one's age.

khaluts(im). Hebrew for "pioneer," the term was used by Zionist movements to refer specifically to Jewish settlers living in agricultural colonies in Palestine or those preparing to settle in Palestine.

khalutsah. Feminine singular form of *khaluts.*

kheyder (khadorim). School where Jewish children begin their traditional education, learning the letters of the *alef-beys* as well as how to read the Hebrew of the Bible and liturgy. "*Kheyder*" sometimes refers specifically to a privately run school, where parents pay tuition to the teacher, as opposed to a *talmud torah*, which is run and funded by the Jewish community.

kitl. Ceremonial white robe, worn by pious Jewish adult men during certain rituals, such as the Passover seder, and sometimes while studying sacred texts.

klaberjass. A card game, also known as *clobyosh* or *bela*, played by either two or three people.

kolkhoz(i). Russian term for a Soviet collective farm.

kvass. A Russian fermented drink, similar to sour beer, made from fermented grain or bread.

kvutsah (kvutsot). Jewish collective agricultural settlement in Palestine. The term is also used to designate a local unit of Hashomer Hatsa'ir or Betar.

makhzor. Jewish prayerbook used on holidays.

mała matura. Literally, "small examination" in Polish; the graduation exam taken after completing the first four years of *gymnasium*. Students continuing to study for two more years at *gymnasium* were then eligible to take the *duza matura* ("big examination"), also refered to simply as the *matura*.

maskil(im). Follower of the *Haskalah.*

matura. Graduation exam taken at the completion of six years of *gymnasium*.

mazhgiekh. Supervisor of Jewish religious practice; the dean of a yeshiva.

melamed (melamdim). A teacher of young Jewish children in a *kheyder*.

melave malke. A festive communal meal held at the end of the Sabbath, which symbolically bids farewell to the Sabbath Queen.

mikve. Ritual bath, in which traditionally observant Jews immerse themselves during rites of purification.

minyan. Quorum of ten adult Jewish males, required for group worship services.

moshavah. A noncollective Jewish agricultural settlement in Palestine.

musar. Religious ethical instruction; specifically, a Jewish religious movement emphasizing the examination of one's moral character, founded by Rabbi Israel Salanter and practiced in East European yeshivas in the late nineteenth and early twentieth centuries.

name-day. Instead of observing one's birthday, Polish Catholics traditionally celebrate on the day of the year dedicated to a particular saint after whom one is named. During the interwar years, some assimilated Jews also held "name-day" parties on the occasion of their birthdays.

Palestinism. Political commitment to promoting Jewish settlement in Palestine, as opposed to other Jewish ideologies, including those of some Zionists, who advocated creating Jewish settlements in other locations.

peye(s). Lock of hair worn in front of the ear by traditionally observant Jewish males.

plugah. Literally, "squadron" in Hebrew; refers to a group of *kvutsot* or local units of Hashomer Hatsa'ir.

Rashi commentaries. Explanations and interpretations of the Bible and Talmud written by the medieval rabbinical scholar Rashi (Rabbi Solomon ben Isaac, 1040–1105). Rashi commentaries have long served as a basic guide to the traditional study of the Bible and Talmud, and they are frequently published with the original texts.

Reb. Traditional honorific title prefixed to a Jewish man's first name.

rebbe (rebbeyim). Charismatic leader of a hasidic community.

rosh-yeshiva. Director of a rabbinical academy.

Sejm. Parliament of the Polish Republic.

shammes. Caretaker of a synagogue or other Jewish community institution.

shikse. Derogatory term for a non-Jewish girl or woman.

shin. Twenty-first letter of the Jewish alphabet, indicating the sound *sh*.

shomer (shomrim). Literally, "guard" in Hebrew, used to refer to members of the Zionist youth movement Hashomer Hatsa'ir.

shoykhet. Official slaughterer of animals for food, who follows rabbinic laws regarding how animals are to be slaughtered and inspected to determine if their meat is kosher.

shule. Progressive Jewish school. Based on the Yiddish word *shul*, which means both "synagogue" and "school," this term is used in various contexts to distinguish a school that is different from more traditional alternatives, such as the *kheyder*.

talles(im). Rectangular shawl with knotted fringes in the corners, traditionally worn by adult Jewish males during worship.

talmud torah. School where Jewish children begin their traditional education, learning the letters of the *alef-beys* as well as how to read the Hebrew of the Bible and liturgy. A *talmud torah* is run and funded by the Jewish community, in contrast to the *kheyder*, which sometimes refers specifically to a privately run school.

tanna'im. Rabbinic sages of the Mishnaic period, ca. 20–200 CE.

tefillin. Small boxes (phylacteries) containing biblical texts (Exodus 13:1–10, 12:11–16, and Deutoronomy 6:4–9, 11:13–21) written on parchment, which are strapped to the arm and forehead with leather bands during weekday morning prayers by traditionally observant adult Jewish males.

tes. Ninth letter of the Jewish alphabet, indicating the sound *t*.

Tisha B'Av. Ninth day of the late summer month of Av, a day of fasting and mourning in remembrance of the destruction of the Temples in ancient Jerusalem.

tosafoth. Later Talmudic commentaries, written in Western Europe between the twelfth and fourteenth centuries CE.

tsholnt. Stew, usually made with meat, beans, and barley, cooked in advance of the Sabbath and kept warm until being served on Saturday afternoon as the main Sabbath meal.

verst. A Russian measure of distance, equal to about two-thirds of a mile.

vov. Sixth letter of the Jewish alphabet, which variously indicates a vowel sound (*u* or *o*) or a consonant (*v*) in Yiddish and Hebrew.

yarmulke. Skullcap, frequently worn by observant Jewish males in keeping with the tradition of covering one's head at all times.

yente(s). Yiddish slang for a vulgar or overly sentimental woman.

Yiddishist. Advocate for the Yiddish language as central to modern Jewish life.

Yotser. Liturgical poetry recited during the morning service on Jewish holidays.

yud. Tenth letter of the Jewish alphabet; in Yiddish, it can either indicate the vowel sound *i* or the consonant *y*.

zloty. Polish currency. In 1930, five zloty were the equivalent of one U.S. dollar.